Nations before Nationali

JOHN A. ARMSTRONG

Nations before

The University of North Carolina Press Chapel Hill

Nationalism

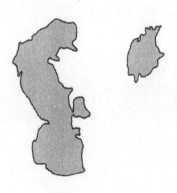

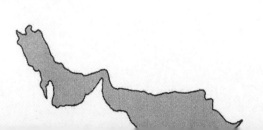

Both the initial research and the publication of
this work were made possible in part through grants
from the National Endowment for the Humanities, a
federal agency whose mission is to award grants to
support education, scholarship, media programming,
libraries, and museums, in order to bring the results of
cultural activities to a broad, general public.

© 1982 The University of North Carolina Press
All rights reserved
Manufactured in the United States of America

Library of Congress Cataloging in Publication Data

Armstrong, John Alexander, 1922–
    Nations before nationalism.

    Bibliography: p.
    Includes index.
    1. Nationalism—History. 2. Ethnic groups—
Political activity—History. I. Title.
JC311.A843   320.5'4'09   81-12988
ISBN 0-8079-1501-2   AACR2

For Janet, Carol, and Kathryn

Contents

Sketch Maps and Schema

Tables

Acknowledgments

When a study has been in progress as long as this one, the author incurs many debts, some explicit, others intangible. Throughout nearly all of my career, I have thought about writing a book on the prelude to nationalism. I took advantage, therefore, of innumerable opportunities to explore facets of the subject with observers better qualified than I. During the past nine years, as my project came into focus, I turned to acquaintances in four continents, some scholars, some not, for advice. Although space limitations require me to confine my express thanks to a few, I hope that all who generously aided me will understand how grateful I am.

My particular thanks go to the organizations that provided the financial support I needed to devote the time and engage in the travel required to complete the book: the Guggenheim Memorial Foundation, the National Endowment for the Humanities, and the University of Wisconsin Graduate School. Expert staffs, especially at the British Library, the Library of Congress, and the University of Wisconsin Libraries, provided indispensable assistance. Throughout eight months of concentrated study in London, Hugh Seton-Watson, Director of the School of Slavonic and East European Studies, unfalteringly encouraged me. My University of Wisconsin colleagues, Murray Edelman, Leon D. Epstein, and M. Crawford Young, made many useful suggestions, as did my former students Kenneth Farmer, Donald Pienkos, and Brian Silver. Kinsfolk and neighbors in my native city of St. Augustine encouraged me throughout the difficult gestation of the manuscript. I owe a special debt to the careful readers of that manuscript, Frederick C. Barghoorn and Guenther Roth. Nor could I have proceeded without the encouragement and expert assistance of Lewis Bateman and other members of the University of North Carolina Press. My deepest gratitude, in this as in all my previous efforts at writing, goes to my wife, Annette Taylor Armstrong, who first edited and then typed the entire manuscript. Trudie Calvert greatly improved the book at a later stage by her skillful, meticulous editing.

No one can essay a work of this kind, spanning so much time and space and addressing so many thorny historical issues, without coming to realize his limitations, not merely of knowledge but of perspective. As an American of West European ancestry and Roman Catholic religion, I would not and cannot divorce myself from my cultural heritage. I have striven to present others' heritages—for such is the essence of this work—in a fair and balanced light, for I regard all of them as precious components of our historical background. But I emphatically absolve all those who assisted me from any responsibility for what is, in the final analysis, a personal interpretation.

J. A. A.

Glossary

Abbasids: second major Islamic dynasty (750–1258), with interruptions; based in Baghdad, with later figurehead continuation in Cairo.

Absolutism: seventeenth- to eighteenth-century European doctrine and practice of relatively unrestricted monarchy.

Achemenids: Persian dynasty, ca. 500–334 B.C.

adab: Abbasid Court culture, Arabic in language, Persian in inspiration.

Afrasiyab: the poet Firdawsi's fictional "Turanian" hero.

agnatic: pertaining to male lineage.

Almohads: Berber mountaineer puritan dynasty in North Africa and Iberia, 1130–1269.

Almoravids: Berber nomad dynasty in North Africa and Iberia, 1056–1147.

Amharic: core ethnic element of Ethiopia and its language.

Ancien régime: prerevolutionary regime in France; by extension the old regime in another country.

Antemurale (*Antemurale Christianitatis*): pertaining to the myth ascribing to a polity the role of front-line defense of Christianity.

arabiya: classical Arabic language.

archetypal diaspora: a dispersed ethnic group that persistently maintains a sacral myth.

architectonic: architectural qualities transcending individual buildings, as in a town layout.

ark: Persian palace quarter.

Arpads: first Magyar dynasty, ca. 899–1301.

Arsacids: dynasty in Parthia and Armenia, second century B.C.–seventh century A.D.

asabiya (*asibiyat*): belief (as in Ibn Khaldun) that solidarities based on blood relationships are decisive.

auctoritas: formal authority, not necessarily accompanied by real power (Latin).

Bagratids: Armenian dynasty (884–1045 and, earlier, as vassals of Moslems); later prominent in Georgia.

banner: Manchu-Chinese organizational subdivision of nomads.

basileus: king (Greek), usually implying, as in *basileus basileon*, "king of kings" or emperor.

Beduin: hot-desert nomad (Arabic).

Bektashi: major Anatolian *sufi* order, connected to Janissaries.

border guard: linguistic symbol for maintaining ethnic distinctiveness.

boundary: tangible or intangible informal border between ethnic groups.

boundary mechanism (boundary maintenance mechanism): symbolic or institutional form for maintaining ethnic distinctiveness.

bourg: a very small town (French).

boyar: landed noble in East Europe (Russian).

Burg (pl. *Burgen*): fortress or fortified town (German; cf. *oppidum*).

Buyids: Shiite dynasty in northern Iraq, 932–1055.

cadaster: land survey for taxation.

cadi: Islamic religious judge.

Caesaropapism: domination of the church by the polity ruler.

caliph: nominal head of the Islamic religion and its universal empire.

calque: formation of new terms by direct, literal translation of the component parts from another language.

cameralistics: eighteenth-century discipline of state economic direction.

capa media: Spanish legally trained officials.

capa y espada: Spanish general governing officials.

Capetians: French dynasty (987–1328) that replaced the Carolingians.

Carolingians: Second Frank dynasty, the founders of the medieval West European empire; reigned 751–911 in East Frank realm, 751–987 in Francia.

Casa de Austria: *see* Habsburgs.

castellum: castle or small fortified town (Latin).

cataphract: pertaining to a heavily armored mounted warrior.

Church Fathers: prominent Greek and Latin Christian theologians of the second through the fourth centuries.

ciuis (*civis*): citizen (Latin).

civitas: city-state (Latin).

Cluny (Cluniac): major Benedictine monastery, center of eleventh-century reforms.

cognatic: pertaining to female lineage.

comitatus: warrior entourage of Eurasian conquest agglomeration rulers (Latin).

Comnenes: Byzantine dynasty (1081–1185), later (1204–1461) rulers of Trebizond.

conquistador: Castilian and Aragonese "conqueror"; by extension, especially to Arabs, any group imbued with a strong conquering mentality.

Conseil d'Etat: council of state in France and Burgundy.

Consejo de Estado: council of state (Spain and other Habsburg dominions).

converso: Iberian Jewish convert to Catholicism.

Copt: Egyptian Monophysite Christian.

corregidor: Spanish royal magistrate for justice and administration.

corregimento: office of *corregidor*.

cossack: originally a semioutlaw on the East Slavic–Islamic frontier, later enlisted by Muscovy or Poland as an irregular soldier.

Court (capitalized): the establishment or entourage of a ruler or religious hierarch; when uncapitalized, a legal tribunal.

coutumes: customary law of a French region, notably the Paris region.

dar: palace quarter (Tunis).

Dar ul-Islam: collective term for territories ruled by Islamic polities, or (in recent times) resembling such polities in the degree of control or intense settlement preserved by Islamic communities.

defterdar: top treasury official in the Ottoman empire.

Dei gratia: by the Grace of God (Latin).

dervish: adherent of a *sufi* order (Persian; the Arabic equivalent is *fakir*).

devshirme: "boy tax" or compulsory recruitment of young males from among Christian subjects by Ottomans for their military and administrative service.

dhimmi: protected non-Moslem subject of an Islamic polity.

diaspora: dispersed ethnic element, constituting a minority in most of its areas of settlement.

diglossia: use of an elaborated code and a restricted code, or two elaborated codes (with one for more intimate, affect concerns) by the same speaker.

domain (of language): social setting in which a speaker or speakers employ a given language.

Donation of Constantine: forged document allegedly conveying sovereignty over the Western Roman empire to the pope.

dragoman: Ottoman interpreter; the grand dragoman was often de facto minister of foreign affairs.

druzhina: Slavic term for *comitatus*.

ecumenical patriarch: patriarch of Constantinople.

elaborated code: language sufficiently developed to be used for "high cultural" purposes.

emir: military commander (Arabic).

endogamy: marriage within a restricted group.

Estates: traditional assembly, by social strata, of a province or kingdom.

ethnarch: leader of an ethnoreligious group.

ethnocentrism: concentration on one's own identity group to the exclusion of others.

exchange relationship: conscious maintenance of a bargaining situation between two elites.

exogamy: marriage outside a restricted group.

Fatimids: Shiite dynasty in North Africa and Egypt (909–1171).

Fertile Crescent: northern edge of Arabian desert, in Mesopotamia, Syria, and Palestine.

filioque: clause in Nicaean Creed concerning procession of the Holy Spirit, diversely interpreted by Catholics and Orthodox.

Flachenstaat: territorial state (German).

four-rivers line: medieval frontier of French kingdom.

Franc-Comtois: native of Franche-Comté, Burgundian territory in Holy Roman empire.

Francia: northern France under late Carolingians.

frontier: geographical division ("line" or "zone") between groups, as established by political or ecclesiastical authority.

Fuggers: major sixteenth-century southern German financiers.

Geblütsrecht: exclusive right of members of a family to rule, because of the mystic power of their blood.

Gefolgschaft: *comitatus* (German).

Genghisids: Mongol dynasty descended from Genghis Khan. Numerous rulers claimed the Genghisid name after he died in 1227.

Geschlecht: family or lineage (German).

ghazi: Islamic warrior in holy war.

glacis: protective zone in front of a fortified area or frontier.

Golden Clan: *see* Genghisids.

Golden Fleece: Burgundian order of chivalry.

Golden Horde: Mongol successor state in the steppes north of the Black Sea and the Caucasus Mountains.

gorod: Slavic term for fortified town or *oppidum*, later extended (in Slavic countries like Russia) to the town in general.

Gospodi: Slavic term for "people of the pact," i.e., a band (as of merchants) bound together by an oath; *see hansa*.

grandee: a high Castilian noble.

grands nomades: nomads who habitually undertake very long migrations, often using camels; cf. *petits nomades*, pastoral nomads.

Great Idea: Phanariot hope of reviving the Byzantine empire by taking over the Ottoman empire.

Great Yasa: *see* Yasa.

Gregorian: Armenian Christian church.

Gubernium (pl. *Gubernien*): "government" or province in the Habsburg dominions; the same term uncapitalized (*guberniya*, pl. *gubernii*) designated a province of the Russian empire.

Habsburgs: thirteenth-century southern German dynasty, Holy Roman emperors intermittently 1273–1322 and continuously (except for Maria Theresa's husband, 1745–65), 1438–1806; also rulers of

Burgundy, Spain (1516–1700), and the Danubian "Austrian" lands (1526–1918).

hadith: a saying attributed to Mohammed.

Hafsid: dynasty in Tunis (1229–1554) claiming the title of Caliph.

Hanafi: Islamic religious law school, dominant under the Ottomans.

Hanbali: Islamic religious law school, predominant in the Arabian Wahhabi movement.

hansa: cohort, as among the peripatetic German merchants; capitalized, roman type, a medieval league of North German mercantile cities.

haraj: system of exceptional tax on Moslem-owned land, or regular tax on *dhimmi*-owned land.

Hellenic: pertaining to Greece or Greek.

Hellenistic: pertaining to Greek civilization after Alexander of Macedonia and its Roman successors.

Hidden Imam: a descendant of Ali and Mohammed who, according to Shiites, will return as savior.

high culture: culture of a complex society, usually developed by an elite.

High Islamic: period of Abbasid caliphate and perpetuation of its culture by later regimes.

High Roman empire: Roman empire of first to third centuries A.D.

Hohenstaufens: dynasty of German kings and Holy Roman emperors, 1152–97, 1212–54.

hoja: chief religious instructor of Ottoman sultan.

Holy Cities: Mecca and Medina (Islam).

Holy Places: Christian shrines in Palestine.

Holy Roman empire: used by contemporaries primarily of official Western Christian empire of late medieval and early modern period, but applied in this work to the entire period from the end of the Carolingian dynasty (tenth century) to the official renunciation of the title of Roman emperor by the Austrian Habsburgs in 1806.

hrad: early Slavic term for "town."

Hulagids: see *Il Khans*.

ideal type: conceptual construct of Max Weber for analyzing historical phenomena.

Il Khans: Mongol successor dynasty ruling Persia, 1256–1335.

Imperial Gaul: territory of ancient Gaul within Holy Roman empire.

Indigenat: right of a noble to maintain status and hold estates anywhere within his sovereign's territories (German).

Indo-European: pertaining to linguistic family including most Europeans, Indians, Persians, Armenians.

ingathering: policy, or claim, of Muscovy of ruling all Orthodox East Slavs.

Iron Gate: mythical route of Gog and Magog, identified with various
    passes through the Caucasus Mountains.
irredenta: an "unredeemed" area regarded by a modern nationalist
    movement as part of its territory.
Ishmaelite: Moslems, or Moslems and Jews together, in Christian usage.
Ismailis: Seventh Imam Shiites, including Fatimids and "Assassins."
Istanbul: colloquial Turkish name (derived from the Greek "in the city")
    for Constantinople under Ottomans, official under Turkish
    Republic.
Jagiellonians: Lithuanian-Polish dynasty, 1386–1572.
Janissaries: slave-recruited infantry of Ottomans.
jihad: Islamic holy war.
Joyeuse Entrée: Burgundian ceremony of ruler's entry into one of his towns.
kaisariya: enclosed market for valuable goods (Arabic).
kalifa: descendant of a Moslem saint.
Karimi: spice merchants in Mameluke Egypt.
kasbah: fortified palace or citadel quarter (Arabic).
Kays: North Arabian faction among Arabs.
Kemalist: Turkish movement associated with Mustafa Kemal's overthrow
    of Ottomans.
khan: Turkic or Mongol ruler.
Kizilbashi: "red head" Shiite dervishes.
koine: a single, elaborated linguistic code, which (as did Attic Greek for the
    various ancient Greek dialects) replaces a family of elaborated
    codes; by extension, any cultural form, like art, that replaces a
    number of closely related styles.
Kuraysh: clans of Mecca region from which a legitimate caliphate is
    supposed to be descended.
Kustantiniye: Arabic and Ottoman name for Constantinople.
Ladin: version of Castilian employed by Jews in the Ottoman empire.
Landnahme: occupation and settling in a region (German).
Languedocian (*langue d'oc*): Romance language of southern Gaul.
langue d'oïl: Romance dialects of northern Gaul.
lesostep: wooded fringe of steppe (Russian).
letrado: originally any educated man; by sixteenth century, specifically a
    lawyer (Castilian).
limes: Roman frontier toward barbarians; by extension, any fortified
    frontier toward a nomadic, barbarian, or unruly neighbor.
limpieza de sangre: purity of blood or descent (Castilian).
lingua franca: a language widely used for intercommunication, but not
    necessarily a fully elaborated code like a *koine*.

literati: Roman or Byzantine men of letters; by extension, any body of persons devoting their attention to literary or linguistic pursuits. The term has largely been replaced in contemporary usage by "intelligentsia."

longue durée: a historical process of long duration, consideration of which provides an extended time perspective in social science analysis.

Lotharingia: intermediate kingdom in ninth-century Frank partition.

Lützelburg (Luxemburg): pertaining to the dynasty of Holy Roman emperors, 1308–13, 1347–1400, 1410–37.

Macedonians: ancient dynasty consisting of Philip of Macedon and his son, Alexander the Great (359–323 B.C.); a dynasty of Byzantine emperors (867–1056), often considered to have been Armenian in origin.

Maghreb: the Moslem "West," that is, North Africa.

Magyar: pertaining to Finno-Ugric founders of kingdom of Hungary.

mahdi: a "purifier" of Islam.

makhzen: Moroccan palace quarter, by extension royal authority.

Malikite: Islamic religious law school, predominant in North Africa.

Mamelukes: Turkic (1250–1382) and Circassian regimes (1382–1517) in Egypt, with continuation under Ottomans to eighteenth century.

Mark: frontier territorial subdivision (German).

Maronite: pertaining to Lebanese Christian denomination in recent centuries united with Rome.

marrano: derogatory term for Jewish convert to Catholicism in Spain.

medressa (*madrasah*): school for Islamic religious law and administration.

mellah: Jewish quarter (Arabic).

men of the law (or of religion): Islamic theological scholars and judges.

men of the pen: administrators of an Islamic polity.

men of the sword: military (often rulers in an Islamic polity).

Merovingians: first Frank dynasty, 457–751.

Mesta: institution of migratory sheep raising in Castile.

mesto (*miasto*, *misto*): newer Slavic terms (equivalent to German *Stadt*) for town.

metropolitan: Eastern Christian hierarch, corresponding to Western archbishop.

millet (*millatyn*, Arabic pl.): Turkish adaptation of Arabic term for religion, especially a religious minority under Moslem rule.

missi dominici: Carolingian traveling inspection officials.

Monophysite: Christian believing that Christ's divine nature was his only true nature.

mother city: North German town from which another town had obtained its customary law and which it used as an appeal instance.

Mozarab: pertaining to Iberian Christians who had lived under Moslem rule and acquired Moslem culture.

Mudejar: pertaining to Iberian Moslems under Christian rule.

mullah: religious teacher, especially in Persia.

myth: coherent belief (true or false) that arouses strong and widespread social affect.

mythomoteur: constitutive myth of a polity.

Nabatean: Syriac villagers before Islam.

natio (pl. *nationes*): nation or ethnic group, but often employed in highly artificial ways (Latin).

Nestorian: Christian "heretical" sect prominent in Asia.

noblesse de robe: French magisterial nobility.

nomad: see *grands nomades*, pastoral nomads, *petits nomades*.

nostalgia: collective memory of symbols conveying intense affect.

oikhonomia: Byzantine and Orthodox principle of temporary renunciation or abandonment of doctrines or rights for reasons of practical necessity.

oppidum (pl. *oppida*): a fortified center, usually a protourban settlement (Latin).

orda: Mongol clan agglomeration or "horde."

Ottomans: Turkic dynasty (ca. 1290–1922), which founded the principal late Islamic empire in the Balkans, Hungary, and the old Islamic lands (also known as "Osmanli").

Ottonians: dynasty of German kings and Holy Roman emperors (936–1002, 1024–1125).

padishah: supreme king (Persian); the preferred title of Ottoman rulers.

pagus: small subdivision, below *civitas*, of the Roman empire.

Pahlevi: Persian *koine* and script, third century B.C. to seventh century; name assumed by Iranian dynasty, 1926–79.

Pantokrator: Christ as Ruler of All (the Universe).

Parlement: high law court in France, especially Paris.

Partitions: division of Poland by its neighbors during the late eighteenth century.

pasha: Ottoman dignitary, especially a governor.

pastoral nomad: shepherd confined to short migrations at the edge of a steppe or desert by the need to obtain water and pastures for his flocks.

patois: a small linguistic unit with transitional zones to neighboring *patois*.

patria: fatherland (Latin).

patriarch: highest church dignity, except for the pope, who is also patriarch of the West.

patriotisme de clocher: parochial loyalty (French).

pays: equivalent to *pagus* (French).

personal law: legal jurisdiction by origins of individuals rather than by territory.

petits nomades: *see* pastoral nomad.

Phanariot: elite Greek of Phanar quarter of Ottoman Constantinople.

pharaonic: pertaining to the pharoahs, the pre-Hellenistic rulers of Egypt.

Piasts: first major dynasty in Poland ca. 992–1370.

pir: *sufi* preacher.

podestà: temporary city dictator (Italian).

polis (pl. *poleis*): Greek city-state.

politai: citizens of *polis*.

posad: merchant suburb of early East Slav town.

potestas: power or effective authority (Latin).

Pravda Russkaya: early East Slav customary law.

proskynesis: prostration before a monarch or God.

Ptolemies: Hellenistic dynasty in Egypt 306–31 B.C.

rayas: "herd animals," non-Moslem subjects of Ottomans.

reconquista: Christian reconquest of Iberia.

regnum (pl. *regna*): kingdom or viceregal territory (Latin).

Reichsapfel: symbol of terrestrial reflection of heavenly dominion in Holy Roman empire, later of rule of terrestrial globe.

Reichskammergericht: Holy Roman empire high court, fifteenth to sixteenth centuries.

Reichsromanen: Romance-speakers of western areas of Holy Roman empire.

restricted code: language used for intimate, affect relations but insufficiently developed for high cultural usage.

ribat: fortified base of Moslem *ghazi* warriors.

rossiisky: general term for East Slavs, later for "all-Russian."

Rum: Moslem term for "Rome," i.e., Byzantium.

Rurikids: dynasty of Rus and Muscovy, ca. 850–1598 (with interruptions).

Russkaya Pravda: *see Pravda Russkaya*.

Sachsenspiegel: North German city law collection derived from Magdeburg.

Safavids: dynasty (1499–1736) that established Shiite Islam in Persia.

Sahil: Syrian coast (Arabic).

Salic law: Frank dynastic law, later basis for most of West European customary law.

Sassanids: Persian dynasty (224–651) that revived opposition to Rome as heir of Hellenistic power.

Schöffen: German town magistrates.

Schöffenkolleg: juridical and administrative guild assembly in early German town, later town council.

Schöffenstuhl: juridical role of town magistrates.
Seljuks: first major Moslem Turkic dynasty, 1077–1302.
senate: ceremonial and consultative body in Rome and Byzantium.
Sephardic Jews: Jews of Iberian origin.
Seraglio: Ottoman palace quarter in Constantinople.
Shafi: Islamic religious law school, of some importance in Arab areas,
    earlier in Persia.
Shamanist: northern Eurasian animistic beliefs.
Sharia: Islamic religious law.
sharif: descendant of Mohammed.
sheikh: Moslem notable or chief (Arabic).
sheikh ul-Islam: highest Ottoman religious authority.
Shia: Islamic sect adhering to the memory of Ali as the true heir of
    Mohammed.
Shiite: pertaining to the Shia sect.
Stadt: German term that replaced *Burg* as the designation for town in the
    eleventh century, influencing parallel changes in Slavic languages.
Stamm (pl. *Stämme*): a Germanic conquest agglomeration, sometimes
    translated as "tribe"; later territorial divisions were ascribed to
    Stämme.
starosta: East Slavic chief or elder, institutionalized in office like a town
    intendancy.
startsy gradskiye: nobles who resided in the early East Slavic towns.
sufi: populist Moslem mystical movements and orders (Arabic, literally a
    "coarse wool garment"); cf. dervish.
suk: market (Arabic); equivalent to bazaar (Persian).
Sunnis: the majority of Moslems, who accept the authority of the early
    Islamic community and its teachers.
symbol: culturally conditioned words, gestures, art objects, and the like
    that succinctly communicate complex meanings.
szlachta: Polish gentry.
Tajik: sedentary peoples of Iran and Central Asia, usually Persian-
    speaking.
Tatar: originally, apparently, a branch of the Mongols; the term is
    commonly applied to Genghisid regimes and their peoples that had
    become Turkic-speaking in the steppe north of the Black Sea and
    in western Central Asia.
theme: military-territorial subdivision of the Byzantine empire.
"tribe": a common but misleading designation for a stable group thought
    to be of common descent; in this work "tribe" is usually equivalent
    to a "conquest agglomeration."
tsarstvo: applied by late medieval Russians to any independent polity.

Tulunids: Moslem Turkic dynasty in Egypt, nominally subordinate to
  Abbasids, 868–905.
Turan: mythical enemy of Iranians, first identified with groups to
  southeast, later ascribed to Turkic elements on northeast frontier.
Ukraine: southwestern frontier area of late medieval East Slavs; italicized,
  not capitalized (*ukraine* or *okraine*), any East Slavic frontier region.
ulema: Islamic religious scholars or collectivity of scholars.
Umayyads: first major Islamic dynasty, 661–750.
umma or *ummah*: the community of all Moslems.
Uniate: pertaining to Eastern Christians united with Rome.
vagina gentium: vagina of nations, identified by late classical Christian
  writers, such as Jordanes, as the source of "barbarian" invaders,
  perhaps in Scandinavia.
vicus: village (Latin).
vizir: minister of Islamic polity.
vulgare aulicum: Italian vernacular used at Court.
wakf: property held in trust for Islamic religious or charitable purposes.
Welsch (*walsch*, etc.): Germanic term for southwestern neighbors of the
  Germanic groups, namely Celts and Romance peoples.
Wend: Germanic term for eastern neighbors of the Germanic groups,
  especially Slavs.
Yasa ("Great Yasa"): Mongol customary law used as dynastic law by
  Genghisids and Mamelukes; each group of clans had a "Little Yasa"
  with a similar foundation in customs.
yayla: running waters and luxuriant pastures (Turkic).
Yemenites: southern Arabian faction among the Arabs.
yeshiva: Jewish religious school and appeals tribunal.
yurt: pastures or landed possessions, as of a clan or dynasty (Mongol and
  Turkic).
zemlya (*zemlja*): land or country; implies people living in the area as well as
  the territory (Slavic).

Chronology

(See also the Glossary for inclusive dates of dynasties)

1250–1000 B.C.	Jewish occupation of Palestine.
ca. 3000 B.C.	Emergence of civilization in Mesopotamia and Egypt.
ca. 2000 B.C.	Indo-European penetration of West Europe.
ca. 1800 B.C.	Mesopotamia united by Babylonian empire.
ca. 1100 B.C.	Appearance of camel nomads.
750–500 B.C.	Age of Jewish prophets.
ca. 500 B.C.	League of Latin city-states.
490–466 B.C.	Persian wars with Greek city-states.
457–404 B.C.	Peloponnesian wars.
306–305 B.C.	Assumption of royal titles by Alexander's epigones.
264–146 B.C.	Roman wars against Carthage.
215–205 B.C.	First Roman war against Macedonia.
125 B.C.	Parthians sack Babylon.
78 B.C.	Cicero studies in Greece.
70–48 B.C.	Pompey prominent in Rome.
58–44 B.C.	Caesar conquers Gaul.
31 B.C.–A.D. 14	Augustus dominant in Rome.
30 B.C.	Roman annexation of Egypt.
6 B.C.	Birth of Jesus Christ, according to most widely accepted scholarly opinion.
64	Execution of Saints Peter and Paul in Rome.
ca. 70	Writing of Gospels.
70	Roman capture of Jerusalem.
180–285	Period of "barracks" emperors in Rome.
224	Foundation of Sassanid kingdom.
232–275	End of "High Roman" empire; invasions and civil wars followed by walling of cities.
252	First capture of Antioch by Sassanids.
284–305	Reign of Diocletian as Roman emperor.
297	Diocletian's transfer of Latin-speaking districts to province of Illyricum.
298	Diocletian separates Aquitania–Gallia Narbonensis from Gallia Lugudunensis.
ca. 300	Conversion of Armenians to Christianity.
ca. 300	Diocletian's administrative reforms.

313	Constantine legalizes Christianity.
321	Arius preaching in Eastern empire.
325	First Council of Nicaea.
370	End of period of usage of Greek in the church in Rome.
376	Huns expel Goths from Black Sea steppe.
378	Battle of Adrianople; Goths defeat Romans.
393	Paganism outlawed by Theodosius.
395	Division of Eastern and Western Roman empires.
400	Lynching of Germanic soldiers by Constantinople mobs.
406	Germanic invasion of Gaul.
406	Stilicho supports Western empire's claim to Latin-speaking provinces in the Balkans.
408	Execution of Stilicho.
ca. 410	Vulgate (Latin) Bible by St. Jerome.
415–419	Visigoth kingdom in Iberia.
421	Transfer, by Theodosius, of Latin-speaking provinces to patriarchate of Constantinople.
429	Naval predominance of Vandals in western Mediterranean.
431	Nestorius condemned by Council of Ephesus.
450	Anglo-Saxon invasion of Britain.
452–453	Hun invasion of West Europe.
457	Establishment of Merovingian Frank dynasty.
486	Clovis, the second Merovingian king, defeats Syagrius.
496–497	Conversion of Franks to Catholicism.
506	"Breviarium Alarici" issued by Alaric II, king of Visigoths in Iberia.
510	Clovis issues Salic law.
527–565	Reign of Justinian I, Byzantine emperor.
ca. 530	Construction of Santi Cosmas i Damiano in Rome.
532	Hagia Sophia construction begins.
ca. 540	Principal mosaics of Sant' Appolinare Nuovo in Ravenna.
548	Dedication of San Vitale in Ravenna.
568	Lombard invasion of Italy.
568–752	Period of Greek and Oriental popes.
ca. 570–632	Life of Mohammed.
617	Sassanids temporarily conquer Egypt.
ca. 620	Construction of St. Hripsimeh near Echmiadzin.
634–642	Arabs defeat Romans and Sassanids in Fertile Crescent and Egypt.
634–644	Reign of Omar as caliph.
661	Foundation of Umayyad caliphate

ca. 873	Disappearance of Twelfth Imam.
893	Use of Church Slavonic in Bulgar kingdom.
ca. 900	Magyars enter Danube Basin.
911	East Carolingian dynasty dies out.
912–961	Reign of Umayyad Caliph Abd al-Rahman in Iberia.
924	Byzantine recognition of papal jurisdiction in Dalmatia.
929	Adoption of caliph title by Andalusian Umayyad dynasty.
933	German defeat of Magyars at Merseburg.
945–983	Buyid Shiite dynasty exercises protectorate over caliph.
955	Germans defeat Magyars at Lechfeld.
960	Byzantine reconquest of Syria begins.
961	Byzantine reconquest of Crete.
962–973	Reign of Otto I as German king.
964	First written text in Italian.
966	Polish King Mieszko converted to Western Christianity.
968	Byzantine recapture of Antioch.
969	Fatimid conquest of Egypt.
980–1015	Reign of St. Vladimir as great prince of Kiev.
987	Hugh Capet, first French king who did not speak German, assumes throne from Carolingians.
ca. 1000	De facto severance of political ties between Catalonia and Francia.
ca. 1000	Poland becomes fief of papacy.
ca. 1000–1080	Culmination of Byzantine use of iconographic hierarchy in churches of Hosios Lukas and Daphni.
1000	Conversion of Magyars to Western Christianity.
1012–1016	Pisan crusade in Sardinia.
ca. 1020	Death of Persian poet Firdawsi.
1050	Hilali Beduins penetrate North Africa.
1054	First formal schism between Eastern and Western Christian churches.
1055	Christian capture of Toledo.
1059	Papal-Norman alliance.
1063	Normans and Pisans conquer Palermo from Moslems.
1066	Normans conquer England.
1071	High point of Byzantine advance in Syria.
1071	Turks defeat Byzantines at Manzikert.
1072–1079	Reign of Alfonso VI of Castile, king of the "two religions."
ca. 1080	Appearance of the "Song of Roland," although the setting of the poem is ca. 778.
1080–1130	Establishment of city-states in northern Italy.

1091	Normans conquer all Sicily.
1096	First crusade to Palestine.
ca. 1100	Completion of transition from Romanesque to Gothic architecture in northern France.
1102	Private documents changed from Latin to Provençal.
1113–1125	Reign of Vladimir Monomakh as great prince of Kiev.
1119	Byzantine force attacks Damietta in Egypt.
1120	Foundation of crusading orders of Hospitallers and Templars.
1145	First written text in Castilian.
1152	Pope Innocent II subordinates the Polish church to the archbishop of Magdeburg.
1155	Last Byzantine effort to reconquer southern Italy.
ca. 1158	Foundation of city of Lübeck.
1162	Destruction of Milan by Frederick I.
1167	Last effective Byzantine intervention in Dalmatia.
1167	Hohenstaufen effort to have Charlemagne canonized.
1172	Private documents changed from Latin to Castilian.
1184	Composition of Armenian Datastangirk legal code.
1186	Foundation of second Bulgarian empire.
1190	Foundation of special German branch of Hospitaller Order; the branch was subsequently known as the Teutonic or Germanic Order.
1193	Private documents changed from Latin to Italian.
1198–1216	Reign of Pope Innocent III.
ca. 1200	Spread of "*Stadt*" terms and Magdeburg law in East Europe.
1204	Western forces of Fourth Crusade capture Constantinople.
1204	Private documents changed from Latin to French.
1209–1213	Albigensian crusade.
1215	Western church requires annual confession.
1217	Papal crown conceded to Serbian king.
1219	First Mongol attacks on Central Asian Moslems.
1224	*Sachsenspiegel* written.
1227	Death of Genghis Khan.
1232	Moslem rule in Iberia restricted to kingdom of Granada.
1237	Polish kings allow German Knights Hospitaller to settle in Poland.
1237–1241	Mongol invasion of East Europe.
1240–1299	Orthodox metropolitan in Halich.
1246	Rus rulers ascribe "tsar" title to Mongol rulers.

1250	Use of French in French royal chancery.
1250–1350	Period when first "filled-up" world was attained in northern France.
1250	Foundation of Mameluke regime in Egypt.
1253	Hafsid dynasty in Tunis assumes caliph title.
1258	Formal French renunciation of sovereignty in Catalonia; severance of major social ties between Catalans and Languedocians.
1258	Last Abbasid caliph in Baghdad killed by Mongols.
1259–1284	Reign of Kublai Khan in China.
1260	Mameluke defeat of Mongols in Syria.
1263	Moscow emerges as autonomous principality.
1270–1290	Maximum Mongol intervention in Rus.
1273	Castilian royal establishment of the Mesta system.
1277	First appearance of Ottoman dynasty in Anatolia.
1282	First establishment of Habsburgs in Vienna.
1291	Formation of Swiss Confederation.
1294	Bohemian reaction against foreigners defeats attempt to found Prague University.
1298	Appearance of Marco Polo's *Merveilles du Monde*.
1299–1327	Orthodox metropolitan of Kiev resides in Vladimir.
1300	Safi ad-Din assumes direction of Azerbaijan *sufi* order.
1312	Final conversion of Golden Horde to Islam.
1313–1341	Reign of Uzbeg, the most powerful ruler of the Golden Horde.
1332–1406	Life of Ibn Khaldun.
1333–1370	Reign of Casimir the Great of Poland.
1334–1353	Construction of the Alhambra.
ca. 1340	Conversion of the Chagatay Mongols to Islam.
1347–1349	Height of Black Death in West Europe.
1348	Foundation of Prague University.
1349	Polish acquisition of Halich.
1351–1381	Separate Orthodox metropolitan of Kiev in Lithuanian principality.
1354	Ottoman invasion of the Balkans.
1362	End of predominant usage of Norman French in English law courts.
1363	Valois dynasty acquires duchy of Burgundy.
1368	End of Mongol rule in southern China.
1370	Tamerlane's first conquests.
1371	Orthodox metropolitan of Kiev becomes resident in Moscow.

1375	Prominence of Armenians in southern Polish cities.
1377	Russian prince Dmitri Donskoy repels the Tatars.
1386	Personal union of Lithuania and Poland, with Lithuanian dynasty and elite converted to Catholicism.
1390	Jagiello I of Poland-Lithuania recruits Cracow Benedictines for Slavonic-rite missionary activity.
1399	Tatars defeat Lithuanians at Vorkla River.
ca. 1400	Construction of Bibi Khanun mosque in Samarkand.
1402	Hus begins preaching.
1402	Tamerlane defeats the Ottomans.
1405	Death of Tamerlane.
1409	Hussite attacks on Germans in Prague.
1410	Poles defeat Teutonic Knights at Tannenberg.
1415	Hus burned as a heretic.
1416–1499	Separate Orthodox metropolitan resident in Lithuania.
1420–1431	Hussite wars in Bohemia.
1431	St. Joan of Arc burned.
1434–1435	Polish law introduced for Galician (Halich) nobles.
1438	Rebellion of Ofen Magyars against German predominance.
1438	Foundation of Khanate of Kazan.
1440–1493	Reign of Frederick III as Holy Roman emperor.
1441	Vasili II intends to offer Moscow as a refuge for the ecumenical patriarch.
1451–1481	Reign of Mohammed II over Ottoman empire.
1453	Ottoman capture of Constantinople.
1456	First Muscovite claim to descent from Vladimir I.
1458–1596	Uniate metropolitanate of Kiev.
1462–1505	Reign of Ivan III.
1474–1534	Intense Tatar raids on Poland-Lithuania and Muscovy.
1477	Death of Charles the Bold; France acquires part of Burgundy.
1492	Spanish conquest of Granada.
1492	Discovery of America.
1492	Appearance of a Castilian grammar, the first in a modern European language.
1499	Shah Ismail begins Safavid expansion.
1500–1617	Construction of Ottoman "imperial mosques."
1503–1515	Ivan III's truce with Tatars.
1510	Establishment of Sunni Uzbeg regime in Central Asia.
1514	Ottomans massacre Shiites in Anatolia.

1516	King Stephen Batory's plans for translating and revising East Slav law.
1517	Ottomans defeat Shah Ismail.
1517	Luther begins an open dispute with papacy.
1518–1521	Beginning of Castilian conquests on the American mainland.
1520–1566	Reign of Suleiman II, the Magnificent, over Ottoman empire.
1521	Habsburg establishment of "Windisch" frontier defense.
1526	Habsburg dynasty acquires Hungarian throne.
1527	Charles V's troops sack Rome.
1529	First Ottoman siege of Vienna.
1530	Coronation of Charles V as Holy Roman emperor.
1539	Official use of French in French law court documents.
1539	Establishment of Orthodox metropolitan in Halich under Polish patronage.
1540	Formation of Jesuit Order.
1541	Ottoman conquest of most of kingdom of Hungary.
1545–1563	Council of Trent.
1547	Official Spanish requirement of *limpieza de sangre.*
1552	Capture of Kazan by Ivan IV.
1556	Charles V abdicates as Holy Roman emperor.
1556–1598	Reign of Philip II of Spain.
1561	Madrid made capital of Spain.
1568	First Polish-language grammar appears.
1569	Philip II secures papal acquiescence in *limpieza de sangre* laws.
1571	Catholic forces defeat Ottoman fleet at Lepanto.
1578	Moroccans defeat Portuguese invasion at Kasr al-Kebir.
1579	Formation of United Netherlands.
1582	Foundation of Academia della Crusca at Florence.
1585	Kiev Orthodox confraternity establishes schools.
1586	First Church Slavonic grammar appears.
1587–1629	Reign of Shah Abbas of Persia.
1589	Consecration of patriarch in Moscow.
1591	Greco-Slavonic comparative grammar appears.
1609	Demands issued by Bohemian anti-Catholic faction.
1612	Habsburg Court removed from Prague to Vienna.
1612–1625	Persian victories over Ottoman forces.
1615	Pro-Czech measures passed by Bohemian Diet.
1616	Habsburg government staffs removed from Prague to Vienna.

1618–1648	Thirty Years' War.
1620	Bohemian nobility defeated at the battle of White Mountain.
1630	Persian loss of Tabriz to Ottomans.
1635	Académie Française founded.
1643–1715	Reign of Louis XIV of France.
1644	Manchu dynasty established as rulers of China.
1654	Zaporozhian cossacks adhere to Moscow.
1656–1678	Köprölü "dynasty" of *vizirs* renew Ottoman power.
1667	The Russian emperor deposes a Moscow patriarch.
1670s	Serb revolt against Austrian Catholic proselytizing.
1682–1725	Reign of Peter I, the Great, of Russia.
1683	Last Ottoman siege of Vienna.
1688	Treaty of Karlowitz; Habsburgs recover Hungary.
1700	Especially severe Tatar raids in Russia and Poland.
1713	Foundation of Réal Academia Español.
1714	Treaty of Rastatt, first major treaty composed in French.
1718	Peace of Passarowitz; Habsburg gains from Ottomans.
1721	South Slavs attracted to Kiev theological study.
1722	Afghan destruction of Isfahan.
1735	Russia compelled to settle for a defensive *glacis* toward Tatars, north of Azov.
1742	Holy Roman empire acknowledges the Russian ruler's claim to the title of emperor.
1750s	Serb appeal to Russia to support Orthodoxy against Austria.
1762–1796	Reign of Catherine II, the Great, of Russia.
1769	Last Tatar raid into Russia.
1770s	Habsburg Germanization of Croatian military frontier schools.
1772–1795	Partitions of Poland.
1774	Treaty of Kuchuck Kainarji between Russia and Ottomans.
1776	Catherine II reduces the Crimea to client status.
1780–1790	Reign of Joseph II of Austria.
1783	Russia annexes the Crimea, ending Russian-Islamic frontier zone except in the Caucasus and Central Asia.
1784	Croatian military frontier mostly retroceded to kingdom of Croatia.
1792–1802	Wars of the French Revolution.
1804–1814	Napoleonic empire.
1821	Ottoman massacre of the Phanariots.

1825–1855	Reign of Nicholas I of Russia.
1830–1840	Ottoman settlement of Kurds among the Armenians.
1835	Last serious Ottoman incursion into the Habsburg dominions.
1848	The "Communist Manifesto."
1860	Uzbek enslavement of Shiite Persians.
1871–1918	The German Second Reich.
1873	All remaining Habsburg military frontier regions incorporated into the kingdom of Hungary.
1877	Russo-Turkish War.

Nations before Nationalism

CHAPTER ONE

An Approach to the Emergence of Nations

Group Boundaries and Ethnic Identification

The aim of this book is to explore the emergence of the intense group identification that today we term a "nation." What, apart from accidents of spatial proximity or the pressure of superior force, has bound individuals together in large agglomerations? Above all, what is the cement that has maintained group identity over very long periods of time?

In exploring such group ties, I do not seek to define general laws as do the natural sciences and increasingly the social sciences. The study of even contemporary ethnicity is, I think, at too preliminary a stage to favor such nomothetic endeavors. Examination of ethnic relations over very extended historical periods is even less suited to the discovery of universal laws, although it may result in the emergence of patterns or typologies in the evolution of nations. To achieve this limited aim, comparisons, often involving phenomena remote from one another in space as well as in time, are indispensable. In my exploratory venture, comparisons are intended to illuminate one historical case by relating it to others. Yet I hope to accomplish more than simple comparisons of patterns. If an extended temporal dimension for generalizing can be found, we must first summarize the relevant historical experience in a way that permits posing specific questions about analogous phenomena. My hope is to reduce some of the complex historical patterns of ethnic identification to shorthand descriptions that will facilitate this immense task.

The focus is upon group identities rather than upon institutional structures such as the state, which has recently constituted the subject of several impressive studies.[1] Because the group identity I term "ethnic" permeates the historical record, my task involves the production of synthetic history. Within the limited scope of my subject, I must provide an overview of Eastern and Western Christendom and Islamic civilization. Why these, and only these, civilizations? An obvious answer is the limitation of time, space, and, above all, of my own grasp. More theoretically cogent is the intimate relationship of these civilizations, based on universal religions derived from the same Judaic tradition.[2] At the same time, one must recognize that patterns derived from such closely related civilizations cannot without further examination be assumed to apply to all human experience.

Within the very extended temporal perspective provided by these civilizations, the key to the significance of phenomena of ethnic identification is persistence rather than genesis of particular patterns. Because of this concern with persistence, my approach differs from examinations of recent ethnic relations. Since the late eighteenth century, nationalism has in many respects become the dominant political doctrine. The right of individuals to choose the state to which they belong, that is, to establish territorial political structures corresponding to their consciousness of group identity, has constituted a principal theme of political analysis.[3] My examination, however, stops at the threshold of nationalism, before the period (varying considerably from one part of Europe and the Middle East to another) when consciousness of ethnic identity became a predominant force for constituting independent political structures. A major objective of my work is, indeed, to provide a perspective in which such historically novel demands posed by nationalist movements must confront a lengthy record of human association in which persistent group identity did not ordinarily constitute the overriding legitimization of polity formation.

A time dimension of many centuries (similar to the *longue durée* emphasized by the *Annales* school of French historiography) is essential for disentangling independent ethnic experiences from the effects of diffusion and mimesis. An extended temporal perspective is especially important as a means of perceiving modern nationalism as part of a cycle of ethnic consciousness. Because the epoch of Absolutism that immediately preceded European nationalism involved, at least for elites, an exceptionally strong rejection of ethnic differentiation, nationalism is often seen as utterly unprecedented.[4] A longer look suggests that widespread intense ethnic identification, although expressed in other forms, is recurrent. For example, Absolutist Enlightenment dispersed the revived linguistic consciousness encouraged by Reformation and Counter-Reformation conflicts. One result has been that modern nationalist thought, succeeding to an age of cosmopolitanism, has sought permanent "essences" of national character instead of recognizing the fundamental but shifting significance of boundaries for human identity.

The importance of focusing on boundaries has been most clearly stated by the Norwegian anthropologist Fredrik Barth.[5] He proposes a social interaction model of ethnic identity that does not posit a fixed "character" or "essence" for the group, but examines the perceptions of its members which distinguish them from other groups. Concentration on these attitudinal boundary mechanisms affords three major advantages: (1) Because ethnicity is defined by boundaries, both the cultural and the biological content of the group can alter as long as the boundary mechanisms are maintained. (2) Although Barth points out that his boundaries may have territorial counterparts, he emphasizes that ethnic groups are "not merely or necessarily based on the occupation of exclusive territories." (3) Barth's boundary approach facilitates consideration of other ethnic phenomena, exotic from the modern European standpoint, such as the use of languages as alternative codes rather than ethnic identifying symbols or prescriptive communication media.

Anthropological historians have been increasingly obliged to confront the fact, implicit in Barth's approach, that groups tend to define themselves not by reference to their own characteristics but by exclusion, that is, by comparison to "strangers." Primitive man, according to this interpretation, was disturbed by the uncanny experience of confronting others who, perforce, remained mute in response to his attempts at communication, whether oral or through symbolic gestures. Terms like "*goyim*," "*barbaroi*," and "*nemtsi*" all imply such perception of the human incompleteness of persons who could not communicate with the in-group, which constituted the only "real men." Usually, in their original application such terms singled out one or two alien neighbors, and, by reference to such aliens, large ethnic groupings came to recognize their own relatively close relationship. Thus the extensive Germanic groups defined themselves as the people "between Wend and Walsche," never using either term to refer to any group that spoke a Germanic tongue. Just as the real referent for Wend shifted, probably, from Finnic reindeer nomads located northeast of the Germanic elements to the Slavs who later occupied the eastern limits of the Germanic sphere, the referent for "Walsche" (or "Welsch") changed from Celt alone to Celt, Latinized Celt, and Roman alike, on the southwest confines of the Germanic world.[6] Hence, in a rudimentary way, the Germanic settlement area was delimited in a territorial sense, although its "boundaries" were very imprecise zones. Similarly, "Turan," among the distant Iranian cousins of the Germanic group, apparently originally applied to the Iranians' dark neighbors in what is now Baluchistan. Considerably later, the referent for "Turan" became the Turkic element intruding into the northeast boundary zone of Iranic settlement.[7]

The French linguist Emile Benveniste is in fundamental agreement with anthropological historians in the conception of the ethnic group as defined by exclusion: "Every name of an ethnic character, in ancient times, was differentiating and oppositional. There was present in the name which a people assumed the intention, manifest or not, of distinguishing itself from the neighboring peoples, of affirming the superiority derived from a common, intelligible language. Hence the ethnic group often constituted an antithetical duality with the opposed ethnic group."[8]

Removing the focus of investigation from the internal characteristics of the group to its self-perceived boundaries is, of course, only a start toward an examination of ethnicity in history. The principal implications of the boundary approach will become clearer in the course of the following substantive chapters. At the start it is important to recognize that the conception of the ethnic group or incipient nation as a group defined by exclusion implies that there is no purely definitional way of distinguishing ethnicity from other types of identity. The boundary approach clearly implies that ethnicity is a bundle of shifting interactions rather than a nuclear component of social organization. It is precisely this complex, shifting quality that has repelled many social scientists from analyzing ethnic identity over long periods of time. Most who have approached ethnicity have also been attracted by the simplifying assumption that each ethnic group occupies an exclusive territory. Once one abandons the principle of territorial exclusivity, one must recognize that the phenomenon of ethnicity is part of a continuum of social collectivities, including, notably, classes and religious bodies. Over a long period of time each may transmute into one of the others. Consequently, I shall be more concerned with the interaction among class, ethnic, and religious characteristics than with compartmentalizing definitions. Nevertheless, there are certain sociological characteristics that, taken as tendencies rather than as categorically differentiating qualities, serve to distinguish the three kinds of collectivities.

Tendencies that have distinguished the major universal religions from ethnic groups will be discussed at several points, notably in chapters 3 and 7. Where, in practice, ethnicity and religion have coincided, groups exhibit the following characteristics: peculiar linguistic features associated with sacral identity; a high degree of endogamy; symbolic border guards such as peculiar architecture, dress, and manners. The dividing lines between class and ethnicity are sharper but harder to characterize briefly. In the premodern period, functional or occupational differentiation from neighboring social or ethnic groups was a prime distinguishing characteristic both of traditional diasporas and of nomads. Generally, however, a lower class (especially in sedentary agricultural societies) cannot constitute a group as persistently conscious of its identity as an ethnic collectivity.[9] The principal reason is that the incomplete lower-class occupational pyramid does not provide an elite with the communications and bargaining skills needed to legitimize the boundary mechanisms of the class, thereby ensuring its distinct identity within a large polity. Lacking the high-culture capacities a counterelite would provide, an underclass has difficulty resisting manipulation by the elites that guard the myths and symbols common to the society as a whole.

Emergence of such a counterelite is especially difficult in sedentary agricultural societies where dominant elites monopolize communication by symbols and supervise the socialization of all members of the polity by inculcation of myths legitimizing the elite's dominance. Nevertheless, it must be admitted that the inabilty of peasants, the agricultural underclass, to develop a persistent identity is a matter of degree rather than an absolute. In chapter 8, the relative importance of language differentiation in such persistence will be explored. Certainly, the presence of very different linguistic patterns among peasants and elites, as contrasted to minor dialect differentiation, made maintenance of a latent but persistently strong identity easier. A major sign of emerging ethnic identification, especially in East Central Europe, has been the appearance of an articulate elite among a mass of peasants hitherto distinguished from other social segments in the polity only by their peculiar folklore and by linguistic patterns restricted to intimate small-group communication.

Once a counterelite peculiar to the incipient ethnic collectivity has developed, it can try to enter into an exchange relationship with the dominant elite of the polity. Indeed, one can posit the potential for such an exchange relationship—although it may be aborted by a *force majeure*—as a major sociological criterion for distinguishing ethnicity from class. In other words, once the occupational pyramid has become complete enough to enable a group to engage in conscious bargaining about its position in the polity rather than incoherent submission to manipulation by the dominant elite, ethnic identification is possible, even where there is no consideration of an autonomous political structure. For groups like diasporas, equipped with unusually sophisticated elites, such an exchange relationship may be crucial for survival. In sum, therefore, there is nothing predetermined about the boundaries that distinguish an ethnic collectivity; but one can point to ways in which these boundaries differ, notably in persistence, from those identifying a class.

Symbol, Myth, and Communication

The discussion so far has frequently referred to symbols and communication, less often to myth; all three concepts are critical to an analysis of the slow emergence of nations in the premodern period. The primary characteristic of ethnic boundaries is attitudinal. In their origins and in their most fundamental effects, ethnic boundary mechanisms exist in the minds of their subjects rather than as lines on a map or norms in a rule book. Both of these secondary effects are, as symbols, major indicators of boundaries. But failure to grasp the way in which culture is expressed by symbols makes it hard to understand boundary mechanisms that are not expressed in material delineations.[10]

Most often symbolic boundary mechanisms are words. Such words are particularly effective as traffic lights warning a group member when he is approaching a barrier separating his group from another. This intense power of a few symbolic "border guards" is illustrated by early Yiddish. It was basically an Old High German dialect, but rigorously excluded certain words in the German environment that had specifically Christian connotations. For example, *sĕganōn*, "to bless," was rejected because it derived from Latin *signare*, "to make the sign [of the cross]," in favor of retaining the neutral form "*bentshn*" from Latin *benedicere*, "to speak well," which earlier Jewish communities had incorporated in Southern Laaz, their Romance dialect. Such verbal symbolic devices safeguarded group identity against penetration of Christian concepts. But, as Suzanne Langer points out, significant symbols also include gestures, drawings, musical sounds, and the like.[11] Sometimes a graphic identity symbol, accepted in a routine manner, suddenly acquires intense significance. For centuries the *Reichsapfel*, a globe surmounted by a cross, symbolized the heavenly sphere in the Holy Roman imperial insignia. When Charles V, already king of Spain ruling lands extending around the terrestrial globe, was crowned emperor in 1530, he used the *Reichsapfel* as a symbol of his reinvigorated claims to universal empire. Though there is no specific evidence that Charles V envisaged his overt use of this symbol as a subtle reflection of the ancient Mesopotamian myth that portrayed terrestrial rule as a reflection of heavenly order, the symbolic resonance of the ancient myth may have unconsciously influenced his audience.[12]

Because the cues conveyed by symbols are signals from one ethnic group to others or among members of the same group, symbolic interaction is a type of communication. Perhaps for my purposes it is simplest to regard symbols as the content and communication as the means by which they become effective. Evidently, as in the case of linguistic border guards, symbols are often established as content generations or even centuries before they are communicated as cues to any given members of a group. Consequently, to an extraordinary degree ethnic symbolic communication is communication over the *longue durée*, between the dead and the living. Here, as in other facets of ethnic identity, the persistence of the symbol is more significant than its point of origin in the past. Persistence is closely related to the incorporation of individual symbols, verbal and nonverbal, in a mythic structure.[13]

Over long periods of time, the legitimizing power of individual mythic structures tends to be enhanced by fusion with other myths in a *mythomoteur* defining identity in relation to a specific polity.[14] Identification of these complex structures as mythic does not imply that they are false, any more than references to religious myths call into question their theological validity. Eric Dardel points out that demonstrable historical validity is not the critical aspect of the *mythomoteur*: "The mythic past cannot be dated, it is a part 'before time' or, better, outside time. . . . Primordial actions are lost 'in the night of time,' what happened 'once' (nobody knows when) goes on in a floating and many-layered time without temporal location. . . . [The myth narrator or epic poet] draws the audience of the story away, but only to make them set themselves at the desired distance."[15] A most significant effect of the myth recital is to arouse an intense awareness among the group members of their "common fate." From the perspective of myth-symbol theory, common fate is simply the extent to which an episode, whether historical or "purely mythical," arouses intense affect by stressing individuals' solidarity against an alien force, that is, by enhancing the salience of boundary perceptions. Consequently, except for the highly differing ways of life discussed in chapters 2 and 4, it is the symbolic rather than the material aspects of common fate that are decisive for identity. Moreover, symbols need not directly reflect the "objectively" most important elements of the material way of life even when it does constitute a sharply differentiating underlying factor.

The Phenomenological Quandary

Ethnic boundaries fundamentally reflect group attitudes rather than geographical divisions. Myth, symbol, communication, and a cluster of associated attitudinal factors are usually more persistent than purely material factors. When, however, one moves from the purely conceptual to the gritty business of investigating specific ethnic divisions, the utility of tangible indicators becomes evident. Geographic boundaries are not only tangible; they possess other important attributes: they often acquire intense symbolic significance, and the direct impact of political action is frequently earliest and strongest in a geographic context. Another reason for concentrating on boundaries is that a specialized social science discipline, geography, has provided a rich array of secondary sources on the physical boundary. For the purposes of this study, the term "boundaries" will be reserved for all relevant informal limits resulting from social processes such as linguistic, folkloric, and economic development, whereas "frontier" will denote borders defined by political action, including the formal action of autonomous ecclesiastical authorities. The distinction between frontier and boundary will become highly important in discussing, notably in chapter 8, the coincidence of one or more social boundaries, such as language isoglosses with political frontiers. As subtypes of the frontier, zone frontiers, which have been the norm throughout most of history, and the line frontier, increasingly significant in the modern period, should be distinguished.

Reference to geographical boundaries and frontiers affords a cogent introduction to the general problem of methodology. The greatest difficulty in studying cultures dispersed over wide ranges of time and space is phenomenological comparability. A brilliant recent analysis by a Czechoslovak scholar emphasizes the peril, even for students of recent nationalist movements, of assuming that phenomena bearing the same names are truly similar.[16] There is, however, the converse danger: assuming that because movements in cultures remote in time or space from modern Europe employ very different terms, the phenomenon of ethnic identification must be absent. A student of nascent French nationalism expresses this danger succinctly: "National sentiment, national consciousness flourished at the start of the modern period. Of course, they were not expressed in the terms of nineteenth-century nationalism. The preliminary goals of our research are to find the appropriate terms, the content, and historical significance of national consciousness during the second half of the sixteenth century."[17]

It is manifestly impossible for a work like the present one, covering many centuries and cultures, to be based on independent deductions from original texts. As Bernard Lewis, a most accomplished Orientalist, has explained, even linguistic knowledge was insufficient for historians dealing with Arabic, Persian, and Turkish sources until they had been published in critical editions accompanied by scholarly elucidations. Up to that time, the danger of misunderstanding the originals was worse than reliance on translations.[18] With my more limited linguistic knowledge, I am wholly dependent, even when I have read critical editions of the "sources" in their original languages or in scholarly translations, upon the expertise of multitudes of devoted scholars. Dependence upon secondary analyses is enhanced by the esoteric, symbolic terms in which much surviving evidence is couched. Such esoteric communication was especially important for groups whose identity was pervaded by sacral concepts. Yet the fact that the content of sacral symbols remained stable over long periods of time throughout large cultural areas provides an immense advantage for the comparativist. Among Christians, elaborate formal definitions designed to preclude idiosyncratic usage in doctrinal matters were adopted at the Second Council of Nicaea in 787. As discussed at more length in chapter 5, such liturgical symbols, strictly regulated in both the Eastern Orthodox and the Latin Catholic churches, came to acquire strong implications for ethnic identity.[19] The persistent constraints that church definitions exerted on ethnic idiosyncrasies in the use of symbols make it possible, as a contemporary historian of Western polity formation explains, to assess subtle shifts in legitimization:

> What synodists tried to express in abstract words, or in legal terms, the coronation rite tried to convey in its rubrics, gestures, prayers, and symbols, that is, by liturgical means. Words could have different significations, but liturgical vehicles should (and on the whole did) have only one unambiguous meaning. . . . For these [rites] had not only to be crystal clear and unambiguous, but also and above all readily comprehensible to even the most dull-witted contemporary accustomed to thinking in only the crudest terms.[20]

The assistance provided by the symbolic code, elaborately reconstructed by recent scholarship, is unusually important in the comparativist's direct observation of visual symbols, which in early Christian churches constituted a kind of "frozen" liturgy. Can the analyst resort to a similar system of visual evidence for Islam, that cultural world so useful for comparison with Christendom? Islamic theology formally eschews the use of symbols.[21] Yet even the lay traveler can discern relationships between one Moslem architectural form, the minaret, and regional ethnic identities. The square Malikite minaret rises above the new as well as the old mosques of Morocco, whereas the mosque of a Cairo suburb retains the intricately decorated polygonal minaret of the Mameluke period, and Turks and Iranians use other forms of minarets to commemorate their own periods of historical greatness.

The Plan of the Work

It should by now be apparent that the exploration this book encompasses must draw on many disciplines. Ordinarily, I advance as evidence expert views only when they appear to reflect the consensus (not necessarily the unanimity) of the latest scholarship on the subject. Rarely do I accept evidence or adopt a position that remains in dispute among specialists.

When I do so, I have tried to make both my temerity and my reasons, deriving from the special perspective of the comparativist, evident to the reader.

I present those aspects of European and Middle Eastern history that I consider to be most important in the overall historical development of ethnicity, or those that are especially relevant for generalization. I assume considerable familiarity with general history, but I endeavor to provide sufficient background (including maps, glossary, and chronology) to enable the reader to place my argumentation in the context of that history. At the close of each chapter, I summarize my principal tentative findings. Such summaries must be understood, of course, in the light of elaborations and qualifications presented earlier.

The aims of this book, I believe, are best served by a form of exposition that avoids two extremes: either a predominantly descriptive treatment of specific countries and epochs, or a propositional summary so abstract as to eliminate the flavor from the historical data without presenting enough of the substance to convince the reader. The middle course I have sought to pursue discusses broad factors that underlie ethnic identity. In the exposition, I proceed from factors that superficially appear remote from the emergence of concrete ethnic identities, yet condition these identities in persistent ways.

In chapter 2, two fundamentally different ways of life, the nomad and the sedentary, are analyzed, not because these ways are ethnic identities, but because the myths and symbols they embody—expressed, notably, in nostalgia—crucially divide nearly all subsequent identities into two groups based on incompatible principles. The territorial principle, slow to emerge, ultimately became the predominant form in Europe; the genealogical or pseudo-genealogical principle has continued to prevail in most of the Middle East. As noted earlier, any effort to compare nations that does not take into account these fundamental differences in perception is gravely flawed, no matter how many superficial resemblances, arising from recent Middle Eastern mimesis of European nationalism, can be found. The subsequent treatment of the dichotomy, Islam and Christianity (chapter 3), pursues and deepens the analysis of nomadic and sedentary ways that have so profoundly affected the civilizations founded on the two great universal religions. Here, again, the aim is not so much to explain particular ethnic identities, although the analysis goes a considerable distance in exploring the bases of Castilian and Ottoman identity, but to determine the symbolic and mythic framework within which more specifically political factors have actually produced such identities.

Chapter 4, therefore, in its analysis of the role of the city, constitutes the first exploration of the impact of a quintessential political structure. Exploration of the effect of towns upon identification requires examination of a very broad range of symbolic and attitudinal data, from the impact of architectonic features on consciousness to the unifying or centrifugal effects of different legal codes. Throughout, the emphasis is upon creation of civic identity rather than the broader social and economic aspects of urbanism treated in the great sociological studies like Max Weber's. Analysis of civic consciousness in the original, etymological sense of the expression is, therefore, a prelude to the topics discussed in chapters 5 and 6—the role of "imperial polities." At this point, the central question becomes, how could the intense consciousness of loyalty and identity established through face-to-face contact in the city-state be transferred to the larger agglomerations of cities and countryside known as empires?

Chapter 5 is devoted primarily to tracing the diverse effects of the Mesopotamian myth of the polity as a reflection of heavenly rule. Use of this myth as a vehicle for incorporating city-state loyalties in a larger framework may have constituted the earliest experiment in myth transference for political purposes. The curious reverberations of this myth in polities variously transformed by Christianity and Islam deserve close scrutiny. Chapter 6 analyzes the impact on identity of more recent and concrete centralizing features of the imperial polity, notably its bureaucracy and its socialization process. Chapter 7 prolongs, in a sense, the discussion by exploring the effects, often congruent with those of the imperial polities but sometimes opposed, of religious organizations on ethnic identity. In chapter 7, as noted earlier, I also grapple with the vexed question of what (if anything) distinguishes ethnicity from sectarian religion.

Finally, in treating the close relationship of religious organization to linguistic adherence, chapter 7 introduces the significance of language for identity in the prenationalist era. I have already suggested that language was rarely salient, and the assertion deserves detailed examination. Beyond that largely negative purpose, however, the detailed treatment of language in chapter 8 is intended to show how diverse were the paths that historical development might have taken. Only by some understanding of the complex "options" that minutely subdivided linguistic patterns afforded before the development of mass communication can the reader appreciate the influence of human intervention, of political action, on the formation of the ethnic identities that actually emerged.

Before turning to the substantive exploration, I must reemphasize the tentative nature of my formulations. Yet I feel justified in undertaking this essay by the remarks of Joseph Strayer, who recognizes that "we are all laymen in most fields of history" and that "if the historian cannot find the pattern men who are less skillful or less honest will make it for him."[22]

CHAPTER TWO

Sedentary versus Nomad:
The Emergence of Territorial Identity

Ethnicity and Way of Life

Mental attitudes, I suggested earlier, have been more enduring than material circumstances of life. In fact, only extreme ways of life appear to lead to ethnic consciousness. The Veniti, from whose name the Germanic groups derived the term "Wend" for their eastern neighbors, were probably perceived as alien not because of their Finnic speech but because of their reindeer-nomad way of life. For less extreme differences, material traits in folk culture are usually not indissolubly bound together. Consequently, it is hard to demonstrate that particular traits in material culture, or even clusters of traits, are related to ethnicity. Some writers, including André Varagnac and Marshall Hodgson, suggest that there is a fundamental similarity among traditional cultures from the Atlantic to India, or even farther.[1]

It is easier to demonstrate that useful material accomplishments diffuse readily, although slowly, without significantly affecting ethnic identities. Such forms as peasant house construction or village layouts that are intimately related to the life cycle, might plausibly become cherished marks of ethnic identity. Some latter-day nationalists have singled out such forms for idealization as, for example, the Ukrainian whitewashed adobe and thatch cottage versus the Russian timbered house. Very possibly, nationalist communication networks can transform such artifacts into symbols of identity. For most of traditional Europe and apparently for other peasant cultures, house and village forms have had surprisingly little affect impact.[2] Early ethnologists vainly endeavored to correlate Swiss ethnic divisions with house forms.[3] In the larger northern European area, boundaries between three basic house and farmyard designs cut straight across the Romance-Germanic-Slavic language boundaries, to say nothing of shifting political frontiers. Furthermore, diffusion of house types exhibits little correlation to other diffusion phenomena, notably high cultural forms, that do tend to carry implications for identity. For example, medieval farmers in France adopted the instrumentally superior German peasant house type at the very moment when German upper classes were adopting French styles.[4] Similarly, the *langue d'oïl–langue d'oc* division in France, which had significance for ecclesiastical but not political frontiers most of the time, was also the boundary between the northern European house and the "Latin" house with curved tile roof. The language boundary has shifted southward, however, whereas house forms have remained stable. In fact, the Latin house covers an entire western Mediterranean zone extending as far as Algeria.[5]

Within Algeria itself, on the other hand, a sharp division prevails between the Latin house and the terrace-roofed house common to most Arab countries. The tile roofs and dispersed village layouts recalling southern Europe persist in certain mountain areas that are now nominally Moslem but retain the Berber language. Arabicized Berbers, when sedentary, quickly adopt Arab houses, even in rainy areas where terraces are inconvenient. These houses are constructed close together in a miniature urban pattern adapted to the seclusion of women.[6] Conversely, Maronite Christian Lebanese, though Arab in language and lineage myths, lack the intense Moslem concern for sequestering women. Consequently, Maronites have turned rapidly to European-style houses.[7] More circumstantial evidence will be presented later. Even the little described above suggests that house and village forms become significant for identity only when a change is related to adoption of some more fundamental way of life.

As in the Berber case, the basic change appears to be adoption of the language and lineage identity patterns of groups like the Arabs who are proud of their nomad heritage. For a nomadic way of life to have had such impact, three complex factors have had to overcome the boundary mechanisms ordinarily maintaining sedentary groups' identities. The impact of Islam, though ambiguous as to doctrine, has been extremely important as a historical force for adoption of nomad identities; the Islamic factor will be explored in chapter 3. Antagonism between real nomads and sedentary groups attempting to maintain their identities, with each acting as the alien element by which the other defines itself, will be explored later in this chapter. When resistance is worn down, however, the sedentary peoples adopt a pseudo-nomadic genealogy as a defense mechanism, thereby completely altering their fundamental identity patterns. The third factor has been the persistent effect of nostalgia, extraordinarily difficult to change, but once altered tending to restructure a group's identity completely.

Nostalgia

Nostalgia can be defined, from the sociohistorical viewpoint, as a persistent image of a superior way of life in the distant past. It is, therefore, a kind of "collective memory" with intense affect implications.[8] As a social form, nostalgia expresses the yearning to return to a golden age, to halcyon days before corruption and equivocation permeated civilized life. Nostalgia, therefore, is—at least in Europe and the Middle East—a syndrome (I use the term in its diagnostic sense) arising from "the heavy burdens imposed by a thousand years of culture."[9] It is also an alleviating response to civilization, taken in the etymological sense to be the social context produced by urbanism. What is most interesting for my purposes is to examine the different appeals nostalgia exerts by recollection of diverse nonurban ways of life. Acting through nostalgia, an earlier life pattern conditions the attitudes of subsequent generations, not, usually, by directly producing boundary mechanisms among ethnic groups but by setting conditions in which such boundaries are perceived.

"Far from being attracted by sedentary life, the pastoral society even when cut off from the desert preserves its ideal," Robert Montagne asserts.[10] Surely this has been true of the Arabs, the most influential hot-desert pastoral people of world history, who throughout their vast migrations preserve "the memory of a lost residence," as André Miquel expresses it.[11] It is not surprising that the Arabs' religion, as Miquel also notes, has consecrated this nostalgia: "Classical Islam is dominated by the thought of a lost paradise, the deep conviction that it was perfect in its origins and that no change was justified except insofar as it conformed to the original model."[12] This orientation to the past, although not unique to Islam, constitutes one dividing line between it and Christendom. Nevertheless, there is a certain ambiguity in the Islamic position. Through its requirement of a pilgrimage to the holy places around Mecca, Islam constantly recalls to its adherents the austere grandeur of the desert.[13] The city in general, however, is the essential locus of a pious Moslem life. Consequently, urbanism can never be condemned as a seat of culture. As a result, the theme of return to a nomadic way of life always partakes of an unreal, dreamlike character. In fact, dreams and dream interpretation have occupied a prominent place in Moslem thought.[14] I agree with G. S. Kirk that there is no such thing as a collective mind, much less a collective dream. Nevertheless, vivid collective experience may be reflected in dreams or, certainly, in the conscious recollection and interpretation of them.[15] Contrasts such as "Islam-shadow-freshness" versus "sun-infidelity-fire" as "symbols suitable to the desert" appear in Moslem oneiromancy as significant indicators of pervasive cultural attitudes.[16]

The symbolic rejection of the desert is not a rejection of the nomad's way, however, for long before Islam he yearned for an earthly paradise in which luxuriant vegatation, shade, and flowing waters would abound—an oasis. The art historian Henri Saladin writes:

> The Alhambra gardens like those of Medinet ez-Zahara [near Cordova] and Morocco were a memory of the Baghdad gardens that themselves derive from the "paradise" of the Sassanid kings. The charms of gardens have always greatly appealed to Arabs. What greater happiness can these children of the desert have, indeed, after torments of heat, thirst, and excessive light and dryness, than to rest under fresh foliage to the sound of splashing water and to be able to cast their eyes on greenery?[17]

Of the four "paradises" identified in early Islamic legend, three were in Iranian cultural areas; the word itself reached the Arabs via the Persians.[18] It is significant, however, that the Arabs regarded the most famous garden, Damascus, as the earthly paradise even before Mohammed's time.[19] Not only did the Umayyad dynasty make Damascus its capital; it embellished the city with the mosque still known centuries later as the "most beautiful possession of the Moslems." This building occupies an exceptional place as a symbol of universal imperial aspirations, which are most strongly expressed in its magnificent mosaics depicting, schematically, the cities or kingdoms of the world. The central theme of the largest panel is, nevertheless, the Barada River that makes Damascus an oasis. It is shown complete with blue waters, overarching trees, and pleasure pavilions.[20]

Nostalgia was not just a folk memory among Arabs. Like most identity themes, it was systematically manipulated by elites. The remnant of the Umayyad dynasty in Spain clung to the memory of Damascus as a symbol of the vanished dominance of the Arab nobility in early Islam. The date palm, uniquely important to nomads and believed to have been made by God from clay left over after Adam's creation, is a prominent theme in the mosaics of the Damascus Great Mosque.[21] Perhaps reflecting on this lost monument, the first Umayyad ruler in Spain composed these poignant lines: "In Rosafa a palm tree just appeared to me, exiled in the land of the West far from the country where its like grew. There, I said to myself, is my image: I too live in distant exile, long separated from my children and my family. Thou grew in strange soil and like thee exile drove me far away."[22] Less exalted poets around the Baghdad Court of the Umayyads' rivals, the Abbasids, also vigorously promoted nomad symbols and ideals, rigorously adhering to pre-Islamic Arabic verse forms and Beduin language. The atmosphere of the desert, where many of the poets had never lived, pervades classic Islamic literature.[23]

In more material ways, Islamic dynasties expressed the attraction of the nomad life style, although declining to an extent after the overthrow of the Umayyads. They had built castles in the midst of hunting preserves at the edge of the Syrian desert, partly to maintain contact with auxiliary nomadic forces, but also because early Moslem rulers felt a nostalgia for great open spaces.[24] Half a millennium later the greatest Arab historian, Ibn Khaldun, who was also a leading adviser to dynasties, expressed a deep ambivalence toward camel nomads, "the most savage human beings that exist," yet the only men from whom true nobility can arise because of their group solidarity (*asabiya*) derived from their pure lineages preserved by desert conditions.[25] Such lingering "desert snobbery" was always an element of Moslem Court life, contributing through its status appeal to perpetuation of nostalgia.[26]

The persistence of nomadic life styles is indicated by the way non-Arab dynasties (mainly Turkic) descended from nomads maintained nostalgia themes. Although fundamentally similar to Arab nostalgia, the Central Asian type differed in certain significant ways from the palm tree–shadow dream of the semitropical desert. The Turkic word *yayla* connoted icy running waters and luxuriant pastures, an "image of paradise" for peoples who recalled the cold, dry, Asian steppe.[27] Even Constantinople Turks expressed such nostalgic yearnings in their frequent outings to the "Sweet Waters of Europe" and the "Sweet Waters of Asia." For the Turk or Mongol, however, the horse rather than the camel (even the two-humped Bactrian) symbolized the freedom of wide open spaces. Freshness was symbolized by the cool mountain conifer rather than the date palm. Long before his descendants became the principal secular force of Islam, Genghis Khan's nostalgia for the hunting and burial grounds of his ancestors centered on this theme:

> It is a region of sacred mountains, this *Burqan-qaldun* which Genghis Khan loved so much that he wanted his tomb to be there. It is the favored locale for legends of the nomad tradition, the great source of waters for Mongolia, whence the Selenga, the Orhon, the Tuula, the Onon, the Kerulen Rivers go their separate ways. Coniferous trees mark out dark patches; pine, fir, cedar, above all the larch, the dominating essence.[28]

Not only did the Central Asian nostalgia have roots independent of the Arabs' nostalgia; the specific tradition flourished even among Genghisids who were remote from Islam, like Kublai Khan, the ruler of China, who "was often nostalgic for nomadic life. Then he moved into the park, where at a selected point a summer palace, a cross between a Chinese kiosque and a Moslem tent (ger) was constructed of bamboo decorated with silk and a pointed rain-proof roof." The kiosque was surrounded by specially planted steppe grasses supporting game hunted with falcons and chee-tahs.[29] It seems safe to conclude, therefore, that important as the legitimiz-ing effect of Islam has been, nomadic nostalgia as a persistent identifying myth can exist independently.

The contrasting nostalgia myth is the sedentary's. He dreams not of the vast spaces but of the security and tranquility of his little plot of earth. Though the subject transcends the scope of this work, it is possible that such contrast is sharpest between nomads and ethnic groups like the Chi-nese, whose cultural tradition (for example, the ruler as "first plowman") is unambiguously sedentary. Both the Jewish heritage of Christianity and the pastoral background of early Indo-Europeans have influenced Europeans' nostalgia in ways rather different from the complications introduced in Moslem nostalgia by Islamic insistence on the city as the focus of religion. At any rate, the difference between the Islamic and the Christian nostalgia myths, as they had evolved by the Middle Ages, was so enormous that their impact on ethnic identities was profoundly divergent.

Numerous students of Old Testament history have noticed the tension between a nomadic ideal and a desire for settled, agricultural life in a "land of milk and honey."[30] The tension theory was strongly yet circumstantially advanced by John W. Flight, who noted how seventh- and eighth-century B.C. prophets expressed nostalgia for the heritage of the desert (Sinai and earlier) as the pure, simple stage of religion.[31] They even prayed that Yahweh would reduce the land "to a condition which will permit only a nomadic existence similar to that of Israel's beginnings," in contrast to the sedentary arts of the "cursed race of Cain."[32] A more elaborate interpreta-tion by a Swedish scholar regards the numinous awe accorded Yahweh as the only means by which the Beduin's pride could be curbed and the heterogeneous Israelites compelled to unite in a sedentary life just as, three millennia later, Wahhabi Moslem puritans united and tamed the Arabian tribes.[33] At the same time, Samuel Nyström recognizes that the complicated background of the Israelites made sedentarization feasible. In contrast to most Arabs they were seminomads rather than *grands nomades* who used dromedaries for ceaseless desert migrations. For the semi-nomad, migrations on foot or donkeyback at the edge of the desert in the company of herds of sheep and goats constituted a much more limited variety of pastoral life. As will appear later, the distinction had critically significant implications. Here it is important to emphasize that pastoral images are far more easily reconciled with sedentary nostalgia than are nomadic memories. The olive tree, the grapevine, even grain fields, become more prominent symbols for the limited pastoralist than the oasis date palm. Because his flocks cannot survive in real desert, the pastoral or *petit nomade* is much more circumscribed in his cherished pastures of hills and valleys (which appear so often in the Old Testament). Nostalgia for the freedom of desert and steppe, if it really survived among the Israelites after Sinai, was almost as incompatible with pastoralism as with agriculture.[34]

Hesiod, the first poet of halcyon days, celebrated more realistically the plowman predominant in the Greece of his time. Shepherds had been replaced by yeoman plowmen in Roman life in Etruscan times.[35] Nevertheless, well before the Christian era the image of the shepherd became almost as recurrent in the nostalgia of Greek and Roman as in the Old Testament. The European pastoral idyll does not even reflect the semiarid hills of the Sixty-fifth Psalm. It simply portrays an occupation, in an agricultural country, imagined to be more attractive than plowing. Moreover, except in Spain (where, as in Persia, the idyll features a cowherd) the shepherd is never mounted. Pastoralism, therefore, is compatible with the Greeks' ideal of a bounded, ordered space and their belief that they were the autochthonous population—a myth that would be meaningless, at least if focused on narrow regions, to the nomad.[36] As a French expert on the Arab world remarks, "Western Christianity is rooted profoundly in the soil. It is sufficient to think of what the popular imagination has made of the nativity: the Savior in a crib on the straw between the ass and the ox, at one side the manure pile and the plow. Isn't this the typical picture of a religion of peasants?"[37]

In other words, European Christians' nostalgia symbolism, within a millennium, has transformed the seminomadic imagery of their Christian origins into a scene from their own ancestral habitat. It would be hard to find a more striking example of the persistence of themes from a way of life profoundly permeating a collective's memory.

Just as Europeans transformed the Nativity into a peasant's idyll, they changed the Old Testament desert "wilderness" into a place of swamps and forests familiar to the sedentary culture. The symbolic dichotomy of "wilderness" as a fearful place yet one of purification was retained; but, because forest and swamp could be cleared and converted to sedentary use, its "frontier" characteristics constituted a challenge to expansion rather than, as did the desert, a constant source of devastating incursions.[38] There are other examples almost as striking. For Christians the Garden of Eden was an ambiguous symbol. To be sure, it had been an earthly paradise, as it remained for the Moslems; but, because it was unattainable by a fallen man, he was in danger of being lured by a counterfeit. Hence Torquato Tasso, at the start of the modern era, rejected a narcissistic, passive paradise as pagan, preferring the city as active grace,[39] a step

Moslem poetry apparently never took despite the central role of the real city for its religion. On the other hand, nostalgia for the simple peasant life could easily become the dominant symbol of a fin-de-siècle European elite that had lost confidence in its ability to rule.

From Sedentary Nostalgia to Territorial Attachment

Considered purely as a recurrent emotion, nostalgia is more significant for class behavior or for literary expression than for group identity.[40] If, however, one believes that collective attitudes expressed in myth and symbol are highly important for identity, the persistent strength of nostalgias with different symbolic content cannot be dismissed. The affect produced by yearning for the simplified life of the sedentary peasant, in particular, appears to have exerted a strong influence on the gradual development of territorial identity in Europe. Anthropologists such as Claude Lévi-Strauss have discovered that spatial configuration is sometimes, though by no means always, "almost a projective representation of the social structure."[41] In the larger, far more complex cultures examined in this work, one would expect to find a parallel relationship to that Lévi-Strauss discovered in small "primitive" societies, but mediated by more complex mechanisms such as nostalgia. The following remarks on territoriality, therefore, are only preliminary. The subject will recur in the consideration of spatial properties of varying types of cities, in the impact of religious organizations, in the informal boundaries of languages, and above all in the activity of imperial systems.

The origins of attachment to specific territories reach far back into the Greek and Roman past, even into the sedentary societies of the ancient Middle East. Terms for "boundary," according to Giorgio Buccellati, indicated the presence of a territorial concept. "Territory," in the sense of a district of a Mesopotamian city, was part of the conceptual framework, along with "government" and "people."[42] As will appear more circumstantially in the discussion of the *polis* in chapter 4, Greek notions of a bounded, ordered space were essentially territorial. The Roman world carried this attachment several steps further. As a French writer emphasizes, "Nothing was more anchored than Latin civilization: as peasants, city dwellers, the Romans and the majority of the conquered peoples thought in terms of boundaries, of returns of fixed amounts. The ground was crisscrossed by boundaries which made one forget the horizon. The labor of centuries drew riches from it, perishable but indefinitely renewable. Latin juridical work was oriented toward the defense of the soil and property."[43]

Roman concern for territoriality left a lasting imprint on West Europe. The effect on Byzantium may have been as great, but eventually was largely dissipated by the Moslem conquest. At an early formative stage of Western society, Latin linguistic development demonstrated a sharp shift from genealogical or tribal designations to territorial concepts. A prominent school of comparative linguistics considers these changes to have accentuated a general Indo-European trend. If that is the case, territorial concepts transmitted by Latin had a strong reinforcing effect on tendencies indigenous to the predominant element of West European population. According to Benveniste,

> The vocabulary reflects this great process of transformation: like *dómos*, the term *oîkos* henceforth becomes the term for habitation. . . .
> We are observing the abolition of the Indo-European social structure and the advance of new terms. The old genealogical names become emptied of their institutional and social meanings in order to become a nomenclature of territorial divisions. . . . Latin is [Indo-European] through its fidelity to old usages, even when its vocabulary conceals new realities; Greek, conversely, is [Indo-European] through the persistence of the primitive organizing model beneath a new series of terms.[44]

Later, Romans, as practical administrators, employed territorial concepts. In a sense, the Roman empire was a vast league of city-states. Rome took upon herself the obligation of fixing precise frontiers among what might otherwise have remained antagonistic units. When *poleis* disputed, the emperor dispatched a central official to investigate the controversial borders on the ground, determine ownership of parcels of land, and make an authoritative ruling.[45] Only in one intractable case did the Romans ultimately recognize a nonterritorial authority. An "ethnarch" chosen from Herod's descendants, the Hillel family, was authorized to appoint officials and act as supreme judge for the Jewish diaspora.[46]

A necessary, though not a sufficient, condition for Roman reliance on territorial division was compact settlement. In earlier eras of the ancient world, as in the Middle Ages, tacitly accepted frontiers were usually sparsely inhabited zones—desert, mountain, swamp, forest. Indeed, such zones were valued as *glacis* protecting against sudden incursions. Apart from the physical difficulty of crossing the zones, enemies with primitive logistical systems could hardly support a considerable force traversing such wastelands.[47] Tacitus noticed that Germanic villages were surrounded by considerable space, whereas Roman villages were contiguous.[48] Nevertheless, the Romans, starting in Italy and extending the system to Gaul, retained old native divisions which the Gauls had sometimes delineated by stone frontier markers. Terming the small division *pagus*, the Romans consolidated it and assigned precise frontiers to it. The city-state (*civitas*) division was superimposed on several *pagi* as a higher administrative level.[49]

Retention of preexisting ethnic ("tribal") units as embryonic territorial attachments turned out to be a critically important reinforcing mechanism. When the Roman empire collapsed, its larger territorial designations retained considerable significance for the successor polities, which based some of their claims on such Roman administrative divisions as Hispania, Gallia, and Italia. Even when these dimly remembered provinces had constituted obvious geographical units, as did the Iberian and the Italian peninsulas, however, the dynamics of polity formation in circumstances of population upheaval and diminished technical and economic capacities produced numerous deviations from the Roman divisions. The complex political reality will be discussed in chapter 5. Here it is essential to emphasize that the coincidence of many factors was indispensable for the development of territorial states. These factors included legitimizing myths and the spread of standard linguistic patterns from administrative centers. The activity of the autonomous church organization, which retained the classic provincial names in its administrative practice, was highly significant. In the thirteenth century, papal tax collectors, each with a strictly defined territory, were major agents of resource mobilization.[50] Not the least of the factors producing territorial polities was the memory of Roman and pre-Roman territorial divisions at the local level.

The persistence of local knowledge of Roman diocesan and *pagi* frontiers has been demonstrated, at least for France, by geographers. Bishops never wholly abandoned the effort to endow these memories with concrete administrative significance.[51] In the near-chaotic conditions of the Germanic invasions and perhaps even more after the collapse of Charlemagne's empire, such efforts were rarely successful. Precisely because frontiers had followed preexisting tribal divisions, they were usually located in natural wastelands. The diminution of population, cultivation, and communications—the retrogression of sedentarization—led such zones to revert to wilderness. During periods of insecurity and uncontrolled rivalry, local warlords once again utilized them as *glacis*.

The role of feudalism in this development is frequently misunderstood. In the core areas of West Europe—France, the Low Countries, and the Rhineland—its gradual consolidation during the eleventh century probably contributed to political stability rather than fragmentation. Because the consolidation of feudalism coincided with intensified agricultural activity, the separate impact on territoriality is hard to determine. For the first time, between 1250 and 1350, a "filled-up-world," to use Pierre Chaunu's phrase, with a population of forty or more per square kilometer emerged in the rich agricultural lands between the Loire and the Scheldt. The peasant always confronted visual evidence of neighbors in the form of other villages' church steeples. As early as the ninth century, every person was for the first time assigned to a specific parish; even attendance at sermons in neighboring parishes was usually forbidden. Nearly all important aspects of life became subjects of ecclesiastical concern within a closely delimited territorial unit in place of the previous lax system. In 895 a decree for the Frank domains required at least five miles (a good visual interval) between an existing parish church and a newly founded one.[52] Consciousness of parochial distinction became a persistent influence on French politics, often expressed as *patriotisme de clocher*, but during the past century more seriously reflected in struggles of lay versus religious schoolmasters. For the feudal period, the impact of this parochialization was unambiguous: each village fief represented a valuable property whose exact extent was, therefore, a matter of material interest. Consequently, as the land filled up, old stone frontier markers were found or new ones were carefully emplaced. Even between somewhat larger units, frontier markers became significant by the fifteenth century, for example, the pillars inscribed in Latin, French, and German that delimited Liège and Brabant.[53] At the village level the definitive, continuous line installed by the Romans on the ground had recovered dominance over the ancient zonal frontier.

Confusion concerning the role of feudalism arises partly from the fact that compact, well-defined villages did not correspond to contiguous territories at the polity level. The nature of feudalism included recognition of territory as a personal possession conveying important political rights, notably legal jurisdiction. It was possible—indeed, it was the rule—for a feudal lord at any level to hold noncontiguous fiefs. As a result, West European polities tended to dissolve into an immensely complicated mosaic of tiny units. On occasion, serfs, like present-day researchers, were confused about the allegiance of a given village; but confusion concerning the adherence of a given strip of farmland to a specific village was very rare.

A town or a village could depend jointly on two or more lords. The lord in turn could hold fiefs in several regions, although powerful rulers strove to overcome such fragmentation. As early as 1244 the French king required his vassals to give up either their fiefs in England or those in France. But nobles holding fiefs in both France and the Holy Roman empire, although no longer required to give personal service to their liege lords, persisted into the eighteenth century.[54] As Marc Bloch points out, however, there is no known case of a territorial unit (village or town) that was

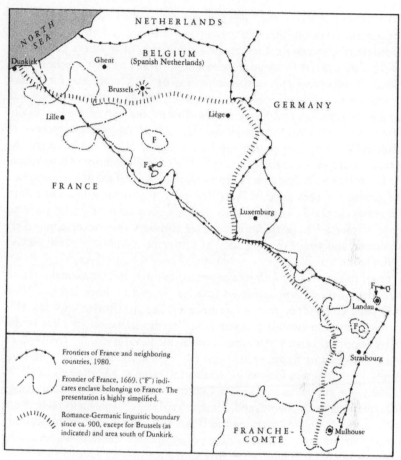

MAP 1. Northern Frontiers of France

subject both to France and to the empire. As a result, Bloch concludes, "the kingdoms . . . were separated by what might legitimately be called frontiers."[55]

Nelly Girard d'Albissin has demonstrated in impressively detailed fashion that the state frontier was difficult to delineate on a map as late as the seventeenth century, although in the north of France the frontier was, with a few exceptions, continuous. Even there it twisted and turned like an American political gerrymander and for much the same reasons. Local interests found enclaves and sinuosities convenient for evading customs duties; statesmen found in ambiguities of fief allegiance useful openings for extending claims backed by superior force. At the same time, Girard

d'Albissin—like the French geographers referred to above—rejects the
conventional wisdom that "'in former periods [that is, before the French
Revolution] concern for the precise delimitation of frontiers did not exist.'"[56] The process of frontier delineation, thanks partly to technical advances in surveying and cartography, was basically complete for France
by the early eighteenth century; moreover, significant social forces had
worked toward this end for centuries. Toward the end of the process of
delineation, however, prominent figures, such as Vauban, in his advice to
Louis XIV "always to preach the squaring, not of the circle but of the
terrain," were very conscious actors.[57] The crucially important conclusion,
for the moment, is that a mutually reinforcing web of sentiments attached
the peasants in core areas of West Europe to well-defined locales or *pays*.
Sedentary nostalgia symbols and, perhaps, Romance linguistic patterns
were reinforced by a tradition of local frontiers that never completely
dissipated and was revived as soon as settlement conditions made precise
delimitation feasible.

From the core area, with its economic, cultural, and occasional political
ascendancy, the concept of fixed frontiers spread to other areas of West
European civilization. As a contemporary Czech historian explains, this
development significantly strengthened "'territorialization' [in place of the
older "personal relationship state"] of the medieval state. . . . *Terra—land*
—zem(lja) became frequent technical concepts in the ninth and tenth centuries . . . with praise for specific territories, often as a 'Promised Land'."[58]
Usually the diffusion was across Central Europe, when areas of stable
settlement gradually converged, often toward the center of natural barriers
such as the mountains rimming the Bohemian plateau. For example, converging streams of colonists—it happened, though the fact was relatively
unimportant to contemporaries, that both streams were German-speaking
—from the two Slavic-ruled principalities of Bohemia and Silesia met near
the crests of the Sudeten Mountains. As each colonizing village established
its cultivated area by clearing forests, the stream of settlement pushed a
few miles farther until the zone frontier was replaced by a line when the
villagers encountered areas already cleared by the colonists coming from
the other side of the mountains. Human efforts, that is, political power relations, were often decisive in determining the frontier at the local level.[59]
On the whole, the process appears to have been remarkably peaceful,
perhaps because after 1400 such continuous line frontiers had become, on
the West European model, the normal expectation. Bohemia did, indeed,
become the first large territorial polity within the Holy Roman empire;
even in the thirteenth century its rulers consciously manipulated its frontiers for political advantage.

Three qualifications are in order. First, the notion of rule over persons or clans, as discussed below, remained stronger in Central Europe than in West Europe. Second, the concept of a fixed frontier at times exhibited precocious power, even in thinly settled areas. For example, in 1374, as the result of arbitration, the frontier of the diocese of Ermland (in Prussia) was surveyed in a seventy-eight kilometer straight line across frozen lakes and open terrain "in a completely modern, American style."[60] Third, a similar development occurred in fifteenth-century Muscovy without discernible imitation of the West. Alexandre Eck notes that, in the fourteenth century, "the territory was generally vast and very sparsely populated. It is highly important to distinguish sharply the personal relations between prince and populations from territorial real-estate relationships," the affair of the landed proprietor.[61] "All these causes combined prevented the territory of a principality from being contiguous; it was characterized by numerous enclaves which interfered with the prince's exercise of authority, diminished the prince's revenue, and greatly complicated the economic and administrative organization of the territory," Eck continues.[62] The clear interest of the prince in eliminating such enclaves led him to forbid his *boyars* (noble landowners) to transfer their holdings to other princes' protection, especially when the latter ruled principalities bordering on his own. Though the *boyars* resisted, the Muscovy Tsar Ivan III was able, by 1504, to stop their defection while carefully maintaining his own practice of "extending tentacles of possessions" into others' principalities.[63] It would appear, therefore, that at the large territorial unit level Russian practices, arising from parallel circumstances affecting sedentary rule, were at least as advanced as those of Western polities. To be sure, the peculiar circumstances of the nomad frontier led to a Russian imperial polity remarkably heterogeneous in ethnic composition. Ever since their pattern of settlement was sufficiently complete, the core Russian lands, on the other hand, have been exceptionally homogeneous in linguistic patterns as well as in their tendency toward continuous line frontiers.

Stamm and Tribe

The severe disruption during the early Middle Ages of the West European trend toward stable sedentary settlement patterns, that is, toward territorialization, is often ascribed to the "tribal" lineage concepts of the Germanic invaders. My explanation has stressed, instead, disruption of communications, recession of cultivated areas, and fragmentation of authority. It is true, however, that the German myth of descent exerted a strong influence on nobles' identity.[64] Consequently, a consideration of what are often called "tribes" and the impact of imputed blood relationships upon an essentially sedentary population is important.

If any word has had a more mischievous impact than "tribe," it is the German term "*Stamm*." Despite a century of scholarly refutations, many educated Germans believe in a continuity between the regional dialect groups they distinguish today and the bands that carried out the invasions, or even the "tribes" Tacitus described. Indeed, the rediscovery in 1455 of Tacitus's *Germania* played some part in stimulating early modern German national consciousness.[65] Equation of *Stamm* (literally "branch," hence "breed" or "stock") to "tribe" brings German popular opinion in line with a widespread misconception that "tribes" are well-defined, persistent ethnic identities, usually held together by biological ties. The first step toward understanding the complicated evolution of European ethnic identity after A.D. 400 is to dispel such notions.

Even the superficial observer of the "barbarian" invasions of the Roman empire (which nineteenth-century German historians termed "wandering of the peoples") is perplexed to see vast hordes strong enough to overwhelm Roman armies appear suddenly, make their *Stamm* name a byword, and then, after a single defeat, disappear altogether or leave incredibly insignificant residues. Many ingenious theories have been advanced, since the days of the early Christian writer Jordanes, to explain such "catastrophes." The theories range from a just punishment of God to a sullen return of the hordes to the "*vagina gentium*" somewhere in Scandinavia. In fact, a simple explanation, adumbrated a century ago but admirably set forth by the German anthropological historian Reinhard Wenskus, clears up the confusion.[66] Only a small nucleus of warriors and their immediate families were really attached to a *Stamm* name, which in turn usually derived from a single leader and his descendants. Often an individual, skilled and lucky in fighting, decided to break with an older *Stamm* leader. His prowess enabled him to attract a new nucleus of warriors (Latin *comitatus*, German *Gefolgschaft*, Slavic *druzhina*). If his cause prospered, this nucleus was joined by masses of uprooted, desperate men; sometimes they joined as extended families, but among Germanic and other Indo-European elements adherence to a war band was often individual.[67] Frequently the original *comitatus* members became the nobility.

Similarity in language and customs were supplementary attractions, but closely related patterns of warfare were probably more significant in distinguishing groups. The East Germanic war bands moved in cumbersome wagon trains and preferred heavily armed cataphract warriors to light steppe cavalry. They used the lance and sword in close combat instead of the archer's hit-and-run tactic of Turkic steppe warfare.[68] On the open steppe the East Germanic methods were apparently inferior, as the Goths' flight from the area north of the Black Sea when Turkic Huns advanced suggests. Cataphract warfare was apparently better suited than steppe cavalry to European conditions including broken terrain and plentiful water; yet the mounted, heavily armored East Germanic warriors could carry out rapid, decisive strokes better than West Germanic warriors, still predominantly on foot. Most Gothic recruits came from other East Germanic groups, but successful conquest agglomerations drew on very diverse sources. Thus the Visigoth leader Alaric was joined in 408 as he approached Rome by swarms of fugitive slaves who must have been very heterogeneous in origin.[69] The Ostrogoths also recruited numerous escaped slaves. Three centuries later, the West Germanic Lombards also recruited heterogeneous elements. Still later, the Slavic Croats and Serbs absorbed undifferentiated elements in Bosnia, according to whether they chose to adhere to Western or to Eastern Christianity.[70] In a very general way, therefore, one can say that all war bands were mixed and tended to become more heterogeneous the more successful they were.

Apart from a stronger tendency to adhere to Turkic (Hun, then Avar) dynastic nuclei, Slavic group organization closely resembled the Germanic *Stamm*. Probably the Celts' and other Indo-Europeans' organizations had been similar at one time. Judging from their ability to repopulate the Balkans, Slavs were apparently more numerous than the Germanic groups. A generous estimate of the number of Ostrogoths is 250,000. Some East Germanic groups, such as the Vandals, numbered only a few tens of thousands even after considerable recruitment among non-Germanic groups. Those who are astonished at East Germanic prowess in encounters with Romans overlook the fact that by A.D. 409 4,000 men constituted a notable Roman expeditionary force. The most successful West Germanic element, the Franks, may have numbered only 60,000, and the Lombards had about 20,000 warriors plus their families.[71]

The initial impulse to *Stamm* formation was thirst for adventure, glory, booty, or even subsistence. As he became successful, however, the leader elaborated and inculcated an identity myth. This myth rarely claimed autochthonous status for the emerging identity group; instead, it ascribed a distant, frequently fabulous origin. This genealogical myth, which essentially was the myth of the *Stamm* dynasty alone, also claimed remote, improbable, but glorious ancestors, such as the Trojans, Magog of the Old Testament, or Germanic divinities. These claims were symbolized by the dragon flag—nearly universal among Germanic groups; by infant skull deformation, borrowed by Bavarians and Burgundians from the Huns;[72] and, above all, by the *Stamm* name with its connotations of descent from a fabulous ancestor. Such descent conveyed the magic of superior blood, which equipped the bearer to rule (*Geblütsrecht*).[73] This superiority was reserved to members of the dynasty; but the prestige of the *Stamm* name was accorded to all recruits. Elite elements competed for a prestigious *Stamm* name. Some dynastic cores (for example, Vandals and Lombards) took special precautions to leave a rear-guard nucleus of the dynasty and its *Stamm* followers in a secure base area before setting out on distant conquest to ensure perpetuation of the *Stamm* if the adventure failed.[74] Occasionally, loss of a single symbolic attribute, such as the Lombards' long beards (the origin of their *Stamm* name), undermined identity, as the Franks doubtless foresaw in compelling their removal.[75] More generally, the force of the myth is evidenced by the fact that third-century Romans reluctantly decided to keep recruits from a single *Stamm* together to enhance morale, despite the obvious risk of concerted rebellion.[76] It is no coincidence that the last real function of *Stämme* organizations (in the ninth-century Holy Roman empire) was also to serve as recruiting agencies.[77] In effect the *Stamm* myth and symbols were always complex devices for recruiting and socializing divergent elements, manipulated (often unconsciously) by the leaders. Generally, however, the complex was very unstable, depending on the leaders' skill and prestige. When these attributes were eliminated by defeat or demonstrative incapacity, the elements of the conquest agglomeration rapidly sought new attachments. As a result, uninstructed observers perceived large *Stamm* formations appearing and disappearing as if by magic.

A large majority of *Stamm* characteristics also apply to nomadic "tribes," and some apply to "tribes" everywhere. Rapid conquest is not always a feasible attraction, but other political initiatives have produced remarkably similar agglomerations.[78] The differences in fighting methods between *Stamm* and Eurasian steppe nomads were noted above. From the sociological point of view, reliance of Turkic, Magyar, and Mongol nomads on archery made recruitment of heterogeneous elements who were accorded full membership difficult because shooting from horseback was a skill that required years of practice. Their clan organization also required adherence by groups rather than by small families or individuals. Arabs, who generally did not use the bow, Turks, and Mongols all tended during periods of defeat to break up into clans. Some clan members were not related by blood, but clans contained sufficiently large nuclei of related members to permit more stable integration than was feasible for the *Stamm*. Among the Turks the clans were at least as ready as individual Germanic warriors were to attach themselves to successful dynasties. Immense numbers of Turks adhered to Attila's Huns, to Genghis Khan's Mongol dynasty, to the pseudo-Genghisid Tamerlane, and to other spectacular leaders, facilely adopting their dynastic myths.[79]

As was the case for Germanic groups, only the dynasty has a real genealogy. The dynastic cores of *Stämme* were more resistant to assimilation, however, and hence tended to constitute more or less independent kingdoms in contrast to the sprawling steppe empires.[80] Residual identity for nomadic clans was ensured, however, by retention of group totems (among Turks and Finns) even when an overpowering dynasty's genealogical myth was accepted. The Turkic totem was the wolf, still retained by the Turkmens, whose identity is remarkably persistent. Kazakh Turks, whose totem, the camel, is apparently the result of Arab influence, seem to be a more recent alignment.[81] Mongols had no totems. The Genghisid "Golden Clan," however, jealously guarded the myth that it was "born of the sky," that is, that the primeval mother was impregnated by a sunbeam. So potent was the Genghisid myth that, two centuries after its origin, Tamerlane consecrated his extremely shaky claim to a share in it by dedicating the principal mosque of his capital, Samarkand, to his wife, Bibi Khanun, a true Genghisid. Tamerlane's own sarcophagus is inscribed with the sunbeam genealogy.[82]

Far more important as distinguishing characteristics were Germanic traits that facilitated sedentarization.[83] The *Stamm* of Tacitus's day had a fixed locale. One recent historian even asserts that "district rule was thus known to the Germanics in their earliest period . . . land and people [with a *Burg*, fortress, as center of territorial rule] belonged together."[84] Despite their generations of acculturation to steppe patterns, the Goths were regarded by contemporaries and subsequent investigators as eager to find a place to settle. Their military operations facilitated this quest because relatively slow wagon movement meant that they could take their families with them and cataphract warfare, in contrast to archery, did not require lifelong specialization. West Germanic groups were even more concerned with securing specific agricultural territories. In the centuries before the invasions, Germanic groups had frequently associated their considerable agricultural activity on the steppe with cattle breeding. Although as warriors East Germanic conquest agglomeration members were reluctant to undertake agricultural labor themselves, their territorial occupation (*Landnahme*) was accompanied by *Leutenahme* (domination of subject populations) to provide an agricultural work force, often Celtic or Slavic in origin.[85] Whereas the prime nomadic concern was for pastures—even when securing them meant destruction of longer-range sources of wealth—Germanic conquerors were anxious to find a realm with sufficient food surplus to support their relatively modest numbers permanently.[86] Consequently, whereas nomads were a constant menace to the very survival of the populations they dominated, the Germanic invaders found it fairly easy to reach an accommodation with the demoralized Roman inhabitants.

In this process of accommodation one group, the Franks, were spectacularly successful, with incalculable consequences for subsequent history. If combined, the most sweeping critiques of the Frank claims virtually eliminate their assertion of ancient origin and continuity. Apparently, the name *"Franci"* (proud, bold) originated with third-century Romans who applied it to all freemen settled in the Rhine-Moselle area and employed as mercenaries.[87] Undoubtedly, most of these mercenaries were of Germanic origin—even the peasant populations of the region became increasingly Germanic in language during the third and fourth centuries. Some authorities believe that this heterogeneous Germanic population may have retained vestigial connections with earlier *Stämme* like the Chatti. High officers called "Franks" had been prominent in the Roman armies throughout the late fourth century.[88] Consequently, it is not astonishing to find the dynasty known as "Merovingian" and its successor "Carolingians" originating as officers of Roman auxiliary forces. The Merovingian family and its *comitatus* carried out a coup d'état in the confused circumstances of northern Gaul in the mid-fifth century. As Karl Werner cogently points out, only after assuming nominal authority well within the old Roman frontier did the Merovingians extend their power into areas across the Rhine. He not only regards the Merovingians as military usurpers, but believes that they were used by the surviving Roman nobility, in a region notorious for centrifugal tendencies, to provide a military executive force and a "front" for the nobles' particularistic rule. It was an age when Germanic styles were in fashion; consequently, the Franks were, perhaps, preferable for these purposes to the short-lived military dictatorship of the Roman officer Syagrius.[89]

About 496, the Merovingian dynasty and its entourage converted to Catholic Christianity, evidently as part of a competition with the far more prestigious Arian ruler of Italy, the Ostrogoth Theodoric.[90] The Franks were the first major Germanic adherents to Catholicism; their conversion fits in with the Werner thesis that their nobility below the dynastic level consisted overwhelmingly of Romano-Gallic aristocrats, not Germanic *Stamm* leaders. The rapid amalgamation of families through intermarriage within the same faith makes it almost impossible to test this hypothesis, however. Children of such mixed marriages and even some of wholly Roman parentage took prestigious Germanic names and adopted the Latin or Romance speech and culture of their mothers.[91] At any rate, it appears certain that the ecclesiastical sees and most important civil offices remained in Roman hands throughout the Merovingian period. The Franks, in contrast to other Germanic groups, readily accepted monasticism, assimilating the monks to *Stamm* categories as the "band [*Gefolgschaft*] of Christ."[92] Consequently, to speak of an invasion, much less a seminomadic invasion of northern Gaul, is very misleading; Werner goes so far as to reject the term "conquest." Even if the Werner view is somewhat exaggerated, the slight, episodic physical impact of the Frank coup appears to be well substantiated. Nothing, therefore, better indicates the legitimizing power of myth than the immense prestige acquired by the Frank dynasties. The fundamental significance of the Carolingian version of the myth was its combination with enhanced papal authority to legitimize a novel political structure for West Europe, as discussed in chapter 5. It is important to clarify the way even the Frank myth, from its inception, reduced the disruption of Roman territorial identity that Germanic rule usually entailed.

The emergence of the Frank dynasties in Roman territory, their continued preference for residences within this territory, their amalgamation with landowners entrenched in Gallic possessions, and their accommodation to the ecclesiastical territorial framework all minimized disruption. The Franks promoted continuity in two more complicated ways. The first was in the crucial field of legal relations. Germanic dynasties and their entourages generally perpetuated personal law, that is, law applying to individuals by their origins rather than because of their residence in a specific territory. This Germanic practice did not represent a sharp departure from custom, for a vulgarized Roman "law of provincial practice" reflected differentiation of Roman provincial elites. Legal particularism emerged in much the same incremental manner that Latin degenerated into provincial Romance languages as centralized authority and classic styles declined.[93] The *coutumes* of Normandy and the Paris region, basically derived from Salic law, provided the fundamental content for a unified territorial law for the core western Frank region, by then known as Francia. But in codifying this law, the Francian authorities followed Roman forms and principles, as did the Visigoths. Ultimately, nearly all West Europe became pervaded by Germanic common law. Salic influences were dominant everywhere (including English common law) except in Spain and in the Lombard content of the *Glossator* school of Bologna.[94] Through the latter channel, Germanic concepts entered the revived Roman law, which later became the standard for most of Europe.

The second, indirect way in which Frank rule promoted continuity of territorial identity was in adaptation of lineage principles. In contrast to legal codification, revision of European aristocratic genealogical principles occurred spontaneously, although it eventually had at least as strong an impact on European identities. Whereas concern for lineage had already diminished among Romans,[95] for Germanic groups the only really significant lineage, as discussed earlier, was the dynasty's.

The peculiar origins of the Merovingian dynasty take on an extraordinary significance in this connection. If, as appears likely, the Merovingians were parvenus even by Germanic standards, they had few stable genealogical patterns to transmit to their entourage nobles. Nobles such as the Carolingian family, who usurped the Merovingian crown in the late seventh century, could rarely trace their lineages for more than a few generations. Nearly half of the high nobles under Carolingian rule were related by blood or marriage to the dynasty, however, including a large majority of those who identified themselves as "Frank." Consequently, it was important for the new rulers not only to continue the Merovingian tradition of identifying the Frank *Stamm* with the ruling dynasty, but to ascribe a specific, sacral locale to both.[96]

The high Carolingian nobility that effectively controlled the empire undoubtedly had extended family attachments; but these were far from stable or regular. Down to the end of the ninth century, descent in the female as well as in the male line was important, as had been the case among earlier Germanic families. These family "clans" bore little resemblance to those of nomadic or "tribal" societies, where genealogical relationships are decisive. Instead, the Frank "clan" derived its prestige almost entirely from its relationship to the dynasty.[97] Probably the family relations themselves were partly artificial, including (as was undoubtedly the case later) persons who preferred to live and work together.[98] In general, ninth- and tenth-century nobles exhibited little concern for lineages. In this respect, the late Carolingian aristocratic families resembled nobles derived from the voluntary association of the *comitatus* in such other European areas as medieval Rus. Neither aristocrat nor commoner had a surname, and Christian names were derived from the maternal line.[99] Higher nobles, dispatched by the ruler throughout the Frank empire, acquired chains of estates across it. Consequently, the noble family of the eighth or early ninth century was no more identifiable by specific estate location than by genealogy. By the tenth century, however, the breakdown of order and communications compelled each family to concentrate in a relatively limited region.

A fundamental alteration in noble identification began, as the Freiburg school of medievalists has demonstrated, around the turn of the millennium. Adoption of the agnatic principle meant that genealogies derived from the male line were stabilized. For some great houses (such as the Welfs) the process was well under way by the eleventh century; for other noble families it was still incomplete in the thirteenth century. By the latter time, paradoxically, the efforts of some great houses, mainly French, to claim Carolingian descent through the maternal line had led to the revival of the cognatic principle (the male Carolingian line had died out in the tenth century, but little effort was apparent for over a century to claim the nimbus of the famous dynasty).[100]

What counted most was the relation of the family to a fixed geographical locale. Usually this point was one of several fortified estates belonging to a family; near it, frequently, the family had endowed a monastery, thereby securing a permanent family burial place. Henceforward the male line was identified with that estate by name and physically by solemn interment. A recent study describes how this process occurred in a prominent German family.

> While their [Welf] power expanded they were tied to a specific place, thereby securing an objective and subjective safeguard, for their local attachment also influenced their consciousness of family. Whereas it had formerly been concentrated on a remote ancestor, this consciousness now became focused on the ancestral graves. Consequently, family consciousness transcended memory. It was present in a visible spot; it was localized. As a result, their origins, which up to that time could be determined only through the ancestor, were finally determined in relation to this specific locale.[101]

Nobles were neither buried like peasants in a parish churchyard nor were their funerals conducted by parish priests. But the nobles depended on a stable territorial locus just as much as (for reasons discussed earlier) the peasants did. Consequently, aristocrats assumed all the associations with a landscape and a rural way of life that, however impractical it may have become, provided the basis for the nostalgia that pervaded their distant descendants among the absolutist Court nobility.

The immense prestige of the aristocracies of the two great successor polities of the Carolingian empire—the French kingdom and the Holy Roman empire—spread the practices of agnatic descent and fixed country seats to the entire West European nobility. This was true of Castile, despite the frontier characteristics of the polity that gave its nobility a peculiar coloration. Another *Antemurale* aristocracy, the Polish, even adopted its genealogical appelation (*szlachta*) from the German word for "family line" (*Geschlecht*).[102] Norman aristocracies in England, Ireland, Sicily, and the Near Eastern crusader kingdoms were, because their lineages were closely scrutinized, perhaps even more "typical" than the "organic" developments of aristocratic orders in France and Germany.

What, then, of the *Stamm* itself? As might be expected, in Francia (northern Gaul) *Stamm* considerations, if one dismisses a confused attachment to the dynasty persisting in the "Frank" designation, were hardly present. There were vestigal attachments to the Visigoths in southern Gaul, to the Burgundians in east-central Gaul, and even to the Lombards in northern and central Italy, for these had been real Germanic *Stämme*, insofar as the term has any meaning. Because the Frank dynasty was dominant in power and prestige and used its authority to assign key posts in other *Stamm* areas to entourage nobles (that is, "Franks"), however, adherence to the other *Stämme* ensured little or no advantage over Romance identification.[103] Consequently, these *Stämme*, like the personal law they once had cherished, rapidly declined.

The situation was somewhat different in the Frank dominions east of the Rhine. Whatever their origins or composition, the Alemanni, the Bavarians, the recently subdued Saxons, perhaps even the central German *Stamm* identified as "East Franks" (Austrasians) had distinct identity myths. In a wholly fictitious form these myths persist even in contemporary Germany; hence they cannot be dismissed as completely insignificant for identity. Their practical import even in Carolingian times was, however, limited and declining. Wholly mythical genealogies, such as the seventh- to eighth-century efforts to trace *Stämme* to Tacitus's catalog, were common among these groups as among the West Franks and other Germanic bands.[104] Not only did the trans-Rhenane *Stämme* suffer in identity from Charlemagne's mistrust and preference for Frank officials (he even kept Frank military units among the other *Stämme*), intermarriage and acquisition of distant family estates proceeded voluntarily because the leading families had no traditions of endogamy.[105]

The effect of frontiers was also important. At first, large transitional zones separated settlements in the German forests, but agricultural clearings progressively reduced them.[106] At the same time, German settlers were rapidly pushing eastward. On the settlement frontier a consciously organized and delimited territorial unit, the *Mark*, predominated. The inhabitants took their name (for example, "*Österreicher*," from the *Ostmark*) from the territory, not from some more or less mythical *Stamm* ancestor.[107] Farther west toward the Rhine, the titular *Stamm* chieftain (*princeps* or *Herzog*) persisted, but he derived his power from family territorial possessions. In addition, great ecclesiastical dominions contended for power. Increasingly, such types of *Flachenstaat* (territorial state) cut across the old *Stamm* divisions, depriving them of significance. Not coincidentally, the division of Germany into territorial states approximately coincided with the emergence of the territorially identified feudal nobility about 1300.[108] By then memory of *Stamm* personal law had been transmuted into identification of regional groups with variations of Salic law. For example, although Martin Luther and certain modern scholars have believed that the *Sachsenspiegel* ("Mirror of the Saxons") was, as its title suggests, the original *Stamm* law of the Saxons, the compilation was really derived via Westphalia from Carolingian law, which had diffused widely because of its adaptability to German urban trade and settlement.[109] Even the dialects that latter-day Germans were fond of identifying with *Stamm* origins actually arose and became delineated primarily by territorial (*Flachenstaat*) frontiers.

Some opportunities to note parallel developments in other European polities will arise later. František Graus has shown how *Stämme* very similar to those Wenskus analyses among Germanic groups were important as starting points for polities among the Slavs of Poland, Bohemia (not Moravia), and the Elbe region. Like the Germanic *Stämme*, the Slav formations rapidly declined. In contrast, the precosity of France as a territorially organized country needs to be emphasized. Under Charlemagne the *Stämme* were still organizations for military recruitment east of the Rhine, whereas large territorial districts were used for recruitment in Gaul.[110] During the century after his death, such large units—Aquitaine, Burgundy, Picardy, Brittany—became temporary bases for considerable autonomous polities (see chapter 6). The influence of their names as identifying symbols for their inhabitants persisted after the regional polities declined. In northern Gallic biographies, regional designations such as "Neustrasian" (Francian), "Aquitanian," and "Burgundian" replaced various Germanic *Stamm*-origin designations in the eighth century.[111] Four centuries later, the medieval epics retrospectively attributed territorial divisions to Charlemagne's western contingents ("Poitevins," "Brabanters," "Normans," "Lorrainers") while retaining *Stamm* designations for the eastern contingents ("Alemanni," "High Germans," "Franconians").[112] Although some of the divisions ("Normans") are clearly anachronistic and others ("Bretons," "Frisians") ambiguous, the overall difference in symbolic identifying terminology, despite the existence in thirteenth-century France of linguistic and political fragmentation as great as in Germany, is apparent. A similar tendency to replace designations indicating rule over people by terms suggesting territorial domination is evident. It is significant that the novel French terminology was, in the early thirteenth century, even applied to the new Latin empire of Constantinople. Baldwin I took the title imperator Romaniae ("emperor of Romania") whereas for centuries the Byzantine emperor had styled himself Basileus toi Romaion (Latin imperator Romanorum, "emperor of the Romans"). As Percy Schramm concludes, "Therewith the territorial principle, which in the West had led to change of the designations *Francorum*, *Anglorum*, etc., into *Franciae*, *Angliae*, etc., was introduced into the East Roman imperial title."[113]

Nomadic Nonterritorial Identity

In the preceding section, I have argued that a new type of territorial identity arose in West Europe during the early Middle Ages, spread by mimesis to East Europe or arose there independently because of similar conditions, and invaded the Byzantine Christian realm by force. The development was by no means irresistible, however, for at the same time a nonterritorial ethnic identity was becoming stronger in the Middle East. The rival process was consolidated and legitimated by Islam; as a result, two sharply different identity models became the hallmarks of distinct civilizations. The Middle Eastern development originated, however, in the profound characteristics of the nomadic way of life outlined earlier.

Numerous anthropologists, as, for example, Jean-Paul Roux, have cautioned against the facile assumption that terrain means nothing to a nomad:

> There was a time when one imagined the nomad to be a man detached
> from all ties with a territory, moving freely across immense zones of
> steppe and desert. . . . Nomadism is neither anarchy nor disorder but
> organized movement over a space which can be vast but clearly
> delimited by custom and treaties or tacit accords between competing or
> related groups. . . . Of course, these spaces of nomadism were fluid and
> their limits changed according to the vicissitudes of history. The absence
> of fixed dwellings and of sown ground plus the habits of seasonal
> movements made the nomads especially inclined to great migratory
> movements which in extreme cases could be intercontinental.[114]

The tendency of nomads to regard any place over which their group ranged as subject to their dominion made stable relations with sedentary elements very difficult even when both groups nominally shared the same ethic. The Moslem historian, Ibn Khaldun, as noted earlier, was extremely ambivalent in evaluating nomads. He recognized their essential role in Islamic civilization, but perhaps even exaggerated their destructiveness.[115] Curiously enough, in the arid central Iranian plateau, it was the medieval Arabs who regarded roving bands of Baluchis with horror.[116] In modern Morocco, religious spokesmen have held it to be more meritorious to fight nomads than infidels. As early as 1195, the Almohad Caliph Al Mansur expressed his regret for having employed the tactic of moving the Beduin Hilalis to Morocco. Sooner or later almost every Moslem regime has succumbed to the temptation to use the ubiquitous nomad agglomerations in such opportunistic fashion. Normally, though, a prime obligation of the Islamic polity is to keep nomads in check. For example, although they themselves were partly nomadic in family background, the long-lasting Mamelukes who controlled Egypt and Syria ordinarily were careful to admit only sedentary Arabs to their ranks, and then only at lower levels.[117]

In such circumstances the development of stable line frontiers comparable to West Europe's is out of the question. Pierre Guichard's recent analysis cautions that

> in complete contrast to European history, where political construction proceeds from territorial particles . . . culminating after mature development and infinitely concrete guarantees in national affirmation, the Maghreb powers were tribal hegemonies, personal chiefdoms, dynastic or ideological expansions which flared up or became extinguished like torches. Their influence was superficial; it extended to a milieu both diverse and diffuse, fragmented but universal in its claims.[118]

The most successful—or least disruptive—solution throughout most of Middle Eastern history has been a kind of symbiosis in which strong rulers based their power on the cities. From the oasis cities, relatively far apart, power radiated as far as the skill and resources of the ruler extended. As will become clearer in chapters 3 and 5, his ability to manipulate Islamic myths to enlist and thereafter to control nomad auxiliaries was critical. Indeed, the ruler himself had often originated as a nomad auxiliary of a previous dynasty. In the hot-desert regions such manipulation of nomad allegiances was favored by the fictive genealogies that bound them to more sophisticated and cautious elements, the caravan merchants. Some of these, like Mohammed and many of his early followers, had even become city merchants. The situation was inherently unstable, however. In depressed times the caravan merchants could regress to predatory activities, as probably occurred with the Hilali Arabs before they reached northwestern Africa. The Zenata Berbers, who had lost their Sahara caravan routes to the Fatimid dynasty during the eleventh century, also turned to depredation.[119] Central Asian nomads, in a somewhat more hospitable natural environment but with fewer contacts with cities, were less inclined to this predatory-symbiotic alternation; but it did occur after the decline of the Mongol empire. Turkmens battled Kazakhs for caravan routes, whereas Chagatays accepted Islam but reverted to pillage.[120]

Because the sedentary polities on the distant edges of the Eurasian steppe (Russia, for a time Persia, above all China) were relatively strong and economically self-sufficient, limited symbiosis in trade but little in agriculture and animal husbandry was feasible. The fragile oasis cultures of the lower Middle East, on the other hand, needed the animal products provided by neighboring nomads, especially the manure deposited after winter grazing on stubble. Overall, however, the results were long-term deterioration of agricultural lands, accelerated by decline in the peasants' social status. Part of this decline was the result of Islamic ideology and more of policies of the Turkic empires. Here it is important to note that, to maintain their self-respect if not their economic interests, peasants almost universally adopted fictive nomad genealogies, rejecting symbols associated with the acceptance of sedentarization as a permanent condition.[121] A systematic study of modern Morocco provides a clear example:

> Before the establishment of the French Protectorate in 1912, the villagers did not conceive of themselves as farmers. Their primary self-conception was either as *wlad siyyed* mediators or rural countrymen, *bidawiyen*, but not farmers, *fellaha*. Even today, when agriculture has become increasingly central to the activities of the village, they see their olive growing as more important than their farming. . . . It is important to emphasize again that even today the villagers refuse the identity of farmer: pastoralist or saint, yes, peasant, no. They are not deeply rooted in their farmland, either by any "mystical ties to the soil" or by any important symbolic elaboration or identity.[122]

The examples just presented suggest that instability of the nomad-sedentary frontier was by no means confined to areas of Islamic-Christian antagonism. Indeed, the Arabs quickly restored a Central Asian *limes* against Turkic nomads. As it had under their Iranian predecessors, the defense had to consist of a zone of fortified oases rather than a line frontier. The massive movement across this frontier by Islamicized Turks in the eleventh to thirteenth centuries was reluctantly accommodated by Moslem regimes; but the vast, sudden incursion by pagan Mongols in the mid-thirteenth century was regarded by Moslem writers as far more dangerous than the European crusaders' fumbling attacks.[123]

Continuity of sedentary concern with nomadic incursions is demonstrated more clearly by East Slavic reactions. Only during their periods of greatest vigor could the early medieval Rus principalities penetrate the open steppe from what is now Zaporozhye to the Black Sea, except for perilous trade and raiding expeditions by river boat. In the early eleventh century, a defensive line was formed along the Dnieper River to protect the trade route to Byzantium, but it extended only about one hundred miles south and west of Kiev, along the Ros and the Zdvizh rivers. Even there it was very unstable.[124] After 1100 the Rus gradually retreated into the forest fringe (*lesostep*), not to reemerge in force onto the open steppe until the seventeenth century.

Rus experience and the later experience of the Muscovite Russians provide significant indications of a notable advantage which the sedentary

European populations on the edge of the steppe had over Middle East oasis inhabitants. Nomads, because of their lifelong experience in deprivation and their skill in mounted hit-and-run tactics, were extremely difficult to cope with in their native steppe or desert environment. Unless expensive defensive barriers were constantly maintained or a powerful field force kept mobilized, agricultural areas without natural obstacles within range of nomad raids—which might extend for months and cover a thousand miles—could not be defended. Even an immense oasis like the Nile Valley could be seized in the initial rush of the Moslem Arab conquerors. The Arab forces, however, were obliged to follow the edge of the desert to avoid bogging down their cavalry in fields half-covered by irrigation water.[125] In the naturally forested regions of West and Central Europe and in East Europe north of the Pripet and the Volga rivers, nomad raiders could not avoid watercourses, swamps, and thick forests. Even the large, skilled Mongol forces failed to capture Novgorod. The Magyars, relying on archery from horseback to paralyze heavily armored Germans, were virtually helpless when rain prevented them from drawing their bowstrings. Insects sapped their horses' strength. After repeated defeats, tenth-century Central Europeans and fifteenth-century Russians learned that steppe raiders were most vulnerable in crossing rivers when returning laden with booty. Fortified outposts at fords could delay the nomads until a pursuing force annihilated them by driving them against a river or lake shore.[126]

Not withstanding such limitations, the Central Asian horse nomads were relatively adaptable to rugged, cold terrain; Mongols even found the frozen forests of northern Russia preferable to summer operations there. Mongols gradually gave up wheels after adhering to Islam, but at first their use of carts and wagons was so extensive that it became an identity symbol—"the families inhabiting the felt wagons."[127] Sometimes carts laden with booty constituted an encumbrance, but as late as the sixteenth century Ottoman and Central Asian regimes adapted wagons to carry field artillery and built wagon-train fortifications similar to those of South Africa and the American West centuries later.[128] Conversely, the dromedary camel was not only a major identity symbol for Arabs and Berbers, but an impediment to their movement in rugged or moist areas. In attacks on Constantinople, a donkey was required to transport the fodder for each camel! Seven centuries later, lack of wheeled transport was a hindrance for Arab regimes trying to compete with their rivals' artillery. Moreover, Arabs and Berbers did not use the bow that made Eurasian hit-and-run tactics so devastating. It appears that a major reason for the rapid loss of Arab momentum in the eighth century was their inability to cope with the colder, more mountainous regions of the Mediterranean basin. Their stable rule in Spain was confined to the southern and eastern river valleys, and they were soon reduced to summer raids in Anatolia.

The digression on physical aspects of nomad-sedentary interaction has been useful to suggest the range of factors—geographical and technological—which this study must treat cursorily. Moreover, the digression is important as an introduction to problems of contrasting identities. When, as throughout most of ancient history, nomads are restricted to the periphery of high cultural areas with great economic resources, their impact on the ethnic identity of large populations is necessarily restricted. The brief discussion of the evolution of the Israelites presented earlier in this chapter serves as a good example of such limitations. From the fifth to the eighteenth centuries, however, irruptions by nomads or nomad-based regimes recurred in major areas of civilization. Some authorities consider that a major reason why West Europe was able to forge ahead economically compared to Moslem and Byzantine civilization was its freedom, after about A.D. 1000, from such devastating invasions.[129] Some suggestions of the secondary effects of nomad ascendancy have already appeared in the discussion of the change in the Middle East peasantry's attitudes. The principal effect from the ethnic point of view was an underlying shift toward identity boundary mechanisms derived from nomad myths. Such mechanisms were tacitly tolerated, often legitimized, and considerably recast by the Islamic creed. Some of the effects will be discussed in the next chapter. Here the focus will be on the peculiarly nomadic content (whether or not operating in Islamic contexts) of identity mechanisms.

By far the most important mechanism is the extraordinary dominance of the genealogical principle. All social groups (at least those encountered in my study) exhibit some concern for lineage. The intensity of nomadic concern is, therefore, the distinguishing feature. Such interest appeared among all groups with nomadic or seminomadic background in the ancient Syrian-Arabian area. Whereas some Israelite tribes derived their names from territorial units, many adopted names of clans or individual leaders. Generally an Arab genealogy was traced back to an eponymous ancestor who may, according to some scholars, have been an animal totem in pre-Islamic times.[130] By Mohammed's period (seventh century A.D.) Arabs regarded genealogical knowledge as their most precious possession, conferring higher status than riches or valor. In the desert then and in some areas today, not to know one's ancestors is equivalent to accepting a "slave lineage." A student of present-day Morocco writes: "The worst tragedy for a group or individual is to have an unknown origin."[131] To Mohammed himself is ascribed the precept, "Learn your genealogies." The early Caliph Omar is said to have added, "Do not be like the Nabateans or the Babylonians. When one asks where they are from, they reply, 'From such and such a village.' "[132]

As these sayings suggest, nomad concern for genealogy was a major legitimizing force in subjugating, then acculturating, the sedentary Semites of the Fertile Crescent. In southern Syria and Lebanon, acculturation to Arab identity patterns had accompanied a slow but cumulatively significant infiltration of Arabs before Islam. Lebanese families acquired their belief in descent from the two basic Arab clans, the Kays and the Yemenites, during this period, and have retained the myth while rejecting Islam.[133] As Guichard's penetrating recent examination of the historical development puts it, the pattern extended to almost the entire Moslem world. Atomization of society into agnatic kin groups prevails even among Moslem populations that do not have remote nomadic ancestors.[134] The concern for finding ancestors has been carried to lengths that appear absurd to an objective observer. Even though becoming devout Moslems, Persians claimed descent from Zoroastrian Sassanid nobles. Conversely, after the Persian poet Firdawsi identified "Turan" with Turkic nomads, many of the latter eagerly claimed descent from the Turanian fictional hero, Afrasiyab. The Sudanese Funj tribe on becoming Moslem asserted its descent from the earliest great Islamic dynasty, the Umayyads. Albanian refugees in the Negev and non-Semitic Somalis alike claim descent from Mohammed himself. The egalitarian Islamic creed recognizes only such *sharif* descent, that is, Mohammed as one's ancestor, as a claim to superiority. The number of his descendants multiplies rapidly—there were four thousand claimants in Baghdad alone by the ninth century. They turn up in the most remote areas. Several recent Moroccan dynasties, for example, have officially claimed "Sharifian" origin as a legitimization of their rule.[135]

Because such claims are neither provable nor disprovable, the force of their presentation, including skill in enlisting learned authorities, the superficial plausibility of the oral traditions, and the real power of the claimants are decisive. In the course of time, political considerations of a broader nature strongly influence acceptance of genealogical claims. Shortly after their conquest of North Africa, the Arabs made a rare exception by admitting Berbers to their armies. Gradually Berbers became Moslems, and all eventually adopted the genealogical identity principle. The earliest and strongest acculturation to Arab principles occurred among Berbers who turned from caravan trading to nomad raiding. First they adopted genealogies linking themselves to Arab nomads like the Hilalis, sometimes while preserving a vestigial Berber lineage. The Berbers then became completely Arabicized in genealogy as well as in language.

It is obvious that what is at stake here is a set of myths, among the most potent structures that have ever influenced identity. Consequently, there is no real incompatibility between the views just expressed and Abdallah Laroui's criticism that "the family model is more territorial than one has admitted; in the long run, one changes genealogy and memories in changing place of residence and the group becomes an agglomeration of men of diverse origins united in a particular locale."[136] Laroui recognizes that it is not real blood relationships but conviction impelled by an intense desire to identify with a more prestigious group that determines the identity myth. Similarly, the European observer, Pierre Guichard, remarked, "It is incontestable that group cohesion is determined only by *consciousness* of this consanguinity, belief in kinship, which is more a social and mental than a biological phenomenon."[137]

Ethnicity is related to two of Claude Lévi-Strauss's basic exchange relationships—symbolic communication and exchange of material values. His third relationship, exchange of women, does not appear salient in a European context because exogamy has been the rule there. Down to the eleventh century, the Western church upheld the drastic impediment to marriage within the seventh degree of kindred. This rule tended to diffuse to Byzantium via the Latins of southern Italy.[138] As a result, nobles developed marriage networks extending all over Romance Europe, with some connections with networks in the Germanic sphere and even in East Europe.[139] Even the peasant was compelled to seek her or his spouse in a distant village. The influences upon identity of such broad contacts have received very little analytical attention though the anecdotal evidence is immense. A basic result seems to have been pressure for outside contacts running counter to the fixed genealogies of the later Middle Ages or to *patriotisme de clocher.*

A more demonstrable result, even after the marriage impediment was reduced to prohibition of marriages within the fourth degree, was the historically precocious development of the nuclear family as a characteristic distinguishing West Europe.[140] The contrast to Moslem practice in exchange of women is succinctly expressed by Guichard: the Oriental takes the prudent course of preserving his values (honor) in marriage, whereas the West European seeks to increase his (in property or prestige) by exogamy.[141] The ramifications of the Moslem practice in terms of seclusion of women, housing, and the like will be touched upon later. Crucial here is that endogamy, although rarely applying to Moslem rulers and in any case incapable of perpetuating knowledge of descent over many centuries, was symbolically tied to the intense concern for genealogy. To practice endogamy, hence to remain in contact with an extended family familiar with one's recent origins, was a powerful force for keeping identity focus on lineage rather than on territory, for providing superficial plausibility for the myth that blood relationships (Ibn Khaldun's *asabiya*) were decisive in human relations.

In suggesting such a connection, one has to confront the basic difference between Arabs and the Central Asian nomads who assumed direction of Islamic political affairs after the first four centuries. The latter were exogamous before conversion and most remained so as Moslems.[142] As noted above, in some respects Eurasian nomads' ready association with dynastic myths of their leaders in large conquest agglomerations was stronger than among Germanic *Stämme*. Clans could rise in a hierarchical order of proximity to the dynasty only by securing, often by force, adherence of new clans, which went to the end of the prestige queue. Moreover, ready acceptance of exogamy meant that proximity to the dynasty, as was the case in the Carolingian *comitatus*, could be secured by intermarriage. Indeed, the prevalence and high significance of the *comitatus* among Germanic, Turkic, Mongol, and Finno-Ugric groups distinguished them from Arabs and Berbers.

Weighing against these similarities between *Stämme* and Central Asian agglomerations was the widespread clan identity of the latter, in which they resembled the Arabs. However remote from the dynasty a clan's lineage might be, it was crucial for identity. The case of the Turkmens, who maintained clans more than other Central Asian peoples despite extensive migrations and frequent shifts of allegiance, has been mentioned.[143] The Kalmyks, although Buddhists not Moslems, retained their clan organization in the seventeenth century after moving two thousand miles to the Volga. They were aware of their remote genealogical relationship with the forest Manchus who conquered China about that time. Such mythic relationships played a minor part in alliances, although the more demonstrable connections among descendants of pre-Genghisid Mongol dynasties were significant for the Kalmyks.[144] The Kazakh groups, which had apparently originated as banditlike offshoots of other Turkic groups, perhaps not very different from the adventurous *comitatus* dissidents of the German invasion period, adopted an Arab symbol as totem, but retained (or invented) a clan organization. Upon meeting a stranger, "a knowledge of the place of one's own group in the genealogical structure of the whole orda [agglomeration] was essential." As among the Arabs, those Kazakhs who were ignorant of their genealogies suffered a drastic loss in status, for only the upper classes knew all the ramifications of the accepted genealogical myths.[145] In this respect the Kazakhs like the Kalmyks were perpetuating a Mongol custom (consecrated by Genghis Khan's "Great Yasa") very different from the Arabs', who admitted no overall hierarchy of lineages. The Yasa classified clans as "White Bones" (rulers, princes, and the like), "Black Bones" (people of middle position such as warriors), and camp followers lacking either of these statuses.[146]

The incentive to maintain genealogies, already strong in Central Asia, was reinforced by conversion to Islam that, despite its egalitarian ethic, was strongly imbued with Arab traditions. The effect is apparent among Anatolian Turks, most of whom are really descended from Greek or pre-Greek inhabitants or from extremely fragmented Moslem groups who came to fight on the Byzantine frontier. Anatolian Turks can trace their ancestors back only a few generations, even in the male line. Nevertheless, pastoral elements in particular exhibit strong interest in remote putative ancestors in Khurasan. The impulse to "tribal" organization was so strong in fifteenth- to sixteenth-century Anatolia that the Kizilbashi dervishes, with membership based entirely on populist religious adherence rather than fictive genealogies, constituted "tribes" that were really territorial divisions.[147]

Just as among Berbers even thoroughly territorialized groups identify by the name of a remote ancestor, the remembrance of an ancestral name, as Lawrence Krader emphasizes, is essential for Central Asian identity. For Berbers, as Laroui admits, "persistence is guaranteed across the generations by the chosen 'name' which no one is free to renounce."[148] In both hot-desert areas and the Central Asian steppes adherence to the fiction of blood relationships across vast expanses of time and space caters to the nostalgia of groups that have accommodated to the nomadic identity principle yet no longer follow a truly nomadic way of life—if they ever did. As long as memory, or what passes for memory, of nomadic ancestors is kept alive, the contemporary Arab, Berber, Turk, or Mongol can dream of a freer, more adventurous life, while scorning the farmer tied to his furrows. Conversely, from the time when ancient Egyptians pityingly remarked that the Asian nomad "does not live in a single place, but his feet wander," to sixteenth-century Russian condescension to Tatars ("Your position is not what it ought to be because you wander as nomads from steppe to steppe") the sedentary peoples have reciprocated this scorn.[149] Contrasting ways of life are so deeply anchored in group attitudes that differences in ethnic identities are almost inevitable.

A Magyar Exception?

Various examples of sedentary groups accepting nomadic identity, originally to escape unbearable pressures, were given above. For a time some of these groups, such as the Berbers, although copying others' identity mechanisms, retained a consciousness of their own ethnic identity. Conversely, *force majeure* (often applied by imperial polities) sedentarized some nomads. Is there any example of a considerable nomadic ethnic group that became sedentary while retaining its identity? The Magyars are a frequently cited instance. An exploration of their myths and historical reality, therefore, may shed considerable light on the interaction of nomad and sedentary influences on changing ethnic boundary mechanisms.

The exploration may profitably, for once, begin with the nineteenth-century nationalist version of the myth. This myth may be regarded as a legitimization of the peculiar rule of the gentry of the Hungarian kingdom over a linguistically heterogeneous population including Magyar-speaking peasants who constituted somewhat less than half of the total. From another standpoint, the nationalist myth was a mechanism for preserving a highly distinctive group culture against leveling pressures emanating from the Habsburg bureaucracy, as discussed in chapter 6. The relationship of the Magyar language to Finno-Ugric was discovered by a German scholar in the eighteenth century. This discovery had little practical application because few of the gentry of the kingdom of Hungary were fluent in the language, preferring Latin but often resorting to German. In the thirteenth century, Latin had become the first official Hungarian written language. Magyar did not become standardized until the sixteenth or seventeenth century. Up to the final generation of the eighteenth century, the language had not developed sufficiently to cope with technical, urban topics.[150] After that period, Magyar was rapidly developed as a symbol of identity, but in the early nineteenth century the gentry urgently required a more powerful boundary mechanism. Hence they embraced the idea that Magyars, alone of the "Turanian" peoples, had preserved their nomadic ways and chivalrous social order on becoming Christian. Such persistence was ascribed to maintenance of a "pure" social order based on the gentry-peasant dichotomy, excluding the "corrupting" bourgeoisie—then mostly German-speaking. Absolutist pressure for Germanification was linked to liberal democracy as threats to identity.[151] Hence the intense interest—a variety of nostalgia—in the early steppe background of the Magyars.

Although at present, philologists question the linguistic association of Finno-Ugric with Turkic and Mongol in a single "Turanian" group, the origins of the Magyars did closely resemble other steppe peoples'. The thesis that there were really two elements within the conquest agglomeration that entered the Danube basin around A.D. 900—a nomadic, warlike Turkic contingent and a relatively peaceful, agricultural core descended from semisedentary Ugric hunters and food gatherers—no longer appears tenable.[152] In fact, most if not all Turkic and Mongol nomads, like the Ugrians, originated in the forest and *lesostep* stretching from the Volga to the Pacific. The Indo-European predecessors of these steppe nomads may have moved from west to east instead of from north to south, but they, too, apparently originated in forested mountains, the Carpathians. Consequently, the origin myths and nostalgia of all Eurasian nomads are similar.

This germ of truth in the nineteenth-century Magyar myth can hardly have been more than accidental. What is more significant is that early Magyars, like Turks and Mongols, regarded hunting, not nomadism, as the most noble occupation. Hunting was linked to the nostalgic emphasis of the Mongols on mountain forests. Apparently, Turkic, Mongol, and Magyar clans became nomads reluctantly, perhaps after a period of rudimentary grain cultivation, when population pressures made hunting, fishing, and food-gathering in the forest an impracticable way of life. In a way, the predicament of these groups resembles that of the Arab who clings to nomadic identity; for the Eurasian nomad, however, there was no possible way back to the hunting stage.[153]

The Magyars spent some four centuries on the Donets–North Caucasus steppe before proceeding in force to the Danube basin, whereas the Mongols made their transition to full nomadism within a few generations. Therefore it was hardly lack of acquaintance with the steppe way of life that prepared the Magyars for eventual sedentarization. The Magyars did, however, have their steppe initiation in far more stable circumstances than did the Mongols. Quite possibly, though, the Magyars resented subjection to the Khazar empire, which provided this stability. Eventually (ca. 850–860) the Magyars were driven out by a more potent agglomeration, the Cumans (also known as Kipchaks or Polovtsy).[154] Apparently, the Magyars maintained, for nomads, an unusually high level of agricultural activity and cattle breeding in river valleys even during their steppe interlude.

In their fundamental identifying myth, however, the Magyars became completely nomadic. They identified with the Arpad dynasty (originally vassals of the Khazars), with deep faith in the mystic power of royal blood or, as early Magyars formulated it, the royal semen. Any Arpad might be called to rule, but the one who succeeded in retaining the crown was perceived as stronger and taller than other men, favored at his accession by a miraculous sign from God. The Arpad ruler was surrounded by a *comitatus* that proved to be a powerful instrument for compelling obedience. It will be recalled that such characteristics, although perhaps less intense, were also common among the *Stämme*; in addition, Magyars had the non-Indo-European attributes of totem and clan division. All of the clans believed that they were related by blood to the dynasty, although some were actually Turkic, notably the Szeklers, who had preceded the Magyars in the Danube basin.

The Magyars adopted the Turkic customs of shaved heads and ritual scars, which struck terror in the sedentary populations.[155] It is not necessary to repeat other characteristics of nomadic warfare which Magyars had acquired on the steppe, except to recall that these methods provided them with easy victories and immense booty gathered throughout most of Europe during the first generation following Magyar establishment on the Danube. Less than forty years after the first major Magyar raid into Central Europe, however, German forces defeated the Magyars at Merseburg (933). Twenty-two years later, a crushing defeat at Lechfeld confirmed German military ascendancy. Among special factors contributing to the Magyar defeats were the use of carts for transporting booty, tying the raiders to surviving roads in a most unnomadlike manner; the rise of the forceful Saxon dynasty in Germany; and, perhaps in the late tenth century, adoption of the heavy swords and armor of their opponents.[156] It is impossible to be sure whether the Magyars perceived this change from steppe archery, which had well served their predecessor nomads (Huns and Avars) in the Danube basin steppes, to be instrumentally advantageous. As noted earlier, the cataphract warrior was indeed apparently superior in Europe proper. Status considerations, however, may have been involved in Magyar mimesis of the ways of the prestigious German nobility. In any case, neglect of light cavalry tactics reduced Magyar effectiveness as either allies or opponents of steppe nomads.

Conversion to Christianity had been the prime condition both for sedentarization and for accommodation with Central European polities. As late as the twelfth century, groups of Magyars had to be compelled by fines to remain in half-nomadic tent or hut settlements grouped around a parish church.[157] A century earlier, the Arpad ruler who converted had had to subdue the recalcitrant steppe nomads. Later, with the help of the *Gesta Ungarorum* written a generation after his death (perhaps by German missionary Bishop Hartwick), the western Magyar aristocracy developed the potent myth of St. Stephen. The Hungarian historian Bálint Hóman refers to Stephen as "a mythic prince who had been lawgiver and founder of clans, uniting in himself the charisma of his heathen ancestors and the concept of a Christian apostolic king ruling through the grace of divine power."[158] As warriors, Magyars relished a major component of the Stephen myth: their role as an *Antemurale* defending Europe against its infidel enemies. Shamanist Magyars probably did not despise a universal religion altogether—their raiders had occasionally shrunk back in awe before Christian shrines. But a very large proportion of the nomadic group was unwilling to give up its way of life. Some major raids occurred after nominal conversion, and a defensive wasteland was maintained as a *glacis* toward the Germans. A great uprising against German influences occurred forty-two years after the conversion. In fact, German polities and the Hungarian kingdom carried on raids and counterraids up to the fifteenth century. Jews and Moslems ("Ishmaelites") were admitted to Christian Hungary to conduct the slave trade.[159]

The difficulty of altering a fundamentally nomadic way of life is indicated by the recurrence of a powerful countermyth (the fourth mythic alternative I have suggested). In this version, the Magyars are not only the successors but the descendants of Attila's Huns, the scourge of Europe; Christian influence has cheated the Magyar of his destiny. An embryonic reinvigoration of this myth occurred during the thirteenth-century Mongol invasions. The Stephen myth portrayed Magyars as Europe's front-line defense, a position that their geographical location rendered unavoidable had they not repeatedly been invited to join the Mongols. Undoubtedly, King Bela I refused initially. He even gave refuge to descendants of the Magyars' antagonists, the Cumans. Ladislas IV, his grandson, and many of his aristocratic entourage, however, were attracted by the Cumans' nomadic way of life, particularly polygamy and plunder. Hóman quotes a revealing passage from the medieval Magyar chronicle:

> "His loyal priest, Master Simon of Kéza, fulfilled the burning heart's desire of the undefeated, powerful Lord Ladislas, the most famous king of Hungary" [by transferring elements of the *Gesta Hungarorum* back to the Hun period]. . . . "Attila," so wrote Kéza, "lived with his people on the broad plain in tents and wagons; he honored the ways of the Medes [nomads] as did all Huns, wore a long beard and esteemed voluptuousness highly. He was generous—holding it shameful to amass gold in his treasury—took great joy in horses, but gave them away lightheartedly, so that he often had only two horses and saddles. But his tent, his bed, and his table were decorated with gold and jewels, he ate from golden vessels and rode in a splendid saddle."[160]

Ladislas called in Moslem Cumans and Nogai Tatars, leading Pope Nicholas IV to authorize a crusade against him in 1286. Four years later, jealous of the newcomers, Ladislas's earlier pagan Cuman allies assassinated him. The steppe countermyth lingered on, nourished by a constant influx of heterogeneous steppe elements, until the Ottoman invasion. At that time a Magyar faction revived the myth in an appeal for an alliance with their "Turanian" cousins—as yet the notion of a relationship was derived from Firdawsi's poem rather than from putative linguistic relationships.[161]

The intricate development of Magyar identity suggests that a recollected way of life is a persistent force, but certainly not always a determining factor. Requiring the legitimizing support of a higher religion, the dominant Magyar elite began sedentarization despite the obvious revulsion of many of their followers, who had no strong opposing religious legitimization such as Islam might have provided for nomadic ways. After the potent myth relating the Magyars to Christendom had been tied to the interests of the new landed aristocracy, neither an ostensibly attractive alliance nor material temptations could displace it. Once turned on, the *mythomoteur* of identity is not easily shut down. Nevertheless, the availability of two very different myths, alternating in intensity, may well have been instrumental in preserving the unusual Magyar ethnic identity, which otherwise might have become vulnerable to recurring pressures for assimilation.

Summary and Conclusions

In most cases, differences in ways of life do not produce strong identity boundaries. Even visibly salient traits like house or village layouts ordinarily cut across ethnic alignments. Ways of life that are extremely different, however, produce underlying attitudes that (although they do not themselves constitute ethnic boundaries) profoundly condition the manner in which such boundaries are perceived. Probably, as such writers as Fernand Braudel have noted, the peculiar mountaineer way of life also tends to produce special attitudes. Except in unusual circumstances, however, the small size and isolation of mountaineer populations reduces their significance and makes them more assimilable than nomads. The "great nomads" of the hot deserts of Southwest Asia, North Africa, and the Eurasian steppe, on the other hand, have clung to ways of life drastically at odds with those of sedentary populations.

Nostalgia is a critical indicator of attachment to a way of life; and the expression of nostalgia constitutes a strong symbolic device for transmitting attitudes deriving from such life patterns. For sedentary agricultural populations—elites and peasants alike—such symbolic transmission has centered on the attachment to specific territories. Like other mass attitudes, the sentiment of territorial identity has been strongly reinforced by political action. Ancient polities and ecclesiastical organizations based on sedentary populations reinforced territorial attachment by precisely delimiting jurisdictions. The momentum of such formal institutionalization is indicated by the fact that geographical frontiers, once firmly established (as were, notably, Roman internal divisions in Western Europe) continued to affect identity consciousness long after the organizations that had created the frontiers had vanished.

The persistence of the sedentary agricultural pattern of identification is demonstrated by the events following disintegration of the Western Roman empire. Germanic, Slavic, and Celtic populations that had invaded the empire or regained their freedom of action adhered to agglomerations suitable for extending conquests. For such conquest agglomerations, which had not passed through a stage of real nomadism, the German term *Stämme* is most convenient. The *Stamm* consisted of a heterogeneous collection of individuals and families who had usually adopted the leading family's genealogical myths as a way of legitimizing their temporary unification. Such, notably, appears to have been the origin of the Franks. After conquering sedentary populations, however, surviving *Stamm* elites became sedentary landed nobles. After the tenth century, elite consciousness of belonging to a *Stamm* distinguished by a genealogical myth was gradually transformed into identification with a geographical location, usually the family estate that contained the ancestral graveyard. In this manner, after prolonged immersion in the European sedentary environment, even elite groups strongly oriented toward genealogical principles of identity transferred their identity attachment to a specific territory.

The persistent influence of the true nomadic way of life produced very different effects on other conquest agglomeration elites. Like the North European *Stämme*, a nomadic agglomeration (frequently but misleadingly termed a "tribe") accepted the genealogical myth of the leader. For Eurasian and hot-desert nomads, however, this myth was a clan rather than a family attribute. The constituent clans of the agglomeration clung to their individual genealogical myth when they adopted the leading family's myth. For hot-desert nomads (Berbers as well as Arabs), intense endogamy, practiced even after a group had become sedentary, strongly reinforced the persistent genealogical myth as the primary identifying structure, in contrast to territorial identity. Eurasian steppe nomads (Mongols, Turks, and Finno-Ugrians) were exogamous, but retained clan genealogical myths (usually symbolized by totems) nearly as strongly as did the hot-desert nomads.

As Eurasian groups like the Buddhist Kalmyks demonstrate, retention of genealogical myths does not depend on specific religious affiliations. Nevertheless, adoption of Islam by nearly all hot-desert nomads and the overwhelming majority of Eurasian nomads constituted a very important reinforcing mechanism. As a universal creed, Islam does not usually recognize superiority of descent. Nevertheless, the Arab origins of Islam deeply influenced its association with genealogical myths. There is no such obvious relation between the origins of Christianity and the religion's reinforcement of the territorial pattern of identity. Early institutionalization of Christianity, however, incorporated the basic Hellenistic-Roman pattern of territorial delimitation. The aspects of this pattern centering on the city-state will be discussed in chapter 4. At this point, it is important to recall the role of the bishop as head of a territorial unit, followed by medieval elaboration of a network of territorial parishes.

Because they originated as a Finno-Ugrian agglomeration formed under intense steppe nomadic influence, the Magyars provide a striking example of the conflicting nomadic and sedentary identity patterns. After establishing themselves in a location where the physical and technological environment made nomadism hazardous for the continued existence of the group, Magyars gradually adopted Christianity. For centuries thereafter, a struggle of sedentary patterns, reinforced by royal and ecclesiastical structures and by Christian myths against inclinations to revert to steppe myths and styles, was apparent. The Magyar case demonstrates the possibility of overcoming the nomadic pattern of identification; numerous instances of the reverse process, by which sedentary peoples have become nomadic, could be adduced. At the same time, Magyar experience demonstrates how hard it is to transform a persistent way of life.

CHAPTER THREE

Islam and Christianity

Islam—The Civilization

The significance of Islam as a legitimizing ideology for nomad identity patterns is inescapable. To assume that such an aspect of a universal religion constitutes its core or is even a major component would be rash in the extreme. In dealing with all religious beliefs, this book emphasizes elements salient for ethnic identity; but the reader should never lose sight of the profound significance of each great religion as a way of organizing man's relation to mankind and, more important, his relation to God. Even in a secular context, the prime historical role of Islam has been to create one of the world's great civilizations. Arnold Toynbee was undoubtedly right, in broad outline, to identify each civilization with a religion that shaped its world view. He was also right in contending that, until the modern epoch, religious identification has usually been far more intense than ethnic identity.[1] The argument of this chapter is that, although in and of itself the Christian-Moslem identity dichotomy was overridingly important, it also shaped and conditioned lesser ethnic identities that became increasingly salient.

In a sense, Islam is the only civilization created by nomads. I have already pointed to the urban caravan-merchant origins of Islam and to the remarkable insistence on the city as the sole completely satisfying locus for religious practice. A recent writer is correct, however, in suggesting that faith in Islam tends to overcome Mediterranean man's fear of the desert. Though the fear of nomads remained, Moslems, in contrast to members of ancient societies, crossed the formidable psychological barrier of the desert, making it a highway rather than an obstacle.[2] By turning their backs on the sea, the Moslems incurred high costs, but they unquestionably opened new avenues for civilization.

The city-nomad accommodation was as significant for what it left out— or opposed—as for what it included and invited. The earliest Islamic empire, the Umayyads, was based on the notion that the founders, the Arabs, were superior and that other groups were to be kept in inferior roles even after embracing Islam. The exception, accorded immediate equality, was the Berbers, who not only had preexisting tendencies to nomadism, but presented no competing culture. Islamic egalitarianism made Arab predominance unstable, for in principle every Moslem is entitled to equal rights wherever he chooses to reside under an Islamic regime. The Umayyads' Abbasid successors were more consistent in applying this principle. Still, as Marshall Hodgson has observed, the Abbasid shift of gravity to the old Persian lands also represented an assertion of superiority: that of the merchant-nomad synthesis over the Sassanid aristocratic-peasant complex.[3] At the cultural level this assertion was not completely effective, for the Fars and Khurassan landed nobility's life styles partially revived in Moslem garb. On the whole, however, Islam did succeed in becoming the only great traditional civilization to reject a rural base. If it had not done so, it would very likely have been absorbed by Persian society as the Chinese absorbed Mongols and Manchus.

Many writers consider the *hadiths* that constitute the fundamental precepts of Islam to have contributed to depreciation of the peasant, as Islamic insistence on urban piety undoubtedly did. The aim of these teachings, however, was not to subjugate the peasant (as he undoubtedly had been subjugated by Sassanids and other polities replaced by Islam) but to elevate him by assimilation to the city to full participation in both society and religion. Such wholesale transformation proved impossible in an economy still tied to an agricultural base. Consequently, new, popular forms of Islam, especially the *sufi* ("wisdom") movement, appealed to peasants. The *sufi* approach, however, was more suitable to pastoralist life styles for several reasons. The preacher (*pir*) was more mobile, because he lacked possessions, than the orthodox Islamic judge (*cadi*), who usually belonged to the property-owning urban stratum. Furthermore, veneration of the tomb of the founder of a *sufi* order is directed, in a characteristically nomadic genealogical manner, by his descendant, the *kalifa*.[4]

The emotional poverty of the Islamic approach to the peasant is also suggested by the peculiar unadaptability of the strictly lunar calendar to the agricultural cycle. The procession of such Islamic observances as the fast of Ramadan through the solar cycle is inconvenient even for observant urban dwellers who, in some years, must abstain from water throughout the long days of the summer solstice. In a rural environment, emotional requirements for sacral recognition of the seasons are compelling. In every Islamic agricultural milieu from Egypt to Indonesia, Moslems join in the seasonal festivals of surviving earlier religions or reincarnate pagan tutelary deities or Christian saints associated with the solar cycle as putative Moslem holy men. "The whole cycle of nature was abandoned to the older traditions," Hodgson remarks.[5] Islamic practice also pressed the interpretation of God as Lord of Hosts to an extreme, as a late Ottoman historian readily admitted: "The new religion made them [Turks] even more daring and eager for conquests. One of the most remarkable effects of Islam is to develop among its adherents love of war and that spirit of proselytism, at once ardent and heroic, which had animated the Arabs after their conversion."[6]

Many analysts have seen the reflection of austere monotheism in Moslem art as in their military spirit. I have already suggested that no architecture remains entirely devoid of symbolism. Where pictorial representation is rejected, forms and monuments themselves become identity symbols. The Word, embodied in the superb calligraphy always favored by Islam, cannot fail to have symbolic significance for the illiterate as well as for the learned believer. The ritual of prayer, as precisely defined as Christian liturgy, has remained even more stable. But Islam abandoned the animal, human, and divine representations essential to nearly all early Middle Eastern religions and transmuted to symbols of monotheism by the mainstream of Christian art. Some regard such "puritanism" as a reflection of Islam's adoption of the emphases of a certain period of Judaic and Christian devotion (embodied in iconoclasm, contemporary with the appearance of Islam) that feared the contamination of anthropomorphism and symbolic representation.[7] Because such representations derived, for the most part, from the rural world, their elimination left an additional void between Islamic practice and the familiar sensual appreciation of the country dweller.[8] In sum, whether these special aspects of Islam reflected its nomadic origins, its antipathy toward the stratified rural society it encountered in Persia, or its hypostatization of a transitory phase of Christian doctrine, they have contributed to the evolution of a civilization based on a unique combination of societal elements.

For centuries, as Hodgson emphasizes, this Islamic civilization was the real center of the ecumene, in contact (as Christianity was not, until the sixteenth century) with all other major societies except, of course, those of America.[9] On its Central Asian frontier Islamic civilization faced steppe peoples who at one point constituted an overwhelming threat. Even as they confronted this threat, however, Islamic thinkers realized that the affinity of their civilization for nomads promised eventual enlistment of the Mongol-Turkic forces. Within a few generations this prospect was realized, although the hidden costs to Islam were high. Islamic relations with the Far Eastern civilization were never intimate enough to constitute a threat to either. With India, however, the threat was one way; Islam periodically expanded by leaps into the subcontinent. No static frontier zone ever developed.[10] Islamic polities occasionally suffered reverses, but the theater of action was entirely in India. Hindu and Buddhist forces never threatened the rest of the Moslem world.

Only on the frontiers with Christian polities—even comparatively small

ones like Ethiopia and Georgia-Armenia—did a relatively permanent frontier zone of resistance and counterattack prevail. Associated with this
military-geographical confrontation was the constant rivalry with a mono-
theistic religion sharing Islam's origins and continuing to operate in the
midst of Islamic polities. Given these circumstances, Christendom was
bound to be the main contrasting environment by which Moslems defined
the limits of their own civilization, just as ethnic groups define themselves
by contrast to neighbors. H. Montgomery Watt has noted the ethniclike
exclusive identity common among Moslems: "Thus in a sense the *raison
d'être* of the Islamic community was its superiority. Moreover, much of the
pride formerly taken in one's tribe became attached to the religious community. This has led to an intense belief in the superiority of Islam and in
the inferiority of other (religious) communities. The Christians and Jews
who had to wear different clothes from the Muslims were made to feel
that that was a humiliation, and this increased the pressure on them to
become Muslims."[11] A recent Moslem writer agrees with much of this
Western assessment: "In the seventh century the Orient suffered from an
ideological and political emptiness. It was this profound need for identity
linked to a superior spiritual aspiration, new and open to the future, which
provided Islam with its opportunity."[12]

A sense of mission, of spiritual superiority, was not, of course, peculiar
to Islam. Christianity had exhibited the same tendency for centuries. One
reason why Moslem superiority appeared to be more salient was that Islam
was more unified in relation to the outside world. Doctrinal cleavages were
present in Islam as in Christendom and occasionally led to bloody clashes.
As is discussed in chapter 7, however, an Islamic sect rarely secured a
lasting power base. Conversely, Christendom was fragmented by such
power alignments, notably between its principal branches: the polities of
Western Europe that recognized the papacy, and Byzantium. Within each
of its specific regions, though, Islam dominated societies that were far
more heterogeneous than were the Christian societies. Numerous manifestations of this nonterritorial distribution of ethnic and ethnoreligious
groups within Moslem regions, small rural districts, and especially individual cities, will be adduced. For the present discussion, the important
aspect of heterogeneity is its impact on Islamic-Christian relations. Hodgson sums up a detailed exposition of the disabilities of Christians under
Moslem rule by remarking that "the most righteous non-Muslim, though
he might win grudging respect, was normally regarded as inferior in status
to any Muslim, however dubious his claim to probity. The feeling was
almost as strong as ethnic feeling and did, indeed, have something of an
ethnic tone to it: a new convert, though he was accepted as a Muslim, was
not always accorded the full respect reserved for those who were Muslim

by birth."[13] Centuries later, when, admittedly, attitudes had hardened, a judicious Ottoman official proferred this measured counsel: *rayas* (non-Moslem subjects, literally "herd animals") must not be overindulged, and sumptuary laws must be enforced; but their riches should not be levied on except for the sultan's service and poor *rayas* should not be oppressed.[14]

It is not the intention of this work to examine the numerous special levies, expropriations of churches, sumptuary restrictions, and plain harassment that constituted a deliberately imposed "state of humiliation" for Christians under Moslem rule. Certainly such impositions were slighter in the first, Arab centuries of Islam. Nevertheless, though the Arabs (as a historian of the conquest of Egypt notes) offered certain guarantees to *dhimmis* (non-Moslem subjects), they never promised religious liberty.[15] Some Christians, notably the Copts and other Monophysite dissidents from Byzantine Orthodoxy, preferred the new rulers. In the Fertile Crescent for several centuries and in Egypt down to British occupation, Moslem rulers depended on Christian clerks and administrators, partly because they were more submissive than free Moslems. Even in the early centuries, however, there were instances of riot and extreme persecution, as under the Fatimid Sultan Hakim in 1007.[16] Two substantial threats hung over the subordinate Christian communities at all times: their women could be induced to marry Moslems, whereas if a Christian male married a Moslem woman both were put to death; a Christian was rewarded for embracing Islam, whereas a Moslem who became Christian was executed for apostasy. It is important to bear in mind that these evidences of intolerance, although no greater than contemporary Christians exhibited toward pagans, "heretics," or Jews, were virtually unilateral as between Islam and Christendom. Whereas Islam ruled immense numbers of Christians, down to the end of the eleventh century Christian rule of Moslems was restricted to small, transitional instances. As a latecomer, Islam had to make inroads on other civilizations—as Watt notes, such expansion was Islam's *raison d'être*. Hence the holy war (*jihad*) was present at the start of Islam, whereas Christian reactions were sporadic and defensive. Carl Becker pointed out, however, that Islam's expansion coincided with an especially intolerant phase of Christianity.[17]

In a strictly doctrinal sense, Moslems always respected Christian tenets. In the first centuries Islamic regimes permitted communication between their Christian subjects and ecclesiastical authorities in Byzantium. Despite early appreciation of the Virgin and Christian saints, later Moslem writers tended to regard devotion to them as idolatrous deviation from monotheism. Conversely, the stylistic exaggeration and apparent illogic of the Koran repelled Europeans, as did Mohammed's polygamy, perceived as "lust" contrary to a "natural law," which Christians could not understand that Moslems rejected. Many of the Christian stereotypes of Moslems originated among Oriental Christians who had a better chance to know Islam, but more reason to denigrate it.[18]

The *Jihad*-Crusade Spiral

Other stereotypes arose during the protracted military struggle between Byzantium and the Islamic empires. It is hard to escape the conclusion that a crusading spirit originated in the Eastern Roman empire long before the term was invented in the West. The long struggle with the Sassanids, who explicitly rejected Christianity in favor of their national Zoroastrian religion, was a tragic prelude to contact with Islam. The Byzantine demand that the True Cross be returned by the defeated Persians constituted a symbolic example of identification of religion and polity. Seventh-century efforts to induce Christian Visigoths to refrain from attacking Byzantine possessions in Spain while the imperial center was engaged in a desperate struggle with the Sassanid enemies of Christendom also testify to such identification.[19] It is hardly conceivable that an empire with strong sacral overtones could react less harshly to an attack like Islam's, overtly designed to replace its Christian universal mission by seizing Constantinople.[20] What is indeed surprising is the belated and intermittent nature of the Byzantine literary polemic against Islam; except during the late ninth and tenth centuries, such ideological defense was largely dissipated by domestic theological disputes.[21] By that time, it is true, Emperor John Tzimisces had, to use A. A. Vasiliev's words, "in aiming to achieve his final goal of freeing Jerusalem," undertaken "a real crusade,"[22] though one that was ended by his untimely death. Over a century earlier, the Emperor Theophilus had vainly proposed a united Christian crusade against the Abbasid empire. Probably the recovery of Crete in 961 had stronger resonance in the Christain world and greater strategic importance than these imperial ventures. The Byzantines, who had long permitted a mosque in their capital, at that time took the step, offensive to Islam, of closing all mosques on Crete.[23] Nevertheless, despite their strong military position lasting well into the eleventh century, the Byzantines did not make a determined effort to regain the Holy Places, and Moslems did not regard the threat as sufficient to warrant a call for renewed holy war.

The significance of the West European assault on Islam in the First Crusade, culminating in the seizure of the entire Syrian coast as well as the

Holy Places, was both strategic and symbolic. As a thrust at the center (or at least the indispensable articulation) of the Islamic world, forcible establishment of crusader principalities was sufficiently alarming. Symbolically, the loss of the Syrian coast (the *Sahil*) painfully inflamed Arab poets' nostalgia for the fertile desert edge, although the supreme garden, Damascus, never actually fell to the crusaders. Up until its conquest, the sacral aura of Jerusalem had been moderate for Moslems, but it became a symbol for the *jihad*. Enormous indignation was aroused by the brutal massacre of thousands of Moslems and Jews in Jerusalem. Such episodes intensely insulting to the opposite faith, as well as morally repugnant, were not unprecedented. At the start of their savage conquest of Crete in 827 the Arabs crucified a captured Byzantine admiral within sight of the coast to terrorize the defenders.[24] But Jerusalem's fall marked the start of an accelerated spiral of mutual antagonism: "'Islam has been entirely expelled from the *Sahil* and from Jerusalem, from that land of Revelation before the mission of the Prophet . . . Jerusalem is full of pigs and wine, the church bell has accompanied the cross there!'" exclaimed the Turkic ruler Nur-al-Din, emphasizing the symbolic barriers dividing Islam and Christianity.[25]

Just as the Palestine crusades constituted as much a symbolic as a strategic threat to Islam, they represented the culmination of a shift of power toward West Europe rather than a really new departure. Nevertheless, the events at the end of the eleventh century confirmed three striking changes. First, Christian naval forces (Byzantine, Norman, and Italian) dominated the Mediterranean. Second, the potential of Western feudalism for mobilizing land armies was considerable. Third, Christians tended to perceive all their enemies as a monolithic, Satanic complex against which holy war became a prime obligation. The lack of real rapport between the Turkic regimes of the Fertile Crescent, the Fatimids of Egypt, and the Almoravids was disregarded in facile extension of the urgent defense of Spain to adventure in Palestine.

The way preachers assimilated the anti-Moslem crusades to war against pagans in Central Europe is more surprising. To be sure, defensive war against such pagan enemies as the Avars and the Magyars had been a duty of Christian rulers since Charlemagne. After defeating the Magyars at Lechfeld, Otto I had tried to extend the Holy Roman empire's frontier from the Elbe to the Oder. He encouraged missionary activity, but did not demand that Christian warriors fight the Slavic Wends as a sacred duty.[26] Some writers have regarded the universalization of the crusade theme in the twelfth century as a projection on external enemies of fear of heresy within the Christian body. An exceptionally violent crusade was eventually directed against the Albigensian heretics in southern France. Certainly the prominence of the theme of Christian unity against all "heathen" enemies past and present, such as the eighth-century Saxons, who were reidentified as "Saracens" in the French epics, suggests that an intensely dichotomized view of the world had emerged.[27]

Up to the twelfth century, there had been localized crusades against the Wends, designed to thwart their savage raids on German settlements. In 1147, however, Bernard of Clairvaux, the most charismatic preacher of his age, assumed the leadership of an appeal with much greater ideological content. He proclaimed that fighting, including necessary killing of non-Christian enemies, was praiseworthy even for clerics (he had in mind the new military Order of Templars). Those who died in battle were to be considered martyrs. "Destruction" of a heathen *natio* (ethnic group) was laudable, as it had been for Moses and Joshua. These novel exhortations were carefully circumscribed to conform to the mainstream of Christian doctrine. A just war against the heathen had to be defensive in its initial impulse. Conversion by force was outlawed; however, conquered heathen might legitimately be prevented from opposing missionary activity. The crusaders' motives had to be pure; "clothed in the armor of faith," they could not admit love of fame, rage, or desire for booty. "The Crusade ideology in no way treated infidels as legitimate game," writes one scholar; the contrast to Central Asian conquest attitudes, as described below, is notable.[28] Destruction of the heathen *natio* implied its elimination as an organized polity, not genocide; all who surrendered were to be spared, but their territory—Bernard specifically used this concept—was to be ruled by Christian authorities.

Internal Dynamics of Islam

Quite apart from the vicious excesses (which he explicitly opposed) that followed Bernard's crusade appeal, it constituted an ideological intensification of the *jihad*-crusade spiral that had already been accelerated by the Christian penetration of Palestine. This spiral was partly responsible for the extreme hostility between the two civilizations that produced a physical scar across Europe that shaped and reshaped ethnic identities. The unprecedented Central Asian incursions of the thirteenth century, however, were still more responsible for the aggravation of hostility. The propensity for irregular attacks of earlier nomad auxiliaries of Islamic regimes had made stable, peaceful frontiers hard enough to achieve. Over the centuries since the foundation of Islam such depredations had tended to subside along the main points of contact with Christendom in western Asia. From the eleventh century on, a peculiar aspect of the Asian nomads converted to Islam counteracted these ameliorative tendencies. Earlier nomads frequently seized captives for ransom, for servile or technical work, or for brides. The pagan Magyars, for example, relied on Slav prisoners for most of their nascent agriculture and acquired many of their wives from among their Christian victims. Unless such nomads had access to major urban high cultures, however, their enslavement of prisoners tended to be self-limiting.[29] Neither Byzantium nor West Europe, sedentary societies using peasants as their work forces, needed extensive slave labor. Although Byzantine emperors did maintain eunuch servants and heathen and Moslem slaves could be held legitimately in Western polities, neither practice was widespread enough to provide a major attraction for slave merchants.[30]

For nomads who entered into a close relationship with Islam, however, an urban culture eager for slaves was at hand. In contrast to ancient civilizations or the postdiscovery offshoots of Europe in America, Islamic civilization rarely depended on slaves for agricultural or handicraft labor. Nevertheless, slaves satisfied three significant needs in Moslem society. The rulers were eager for administrative personnel more submissive than free Moslems and less opposed to Islamic tenets than were *dhimmis*. A reliable soldiery detached in its background from the turbulent nomads and the recalcitrant Moslem urban population was essential. Male slaves, especially if they could be trained from youth, appeared to provide an ideal source of recruitment for these requisites of stable rule. From the Abbasid caliphate and the Andalusian Umayyad regime on, such slaves were critically important, but their numbers were relatively low compared to the slave populations of first-century Rome or eighteenth-century tropical America. Altogether, slaves in the tenth century accounted for only 1 to 2 percent of the Islamic population, according to recent estimates.[31]

The second function performed by slaves for Islamic society, though also involving relatively small numbers, was equally significant. Conspicuous consumption of sex partners, mostly female, became a status symbol for top Moslem elites from the first days of the Arab conquest. This practice represented a departure from pre-Islamic circumstances, when Beduin clans in their fierce raids on one another rarely harmed or enslaved women and children.[32] Throughout later history, indeed, economic stringencies rarely permitted the typical Moslem to acquire a second wife much less an entourage of women ("harem"). But victorious military or political leaders became able to indulge their sensuality freely, though it appears that the symbolic significance of acquiring women from the vanquished was more important than "lust." Not only had Mohammed formally sanctioned polygamy, he openly kept concubines. Evidently, he conceived this practice to be a prolongation of the Semitic patriarchal style and cautioned his followers to treat their women equitably. The combination of rapid conquest and sacral example strongly established the harem status symbol in the beginnings of Islam.

As the nomadic traditions declined in the urban, status-oriented world of the Abbasid, Fatimid, and Andalusian Umayyad caliphates, and still more in subsequent regimes, the male's control of a large female household became an accepted concomitant of high rank. The difference between the Moslem and the Jewish practical ethic on this issue is undramatically but emphatically illustrated in the Mameluke Cairo documents which S. D. Goitein has meticulously analyzed. A Moslem mother, not atypically, considered the gift of a comely slave girl for her widowed son to be a meritorious act, whereas a single Jewish male who even lived under the same roof with a female slave was subject to excommunication by his community.[33] No doubt there were lax practices among Jews as among Christians, notably in Mediterranean coastal communities where Moslem women slaves were available; but it was impossible for concubines to become regular status symbols among adherents of these religions. Sexual conspicuous consumption would have been derisory if it had not been monopolized by the master, thus the high-status Moslem also required harem guardians. In the nature of things—a rare occasion when this phrase is appropriate—such guardians had to be eunuchs, therefore males enslaved as boys.

The third category of slaves, ordinary domestic servants, may have been as numerous as the other two groups combined, though still a small proportion of the total population. Christian and Jewish households as well as Moslems used domestic slaves in proportion to their economic resources. The tenets of Islam made such slavery unusually mild and afforded strong prospects of emancipation and advancement to converts.

The situation just described constituted part of the dynamic of Islamic civilization. Moslems were the principal customers for German Christian warriors and Swedish-Slavic traders who enslaved pagan Slavic and Baltic captives. Because they were able to maintain reliable family connections on both sides of the Islamic-Christian frontier, Jews and "heretical" Christian communities (at first Nestorians, later Armenian Gregorians) were the principal slave merchants. Jewish depots and Nestorian monasteries were important "eunuch factories," as Maurice Lombard's convenient map (designating each center by a scissors symbol) demonstrates.[34]

Christian churches forbade trade in Christian slaves, although the Genoese violated the precept down to the fifteenth century. In principle, Moslems could not acquire other Moslems as slaves. Consequently, as conversions to the two universal religions spread, the source of Moslem slaves (apart from black Africans) tended to be the enemy Christian populations. As a result, attacks on Christian territories became not merely a religious duty but a lucrative venture. Even if the *Dar ul-Islam* (the collective term for Moslem-ruled territory) could not be expanded, the attackers were almost certain to seize captives who could be sold profitably. Guichard identifies this development even in the early centuries of Islam:

> One should note in this connection the importance for the Occident of the slave "razzias" carried out following the conquest of North Africa and Spain, then within the framework of expanding Andalusian and North African piracy along the European coasts, as well as in the commerce with the Frank world. . . . It is evident that these facts had to correspond to a demand for slaves, i.e., to preexisting social forms and customs.[35]

The demand for female slaves was especially strong because pre-Islamic society permitted concubinage, which expanded rapidly during the conquest.

The acceleration over time in the extent and harshness of slave raids appears to have resulted from three factors: increased despotism of rulers and their neglect of early Islamic norms; brutal disregard of human life by the Eurasian steppe nomads and their Genghisid descendants; and imitation of the Court styles of Moslem Genghisid regimes by other Islamic polities.[36] The main alarm throughout Christendom was sounded as a result of slave raids, unprecedented in extent, that catered to the vastly expanded market in Ottoman Constantinople. A Moslem historian notes that huge harems and entourages were more characteristic of Ottoman and Chinese monarchs than they had been of the relatively modest Arab caliphs. A papal emissary charged that two hundred thousand captives had been taken in the Holy Roman empire during the long reign of Frederick III (1440–93).[37] During the same period, Tatars raiding the Russian principalities found that captives, who could be dispatched on foot all the way to the Black Sea slave emporiums, were their most valuable booty. In 1713 a Crimean Tatar raid on the relatively thinly settled Kiev area took off fourteen thousand prisoners.[38] Often Ottoman forces on the Habsburg borders preferred ransoming peasants needed by their Christian lords rather than transporting them to distant Constantinople, where the more accessible East Slavic and Caucasus slave reservoirs made competition too difficult. In a major campaign like that against Vienna in 1683, however, the Ottomans welcomed Crimean Tatar auxiliaries who led off numerous captives for sale.[39] Such recurrent threats did not oppress Christians alone. By 1400 rulers such as Tamerlane, proud of their steppe origins, had violated Islamic precepts by enslaving subject Christians (*dhimmis*) and even fellow Moslems. As they did on the Christian frontier, such brutal practices continued far into the modern period. Down to 1860, Uzbek seminomad raiders were still enslaving Persian sedentary captives on the dubious ground that, as Shiite schismatics, they were legitimate prey.[40]

The Frontier: An Overview

I fully agree with Norman Daniel's remark that "the physical frontier was not very clearly marked and was easily crossed. The frontier that divided the mental attitudes of Christians and Muslims was emphatically defined and crossed only with the greatest difficulty."[41] Nevertheless, the geographic frontier was there. Its presence is still almost tangible, and its ramifications are highly significant. One great Western nation, the Castilian, owed its *mythomoteur* to this frontier; the most powerful Islamic regime ever known, the Ottoman, derived much if not most of its legitimization from the *jihad*. Identities in other polities, not primarily crusader or *jihad* in origin or in legitimizing myths, can be understood only in relation to the frontier. Some of these polities, like the Habsburg empire, have vanished, but the early interaction with Moslem enemies continues to reverberate in the consciousness of Poles and Magyars. Present tensions between Serbs and Croats, though their origins are remote, are largely a by-product of the Ottoman frontier. Most important, the Russian imperial complex cannot be understood apart from its steppe experience. Numerous scholars have investigated these subjects intensively. Without their meticulous studies, I could not attempt an overall comparison. Certain comparative analyses have been invaluable guides, notably Andreas Angyal's recent study of East European baroque, Charles Dufourcq's and Fernand Braudel's comparison of developments in the western Mediterranean, Max Kortepeter's examination of the East European–Caucasus region, and above all William H. McNeill's *Europe's Steppe Frontier*.[42] Except for its greater extension in time and space, my analysis could add little; in comparative examination, however, such dimensions are crucial.

A few words concerning the frontier, invisible but very tangible, that always separated Islam from Christianity on the waters of the Mediterranean, are needed. Nearly all of the phenomena—extreme insecurity, threat of enslavement, deep raids, shifting lines of influence—were present at sea as well as on land. Except during brief periods, however, Christian naval forces were ascendant. Byzantium, in contrast to the High Roman empire,

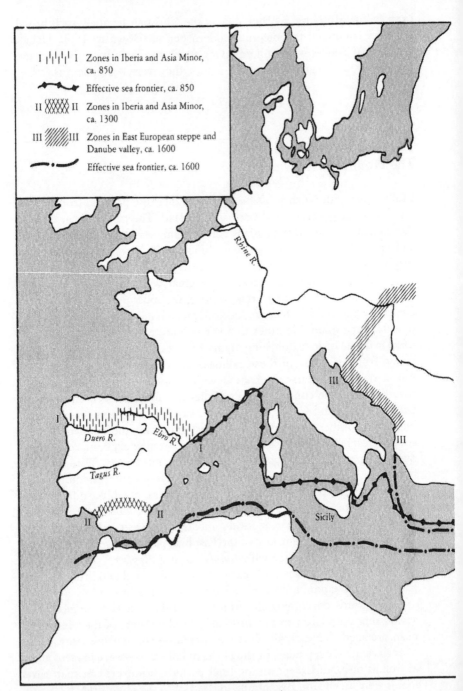

MAP 2. Frontier Zones between Islam and Christendom

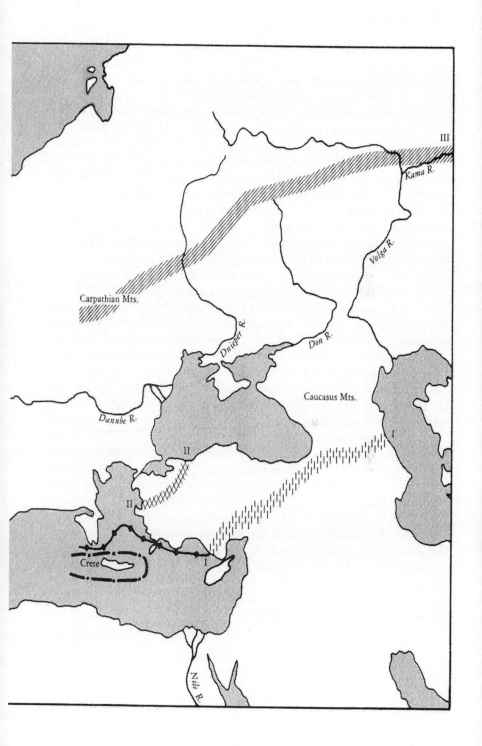

Carpathian Mts.

Kama R.

Volga R.

III

Dnieper R.

Don R.

Danube R.

Caucasus Mts.

II

I

II

Crete

I

Nile R.

was essentially a thalassocracy. Two brilliant studies (one by a German, the other by a Frenchwoman) have shown how Byzantium maintained that stance until the eleventh century, when the Italian city-states (to be sure, in no amicable manner) took up the relay.[43]

In contrast to the sea, the land frontier zone between Abbasid caliphate and Byzantine empire presented in embryo all the characteristics of more active frontiers, despite the relatively low intensity of the *jihad*-crusade spiral. It was not a line, but a constantly shifting zone. After 718 the Arabs had little prospect of major permanent advances. Until the mid-tenth century, however, they launched huge razzias into Asia Minor every summer and occasionally in winter. Apart from acquiring booty, these raids were designed to devastate a zone that could serve as a *glacis* for defense against Byzantine counterattacks. Both directly, through depression of agriculture and ruin of *poleis*, and indirectly, through enhanced landlord domination and Byzantine employment of rapacious mercenaries, Arab raids sapped the strength of the most important Byzantine region.[44]

In the broad frontier zone similar populations, often transplanted forcibly or recruited from afar, developed on both sides. The two sides were not always distinguished by religion, for the Abbasids excepted from taxation some border warrior elements who remained non-Moslem, whereas dissident Arab tribes fled to Byzantine territory. Both sides used Turkic mercenaries and adventurers, although those in Byzantine service were usually pagans from the Black Sea steppes. Both sides developed Greek-language epics, and Moslem antipathy to images was apparently reflected by intense iconoclasm on the Byzantine side.[45]

As Christian rulers attempted elsewhere when confronted by the unending drain of Moslem frontier warfare, the Byzantines ultimately set out to terminate their debilitating losses by pushing the zone away from fertile Christian areas back into the desert. Between 960 and 1071 the reconquest was largely successful. Although Byzantine power in the old Semitic areas beyond Antioch remained fragile, the reconquest of Cilicia and much of Armenia effectively excluded Moslem attacks on the Byzantine heartland until the arrival of the Seljuk Turks. Then, after extreme vicissitudes during the late eleventh century, the frontier zone became established on the coasts of the Anatolian peninsula and at the edges of the last remaining Byzantine foothold in the northwest.

The Iberian Frontier: The *Conquistador Mythomoteur*

All Mediterranean peninsulas are vulnerable to nomad attacks because their scanty rainfall supports fragile vegetation. Xavier de Planhol has emphasized that there is nothing "natural" about the Islamic nomad conquest of Asia Minor, for even the interior around the salt lakes once supported sedentary agriculturists.[46] Today the traveler sees a landscape not much different from the steppes of Iran or Jordan. The fundamental reason for the loss of the region to agriculture was that Byzantine forces, even before their great defeat at Manzikert in 1071, were unable to prevent hostile nomad incursions that destroyed crops by grazing, carried peasants off to slavery, and strangled the cities. Asia Minor is especially vulnerable because its open end extends into the Middle Eastern deserts. It is not generally realized that, apart from its sheltered location, the Italian peninsula is almost as fragile. Arab incursions from the sea by necessity excluded significant nomad participation even in Sicily and Sardinia, however. Transhumant pasturage, common throughout the central, semiarid plateau (Abruzzi) as recently as two generations ago, required broad passages for flocks coming down to the plains for winter feeding. Friction between migrating shepherds and sedentary cultivators had been endemic since Roman times. Lacking true nomadic traditions or religious legitimization, however, the shepherds could not become an organized menace.[47] The Balkan peninsula, on the other hand, has experienced successive regressions of sedentary elements (Vlachs, Albanians, Slavic mountaineer shepherds) to seminomadic ways of life. Only their separation from Central Asian nomad reservoirs (a result of Safavid interposition) prevented the Ottoman Turks from promoting more serious nomadic incursions in the Balkans. A third peninsula—for the Maghreb from the Gulf of Gabes to the Rif mountains really constitutes a Mediterranean peninsula—was completely overrun by nomads. The most extraordinary fate was reserved, however, for Iberia.

Although they retained a nostalgia for the desert and the oasis, by the time the Arab conquerors crossed the Straits of Gibraltar, they had left behind their nomadic styles of fighting and living from flocks. Consequently, they ceased to disrupt agriculture. Apparently, their Berber recruits far outnumbered the Arab leaders of the invasion. Although the initial Berber contingent included some Zenata nomad elements, such elements did not become dominant until the period of the Almoravids and the Almohads.[48] Moreover, their factionalism rarely permitted the Berbers to act as a united force. A revolt in 741 was suppressed by Syrian

Arab troops from Africa. Urban Arab or Arabicized elites were always dominant except, briefly, during Almoravid rule. It is significant that the early Berber invaders were not from camel-nomad tribes; only the Almoravids and their Mauretanian auxiliaries, three centuries later, were *grands nomades*. Even then, according to one recent historian, the sedentary Moslem kinglets preferred the Almoravids as less disruptive nomads than the alternate source of aid against Christendom, the Arab Hilalis.[49]

In such circumstances, a strange reversal of roles took place in Iberia. The skilled, urbanized Arab elites quickly seized the parts of Iberia that had appealed to the Romans—the southern and eastern coasts and the great Guadalquivir and Ebro valleys. Here were nearly all the significant cities and productive farmlands. For two centuries the dense preexisting population was well treated. Although a majority evidently remained Christian and Romance-speaking, enough became Moslem Arab in culture to provide, along with the rapidly Arabicized sedentary Berbers, a heavy reinforcement for the initial Arab invaders. Numerous Jews, gradually shifting from the Aramaic language to Arabic, also reinforced the Arab mercantile stratum. Consequently, an unusually prosperous, culturally brilliant urban society developed in Andalusia, based on an agriculture that was more extensive than the usual Moslem oasis cultivation. But this civilization included only a small part of the peninsula.

The Arab conquest necessarily extended to the center of Iberia, notably the symbolically significant Visigoth capital, Toledo. The first rush also nominally subdued all except the extreme northwestern mountains, which, probably, no previous government had thoroughly penetrated. There a Gothic elite remnant mingled with the Basque and Cantabrian indigenous population. Irregular warfare with the Moslems probably never ceased; in 791, only eighty years after the Arabs' conquest had begun, Alfonso II defied them by claiming to be king of Andalusia. In other words, almost from the start, as Ramon d' Abadal i de Vinyals contends, the claim to recover all the Iberian peninsula constituted a *mythomoteur* of the *reconquista*.[50]

The Christian remnant was neither nomadic (it included some semi-pastoral mountaineers) nor barbarian (although simplified, its Visigoth church architecture was impressive). Compared to the brilliant Moslem Andalusian culture, however, the Christians' was, to say the least, impoverished. Moreover, no Christian force could face a regular, determined Moslem army in the field. A century and a half later, unified under a capable Umayyad caliph, Abd al-Rahman, the Moslems were able to drive right across Christian Iberia to its symbolic heart, Santiago de Compostella. The Christians thus resorted to a tactic that strangely resembled the nomads'; one prominent historian has aptly written that "the weapon of the *reconquista* was transhumance."[51] The Christian internal economy depended on flocks, herds, and horses—property that could be evacuated quickly when a superior Moslem force appeared, yet could advance as quickly. Of course, these movements were not the same as desert or steppe migration. Nevertheless, over the centuries necessary for the reconquest and for three hundred years thereafter, Iberian shepherds moved their flocks up to four hundred miles along broad, royally protected routes. Forests along the way were denuded by sheep and goats, with subsequent erosion. A high degree of friction between shepherds and sedentary farmers, although both were Christian, was endemic to the "Mesta," as this transhumant pattern was called.

Some authorities ascribe a Berber origin even to the name "Mesta." Certainly many of the Christian styles of pasturage and mounted warfare were borrowed from Berbers, whom the Moslem regimes assigned as frontier guards. In the Duero valley and the upper Ebro valley, the principal scenes of frontier conflict until the eleventh century, the majority of the Berbers appear to have been sedentary mountaineers, probably less habituated than the Christians to this type of warfare. As early as 750, the frontier region became an immense zone of raids and counterraids. By the tenth century, a no-man's-land from the Central Sierra to the Asturian Mountains (about 150 miles) was too devastated to provide fodder for an advancing army.[52] After Christian reverses following their advance beyond the Tagus River in the eleventh century, their legendary hero, the Cid, devastated a similar area south of Toledo. During the fourteenth to fifteenth centuries, a smaller devastated zone half surrounded the remaining Moslem kingdom of Granada.[53]

In contrast to the Byzantine-Arab frontier zone, raiding tended to favor the Christian cause in Iberia. It is true that the Arabs desired a devastated *glacis* there, too; but their wealth was so superior to the Christians' that Moslems inevitably suffered more from deep raids. The Christian position differed completely from that of a real nomadic aggressor, however, in the use of fortified positions as nuclei for permanent, sedentary settlement. The dominant polity of the Iberian future, Castile, took its name from such castles; the term *"frontera"* originated as a chain of border forts. The terrain favored this tactic. In most circumstances the northern Iberian climate and terrain also favored the armored knight, one type of Castilian and French warrior, against the lightly armed Berber frontiersman, in contrast to nomadic superiority in a truly dry, open steppe or desert.[54] Consequently, except when confronted by an overwhelming Moslem concentration, Christian forces could maintain liaison between their fortifications more easily than could regular Arab forces, hence could provide more protection for agriculturists. Thus the Castilian fortified frontier advanced from the Asturian Mountains to the Duero, then in the eleventh century in a leap to the Tagus. In a sense, the Christians enjoyed advantages of both nomad and sedentary tactics in the peculiar Iberian environment.

The price they paid was transformation of the mentality and the identity of the leading Christian element, the Castilians, in a manner unprecedented in West Europe. Frontier shepherding attracted men with characteristics not dissimilar to the nomad's: ardent, strong, inclined to mysticism, warlike, anarchic, with low attachment to specific pieces of earth, hence always hungry for conquest and booty.[55] Alone among Western societies, the Iberian found taking of Moslems as slaves to be worthwhile. In contrast to Moslem practice, most were employed in agriculture, where serf labor eventually proved more profitable.[56] The Christian towns depended heavily on booty from raids, as well as on stock breeding.

The tendency of frontier populations to develop similar characteristics is further exemplified by the extensive uprooting and mixing of the Iberian populations. As noted above, the early Christian mountaineer kingdoms were of mixed ethnic origins. In the eighth century, settled Christian populations tended to flee the advance of the rude northerners or at least to accept evacuation arranged by their Moslem rulers.[57] A century later, Moslem restrictions on their religion led Christians to migrate en masse to the Duero River frontier. These "Mozarabs" became the dominant cultural element in Castile, providing its architectural, literary, and Court styles adapted from Moslem culture. In this way the second myth of the Castilian polity—the first having been simply the desperate defense of independence and Christianity—assumed visual form. The new version regarded the Castilian ruler of León, Alfonso VI (1072-79) as a supranational ruler. Two centuries later another Iberian ruler, James of Aragon, advanced a similar formula, claiming to be "ruler of the two *millatyn*," an Arabic word denoting "religion," but also implying "ethnic." As the myth was elaborated, the Iberian rulers asserted Christian dominance, but only in a pluralist society that tolerated a separate Moslem way of life including religious practice and community tribunals. The concept and the reality embraced not only Christians and Moslems but numerous Jews.[58]

Such tripartite division did not exhaust the acknowledged diversity of the Iberian kingdoms during the eleventh to fourteenth centuries. A great influx of Frenchmen—crusaders, Cluniac monks, pilgrims, adventurers, simple artisans, and farmers moving to a less crowded land—continued as late as the seventeenth century.[59] By then there had been an additional influx of Italians, principally Genoese, who dominated banking and were involved in ocean exploration. By the eleventh century, the majority of Christians in the Christian kingdoms were descendants of former subjects of the Moslems. They constituted in effect a separate ethnic community, speaking a Romance dialect heavily influenced by Arabic and maintaining their Mozarab styles. Except for the Basques, all Catholic elements coalesced fairly rapidly. Dialect areas in each kingdom were at first interpenetrating. Later they corresponded very closely, in the center and south of the peninsula, to the political divisions, especially those between the three *reconquista* kingdoms—Castile, Aragon, and Portugal.[60] The major dialects, however, remained as distinct (see chapter 8) as any Romance tongues. In addition, Castile derived its Mudejar architecture from the Cordova style of the Umayyad caliphate, whereas Aragon adopted the more austere Almohad style characterized by brick and colored tile *entrelacs*.[61]

In their heterogeneity, the Iberian kingdoms resembled the typically variegated populations governed by a Moslem regime. By the late thirteenth century, Granada, the only Islamic polity, also had a population heterogeneous even by Moslem standards. It included Berbers (nomad and sedentary), Moslems long settled in Spain, speaking Arabic and known as "Andalus," Christian renegades, and Jews.[62] To ascribe complete tolerance to Moslem Iberian regimes would be misleading, however. Periodical persecutions had occurred before the twelfth century, when the fanatic Almohad suppression threatened the survival of Andalusian Christianity and wiped out the remaining Christian communities in North Africa. Unquestionably, too, the *jihad* spirit was reflected in the extreme importance, by the end of the twelfth century, of Christian military-religious orders—Santiago, Calatrava, Alcantara—resembling the *ghazi ribat* strongholds, although directly modeled on crusader orders like the Templars.[63]

Moslem example does not seem to have been the principal force displacing the second version of the Christian myth. Increasingly during the Middle Ages, Iberia became an anomaly among the religiously unified Christian polities of the West. By the time Castile and Aragon were unified at the end of the fifteenth century, their elites felt a certain discomfiture at European jibes at the mixed religious background of Spaniards. The tolerance of a pluralist society appeared to be incompatible with the mythic claim that Spain had constituted the earliest *Antemurale* of Christendom. During the sixteenth-century French wars of religion, even the Catholic faction charged that "for Spain as a whole two out of three are Jews, *Marranos* [a derogatory term for converted Jews], Mohammedans or Saracens, that is, Granada Moors," according to sixteenth-century French opinion that Myriam Yardeni reports.[64] Spanish elite intolerance was heightened by a belated but intense flourishing of chivalric romances. Despite the obvious compatibility of the *chevalier* (*caballero*) and the seminomadic warrior styles, Christians considered Moslems to lack "knightly consciousness" even when they were prepared to fight for a Christian king.[65]

Examples of intolerance had been associated with Castilian warrior heroism—the Cid, in contrast to the royal authorities, closed mosques in the eleventh century. By the sixteenth century, not even long-expropriated mosques were safe from mutilation. An incongruous Gothic chapel was introduced into the finest Moslem monument, the Great Mosque of Cordova. By then Gothic architecture, adapted from French and Burgundian styles to replace the Mozarab type, had become a prime visual symbol of the third myth: the Most Catholic purity of the united Spanish kingdoms. In "purifying" its architecture, Castile was belatedly taking a path Aragon had followed for two centuries. As Robert I. Burns diagnoses the situation, "Something more imposing, more aggressively Christian was required. . . . Here, then, since Aragonese Gothic was not so advanced as Castilian, there would be no Burgos or León or Toledo Cathedral. . . . On the other hand, there would be no regression of Gothic influence in face of an upsurging Mudejar art, as happened in the contemporary Castilian conquest."[66]

Like the fourth Magyar myth discussed in chapter 2, this Iberian version was heavily inspired by gentry interests. The strong Jewish merchant stratum and the large element of *conversos* (converted Jews) in administration, the law, even the high nobility and clergy, were the target, just as Germans were the target of the early nineteenth-century Magyar myth. For Christian Spain there was a real threat to identity from the immense power of the Ottoman empire, just as a more insinuating though milder threat to Magyar identity arose from the Germanizing Habsburg administration. Moslem notions of genealogy also permeated the Spanish myth, leading to a concept of purity of descent (*limpieza de sangre*) virtually unknown elsewhere in Christendom. Fundamentally, the drive for purity at many levels represented a victory for the numerous gentry, which in some Castilian areas included all who could afford to serve as mounted warriors, over the upper-class, cosmopolitan, pluralist myth.[67]

As numerous writers have noticed, by far the most striking expression of the third myth's influence appeared in the real-life epics of the *conquistadores* in America. Not only did life imitate (in the best and the worst senses of the verb) the chivalric romance, the *conquistadores* themselves were drawn disproportionately from the transhumant petty gentry and shepherds of Estremadura.[68] Their lack of the usual sedentary attachment to particular pieces of soil made them easily mobilizable for restless adventures over a space comparable only to that traversed by the first Arab *conquistadores*. Lacking any real nomadic way of life or clan reservoir, however, the Spanish conquerors soon settled down to exploit their gains. Reverberations of the frontier identity myth persisted, as M. Crawford Young has noted, in the sharp line drawn between indigenous non-Christians (undifferentiated by "tribe") and Christians.[69]

In the final stage, the third mythic version became the sole *mythomoteur* for Spanish identity to a degree unparalleled in Magyar history, where competing myths continued to interact. The result in Spain was physical elimination (by death or expulsion) of a large majority of Iberian Jews and Moslems. The remaining Christian population of Spain was unusually intense in its ethnoreligious identity. But the problem of heterogeneous ethnolinguistic elements has never been fully solved there. The formal union of Aragon, which included a Catalan-speaking majority, with Castile appears to have been a "historical accident" when compared to the abortive attempt at union between those two kingdoms and Portugal, which was not notably more distinct from them than they were from each other. One explanation is that the Aragon-Castile union, late as it was, occurred just in time to be sealed by the final episode of the *reconquista*. Portugal, on the other hand, not only did not share, as part of an Iberian unified polity in the *Antemurale* myth, but had time to develop its own saga of overseas conquest.

The Great Steppe: A Frontier of Conflicting Myths

There is nothing novel about a comparison between the Iberian frontier with Islam and the Russian steppe frontier. Many historians, such as Pierre Chaunu, have noted the parallels.[70] I have not, however, encountered any systematic effort to compare the two cases. Much of the detailed, objective literature that permits one to undertake such a comparison has appeared fairly recently. The fact that the two lengthy frontier experiences are separated geographically, culturally, and temporally makes the comparison difficult but potentially highly valuable.

Although its aftermath was very important, the Iberian frontier ended in 1492 after seven and one-half centuries of existence. The East Slav steppe frontier probably emerged as early as the Iberian; but it did not become a Christian-Moslem frontier until the final conversion of the Golden Horde dynasty to Islam in 1312.[71] The Russian frontier ended—except in the Caucasus—in 1783. Its span was, therefore, somewhat shorter than the Iberian, but the periods involved are of the same magnitude and impact.

If one makes allowance for the different scale of forces and distances involved, the way Genghis Khan's Mongols overran the Rus polities immediately after 1241 resembles the Arab conquest of Spain. Novgorod submitted nominally but remained unconquered, as did a few lesser principalities in the Carpathian region (Halich) and the northwestern forest-swamp area. Concentrated Mongol forces could penetrate almost any part of the Rus-settled area, just as the Umayyad forces until the mid-tenth century could traverse Christian Iberia. The Mongols found the swampy forests hardly more attractive than the Arabs found the northern Iberian mountains. Consequently, they rarely disturbed the Christian principalities, which paid heavy tribute. Apparently, Mongol armed intervention was most frequent during 1270–90 when two large hordes were based near the Dnieper River.[72]

The "Tatar yoke," although burdensome and humiliating, was predictable, hence more endurable than many other nomad incursions. In contrast to Arab domination in Spain, which never overcame a nucleus of fierce Christian resistance, the Mongols were able in a few years of unprecedented destruction to inspire such awe that the East Slavs regarded them as the biblical Gog and Magog destined to conquer the entire world except Ethiopia. Alexandre Eck portrays the lasting impact on Slavic psychology. "The crushing military defeat inflicted on Russia by the Tatars had brought about the debacle of this authority [of the grand princes]. The terror which the invaders inspired remained profoundly anchored in the souls of the generations which had experienced the debacle. This terror was transmitted to their descendants. The Tatars were considered to be invincible beings. For more than a century no idea of organized resistance could even begin to arise in Russians' minds."[73]

Pressures resulting in the breakdown of this tolerable equilibrium came from four directions. In the late fourteenth century, the conversion to Catholicism of the Lithuanian dynasty (the Gedymids or Jagiellos) and its assumption of the Polish crown produced a powerful *Antemurale* state eager to extend its rule to most East Slavs. The almost impregnable forest and swamps protecting the Polish-Lithuanian bases and their West European technology enabled them in the mid-fourteenth century to challenge the Golden Horde Moslems by extending armed settlements into the Dnieper *lesostep*.[74] The Polish-Lithuanian Catholics were, however, perceived as enemies by the Russian Orthodox princes, who often preferred Tatar alliances.

Russian rebellion against the Tatars constituted a second factor. The Moscow princes' defeat of the Golden Horde at Kulikovo in 1380 may have prepared for the decisive blow to Golden Horde prestige that constituted the third factor upsetting the equilibrium. The direct blow, however, was dealt by Tamerlane, in repeated victories between 1391 and 1395. From that time on, the Tatars had to turn to Lithuania and Moscow for firearms, a technological advance nomads could not counter from their own resources.[75]

The fourth factor was Ottoman capture of Constantinople, followed a few years later by the seizure of the Genoese colonies on the south coast of the Crimea. This step not only provided a Moslem alternative source of firearms, but offered to the Crimean Tatar khanate, the partial successor of the Golden Horde, an inexhaustible market for slaves. Maintaining much of their own nomadic heritage and enlisting the completely nomadic Nogai Tatars, the Crimean elite turned avidly to booty raids, even ransacking Ottoman territory when they were allowed to transit it.[76] Until the Ottoman conquest was consolidated, about 1474, the Crimean Tatars had been turning to sedentary ways. From that date until about 1534, they carried out thirty-seven raids on Poland-Lithuania. The average interval of one and one-half years was as short as between the most intensive Mongol attacks in the thirteenth century and only one-tenth as long as the interval between Golden Horde incursions into the Russian principalities during the period of stabilization.[77] Moreover, the character of the raids changed; instead of the slow, rather disorganized horde movements typical of nomadic clans, the Crimean Tatars dispatched systematic cavalry raids of one to twenty thousand men. Defeats or negotiations secured some respites (notably Ivan III's success of 1503–15, which did not, however, protect Poland). The large-scale raids continued down to 1769, with exceptionally severe attacks around 1700.[78]

This account suggests that the picture of a steady Russian advance once the "Tatar yoke" was broken in the fifteenth century is misleading. The real but peripheral advances in Siberia, deliberately emphasized by Russian official propaganda from 1589 on, obscured the constant drain of the southern frontier and its traumatizing effect on East Slav mentality.[79] Fear of disaster from the steppe remained constant for a large proportion of the populations of Muscovy-Russia and Lithuania-Poland alike. Yet the pressure to move into fertile lands farther south was compelling. Both Christian monarchies used fixed but discontinuous fortifications, taking advantage of river lines and closing the gaps between them. For many years the Russian line ran along the Oka River to the Volga. Then it was advanced to Orel-Mtsensk-Seversk, where it remained until the mid-seventeenth century. No fixed defense line on the edge of the *lesostep* could close the tongues of open steppe that facilitated nomad advance. One corridor extended as far as Tula, only a hundred miles south of Moscow, opening the latter's suburbs to devastation more than once. A second corridor, from the Dnieper near Pereyaslav deep into Volhynia, had enabled the Cumans to cut across the Rus lands in the late twelfth century; from the fifteenth to the seventeenth centuries, it posed a threat to the heart of the Polish–East Slav acquisitions.[80]

The response of both Poland-Lithuania and Russia was to organize semioutlaw bands of frontiersmen known as "cossacks" as irregular light troops. They could meet the steppe cavalry on its own terms, but won advantages primarily by skillful use of the rivers that dissected the steppe. Boats mounting small cannon were invincible to steppe bowmen. Even wagons with firearms tended to offset the special archery skills the nomads maintained. The cossack zone of operation was called the "Ukraine," that is, the frontier region, whether in Poland-Lithuania or Russia. Indeed, there were transitory "Ukraines" or "Okraines" elsewhere on Slavic borders.[81] Like the Russian rulers, nearly all of the cossack leaders were Orthodox. In sharp contrast to Castile, where both church and polity were penetrated by the frontier mentality, however, the cossack frontier personalities could never dominate the strictly centralized Russian state. The Don cossacks remained relatively tractable to the Russian tsar's administration. The Zaporozhian cossacks, farther west, chose allegiance to him after rebelling against Polish religious and social oppression, but remained dissatisfied. The special cossack customs, above all their myth of a free, adventurous republic of warriors, became a major component in the slow emergence of a distinctive Ukrainian ethnic identity. Conversely, the defection of the Zaporozhian cossacks from Poland (1654) constituted a significant stage in the deterioration of Poland's position as the principal power of the Slavic world and as Christendom's eastern bulwark.

The emergence of Ukrainian identity was only part of the very complex way myths and ethnic identity were shaped by the steppe frontier experience. The Soviet historian S. F. Platonov suggests that East Slavic settlers' need to be ready to abandon a given settlement on approach of nomad raiders led to mobility and simplicity of habitation conducive to formation of a single state and church. Certainly the need for portable goods that could be saved from enemy raids constitutes a point of resemblance between Iberian and Russian Christians that may have inculcated in both a tendency to risky, distant imperial ventures. Like the Castilian and the Aragonese monarchs, the Russian tsars also prided themselves on being heirs of two great traditions. For the Russians, these were the city-centered Orthodox culture and the steppe empire tradition. In the latter role, tsars, like earlier Iberian monarchs, readily enlisted Moslem princelings as frontier buffers.[82] Because of their distance from Moslem cultural centers and their relatively recent adherence to Islam, it was possible in Russia—as it rarely was in Spain—to assimilate such protégés to the Christian nobility. Moreover, given the amorphous nature of steppe alliances, the Russians were able to use nomad to curb nomad.[83] The largest-scale success achieved by this policy was enlistment, in the late seventeenth and the eighteenth centuries, of the Buddhist Kalmyks for defense of the lower Volga region against Moslem nomads. The unreliable nature of the Kalmyk alliance, however, induced the tsarist authorities to tolerate a strong seminomadic Moslem group, the Bashkirs, in the southern Urals as a potential curb on the Kalmyks.[84]

As Jaroslaw Pelenski has brilliantly demonstrated, the fateful assumption by the Russians of the steppe heritage began with Ivan IV's conquest of Kazan in 1552.[85] Kazan was no ancient Moslem polity. It had been founded only in 1438; but its khan purported, like other heirs of the Golden Horde, to be a Genghisid. Acquisition of his realm (*yurt*) brought the Russians into sharp formal conflict with other Genghisid claimants, notably the Crimean Tatars; it also afforded the tsars an opening to claim a special place in the succession to steppe empire. Instead of formally dissolving the Kazan polity, the Russians continued to style it the "Tsarist State of Kazan," an assertion of title to the Moslem heritage paralleling the Iberian monarchs' claim to be "rulers of the Two Religions." Islamic law was conceded to the Kazan Moslem population until the eighteenth century, but (as in Valencia) only the numerous Christian immigrants were accorded full rights. It is notable that the impetus for the Kazan conquest not only came from popular aversion to slave-raiding, but was legitimized by crusader themes—"a holy war against the infidels who 'spill Christian blood and defile and destroy churches.'"[86]

Practically, though the conquest cleared the road to Siberia, it did little to diminish the steppe danger. From the seventeenth century on, the constant aim of Russian rulers was to eliminate this perennial drain by conquering its base, the Crimea, thereby attaining a frontier on the Black Sea. But it was extremely difficult to move the frontier across the open steppe by stages. At the end of the seventeenth century, an insecure "Belgorod line" near the present northern frontier of the Ukrainian S.S.R. was established. Peter the Great did not even try, in his treaties with the Ottomans and their Crimean vassals, to define a line frontier, for the Russians knew from their experience with Kazan that such a stable, fixed division of territory was impracticable. As late as 1735, the Russians had to settle for a defensive desert *glacis* north of the Sea of Azov. In the meantime, both cossacks and Tatars frequently violated whatever accords had been formally achieved.[87]

The preferred solution had to await a decisive weakening of the Ottoman empire and a rise of the relative weight of the Russian empire in the European balance. In 1776, Catherine the Great was able to insinuate a client as khan of the Crimea, but her ministers recognized in advance the precarious nature of such a step: "The easy means that the Turks have of influencing the country and submitting it to their power, the pillaging and other crimes peculiar to the Tatars that are carried out in our neighborhood and Poland's would soon give rise to new conflicts."[88] In fact, Russia formally annexed the entire Crimea in 1783.[89] The conquest of the Crimea was a turning point in Russian history; but the net result was not very different from the Catholic monarchs' conquest of Granada. Moslem raids on the Iberian coasts continued to constitute a menace, especially in conjunction with the rebellions of unhappy Mudejar subjects of Spain. Conversely, after 1783, Russia never had to face serious Moslem raids from across the Black Sea. Russia did, however, confront a potentially more serious continuation of the Islamic-Christian frontier by land, eastward into the difficult terrain of the North Caucasus. Even while mopping up the Crimean bases, Russian authorities feared that harsh treatment of the Nogai nomads would drive them into refuge among the Moslem mountaineers of the Caucasus.[90]

The peculiar myth complex of the tsarist state suggested a solution to the Caucasus problem, but it entailed further complications. On the opposite side of the main Caucasus range Christian princes, nominally Georgian Orthodox but ruling numerous Armenian Gregorian subjects, led a precarious existence as enemies or vassals of their Moslem neighbors. As early as the sixteenth century, Russian agents were in contact with these princes. By the late eighteenth century, the mythic role of the tsar as protector of the Orthodox required him to go to their aid. One of their principal grievances was an annual tribute, extorted by Moslem Lesghian mountaineers, of girl and boy slaves to be dispatched to Constantinople.[91] The instrument for affording tsarist relief was at hand in the Kuban cossacks, actually the turbulent Zaporozhian cossacks transplanted to the North Caucasus after they were no longer needed along the Dnieper.[92] In a complicated series of maneuvers, Russians asserted their suzerainty over the princes of Georgia, then reduced the region to an integral part of their empire. Georgian ethnic identity, like the Armenian, long predated East Slav identity; consequently, both groups proved too intensely self-conscious to be acculturated by Russian imperial policy.

There, as in the Ukraine, the circumstances of the Moslem-Christian frontier produced or intermingled ethnic identities in a manner that immensely complicated interactions among the populations of Christian polities. In a sense, the Russian frontier has had a more permanently disintegrative effect on its polity than did the Spanish. The most intractable ethnic problems of Spain—Basques and Catalans—predated the impact of the frontier with Islam, although coping with this impact may have thwarted Iberian rulers' integration of these diverse elements. On the other hand, the dominance of the frontier question produced a high degree of Iberian integration around the *Antemurale* myth common to Castile, Aragon, and even in some degree to Portugal. Russian championing of Orthodoxy, on the other hand, had some influence on integrating Ukrainians, but it also led to acquisition of the two indigestible Caucasus Christian ethnic collectivities.

The Russian empire permanently acquired Moslem elements that have been even less digestible. The Kazan Tatars at first occupied a position remarkably similar to the Mudejars'. Like the Castilian and the Aragonese kings, Ivan IV immediately eliminated the Moslem "noble" stratum. Like the Mudejars of Valencia, the Tatars (apart from a nomad remnant, a thoroughly urban group) withdrew to agricultural activity, often as serfs of Russian land grantees, like the Moor serfs of Aragonese nobles and religious orders. Maintenance of distinctive Moslem family patterns and religious practice was evidently considered to be a minimal surrogate in both instances for actually living in the *Dar ul-Islam*. The fraction of the Crimean Tatar population (one-third to two-fifths) that did not take the relatively easy emigration route to the Ottoman empire likewise retreated to mountain farming and horticulture, though these occupations were uncharacteristic for Moslems of nomadic descent.[93] In 1944 this tenacious ethnic fragment was dispersed, but the Kazan Tatars increased numerically and, as merchants indispensable for the Russian–Central Asian trade, manipulated their way into a relatively strong position.[94] In contrast, seventeenth-century Spain "solved" its Moslem problem by wholesale deportation.

The Habsburg Military Frontier

The strength of the Ottoman empire, the prime factor in the intractable nature of the Russian steppe frontier after 1474, presented Catholic Central Europe with a problem just as serious. Whereas the Ottoman regime never had any proximate intention of subjugating the East Slav territories, the Ottoman sultans—this is the familiar title, though they preferred "padishah"—had a very real prospect of conquering much of East Central Europe.[95] Their conquest in 1541 of the greater part of the Hungarian kingdom (acquired by the Habsburg dynasty in 1526) transferred a part of the problem of dealing with an aggressive Moslem neighbor, on the Carpathian frontier, to the Poles. But the main zone of contention remained the strategic region from the Hungarian plain to the Adriatic. The zone is located in a relatively thickly settled region with natural obstacles, including mountains near the sea and broad rivers that traversed the Hungarian plain. The Habsburg wasteland *glacis* was narrower than in Russia or even in Iberia, but it was crucial to the Ottomans as a jumping-off place for penetrating the heart of Christendom. Whether or not the zone actually represented the extreme limit of Ottoman power, it became apparent by 1600 that it lay at an equilibrium point between the great contestants.[96] Although a minor retreat would not have threatened the heart of their empire, the Ottomans' legitimizing myth obliged them to stand fast. Hungary was an integral part of their dominions, complete with towns containing mosques, in contrast to the vassal status of the Black Sea steppe. Any substantial retreat, therefore, would entail a surrender of part of the *Dar ul-Islam*. A historian of the Habsburg empire, Friedrich Walter, cautions, "It is basically incorrect to speak of 'boundaries' of these parts of the old Kingdom of St. Stephen, for they were only 'fluid demarcation lines.' According to the Turkish view, indeed, a land once conquered by the Moslems' sword could never be allowed to return to a Christian ruler. Hence the Sultan concluded no peaces, but only voluntarily respected an armistice that he might renounce at any moment."[97]

The crucial implication of this conclusion is that a regularly organized Moslem regime could no more assure a stable frontier with Christian neighbors than could Moslem steppe nomads. On their frontier with the Habsburgs the Ottomans occasionally did use Tatar auxiliaries; but more commonly Balkan Moslem recruits equally eager for booty were employed. The governors (*beglerbegs*) themselves consistently failed to observe armistice treaties. Up to 1600 they constantly attacked in order to prevent a consolidation of the Habsburg fortified frontier that would have impeded future large-scale advances. After that date, except for the great attack on Vienna in 1683, raids were primarily for loot. Given the Ottoman system of having its troops live off the enemy, whether formally belligerent or not, such raiding was indispensable for maintaining the Ottoman military posture.[98] Except in the deep penetrations of major campaigns, slave taking was a minor business, because distance and sparse pickings precluded competition with the Crimean and Caucasus wholesale slave traders. A historian of this frontier, Gunther Rothenberg, writes that "a period of formal peace only thinly veiled a state of constant border war. The numerous irregular troops maintained by the Ottoman border governors continued to harry 'the miserable peasantry with their ceaseless raids, plundered their property, and carried off into captivity the peasants, their wives, and their children.' "[99] A vigorous Habsburg response was not only a strategic necessity to protect Vienna and the Adriatic coast but a prime element in the Habsburg *Antemurale* myth. Apart from their family connection with the Castilian *Antemurale* kingdom, the Austrian Habsburgs based their claims to the crowns of Hungary and Croatia (a subkingdom) on their readiness to defend Christendom. In 1521, therefore, the hereditary Austrian lands closest to the scene of operations resolved to set up a "Wendisch" (that is, Slav) defensive frontier.[100] The intense symbolic significance of this frontier is suggested by the literary and personal connections that it developed with other European struggles against the Ottomans. A recent Hungarian study notes that

> Hungarian literature and the history of ideas of this period contain gripping documents on these struggles; but the South and East Slavic literature is also not devoid of gripping testimonials. . . . The heroic battle themes, which are often adventurous; the strong persistence of religious connections and medieval chivalric themes which we find in "the world of border fortresses" made a "baroquization" of this sphere easy. The baroque, penetrating from the south and west, encountered here a life style which was in many respects similar. . . . Moreover, we can draw on the quite analogous Spanish case. . . . It is so to speak symbolic that many Spaniards also participated in the struggles against the Turks in the sixteenth and seventeenth centuries [in Croatia].[101]

As on the Oka frontier of Muscovy, regular troops were employed for garrisons, but light forces were indispensable for closing the gaps between fortifications. Even the pre-Habsburg Hungarian kings had welcomed Serb recruits on a small scale. The masses of Orthodox Serbs fleeing Ottoman oppression in the sixteenth and seventeenth centuries provided a large reinforcement for the Croatian frontier defenses. Because only remnants of the old Croatian kingdom remained under Habsburg rule, employment of Serbs was inescapable. Their settlement meant, however, that the fairly clear, stable linguistic and cultural boundary (see chapter 8) separating Orthodox Serbs and Catholic Croats became hopelessly confused. At an early stage the Croat Estates expressed fear for the dissolution of the regular territorial order.[102] From the standpoint of the Habsburg myth, however, Serb enlistment provided a certain support for the verbal initiatives for liberation of all Balkan Christians. Another aspect of the Habsburg myth—the preoccupation with championing Catholicism—worked at cross-purposes, however. Serb settlers were driven to revolt in the 1670s by pressures emanating from local administrators and Jesuit clergy to accept a Uniate relationship with Rome. The central Habsburg authorities usually tried to shield the Orthodox from such proselytism. The regimental organization of their military colonies, each complete with Serb officers and cultural facilities, fostered the emergence of an educated Orthodox lay elite. A Serbian metropolitan at Karlowitz was recognized as "ethnarch," leader of the community. Despite the hostility of Ottomans and Habsburgs, Serb connections could also be maintained across the frontier zone, with a significant effect for maintenance of Serb identity.[103]

After their abortive second siege of Vienna in 1683, the Ottomans' power receded so rapidly that the Croatian military frontier became a backwater. A large part was retroceded—including its latent ethnic antagonisms—to the kingdom of Croatia in 1784. New fortified frontiers were required to guard the reconquered Banat of Temesvar and Transylvania. Indeed, the last serious Ottoman incursion into the Habsburg realms occurred in 1835, and the latter two frontier regions were not formally reincorporated into the kingdom of Hungary until 1873.[104] The effect of the Transylvanian military frontier was to stimulate Orthodox "Vlach" (Rumanian) ethnic consciousness. In Temesvar, which had been a part of Hungary proper, military colonization produced an ethnic mosaic in a region that had, apparently, been uniformly Magyar. In addition to Rumanian Orthodox settlers, mainly in the eastern section, and Serb refugees in the west, returning Magyars and German-speaking veterans of the Habsburg army appeared. The latter settled in "Suabian" villages and followed their own customs. The Orthodox colonies were at a "prenational" stage, mainly distinguished by religious communities distinct from the Magyar Catholic elite. As early as the 1750s, Serbs appealed to Russia to protect their Orthodox privileges and began to have some concern for Slavic solidarity.[105]

The lasting effect of the Moslem frontier, therefore, was to upset population in the middle Danube valley, which had been almost homogeneously Western Christian, although increasingly divided between Catholics and various Protestant denominations. The injection of Orthodoxy was enhanced by Habsburg acquisition during the late nineteenth and early twentieth centuries of Bosnia-Herzegovina, a move taken in part to eliminate a salient left over from the frontier hostilities. Habsburg administrative pressure in the 1770s to make all instruction in military colony schools German heightened tensions. Renunciation of new conquests that might destroy the Ottoman empire that by the start of the nineteenth century seemed to the Habsburgs an important offset to Russian power also tended to make the position of the frontier regiments equivocal. During the nineteenth century, they were increasingly employed, like the Russian empire's cossacks, for internal security rather than for defense against an enemy of Christianity. As a result, the *Antemurale* element of the Austrian Habsburgs' myth not only declined but in some ways became an anachronistic encumbrance.[106]

Frontier Legitimacy: The Ottoman Case

References to the involvement of the Ottoman legitimizing myth with upholding conquests have already appeared. The role of the frontier with Christianity in this myth goes far beyond defensive requirements. Scholarly authorities disagree sharply on the relative importance of the *jihad* component of the myth, but it is beyond dispute that it was far more important for the Ottomans than for any other major Islamic polity. The *ghazi* (*jihad* warrior) tradition set in motion a *mythomoteur* that impelled the Ottoman empire toward adventures abroad—to become a kind of "warfare state." A large, steady influx of slaves was basic both for maintenance of the administrative apparatus and for elite status. The self-image and self-confidence of elites was inextricably bound up with conspicuous consumption of sex partners. Maintaining the loyalty and discipline of the top-heavy military apparatus required regular expansion or, at the very least, constant irregular raiding.

Understanding the role of the *ghazi* frontier is enormously complicated by the *parti pris* of some leading scholarly analyses. Ernst Werner's critique of "Kemalist" Turkish historians' exaggeration of the nomad origins of the Ottomans is plausible. As a recent Turkish study indicates, the return to emphasis on Central Asian ties actually began among Ottoman elites as early as the 1860s; it appears very likely, therefore, that subsequent historiography was influenced by this emphasis.[107] But Werner's own interpretation is too heavily influenced by Leninist insistence on finding "feudalism" in all evolving societies. Both approaches offer some corrective to the Eurocentrism of earlier studies, however, especially the nineteenth-century classics by Leopold Ranke, Joseph von Hammer (Purgstall), and Johann W. Zinkeisen.[108] For a nonspecialist to enter this complicated historiographical dispute is dangerous. I am impressed, however, by the slight extent to which these vigorously defended positions really differ in evidence adduced. I suspect that the historical record these scholars have so diligently established can support an interpretation that combines the essentials of their competing views.

There is no serious disagreement concerning the geopolitical framework of the Ottoman experience. After the battle of Manzikert (1071), Anatolia was overrun by Turkoman nomads, whom Werner estimates at 550,000 to 600,000 in number, pursuing the typical steppe pattern of expansion into sedentary areas.[109] In addition, they were inspired and legitimized by the *jihad* concept, which they had adopted on conversion to Islam a few generations earlier. The leading Turkic dynasty, the Seljuks, although dependent on the military capacities of these "tribal" warriors, rapidly adopted High Islamic patterns of despotic rule, including the invention or large-scale adaptation of such centralized administrative-religious institutions as the *medressa*. In Anatolia the Seljuk power base was around Konia, far to the southeast of the principal remaining Byzantine centers. Consequently, *jihad* participation became increasingly peripheral both to Seljuk legitimacy and Seljuk policy, which stressed expansion in the Fertile Crescent. After 1259 the Seljuks were weakened by Mongol pressures. The *ghazi* tradition devolved on semiautonomous frontier bands.[110]

The Ottomans officially claimed to have once been Seljuk vassals; but an early seventeenth-century Ottoman history places their appearance (as "descendants of Japhet") in Anatolia in 1277, when Seljuk authority was already vestigial.[111] At that time, the Ottoman ("Osmanli," from the eponymous ancestor) band on the Byzantine frontier, Werner notes, comprised only four hundred families. Here, it seems to me, is one key to understanding apparent historical contradictions. A group this size, formed as a *comitatus* around a single clan or family and adhering to its dynastic myth, is the typical beginning of a *Stamm* or nomadic conquest agglomeration. Not until two centuries later did this Ottoman agglomeration finally absorb competing bands in Anatolia. The Ottomans experienced great difficulties in competing with Tamerlane's successors, who stressed their fictitious Genghisid genealogies, for the loyalty of Turkic elements; a more appealing legitimizing myth was crucial for Ottoman success. Paul Wittek notes that the Ottoman dynastic genealogical myth was very sketchy until this later stage (ca. 1400) of Turkic amalgamation: "This contact made them conscious of their Turkic character. The Sultan assumed the national title of '*khan*,' and was provided with a genealogy which related him to the most noble of Oghuz tribes. The Ottoman state appeared as the continuation of this tribe. If all this was only fiction, the very introduction of this fiction into tradition is an extremely important historical fact—it belongs to a first 'national' movement which was manifested by numerous other traits and had lasting consequences."[112] In terms of the myth-symbol interpretation I employ, then, the fifteenth-century Ottomans elaborated a new genealogical myth. The myth appears to have stimulated the Ottoman Sultan Mohammed II (1451–81) to believe his dynasty, as the heir of Oghuz, was destined to rule the world. Thereafter, as in the *Stamm*, only the padishah's genealogy counted.[113]

In contrast to most successful Eurasian conquest agglomerations, however, the Ottomans developed their genealogical myth not at the start of conquest but at a very advanced stage. The departure from the norm was possible, I think, because of the peculiar nature of the Moslem-Christian frontier and the Ottomans' extraordinary skill in exploiting the opportunities it afforded. Following the mid-thirteenth-century Mongol disruption, a new mass of Turkomans moved into Anatolia, providing manpower for enhanced Moslem attacks on the remaining Byzantine area around Nicaea. Just what proportion of these new arrivals were from Central Asia, as compared to those who had been occupying parts of Iran, is disputed. Descriptions of the newcomers as "savage tribesmen" appear exaggerated, if only because the very fragmented groups resembled small war bands or clans rather than the large agglomerations to which the term "tribe" is usually applied.[114] Moreover, the Turkic arrivals appear to have supported themselves by booty in contrast to pastoralism to a greater extent than most nomads did. Finally, and most important, the larger organizational forms of the frontier Turkomans derived from *sufi* dervishes, notably the Bektashi or "white cap" order. Although the latter may not actually have provided military structures, dervish preachers certainly inspired the Turkic elements to united, relatively disciplined combat against Christian regimes, that is, to *ghazi* warfare organization.[115]

The Bektashi were Turkic in origin with fairly recent steppe traditions. Therefore, their special appeal to men of similar background, in line with the populist character of the *sufi* movement, is not surprising. Nor is it astonishing that the deviations from orthodox Islam which the Bekhtashi encouraged were greater, in the *ghazi* situation, than the adaptations of Islam to popular milieus *sufi* preachers usually made. The principal doctrinal deviation, which orthodox or High Islamic culture later combated, was forced conversion. This practice was related to an unrestrained exploitation of non-Moslems going far beyond the "state of humiliation" imposed by earlier Islamic regimes. A frontier romance originating among Danishmend *ghazis* of the fifteenth century proclaimed: "We are the wolves and they [Christians] sheep. . . . Did a wolf ever renounce enjoying a sheep?"[116] Fundamentally, such ruthlessness derived from the traditions of the Central Asian steppe (note the significance of the Turkic wolf totem) and the recent example of Genghis and Tamerlane. The populist Islamic insistence on conversion or death provided a necessary legitimization. A dervish leader's remarks implicitly recognized the ruthlessness of his followers: "For this construction [of a garden wall] thou must employ Greek workers, for the building of the world is work of the Greeks . . . the annihilation of the same world, on the contrary, is reserved for the Turks."[117]

From this point of view, the "contradictions" scholars have perceived in fourteenth- and fifteenth-century Ottoman attitudes appear to be relatively slight differences in emphases deriving from changing circumstances and personalities attached in different ways to both the *ghazi* and the steppe traditions. Werner is no doubt right in pointing out that in the early fourteenth century the Ottoman dynasts, having become the military leaders of the Turkic elements organized by the Bektashis, glorified their Turkic forefathers even when their names did not suggest that they had been Moslems. Murad II (1421–51) was considered a throwback to tribalism because he was illiterate and erected pyramids of skulls of his defeated enemies; but until 1583 Ottoman armies occasionally reverted to this practice in fighting the Safavid dynasty. If Murad indeed carried out human sacrifices on the graves of Turkic heroes, he was, of course, violating fundamental Islamic precepts.[118] But other elements of steppe tradition, such as the belief that a rug is sufficient furniture or the retention of *"askerg"* (soldier) as a title even for sedentary townsmen to distinguish them from despised elements like the Greeks, are general features of nostalgia among sedentary Moslems.[119]

Without *ghazi* legitimization the Ottoman dynasty could not have enlisted fragmented Turkic elements for the concentrated attack on Byzantium which the Ottoman geographical location favored. Without the single-minded concentration on attacking Christian lands, including the move to the Balkans in the late fourteenth century, the Ottomans could not have maintained *ghazi* solidarity. Their earliest chronicle stressed this myth: "Why have the Ghāzīs appeared at the last?. . . . Because the best always comes at the end. Just as the definitive prophet Mohammed came after the others, just as the Koran came down from heaven after the Torah, the Psalms, and the Gospels, so also the Ghāzīs appeared in the world at the last [Ottoman rule]."[120] One of the major ceremonial symbols of Ottoman rule, the investiture of a sultan, included presentation of a saber, the symbol of a nomad horseman, by the *kalifa* of a dervish *pir*, nominally acting as representative of the long-defunct Ottoman suzerain, the Seljuk sultan, but actually combining the *ghazi* and the nomad legitimization myth in his act.[121]

In effect, this ceremony combined three myths crucial to the Ottoman polity: continuity with High Islamic orthodoxy; dervish *ghazi* spirit; and steppe military valor. None disappeared entirely during the empire's history. The special relation to the Tatars and the practices of regular military organizations outlined above always retained a steppe connection. The *ghazi* dervish spirit was reinvigorated by conversion in the seventeenth century of most of the Albanians, who thenceforward provided many of the most vigorous statesmen and warriors.[122]

If one accepts this interpretation, the Ottoman version of the High Islamic legitimization was not much more contradictory as myth to the *ghazi* and the steppe mythic versions than they were to each other.[123] Peter Sugar sees a sharper clash between a *ghazi* faction seeking populist dominance and a commercial interest encouraging more systematic conquest in order to stabilize Balkan trade routes.[124] Sugar recognizes, however, that the *ghazi* spirit was a valuable instrument for merchants attached to High Islamic culture. As was noted in discussing Hungary, the role of the padishah as defender of the *Dar ul-Islam* could not be renounced under any of these mythic versions. In earlier stages of imperial consolidation, shifts in emphasis were probably decisive. Acceptance of High Islamic (*Sharia*) ethics made it possible for the Ottomans to conquer the sedentary Byzantine population around Nicaea without the complete disruption the *ghazi* unconditional demand for conversion would have entailed. Adoption of the old Islamic institution of a professional mercenary army provided the Ottoman rulers with a loyal instrument to curb turbulence of either nomads or dervishes. The first step toward forming such a force was the enlistment of Christian prisoners and deserters in a small, impermanent "Janissary" bodyguard. Significantly, the Janissaries (after considerable transformation) were assigned a dervish patron saint.[125] Later, as the largest body of regular infantry in Europe, they enabled the Ottoman army to make sweeping conquests without failing, as steppe conquerors so often did, to consolidate their hold on the ground.

Johann Zinkeisen noted this tradition in 1840 in a passage that presents a precocious paradigm of the interpretation of incremental policy making:

> It is indeed true that the first campaigns of the Osmans in Europe, taken individually, not infrequently appear to be planless, confused freebooting and destruction expeditions. They win provinces, only to lose them. . . . But if one keeps the entire perspective in mind, one cannot mistake the fact that the growth of the Ottoman Empire proceeds in almost regularly expanding circles. It resembles a plant which expands each year without losing strength as a result. On the contrary, both through their mutually supporting relationship, are very closely connected. Moral and material unity is the vital principle of the Osmanli Empire from its very first period. That is the basis of its strength, its superiority, particularly to the principalities of Asia Minor. From the start no new permanent conquest was made that did not rest on an early, secure foundation, a strong bulwark. The Hellespont was not crossed by the Osmanlis until their rule in Asia Minor had been firmly entrenched.[126]

Such step-by-step consolidation of gains in sedentary areas provided the Ottoman empire with a high degree of military stability and an economic base that was not quickly exhausted. The *devshirme*-Janissary complex also permitted (as discussed in chapter 6) a degree of administrative centralization based on a permanent capital that was unusual in Islam. Only the stability and centralization that the peculiar Ottoman adaptation of the frontier opportunities produced could have altered the evolution of southeastern European ethnic identity by direct and indirect effects on population movements and manipulation of preexisting myths. On the other hand, only the adoption of a High Islamic legitimizing myth could have reconciled the populations of southwestern Asia to four centuries of Ottoman rule.

Summary and Conclusions

Each of the two great universal religions that came to dominate the Mediterranean world by the early Middle Ages provided a legitimizing myth for a distinctive civilization. As was discussed in chapter 2, circumstances related to the formation of these civilizations but not intrinsic to their teachings associated the two civilizations with two equally distinctive ways of life: Islam with the nomadic way, Christianity with the sedentary. As the legitimizing myths developed, the sharply differing identity components derived from the two ways of life interacted with doctrinal cleavages between Islam and Christianity to produce two intensely opposed identities. As frequently occurs when different creeds become the legitimizations for societies that are sharply opposed in interests and attitudes, doctrinal cleavages became salient in men's consciousness, whereas shared doctrines were minimized. Indeed, their common origins as well as their geographical proximity made the Islamic and the Christian civilizations the major negative reference points for one another. In this respect, the two civilizations resembled on a grand scale ethnic groups that commonly define themselves by reference to out-groups. All Moslems conceived themselves to be united, at least in contrast to neighboring Christians. Christians, usually on the defensive, often adopted a similar minimal identity criterion. In this way, the two great religious civilizations interacted over the centuries to perpetuate and to redefine each other's identity in terms that may be characterized as "supraethnic."

As in the typical ethnic interaction, the exclusionary relationship of Islam and Christianity was not confined to attitudes. Violent conflict was common where the two civilizations, organized in polities, encountered one another physically. Although the course of this conflict was complicated, it tended toward a spiral of intensifying antagonism. The spiral movement was greatly accelerated by the intrusion into the eastern areas of the two civilizations of Eurasian steppe nomads—Seljuk Turks, Mongols, Chagatay Turks. Apart from their larger numbers and more frequent incursions, the Eurasian nomads' value systems manifested a harsher attitude toward sedentary populations than had Arabs of the original Moslem conquest. The Eurasian steppe attitude led to immense depredations directed against sedentarized Moslems. Nevertheless, the fundamental affinity of Islam for the nomadic way of life, evidenced in nostalgia forms that contrasted with peasant patterns, led most steppe nomads to become Moslems themselves a few generations after their conquests. The mainly Turkic converts retained their identity based on genealogical myths and much of the steppe tradition of ruthlessness, but directed their further depredations primarily, though not entirely, against Christians. The converts adopted specific values from earlier Islamic civilizations, including slaveholding as a form of conspicuous consumption, that affected their continued depredations. Slave raids became a major motive for accelerated conflict with Christians.

The spiral of antagonism was also accelerated by Christian reprisals. The effect was creation of a broad frontier zone of insecurity between Islamic civilization and Christendom. Moreover, the concept of defending this frontier provided an intense legitimizing myth for major polities on both sides. For the Castilians and the Ottomans, frontier championship of their respective religions became the main component of the constitutive myths. For the Habsburg version of the Holy Roman empire, for Byzantium, Poland, Hungary, Russia, Aragon, Safavid Persia, the Mameluke empire, and lesser polities, frontier defense became a major element of the *mythomoteur*. The customary term for a polity based on the Islamic frontier myth is *ghazi*; for the corresponding Christian polity it is *Antemurale*. Injection of steppe conquest values intensified later versions of the *ghazi* myth; but adoption of either version of the myth tended to produce an intense identification of polity and dominant population elements, mass and elite alike. On both sides of the frontier, groups tended to mimic each others' values and behavior patterns, while remaining hostile. Castilian *conquistadores*, especially, adopted many Moslem and nomadic patterns. The frontiersmen tended to perceive themselves as "chosen" or superior to other populations of their own faith. Consequently, the frontier groups evolved a precocious national identity within the broader religious identity.

At the same time, the region of frontier conflict became a "shatter zone," to borrow a term originally applied to East Europe between the world wars. The populations, of diverse religious and cultural backgrounds, had been transplanted or realigned politically during the protracted hostilities. Such notably was the situation of Catholic and Orthodox populations on the Habsburg-Ottoman frontier and for various Moslem and Christian groups along the Russian frontier with Islam. Even when religious differences were not present among the peoples on one side of these frontiers, the perilous frontier experience itself sometimes produced significant consciousness of identity, as among Ukrainians. Incorporation of diverse, intermixed elements of these types in an empire whose myth they did not fully share produced, in turn, a persisting legacy of interethnic tension within the major polities of East Europe and the Middle East. Throughout a broad zone including Iberia, the Danubian basin, the Balkans, Asia Minor, the Caucasus, and the Black Sea steppe, therefore, the clash of Islam and Christendom constituted a major factor in the emergence of special types of ethnic identity.

CHAPTER FOUR

Polis and *Patria*

Civic Identity and Urban Civilization

"These [medieval] towns were the West's first 'fatherlands.' And certainly their patriotism was for a long time to be more coherent and much more conscious than territorial patriotism, which was slow to appear in the first states," writes Fernand Braudel.[1] Citizenship, as the derivation of the word suggests, began with the experience of intimate participation in a small political entity. The intense identity this participation fostered became, after many vicissitudes, the basis for many if not most broader identities. Indeed, it seems probable that, as Emile Benveniste argues, the fundamental concepts of territorial habitat and city were inextricably mingled for Indo-Europeans at a very early stage of their historical evolution:

> In fact there are terms, a series of terms, which comprise the extent of a territorial and social division of varying dimensions. From their origin, such territorial organizations appear to have been rather complex; each people has a distinctive variety of them. Nevertheless, one can specify one term for a considerable area in the western part of the Indo-European world. In Italy—apart from Latin—this term is represented by the Umbrian word *tota*, which means "*urbs*" or "*ciuitas*," "city" or "city-state." ... They did not distinguish between city and society, which were one and the same concept. The limits of the organized group's habitat marked the frontiers of the society itself.[2]

The city, therefore, was the original *patria*, and "patriotism," although a neologism only a little older than "nationalism," constitutes a logical and perhaps psychological extension of the old concept of civic identity.

Where, then, does this leave the Islamic world? Because among Europeans—or Indo-Europeans—the city reinforced or even originated territorial identity, is the city as a highly developed social institution irrelevant to Islamic identity? Certainly not insofar as the Islamic civilization is concerned. Braudel points out that large cities are the "hothouses of every civilization. Furthermore, they create an order."[3] Because Islam produced several large urban centers during the centuries (seventh to sixteenth) when West Europe had none, it would be anomalous to suggest that the city was unimportant to Islamic identity as such. In fact, the faith itself requires an urban environment for its fullest expression. Although descended from a line of caravan merchants, Mohammed made two successive Arabian cities his base of operations. Prior to the crusades, city merchants dominated all Moslem religious scholarship, despite Beduin antipathy to the talkative *suk* ("market," *bazaar* in Persian) and aristocratic Persian contempt for commerce.[4]

The basic difference was between Moslem attachment to urban culture as such and European particularist loyalty to specific cities. According to Islamic norms, a believer is a full "citizen" of any Moslem polity in which he chooses to reside, and he is therefore in principle at home in any city of the *Dar ul-Islam*. Only gradually, after the ninth century, did the city lose its dominant place in Islam, as Central Asian steppe mercenaries and invaders undermined merchant-scholar predominance. One turning point in this process was the replacement, in 1422, of *Karimi* (spice merchant) activities, a vigorous although late expression of Arab mercantile enterprise, by a Mameluke state monopoly.[5] Most authorities somberly note that the decline of the urban merchant culture coincided with stagnation of Islamic civilization as a whole.

Even in decline, urban culture remained essential for Islamic identity. Elsewhere, the persistence of the city as a focus of identity, even after its economic utility was undermined, is remarkable. Residents of small places in Italy accorded legal status as towns in medieval times jealously clung to the designation *cittadino* to avoid the pejorative *contadino* (countryman). On the Gulf of Lyons coast, in southern Spain, in Tunisia, networks of cities persisted after their economic functions in the Roman empire had dissipated.[6] The remarkable persistence of urbanization is further demonstrated, a millennium later and many thousands of miles away, by a tiny but intensely urban center in the Brazilian highlands. The American anthropologist who studied this town concludes:

> Once a society reaches the stage of technology and social organization in which a large number of people can be freed from food-producing activities and occupational specialization becomes feasible on a large scale, there is little likelihood of reverting to more homogeneous arrangements. . . . A specialized economy evidently tends to respond to a threat to its particular specialties by developing new specialties. Urbanism, in this sense, is a one-way road, from which once having embarked upon it, there is no turning back. . . . They refuse to admit that they are of the country and hence the wilderness all but engulfs them. They despise the work of the peasant and see in him the destroyer rather than the creator of civilization.[7]

Significantly, the sociological analysis just quoted is based on observation of a transatlantic offshoot of Mediterranean culture. Not only are differences between Mediterranean urbanism and the Moslem variety apparent, but there are also significant similarities. Although divergent attitudes toward urbanism in North European and Mediterranean cultures are important, the persistence of urban images is remarkable in the north, too.[8]

In a sense, therefore, the city constitutes a third way of life, as ineradicable and as permeating as nomadism or sedentarism. As indicated above, the impact of the city differed psychologically in different cultures; the total impact of the urban pattern was also affected by the sheer weight and distribution of the phenomenon. The modern recourse to an overall index of urbanization derived from the proportion of city dwellers to the total population tells only one part of the story. Distribution of urban centers has been equally important. As Table 1 indicates, despite Islam's creation of large cities, the total number was small in proportion to the huge expanses incorporated in Islamic civilization. In Persia, largely urbanized before the advent of Islam, density of cities was only one-third to one-half as high as in the Roman empire or medieval or early modern Germany. In Moslem countries, where steppe and desert were far more prominent than in Persia, density must have been correspondingly lower. In fact, both the size of individual cities and the scarcity of cities of any type were concomitants of the caravan trade complex that was the economic basis of Islamic civilization. Each oasis tended to have a single city, the node of a trade network that provided wealth sufficient to sustain artisanry and mercantile activities on a scale rarely attained in Europe until modern times. For

Table 1. Density of Urban Network

Region	Period	Number of Cities	Approx. Sq. Miles per City
Iran	20th century	100	6,000
Iran	pre-20th century	400	1,500
Roman empire	6th century	900–1,200	700
Italy	ca. 1200	200–300	400
Germany	15th century	3,000	100
Germany	ca. 1800	4,000	70
European Russia	ca. 1700	200–250	8,000
Russian empire	1787	500	4,000

Sources: Rörig, p. 75; Walker, p. 32; estimate for Iran based on Bémont, p. 32; see also Dagron, *Naissance d'une Capitale*, p. 60; Claude, p. 12; Waley, pp. 7ff.; Hamm, p. 13; Miliukov, p. 134; Rozman, p. 97.

example, in 1500 the urban population of Egypt, concentrated in a very few cities, was about one-fourth of the country's total, whereas the three thousand German "cities" (average population four hundred) of the same period contained only 10 percent of that country's total. By 1740, the average German town had attained only two thousand population.[9] Contemporary Italian cities were considerably larger.[10]

The low density of cities in early modern Russia, on the other hand, is a function of low agricultural development, the result in part of devastation by steppe nomads. But the small number of cities was not offset, as in Islam, by the presence of unusually large mercantile centers, and the Russian urban population apparently reached only 3 percent of the total. As a German scholar notes, a thick network of European cities developed step by step as the increase in density of agricultural population provided the basis for enhanced local trade.[11] In Russia and the Middle East, urban centers relied on long-distance trade, which could produce quicker growth but was inherently fragile.

The City as Architectonic Symbol

Although the importance of the economic role of the city has required a brief look at the fundamental differences in distribution of urban centers, this role is only indirectly significant for identity questions. Much more salient is the role of urban space. Central among the spatial aspects is the visual impact, that is, the architectonic quality. Claude Lévi-Strauss suggests the importance of the subject: "Spatial configuration is the mirror image of social organization . . . while among numerous peoples it would be extremely difficult to discover any such relation, among others (who accordingly must have something in common) the existence of a relation is evident, though unclear, and in a third group spatial configuration seems to be almost a projective representation of the social structure."[12] Art and even architecture, considered individually, can refer to the agrarian countryside, the pastoral hills, or the nomad's wastes, but they cannot significantly transform the natural landscape. A man-made "landscape" might, as in Tuscany, extend a little distance into the countryside; but in premodern periods true architectonic space in the sense of a total visual environment was perforce limited to areas of highly concentrated settlement. Even when such a settlement was not truly urban, it assumed the symbolic role of a city. Consequently, the Absolutist palace complex, like the pre-Islamic ordered space of the Javan royal castle which Clifford Geertz describes, is all symbolic "heavenly cities."[13]

The significance of the earthly projection of the heavenly city for imperial rule will become evident later. It is interesting to note that this symbol, like architectonic space itself, apparently originated in Mesopotamia. In Greece, however, the expression of architectonic order influenced physical layouts and man's conception of them to a far greater degree.[14] Hellenic reality expressed its ideal of ordered, bounded space, which it was unable to extend fully to the countryside, in the architectonic harmony of urban public space. Characteristically—it is not only the owl of Minerva that flies at dusk—model cities proliferated as classic Hellenism gave way to the geographically broader, materially richer Hellenistic civilization. Alexander the Great regarded the city as the common home of all humanity. It was appropriate, although not precisely his intention, that the greatest city named after him should have expressed this theme in its architectonic quality. The basic elements of Alexandria, like other Hellenistic cities, were colonnaded streets leading to broad squares before the palace and the temple. Two great axial thoroughfares, likewise colonnaded, led from city gate to city gate and from land wall to harbor.[15] All of these spaces facilitated public expression of civic loyalty.

Throughout the Hellenistic world, including its Roman prolongation, the essential architectonic characteristics were perpetuated even though individual architectural attainments necessarily varied in size and quality. The effect and, apparently, the intention was to create a visual space in which the citizen, drawn to outdoors participation, would consider himself to be a unit in a harmonious whole. Space was designed to be impressive but not overwhelming, enriching but not incomprehensible. Centuries of Roman rule eroded the significance of municipal participation and placed unbearable burdens upon the most active citizens. Nevertheless, the enduring success of the architectonic accomplishment of the *polis* is demonstrated (as Dietrich Claude's penetrating analysis concludes) by the profoundly depressing psychological effect on its citizens produced by "barbarian" destruction of their city's physical components.[16] Some art historians perceive an echo of this shock, a nostalgia for the declining *polis*, in the two-dimensional but monumental mosaic decoration of sixth-century Italian churches, notably the approach of saints to the Savior in Santi Cosmas i Damiano of Rome and the portrayals of the cities of Classe and Ravenna in Sant' Appolinare Nuovo. Otto von Simson writes,

> Of this interrelation of political and theological concepts Sant'
> Appolinare Nuovo provides an example no less interesting than San
> Vitale. The ancient city-state, strange though it may seem, received its
> last apotheosis in this sixth-century basilica. Not only does the nave

evoke the memory of classical cities to convey the vision of the heavenly one; not only does the procession of virgins and martyrs recall the epiphany pageants of ancient citizenry; but the selection of this ceremonial for the expression of religious worship is most revealing, for that pageant bespoke not only the submission of the ancient city to the ruler but also her autonomy.[17]

Claude has also analyzed the gradual determination of this profoundly moving visual unity even in core Byzantine areas, where violent upheaval was less prevalent than in the West. Even during the reign of Justinian I, only two generations prior to the Moslem conquest, the process was still far from complete. The Moslem invasion entailed little immediate destruction, but it accelerated the process of deterioration. This process has been carefully traced on the ground in cities like Damascus, where even the inexpert visitor can readily discern the principal elements of disintegration. As the urban economy and population declined and municipal participation appeared less meaningful, the great ceremonial spaces became redundant. New constructions blocked the thoroughfares from walled-up colonnade to colonnade, leaving only the parallel footpaths beneath the columns. The geometrical forum gave way to irregular, rounded marketplaces. The Street Called Straight, supremely monumental during the Hellenistic age, can still be traced—but it is neither straight nor monumental.[18]

Damascus is a common starting point for comparative analysis because, although it has remained an important urban center longer than any other city, its layout has undergone extreme alteration. The social bases of this transformation will be examined at the end of this chapter. Here the essential objective is to establish the relative extent of architectonic change and its potential resonance for identity. Scholarly opinion is sharply divided on the reasons for the emergence of a distinctive Islamic city layout, but no one questions the sweeping change in appearance of the cities Islam inherited from the Hellenistic world.

The principal difference between the Moslem and the Hellenistic city was loss of architectonic quality, the visual unity of the public areas. The Moslem city has no central square; its narrow, crooked thoroughfares are bordered by blank walls or makeshift stalls; imposing gates, often intricately decorated, lead into caravan camping grounds rather than ceremonial avenues. Except for glimpses of these gates, the city walls, and the numerous minarets, the passerby has no visual orientation to the city as a whole. If he departs from the main thoroughfares, he passes almost imperceptibly into a walled-off residential quarter, then into a labyrinth of twisting, dead-end alleys closed in by walls completely blank except for narrow, closed doors. In its concern for individual rather than public rights Islamic law fails to discourage the gradual elimination of public outdoor spaces.

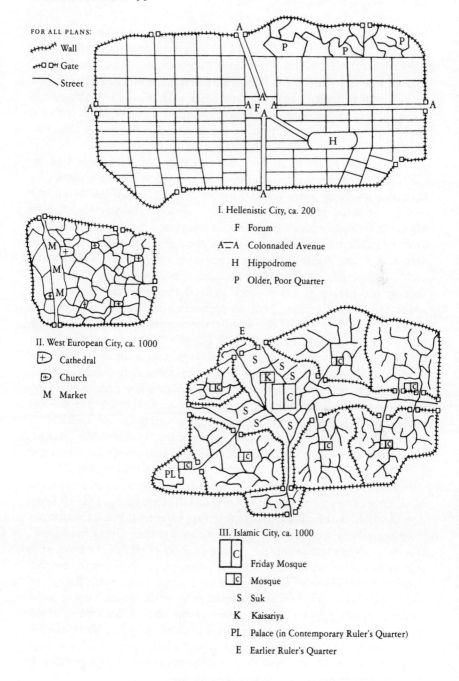

FOR ALL PLANS:

   Wall

   Gate

   Street

I. Hellenistic City, ca. 200

F   Forum

A—A Colonnaded Avenue

H   Hippodrome

P   Older, Poor Quarter

II. West European City, ca. 1000

  Cathedral

  Church

M Market

III. Islamic City, ca. 1000

C   Friday Mosque

c   Mosque

S   Suk

K   Kaisariya

PL Palace (in Contemporary Ruler's Quarter)

E   Earlier Ruler's Quarter

MAP 3. Hypothetical Transformation of a Typical Hellenistic City

On the dead-end streets, overhanging balconies and other encroachments are permitted by the Malikite school, although the consent of all abutting property owners is required to open a doorway into one's own house.[19] Both dead-end streets and thoroughfares have been blocked or narrowed by powerful property owners without legal authorization. Notables had lavish residences, but no display except for intimate guests; blank walls hid their exquisite private courtyards even from passersby in the dead-end streets.

Private space, on the other hand, was exceptionally well arranged. In the *suk* each type of merchant had his shop on a specific street or in the secure *kaisariya*; dwellings were separated from business areas. Above all, the principal mosque and its great courtyard, although completely shut off physically from the city, constituted a meeting place for individuals and the locus of public proclamations as well as the obligatory place of common prayer on Friday. Apart from these functions of the mosque, available only to Moslems conforming to the particular orthodoxy of the polity, very little in the nature of urban space defined the inhabitant as part of a municipal whole. Certainly, Moslem authorities did not plan the irregular appearance of their cities. Apparently, the streets of the Arabian Holy Cities had neither dead ends nor blank house walls. Cairo and Samarra in Iraq, for example, were originally laid out as geometrically as the Hellenistic cities. Archaeological evidence from Fustat (near Cairo) demonstrates, however, that the loss of regularity began within a few decades after the town was founded. Similarly, although Byzantine Constantinople had lost some of its regularity and monumental spaces during the eleven hundred years between its foundation and its capture by the Ottomans, the crooked, irregular street pattern with frequent dead ends that developed during the following four hundred years had no precedent in its earlier phase.[20]

In some respects, the Islamic urban layout appears to be a reversion to Mediterranean patterns that preceded the Hellenistic or even the Hellenic period. Strabo asserted that the confused appearance of Punic foundations in southern Spain contrasted with the regularity of their Greek neighbor.[21] It is by no means certain that the poorer quarters of Hellenistic cities were regular in appearance; those of the Egyptian *nome* certainly were not. An authoritative study of ancient Egyptian civic affairs comments: "Except for one or two broad streets which most often were the *dromoi* ending at the entrance of the temples and a square, usually also in the vicinity of the sanctuaries of the gods, it was only a jumble of streets (*odoi*), alleys (*rumai*), and winding dead ends (*laurai*). . . . Nevertheless, one should not exaggerate the contrast between the native [Egyptian] cities and the poor quarters of the metropolises or even of the city-state."[22]

Whatever the sources of the Islamic urban pattern, the differences between it and the medieval Christian city in a frontier region like Spain were so striking as to constitute a virtual phenomenological barrier to appreciation between the two civilizations. After their reconquest, northern Spanish visitors to Malaga and Granada were amazed at the narrow, gloomy streets lacking impressive house façades. Conversely, a twelfth-century Moslem visitor to Avila and Segovia thought they must consist of mere juxtaposed villages, for each household had its own pasture.[23] The northern Castilián town was not entirely typical of twelfth-century Europe. The large open spaces were convenient for the semipastoral economy, and the recent incorporation of villages within a single protective wall resulted in a few dead-end streets. As yet the central plaza, derived from Italian models, hardly existed.

North of the Pyrenees and the Alps, towns were more crowded. A few scholars have considered the obvious departures from the Hellenistic ideal in northern Europe to be comparable to the Islamic developments.[24] Such views, however, appear to derive from erroneous conceptions of the fundamental Moslem irregularities. To be sure, European streets were only a little wider than those of Moslem cities and often as crooked. But European towns had very few dead ends; with the exception of certain Jewish "streets," quarters were never walled off. Richly decorated patrician houses surrounded the central square. Although the public space in front of the cathedral was only a little more ample than the area before the great mosque and public markets were poorer and less organized, the nave of the cathedral and its spires, rising above other churches, constituted a visual symbol of unity reinforcing the role of the cathedral building as a sacral and public gathering space for all citizens.

European urbanism as a pattern of visual regularity revived first in Italy. Growth of concern for architectonic quality coincided with the growth in the economy and the size of the urban population, in contrast to the deterioration in visual unity that accompanied Islamic urban expansion. Early medieval Italian towns—the port quarter of Genoa retains such characteristics—were as cramped and crooked as their northern European counterparts. As soon as increased wealth made improvement possible, architectonic regularity became a major civic objective: "It is a matter of honor for each city," declared the Sienese, "that its rulers and officials should occupy beautiful and honourable buildings"—in this instance even to the point of competing with ecclesiastical structures.[25] More commonly, care was exercised to make the *signoria* palace and the cathedral harmonize visually: "The outward appearance of the city was treated as a unity and men were employed to foster it as a whole."[26] Street regulations were designed "to prevent those who build from trespassing on public streets or on any of the rights of the commune."[27]

Elites in the Italian cities were highly conscious of the significance of architectonic unity for fostering intense identity with their miniature states. "A great deal of visual propaganda, in fact, was entrusted to artists and this form of publicity was taken very seriously. . . . It is important that a great deal of art was 'official' art, and this may help to explain the comparatively slow development of change in taste during this period."[28] It is notorious that internal strife was fierce within each city. Each great house was a fortress, often including a disproportionately higher tower for defense. There were, however, no walled-off quarters. Common concern for the encompassing city walls was intense in symbolic as well as in practical manifestations. The Roman forum was revived or a new central piazza was established for the great religio-civic celebrations such as the Easter fireworks at Florence or the symbolic marriage of Venice and the Sea on Ascension Thursday. Rivalry in the pageantry of civic affairs rather than seclusion in separate quarters was the hallmark of "clan" division in the Italian city.

The City as State

In constitution as in visual unity the Italian city-state was the worthiest heir of the *polis*. Both were essentially little self-contained polities. Both attained—despite their intense factional disputes—a degree of civic identification and participation that has rarely been equaled in larger polities. It is reasonable to call this phenomenon "patriotism" and therefore to regard the city as the first *patria* of the West just as the *polis* was the first focus for identity in the ancient world. For the numerous *poleis* of the Mediterranean shores, the period 338 B.C. to about A.D. 200 was one of material expansion but slow deterioration of real independence and civic consciousness. For the Italian town, the period from about A.D. 1000 to 1500 was a time of spectacular economic growth, civic awareness, and attainment of sovereign status. In that half-millennium the Italian city attained what the Greek *polis* had received as its birthright: extension of its territory to a small but vitally important rural area. This combination of strictly urban and rural districts was the Hellenic ideal. The urban-rural unity constitutes the underlying significance of bounded, ordered space. Indeed, the intense concentration of identity in a small, self-sufficient world is what makes the English term "city-state" so inadequate as a translation of *polis, civitas,* or *cité*.

According to the German scholar Ernst Kirsten, the *polis* arose when merchants and artisans built up a "lower city" beside the defensive citadel (*polis*) of an agricultural population.

The problematic of city and countryside is, moreover, one of the basic questions for determining the nature and development of the medieval and modern periods in the entire European area and consequently may provide additional indicators for deciding the problematic urban character of the antique settlements. To put the matter succinctly, it may provide the answer to the question: May *polis* be translated as "city," and for what period and in what manner is the concept of "city-state" applicable to Greek antiquity?[29]

Kirsten answers his own question by pointing out that the citadel, the lower city, and the environing plowland that provided the essential food supply were part of the *polis*, and the inhabitants of all three areas were citizens (*politai*). Benveniste notes that starting from the opposite assumption—that the *civitas* was where the citizen (*ciuis*) lived—Romans arrived at the same unity of urban space and surrounding countryside.[30] The test of the indispensable unity for the Greeks, though, came when a wholly new, colonial town was to be established: despite obvious commercial or strategic advantages, a *polis* was rarely founded unless it could have agricultural land sufficient to support it. The colonists were primarily peasants rather than merchants. Hence Greek colonies were usually confined to areas of Mediterranean vegetation suited to their farming methods, avoiding thick forests and steppes on most of the Black Sea coasts or the extremely narrow, infertile shores of the Adriatic.[31] Indeed, Alexander himself is reported to have recoiled at the notion of founding what became Alexandria "by" Egypt on a barren sand strip: "A city without fields and their products gathered within its walls cannot develop, nor without abundant food supply can it have a numerous population or protect its inhabitants without resources."[32] The Hellenistic kingdoms nevertheless began the process of separation of city and countryside by withholding full citizenship from the non-Hellenic peasants. The Romans, too, were less exacting in choosing environments for their colonies. Gradually, the countryside became dependent on wealthy urban landowners. During the invasions period the latter retired, as protofeudal lords, to fortified country estates independent of the cities. The tradition of the city as an autonomous territory persisted, however. *Poleis* were increasing in number and subdividing the territory of Asia Minor as late as the sixth century, following the late Roman maxim: *Territorium est universitas agrorum intra fines cuiusque civitatis* (a territory comprises all the fields within the confines of a given city-state). Kirsten believes that this ascription of all territory to specific cities essentially prevailed in the Byzantine empire until its areas were overrun by Slavs and Seljuk Turks.[33]

The northern Italian regions where the new medieval city-state grew most vigorously must have retained little explicit awareness of Greco-Roman traditions. Still, Mediterranean culture is imbued with the notion that city and countryside should form a jurisdictional unity. Cities in southern France and Catalonia-Aragon shared many of the Italian city-state characteristics. A basic consideration was restriction of citizenship to the number of active adult males small enough to permit personal acquaintance —about five thousand. Such Greek mercantile cities as Athens had total populations greatly inflated by slaves and aliens. Italian cities, including a smaller number of such dependents, ideally could not exceed fifty thousand total population.[34]

The situation of the peasants in the countryside surrounding the Italian city was ambiguous. Early city communes often acquired rural territories dominated by landholders, including an important gentry and perhaps "mountaineer clans." Not surprisingly, such elements insisted that the serfdom in the countryside be upheld by the urban commune. The city's population became increasingly recruited from its own rural districts; laborers and craftsmen who acquired full citizenship retained their peasant farms. Eventually, the communes freed all serfs on their territories, thereby constituting a uniform legal jurisdiction for city and countryside; but urban residence remained the usual prerequisite for civic participation, whether by erstwhile rural gentry or craftsmen in the politically important guilds.[35] Stratification derived from wealth, including ownership of urban as well as rural real estate, was important as the rich mercantile element accommodated to gentry life styles. This life style increasingly involved expensive legal education to equip sons for civic office. The main concern for the commune as a whole was to acquire enough territory to assure adequate food, for without self-sufficiency formal independence from greater feudal nobles and ecclesiastical overlords who had previously exercised suzerainty over the towns would have been ephemeral.[36]

Not surprisingly, the Mediterranean city-state maintained numerous sacral symbols that recalled the cult of tutelary deities in the ancient *polis*. Feast-day devotions to patron saints were prime occasions for expressing civic unity. Banners with religious motifs provided symbols of guild or clan rivalries but also served as stimuli to civic patriotism, especially in fulfilling the general male obligation for military service. The medieval Christian city-state had a special reason for emphasizing its semisacral character. In West Europe only royal authority was fully legitimate. The myth of Rome as "patrimony of St. Peter" provided, however, an alternative legitimizing model for the republican commune. Venice, for example, officially became the "patrimony of St. Mark," with the doge (on the model of the pope) merely the saint's terrestrial representative. Strenuous efforts, including the ravishing of St. Mark's body from Alexandria, were devoted to symbolic fortification of the myth.[37] As will appear in chapter 5, such myths were essentially similar to the legitimizing myths of monarchical rule as a Christian trusteeship for a particular purpose. Consequently, although the legitimizing myths of the city-states often helped maintain their independence for long periods, such myths also acted in many cases as a preparation for adopting myths of broader polities.

The contrast to the medieval Moslem city does not require great elaboration at this point. The Christian Mediterranean city recruited its population from a small surrounding territory, usually under its own jurisdiction. There was intense pride in local ancestry and little interurban migration.[38] For a citizen "to eat the bitter bread of exile," in Dante's words, was the worst of punishments. The Moslem city dweller's attitude was diametrically opposite. He asserted when possible a genealogy linking him to a city at the opposite end of the *Dar ul-Islam*.[39] For example, an Andalusian, perhaps really of pre-Islamic Iberian descent, would cherish putative ancestry in Samarkand. Resettlement of individuals such as Ibn Khaldun in urban centers distant from where their immediate forebears had been notables was frequent.

There were a few exceptions to this indifference to civic roots—notably the proud, inbred merchant stratum of Fez. Its case is justly celebrated because of the exceptional preservation of the Fasi physical and social order. The town was founded by remnants of an established Roman municipality. Its invulnerable water supply minimized dependence on outside authorities.[40] Successive Moroccan dynasties appended *kasbahs* or palace-citadels even to Fez, however. Such isolation of citadel from city dwellers, eliminated in Greece and West Europe at an early stage of urban development, remained a key characteristic of the Islamic city. The *ark* (Persian), *dar* (Andalusian-Tunisian), or *makhzen* (Moroccan) is the seat of royal or gubernatorial authority physically removed from the town and politically aloof from townsmen's participation. In a religiously homogeneous city like Fez cooperation among notables representing the diverse quarters is feasible. In the Moslem city, each quarter normally provides its own police protection, welfare, schools, and public utilities (notably baths) without day-to-day intervention by higher authority. Even in more heterogeneous cities, the murmurs by men of the dominant sect during Friday services or in the bazaar deserve the urgent attention of the authorities. For example, the inhabitants of Herat refused to obey a proclamation in the bazaar to man the city walls as Tamerlane approached. Almost invariably, however, protests are made in the name of religion rather than as expressions of specific civic solidarity—which is as hard to detect as visual symbols of municipal unity.[41] As Georges Marçais remarks, some sentimental attachment to the cult of specific Moslem saints is associated with the city; but even a "former capital like Kairuan, Tlemcen, or Fez does not represent for the people who live there a 'glorious' past that they should be proud of."[42]

In certain respects, the Moslem city's relationship to the environing countryside—usually more or less an oasis—resembled that of the Hellenistic city. Economically, the Moslem villages depended even more completely on the nearest city. Urban notables (intermarried families of the *ulema* [religious scholar], mercantile and assimilated ruling elements) owned the soil that provided essential provisioning. There were, however, basic differences. Landowning was occasionally a social asset, but did not determine status in an Islamic society. The city population, lacking numerous ancestral roots in the adjoining countryside, had virtually no affect ties to the village. Especially when the land was held in trust (*wakf*) by religious institutions, administrators made little effort to improve the village's economic circumstances. Usually villages were even denied walls that might have provided some security against nomadic incursions. Urban Moslem incompetence in dealing with peasants was so notorious that in Egypt, where agriculture was highly important, the rulers relied on non-Moslem minorities like the Copts as intermediaries.[43]

Typically, the landowner not only regarded the peasant as a social inferior inadequate in religious training and practice, but also beneath consideration as a marriage partner. On the other hand, a peasant who managed to escape the web of village obligations (complete ascription to the soil did not arrive until the thirteenth-century Mongol Il Khans) and became a permanent urban resident, even in a humble occupation, had crossed the threshold to full participation. Accumulation of modest property and good religious education would make his children fully acceptable to the upper strata of most Moslem cities. Confraternities and *sufi* orders that had rural as well as urban members sometimes smoothed the transition. On the whole, however, such organizations did more to join distant cities than to tie a given city to its surrounding countryside. A Soviet scholar—writing under Stalin—has made a careful quantitative analysis of familial relationships in Il Khan Persia. His conclusion appears to grasp the general Middle Eastern situation pithily, if with some Leninist overtones: "In the city and the dependent rural district one and the same strong groups of the feudal class—rural-urban officials and clerical notables—held power by economic, juridical, or ideological means over the broad masses of the urban and rural lower strata."[44]

Divergence of the northern European city from Christian Mediterranean adherence to antique models was almost as striking as the Moslem alternative. Deterioration of early medieval urban life was much more extreme than in the Mediterranean region. Only the ecclesiastical sees, whether prolongations of Roman centers or new foundations, maintained a vestige of urbanism. Bishoprics were generally located at communications nodes; diocesan and archepiscopal provincial synods maintained some regular intercourse. The bishop's Court drew together a staff of officials and secular knights, which in turn attracted little colonies of merchants as soon as enough commerce had developed to justify their settling in one place. Often the ecclesiastical sees were little more than fortified monasteries, especially during the ninth- and tenth-century Magyar and Viking invasions. The more powerful forces, the landed nobles, had no particular attraction to living in such poor centers, preferring strongholds descended from Gallic *oppida* or German *Burgen*.[45] On the contrary, Germanic populations tended to resent crowded city conditions. Their ruling strata remained rural; as a result, Germanic culture retained a rustic flavor, in contrast to the cultures of the Mediterranean region.[46]

Such cities as arose in northern Europe, in contrast to both the Mediterranean and the Islamic worlds, usually developed apart from and often in opposition to the dominant secular forces. The conventional interpretation, applicable to the Low Countries, Scandinavia, Germany, and some Slavic areas, but not so readily to northern Gaul, is that the city arose when merchants who had traveled about in strong bands bound together by oaths (Gothic *hansa*, "cohort"; Slavic *Gospodi*, "people of the pact") found that there was enough commerce in communication nodes to justify settling down. The merchants' acquisition of sufficient literacy to keep records also facilitated dispatch of agents in lieu of personal travels. Being stronger and better organized in new urban guilds modeled on the *hansa* than were local shopkeepers, the newly sedentarized merchants took over municipal authority from the bishop's officers. Often the new masters of the city had at least verbal support from a distant monarch, whose authority did not penetrate individual towns but who had a strong interest in mobilizing resources through mercantile activity.[47] Edith Ennen notes, however, that "the merchant guild has left no lasting trace of its influence on the development of the town commune" except for the bare concepts of community organization, public meetings, and action against the titular suzerain, usually an ecclesiastic. All active organization, she believes, was carried out by very different types of craft guilds or by a popular juridical and administrative assembly, the *Schöffenkolleg*.[48]

A wider range of scholarly agreement emerges on other suggestive issues. The northern European city wall played an exceptionally critical role in symbolizing civic identity. As a symbolic as well as a physical boundary mechanism, the wall was analogous to the frontier zone. Hellenistic *poleis* had been walled at their inception as *oppida*. Some retained walls until the Roman period, although Sparta felt secure enough to do without them. The erection of new walls, often with a more restricted circumference, during the third century was a sign of the decline of municipal security. Throughout antiquity, however, public buildings and the colonnaded thoroughfares remained more important symbols of urban life than did walls.[49] Their impact on citizens' consciousness was probably higher in the Italian city-state and possibly in the Islamic city, where security from nomads was essential. In the Islamic case, however, walls were ordinarily ineffective against the intrusion of a powerful, organized regime.

For the northern European town, confronted by petty but greedy landed nobles, the wall was a constant symbol of liberty. *Stadtluft macht frei* (city air makes one free), a maxim originating in the half-Germanic Meuse valley during the eleventh century, became a legal principle guaranteeing liberation from serfdom for a man who maintained uncontested residence for a year within a city's walls. In contrast to the Italian city, the northern city forbade nobles to maintain fortified residences within its walls. Usually even the ecclesiastical suzerain withdrew to a fortified abbey or other nearby residence.[50]

The converse of the maxim quoted above was also widely applied: *Dorfluft macht eigen* (village air makes one into property). Outside the walls the burghers were subject to the jurisdiction if not the actual possession of feudal lords, in sharp contrast to the Italian or Hellenistic citizen who, in effect, owned and governed the environing countryside. The exclusion of the northern city's jurisdiction from rural areas was not entirely a result of the town's defensive origins. In the late Middle Ages, numbers of individual towns, principally in the rich but disunited zone from the North Sea to Switzerland, did try to acquire sufficient territories to make them economically and demographically strong enough to resist neighboring territorial princes. Nuremberg, for example, struggled against the Franconian branch of the Hohenzollerns during the fifteenth century to acquire rural areas. By 1500, Erfurt in Thuringia owned eighty-three villages. Still, the extent of this territory—two hundred square miles—was derisory in comparison with the larger Italian city-states. Most German cities were far less successful than Erfurt.[51] By the mid-sixteenth century even the more powerful cities like Strasbourg were on the verge of subjugation; it vainly sought to join the Swiss Confederation, the only example of a permanent league (including rural as well as urban cantons) until the United Netherlands.

One reason why the northern European city was so restricted in extent was that, even in Switzerland, it denied citizenship to its rural subjects. Similarly, town guilds jealously excluded country merchants. Of course, wealthy townsmen invested in a purely private way in rural property. Even patrician families in important towns like Augsburg and Ulm apparently did not realize, as did the Fuggers, that landed possessions provided an assurance of stable status.[52]

Recruitment of population locally was a major source of civic stability for both the *polis* and the Italian city-state. In contrast, Lübeck, a major German town, recruited its early population from distant regions, although it did not originate as a settlement of wandering merchants. Between 1158 and 1259, 31 percent of Lübeck's settlers had come from Rhineland-Westphalia, 17 percent from other distant regions, and 29 percent from Lower Saxony, some hundred miles distant, leaving only 22 percent from neighboring Holstein, Lauenberg, and Mecklenburg. Newer Hansa League towns around the Baltic recruited heavily from Lübeck. Indeed, family origins and continued ties were sources of pride for the Baltic German bourgeoisie as late as the nineteenth century.[53] As among the Moslems, such distant family ties were undoubtedly stimulating in many respects. After the brief period of Hansa League ascendancy, however, Baltic emphasis on such intercity attachments tended to erode the impact of one's own native city as a source of identity.

In another significant way towns like Lübeck in the far north did start to contribute to new types of identity. Apart from its own military and economic strength, every northern European city depended on privileges guaranteed by law, such as the right of asylum for peasants. As boundary mechanisms distinguishing urban from rural identity, such legal privileges were as important as physical walls. The privileges had begun as concessions of territorial jurisdiction by the Holy Roman emperors during the tenth to eleventh centuries at a time when *Stamm* law generally prevailed in Germany. By the fifteenth century, standardization of Roman law jurisdictions by territorial princes constituted a major instrument for undermining city autonomy. In between these periods, the northernmost German cities (parallel efforts in the south were relatively trivial) carried out an interesting attempt to establish systematized legal jurisdictions encompassing numerous cities. Two great systems developed, both basically derived from Frank Salic law but elaborated as the common law of cities.

The Magdeburg system assembled in the *Sachsenspiegel* (1224) was much more extensive, but was relatively unimportant in establishing autonomous identity. Indeed, Magdeburg law was readily admitted by territorial lords controlling minor cities in the German eastern frontier zone because the legal system did not diminish the lords' essential control. Poland accepted Magdeburg law because, though not incompatible with lords' jurisdiction over small towns, it generally favored the interests of the crown. For similar reasons, Magdeburg law was even perpetuated in some Russian cities acquired from Poland.[54] Handy written versions in Low German and Latin, as well as a later translation into Polish, enhanced the utility of Magdeburg law. The magistrates (*Schöffen*) of the city of Magdeburg readily issued "opinions" (they were little more than conclusions) on request. They were not binding, however, and a city adhering to Magdeburg law could ask for an opinion on the same or a different case from another *Schöffenstuhl* (city magistracy) in the Magdeburg system. In this capacity, Halle, Leipzig, Breslau, and Kulm were about as important as Magdeburg itself. In 1356 the Polish king forbade his Magdeburg law towns to appeal to any German "mother city" and established an alternative magistrate panel composed of representatives of towns in Poland. As early as 1315 the Margrave of Brandenburg had instituted a similar requirement.[55] Even among German migrant settlements, adoption of Magdeburg law had little to do with the origins of the colonists. Adoption generally represented an effort of territorial overlords, notably the Teutonic Order, to introduce a uniform, easily manageable law to supersede diverse and obsolescent customary laws the settlers had brought with them.

The portentous effect of the export of Magdeburg law to the non-German kingdoms of East Europe was the sharp formal line it drew, in accordance with the traditions of the German towns where it had originated, between town and countryside. The law was sometimes extended to neighboring German settler villages, which the territorial lords hoped to stabilize in order to provide a reliable food supply and demographic recruits for their towns. But most Slavic and Magyar peasants remained under a different, native customary law that sharply separated them from the neighboring towns. When, later, some of these peasants were granted Magdeburg law, it hardly constituted a privilege because it consolidated the feudal rights of their lords.[56]

The impact of the second great northern German system, Lübeck law, was very different. It, too, was a sharply restricted town law, rarely if ever extended to rural districts. Lübeck law was derived in the early eleventh century from the Salic Frank law of the Cologne-Soest area; its substantive differences from Magdeburg law in either private or criminal matters were slight. But Lübeck law provided distinct safeguards against territorial lords' encroachments on the hundred cities that adhered to it. In the first place, the Lübeck city council jealously reserved the right to render opinions. All "daughter cities" were forbidden to seek opinions elsewhere, with the sole exception (after 1400) of the Reval magistracy, which was admitted as an appeal instance because of the great distance between Lübeck and the East Baltic towns.[57] Until 1586—two and one-half centuries after the *Sachsen-*

spiegel—there was no complete written version of Lübeck law. Even then, only a defensive, conservative version of the predominantly oral tradition appeared in print. Consequently, Lübeck law was more successful in resisting the intrusion of Roman law elements that tended to favor territorial lords' jurisdiction. Family connections of the Baltic cities and their maritime positions also strengthened them against encroachments. By retaining their Lübeck affiliation, towns like Elbing in East Prussia long resisted the pressures of their Teutonic Order overlords who wanted to introduce a variety of Magdeburg law.[58] In East Baltic areas, however, Lübeck affiliates were undermined by the total lack of *rapport* with the environing countryside, which was alien in language and customs as well as in law.

German legal historians, such as Paul Koschaker, have made a convincing case that northern German city law, like English common law (which was also ultimately derived from Frank Salic law) could have developed as an adequate modern legal framework.[59] Most authorities now appear to agree that the fundamental reason why this did not occur was lack of a powerful central authority in Germany equipped with law courts and a professional bar such as fostered the *coutumes* in Paris and the common law in London. Early use of Roman canon law in church jurisdictions and the appeal of Roman law theory to large bodies of university-trained jurists were also important factors.

For Lübeck law specifically, with opinions always rendered in Low German, the decline of that linguistic pattern as an elaborated, high-status code was serious. As Thomas Mann illustrates in *Buddenbrooks*, civic pride remained intense in Lübeck itself throughout the nineteenth century. But by that time, it was obvious that the strong civic consciousness the isolated city-state had produced was being transmuted into a broader modern national identity.

German scholars have been particularly concerned to examine the mechanisms by which their heritage of municipal autonomy became relevant for the development of larger polities. Georg von Below showed several generations ago that in strictly institutional terms the carryover was modest. The German territorial states that emerged in the fifteenth century had administrations, like those of most of West Europe, modeled on France. Not many of the municipal officials transferred to the service of territorial princes. The most significant influence of the city as an organizational model came much later, in the welfare activities neglected by early territorial states that became indispensable in the nineteenth century.[60]

Under emerging Absolutist states elsewhere (Burgundy, France, to a lesser extent Spain and Austria) bourgeois alliance with the monarchs was probably decisive in enabling the latter to mobilize resources and overcome noble particularism. Such bourgeois, however, like the French *no-*

blesse de robe, quickly transferred their allegiance from specific towns to the royal polity, which they then reshaped as a focus for civic identity. In the process, individual cities were reduced, apart from their economic activity, to the level of provincial administrative centers.

In Germany (essentially the non-Italian portions of the Holy Roman empire) there were only eighty imperial cities by 1500, half of them in the small southwestern region, Suabia.[61] The remaining 2,900 towns were already subject to territorial princes. Consequently, their material resources contributed to the strengthening of those smaller polities, thereby delaying broader German unification. It appears that very little transfer of affect from town to principality occurred even in strong eastern frontier polities such as Austria and Prussia. Such polities relied for active support primarily on a disciplined landed nobility, gradually injecting bourgeois officials who lacked the strong esprit de corps of the French *noblesse de robe*. Stein Rokkan has suggested that the very strength of economic activity and municipal consciousness in the area of dense urban development from northern Italy through the Rhine valley to the Low Countries hindered the emergence of strong territorial states there.[62] Apart from precocious developments as in the United Netherlands, Switzerland, and England, myths of civic solidarity and symbols of commoner participation in politics apparently had to await the period of modern nationalism, when the adaptation of urban culture to spectacular economic growth made the city dweller the salient component of the polity.

The dichotomy in northern European consciousness between town and countryside persists, nevertheless, as a significant secondary identity component. A major theme of Edith Ennen's work is the way the early Germanic aristocratic attachment to rural seats has been perpetuated by symbolic ascendancy of rural values. In contrast, the Mediterranean nobility at a very early stage moved into the towns: "The social-historical peculiarity of the southern European city was to be the seat of the nobility, just as its constitutional peculiarity was based on the concept of city resident and city district."[63] The urban patricians not only dominated the Italian countryside but actually transformed the appearance of Tuscany and parts of Lombardy into something resembling urban architectonic regularity.[64] The individual city as such, subsuming all active elements rather than a particular class, the bourgeoisie, remained the focus of southern European identity just as the *polis*, in very different ways, constituted the sole focus for the antique world and for Islam. From this perspective, it is the northern city that is "peculiar," as Antonio Garcia y Bellido implies and an associate, Fernando C. Goitia makes explicit: "For us, direct heirs of the full Greek and Mediterranean tradition, the city therefore has a preponderant character which it does not have, for example, in English civilization."[65] A penetrating English examination makes almost the same point: "For it is a critical fact that in and through these transforming experiences English attitudes to the country, and to the ideas of rural life, persisted with extraordinary power, so that even after the society was predominantly urban its literature, for a generation, was still predominantly rural; and even in the twentieth century, in an urban and industrial land, forms of the older ideas and experiences still remarkably persist."[66]

Urbanism in the Shatter Zone

The strongly sedentary inclination of East European Slavic populations, as suggested in chapter 2, was not fundamentally different from West European attitudes. As *Stamm* or "tribal" characteristics dissipated during the Middle Ages, therefore, large rural areas were settled by groups that were very much alike in way of life, linguistic patterns, and symbolic attachment to diverse dynasties even when (as was still the case in most of West Europe) administrative penetration by such nominal rulers was rudimentary. Although at the time largely latent as identifying forces, these factors constituted potential bases for large-scale ethnic units. The differentiation among core elements of Poles, Russians, and ultimately even of sedentarized Magyars was often less than it was among similar Western groups. It is true that the Islamic-Christian frontier zone exerted a traumatic influence. Perhaps, however, the dramatic effects of this influence could have been limited to peripheral areas of East Europe had it not been for preconditioning circumstances that facilitated the emergence of East Europe as an ethnic shatter zone. The most salient of these preconditions was the peculiar development of the city as an alien cultural element.

Unquestionably, the fundamental reason for the intrusion of diverse ethnic elements into medieval East Europe was its urgent economic and technological requirements. Some historians have emphasized the *Drang nach Osten* of the Germans as a conscious although incremental political and ecclesiastical force. As indicated in chapters 6 and 8, conscious plans for German expansion did appear sporadically. Nevertheless, major East European elites—Magyars, Poles, Czechs, Croats—were able to develop strong dynastic polities based on the early French model and supported by the papal Curia. No doubt such dynasties needed to mobilize economic resources and enlist advanced technology in order to safeguard their position against the neighboring Germans; but they also required such advances for protection against steppe incursions and, indeed, against each other. Their circumstances resembled those of strong twentieth-century Third World regimes. At times, the latter may perceive reception of Western technology to be a defense against Western imperialism, but in reality advanced technology is more often sought to provide material awards for supportive elites or to compete with other Third World regimes. In much the same way, Polish kings sought German colonists for the Carpathian area to counteract encroachments by settlers from the kingdom of Hungary. St. Stephen of Hungary is said to have recommended "guest and foreign peoples" to his son and heir because "they are very useful, they bring varied values and customs, weapons and knowledge with them, all of which ornament the Royal Court and make it splendid, while frightening the haughty foreigners. For weak and defenseless is a country which has but a single language and uniform customs."[67] Thus, from their inception, the East European dynastic myths carefully provided for multiethnic polities that would maximize the dynasties' strength.

The East European dynasties secured advanced techniques where they could, preferably (like sophisticated Third World regimes) from the most distant Western sources they believed to be least dangerous. French and papal ties were valuable not only for legitimizing ideologies but as models for ecclesiastical organization and cultural development. The Rus polities drew on Byzantium, the Adriatic Slavs adopted Italian techniques, and Scandinavian influences were important along the Baltic. A large share of the Holy Roman empire settlers were in fact *Reichsromanen* (Romance-speakers from its western fringe) rather than Germans. Nevertheless, the major material requirements of the East European polities as well as many cultural advances were obtained from Germans. A relatively small part of these services was in the form of peasant settlements, although even these were ultimately decisive in altering the ethnic identity of Silesia, the Bohemian fringe, East Prussia, and the Elbe-Oder region. In all except the last of these, which was conquered by the twelfth-century crusade, Christian Slavic princes urged German immigration. Such dynasts required agricultural settlers, and the Germans were renowned for their advanced techniques in reclaiming mountainous and swampy areas.[68] At times, such techniques could be borrowed without accepting settlers, as in the utilization of advanced German village and house forms. Indeed, many of the German agricultural colonists who moved into strong, relatively well-integrated kingdoms like Hungary and Poland were assimilated after a couple of centuries.

The second requirement of the East European polities was for mining, which was so closely related to German agricultural reclamation in mountainous regions that the two terms became synonymous. Miners usually settled in towns. Consequently, exploitation of mineral resources merged with the prime requirement for economic development—urbanization. To urbanize quickly and efficiently, East European polities required Germans; but the satisfaction of this short-term need had far-reaching social implications. For two generations historians, mainly Germans on one side and Polish, Czechs, and Magyars on the other, have been debating the question of whether "real" cities were present in East Central Europe before German settlers arrived. Russian historians have been less concerned, for their parallel debate about the role of the Swedish Varangians in polity formation does not focus on urbanization. Precisely because the Rus situation is less controversial, emergence of towns there may throw light on developments in East Central Europe. In both regions the first organized, concentrated settlement consisted of a citadel as place of refuge. It was known by such Slavic terms as *gorod* or *hrad*, corresponding to German *Burg*. Apart from the fact that a bishop or the equivalent was rarely in residence, such *oppida* (to use the "neutral" Latin term) developed suburbs of sedentary merchants very much as the embryonic Western towns had about a century earlier. In the eleventh century, the suburbs of the most important East Central European *oppida* were transformed by the influx of Western settlers, predominantly German. German historians argue that a major change was from a crowded, disorganized layout to a geometric, planned settlement around a central marketplace. There is no doubt that the eastern settlements were far more regular in plan than the Rhenish towns, which had grown up "spontaneously." The argument that such planned urban space containing relatively low population densities could not have developed from the Slavic suburb is hard to refute.[69]

Another line of German historiographical argumentation seems less decisive, although it is suggestive. At this very moment of history, Czech, Polish, Ukrainian, Slovene, and Croat replaced their old noun forms connoting *oppidum* with new forms derived from "place"—*mesto, miasto, misto*. Although just as Slavic in their roots as the old terms, these changes precisely paralleled the German change a little earlier from *Burg* to *Stadt*.[70] Consequently, the implication of a linguistic calque reflecting intense cultural influence in the sphere of urban development is strong. It is important to note that the calquing process occurred only in Slavic regions dominated by Western Christianity. Regions deriving their ecclesiastical culture from Byzantium retained the old terms. Moreover, the appearance of the new terms for "town" coincides (ca. 1200) with the spread of Magdeburg law in the same regions, at first to merchant suburbs, then to towns as a whole. It is fairly clear, too, that the Magdeburg law privilege was necessary at that time to guarantee a settlement's autonomy from local Slavic nobles.[71]

Large-scale German foundation of cities in both Poland and Hungary occurred before the Mongol invasions of the mid-thirteenth century, but was especially vigorous after that disruption. Germans founded thirty-eight towns in north-central Poland during the thirteenth century, fifty-three in the fourteenth century. One writer estimates that 20 to 25 percent of the kingdom's population was German by that time, with Germans very likely constituting a large majority of the urban dwellers. Another investigation finds that 80 percent or more of identifiable names of urban individuals were German.[72] German predominance in Hungarian cities was probably even greater. In 1438 the Magyar population of the principal city, Ofen ("Etzelburg" in German, now part of Budapest), rebelled against German dominance and received parity in the city council. Soon thereafter the role of Germans receded in the towns, partly through assimilation (as indicated by the decline of recorded German names) but to a greater extent, apparently, because of an influx of Magyars and Slovaks from the surrounding countryside.[73]

In Central Hungary the principal cause of the decline of the towns or, more accurately, the replacement of German burghers by Ottoman Turks and their Orthodox Greek and Serbian subjects, was Ottoman conquest. After the expulsion of the Moslems at the end of the seventeenth century, the almost depopulated cities required a new German influx. These settlers also began to assimilate to the extent of adopting Magyar names. This symbol of reidentification apparently satisfied Magyar elites until the nineteenth century; they did not use Magyar themselves. Until the nineteenth century, town records were usually kept in Latin, but the common language of urban affairs was German.[74]

Polonization of German burghers was earlier and more intensive. The prestige of the *szlachta* (gentry) led patrician German families in the cities to become acculturated socially in the fourteenth and fifteenth centuries, although they kept their separate legal status. During the first half of the sixteenth century, German urban families eliminated another symbolic boundary mechanism by changing their names to Polish forms. They apparently also adopted the Polish language. Thenceforward only Protestant German immigrants retained a sharply distinct identity.[75]

The overall tendency in both Poland and Hungary (despite the extreme Turkish disruption in the latter) was for the identity of dominant aristocratic elites formed around powerful dynastic myths in the eleventh century to extend to all Catholic inhabitants. In some respects, the city was a weaker institution than in West Europe, for it had been established on the dynasty's invitation and needed more support from the rulers against nobles' encroachments. For example, city walls were urgently required to repel (with royal assistance) steppe invaders, but there is little evidence that they constituted effective barriers against local pressures. The economic resources of the towns were so significant for enhancing royal unifying efforts that one might have anticipated, as in the West, a merging of city population with sedentary nobility and peasantry to constitute a single national identity. In the West, the bourgeoisie transferred its intense civic loyalty to the larger entity, first the Absolutist state, then the nation state. The fairly smooth assimilation of Polish-German burghers suggests that such a development was not out of the question in East Central Europe. But intense disruptions by steppe invaders, the relative lack of attraction of the native elites' linguistic codes, and the recurrent influx of new German immigrants made assimilation problematic in Hungary from the start. In either country, complete assimilation of the bourgeoisie would have provided the nucleus of a middle class within a unified ethnic identity. Understanding why such assimilation did not occur requires a more complex explanation than the usual assertion that the towns of East Central Europe constituted, from their origins, "alien" elements.

A subtle but critical factor was the failure of royal power to subdue aristocratic particularism. As indicated above, the attraction of gentry styles and authority was related to early assimilation (semiassimilation in Hungary) of the German bourgeoisie. On the other hand, gentry authority limited the role of the monarchies as unifying forces compared to Western polities. A full explanation of why the gentry was stronger in East Central Europe would transcend the limits of my study. It should be noted, however, that particularism did not usually constitute an insuperable barrier to eventual assimilation of the bourgeoisie to the overall national identity in the West, as the case of the highly particularistic Lübeck burghers demonstrates. More decisive was the development of gentry myths that proclaimed their life style to be "purer" and "superior" to that of the city or any occupations associated with it. The "fourth myth" of the eighteenth- to nineteenth-century Magyar gentry (see chapter 2) fits this pattern. A century earlier, Polish gentry evolved a similar myth of an easygoing, free-spending, chivalrous, "Sarmatian" life style. A nineteenth-century Austrian scholar comments: "Nobles, even starving ones, treated the richest and most respectable city people with boundless scorn; the latter regarded being burghers as a distressing evil and sought to get out of the status at all costs" by buying patents of nobility.[76] This xenophobic and antiurban myth appealed to the lesser nobility throughout East Central Europe. In contrast, contemporary German, French, and British petty nobles were moving toward accommodation with bourgeois values.

Both the real power of the gentries of Poland and Hungary and their potent myths were related to the continued economic and technological underdevelopment of these countries. The critical effect of this underdevelopment was to perpetuate the requirement (recognized by king, higher clergy, and great nobles alike) for new, relatively modernized urban elements. In Hungary during the late eighteenth century this requirement led to a new influx of German burghers that postponed and complicated ethnic homogenization. In Poland the requirement was perhaps less intense but developed much earlier. Just at the time when the German patricians had become assimilated, the Polish kings admitted large numbers of Central European Jews. In 1500 the total number of Jews in Poland-Lithuania was only 30,000. By mid-seventeenth century there were about 400,000, some 5 percent of the total population; by 1764 Jews numbered 750,000, nearly 7 percent.[77] Given the dominant religious assumptions of the time—Jewish as well as Christian (see chapter 7)—Jews were utterly unassimilable. A large portion constituted market-center nuclei for artisanry and shopkeeping. Overseer occupations on great estates employed many others. By the seventeenth century, Jews also constituted a significant share of the populations of the larger towns.

Because of the immense tragedies that engulfed the Jewish population of these regions in later centuries, it is easy to regard their position in Poland-Lithuania as unique. Nevertheless, as brief examination of the position of the Armenians suggests, the diaspora phenomenon (which will be treated at greater length in chapter 7) is by no means purely Jewish. As early as 1375, Armenians were prominent in southern Polish cities where they became especially valuable for long-distance trade, via family connections, with Persia and the Ottoman empire. A considerable number became Catholic, but many remained unassimilable as Gregorian "heretics." By 1589, twenty-two of the "rich" merchants of Lvov were Armenian, as contrasted to only eight Catholics (Poles and assimilated Germans) and six Ruthenian Orthodox or Uniates. The corresponding figures for "poor" merchants were nineteen, two, and three.[78] Jews were not yet prominent in this large town. As early as the fourteenth century, the Armenians were granted a separate community tribunal system, using the Datastangirk code of 1184 administered by a council of elders. By royal command, the code was translated into Latin shortly after 1519, but it continued to constitute a major boundary mechanism, closely linked to the distinctive religious organization headed by a Gregorian bishop. It is highly significant that, by the eighteenth century, Lvov Armenians used their ancestral language only in the liturgy, employing Polish for commerce and apparently within families.[79]

Jews also retained a separate legal system attached to their religious organization and used a nonsacral language (Yiddish) for daily affairs. The Ruthenians, Orthodox East Slavs most of whom became united (Uniate) with Rome in the Lvov region during the late sixteenth century, retained a distinctive court jurisdiction based on the *Pravda Russkaya* (the collection of customary laws originated in eleventh-century Kiev) as well as separate religious organizations, including an Orthodox metropolitan and a Uniate metropolitan heading the Catholic Slavonic rite.[80] Certainly retention of their ancestral language was somewhat stronger among these recent rural arrivals than among Jews and Armenians, but the upper stratum rapidly Polonized. Consequently, it is totally erroneous to regard language, as a barrier to communication, as a major factor in the unassimilability of the towns. Religion was crucial, but it was powerfully reinforced by the separate legal systems. In cities like Lvov, the Magdeburg law was virtually confined to the Catholic element, although its forms and principles strongly influenced other legal systems.[81] Renunciation of one's particular legal allegiance meant not only religious apostasy; in most cases it meant exclusion from an established urban occupation. A German scholar emphasizes the complexity of the problem:

> In this sphere, national and religious questions were interconnected. Artisanry in the cities was divided along religious and national lines, either through acceptance of the principle of parity in all relations or by separation of the guild along religious and national lines. From the religious standpoint the Catholics, Greek-Uniates, and Greek-Orientals (non-Uniates) were most significant, from the national standpoint, Poles, Ruthenians, and Armenians. Jews had a peculiar position, generally outside the sphere of city law; very rarely do we encounter guilds based on Jewry.[82]

The East Central European town (for I believe Lvov was not highly exceptional), therefore, contained a set of very powerful mechanisms mutually reinforcing the boundaries between distinctive groups. In itself, the history of the German settlement with its introduction of a separate (Magdeburg) law for urban people was not decisive; but it constituted a potent precedent, readily accepted by both the crown and various later settlers, for according special tribunals to each distinctive element. Insofar as the newer elements, in contrast to Catholic German settlers, were religiously unassimilable, the precedent led to a reinforcement of urban segmentation. In this sense—and not, as mentioned earlier, in their origins—"the cities thus constituted islands of foreigners in the heart of a country most of whose laws did not apply to them," as a French scholar wrote.[83]

The "island" nature of the city was a more direct product of German settlement. As indicated earlier in this chapter, Magdeburg law, developed as a part of the struggle of the German bourgeoisie for autonomy, sharply separated town and countryside. Generally Polish law, adapted from *szlachta* customs, continued to prevail for nobles and peasants. Consequently, the notion of separate jurisdictions for urban and rural elements, even when they were of the same religion (and increasingly both Polish-speaking) was established at an early date. As the towns filled with unassimilable religious groups, perpetuation of this division was almost automatic, but it entailed a far sharper identity cleavage. Consequently, a single high culture and a unified identity became virtually unattainable, although sheer linguistic barriers to communication were by no means insurmountable. In the Hungarian kingdom developments were somewhat different, primarily because the urban majorities remained German-speaking and religious divisions tended to be cross-cutting. It appears, however, that earlier precedents of urban distinction from the countryside contributed there, too, to resistance of Slovak and Rumanian urban immigrants to Magyarization. The effect of the large influx of Jews, who largely replaced Germans as the dominant urban ethnic component in the nineteenth century, was more complex. Whereas the Germans had retained their native language while accepting the symbols of Magyarization represented by name changes, Jews readily acculturated in both respects. By the nineteenth century, however, the Magyar gentry's myth opposing urban occupations prevented more than a fragile alliance between it and a strongly urban life style such as Jews—even the minority who converted to Christian denominations —represented. Consequently, although in very complex ways, the "island" character of Hungarian cities remained as pronounced as the Polish phenomenon.

A brief look at developments in the Orthodox East Slav regions will illustrate both the powerful tendencies toward heterogeneous urban populations present throughout economically underdeveloped East Europe and the way that a strong, unified polity could overcome such tendencies. The similar origins, as *oppida*, of Rus and other East European cities have been noted. The *posad* for merchants developed alongside the prince's fortress (*gorod*), although native Rus merchants may (at Kiev) have resided in the *gorod*.[84] The attraction of the great river routes to the Orient meant that merchants were very mixed in origin. Armenians appeared as early as the eleventh century. The first Jews were also said to have arrived from Germany at that time. They formed a suburb called Zhiddy—later the Ukrainian term for "Jews," but opprobrious in Russian. Jewish merchants from the Turkic Khazar kingdom had a separate suburb called Kozar. Germans, Tatars, and Greeks were also present.[85] Rus urban agglomerations differed in two basic ways from Polish and Hungarian towns, however. Each community apparently governed its own internal affairs, but the prince, often resident in the citadel with his powerful *druzhina* (*comitatus*), maintained a tight control over all townsmen. Meetings and enforcement activities of the communities were primarily to carry out his orders. Some nobles originating in the *druzhina* resided in town as *startsy gradskiye*, tending to blur the distinction between town and countryside. The principles of the *Pravda Russkaya* also prevailed in rural areas by 1200.[86] Non-Orthodox religious groups in the towns retained their own legal systems.[87] Although there is little or no evidence that the practice derived from Byzantine legal norms, Rus perpetuated the *polis* concept of a unified town and surrounding countryside, but diverged from it in segmentation.

Cities in the northwest, such as Pskov and Novgorod, lacking princes, allowed much greater scope to communal authority. Established, property-owning Rus citizens governed through a popular assembly in each town. A great mass of poorer artisans and laborers were excluded—as in the *posads* elsewhere or, indeed, in the *polis*—from participation, however, and influential foreigners ("Goths"—that is, Swedes and Germans) had separate quarters with autonomous jurisdictions. Novgorod's authority extended to an immense territory in the far north, although one with few peasants.

As the East Slavic towns painfully emerged from the Mongol invasion, relations between urban and rural areas were somewhat modified. In the lands acquired by Lithuania, town jurisdiction (influenced by Magdeburg law) was confined to the area within the walls, although some towns tried to maintain claims to territorial jurisdiction. Conversely, the royal intendant (*starosta*) or, in smaller cities, the noble landlord, imposed so many burdens through taxes and military obligations that townsmen were almost enserfed.[88] A similar emphasis on defense, especially near insecure frontiers, gave the military governor comparable authority in Muscovy and other Russian principalities. Ivan III suppressed the aristocratic merchant republic of Novgorod as incompatible with his autocratic rule.[89] Merchants in Muscovy generally attained a strictly regulated status apart from rural serfs, but the towns as such had no separate legal status. The military governor's authority usually extended, in accord with the old Rus practice, to an entire district, although the town had a separate intendant.[90]

For several centuries, Russian cities retained a heterogeneous ethnic composition. Jews were almost always excluded, and Christian Ottoman subjects (Armenians and Greeks) were forbidden entry by the sixteenth century. The only major exception was Astrakhan, essentially a trading and military outpost on the route to the Orient. There, in 1625, the governor ordered construction of a separate quarter for Armenian, Persian, and Bukharan merchants; the numerous Indian merchants already possessed their own quarter.[91] In conquered towns like Kazan, the Tatars were compelled to withdraw to outlying areas if they did not do so voluntarily. Consequently, in contrast to Polish towns, Russian towns held few non-Christians by the sixteenth century. The large, highly important foreign element consisted predominantly of West Europeans, including mercenar-

ies, artisans, and merchants. Often, as at Moscow, they were lumped together in a "German suburb." A large majority appears to have been
Protestants, who assimilated steadily (in Moscow and other interior cities)
throughout the seventeenth and eighteenth centuries. Consequently, there
was a good prospect for the development of homogeneous towns, at least
in Russia proper. Peter I's foundation of St. Petersburg as a deliberately
cosmopolitan capital, together with the acquisition—simultaneous but
partly fortuitous—of a tightly organized, self-conscious German burgher
and aristocrat element in the Baltic provinces, decisively reversed this
trend.[92] Peter's move, along with privileges granted German immigrants
and the Baltic ethnic enclave, in effect recognized the continued need of
the underdeveloped country for foreigners. A competing myth and a supporting socialization process emerged around Baltic German institutions.
These institutions produced a supply of modernizing talents which the
dominant Russian socialization patterns did not encourage. As a result,
however, the Russian city, which on the threshold of the modern era was
becoming "purely Russian," experiencing "almost no confrontation with
other ways of life,"[93] entered the era of nationalism with a sharply segmented population. Acquisition, about 1800, of the heterogeneous Polish
cities and towns in such areas as Georgia-Armenia immensely complicated
the urban ethnic composition of the empire.

The Multiethnic City as Norm

Evolution toward homogeneity in the West European city has been neither
smooth nor costless. Towns in early Frank Gaul had quarters for specific
Germanic groups that, as noted in chapter 2, still maintained personal law
privileges. More important were the numerous Syrians and Jews who had
penetrated the Roman West as merchants. There seems to be little doubt
that these two groups were distinct. Syrians were especially hated by
native Romance populations for taking over what commerce remained
after the invasions. But all—Romance, Frank, and Syrian—were subsumed in the same Catholic church organization. By about 800, Syrians
ceased to be noted separately, although Jews remained distinct, providing
important commercial links with the Moslem conquests to the south.[94]
Jewish quarters, usually regarded as concessions to Jewish worship and
community solidarity, existed in all major West European towns until the
crusades. Then the Jews were attacked by fanatic mobs, and over the course

of several centuries nearly all were expelled. Most survivors emigrated to Poland-Lithuania. Jewish communities remained in a few major Italian centers, Venice, for example, which also had Armenian and Greek Orthodox communities with their own churches but without full citizenship.[95]

The disappearance of ethnic minorities in West European towns was an unusual phenomenon, although the contemporary Byzantine situation was not dissimilar from that of the cosmopolitan Western centers like Venice and Rome. In neither West Europe nor Byzantium was urban homogeneity altogether explicable as the result of religious pressure. The developments are closely related to the elimination of distinctive personal legal affiliations. In the Eastern Roman empire the Christian church had even frowned on "circus" factions because it feared that they might become covert bases for heresies or pagan survivals. The extraordinary strength of the bishop in the vestigial Western town must have worked for unification. Certainly one reason Frank amalgamation of Germanic and Romance elements left no room for distinctive urban ethnic affiliation was that surviving Germanic elements other than the Franks were, or in recent memory had been, Arian. Later, the complete solidarity of the small bourgeois stratum against the powerful aristocratic forces of the countryside was almost the precondition for the town's survival as an autonomous unit. Historical evolution produced, for all these and possibly other reasons, a Western society that was segmented horizontally by class—with the bourgeoisie most salient—instead of vertically by ethnic groups, each with its own status pyramid. The sole exception was Iberia, resembling, as a frontier society, the complex East European urban ethnic alignments. Just as East Europe required an influx of Germans with commercial and technological skills, underdeveloped Iberia received French, Flemings, and Genoese down to the seventeenth century. But whereas Poland—another Catholic country with an *Antemurale* myth—was attracting Jews, the united Spanish kingdoms were persecuting and expelling them. In both instances the crown and high secular and ecclesiastical lords perceived a need for Jewish enterprise. In Spain the intense ethnocentrism of the gentry overcame such elite forces, whereas in Poland the gentry, although scornful of urban occupations in general, did not actively oppose Jewish immigration. In both countries peasants appear to have resented Jews (it is said that they could not remain in Polish Catholic villages as contrasted to Uniate villages) but exerted little direct influence on the composition of the urban population.[96]

Up to the 1490s, the Spanish urban pattern resembled the Moslem city more than West European cities. As long as Moslems and Jews remained in Spain they were legally restricted to separate quarters, although the regulations were not always enforced. But distinctive quarters for Christian elements such as the "Franks" rapidly dissolved. The critical boundary mechanism there as elsewhere consisted of separate legal status. Both Jewish and Moslem minorities cherished their own community tribunals.[97] As indicated earlier, Iberian rulers at first willingly conceded such privileges, for they took pride in ruling a multireligious population.

Such pluralist patterns had been present, although by no means the rule, in the eastern Mediterranean prior to the emergence of Islam. Greeks, Jews, and Egyptians had lived under separate laws and partly in distinct quarters in Alexandria and other Egyptian cities. The capital of the Sassanid empire consisted of a cluster of cities: Ctesiphon was the principal element, with some Jews as well as Zoroastrian Persians; a larger Jewish group and the heads of the tolerated Christian churches lived in Seleucia, a Hellenistic foundation; the imperial palace-city, Aspanbar, was virtually closed to all except Zoroastrian Court circles.[98]

It remained for Islam to raise the segmented city to the standard type. Many observers have seen this development as a reflection of pre-Islamic nomad tendencies, including the tendency to factional conflict.[99] Arab occupying troops were quartered in special districts of conquered cities or in separate garrison towns.[100] The most famous Abbasid caliph, Harun al-Rashid, and the first prominent Moslem ruler of Egypt, Ibn Tulun, both are said to have built their new capitals to escape factional turbulence. In addition, Moslem rulers felt obliged to establish separate quarters for factional groups in older cities to minimize destructive quarrels. The phenomenon is not confined to Arabs; special quarters were set up for Turkic genealogical or pseudo-genealogical alignments.[101] Usually, however, genealogical affiliations among Moslems adhering to the same sect or school of law do not lead to residential segmentation. Thus Berbers and Arabs mingle in most North African cities, with the former readily assimilating. As noted earlier, in the purely Arab Malikite city Fez, cooperation among representatives of different quarters presents few problems.

Various other explanations have been advanced. A recent ingenious interpretation has ascribed the narrow, twisting Moslem street layout to the absence of wheeled vehicles. If this transportation factor were in fact causally decisive, it would go far to explain how dead-end streets and separate quarters arose. Richard Bulliet demonstrates that wheeled traffic disappeared wherever Islam was dominant and makes a good case for the proposition that pack animals were economically advantageous in desert and steppe conditions. Consequently, he continues, caravan competition drove out wagons and carts in large regions adjoining the steppe-desert area.[102] It may well be, too, that the symbolic significance of the camel (although within cities the principal pack animal is the donkey) for the Arab, and by diffusion for all Moslems, was important. It seems to me, however, that here is a clear instance of an interpretation that has uncovered a necessary but not a sufficient condition. A strong economic need for streets broad enough for wheeled traffic, such as appeared in early nineteenth-century Cairo, would make a labyrinth of streets intolerable; hence strict segregation by quarter would be difficult if not impossible. Streets of modest width with fewer contortions than those of the Moslems, minimizing dead ends, are, however, as Hellenistic and medieval European cities demonstrate, compatible with very little wheeled traffic.

Alternative explanations stress the need for shade, protection against cold winds, and the like; they are hardly adequate to explain such a widespread phenomenon as urban segmentation. Emphasis on the Moslem as an urbanite at home anywhere in the *Dar ul-Islam*, laxity of legal concern for public thoroughfares, and other social factors appear to have been more important preconditioning factors. Both of the latter factors are social tendencies related indirectly to the Islamic life style. This life style depends on the integrity of the special type of family prevalent in Islam, particularly on the privacy of the harem. The concern, noted in chapter 2, for feminine integrity, which is rooted in the Arab concept of honor, has diffused widely in Moslem countries. Fear of violation of the harem has been realistic, considering the endemic instability of regimes and the threat of incursions from steppe or desert. As recently as 1936, a French observer noted that "a feeling of fear dominates the interior topography of Damascus, a sentiment of fear which makes security the principal preoccupation. This explains in part an urbanism that does not appear to result in a conscious layout."[103] Security against surprise attack is greatly enhanced when several families, related by clan, sect, or guild brotherhood ties, live in a maze of branching streets with a single exit barred by a gate. The intensive social life fostered by such a quarter greatly differs from European concepts of family parties; it frequently involves women's visits across the terraced roofs and, on women's day, in the public baths of the quarter. For men, encounters in the bath, the coffee house, the local *suk*, and the street are frequent.

Some support for the interpretation that concern for the integrity of the life style dominates is provided by consideration of the very different housing patterns in Ottoman Turkish cities. Overwhelming military superiority banished insecurity from external threats, hence cities were unwalled. Houses were built of wood, often with windows on the street. But the windows were heavily shuttered to maintain privacy, dead-end streets blocked by barriers constituted separate quarters, and many districts were in fact restricted to Sunni Moslem residents with uniform life styles.[104]

Clearly, the Moslem system of neighborhood quarters was extraordinarily adapted to the presence of sharply distinguished ethnoreligious elements. From its inception, Islam, as a newcomer, confronted many non-Moslem groups. On the whole, such groups have been more persistent in the city than in the countryside. Apart from urban segments of predominantly rural groups like the Copts and Maronites, for several important groups (Jews, Greeks, more recently Armenians) the urban portion has constituted the heart of the ethnic community. Separate quarters for non-Sunni Moslems developed under the Abbasid caliphate, as Dominique and Janine Sourdel emphasize: "Social barriers were added to confessional distinctions to produce a compartmentalized and cramped city, incapable later on (up to the modern era) of development, except through major political revolution, from its excessively rigid framework."[105] The establishment, centuries later, of separate guilds for different religions enhanced the divisive effect. Nevertheless, it is notable that separate residential quarters were rarely legally prescribed for religious minorities. Most Jews in Mameluke Cairo did in fact inhabit a few quarters, but in principle they could live anywhere. In the interior of Ottoman Constantinople most Jews lived in the Haskeray quarter, but there was no rule prohibiting them from residing elsewhere. Greeks gradually moved to the Phanar district on the Golden Horn. Armenians lived for the most part in the southwest near the Castle of Seven Towers, though they were not legally restricted to that area.

As one nineteenth-century observer notes, however, Moslem Turks tended to move out when Jews or Christians moved into a street; their presence was "inconvenient" (no doubt as role models) for Turkish women and children.[106] Given the ascendancy of the Turks in status and power, one can hardly doubt that their exclusivist attitude exerted a strong influence on non-Moslems' choice of residence. In any case, the multitudinous quarters of Moslem cities were usually easily identifiable by ethnicity. There were three Greek, three Slav, and three Gypsy quarters among Ottoman Belgrade's thirty-eight subdivisions in the eighteenth century. Copt, Jewish, Greek Orthodox, and "Frank" quarters were among the fifty-three of Cairo in the same period. Valencia retained distinctive Moslem and Jewish quarters among the twenty-four city districts which the Christian conquerors took over. A city like Fez, entirely Moslem except for the Jewish *mellah*, was almost as minutely subdivided, however, with eighteen quarters at the opening of the twentieth century. The overall effect has been a profoundly different although no less durable and emphatic way of partitioning people than is familiar in European experience.[107]

Summary and Conclusions

The two preceding chapters analyzed inherently dichotomous aspects of ethnic identity: sedentary and nomad, Moslem and Christian. Analysis of the role of the city in ethnic identity calls for a somewhat more elaborate presentation. I shall, therefore, present my conclusions as a formal typology. Let me reemphasize that everywhere (in the periods and regions I have examined) urbanism is essential to civilization. The reader should be aware that my typology treats only the relevance of this immense urban phenomenon for ethnicity. Even within that limited context, some urban effects (notably that of the capital city discussed in chapter 6) are not subsumed in this typology. The departures of my typology from classifications like Max Weber's, which do cover the broader aspects of urban experience, should not, therefore, be surprising.

In classifying the impact of different types of cities upon ethnicity, three salient criteria can be identified: (a) strong civic consciousness, expressed in the symbolism of architectonic unity as well as in more direct social participation; (b) territorial extension of the city, by legal jurisdiction and by residence of elites, to a surrounding rural district; and (c) sharply separated ethnoreligious elements, often distinguished by residential segregation but always identified by other boundary mechanisms such as distinct legal codes. If each of these three criteria is taken as a dichotomous variable, their combination produces, logically, eight distinct city types. As indicated below, however, two of the historical types are weak and transitory, and the historical evidence for two other types is uncertain.

(A.) Strong civic consciousness, territorial extension, and *lack* of segmentation (+a, +b, −c) characterized the *polis*, including at least the early phases of the Byzantine city and the Italian city-state. The intense identity produced by the city-state was not directly transferable to a broader ethnic identification, but may have prepared the way for such identities.

(B.) Strong civic consciousness, lack of territorial extension to the countryside, and lack of ethnic segmentation (+a, −b, −c) characterized the northern West European city. Intense burgher identification was transferred to modern nationalism, as its major source component, and was conducive to strong class divisions within a single ethnic identity.

(C.) Strong civic consciousness, lack of territorial extension, and ethnoreligious segmentation (+a, −b, +c) characterized the Iberian city of the late Middle Ages. This combination proved to be unstable and was replaced by Type B when non-Christian urban elements were eliminated.

(D.) Weak civic consciousness, territorial extension, and ethnic segmentation (−a, +b, +c) characterized the Islamic city and some of its Middle Eastern predecessors. Although identification with urban civilization in general was intense, identification with any particular city was very low, consequently there was no transfer to a broader ethnic identity.

(E.) Weak civic consciousness, territorial extension, and lack of segmentation (−a, +b, −c) characterized the Russian city of the late medieval and the early modern periods. The type is weak both in its recurrent tendency to segmentation and its unstable extension of city jurisdiction and elite control to the countryside. The Russian type therefore tends to become similar to Type F (though rural elites never developed a strong myth of hostility toward the city) or a hypothetical Type G (−a, −b, −c), which is not generally found in European or Middle Eastern cities, but is perhaps exemplified by the Egyptian *nome* or some Far Eastern cities.[108] The impact of urban society on general ethnic identity is vestigial.

(F.) Weak civic consciousness, lack of territorial extension, and ethnic segmentation (−a, −b, +c) characterized the Polish and Hungarian cities. Lack of civic consciousness plus segmentation precluded the impact on national identity that was exerted by this type's nominal model, the West European city. Consequently, the society's class divisions were fundamentally different from West Europe's, and internal ethnic divisions remained more intense.

The implications of this typology are sweeping, although less so for the origination of specific ethnic identities than for their relationship to emerging polities. In some sense, most of the identities associated directly with towns existed prior to the development of specific types of urbanism. Such was the case for diaspora urban elements, especially Jews and Armenians; it was also true of groups like Greeks, East Slavs, and Germans that were minorities only in particular clusters of cities. The forms of urbanism decided, in considerable measure, whether such minorities would remain "undigested" or would assimilate. Perpetuation of specific forms of urbanism (or the myths and traditions associated with them, notably in legal practice) went a long way toward determining whether burghers would constitute a homogeneous stratum capable of assisting the development of a strong polity. Such a polity in turn produced, around intense legitimizing myths, the powerful ethnic identification that characterizes modern Europe.

CHAPTER FIVE

Imperial Polities:
The *Mythomoteur*

Myth Transcendence in the Compound Polity

Modern focus on the nation-state often assumes that it is "natural," that it reflects inherent qualities of the people it governs. In this view, the state is, or should be, the dependent variable, whereas "innate" national characteristics constitute the independent variables. A more sophisticated interpretation reverses the relationship: modern nations are more frequently the creations of states than the opposite. I consider this second interpretation more appropriate, for focus on the prior existence of the state or polity emphasizes politics as a critical independent variable. Unless pursued carefully, however, the interpretation of ethnicity as a product of a specific institution like the state can be misleading. The danger arises from two quarters. First, emphasis on the state tends to produce a myopic perspective. The analyst is apt to locate institutions in earlier eras that superficially resemble those familiar in his own time, then ascribe critical causal roles to such institutions. In fact, polities very different in all superficial respects from current sovereign states have constituted the institutional frameworks in which the political variable produced strong identities in past ages. Second, even if earlier polities were fairly uniform and recognizable as "states," one would still have to confront the question of how and why certain polities produced strong, durable identities whereas others disappeared quickly. Definitive answers to such questions, which have puzzled generations of scholars, are hardly attainable. I hope, however, that attention to structures that have defined polities, to their legitimizing myths and the complex symbols disseminated by their communication networks may provide more insights into the specific process of ethnic evolution than have most efforts to investigate state-building in general.

In contrast to an investigation of ethnic identity, efforts to explain the origin and persistence of an institution such as a polity involve direct consideration of the constraints imposed by the economic and technological capacities of the period. Such questions as the polity's ability to mobilize material resources and the degree of penetrability an administration can achieve are important for my treatment, but a full consideration of them would greatly exceed the scope of this work. My investigation of polities, therefore, like my discussion of cities, has limited objectives in comparison to the excellent works that in recent years have examined state-building as a holistic process.

I prefer "polity" as a general term because of the heavy legal baggage the word "state" carries; I reserve the latter term for the last four or five centuries in the West. There are, of course, several kinds of polities. In this respect as in many others, Shmuel N. Eisenstadt's typology is a useful guide. His types of "primitive political systems" and "modern societies" are both peripheral to my interests. All but two of his remaining five types are "empires."[1] Of these two, I have examined one—the city-state—and shall deal with "feudal systems" very briefly in this chapter. The focus of the chapter will be on the three "empires": the "patrimonial empire," which is peripheral to Eisenstadt's interests but very important for mine; "nomad or conquest empires", which were discussed briefly in chapter 2 and will reappear in these pages; and "centralized historical bureaucratic empires," which will be a major subject of this chapter and the primary focus of chapter 6. In this last emphasis I agree with Eisenstadt, whose main concern is the functioning of empires as complex centralized systems; but my interest also extends to periods when polities were too embryonic to support centralized bureaucracies or when such complex institutions were in a phase of regression. I must trace the impact of informal social institutions, notably the myth-symbol complex, even during periods when centralized institutions were scarcely functioning.

Neither Eisenstadt nor I regard the concept of "empires" as coextensive with "states" or "polities." "Empire" implies, at the very least, "large state" or "large polity."[2] From the geopolitical standpoint, the various types of polities constitute a continuum. Athens and Venice were very successful city-states that became empires, and it is easy to envisage how Lübeck might have become the master of a Hansa empire. Numerous steppe agglomerations arose, engaged in more or less extensive conquests, then vanished. Only a few—notably Attila's Huns and Genghis Khan's Mongols—established what Eisenstadt aptly terms "conquest empires." To satisfy my concerns, however, I must proceed beyond consideration of the imperial polity as part of a continuum and grapple with the peculiarities of its identifying myths. After examining varieties of imperial myths, I can turn (in the following chapter) to the special institutional aspects of imperial polities that exert a strong influence on ethnic identity, namely the symbolic and communications role of the capital city and the centralized bureaucratic administration as a creator and propagator of identity myths.

Consequently, I cannot be content with a definition that treats an empire as a polity embracing diverse peoples, for such an approach would tend toward circularity of reasoning in examining the influence of the polity on identity. Nevertheless, one should not dismiss the insights implicit in this conventional notion, expressed throughout millennia, from Achemenid Persia to Haile Selassie's Ethiopia, by the proud title "king of kings."[3] The conventional wisdom implies that an imperial polity presupposes the prior existence of smaller but durable polities. To put the matter another way, in any meaningful sense of the term, an "empire" is not merely a large polity, but a compound polity that has incorporated lesser ones.

Even such a minimal definition has significant implications for investigating the intangible boundaries of an empire as defined by its myth-symbol complex. Because these boundaries include groups possessing distinct identity myths, the imperial polity—if it is to be stable—must either erase or transcend them. Even where identity myths based on characteristics like language are latent, the presence within an empire of such alternative myths associated with memories of earlier polities poses serious problems for the imperial elite. Erasing the memories except through substituting a more powerful, transcendent myth is virtually impossible. A small polity like a city-state can rely, to a considerable degree, on visual contiguity and personal acquaintance to support the myth that its inhabitants (really its elites) constitute within the bounded space of an Athens or a Carthage the only significant reference group. In a way, the degree of ethnocentric self-confidence of such city-states is not very remote from the "primitive tribe's" conviction that its members are the only "real men." Such convictions could even be sustained in a large, sophisticated, but very homogeneous and isolated polity such as pharaonic Egypt. The imperial elite that dominated an agglomeration of clans and *poleis*, however, had to produce more compelling beliefs. The myths it produced maintained, therefore, that its imperial polity constituted the inescapable framework for existence, that its boundaries, physical and mental, constituted the limits of meaningful identity.

Ancient Imperial Universalism

The very first historical polities in Mesopotamia that absorbed preexisting city-states confronted this problem. Giorgio Buccellati points out that the "unity [of each component city] was a *consequence* of common residence in the same territory and of being under a common ruler rather than being an *antecedent* of the political structure, or even less, a *cause* of its existence." The city's unity—in contrast to that of the nomads united by fictitious gene-alogies—centered on a myth of city-gods whose representative was the king.[4] Transfer of the individual city's mythic identification to the larger polity was accomplished by a potent myth that turned the city-gods into subordinate members of a supernatural universe parallel to and controlling its terrestrial reflection, the empire. The process can be summarized from Thorkild Jacobsen's vivid reconstruction. The only truly sovereign state is the universe governed by the assembly of gods. This polity and its human population created to serve gods embraces Mesopotamia, with its secon-dary power structure (each city-state) serving primarily economic pur-poses, that is, the self-expression of each god in ritual, as the estate of some great god. The "national state" (the empire) has the political function of police force for the universal heavenly state. In effect, the ruling body of the latter is an assembly of gods under Enlil, which must approve each city-god's appointment of human stewards. The "national state" or empire was the executive committee on earth of the gods' assembly. Various astrological symbols, notably the sun and the moon, conveyed this myth. They were perpetuated on the coins and in the coats of arms of later secular and ecclesiastical rulers with universal pretensions who often did not know their origin. Franz Kampers, a close student of the imperial myth, even maintains that "all imperial insignias can, consequently, be identified unequivocally as successors of Babylonian cosmic symbols."[5] Mason Hammond sums up the external side of the transfer process suc-cinctly: the Akkadians began and the Assyrians completed (in the ninth century) the city's transition from "an independent center to the tool of territorial empire builders, an eminently useful administrative tool but no longer one that was central to the mentality of ruler or subject. . . . The urban center remained, or in the case of later invaders became, central in the consciousness of ruler and subject alike. Proof of this is that the civilizations of the Babylonians, Assyrians, and neo-Babylonians were pre-served in folk memory and in literary sources with a strong urban flavor."[6]

The culmination for the ancient Middle East—although constituting a certain departure from the urban emphasis of earlier Mesopotamia—was the Achemenid Persian empire, which came closer to achieving domina-tion of all civilized regions known to its inhabitants than had any previous empire. Subsequent conquerors to a very considerable extent had to de-fine their accomplishments by relation to the Achemenid achievement. To the Hellenic world, which achieved self-confidence by turning back the Achemenids' attack, their empire remained the supreme reference point for imperial rule. Consequently, the Macedonian dynasty's transcendence of the city-state order had to rest mythically as well as physically on the conquest of the Persian empire.

The empire of Alexander of Macedonia, as a political structure, was one of the most ephemeral of achievements, but his myth was among the most enduring. The essence of that myth is that through conscious design Alexander amalgamated nearly all civilized mankind into a single polity. Every group or individual enjoying complete human potential was part of the universal empire except for a few polities near the World Ocean like Carthage, which the myth asserted (probably erroneously) Alexander had intended to absorb. From Alexander's time on every empire-builder in the Hellenistic tradition proclaimed the intention of continuing his mission of unifying all mankind. There were, to be sure, far less ambitious rulers. Some of Alexander's own successors, notably the Ptolemies, did not pretend to universal empire. It is significant that the Ptolemies' base was Egypt, the part of the ecumene that was most self-sufficient yet virtually devoid of city-states. Consequently, Egypt alone did not require a potent superordinate myth to replace particularistic myths of its components. By their policy of self-restraint, the Ptolemies laid the foundation for a system of polities interrelated through a balance of power; such a system has constituted a recurring alternative to the model of universal empire.[7]

A second alternative emerged in the form of the revived Persian empire under the Sassanids. Their myth of the *basileus* or king of kings was essentially a counterlegitimation based on resurrection of the Achemenid protouniversal myth to challenge the Roman-Hellenistic successors of Alexander. Apparently, the Sassanid kings realistically assessed their limitations; complete supplanting of the Roman empire may never have figured in their calculations.[8] As a result, their myth tended to envisage a dualistic universe in which Rome and Persia shared the imperial mission.[9] Rome recognized the Sassanids not only as its principal opponent but as one worthy of a place of esteem in the "family of nations." As early as Diocletian (ca. A.D. 300), Roman Court ceremonial and its artistic representations, such as a procession of kings in Persian costumes, copied Sassanid models. Neither the Roman nor the Byzantine elites, however, really accepted the shared universal mission. In a fundamental sense, the Roman ideology did not recognize rights of other polities. In contrast to later empires, the Roman rulers at the height of their powers did not take brides from outside their realm. In the early seventh century, when they had at last defeated the Sassanid attacks, the Roman-Byzantine emperors finally assumed the *basileus* title as a symbol of their unique claim to empire.[10] But six hundred years earlier, Ovid had written, "For other peoples land is given with fixed limit; the extent of the Roman city and world is the same."[11]

At the height of their imperial glory the Romans' imperial claims did not extend beyond the early Mesopotamian model. That is, the city-gods of Rome assumed an elevated place in the pantheon of gods from all of the city-states of the empire. Deification of the emperor began as early as Augustus, who used Egyptian models developed by the Ptolemies, notably such attributes as "Helper," "Healer," and "Benefactor."[12] As Alexander had, Augustus "created" cities as a manifestation of his divine attributes. Legally, the empire was considered to be the property of the emperor; hence he might choose his successor. Later emperors emulated Augustus and sometimes claimed descent, natural or adoptive, from him and Caesar. The concept of *Geblütsrecht*—restriction of supreme rule to a single royal dynasty—was fundamentally foreign to Roman thought. The frequent "election" of "barracks" or "Praetorian" emperors in later centuries made it essential for such parvenus to assert that fortune rather than descent was a sign of the favor of the gods. In a more formal sense, the ability of a pretender to reside in Rome and to receive the acclamations of its inhabitants and the decrees of accession of the Senate (even if the latter was acting under pressure) and the ceremony of *Adventus Augusti* all constituted a claim to legitimacy.[13]

The concept of terrestrial rule as a mirror of the heavenly hierarchy was perpetuated but, in an age of increasing skepticism, probably lacked the psychological force it had exerted in ancient Middle Eastern polities. Emphasis on Rome as a city immeasurably superior to all others apparently carried more conviction because, prior to the fourth century, its unprecedented success and its dazzling architectonic and ceremonial embellishments were manifest. François Paschoud has traced the power of such themes in Roman literature even during the fourth-century period of decline. Despite the anachronism of the assertion, Rome was still held to be the largest city of the world. Above all, Rome was universal, the Mother of all other cities. Wherever he might be, the Roman citizen was in his fatherland. As insecurity increased, the claim to universality was imbued with a compensatory secular character. Rome, the myth assured its subjects, represented the perfect equilibrium between force and law, hence was the creator and guarantor of peace. To be sure, the predominantly pagan literary men still maintained that peace depended on a secret pact with the city-gods; as long as the Romans kept their part of the bargain peace would be as eternal as the city itself.[14] Heinrich Dannenbauer suggests, however, that by that time Rome's claim to universality appealed primarily to the elite acquainted with Stoic philosophy rather than to the masses among whom earlier sacral myths had had the strongest resonance:

The concept of the unity and indissolubility of the empire did, indeed, attract the top ten thousand—high officials and officers, the aristocracy, and the rich educated citizens who administered the cities. Pride in the great past dominated them, and it would have been inconceivable to them for Rome no longer to be the midpoint and mistress of the earth. The "Rome Aeterna" and "Aeternitas Imperii" of the monuments and coin inscriptions were no empty formulas for them. It was more than patriotism, which could not and would not conceive of the downfall of the fatherland, hence closed its eyes to reality; it was a faith, a religion.[15]

The faith of the elite was not sustained by custom and pride in office-holding, which continued in aristocratic circles to be regarded as a natural duty, alone. Elite identification with the empire as a whole was strongly reinforced by material interests in estates scattered throughout its territory and personal attachments arising from constant travels on official and private business. Retreat of elite members to estates in specific provinces was accompanied by decline of their loyalty to the empire. This decline, apparently, was the source of provincial legal particularism and ultimately of the willingness of Roman senatorial aristocrats in fifth-century Gaul to sponsor whatever mercenary force afforded a prospect of stability.

Contemporaries and subsequent investigators alike have been impressed by the extent to which the Roman empire, for the immense majority of its subjects, rested its claims on achievement of peace and prosperity as contrasted to the intense civic identification of the city-states it had subsumed. " 'Patriotism,' " as defined by the late Roman rhetoricians whom Emilienne Demougeot examines, "ultimately assumed, although it was the affect content of national life, the form of love for and defense of a culture and a way of life considered to be superior rather than of a territory or of the independence of a collectivity."[16]

The fragility of any identity myth resting on a claim to a superior way of life, unless that way is anchored in very profound affect symbolism expressed as nostalgia, has already been discussed. If the myth merely asserts, as Rome's increasingly did, that life is better under the aegis of an imperial polity, a series of reverses can completely undermine the basis of loyalty. Nevertheless, an attainment of peace and prosperity as durable as Rome's creates a nostalgia of its own. In many ways, the persistent yearning to renew or recreate Roman universal imperialism has been stronger than the willingness to defend the imperial polity while it was still a going concern.[17]

Islam: Identity of Faith and Imperium

It may seem incongruous to turn from Roman imperialism to the special brand propagated by Islam rather than to Rome's natural heirs in Byzantium or its putative heritors in the Christian West. Here, however, the technique of comparing least-like cases comes into its own. In conquering force, in territorial extent, and in self-confidence, the Islamic imperial polities most closely resembled the Roman. Their mythic basis, on the other hand, is as remote from Rome's as can be found among civilizations derived from the Middle Eastern–Hellenistic tradition. Building on the Middle Eastern myth of a terrestrial hierarchy reflecting the order of the gods, the Hellenistic monarchies, followed by Rome, had gradually reconstructed their myths on a secular basis. Islam emphasized universalism as a sacral mission to a degree that the ambiguities arising from the intimate relationship of the Christian empires to Roman secularism simply did not admit. The Islamic empire, therefore, presented in boldest contrast the image of a universal religion clothed in the forms of imperial domination, instead of the late Roman version of a secular religion of material achievement adorned by vestigial concessions to a declining pagan faith.

To be sure, there are deep ambiguities in the Islamic concept of empire; but they arise in a very different manner from the ambiguities that have plagued Christian polities. As a sympathetic writer has recently noted, Islam makes no provision for a secular polity: "Politics in Islam is neither a power concept nor power itself, nor a search for an organizing principle for society (conceived as a body politic); rather it is pure nostalgia for the primitive period plus a mobilizing force for defense."[18]

On the other hand, although for a Moslem religion is the only motive force worth considering, there is no structure in orthodox Sunni Islam capable of directing a theocracy in the ordinary sense of the term. Consequently, the Islamic ideal does not envisage religious rule, either. In the first two centuries the caliph, as successor of Mohammed and head of the faith, was lawgiver. But several fundamental factors prevented even the early caliphs from acting like true theocrats. To a much greater extent than Mohammed himself had been, the caliphs were leaders of desert conquest agglomerations. The great razzias they launched unexpectedly conquered vast countries. Because forceful conquest was not only compatible with Islamic teaching but enjoined for Moslems confronting recalcitrant non-Islamic polities, the new role was not inherently incompatible with that of supreme religious leader. But military leadership was at the least a distraction for a spiritual director. The unavoidable involvement in seizure of power from rivals, maneuvering among rival factions of Arab soldiery, and maintaining Arab domination over other groups were dubiously, if at all, compatible with early Islamic teachings. In fact, such activities very closely resembled the age-old practices of imperial rule.

Such incompatibilities in the role-set of the caliph emerged sharply during the conflict of the Umayyad family with the descendants of Mohammed's daughter Fatima, Ali and his son Husayn. In effect both sides claimed supreme authority in order to employ it for political purposes. Muawiya, the first Umayyad caliph, was able to win by gaining the support of the Syrian Arab faction through the typical political payoff of perpetuating their dominance by shutting off immigration from Arabia.[19] Muawiya sought to legitimate his rule by warfare against Byzantium—an imperial mission—rather than by primarily religious methods. As H. A. R. Gibb writes: "The Umayyad Caliphate, however, in its attitude to the Empire, was much more than a provincial successor state. The two facets of its policy, the military assault and the administrative adaptation [in matters such as coinage], point clearly to the real ambition of the first-century Caliphs, which was nothing less than to establish their own imperial dynasty at Constantinople."[20] To conquer "Kustantiniye," as Mohammed had supposedly prophesied, was symbolic; to assume the mantle of universal empire by doing so would have been the culmination of the Islamic mission. This intention was explicit, and competition in symbols constituted a preparation for it: "We are on the frontier," an early caliph's governor in Syria is supposed to have written him, "and I want to compete with the enemy in military pomp as witness of the prestige of Islam."[21]

After their defeats at Constantinople, the last Umayyad caliphs were already shifting their orientation eastward. The Abbasid dynasty that overthrew them established its seat in Baghdad, terminating Syrian Arab domination and reducing Arab ascendancy in general. Most significant was the Abbasid turn to Sassanid models of rule. Abbasid dependence on Persian advisers and propagandists, converted to Islam but descended from Sassanid official families, became important. The Persians endeavored to construct an ideology that would enhance the prestige of their own tradition by casting Islam in the role of successor to the Sassanid struggle against the world hegemony of "Rum."[22] In the new myth they developed, Mesopotamia rather than Constantinople became, in accordance with old Persian traditions, the center of the world.[23] Just as the Roman myth acquired credibility because of its city's splendor, the Mesopotamian version of the Islamic myth was nourished by Baghdad's wealth, population, and architectural adornment.

The new myth encouraged a fundamental shift toward pre-Hellenistic Middle Eastern forms assimilated by the Achemenids and passed on to the

Sassanids. The effect of such models on administration, religion, and language was highly important for Islamic ethnic alignments, as will appear in later chapters. Here it is important to stress the impact on styles of rule as well as on the myth itself. Instead of remaining a military or clan leader, the caliph became (in what is often called the "High Islamic" manner) a remote despot. The legend of the good Caliph Harun al-Rashid, who walked Baghdad's streets in disguise, expressed the omniscient benefactor element of the myth. More often the ruler exercised his power from the seclusion of his palace, surrounded by the accoutrements of ancient Mesopotamian splendor.

After 195 years of rule, the Abbasid caliphs were replaced de facto by the Shiite Buyid dynasty, although they briefly regained a measure of power. In the tenth and eleventh centuries, various claimants to the title of caliph appeared in Africa, notably the powerful Shiite Fatimid dynasty in Egypt. The lingering respect for the requirement that the caliph descend from the Kuraysh clans of the Mecca region, however, together with the memory of their former magnificence perpetuated the formal rule of the Abbasids for six more centuries. All acknowledged that the caliph had a duty to protect Islam and to act as supreme judge when necessary. Although scholars (the *ulema*) held that even the ruler could not innovate or abrogate laws, in fact the plea of necessity led caliphs and other Moslem rulers to decree harsh, arbitrary punishments to uphold their absolute authority.[24] As Marshall Hodgson writes, the Abbasid caliph, although theoretically denied the position of God's vice-regent, actually assumed the Sassanid Mesopotamian role of "shadow of God on earth."[25]

The subsequent history of the Abbasid dynasty is interesting principally as an indication of the nostalgia for universal legitimacy in Islam. For two and one-half centuries putative descendants survived as figureheads of the Mameluke rulers in Cairo and briefly thereafter under Ottoman protection. After that, the title remained in abeyance until the late nineteenth century, when the Ottoman sultans added the title of "caliph" to their preferred style of "padishah," apparently inventing a legend that the last Abbasid had willed the caliphate to them.

These details are interesting mainly to show how events in an area as far-flung as the Islamic conquests precluded maintenance of a truly secular authority that could match the religion's claims to universality. Even the early Umayyad caliphs, at a time when Arab conquering armies represented the sole sources of power, were unable to obtain more than nominal allegiance in such peripheral areas as Iberia. Relying entirely on land routes—no single Moslem navy ever dominated both the eastern and the western Mediterranean—the Islamic empire had an impossible control task, even as compared to the later Roman empire. Here, it seems obvious, was a case where technological and economic limitations set restrictions on the scope of imperial rule. The ambiguities of the universalist myth also posed problems. Even orthodox Islamic teachings made no definitive provision for solving persistent dynastic conflicts. The caliph was the legitimate source of political as well as religious authority, but he was never regarded as the sole source. The problem was to define authoritatively how much power might be exercised legitimately by a de facto ruler other than a caliph.

Apart from claims to the title of caliph or to investiture by him, Moslem rulers resorted to several legitimizing devices. The *ghazi* role discussed in chapter 3 was the prime alternative because a strong ruler was not only imperative for fighting infidels but attracted the most vigorous warriors. Religious revival (the *mahdi* claim) has been important throughout Islamic history for similar reasons. The Shiite claim, incompatible with any Sunni theories, is a more extreme demand for legitimacy (discussed in chapter 7) on the basis of millennial religious revival. A special claim used by Fatimids and Mamelukes alike was based on the role of protector of the Arabian Holy Cities. Some dynasties, like the Hafsids of Tunis, resorted to investiture as *emir* (ruler) by the *sharif* (descendant of Mohammed) of Mecca.[26] Other dynasties, notably in Morocco, have advanced genealogical claims to be *sharif*. The Genghisid legitimization claims, although incompatible as such with Moslem orthodoxy, whether Sunni or Shiite, were a real force in Asia during the fourteenth and fifteenth centuries.

The multitude of cross-cutting claims to legitimate authority combined with the impotence of any central authority, after the decline of the Baghdad caliphate, to adjudicate them, led Moslem regimes to resort to an extreme version of the "Grace of God" theory. By the eleventh century, Moslem scholars accepted the "law of necessity" not merely as a cover for decrees by a caliph but as a legitimization of de facto authority in general. As the power of the caliphate declined, usurpers, installed originally by military force, often came to be regarded as "blessed by God."[27] The phrase "blessed by God" is equivalent to *Dei gratia* (Grace of God) in Europe; the origins of the phrase go back to the fifth millennium B.C. Middle East, where it expressed personal humiliation and devotion.[28] Gradually, the Grace of God concept was elaborated to require that the ruler maintain order in accord with the *Sharia*, assist religion, and support the *jihad*. If he did these things he was considered a legitimate authority whom all good Moslems were obliged to obey even if he ruled only a portion of the *Dar ul-Islam*. As a result, the Mesopotamian myth of a terrestrial order paralleling the divine order adopted by the Abbasid caliphs was ultimately applied to any strong, stable ruler—"caliph within his territories," as an Ottoman *vizir* (minister) pronounced in the sixteenth century: "The Prophet said, 'The Sultan is the Shadow of God upon earth, with whom every wronged one takes refuge.' He said also, . . . 'Obey the Sultan, even if there is appointed to command over you an Abyssinian slave.'"[29]

Resort to the Grace of God theory solved the immediate problem of obedience for inhabitants of a region ruled by a Moslem reasonably in accord with Islamic law. From a broader standpoint, the "solution" posed three additional problems. First, the continued insistence on the inseparability of religious and secular authority complicated frontier relations with non-Moslem polities. The most famous historical instance is the Treaty of Kuchuk Kainarji (1774). The Russian negotiators assumed that Turkey had renounced sovereignty over the Crimean khanate, only to discover that the latter insisted on maintaining subordination to the sultan. "We, all the Tatar people, thanks be to God, are of the same religion and Moslem law as the Sovereign and Supreme Caliph of the Moslems, the Emperor of the Ottoman Porte. Because of our religion and our law, it is proper for us to renounce this liberty [from the Ottomans as guaranteed in the treaty]."[30] As a result, as noted in chapter 3, the Crimea was lost to Islam altogether, for the indignant Russians simply annexed it.

A second problem, present everywhere that a Grace of God theory prevails, is how to determine whether a rebel has acquired the right to usurp a throne, at what point his authority is sufficiently established to command religious obedience. The third problem was more acute in Islam than in Christendom, where even Grace of God theorists recognized that separate polities as such enjoyed legitimacy. Within the *Dar ul-Islam*, on the other hand, there was no legitimate basis for division; any Moslem sovereign might seek to extend his dominion over any or all other Moslem polities.[31] To be sure, the *ulema* often sought to avoid such fratricidal conflicts. The Ottoman *ulema*, however, urged their sovereign to fight Tamerlane, a vicious usurper of power. A century later, a Sunni *mullah* of Isfahan in Persia urged the sultan as "King of the Caliph's Throne" to continue war on the Shiites rather than on the Sunni Mameluke regime. In the eighteenth century, on the other hand, some Ottoman *cadis* (judges) denounced the seizure of Persian provinces even though they had been ruled up to then by Shiite infidels.[32] As might be expected from a power-oriented, ruthless dynasty that confronted, over the centuries, such conflicting ethical advice, the Ottomans proceeded to seize such Moslem polities as they could. After swallowing up the Mameluke empire, they returned to nibbling on the Persian realm.

The intrusion of Central Asian steppe nomads into the Moslem world exacerbated the contradictions inherent in the Islamic concept of the imperial polity. As was discussed in chapter 2, Turkic groups maintained a strong traditional belief in their right to rule wherever they could prevail. The early success of Turkic mercenaries as agents of established Arab polities greatly enhanced such self-confidence. Nevertheless, it appears that the most prominent Turkic conquerors of the eleventh century, the Seljuks, accepted standard Islamic legitimizing myths. Not surprisingly, a *hadith* was discovered to facilitate this linkage: "I [Mohammed pronounced, as God's mouthpiece,] have an army in the East which I call Turk, I set them on any people that kindle my wrath." It is equally unsurprising that an opposite *hadith* had appeared in the mouths of the ninth-century enemies of the Turks, referring to them as "the small-eyed, red-faced, and flat-nosed Turks with faces like shields clad with sinews one above another."[33] The principal Turkic effect on the Islamic imperial myth down to the thirteenth century seems to have been a certain enhancement of the opportunism and ruthlessness lurking beneath the Grace of God concept and a heightening of *jihad* propensities. But, because both these tendencies appeared independently among fanatic Moslem regimes (notably the Almohads) in the contemporary Maghreb, one may infer that the problems associated with the Islamic legitimizing myth tend to accelerate internal conflict everywhere. Indeed, this spiral resembles that accelerating Moslem-Christian frontier conflict, and both spirals appear to derive ultimately from the nomadic background of Islam.

The immense increase in turbulence and ruthlessness following the Mongol invasion posed problems of a different magnitude, however, from those arising from successive nomadic regimes in such areas as North Africa. Genghis Khan's extraordinary military and political abilities enabled him to seize upon an instant in history when the steppe clans were ready to join an immense conquest agglomeration. The intense self-confidence he instilled in this agglomeration resembled the achievements of steppe leaders since Attila. A modern Turkish historian argues that the concept of universal dominion among the Central Asians derived from the shamanist belief that God had created the Turks to inherit everything between the blue sky and the black earth.[34] Other scholars believe that Persia and Rome may have provided notions of universal dominion. It is worthy of note that Nestorian Christian Uighur chancery scribes actually formulated, if they did not invent, Genghis Khan's ideology. The formula, "rule of the Four Parts of the World," which the ancient Middle Eastern kingdoms derived from Syrian-Arabian pastoral nomads, strikingly resembles the Four Directions of the World claimed by Central Asian conquerors.[35]

It would seem, nevertheless, that the latter formula was obtained, at least in the first instance, from China. Nearly all scholarly authorities agree that it was the immense prestige of the nearby Chinese sedentary civilization that decisively shaped the Mongol myth. According to Bertold Spuler, Genghis's "first desire was to give a legal basis to the power which his success had embodied in his person." He found the appropriate formula in the slogan, "*one* sun in heaven, *one* Lord on earth."[36] Marco Polo noted that Genghis's successors proclaimed, "through the strength of the great god and the great grace which he has given to our empire, be the name of the Khan blessed, and may all who do not obey him die and disappear."[37] The affinity of such formulas to Moslem and Christian Grace of God theories is obvious. Even for the Mongol rulers who had converted to Islam, however, China remained the dynasty's greatest acquisition. China's ruler, the Great Khan, developed the cult of Genghis as founder of an autocratic universal empire. Kublai Khan provided a fixed date related to the pastoral cycle for commemorating Genghis, a practice incompatible with the Moslem calendar but suited to the Chinese agrarian cycle.[38] The veneration of Genghis's tent and his remains in a golden pyramid was instituted under the Chinese khan's patronage. In the fifteenth century, when Mongol rule in China was drawing to a close, Buddhist monks became the custodians of the Genghis cult.[39] Using the symbolism of lances and banners placed before the ruler's tent, Buddhist Kalmyk Mongols carried the Genghis myth as far as the Volga.[40] Buddhist legitimization was extremely important both for Mongols, who believed that the seventeenth-century Manchu dynasty in China would carry out the mission of ruling the universe, and those Dzhungarian Mongols who tried to establish a competing empire.

Unquestionably, however, Genghis's adaptation of the Chinese universal imperial myth was designed to legitimize his own dynasty's claims. These claims were based on *Geblütsrecht*, specifically, the sanctification of a special lineage (the "Golden Clan") in the manner usual among steppe groups. Genghis's "Great Yasa," based on Mongol customary law, was designed to consecrate the monopoly of absolute power in the Golden Clan. All Mongol conquests were regarded as its property, or *yurt*. Although his heirs were separately assigned the four directions of the empire, the Yasa counseled them to maintain unity, refrain from killing Golden Clan members, and keep up nomadic customs, especially lifelong practice in the archery that gave them military superiority. The current supreme ruler was to be designated by a great assembly of lesser clan leaders, even including sedentary allies, from among Golden Clan males. In practice, the Chinese branch acquired a purely nominal ascendancy, whereas the various parts of the empire were governed as independent realms.[41]

Direct offshoots of the Golden Clan are important historically. The Il Khans (or Hulagids) of Persia introduced into the Islamic world the formal ascription of peasants to the soil, probably as an extension of the compulsory retention of nomad clan members in their military units rather than in imitation of feudal serfdom. Following their Persian ministers' advice, the Il Khan rulers claimed the title of padishah and the heritage of Sassanids and Abbasids alike. The Golden Horde Khanate of the Black Sea–Central Asian steppes also adopted Islam and some of its legitimizations. The most striking Genghisid succession claims were less direct. Tamerlane began his career of conquest, only less extensive than Genghis's, over a century after the latter had died. Tamerlane had extremely tenuous claims to being an heir of Genghis, but he did rely on partly pagan Chagatay Turkic clans that had been a part of the original Mongol conquest agglomeration. His extreme use of terror, uprooting of sedentary populations, and attacks on fellow Moslem princes were related as much, probably, to his followers' inclinations as to his own adherence to the Genghisid model. The desire of newer clans to rise in the hierarchy, added to the usual nomad thirst for conquest, constituted strong motivations for all Genghisid steppe rulers to pursue constant warfare.[42] Tamerlane used both the Grace of God theory and the *mahdi* puritanical theme—other regimes, he asserted, were lukewarm in Islam—as justifications.[43]

The relationship of the Egyptian Mamelukes to the Genghisid myth shows, on the other hand, how ambivalent its effects could be. Prior to the Ottoman Janissaries, the Mamelukes constituted the most prominent of the slave armies endemic in the Moslem world. Their greatest ruler, the thirteenth-century Sultan Baybars, introduced the Great Yasa as the special law of the Mamelukes. The essential elements of the Mameluke imperial myth survived a sweeping change of recruitment at the end of the fourteenth century. After that time, nominal slaves (often young men whom their families had dispatched to seek their fortunes) were recruited from among Caucasus mountaineers. These "Circassian" Mamelukes retained Turkic as a secret language, used the tent mosque symbolic of nomadic warrior origins despite their sedentary life, and favored such nomad customs as drinking *kumiss* (fermented mare's milk).[44] An essential legitimizing element of their myth was, nevertheless, defense of sedentary Egypt, Syria, and the Holy Cities against both Mongols and crusaders. After Sultan Baybars's victory over the Mongol armies in Syria, Islamic poets celebrated the Mamelukes as Islam's principal defenders.[45] Nevertheless, the Mamelukes retained links with the Genghisid Golden Horde as part of the Middle Eastern balance of power. Throughout the late thirteenth and early fourteenth centuries its rulers' assent was also essential for Mameluke recruitment of Kipchaks. In return, the Golden Horde requested from the Mamelukes, as guardians of the caliph, the supreme *jihad* symbol, the Black Banner of the Abbasids.[46]

Interesting and durable as the Mameluke imperial myth was, it left few lasting traces on the ethnic identity of the subject Egyptians. The same verdict applies to nearly all Moslem imperial polities. Either they were part of the larger Arab or Turkic identity or (like the Golden Horde or the Andalusian empires) these polities were ephemeral. The most that can be asserted is that persistence of a polity like the Mamelukes' or some of the later Moroccan regimes in a well-defined geographical area may have constituted some basis for future regional identity. Because Egyptian concepts of geographic distinctiveness and unity were stronger before Islam (that is, before such concepts became intermingled with the idea of Egypt as a center of Arabicism) and the Moroccan polity is still fragile, however, even such indirect effects are problematical. The special relation of the Persians to their imperial past requires more exploration in chapter 7 together with its effect—as an alien boundary-defining element—on the Ottoman Turks.

As suggested in chapter 3, the Ottoman legitimizing myth was very complex. Apart from the *ghazi* and nomad elements, the Ottomans were careful to maintain a minimal conformity to the High Islamic myth stressed by the *ulema*. Consequently, it is difficult to subscribe to views advanced by scholars such as Arnold Toynbee that the Ottoman empire was the "universal state" of the "Byzantine family of nations." Greeks desperately endeavoring to reach an accommodation with their conquerors would, of course, have liked to promote such a denouement. One prominent Byzantine scholar termed Mohammed the Conqueror the true "Emperor of the Romans," called by God to Constantine's throne.[47] Down to the end of the nineteenth century, Moslem writers occasionally reciprocated these sentiments. Halil Ganem, for example, wrote: "The Islamic religion, which one cannot deny has a truly grand character and elevated morality, constituted in fact a very sharp line of demarcation between East and West, a sort of Chinese wall which [sixteenth-century Sultan] Suleiman sought to break down by being crowned king of Hungary and by . . . close alliances with European powers. . . . But the fanatic party led by the *ulema* . . . soon re-erected the wall."[48] More recent Turkish historians, on the other hand, as a German art historian notes, even depreciate the influence of the Byzantine imperial architectural heritage; but the Ottoman mosques, as visual symbols of empire, constitute the only real perpetuation of the Hagia Sophia style.[49] At a literal level, the Ottomans, while of course retaining the Byzantine capital city, rejected specific Court mythic formulas.

Christianity and Imperial Polity: The Eastern Accommodation

The relation of Byzantium to the Moslem imperial concept suggests one reason for turning to a consideration of Eastern Christians' accommodation to the imperial myth. There is an even more compelling reason for examining this relationship before analyzing the peculiar Western concepts of Christian empire. Byzantium *was* Rome. It was not merely an heir of Roman secular universalism; the introduction of Christianity is, many scholars agree, the only major distinction between the empire that governed the Mediterranean world from Rome and its continuation in Constantinople. The change of capital and administrative machinery are nonetheless significant, as will appear in chapter 6. The mythic adaptation was critically important not only for its impact on the Roman polity but as a starting point for other Christian accommodations to empire.

Because the Christian religion claimed to be universal, accommodation to the universalist aspect of the Roman empire was easiest. Even before Christianity triumphed, the universality of the Roman empire was regarded as a providential arrangement for the spread of Christian teaching. After Constantine, the empire became God's chosen realm of peace, a fundamental part of the divine plan for history and precursor of the ultimate Christian ecumenism.[50] Such absolute insistence on a universal mission posed a problem for the Hellenization of Byzantium and for its relations with the Western Church. The sense of mission also posed a severe, possibly fatal geopolitical problem. To maintain its claims to universality, Byzantium had to govern Rome (which, at least juridically, it did as late as 772)[51] and the West. This task exceeded the powers of the empire once it had become Christian, for the Germanic invasions irreparably disrupted the western provinces. Justinian I, nevertheless, aimed to win back all lost territories "to the borders of both Oceans."[52] Nominally he succeeded by reconquering an Atlantic coastal strip of southern Iberia, but he may have fatally depleted the empire's resources. Nevertheless, Justinian's successors up to 1155, when Byzantium was on the verge of disaster, insisted on attempting to regain Italy and perhaps more distant lands in the West.[53]

The Byzantine universalist myth did pose a certain problem for sincere Christians. The most profound spiritual reservations, expressed eloquently by Saints Augustine and Jerome during the fifth century, cannot be treated here. An enduring problem related to ethnicity was the identification of Christianity and a specific secular order. Not only did the empire have a universal mission, being *in* and *of* the empire was equated with being

Christian and civilized. Separation from the emperor was the unforgivable sin. Consequently, the myth catered to the strong xenophobia of the Byzantine population, especially its hatred of the Germanic groups. This hatred led to the death penalty for intermarriage and ultimately to a shocking massacre of Germanic auxiliaries in Constantinople in 400. A German writer, Count Alexander Schenk von Stauffenberg, has even interpreted this extreme anti-Teutonism as a secret ideology of pagans trying to reverse Constantine's Christian universalism. But writers who were at least nominally Christian described Germanic people as animals worse than pagans.[54] It is hard to separate such dislike from the orthodox Christian horror at their Arian heresy. A Gallic bishop who was a precursor of the Western church's policy of reconciling Roman and Germanic elements stipulated that the latter would have to become orthodox before being accepted by Romans.[55] Nevertheless, in the East brigandish Isaurians were accepted as loyal imperial servants and ultimately as emperors because they dwelt within the empire. Conversely, Christian writers demanded that all Germanic elements be expelled beyond the Danube. Such facts were indeed hard to reconcile with ecumenism.[56]

The relationship of orthodox Christians living outside its frontiers to the empire as the universal realm of God also caused complications, aggravating tendencies to heresy, notably among the Armenians. A partial solution, as Byzantine strength declined, was relaxation of the imperial demand for real power (*potestas*) over other Christian polities provided that they conceded formal authority (*auctoritas*) to the emperor.[57] Franz Dölger describes the supple tactic: "In time of need Byzantium was always . . . inclined to disregard temporarily, for practical reasons, measures which in times of strength she did not hesitate to attack with heavy artillery. They referred to this practice by the expression '*oikhonomia*' borrowed from Christian salvation theology."[58] To preserve *auctoritas*, the ancient Middle Eastern concept of a hierarchy of terrestrial powers corresponding to a heavenly hierarchy—employed by Rome centuries earlier—was garbed in Christian dress. A family of kings, all related to the emperor by degrees such as "son," "brother," and the like, corresponding to the favor he was prepared to extend to them, was elaborated for protocol purposes. Even pagans such as the Sassanid rulers were admitted; but orthodox Christian "relatives" were required to have their churches mention the Byzantine emperor in their prayers. In the last desperate centuries concessions went so far as to invent titles like "Colchis Emperor" for the rival Greek polity in Trebizond and to acknowledge its ruler's right to appoint bishops.[59]

Mention of the emperor suggests the crucial role of the sovereign for the Byzantine universalist myth. Indeed, some historians consider that the pressing need to maintain the pagan emperor's divinity cult, the last sacral component of the Roman myth, was the principal motive for persecuting Christians.[60] Transformation of the myth of universal empire without retention of the sacral role of the ruler was inconceivable for early Christians. The alternative—regarding an ecclesiastical figure as the vicar of Christ—gradually adopted in the West was hardly considered, although the honorary primacy of the pope as successor to Peter's episcopal ministry in Rome was acknowledged by Byzantium at least until the tenth century. The main Byzantine accommodation, however, was to acclaim the secular ruler as Christ's vicar.[61]

Powerful support for the thesis that the Christian emperor derived his mythic role from an adaptation of the ancient concept of parallel heavenly and terrestrial hierarchies is provided by Byzantine architecture. As the art historian André Grabar writes, a new movement like Christianity was obliged to adapt themes from older cults, however much it might reject their principles. Oriental motifs reflecting the Mesopotamian dual hierarchy concept had been introduced into Roman official art centuries before Constantine as part of what Franz Altheim terms the "artistic *koine* [common vocabulary] of the Orient."[62] These themes penetrated Christian monuments designed to deliver the message that the emperor was God's vicar, such as Justinian I's foundations in Ravenna and Constantinople, as Deno Geanakoplos notes: "In general, then, it may be said that the emperors' building of religious structures constituted an instrument, not only for the furthering of imperial control over the church but, through imperial insistence on ecclesiastical unity as reflected in their building policy, for promoting the ultimate aim of the unity of the empire itself."[63]

As the central-plan church building became dominant during the period following the iconoclast interval of the seventh to eighth centuries, its decorative arrangement strongly resembled the Mesopotamian heavenly hierarchy. Christ as the Ruler of All (Pantokrator) always appeared in mosaic or fresco in the central dome. The principal events of his life appeared along with his mother and the apostles in the next lower rank of pictures. Farther down came lesser saints. The most detailed art historiographical analysis contends, moreover, that these precisely prescribed portrayals were a culmination of earlier Christian symbolism, but at the same time embodied a new emphasis.[64] The Pantokrator image, derived from the ancient Middle East via Magian motifs,[65] was the heavenly counterpart of the emperor who, as archpriest and priest-king (roles explicitly based on Old Testament models) alone among laymen could penetrate the central portion of the church during the mass. In a somewhat similar manner, the Oriental custom of prostration before a ruler (the *proskynesis*) is portrayed above the main entrance to the nave of Hagia Sophia as the supreme gesture of absolute subordination of the earthly ruler to Christ. But the emperor was in turn entitled to the same complete obeisance from his subjects. More concretely, the emperor's universal mission as terrestrial savior was considered to constitute justification for his intervention in any polity, Christian or non-Christian, if the safety of Christians was at stake.[66]

The elevation of the emperor's role to that of vicar of Christ did not remove all human restraint upon him. The Roman law tradition included an element of natural law limiting all human authority.[67] The logic behind such restraints was very different from that of the Islamic *Sharia*, but the residual effect was not wholly dissimilar. Some authors have even contended that true "Caesaropapism"—domination of polity and church by the emperor—was absent. In the later centuries of Byzantium the emperor rarely deposed patriarchs of Constantinople, whereas one patriarch excommunicated an emperor.[68] On the other hand, no ecclesiastical authority, neither the Constantinople patriarch, nor the four Eastern patriarchs conjointly, nor a church synod, ever tried to depose a Byzantine emperor. Consequently, Christians faced a dilemma somewhat similar to the Moslems'. The emperor was nominally elected by acclamation. His coronation and anointment by the patriarch constituted mere symbolic expressions of the Divine Grace he had already received.[69] Once he was installed, no earthly authority had the formal right to remove the emperor; rebels were denounced as traitors and sinners. On the other hand, a successful rebellion, like a usurpation in an Islamic regime, was perceived to be the result of God's will. The church recognized this divine sanction by proceeding with the coronation ceremony.[70] In contrast to Islamic difficulties with the Grace of God theory, however, Byzantium had no problem with the extension of the emperor's claims to other polities, for this was never usurpation because he was by right the universal ruler, entitled to intervene in any polity. Byzantium also never faced the problem Islam encountered from the Genghisid intrusion of alien rulers, for no person who was not already a Byzantine subject ever became emperor.[71]

The implications of the accommodation of Byzantine Christianity to the myth of universal empire will become clearer after consideration in the next chapter of the influences exerted by the capital and the bureaucracy. Without a prior understanding of this accommodation, however, one could not proceed to exploration of the special accommodations attained in Russia and West Europe. The direct impact of the Byzantine myth of empire on Russia has been exaggerated. There were at least five major components of the Russian imperial myth. In contrast, for example, to the successive nature of Magyar myths, until the nineteenth century the five Russian strands were mutually reinforcing. The first component by time of origin (at least as a major theme) was "ingathering of the Russian lands."

Much confusion has been generated by fifteenth- and sixteenth-century use of *"tsarstvo"* by Russian propagandists. The obvious derivation of the term from "Caesar," a Roman imperial title, suggests that the usage was meant to advance a universalist claim. In fact, however, as Michael Cherniavsky has shown, from 1246 on Russians called many independent rulers, notably the Mongol khans, "tsar." Assumption of the title was, therefore, a corollary of Ivan III's formal declaration of independence from the Genghisids.[72] Probably more significant in the minds of Russian Court circles, the title represented an assertion of Muscovite claims to the heritage of pre-Mongol Rus against the Jagiellonian dynasty. About 1456 the Moscow princes' genealogy was for the first time traced to Vladimir I of Kiev, the "tsar" or "New Constantine who baptized the Russian land," and through him to Rurik, the founder of the dynasty. It followed that such *"Russian zemlya"*—a vague term embracing people as well as territory but not necessarily implying centralized rule—was the "patrimony" of the Moscow princes. Their use of *"tsarstvo"* implied an intention to exert stronger control over the *zemlya*. It was a claim reflecting the *Geblütsrecht* or dynastic rights of the Rurikid family versus the Jagiellonians, henceforward regarded as usurpers of Rus.[73]

Especially among Slavs and Scandinavians, the sainthood of the dynastic forefather provided a strong reinforcement of pre-Christian dynastic solidarity. Consequently, St. Vladimir's patrimony was indissolubly linked to the fact that the "Russian land" was Orthodox Christian. By the fifteenth century (as discussed in chapter 7), the split between the Eastern Orthodox and the Western Roman Catholic churches was extreme. As a result, emphasis on Orthodoxy constituted a second major theme of the Russian myth. A claim to St. Vladimir's heritage, sometimes joined to the assertion that Moscow was the "second Kiev," also reinforced the challenge to the Jagiellonians.[74] Apparently, Ivan IV would even have preferred war with them to war against infidel Kazan.

After the conquest of Kazan, Ivan used his new title of "tsar" of its *yurt* (which emphasized rule over people more than did *zemlya*) to back up his claim to the Slavs whom the Lithuanians had taken over from Mongol rule. As a third distinct element of the Russian imperial myth, incorporation of Kazan in Russia was most important as the first fateful step, within the dynamic of the Islamic-Christian frontier, beyond the ethnic territories of Russian nationality. As Jaroslaw Pelenski has pointed out, "This conquest signalled the transformation of Muscovite Russia from a centralized national state into a multinational empire, a development of crucial importance for the subsequent course of Russian history."[75] Symbolically, the change was reflected in the fantastic architecture of St. Basil.[76] Like all northern Eurasian dynasties, Rurikids and Genghisids alike believed in *Geblütsrecht*. Something closer to the myths of Christian empire was also essential for Russians.

One returns, therefore, with the notion of cosmic empire, to the fourth mythic theme, the Byzantine heritage. Certainly St. Vladimir and his descendants in Kiev had never tried to usurp Byzantium's universal empire, although his pagan forebears had rather naively demanded that Byzantium pay tribute or withdraw from Europe.[77] The Kiev princes had never claimed the title of *basileus*. They were content to exercise a de facto sovereignty with considerable support from the Greek heads of their church, who considered it important to avoid fragmenting the Orthodox Rus commonwealth. Even during the thirteenth to fifteenth centuries, when the Rus church enjoined obedience to Mongol "tsars," it reserved the supreme place for the ruler in the liturgy for the Byzantine emperor.[78] The appearance during the fifteenth century of prophecies fortelling a greater role for Muscovy is related to two developments. The most obvious was the need for a strong Orthodox polity at a time when Byzantium was virtually reduced to a single, harassed city. Thus Prince Vasili II (1441) wrote (the letter was never dispatched because of conditions in Constantinople) to the ecumenical patriarch to offer Muscovy as Orthodoxy's bastion, while promising always to seek his blessing.[79] The other factor leading to enhanced Muscovite claims was a "second wave" of South Slav immigration consisting mostly of Bulgarian monks arriving in fifteenth-century Russia as refugees from the Ottoman advance. The proximity of the Bulgar polity to Byzantium had meant that its independence was difficult to maintain on a purely de facto basis.[80] Consequently, the Bulgar myth continued to include the notion, not of rejecting the universal empire, but of replacing it. Thus Bulgars referred to the capital, Trnovo, of the second Bulgarian empire (1186–1330) as "Tsargrad" and developed the legend that it was to be the "Third Rome," the "imperial bastion of refuge" after the decline of Constantinople. It was this myth that the immigrant Bulgar clerics attempted to transfer to Moscow. But even Ivan IV in his triumph declared that he had no claim on "the realm of the whole universe."[81]

Perhaps it is safer to conclude, as Dmitri Obolensky seems to imply in his impressive examination of the "Byzantine commonwealth," that the disappearance of a Byzantine emperor cleared the way for a Russian emperor as national ruler rather than as heritor of the universal mission. Only two generations before the Ottoman conquest, the Constantinople patriarch had assured the Russian princes that "it is impossible for Christians to have a Church and no Emperor."[82] The logical implication was that any considerable independent orthodox polity surviving the death of the last Byzantine emperor had to find a replacement. That is what the Russian polity did under Ivan IV. The four Eastern patriarchs in effect endorsed his move by agreeing to the consecration (1589) of a fifth patriarch for Moscow.[83] Moreover, Russian propagandists invoked a kind of Grace of God theory for the advent of Ivan by asserting that Byzantium had fallen as a punishment for its sins.

The emergence of the sole remaining Orthodox emperor as a ruler who renounced universal dominion constituted a major step in the transformation of the imperial concept throughout Christendom. Henceforward the sacral mission of empire was to consolidate peoples united by religion, history, and culture. This development accounts for what observers have described as Russia's "precocious nationalism." The altered concept also made it possible for Russian rulers to turn away from the defunct "Byzantine commonwealth" toward guarded participation in the society of "sovereign states" that had emerged in Europe. The leading role that Russia acquired in this concert was, in fact, the basis for the fifth mythic strand that sustained the empire for three centuries. Ivan IV refused to join the Catholic powers in a crusade against the Ottomans because he preferred acquisition of the Rurikid heritage to an adventure designed to establish hegemony over Balkan Orthodox Slavs.[84] When the Russian title, *Imperator Vserussky* was accepted by the Holy Roman emperor in 1742,[85] the step amounted to recognition of the concept of multiple empires. Only two generations later, the Habsburgs decided to renounce their own vestigial universal claims. As strong a Russian autocrat as Nicholas I, in the mid-nineteenth century, was disturbed by the Slavophile proposal that there was something unique and inimitable about a Russian Christian empire. He preferred to consider himself to be a European emperor, one of a family of rulers, rather than to revive the notion of universal mission.[86]

The principal utility of the imperial title, the Third Rome concept, and the Moscow patriarchate to Russian rulers quite possibly had been the consolidation of autocratic centralism in the sixteenth century.[87] Absence of a Roman law tradition like the one that had restrained the Byzantine emperor enabled the Russian rulers to become more complete autocrats than the Byzantine emperors, as did the *Geblütsrecht* concept reinforced by the Mongol steppe heritage. The tsar's drastically enhanced power over the church, as evidenced by even a weak tsar's ability to depose a patriarch in 1667, constituted an important component of autocracy. Peter I's elimination of the patriarchate (significantly, he applied Lutheran theories of temporal supremacy rather than resorting to Byzantine precedents), signaled the attainment of Caesaropapism such as the Byzantine myth had only adumbrated.[88]

The Myth of Empire in West Europe

The Byzantine way of accommodating Christianity and universal empire was the starting point for developments in the West as well as in Russia. The two roads led, however, in almost diametrically opposite directions. In Byzantium the universalist aspect of the imperial myth, at first rendered more potent by Christian teachings, gradually declined through the *oikhonomia* of admitting the real independence of other Orthodox polities, then by the development within the framework of Byzantium of a precocious Greek nationalism. The myth of a single supreme terrestrial ruler remained in Byzantium to the end, however. In Russia, the power of the ruler attained new heights internally, but truly universal pretensions were renounced in favor of a broad but limited sphere of expansion. For the West, the ideal solution was a universal secular empire protecting a universal spiritual domain and in tutelage to the latter. In practice, the balance between secular and ecclesiastical forces permitted the emergence of a Western polity separate from both church and empire, followed by an entire series of competing polities that became the European state system. In the West, moreover, an emperor, unless endowed with great charisma, was restricted by material limitations, legal traditions, and ecclesiastical power to an extent rarely encountered in other imperial polities.

To understand, even in outline, how this complicated interplay developed in the West, one must envisage the situation in Rome in the eighth century. The Catholic Merovingian kingdom had been a welcome development for the popes amid the disorder of the sixth century; but Byzantine force was intermittently available in central Italy until the eighth century. Tensions between the papacy and the Byzantine emperor because of iconoclasm were increasing, but down to the middle of that century the popes did not dispute the emperors' temporal authority in Rome. By the end of the seventh century, however, the de facto Carolingian ruler of the Frank kingdom, Charles Martel, was providing aid to the papacy. In 754 the alliance was formalized when the pope urgently required Frank aid against rapacious Lombard nobles, whereas the first Carolingian formally to assume the throne, Pepin, needed a source of legitimization.[89] The lingering force of Germanic *Geblütsrecht* favored a Merovingian successor, despite the obvious incompetence of that dynasty. The Merovingian dynastic myth, which attributed to them (hence to Franks in general) descent from the Trojans, replacing the pagan gods of the earliest myth, preserved a measure of potency. Consequently, Pepin found papal approval a valuable justification for his usurpation. Pope Paul conferred the title of Patrician of Rome and other titles on Pepin, pronouncing him chosen by God before all other kings. Paul also termed the Frank realm a new Kingdom of David. The Frank people, he said, had a special place inscribed in heaven because of its aid to the church, similar to the place the people of Israel had held.[90] Such endorsements took the place of the Germanic legitimization principle, but implied neither a universal mission for the Franks nor formal sovereignty for the pope, although the formulas certainly expressed his de facto independence from the Christian Byzantine emperor. The Roman liturgy included prayers for the Frank king as its real protector without, at least until 772, wholly neglecting the distant emperor.

Pope Leo III's coronation of Charlemagne as emperor on Christmas day, 800, instituted a new relationship between papacy and secular empire.[91] An obviously inspired acclamation in rhythmic chant by the congregation satisfied the sole formal requirement for the elevation of a Roman emperor —that divine sanction be expressed through the voice of the people.[92] The popes had been trying for centuries, apparently, to assume a more substantial role in the coronation of Byzantine emperors. Charlemagne's crown, so evidently a gift of the papacy, could serve as a valuable precedent. Anointment had been instituted some centuries earlier. This sacral ritual strengthened the church's role in the choice of the emperor. Thenceforward, the carefully formulated rubrics inextricably involved high ecclesiastics (not always the pope) in every solemn elevation of a sovereign to the "anointed of God," protected against profane attack. But, in contrast to the situation in Eastern Christendom or Islam, a superior ecclesiastical power reserved the right to declare the ruler unfit and to absolve his subjects from their sacred duty of obedience.[93] Charlemagne himself apparently accepted the idea that the church was to be the tutor of rulers, as rulers were of their people.[94]

Charlemagne's recent role as a patron of the Holy Places in Palestine gave him a special aura,[95] although his personal morality (that is, his bastards) thwarted later German attempts to have him canonized. After some territorial concessions from Charlemagne, the new Byzantine emperor, Michael I, recognized him as *Imperator Augustus*, while carefully reserving the Greek version of the title (*Basileus toi Romaion*) for himself.[96] For Charlemagne, who already (at least according to some scholarly opinion) regarded himself as the ruler of a definite territorial unit, this distinction was perhaps acceptable. He was "apostrophized as the one called upon by Divinity to govern the *regnum Europae*," with Europe's boundary defined by the extent of Roman Christianity, for, according to Walter Ullmann, "Charlemagne was not the Ruler of the Romans, as the Byzantine Emperor designated himself, but a Ruler of a territorial unit, the Roman empire, of which the vital ingredient and cementing bond was the Roman-Christian faith. This is a distinction which as yet is hardly appreciated."[97]

As subsequent events showed, the Byzantines intended the gesture to be a personal concession to Charlemagne. Indeed, it is not certain that either the pope or Charlemagne intended the imperial title to be perpetuated in the West, much less to remain in his dynasty. His arrangements of 806, based on the specific Germanic version of *Geblütsrecht*, for partitioning his dominions among his sons appeared to disregard the possibility.[98] For about two decades the imperial title was shared by his heirs, but eventually the ruler of the East Frank kingdom was recognized as entitled to the imperial throne. After the eastern branch of the Carolingians died out in 911 (it had been displaced as ruling house a generation earlier) the title was in abeyance until the Ottonian dynasty at the end of the tenth century, but some residual claim of the eastern kingdom persisted.

Otto III, whose mother was a Byzantine princess, may have aspired to truly universal dominion. Certainly he and other emperors (whom for convenience I shall term Holy Roman emperors, although the title was not generally used until the late Middle Ages) aimed at expanding their influence eastward to all princes accepting Western (Catholic) Christianity. On the other hand, Holy Roman emperors, although asserting their claim to be emperor of the Romans (*Imperator Romanorum*) were always ready to recognize the equality of the Byzantine emperor as *Imperator Grecorum*. Consequently, the Western concept at its broadest was limited to a claim to be one of two legitimate Christian emperors.[99]

The French Exception

Far more serious as a practical limitation was the renunciation of any claim to universal empire—except in terms of purely formal precedence—over realms west of the final ninth-century Carolingian partition line. The West Frank kingdom, "Francia," soon to become known as "France," was not formally an empire, but it was equal to the Holy Roman empire in all practical respects. Several factors combined to produce this situation, so important for future European development. Francia, incorporating most of Gaul, was the richest part of Europe. Given the military successes of the Ottonian dynasty and its German successors and the fragmentation of Francia, however, only a dynastic accident ensured the latter's complete independence—the survival of the Francian Carolingians beyond the extinction of their eastern cousins.[100] In 911, when the last of the eastern Carolingians had died, Charles of Francia styled himself *rex Francorum*, king of the Franks. The Capetian dynasty, which succeeded the Francian Carolingians in 987, dropped this implied claim to the entire Frank realm. Throughout the Middle Ages, however, intense confusion over the meaning of the Franks' heritage persisted. Their name and their original seat were in the west, yet Charlemagne's old capital, Aachen, and his imperial title had gone to the east.[101] Innumerable symbolic devices were used by the French and the German sides to compete for the position of true heirs. Emperor Frederick I "discovered" Charlemagne's bones at Aachen and revived the town as sacral capital. The French royal burial ground was associated with St. Dionysius (Denis), a mythical counselor of Charlemagne.[102] French epics retrospectively assigned to the various French provincial contingents the leading roles in Charlemagne's army, while ignoring the fact that the Franks had been Germans. German Romanesque architecture resisted for a long time the twelfth-century French Gothic just as German monastic practice resisted French innovations. As language consciousness developed, a bad pun was advanced in France: "empire" meant *en pire*, "the worst."[103]

The critical development that sealed the independence of France regardless of the ups and downs in its rivalry with its neighbors was the symbiosis of episcopacy and hereditary monarchy. This unique cooperation resembled the alignment of the first Carolingians with the popes, but it was more national or at least protonational. The initial Francian advantage derived from the highly educated and perceptive qualities of the western bishops under the last Carolingians. The bishops developed the ideology of royal power by Grace of God, transmitted in the coronation ceremony by ecclesiastical anointing, on the model of Charlemagne's imperial accession.[104] The influence of the bishops, particularly their ability to elect and secure the acceptance of strong kings, was enhanced by the dangers posed by the Norman invasions. Because there was no permanent primate of France, the bishops constituted an oligarchy. At the end of the tenth century, however, by backing Hugh Capet as successor to the moribund Carolingians, the archbishop of Reims established his cathedral as the permanent coronation site.[105] Even more important by the late thirteenth century was the bishops' acquiescence in complete heredity by male primogeniture without even the form of an election. To ensure undisturbed succession to the French throne, the eldest son was crowned during his father's lifetime. The Capetians maintained a claim to descent from Charlemagne in the female line, but carefully excluded foreign princes who might claim the French throne through their mothers by the rule

"*Femme ne succède pas à la couronne de France.*"[106] Consequently, the kingdom was established on a basis that preserved some of the magic aura of the *Geblütsrecht*, though purging its potential for conflicting claims and external intervention.

The significance of the French development is highlighted by the problems faced simultaneously by the Holy Roman emperor. Lacking the power to secure an undisputed succession, the eastern bishops and imperial candidates repeatedly appealed to Rome, thus perpetuating the concept of tutelage.[107] The position of emperor remained elective; although primogeniture in powerful dynasties appeared, none was long-lasting. The popes generally preferred elective monarchies, for they afforded the possibility of rejecting a monarch hostile to the church.[108] Nevertheless, German emperors, most notoriously the strong Hohenstaufens, repeatedly clashed with the papacy over the scope of their respective imperial missions.

In contrast, the French kings, despite strict heredity and stronger claims to independence, usually avoided outright clashes with the papal Curia. Undoubtedly, a major reason was power politics in the simplest sense of the term. French monarchs were relatively distant from Rome and, until the thirteenth century, were less powerful than the Germans. Consequently, the popes could afford to tolerate the French as counterweights. Another major factor was the lack of potential for direct clash between the French myth of royal sovereignty and papal myths asserting feudal suzerainty over all Christian princes. The French publicists were careful to phrase their assertions in such a way as to constitute, in form at least, an exception. Thus the alleged Roman law maxim, *rex est imperator in regno suo* (the king is emperor in his own kingdom), used to assert sovereign authority subject to no external review was based, at times, on the claim that the French alone among European peoples were descendants of Trojans— a myth developed by the Franks at least by the fifth century—who had settled outside the confines of the Roman empire. Consequently, the argument implied, France could not have been a part of the "Donation of Constantine" to the popes.[109] By the thirteenth century, even Innocent III had to be content with a different conception of ruler consecration for the king and for the emperor. The pope recognized that the French king was directly related to God, but still asserted that the pope was intermediary for the emperor.[110] Imperial legalists at Bologna University recognized, a century later, that the kingdom of France was "exempt" from the pyramid of Roman law jurisdiction culminating in the emperor.[111]

The peculiar position of the French king directly affected the special role of the French people, then, as it gradually emerged, the French state in the modern sense of the term as Percy Schramm explains:

The concept of the state. . . . also became the concept of the French nation. The monarchy formed the nation and the nation formed the monarchy—a give and take which is so close that it is no longer possible to untangle it completely. But its results are apparent: the "*religion royale*," as a medieval author called it, a unique "status" which the Middle Ages ascribed to the French king still prevailed under Absolutism. "France," as Renan expressed it in a striking sentence that has often been quoted, "had created an eighth sacrament which was administered only at Reims, the sacrament of royalty."[112]

Joseph R. Strayer sums up one side of the process by the phrase, the "Capetians had to invent the France which they claimed to rule." "The French," Strayer continues, "earlier than any other continental kingdom, solved the problem of the 'mosaic' state, that is, a state put together out of provinces which had strongly autonomous cultural, legal, and institutional traditions."[113] To describe the process in terms used at the beginning of this chapter, a precociously successful compound polity arose in what had been the fragmented western part of the Franks' realm.

One factor, certainly, was the residual legitimacy of Charlemagne's governors as well as his royal heirs. A recent study argues that the ninth-century disintegration of his realm did not arise through usurpations, but through nobles who had been legitimately appointed as viceroys becoming virtually independent.[114] In view of the fact that such appointments were often made as an inescapable expedient to retain loyalty by territorial awards after external conquest had ceased, the practical distinction is not great. A strong case has been made that quasi-independent principalities evolved to as great dimensions as tenth-century economic and technological circumstances permitted, by a process of trial and error or even through survival of the fittest.[115] There was further disintegration in the eleventh-century "second wave" of autonomous county formation. I should not, therefore, wish to convey the impression that all, or even the most significant, developments can be explained by mythic influences. The strongest factor enabling France to emerge as a united polity in the late Middle Ages may well have been the fact that disintegration peaked in the eleventh century, when the international environment was benign enough to allow regrouping of forces for a second chance.

Nevertheless, remnants of the Carolingian legitimacy myth do appear to have exerted considerable influence. The same scholar who detects a thread of viceregal legitimacy finds that these same ninth-century personages rarely expanded beyond the frontiers of the regions (*regna*) they had been allotted originally.[116] More important, it appears, was constant reinforcement of the theme, introduced in Pepin's and Charlemagne's reigns, that the Franks (that is, the French) were a chosen people because their kingdom was a terrestrial parallel of the Kingdom of Heaven, just as their monarch was the earthly type of Christ himself, ruling the Frank ("free") kingdom that truly exists only in heaven, but which France resembles. At the end of the thirteenth century, Pope Boniface VIII sanctioned this concept in proclaiming that "like the people of Israel . . . the kingdom of France [is] a peculiar people chosen by the Lord to carry out the orders of Heaven."[117] Byzantine Christianity at its height did not reflect the ancient Mesopotamian myth more faithfully.

A final point of immense importance was the early linkage between this sacral kingdom and specific territory. The basic reasons why concepts of territoriality arose among both peasants and nobles in West Europe, particularly in the densely settled regions of northern France, were discussed in chapter 2. In France, royal authority was early exerted to secure definite frontiers and to acquire as much jurisdiction as the circumstances of the age permitted within such physical limits. The basic frontier after the final Carolingian partition remained for six centuries the "four-rivers line" along the Scheldt, the Meuse, the Saône, and the Rhone. This frontier was a long way from the classic concept of Gaul or even the present "hexagon" achieved by Vauban, Colbert, and Louis XIV.[118] But the rivers line lasted long enough to fix firmly in men's minds the concept of a definite state frontier.

For the purposes of this study, it is unnecessary to trace the strengthening of the French king-state-nation complex during the late medieval and the early modern periods, particularly the wars of religion. It is necessary to emphasize only that this process, despite external disruptive forces, was almost continuous in contrast to extreme fluctuations in the fortunes of the German imperial idea. A much more important theme for my purposes is the impact of the French model on other nascent European polities. The Frank nobility provided at least part of the ancestral stock for most European aristocracies, and therefore its myths and traditions were widely diffused. Consequently, the ideology embodied in the French coronation rubrics became the common property of the European family of monarchs.[119] In the symbolic intricacies of this myth, building upon but transcending *Geblütsrecht*, appeared the principle of primogeniture, not always restricted to males. The preeminence of French culture, Gothic architecture, and the prestigious language was an extremely important auxiliary. In the later Middle Ages, when the prestige of the French Court and the French administration connected with it had become firmly established, there was no real doubt about the close relationship of the culture and the kingdom that provided the basic models for most polities of Western Christendom. In sum, a Europe of nations would have been inconceivable without the peculiar combination of circumstances that first produced a France.

Revival of the Imperial Ideal

Despite innumerable reversals caused by political or external circumstances, French consciousness constantly evolved toward a stronger, more precisely bounded identity. The concept of empire in the West, on the other hand, appears to have had a cyclical aspect. Europe, Walter Ullmann writes, "was not a geographical expression, but denoted a perfectly well understood conceptual structure characterized on the one hand by the multiform if not heterogeneous complexion of the inhabitants under Carolingian rule, and on the other hand by the unifying cement and cementing bond of Roman-Latin, Western as opposed to Byzantine, Christianity."[120] The road from this ninth-century peak in significance of the imperial framework, through the Ottonian, the Hohenstaufen, and the Lützelburg reinvigorations of Holy Roman imperial force and myth is too complicated even to be outlined here. The remarkable imperial revival of the early sixteenth century cannot, however, be dismissed without closer scrutiny.

In 1519, a new Charles was crowned Holy Roman emperor; his minister, Mercurino Gattinara, asserted without fear of contradiction that Charles V was the head of the most nearly universal monarchy that Christendom had ever known.[121] There was not to be another like it. Indeed, Charles's election probably owed something to German national sentiment, revived to some degree by the resurrection of Charlemagne in humanistic research. Yet these same humanists realized that the imperial election conveyed title to rule over a shadow.[122] Nevertheless, the humanists continued to prophesy: Charles V would become ruler of Gaul, he would vanquish the Turks, he would liberate the Holy Sepulcher. Everywhere the universal myth was revived, for some a threat, for others a promise of safety. Even among Protestants, Heinz Duchhardt writes, a belief lingered "that the empire was not merely a secular structure, but had a spiritual function as well, that in theological history it constituted one of the powers with the theocratic and sacral quality of the Prophet Daniel's four universal monarchies, the earthly manifestation of the Divine Empire, encompassing Heaven and earth."[123] How did such a spectacular upsurge in imperial fortunes appear on the horizon, and why did it not survive Charles and his son Philip II?

Very mixed in ancestry, in sentiment Charles was a Burgundian Frenchman. No stronger example of nostalgia was ever recorded than his yearning for his ancestral city of Dijon: "If at the hour of our said demise our Duchy of Burgundy has been reduced to our obedience, we wish our said body to be entombed in the conventual church of the Carthusians in our city of Dijon in the said Duchy of Burgundy, by and with the bodies of our deceased predecessors."[124] The poignant testament indicates why the central aim of Charles's policy was defeat of France. It also points to his strongest positive sentiment, dynastic reverence. As did every other great noble house, the House of Austria (Habsburg-Burgundian dynasty) looked to its endowed churchyard burial place for its prime source of identity.

The Burgundy that constituted Charles's nostalgia, then, was first of all a family, a tradition, then a place, all united in a brilliant episode of history as ephemeral as Charles's own universal empire was to be. By the late fourteenth century, through the usual combination of luck, prudent marriages, and military skill, the dukes of Burgundy had assembled a relatively small but rich and strategic cluster of fiefs comprising, essentially, the modern Low Countries, extreme northern France, and a large chunk of east-central France. This was the classic intermediate zone where strong cities and coveted trade routes had precluded unification since the ninth century. Memory of the Burgundian kingdom that had preceded Frank rule in the area was vestigial. Juridically, the new Burgundian possessions had the considerable advantage of lying on both sides of the frontier between France and the Holy Roman empire. Because the empire was weak, it and the English could, up to Charles the Bold's fatal defeat in 1477, be used to weaken France. For example, Emperor Frederick III offered to make Charles the Bold a king, although only of his imperial fief of Brabant, not of a Lotharingia revived from the ninth-century Carolingian partition as Charles had requested. Still, the hope of a union of three kingdoms— Frisia, Flanders, and Burgundy—under a single monarch remained.[125] The problems were severe: particularistic nobles and cities, lack of secure communications, above all the overwhelming power and attraction, if ever it should be freed of distractions, of the French monarchy. An earlier emperor, Sigismund, perceiving the danger, dryly warned the Brabant Estates when they were on the point of accepting the Burgundian dynasty: "You wish, then, to be French."[126]

Before Charles the Bold's rashness reduced the Burgundian possessions in France to a shadow, the dynasty created a myth embodied in peculiar institutions that persistently influenced Europe's future. The most striking institution, combining symbols of knightly valor from the Old Testament (Gideon) and classic antiquity (Jason) was the Order of the Golden Fleece. The order served as a socializing mechanism for the high nobility, including ministers of state. Its prestige among the European nobility also served to offset, in some measure, the immense, intangible attraction of France. Still, with its crusader style—Charles the Bold himself had planned to lead a new crusade—the order was already an archaicizing mechanism, "the last flower of the chivalrous cult of the ladies," as a German historian calls it. Preference for Latin instead of French, use of a solemn, magnificent Court etiquette, the *Joyeuses Entrées* of the sovereigns into Flemish towns—all reflected in one way or another the Burgundian dynasty's attraction to the past.[127] The style had melancholy, occasionally macabre aspects that reflected, according to Pierre Chaunu, the intense psychological effect of the Black Death. These moods made Burgundian themes attractive, later, to Spain as its population drained away to America.[128] Neither the archaicizing element nor the solemn foreboding constituted, one may suspect, very auspicious forms for reviving the Christian empire.

The myth Burgundy transmitted to Charles V was archaicizing; it was not entirely obsolete. The danger that confronted the Christian order from the Ottomans, who had just absorbed Byzantium, was undeniable. The Turkish forces had already penetrated the possessions he had inherited from his paternal grandfather, the Emperor Maximilian I, and their fleets were threatening the shores of eastern Iberia and southern Italy, which he had received through his maternal grandfather, Ferdinand of Aragon. If the myth of the last flower of crusading chivalry could turn back this threat—in a sense it did—chivalry, for once, would not be mobilized for a lost cause.

The Burgundian heritage enormously complicated Charles's mission in other respects. As will appear later, the cultural diversity of his subjects made harmonious direction of affairs very difficult. The sheer geopolitical problems were staggering. In fact, Charles confronted on a European scale the dispersion of resources and fragility of communications that had been the nemesis of the Burgundian dynasty within the narrow region from the Jura Mountains to the North Sea. Given the availability of Fernand Braudel's marvelously circumstantial exposition of these communications problems, it would be ridiculous to discuss them in detail. The special problem Charles coped with was his personal center of operations. His heart was in Burgundy, but he realized that both the principal military resources and one of the two most threatened frontiers lay in Iberia. Consequently, although he resided there for only part of his reign, he gradually adapted his outlook to the peninsula's.

Probably the most serious complication arose from Charles's own determination to reduce France. Today French historians such as Braudel are sufficiently generous to admit that the concentration of force in the French kingdom was so great that all the resources of Charles's widely dispersed possessions were required to offset it. France's ambiguous attitude toward the Ottoman menace makes his desires to restrict French power all the more comprehensible. At the beginning of Charles's reign, at least, it appears that he was not intransigent, for his Flemish advisers headed by Chièvres (Guillaume de Croy) were generally as pro-French in attitude as they (and Charles himself) were Francophone. But the myth of a reunited Burgundy plus the pressure from some of his advisers to humble France triumphed.[129] Gattinara, although a Piedmontese who had served in French-speaking "Imperial Burgundy," replaced Chièvres's policy by an aggressive ideology based on a universalist myth more inclusive than the Western empire had previously experienced. There was to be "One Flock and one Shepherd," Charles, in the terrestrial order. Although the emperor was to exert only a sacral, moral, and legal authority over "independent" states, he was to make no exception for France, which was to be incorporated forcibly, if necessary, in his world order.[130]

Charles's imperial mission was further complicated, before much of his reign had passed, by the necessity of dealing with the northern European "heresies." He and Gattinara did not try to avoid this task, which they conceived to be incumbent on a Christian emperor. At the same time, though devout, neither was exactly propapal. Charles was one of the few European monarchs who ever imprisoned a pope. Gattinara revived Dante's antipapal *De Monarchia* and modeled the Christian empire on Justinian's Byzantine revival, implying a secondary position for the Roman pontiff.[131] The concept of a new universal empire, like the Byzantine empire from Justinian's time through the Isaurian dynasty, led to emphasis on the Mediterranean, although three of its critical theaters of action were in northern Europe. Defense against the Turks and maintenance of communications across the Mediterranean and the Atlantic required a thalassocracy. Charles was somewhat less successful than Justinian in securing command of the sea, and his son Philip II suffered grave reverses.

The ability to attract elites is an acid test of an imperial myth. The new imperial myth etched individual characters deeply, but failed to dominate a broad enough surface. Gattinara, naturally, would have preferred to center the new world order on Italy, which in culture and riches exceeded Charles's other domains. Italy also had the inestimable advantage of proximity to Germany as well as to the Mediterranean. The division of the Casa de Austria's titles between Charles's son Philip and his brother, the Emperor Ferdinand, eliminated this option. The difficulty for a single ruler of controlling such a far-flung empire constituted an obvious ground for this division. Moreover, the Habsburgs, like some other great German families, still preserved enough of the *Geblütsrecht* tradition of dynastic collective inheritance to make departure from primogeniture acceptable.

Spain continued to exert an enormous influence in Central Europe, however. During the first phase of the Thirty Years' War (the 1620s), "Spanish" troops (including Walloons and Italians trained on the Spanish model and commanded by Spaniards) constituted a majority of the imperial army in Bohemia. The officers even referred to the Spanish monarch as "our king."[132]

Philip II was a Spaniard by upbringing and by temperament, introducing such titles as *Rex Hispaniorum* and *Roi des Espagnes Catholiques* into his documents. His minister, Antoine de Granvelle, was a Franc-Comtois who mistrusted Spanish judgment. He wrote that "the Spanish . . . want to meddle in everything; but many of them know neither the province [Netherlands] nor the attitude of its inhabitants, nor affairs in general. . . . One will get nowhere with the Spanish and Italian officials." On another occasion he commented that "the Castilians want everything. I fear that they will end by losing everything."[133] But the Castilians, with their ardent frontier mentality, considered themselves to be Philip's only loyal subjects; consequently, they thought they were entitled to all leading positions. Leaving aside the Netherlands, the principal damage appears to have been caused in Italy, where Sicilian and Neapolitan nobles skilled in governance desired to maintain autonomy within the personal union with Castile.

A basic difficulty was the failure of Philip II's Spain, once it was formally divorced from the Holy Roman empire, to present a legitimization for maintaining its far-flung de facto empire. The very term "empire" was not and could not be formally employed for Spain by servants of the Casa de Austria, which already ruled the only legitimate Catholic empire. Consequently, the sagacious Italians had to resort to the design of Thomas Campanella, more grandiose than Gattinara's had been, or to mundane defense of a "beneficent empire," the virtues of personal union, and administrative necessity.[134] If, as suggested at the start of this chapter, promises of peace and prosperity were insufficient to sustain the morale even of the venerable Roman empire's subjects once it had encountered severe reversals, one can easily understand how a new Spanish empire, facing intense stress, could not mobilize elite forces with such bland themes. The Mediterranean sphere of the Spanish empire, patiently assembled during the course of two centuries by Aragon, was almost inevitably dominated, then alienated, by the dynamic but abrasive Castilian frontier myth.

The Holy Roman imperial title remained in the Austrian branch of the Habsburg dynasty for nearly three centuries, until the formal renunciation in 1804. This lengthy possession of the title was the result of converging circumstances that elevated that branch to the role of *Antemurale* defenders of Christendom at the same time as the Spanish branch was adopting the Castilian version of the frontier myth. Throughout the fifteenth century, Habsburg dynasts had tried to unite the crowns of Bohemia and Hungary with their own relatively small possessions on the eastern frontier of a Christendom threatened by Ottoman advance.[135] Clever diplomacy, backed by the obvious benefits that the immense Spanish and Burgundian resources of the dynasty might provide for resisting the Turk, finally (1526–27) brought the Bohemian, Hungarian, and Croatian Estates (the last nominally subject to the kingdom of Hungary) to accept Ferdinand as their king.[136] It is important to note that this event occurred decades before Ferdinand succeeded Charles V as Holy Roman emperor. In effect, therefore, a new autonomous Habsburg realm of great extent and symbolic importance arose alongside the Burgundian imperial myth.

Ferdinand himself had been brought up as a Spaniard and had adopted Spanish customs such as primogeniture, which was useful as a device for consolidating his East Central European realm.[137] From the start, the principal concern of the Austrian Habsburgs was to unite their diverse and geographically sprawling possessions into a strong centralized monarchy. The need of such strength to resist the Ottomans was the Habsburgs' principal legitimization. Throughout the sixteenth century, however, emphasis on centralization shifted toward reducing the privileges of the provincial nobilities inclined to Lutheranism. The strong Habsburg Catholic allegiance was reinforced by such Spanish Jesuit counselors as Juan Mariano as well as by Spanish troops.[138] Furthering aristocratic homogenization was also a motive behind the prohibition of formal correspondence and contacts among these dominions. Throughout the preceding century, the Estates of Austrian Crownlands and occasionally Bohemia had acted as members of a confederation for concerting defense measures. Useful as these steps had been, by the mid-seventeenth century, Vienna authorities felt strong enough to insist on centralized decision making.[139]

Summary and Conclusions

Through the transfer of identification from smaller constituent units to the compound or imperial polity, myths and symbols have an intense impact. Because polities are formal organizations of a highly articulated and relatively stable type, indicators of such myths and symbols in architecture, rubrics, and insignia are especially important. Such indicators, moreover, are characterized by extraordinary persistence in time and diffusion in space.

In promoting the identity transfer that was essential for their own persistence, imperial polities of the medieval and early modern periods were, albeit unconsciously, following a model established at the dawn of civilization in Mesopotamia. Transcendental myths attributing universal sacral qualities to the empire by asserting that it was the terrestrial reflection of divine order had been potent instruments for transforming collections of minor polities, mostly city-states, into large, compound polities. Later imperial polities in the ancient Middle East and the Hellenistic period systematized this legitimizing *mythomoteur* on a quasi-secular basis. The Roman empire constituted the culmination of this dilution of a sacral myth by appeals to the supreme value of order and prosperity.

No empire created on the ruins of the ancient Roman empire or in adjacent regions could avoid coping with the residual aura of the Roman myth. Yet acceptance of it by either of the great universal religions (Christianity and Islam) required significant adaptations. Such adaptation was essential even in Byzantium, the direct heir of Roman imperialism, for the Byzantine polity had been fundamentally altered by Christian values. The solution was to reject divinity of the emperor, yet ascribe to him alone the role of vicar of Christ ruling a universal terrestrial polity paralleling the heavenly kingdom.

The Islamic imperial myth developed very differently. Islam as a religion was not concerned with the existence of polities as such. Rather, the universal religious mission of Islam was conceived in a manner that required more direct political and military action than did Christianity as a religion. Consequently, the first requisite of an acceptable Islamic polity was its implementation of this mission, including expansion of the domain of Islam. Within the broad limits of this requirement, various claims to legitimacy were asserted—genealogical, manifestation of the Grace of God, protection of the Holy Cities, and the like. Fundamentally, such claims to legitimacy by a particular ruler or regime did not differ very much from rulers' claims to dominance of a given polity in Christendom. The principal difference has been that all polities as such in the *Dar ul-Islam* are regarded as contingent. All Moslems, in theory, are citizens of any Islamic polity in which they chance to reside. A given Islamic ruler has just as much or as little right to extend his power to other Islamic polities as he has to acquire power in the polity where he began his rule.

In contrast, Christian practice has established a presumption, varying in strength, of the legitimacy of any stable, autonomous polity. For Byzantium this presumption became increasingly the rule in practice although the primacy of the emperor-vicar was never formally renounced. For the Russian Orthodox polity, despite sweeping claims derived from steppe rulers as well as from the Byzantine and the Slavic traditions, acceptance of a limited imperial status in a community of polities always constituted a major modification of the imperial myth of universality.

From its origins in the formal break with Byzantine hegemony at the end of the eighth century, the West European imperial myth made still broader concessions to the coexistence of polities. In effect, the Carolingian empire and its successor, the Holy Roman empire, claimed no more of the imperial heritage than precedence over other sovereign rulers. The position of the pope instead of the emperor as vicar of Christ placed the Western empire in tutelage. The popes persistently and with a measure of success asserted the right to confirm the emperor, to instruct him in his duties, and in the extreme case to depose him. These limitations, and many others of a more material nature, tended to make the imperial myth cyclical in strength in West Europe. Two high points were the Carolingian empire of the eighth and ninth centuries and the sixteenth-century Burgundian revival. For two centuries thereafter, nevertheless, the imperial myth constituted an important element of Austrian Habsburg claims. Conversely, once separated from the Holy Roman crown, the extensive de facto empire of Spain lacked the legitimacy that other professedly Christian imperial polities have usually enjoyed.

A major factor in the decline of imperial claims and the concomitant emergence of a West European state system was the balancing policy of the papacy. The intense sacral legitimacy, which popes conferred on the early Carolingians as protectors of Christ's vicar, was not allowed to pass undivided to their imperial successors. Instead, the popes turned to the more distant yet powerful branch of the western Franks, that is, to what became the kingdom of France, endowing its rulers with the aura of protectors of the vicariate, often in opposition to the Holy Roman emperors. The acumen and prestige of the French hierarchy, often working independently of the papal Curia, reinforced the exceptional role of the French kings. A complex set of historical circumstances, notably including the concept of parity between legitimate heirs of the Franks in west and east, facilitated this division of authority.

During the Middle Ages, the French kingdom successfully asserted formal independence from any secular authority, notably the emperor's, and factual independence from the papacy. This success led major secular rulers in West and East Central Europe to model their own claims for independence on those of France. The superlative prestige of French culture and papal encouragement of independent polities generally favored such mimesis. At the same time, other secular rulers bolstered their legitimacy with other myth components, notably the *Antemurale mythomoteur* discussed in chapter 3. But recurring Holy Roman imperial structures also used this myth of defense against Islam, in cases like that of the Habsburgs' with great temporary success.

How effective the competing mythic structures were in promoting stable polities depended on the capacity of the myths to supersede the particularist myths of diverse elements in the compound polities. Apart from the coherence of the *mythomoteurs* themselves, such capacity depended in large measure on three sets of factors: the relationships between gentry and burghers outlined in chapter 4; the assistance or resistance presented by penetrative ecclesiastical organizations treated in chapter 7; and the dynamics of centralization discussed in the pages immediately following.

CHAPTER SIX

Imperial Polities:
The Centralization Imperative

Capital Cities as Symbols and Administrative Centers

The seventeenth-century trend toward centralization was part of a general European movement toward Absolutism. As such, it represented a subtle but fundamental departure from the concept of universal empire as a supranational hierarchy of authorities. This concept had characterized Western Christendom since the ninth century. The Habsburg measures noted at the end of the last chapter, like Absolutism itself, were a prelude to the centralized sovereignty of the nation-state. Although this imperative for centralization was new, at least in its intensity, in West Europe, it had a long history in the bureaucratic empires of the Mediterranean world as well as in polities farther afield. Consequently, before proceeding to a more detailed discussion of the factors pushing the Habsburg empire to become a nationalizing force despite the dynasty's sincere desire to preserve supranationalism, it is essential to review earlier experience.

The long discussion of the evolution of imperial myths began the exploration of the complex relationship between the universal missions that legitimized polities and the myth transformation that enabled them to become stable entities limited to specific territories. The dynamics of this process involved, especially, transmission of the changing identity myth to governing elites. The process of systematic socialization for bureaucratic careers, reinforced by experiences within the administration itself, will be the primary concern of this chapter. First, however, the role of the capital city, which constitutes a connecting link between imperial myth and imperial administration, requires brief review.[1]

The early emergence of the city as a center of identity made it attractive as a focus of the myth of a larger polity. If the sacral connotations of the city-state could be transferred to a single principal city among several cities in a polity, the task of reorienting loyalties would be half solved. Moreover, if the tradition of organizing urban space to provide a ceremonial setting for civil loyalties had already been developed, the arrangement of grander architectonic qualities for a capital became a natural further step. No matter how slight a group's attachment to urbanism, the choice of a permanent location for sacral objects necessarily required accepting some of the symbolic connotations of the city. It has been argued, for example (see chapter 3), that David's use of Jerusalem, despite his effort to avoid the styles of neighboring Semitic city-states (he always used the title "King of Israel," a people, rather than "King of Jerusalem"), involved a fundamental change in the identity of the Jews. Instead of being a seminomadic people with their most precious possession, the Ark of the Covenant, accompanying them on their travels, the Jews acquired a sacral locus that, as discussed in the next chapter, became the core of their identity.[2] Similarly, even *grands nomades* like the Mongols inevitably felt a pull toward a central place like Karakorum where the relics of their great leader were kept. In China Kublai Khan (like the Umayyads at Damascus) kept a huge hunting estate on the edge of the steppe, but he was drawn to the attractions of a fixed capital, as were his cousins, the Il Khans, after a couple of generations of tent camp on the Azerbaijani steppe.[3]

As the chief of a confederation of city-states, ancient Rome became the symbol as well as the seat of a sedentary empire. It is tempting to project a straight-line development from an early Roman empire revolving about that great capital to a late Roman empire centering on Constantinople. In practical, as contrasted to symbolic terms, however, the development was not straightforward. By the third century, the emperors were convinced that proper defense required their own regular movement among a series of capitals closer to the far-flung frontiers. The change in locus of imperial authority was made easier by two factors. First, the republican traditions of Rome had precluded complete physical domination of the city by the rulers, despite the increasing importance of the cult of their persons. The Capitol for the Senate and the Forum for the people both constituted alternative symbols of authority, whereas the imperial "palaces" (on the Palatine Hill) had developed out of Augustus's private residence. Only after centuries of autocracy did the emperors venture to imitate the Oriental "royal house." Second, the central administrative machinery was skeletal. Of the top ten thousand functionaries and aristocrats mentioned in chapter 5, only a few resided in Rome. The majority were deployed in the provinces for military or gubernatorial tasks or were involved in the basic lower-level administration entrusted to component *poleis*.[4] Until the second century, on the eve of the rulers' adoption of peripatetic capitals, their subjects did not expect the emperor to be very active. In modern terms, Roman expectations did not require a considerable degree of administrative penetration. Consequently, the small administrative apparatus could, without overwhelming inconvenience, accompany the emperor from Trier to Milan, to Sirmium, to Split, to Antioch, or to towns like Nikomedia near the Bosphorus that increasingly attracted early fourth-century rulers. Nevertheless, there was a cost; as a close student of the subject expresses it, "the Court [through its peripatetic, garrison characteristics] clearly reveals that the monarchy was imperfect by nature, that it had not yet acquired sovereignty."[5]

Medieval European polities were exposed to the same problem of converging dangers and to the additional problem, posed by a primitive economy, of provisioning a ruler, his Court, and his military escort. As a result, nearly all European princes remained peripatetic until the thirteenth century. After that there does not appear to have been any correlation between level of economic development and establishment of a fixed capital. Although it later shifted to Cracow and after that to Warsaw, the economically underdeveloped Polish kingdom had a seat in Gniezno by the thirteenth century, whereas the French monarchy was not permanently directed from Paris until late in that century. Possibly the sheer burden of attempting to control a country as large and well-developed as France by technically primitive methods had something to do with this lack of correlation. The ability of the French rulers to perambulate within a convenient circle of domains in the rich central districts of the Ile de France and Touraine also may have postponed a fixed capital.[6] By the time the kings did settle in Paris, the city was so widely recognized as a symbol and a cultural center that it rapidly became the focus of protonational identity. By the early thirteenth century, the famous theological and legal schools of Paris had given France the reputation as the *studium* of Christendom, to use Alexander von Roes's term.[7] The "Song of Roland" made Paris Charlemagne's capital instead of his real center at Aachen. The proximity of the royal burial ground at St. Denis provided a measure of sacral aura. After the capital was established in Paris, the Parlement (high law court) became the principal secular legitimizing institution by codifying the *coutumes* as an alternative to Roman law derived from Italy and by litigating frontier jurisdiction cases. Even a century later, the Paris elite hesitated between the king of France and his Burgundian-English opponents, but by the end of the fifteenth century, the Paris bourgeoisie provided the strongest support for royal centralism. The bourgeoisie maintained this position, combined with Gallican-flavored Catholicism, throughout the upheavals of the sixteenth and seventeenth centuries.[8]

The French contrast to capital city developments in all of the putative Western imperial polities is striking. It is easy to understand why the Holy Roman empire of the Middle Ages did not develop a fixed capital. In the ninth century, centrifugal frontier demands and the lack of an agricultural area rich enough to support the apparatus of the Court required its annual migration from the Regensburg region to the Mainz-Frankfurt-Worms triangle, then on to Trier. Without their own residences, the emperors had to use bishops' palaces in these cities, in addition to Bamberg, Wurzberg, and Speyer, and to draw on imperial estates for provisioning.[9] It is harder to understand why even powerful emperors did not attempt to establish a fixed capital. Aachen was elevated as a symbol of the Carolingian heritage by the Hohenstaufens, but Frederick II and his Court led an unsettled life, moving from one city to another in the Italian peninsula.[10] His obvious preference was Palermo, but it was much too peripherally located to become the regular capital. One reason for the apparent indecision of the emperors was that a permanent capital in either Germany or Italy would have identified the Holy Roman Empire too closely with a single element of its power base, whereas a country as large as France was already cohesive enough to tolerate a single center. In other words, a capital could be a strong force for integration, but it required a threshold level of integration before it could become established.

During the later Middle Ages, powerful particularistic forces—which had arisen in part because there was no strong directing center—enhanced the barriers to concentration of Holy Roman imperial authority in a single spot. Latter-day German governments, in fact, still have to reckon with this heritage. The sixteenth-century imperial high court, the Reichskammergericht, for example, was located in Speyer, not far from the imperial chancery directed by the archbishop of Mainz, but close enough to the Calvinist Palatinate to cause Protestants to press for keeping the court where it was, away from the centers of Habsburg authority.[11] As Ludwig Schmitt points out, the absence of a capital had incalculable effects on central authority, depriving it of a large, stable professional staff or regular archives and of a systematic administrative tradition.[12] Only one point in the imperial cycle was fixed: the emperor's burial place in Speyer.

It is more puzzling that the Burgundian dukes were unable to develop a capital. No concatenation of disparate territories ever needed a directing and symbolic center more than theirs did. Dijon, the dynastic burial ground, was too distant to exercise control over the richer Flanders area. Resenting the privileges of the university in the imperial city of Besançon, not far from Dijon, the dukes proceeded to create still another center of attraction at Dôle in Franche-Comté by establishing another university there to train their officials. In the Low Countries the dukes preferred the small city of Malines, but Charles the Bold, in particular, moved about perpetually. To maintain some sense of continuity, he resorted to the pathetic surrogate for architectonic symbolism of taking along tapestries depicting the legendary feats of the heroes of the Golden Fleece.[13]

Charles V inherited the centrifugal associations of his Burgundian ancestors. His Spanish and Italian possessions not only required additional capitals, but had their own peripatetic traditions. Curiously enough, a millennium earlier the Visigoths had grasped the importance of establishing a central Iberian capital at Toledo. During the eleventh century, Castilian monarchs devoted their energies to regaining this symbol of Hispanic continuity, but within two centuries they had removed their principal residence to Seville. Charles not only inherited these two capitals, he built a ponderous palace in Granada, where he wanted to be buried if Dijon proved impracticable. Nevertheless, most of the sixteen years he spent in Spain were consumed in peripatetic northern capitals such as Valladolid, Zaragossa, and Barcelona. Philip established the Court at Madrid, not far from the geographic center of the peninsula, in 1561. Characteristically for a Habsburg, he was concerned to locate this headquarters near his chosen burial place, the Escorial, even though Madrid was a poor little town that had to be built up almost from scratch.[14] Luis Cervera Vera outlines the consequences:

> In the first period of the Austrian dynasty, the perambulating
> Court resembled an encampment. Power required vigilance. Its price
> was personal supervision of the nation. But, with the passage of the
> years, the archives, the correspondence, and the functionaries became
> too numerous for such moves from one place to another. The necessity
> of a capital for the central power and the bureaucratic apparatus arose.
> As a result, national life was governed in a unified manner, and the royal
> power was centralized in a way that led to unification of the customs,
> sentiments, and needs of the Spaniards, as reflected in the urbanism
> of the period.[15]

By the time all of this was accomplished, however, other factors had eliminated Spain as a serious contestant for empire.

The image of the Habsburg dynasty has become so identified with nostalgia for *Belle Epoque* Vienna that it is difficult to recall that the Austrian Habsburgs settled on a permanent capital two generations later than their Spanish cousins. Vienna had been associated with the dynasty since 1282, but the rulers followed the usual custom of moving from place to place with their Court. Habsburg emperors resided in Prague, which in the fifteenth century was the great imperial city.[16] Maximilian I preferred various central German cities. After acquiring the Hungarian crown, Ferdinand I is said to have determined to keep his capital in Austria; but Rudolph II moved the Court and the principal administrative offices to Prague. The imperial residence moved back to Vienna in 1612, but the staffs were not returned until 1616. Even in subsequent years emperors yielded to requests from Prague for shorter periods of residence there.

The 1630s, or in some respects even the 1680s following the last Ottoman siege, represented the first concentrated imperial effort to embellish Vienna.[17] By the end of the first decade of the eighteenth century, the city had become renowned as an Absolutist Court center ahead of Paris.[18] Then Louis XIV's creation of Versailles made his successors' Court establishment the model of all Europe. Norbert Elias has written the best analysis of the peculiar relationship of the Absolutist garden-palace capital to traditional urbanism. The Court was the primary focus of rule and activity; the country as a whole was secondary. Court nobles lived in the city, which had some effect on their lives, but because they had country seats in addition, they were less attached to it than citizens with urban occupations. "This peculiar situation, a firm attachment to their [aristocratic] society that was their real homeland, along with a relatively transient local attachment, was not the least of the factors that determined their characters and their house styles alike." As a result, Court aristocrats, in contrast to real bourgeois, became pioneers in modern social alienation —hence their nostalgia for the countryside.[19]

This peculiar outcome of the adaptation of the urban *patria* to Absolutist centralization had certain analogies in the Moslem world. As noted earlier, dismay at local turbulence induced the Abbasid caliphs to remove their capital temporarily from Baghdad to Samarra. Probably lingering respect for the old Persian belief that Iraq (Mesopotamia) is the center of the world made the role of any particular capital in that area seem relatively unimportant. The more usual reason for building a new capital was magnificence—the desire to symbolize a new dynasty's power in visual form. The Moslem symbols were not, as a rule, architectonic harmony in urban layout, although some dynasties did attempt such forms for brief periods. Usually the solidity of the walls and the size of the palace quarter itself provided the symbols of dynastic accomplishment. Moslem dynasties rarely lasted more than a few generations, and capitals proliferated, but Khaldun's assertion that old capitals generally fall into ruin is somewhat overdrawn.[20] Often construction of a new palace quarter adjacent to an existing city met the need for dynastic magnificence, because the walls of the quarter served both to isolate the ruler from the potentially rebellious residents and to symbolize his strength. Fez, for example, had appended to it the entire city "Fez-the-new" as well as various *kasbahs* to house tribal garrisons for successive dynasties.

Cairo illustrates the same process on a larger scale. The Arab conquerors who wished to develop an inland capital at the first practicable crossing of the Nile south of the Delta waterways settled near the Roman city of Babylon. Their garrison town, Fustat, was supplemented in the ninth century by a new capital around the mosque bearing the name of a de facto ruler, Ibn Tulun. The old Cairo that exists today is a Fatimid foundation. A new Sunni dynasty started a huge citadel complex farther east; the Mamelukes elaborated it. Whereas Fez has remained one of several alternative Moroccan capitals, each constructed by a new dynasty, Cairo, as an integrated urban agglomeration for thirteen hundred years, demonstrates that successive Islamic regimes are able to maintain a fixed capital location. Indeed, both in size relative to the total Egyptian population and in concentration of wealth and military force, Cairo is an outstanding example of the single dominating city such as Europe did not know until the eighteenth-century expansion of London and Paris. Certainly the continuous, imposing position of Cairo has constituted the principal remaining symbol of a separate Egyptian identity under Islam.

The other outstanding example of a single dominant Islamic capital is Constantinople, which had been a great city for eleven hundred years before the Ottomans acquired it. Nevertheless, the city they conquered had already been reduced, demographically, to the dimensions of a provincial town. Within a generation the sultans restored Constantinople to half a million population, approximately its Byzantine maximum, by ruthless deportation (largely as slaves) of the remaining Greek inhabitants, quickly followed by repopulation by Greeks, Armenians, and Sephardic Jews as well as Moslems. Such wholesale, compulsory transfers of urban populations are characteristic of Islamic polities, which borrowed the practice from the Sassanids. But it is more difficult to assess the significance of Constantinople as an influence on Ottoman or Turkish identity. The Seraglio (palace complex) and its gate (the Sublime Porte) soon became bywords for Ottoman power. In fact, all intrigues and factional clashes did revolve around that quarter of Constantinople.[21]

The Ottomans' lukewarm attitude toward Constantinople nevertheless presents a striking contrast to the intense identification Byzantines had with the city. After Constantinople had been captured by the Fourth Crusade, the emperor in exile nostalgically promised to regain "our first and ancient seat, the Paradise, the city of the All-Powerful situated on the Hellespont, the city of our God, the jewel of the earth, she who is desired by all the peoples of the earth and is renowned in the entire world."[22] When one of his successors, Michael VIII, finally recovered the capital, he was hailed as a "New David," a "New Constantine," who had regained "New Zion."[23] Even after allowance for rhetorical hyperbole, these sentiments appear to clash with the Christian concept of the unsanctified, transitory terrestrial city. Constantine himself had been careful to embellish the real Jerusalem as much as his new capital, which some contemporaries regarded as his caprice. Succeeding emperors, however, concentrated the relics of early Christianity (such as the True Cross) there, constructing magnificent churches to contain them. The Hagia Sophia, to many still the supreme achievement of Christian architecture, acquired a mystic aura soon after it was built. The importance of the imperial palace was greatly increased compared to its modest situation in old Rome. The Forum and the Hippodrome constituted symbolic public spaces that preserved a reduced measure of popular participation.

Above all, its great walls symbolized the unique position of Constantinople as an impregnable city at the junction of the most important land and sea routes of the Mediterranean world. An endless debate continues as to whether this invulnerability prolonged the life of the Roman empire for a millennium or led to its piecemeal loss by focusing all attention on a single city.[24] In a purely strategic sense, the advantages of the location were so great that dispute appears futile; besides, a few emperors did carry on campaigns hundreds of miles away, sometimes very successfully, occasionally disastrously. The concentration of affect resources on the myth of the city is another matter, more difficult to assess. If the remarkably rapid transfer of the Roman myth of Constantinople had not occurred in the fourth century, it is questionable whether any imperial power could have survived. For the first century after its foundation, Constantinople was modestly termed the "New Rome." After 451 (the Council of Chalcedon) the new capital was frequently called the "Second Rome," implying an essential transfer of imperial aura from decaying old Rome.[25]

It is significant that this aspect of the myth of Constantinople began with a church council. The new patriarch of Constantinople rapidly emerged as the most prestigious of the four Eastern patriarchs. He ultimately assumed the qualification "ecumenical," although conceding (until the eleventh century) precedence to the patriarch of the West, the pope. A prophecy held that the Second Rome would endure until the end of the world; some even added that presence of a Christian at the Last Judgment depended on his or her adherence to the empire.

The idea of the city as the focus of an identity (which Ottomans could accept only in a restricted sense) spread throughout the East European sphere. With nearly three hundred years of existence as the center of an independent "empire," Trebizond, at the opposite end of the Black Sea, had enough time to demonstrate the influence of the Great City model. Trebizond's rulers, the Comnenes, had first established their kingdom as a base for regaining Constantinople for their dynasty. Within a short time they made the town, with its strong encompassing walls, its great church, Our Lady of the Golden Dome, and its concentration of civil and military officials, the only really important part of their dominion.[26] Similarly, the Bulgarian tsars tried to embellish their capitals to compete as "Third Romes" with Constantinople.

Although the myth of Moscow as the Third Rome has been greatly exaggerated, the massive Kremlin complex outdid Constantinople in concentrating secular and religious monuments.[27] A curious example of the influence of the Great City myth is provided by the efforts of Russian writers to find "seven hills" in the flat terrain of early modern Moscow to complete its resemblance to the two preceding Romes. Peter founded his new capital to set a distance between the dynasty and the complex of "antiquated" myths that had developed around Moscow. Orthodox prayers referred to St. Petersburg as the "Tsar's city," however, the term that had been used for Moscow, suggesting an inclination to move the "Third Rome" once again. The enduring tension between alternative capitals since that time has drawn the Russian polity in certain respects closer to the arbitrary associations with ruling powers that characterized the ancient Orient and Islam than to the single city tradition. From the sixteenth century on, Russian writers tended, moreover, to identify the Third Rome not exclusively with Moscow, the city, but with Russia as an entity: "The woman clothed with the sun [Apocalypse 12] . . . fled to the *Third Rome which is the New Great Russia.*"[28]

From Imperial Administration to Precocious Nationalism

Whatever the ultimate effects of the diffusion of Constantinople's example may have been, it is certain that the actual concentration within the city of an administrative machine unprecedented in its centralized organization, hierarchical order, regular socialization, and cultural quality exerted an immense influence on subsequent imperial structures. I suggest that a fundamental reason why Constantinople as a city and Byzantium as an imperial tradition distinguishable from Rome's heritage gained ground so quickly was precisely this shift from an exiguous, peripatetic central administration to a huge, firmly articulated bureaucracy. The rise of Constantinople is the more remarkable because the local traditions of its predecessor *polis*, Byzantium, were trivial. Moreover, the inhabitants of fourth-century Constantinople were recruited from the entire Roman empire. One might have expected the result, however favorable the city's location and however determined its imperial patrons, to resemble heterogeneous Oriental foundations. Instead, Constantinople quickly developed one of the most intense local patriotisms in history.

Constantinople did have a striking precedent as a heterogeneous megalopolis. Prior to the rise of Constantinople, Alexandria, not Rome, was the real leader of the Mediterranean world in culture as in commerce. Even today the entirely reconstructed city preserves some of old Alexandria's aura in references by the Greek poet C. V. Cavafy to "the City." Ancient "Alexandria by Egypt" had a population consisting of Greeks, Jews, and Egyptians, but in contrast to Constantinople's rapid welding of its diverse elements into an intensely self-conscious civic population, Alexandrines remained divided ethnically. After the Ptolemies, however, the city lacked the amalgamating influence of a great imperial bureaucracy.

Paradoxically, Egypt itself, the rich, almost completely unurbanized Nile Valley, was the seat of the earliest and most refined bureaucracy of the Roman empire. Augustus and his successors reserved Egypt for their personal control, for reasons a French scholar succinctly analyzes: "For his Egyptian subjects, the emperor was an absolute monarch who exercised sovereign disposal of all the resources of the country. This conception, which later would be extended to the entire empire, applied to Egypt alone. It was the heritage of the previous dynasties, but the emperor of Rome had no cause to modify it, for it served his interests too well."[29] The basic features of the Egyptian bureaucracy, rural except for the prefects and governors and their staffs in Alexandria, were the following: (1) strict hierarchical organization; (2) rigorous concentration on extracting the taxes in kind required to support the imperial capitals; (3) use of paid, trained scribes to supervise tasks such as the cadaster (land survey); (4) reliance for actual tax collection (during the Roman period) on local small proprietors bound hereditarily in "liturgies." Neither the governor, commanding the garrison and entrusted with certain minor administrative affairs, nor local notables were allowed to influence in any way this grain collection, which constituted a principal resource of the empire.[30]

The Egyptian bureaucracy had long been a model for the entire Hellenistic world. When the Emperor Diocletian decided to reform Roman administration at the end of the third century, after severe disruptions of the laxer system inherited from the early Roman empire, it was natural for him to turn to Egypt.[31] His principal innovation was to bind municipal officials throughout the Roman world in liturgical service and to ascribe all peasants, as in Egypt, to the soil of their native villages. Alexandria, still the greatest commercial metropolis, had already provided a model for expanded Roman municipal and police services.[32] Both types of innovation required recruitment from heterogeneous sources of a mass of professional administrators. In contrast to the old Roman senatorial aristocracy, the upper, ennobled levels of the new apparatus, although usually wealthy from landholdings, pursued regular bureaucratic careers. Such men had little attachment to the cult of Rome's local deities and lacked the senatorial spirit of independence from the empire. Constantine and his Christian successors implanted this new corps in Constantinople, creating a new senate that soon rivaled Rome's in prestige. It is still another irony of history that the new elite which Diocletian, the fierce persecutor of Christianity, had created played a major role in making possible the official institution of Christianity.[33]

From Diocletian's time until the end of the empire, eleven hundred years later, changes in administrative organization and practice were incremental; but over time the increments led to fundamental transformation. Although titles changed over time, offices were always strictly ordered by rank, and official rank usually determined social status. In the later empire, sons of officials became obliged to follow their fathers' professions, but other recruits were drawn from the merchants, the liberal professions, and younger sons of administrators. Apparently, an official career provided a major avenue of social mobility for these strata.[34] A modern Greek historian finds men of humble origins as late as the eleventh century starting careers by securing university instruction.[35]

The social stratification of the bureaucracy is important to my subject only insofar as examining it throws light on increasing ethnic identification. Here the crucial question is what kind of socialization accompanied hereditary recruitment? Through the reign of Justinian I legal education was standard, whether acquired in the Constantinople law school or in Berytus. The latter, significantly, was a Latin enclave in Syria, for the law was Roman in language and substance. Indeed, justice and military administration remained the strongholds of Latin usage. For the emperors, continued use of Latin was important for maintaining a prestigious link to the earlier Roman empire.[36] Besides, up to Tiberius (698–705) there was no native speaker of Greek among the emperors; the Comnenes (1081–1185) were the first thoroughly Greek rulers. Justinian was an Illyrian, from a backward but ardently Latin region. Latin was his personal linguistic preference as well as a symbol of his role as restorer of the Roman empire.[37] But Greek had been permitted for official use a century before him, and only his top officials were fluent in Latin.[38] Consequently, even Justinian found it necessary to publish a Greek version of his laws. By the seventh century, an influx of Greeks from Asia and the inundation of the Latin Balkans by Slavic invaders drastically shifted the balance of the empire's remaining population. Greek became the language of state soon afterward, although ceremonial formulas in Latin, gradually Hellenized in alphabet and grammatical construction, were retained.[39]

The loss of knowledge of Latin was apparently at least one factor leading to the elimination of legal requirements for administrative posts, hence to closing of the law schools. Top positions ceased to require specific training, whereas the remaining general educational requirements became predominantly literary. Some educational preparation for bureaucratic careers was obtained in the patriarchal school. Because, as discussed in the next chapter, the Byzantine church was the foremost institution for promoting Greek, this change affected elite socialization. Other aspiring officials received their educations in secular classics that inculcated a deep pride in the Hellenistic heritage of the students.[40] Some legal education apparently persisted until the tenth century, when a new law school was opened, lasting until about 1060; its dean was required to know Latin. This minor Latin revival coincided, however, with a much more general revival of Greek classical learning under the Macedonian dynasty. The revival heightened the prestige of Greek culture, whereas law, although still basically Roman in substance, had become so dogmatic centuries earlier that it was not stimulating intellectually.[41]

By the fateful year 1204, when the Byzantines were enraged by the "Latin" crusaders' capture of their capital, the ground was prepared for a massive reaction that would turn the elites toward a new national model. Apart from the intensely Greek clergy, which on religious grounds objected to the pagan term "Hellene," this reaction meant a spiritual return to the independent Greece that had preceded the Roman empire. The earliest Roman emperors had been strict in demanding Latin in official communications. Claudius, for example, deprived a Lycian petitioner of Roman citizenship for failing to understand a question in Latin.[42] Even at the height of the empire (ca. A.D. 150) Greek writers, although referring to it as *"imperium nostrum,"* tended to deemphasize the specific Latin qualities of the empire by concentrating on its universal mission.[43] In the course of the Byzantine period, literary images gradually dropped all Latin references. Xenophobic ethnic stereotypes, modeled on classic epithets, had appeared even before the Byzantine clash with the crusaders: "round-faced Slavs," "bold Armenians," "arrogant Franks."[44] At Nicaea, after the crusader conquest of Constantinople, the literati demanded that the emperor-in-exile entitle himself "king of the Hellenes." Two centuries later the last emperor was mourned as "Constantine the Hellene."[45]

Once the Ottomans had subjected Byzantium completely, "Rum" and similar derivatives from "Roman" became "slave names"; hence recourse to the proud alternative identification "Hellene" was almost mandatory. Several writers have suggested that, as early as the thirteenth century, a precocious Greek nationalism arose, leading directly to the kingdom of the Hellenes of the nineteenth century.[46] Certainly this line of interpretation has validity. Not all conquered societies, especially in the Middle Ages, developed nationalism, however. One wonders by what processes this occurred among the Byzantines. Moreover, the process by which an empire founded by a Latin city-state became transformed in the course of a millennium and a half into an intensely Hellenic, anti-Latin structure is fascinating in itself. For my purposes, it is most important as an example of the ability of powerful imperial institutions, especially clerical, civil, and military bureaucracies, to produce a momentum toward a specific ethnic identity. Certainly the perceived requirements of Byzantine administration had an enormous feedback effect on formal education and on the socialization processes generally. As the carriers of the imperial ideal, Roman aristocratic officials had been the last determined supporters of the empire in the West. In thirteenth-century Byzantium, the official class—by then a service nobility of Greek culture—was equally concerned to preserve an empire that upheld its raison d'être both in career security and in symbolic terms. If officials did not provide most of the propagandists for a return to Hellenism, as educated, urbane men they must have provided the most appreciative and influential audience.

The dynamic by which the imperial administration switched cultural sides was unintended. Each small step was incremental. It is not clear whether Constantine wanted to Latinize the East by putting a Latin capital there, but the immediate impetus from an influx of Latin-speaking officials was in that direction. Very quickly, however, the strong cultural influence of Hellenism was felt among the rootless Constantinopolitan elites. Friction with the haughty, half-pagan Roman aristocracy and dislike of "barbarian" generals allied to it were intense by 400. As discussed in Chapter 7, ecclesiastical friction developed more slowly but ultimately became more massive. "Historical accidents" like the loss of part of Illyria to barbarian invaders are often said to have played a role; but was it really an accident that Byzantine statesmen pushed the Goths westward, thus starting a chain of disruptions across the Middle Danube? Population losses from these events reduced the potential supply of Latin-speaking officials. No one advocated abandoning Latin, but exigencies of recruitment made the language hard to maintain. A highly centralized, hierarchical bureaucracy depended on uniform role expectations. Ease of communication and, above all, predictability of behavior within the administration required an intense, formalized socialization. A hereditary, aristocratic service nobility was likely to become imbued with concern for technique and style. If the law was not easily intelligible, literary classics transmitting an overwhelmingly Hellenist message were the only available alternative curriculum, except for the writings of the Greek Church Fathers. Gilbert Dagron believes that Latin did, in fact, constitute a realistic alternative at the start of Byzantine bureaucratization. The moment in the mid-fourth century when a choice could be made was fleeting.[47] The initial choice produced a momentum for use of Greek that became increasingly difficult to overcome. As the Hellenist curriculum became firmly established, it in turn created an imperial elite with a steadily intensifying ethnic identity.

Segmented Imperial Administrations

None of the great Eastern empires adhered to the Byzantine bureaucratic model either in its strict hierarchical unity or in the homogeneous recruitment and socialization of its members. Consequently, the impact of imperial administration upon ethnic consciousness in those empires was very different. As indicated earlier, the Russian empire was the only large, stable polity equipped with a myth conducive to claiming the complete Byzantine heritage. The development of an autocracy more extreme than Byzantium's did not, however, produce a comparably skilled and integrated bureaucracy. I have dealt with the peculiar evolution of the Russian imperial administration at length elsewhere; hence I shall summarize its differences in ethnic identity from Byzantium briefly.[48] Down to Peter I, Russian administration, although hierarchical, was poorly developed in the technical sense. General education, let alone legal and technical skills, was scarce among available administrative recruits, who were predominantly Russian. During the eighteenth century, this deficiency was in some measure overcome by training generations of Russian elites in Westernized institutions associated with the cosmopolitan capital, St. Petersburg. As I pointed out chapter 4, however, the underdeveloped economy required more urban recruits equipped by prior socialization for professional, administrative, and entrepreneurial activities than the Russian population could supply. Acquisition of the Baltic provinces provided a source of extraordinarily capable German recruits who supplemented German families already living in Russia proper or who immigrated from Germany. The Polish Partitions provided a somewhat less significant flow of Polish recruits. Later, despite harsh restrictions, capable Jewish entrepreneurs and professionals supplemented the empire's resources. For all of these non-Russian recruits, early socialization based on family backgrounds and informal training and often on special religious schools produced qualities that were still rare in the Russian culture.

As a result, the ethnic composition of the Russian imperial administration and paragovernmental services like the *zemstvo* welfare activities became heterogeneous ethnically some two to three centuries after the empire was founded. The contrast to Byzantium, where elite ethnic homogeneity had emerged by a comparable period (sixth to seventh centuries) is strong. In Russia the ethnic heterogeneity of the administration persisted for a generation after the establishment of Soviet rule, that is, into the mid-twentieth century. This heterogeneity considerably complicated the process of developing successive myths to legitimize the Russian imperial polities.

Moslem polities that might have derived their administrative models from Byzantium (as, to a minor degree, they derived their imperial myths) also developed heterogeneous administrative elites, but for different reasons than the Russians did. Islamic imperial administration is generally not only heterogeneous but intentionally segmented. Although they were in other ways attracted to Byzantine models, the Ummayads drew more heavily on Sassanid administrative experience. Thereafter, the Abbasid adaptation of Sassanid models became the predominant source of administrative lore even for regimes distant from Persia, like Ibn Tulun's in ninth-century Egypt. Moslem rulers of Egypt retained the pharaonic-Hellenic land cadaster to draw taxes from peasants tied to the soil (an exception at this stage of Islamic history), but the actual collection resembled the *haraj* system developed by Persian officials of the caliphate to enable them to tax Moslem-owned land in Iraq.[49] Bureaucratic experience had, in fact, been constantly interchanged between Persia and Egypt ever since the Achemenids ruled both. Roman and Sassanid administrators also copied freely from each other. Moreover, the pre-Moslem Persian administrative elite was probably as ethnically homogeneous as the Byzantine.

In itself, therefore, Moslem emulation of Sassanid organization did not sharply distinguish Islamic administration from the Byzantine tradition. What appears to have been much more significant—the scholarly evidence is sketchy—were the myths, styles, and terminology of the Sassanid system, which hypostatized roles that elsewhere were regarded as purely instrumental. The Sassanid Court hierarchy, although depicted in Zoroastrian terms, was derived from the Mesopotamian concept of a terrestrial order paralleling the empire of heaven encountered earlier in these pages. In the heavens, five planets of Ormuz's empire corresponded to five ministers around the throne of the terrestrial monarch. These ministers symbolized judges, the monarch's tongues; priests, his ears; warriors, his hands; internal officials, his eyes (spies); and finance officials, his nose (as of a bloodhound!).[50] Moslem admiration of such imagery extended to the Sassanid Court etiquette, its ceremonial titles, and even the concept of King Khrosoes as the "last good king." Emulation of the system apparently nurtured a Moslem tendency to conceptualize the work of government as segmented.

A second, more direct force for segmentation was the great difficulty that would-be despots in Islam encountered in employing free Moslem officials. The haughty factionalism of the Arabs, especially evident among princes related to the dynasty, made them unserviceable. Later, *Sharia* restrictions on arbitrary treatment of Moslem freemen, although frequently violated, discouraged rulers from relying upon them. The rulers' resort, which continued until modern times in Egypt, for example, was to use non-Moslems. These recruits were necessarily submissive and often came from families with pre-Islamic traditions of administrative service. Employment of such secretaries in major posts in Baghdad aroused considerable Moslem resentment, even when some of the officials (especially the Zoroastrians) converted to Islam. It is significant that the top post of grand *vizir* developed in these first centuries of Abbasid rule. The position was by no means entirely Persian in origin, nor was it necessarily held by men of Persian tradition; the greatest "dynasty" of Abbasid *vizirs*, the Barmakids, originated as Buddhist monks in Central Asia. Still, a caliph exclaimed: "The Persians ruled for a thousand years and did not need us (Arabs) even for a day; we have been ruling for one or two centuries and cannot do without them for an hour."[51]

At the start of the Abbasid caliphate, therefore, an ethnoreligious division emerged in Moslem administration. On one side were Arab military commanders and "men of the law" (*ulema*, religious leaders), part of the administrative apparatus because Sunni Islam does not acknowledge separation of law and faith. On the other side were Persianate officials, Nestorian, Zoroastrian, or converts for the most part, though some were Orthodox Christians from conquered Byzantine territory. The chancery styles were derived from the Persian rhetorical tradition, with little concern for the forms (although the content was usually respected) of Moslem law. Such a dual administration obviously could not transmit a unifying myth based on a single pattern of socialization. Very quickly—at least by the ninth century—the turbulent Arab levies and their commanders were replaced by Turkic mercenaries, sometimes recruited from slaves. As a result, a threefold division arose. Because military officers usually were the governors of provinces, clever caliphs could use them as counterweights to the secretaries and *vizirs* of the central administration, whereas weak rulers had virtually to concede independence to such satraps. A similar process occurred in the Maghreb, although there after the eleventh century it was the Andalusian Moslem officials who were sharply divided from Almoravid, Almohad, and other military elites, also mostly Moslem speakers of Arabic, but with otherwise very different backgrounds and socialization.

When a Turkic regime, the Seljuks, actually assumed supreme power in the Fertile Crescent, it introduced reforms that resulted in a new dual cleavage. The slow conversion of non-Moslem-educated elements was consolidated by the introduction of the *medressa* or training school, which subsequently spread to all Islamic polities. Although this institution was developed primarily for training administrators, it employed *ulema* instructors who taught a curriculum based on Islamic law supplemented by enough literary and "practical" subjects to suit future officials. The grand *vizir*, Nizam al-Mulk, who invented (or at least transformed) the *medressa*, was a Persian bureaucrat by training; consequently, the new institution represented a further advance for Persian styles. Because future "men of the law" themselves attended the *medressa*, the cleavage between administration of justice (apart from the ruler's arbitrary dispensation outside the scope of the *Sharia*) and administration by "men of the pen" was bridged. On the other hand, the gap between both these groups and the Turkic military widened. For example, in a relatively unstable polity like the "White Sheep" regime that governed in the fifteenth century, no urban, Persian-speaking notable ever held a military post; but no Turkic military chief ever became a "man of the law."[52] The division of roles, however, permitted stable relations when a polity itself achieved stability.

The Mameluke regime, based on a single capital and governing a rich territory with relatively stable frontiers, constituted a culmination of Islamic administrative practice that influenced subsequent polities, notably the Ottoman empire. As indicated earlier, the Mamelukes themselves, monopolizing the role of "men of the sword" and sometimes assuming the role of grand *vizir* as well as that of sultan, were always sharply differentiated from the mass of the population. Not only was their slave recruitment background a strong distinguishing feature; their Turkic myth was rigorously respected both by their own members and by the subject population. Some *vizir* roles, and, of course, the entire regular legal administration, were filled by "men of the law," *cadis*, headed by grand *cadis* in Cairo for each of the four Islamic law schools. Routine administration and the crucial financial affairs were entrusted mainly to Copt or Jewish officials, although Maronite Syrians were later introduced under Ottoman suzerainty. Even this threefold division did not exhaust the segmentation of practical administration. The spice merchants (*Karimi*), Moslem Arabs, for a period during the fourteenth and early fifteenth centuries exerted strong indirect influences on financial administration and diplomacy.[53]

The Ottomans complicated this segmented administrative tradition still more. Their apparatus was the most imposing developed by a Moslem regime, but its socialization and recruitment remained compartmentalized formally and informally. The effort to abstract a reliable military force from the Turkic *ghazis* and clan levies discussed in chapter 3 eventually led to the *devshirme*, a "boy tax" levied on Christian families (mainly Balkan Slavs).[54] Every three or four years some twelve thousand boys were compulsorily removed from their families. Although estimates vary somewhat, a reasonably strong scholarly consensus puts the annual influx of recruits at two to four thousand, matched by about as many very young men sold into the sultan's service by the Tatars, Caucasian mountaineers, and Barbary pirates. Whereas adult male captives could be used only as soldiers, boys taken under the *devshirme* system were young enough for complete resocialization and training in a variety of skills.

The number in training was large—one estimate puts it at fifty thousand at any one time—because "wastage" was heavy. The process lasted about fourteen years, involving a pyramid of schools that facilitated screening out the most capable and adaptable for promotion. Most young men ended up in the Janissaries, the regular infantry force that constituted the backbone of the Ottoman armies. Altogether about one hundred thousand "slaves of the sultan" were in service at any one time. By the end of the eighteenth century, they and their descendants may have numbered over a million, a substantial fraction of the Ottoman Moslem population in the core areas of central and western Anatolia and the southern Balkan peninsula.[55]

Janissary military commanders constituted a significant elite. The much smaller number of boys who eventually attained administrative rank as "men of the pen" were even more important for maintaining the Ottoman myth. In the seventeenth century, the critical treasury chambers were nearly all manned by slaves. Not only was the treasury the key to supervising resource mobilization; its three *defterdars* often later obtained gubernatorial posts, then, if successful, returned to the Seraglio as grand *Vizir*. This top position was almost incredibly perilous. Some two hundred men passed through it between 1376 and 1829, usually facing execution for some failure, real or concocted, after a year or two. A dervish sheikh, with the privileged insolence his status allowed, is said to have replied to a *vizir*'s question as to who was the most foolish of men: "You, O mighty vizir. For you have done everything in your power to gain your office, although you rode past the bleeding head of your predecessor, which lay in the same spot as that of his predecessor."[56] Nevertheless, the Ottoman career official had a high conception of his functions, as a *defterdar*'s memoir of 1703 suggests. The grand *vizir*, he wrote, should be given unrestrained power during his term of office but should treat the *ulema* and the ministers of the Divan respectfully, especially the *defterdar* of the imperial treasury who engages in the most important labors of the "art of the pen."[57]

Unfortunately for the future of the empire, the real devotion to duty that shows through such counsels was not translated into efficiency. By about this time (1700), the *devshirme* system ceased to be significant.[58] Its graduates, customarily allowed to establish families but at first forbidden to introduce their sons into the service, were gradually allowed this privilege. Other free Moslems—for the offspring of the sultan's powerful "slaves" were all free—also wheedled their way into the Seraglio schools, thus minimizing the difference between these institutions and the ordinary *medressas* in which "men of the law" trained. Indeed, the *ulema* (headed by the *hoja*, who had instructed the sultan) always conducted Seraglio teaching, apart from military subjects. On the surface, the curriculum was impressive. In addition to Islamic law and the great languages (Arabic, Persian, and the peculiar Ottoman form of Turkic), the young men learned something about diplomacy, war, and even the nomadic traditions of the Ottoman dynasty.[59] Up to the middle of the seventeenth century, forty-eight out of sixty grand *vizirs* and corresponding proportions of other high officials had been trained in the Seraglio schools.[60] Apparently, the socialization process, both before and after the influx of free Moslems, was effective in producing loyalty to caste and to the concept of Ottoman rule, although such loyalty did not always preclude rebellions to secure privileges.

For the "slaves" the Seraglio was too secluded to produce men with a wide knowledge of the world. A sympathetic observer admits that officials in charge of foreign affairs sometimes did not know even the location of important foreign countries. Free Moslems were so attached to their Islamic life styles that they could not be induced to spend enough time in diplomatic posts in Christian countries to learn the languages.[61] The expenses of the luxurious life style fostered by the Court provided a constant temptation for official corruption, especially for middle-aged pashas in gubernatorial posts who hoped to return to Constantinople. Because the average tenure of the 26 governors-general and the 163 provincial governors was only one or two years, and their property could be confiscated following their deaths, insecurity increased the temptation to seek quick profit by corruption.[62]

In the two critical areas of diplomacy and resources mobilization, therefore, the Ottoman system produced officials who were increasingly unprepared to meet the demands of an empire exposed to competition with the modernizing polities of Europe. As a result, the imperial system was in difficulty from the sixteenth century on and proved to be utterly inadequate during the eighteenth century. The immediate expedient was recourse to non-Moslem subjects of the sultan. High Ottoman personages had never hesitated to resort to non-Moslem experts when they considered the need sufficiently pressing. Jewish and Christian physicians were always close to the sultan, not only because he feared for his own health, but because his conspicuous consumption required diligent supervision of the harem. A sixteenth-century anecdote illustrates this prestige concern: "They are all cut off at the level of the belly ever since Suleiman II, while in the country one day, saw a gelding trying to mount a mare. He deduced from that that the Eunuchs who guarded his wives might be able to amuse their passions; he took the remedy of having everything cut from them, and his successors have observed the same rule."[63]

For a half century after the conquest of Constantinople, the sultans even kept on Greek administrators in major offices. A little later, the rulers turned to a succession of informal administrations operated by non-Moslems for performance of the tasks that were beyond the capacities of Seraglio-trained officials.[64] This expedient resembled the introduction of non-Moslem officials into the regular administrations in earlier Islamic polities, but because accompanied by ruthless punishments and humiliating restrictions, it was more debilitating. In diplomacy, reliance on Greek grand dragomans, nominally interpreters, really exercising the powers of foreign ministers, made some sense in view of the Phanariot elite's identification with opposition to Western Christian powers. Probably the Phanariots always retained a vague hope of assuming power within the framework of a nominally Ottoman empire, then transforming it into a new Hellenic Byzantine imperium—the "Great Idea." Intensive socialization in the religious schools, including a modified version of the patriarchal school that had intermittently dominated Byzantine administrative training, inculcated a sense of solidarity among the Phanariots. But such education, notably superior to the Ottoman standard, made the Greek *millet* (religious minority) increasingly impermeable to Ottoman legitimizing myths. The emergence of a Russian Orthodox imperial polity on the Black Sea in the late eighteenth century seemed to the more impatient members of the Phanariot elite to offer an immediate opportunity for achieving the goal of a revived Hellenic empire. The invasion from Russian territory carried out by the Phanariot Alexander Ypsilanti led to an Ottoman massacre of the leading Greeks in Constantinople. A small Greek kingdom was established somewhat later with Western assistance. The presence of such a nucleus of disaffection made the sultans determine not to let the Phanariots regain control of Ottoman diplomacy. Nevertheless, attempts to attract Moslem students to new Western-model schools such as the Galataseray

Lycée proved a failure throughout the nineteenth century. Consequently, the Ottoman empire had no source of fully qualified recruits for urgent diplomatic tasks.

Just as the Greeks at the end of the seventeenth century had replaced Sephardic Jews in providing surety bonds and administrative skills for the *pashas* nominally charged with tax collection, Armenian bankers came to the fore in the early nineteenth century.[65] By the 1870s, however, Ottoman mistrust (fueled by Armenian nationalists' attraction to Russia) also undermined these bankers' position.

The review of Moslem experience with centralized imperial administrations suggests that no design produced by an Islamic polity provided an organization sufficiently unified to elaborate and diffuse a single myth of ethnic identity, much less to introduce one. Many Kemalist nationalists in Turkey ultimately resorted to a version of the Turkic genealogical myth that had been a minor component even of the first stages of Ottoman rule. No doubt the memory of past Ottoman grandeur has been a significant latent component of Turkish nationalism. The necessity of rejecting or distorting elements like the *devshirme* and imperial mosque architecture makes contemporary Turkish nationalist use of the Ottoman theme awkward, however. For other twentieth-century Moslem regimes, religious differences such as the Shiite-Sunni cleavage or even symbols of less significant cults such as the Malikite minaret appear to be more readily available for myth-building than are memories of imperial polities. For most areas, the genealogical myths with their nomadic associations remain the most significant foci of identity.

Reverberations of Imperial Administrations in the West

Whereas the Islamic world failed to utilize imperial administrations for building identity because expediency and religious fragmentation induced rulers to construct segmented elites, Western imperial polities seeking to construct supranational elites have failed repeatedly. In the current tendency to produce monoethnic administrative elites, the West resembles Byzantium rather than Islam or Russia. But the process by which Western universal empires have been transformed into national or protonational institutions has been even more tortuous than in Byzantium.

Analysis of patrimonial empires (to return briefly to S. N. Eisenstadt's basic categories) can be reduced to a minimum at this point; in contrast to the significance of this type for myths, administration as an institutional force was slight among them. Charlemagne could not develop a stable centralized administration in the deteriorating economic conditions of his time. Given the circumstances of the early Frank rulers, the institution of *missi dominici* was admirable. In effect the *missi* were roving plenipotentiary inspectors (half were bishops) assigned for one year to each of the major regions of the empire. In these regions, entourage nobles, descendants of the *comitatus* and often related by blood or marriage to the dynasty, were assigned as counts or viceroys. The monarchy moved these governing officials about occasionally, encouraging them to acquire widely dispersed estates, to intermarry, and thereby to acquire interests in all parts of the Frank realm. What little trained staff existed was provided by clerics working under bishops. In the chaotic conditions of the late ninth century, the Carolingian system regressed to patrimonial regional rule deriving a degree of legitimacy from the original royal appointments. Holy Roman imperial administration, like the administrations of the separate polities down to the twelfth century, probably did not even attain the level of sophistication—much less efficacy—reached by the Carolingians.[66] The more effective medieval Western administrations (Norman England, Norman and Hohenstaufen Sicily, the Roman Curia) were limited in scope territorially or otherwise. French development was broader in scope but until the seventeenth century did not produce a bureaucratic system comparable to Byzantium's at its apogee.[67]

When Charles V moved to Spain, the Burgundian administration, derived almost entirely from earlier French models but in some ways more advanced, provided the core of his regime. His council included five Flemings, three Burgundians, and only five Castilians in 1517–20. As indicated in chapter 5, the council was directed by the Fleming Chièvres, but the Piedmontese Gattinara became increasingly important as grand chancellor. Apparently, Gattinara had no desire to enhance Castilian participation; but when the council was formally reconstituted in 1520 as the Consejo de Estado, their number increased to six at the expense of the Burgundian contingent.[68] The Habsburgs' practice of governing each of their domains by officials drawn from another (for example, Austrians in Suabia) came up against an intense protonationalist Castilian identity derived from the frontier myth partially shared with the Aragonese. Though insisting that they were the only men loyal enough to govern, Castilians and Aragonese actually rebelled, at least passively. As an official under Philip II wrote concerning the viceroy, the Duke of Alba, "It was his aristocratic instinct to aid despotism, as long as he himself did not suffer from its effects," notably in respect to the "liberties" of Aragon cherished by Alba.[69]

The strength of the Spanish administrators derived not only from their unity vis-à-vis the heterogeneous officials whom Charles and Chièvres had brought into Spain, but also from the thorough Spanish training in law, chancery practice, and military administration. The *corregidores*, royal district magistrates for justice and administration, were practical men, often soldiers, relying when necessary on deputies trained in law. Other general officials (*capa y espada*) had to be literate in Latin though not necessarily in law. The *capa media* lawyers included many converts from Judaism trained at Alcala University whom the Franciscan Cardinal Ximinez Cisneros had introduced to break the monopoly of lawyers from the Thomist Salamanca University. Spanish administration drew on a tradition of widespread higher education, especially in law, stronger than in France, England, Burgundy, or Germany. As early as 1600 there were thirty-one universities in the Iberian peninsula enrolling a significant proportion (about 5 percent) of young men.[70]

Burgundian and French experience had demonstrated that legally trained administrators were essential to curb the particularist tendencies of the high nobility. A noted German analyst of this phase of administrative development writes that the officials trained in law "carried the gospel of law and order, official duty and centralization with almost religious fervor . . . against feudal reaction (at the start of Charles V's reign [in Burgundy]), which used the slogan 'Whoever makes a judge of his serf cannot live without dishonor.'" But it had become just as evident that an administration composed entirely of lawyers was inadequate for practical financial direction: "The long-robed counselors have never had occasion to learn the affairs of the ruler's domains and finances."[71] In Spain, Charles was fortunate to have available the important category of chancery secretaries without legal or even university educations, who began their careers as scribes learning from previous secretaries who were often their relatives, then moving up to high posts. As another German historian observes, "These secretarial dynasties exerted a most devoted and conscientious effort to maintain and develop political traditions and techniques, particularly those embodied in modern correspondence."[72] It is fairly evident that taken as a group the types of officials just described, nearly all of middling origin although divided on *converso*-gentry lines, constituted as in Byzantium the core of a highly resistant ethnic identity.

In Burgundy, Charles and his predecessors had learned to live with the high nobility who (in contrast to France at that early period) continued to dominate the principal offices and to sit as of right in the Conseil d'Etat. Shortly before Charles left for Spain, the power of the high aristocracy was slightly curbed by the introduction of a privy council to bypass the anachronistic Conseil d'Etat, but the chief minister remained a top noble.[73] In Spain, Charles and Chièvres had little difficulty curbing the great nobles (*grandees*) by using officials of more humble origins as, for example, Ferdinand of Aragon's secretary Pedro Ruiz de la Mota.[74] A strikingly parallel recession of *grandee* influence was occurring simultaneously in Spanish internal affairs, with the high aristocrats unable to defend the tolerant policy toward *conversos* against intransigent gentry imbued with the frontier myth. Many *conversos* (often the vanguard of the Inquisition) were, to be sure, able to adhere successfully to the "pure-blooded" gentry faction of the official class, but the last vestiges of the old myth of a supranational Spanish monarchy were eliminated. Consequently, the policies Charles V had employed in Burgundy to deal with feudal particularism proved in the long run to be wholly inadequate to subordinate the Spanish officials with their strong esprit de corps. Through his own skills in law and chancery manipulation and by timely concessions in appointment to Spanish offices, Gattinara was able to maintain control of foreign policy. To secure adoption of certain specific policies advanced by his minister, however, Charles had to resort to such extraordinary measures as threatening to remove his residence from Spain to Italy. As soon as his son Philip II succeeded to the throne, a virtual bureaucratic revolution occurred in which the entire composition of the Consejo de Estado became Iberian.[75] The reverberations in Flanders and Italy, emphasized in chapter 5, ultimately undermined the Castilian myth of universal rule.

A very similar tendency for the administration to develop such strong protonationalist identity that it became incapacitated to act as an instrument of supranational rule eventually appeared under the Austrian Habsburgs. Although gradual, the development in the Austrian dominions is striking because the dynasty there, in contrast to Philip II's voluntary acceptance of Castilian identity, consistently encouraged a supranational legitimizing myth. A constitutional historian of the Habsburg monarchy, Hermann J. Bidermann, wrote that "if Ferdinand I had acted like a German prince, giving Germans precedence, if he had organized his administration on that basis (putting non-Germans in the shadow, artificially promoting the German language, etc.) the present Austrian united state (*Gesammtstaat*) would have remained a concept of pure fantasy."[76] Instead, from the sixteenth century to the late eighteenth century the monarchs deliberately chose a Court language that no large body of their subjects spoke. The dynasty emphasized its Franco-Burgundian origins rather than its German background. At Court Spanish styles were preferred, not to curry favor with real Spaniards, but to avoid giving precedence to any ethnic group (*Volksstamm*) living in the Austrian domains.[77]

Indeed, as Bidermann points out, Ferdinand I, himself educated in Spain, nearly faced the same kind of rebellion from his German subjects for employing a Spanish treasurer, Gabriel de Salamanca, as his brother

Charles V had confronted for using Low Germans (Flemings) in Spain. The "Welsch" Salamanca was sacrificed, but the Austrian effort to maintain a cosmopolitan administration was temporarily more successful than the Spanish Habsburg experience.[78] Ferdinand's first task was to assemble a body of officials to enforce unified rule against the particularist nobles, increasingly affected by Protestantism, who were entrenched in provincial Estates. He began the process—which later became the principal weapon of Absolutist monarchs—of enticing the nobility to his Court through symbolic rewards and financial favors. After a time, their Court entanglement deprived the nobles of their local bases for resistance.

At the administrative level, German was dominant in the sixteenth-century Habsburg chancery, but French (not Latin) was also widely employed. Some Burgundian officials were imported, as were graduates of Italian university law schools. German officials, although apparently receptive to Slav and Magyar recruits who could be assimilated, hated all "Welsch" administrators—perhaps because the Romance were more capable competitors.[79] Because more legally trained officials were required than the Austrian domains could supply, the hereditary imperial chancellor, the archbishop of Mainz, acted as a major recruiting agent, drawing on the numerous southern and central German universities. But the bourgeoisie who did supply recruits from the Habsburgs' own territories were also almost all German-speaking. Probably the mere fact that the Habsburgs constituted a single imperial dynasty for nearly five centuries also enhanced the tendency to recruit a homogeneous body of high officials. The uncertain nature of succession in the ancient Roman empire had led to a tendency for each new dynasty to bring in a coterie of high officials from its base territory, for example, Iberia or Illyria.[80] Similar trends appeared in the Holy Roman empire and, indeed, in the modern Soviet and American polities as the de facto head of government changed. Conversely, the individual ruler in the earlier modern Habsburg empire in Austria—in contrast even to its Spanish branch—had little need to replace his predecessor's principal lieutenants.

The events of the early seventeenth century, starting with the suppression of the Austrian provincial nobility and continuing during the Thirty Years' War with the purge of the predominantly Protestant nobility of Bohemia and Moravia, in the Habsburg perspective constituted moves toward a supranational if not a universal empire. It has recently been argued that this purge, regarded as a net rate of attrition of the preexisting nobility, was not significantly different from the considerable turnover (some 70 families per decade) experienced by the Bohemian nobility during the sixteenth century. But of 417 new families entering that nobility during 1621–56, nearly one-half were Germans, mainly Alpine and often of bourgeois origin; 43 were Italians, 20 French, and 18 from Spain or the Spanish Netherlands.[81] The overwhelming Catholic contingent—including many who were more or less soldiers of fortune—came from all parts of Europe. Such a heterogeneous body obviously provided good material for an imperial elite severed from local attachments. Throughout the following century, the monarchy diligently endeavored, with considerable success, to transform the nobility into a bulwark of the Austrian system. Because the raison d'être of the new nobility was defense of Catholicism, Jesuits (until their expulsion under Joseph II) and other religious orders directed its education. In line with Burgundian tradition, the Austrian Habsburgs resorted to archaicizing mechanisms. Adult socialization centered on the Vienna Court, where French was the stylish language. In practice, however, the diverse nobles of the western domains communicated among themselves in German by the mid-seventeenth century; only the Hungarian nobility clung to "kitchen Latin."

One price exacted by a socialization that stressed archaicisms was, as in Burgundy, maintenance of noble ascendancy in high offices, in contrast to gentry domination in Spain a century earlier. Wilhelm Roscher, an early student of Habsburg institutions, believed that

> the decisive significance which the Austrian state always attributed
> to the nobles, especially high nobles, is largely a result of the view that
> while no Austrian nation as a whole could be formed, a general Austrian
> nobility could be established. Consequently, the upbringing of the no-
> bles (as a foundation for general development) needed to be furthered
> by a group of institutions, mostly connected to the Sovereign House,
> such as the Theresa Knights' Academy, the Noble Guards, the
> clerical chivalric orders, etc.[82]

Officials of middle-class origin became increasingly dominant in the *Gubernien*, the territorial framework for unifying the western domains. Nevertheless, nineteenth-century memoirs by Austrian administrators of humble origin expressed resentment of nobles' privileges.[83]

Class cleavage in the administration generally did not affect ethnic adherence because bourgeois recruits were even more German in language than the nobles. As recruitment of Holy Roman empire knights from southwest Germany declined, literate noncommissioned officers had to be obtained from northern Germany. The army continued to be a major centralizing mechanism, which meant, therefore, additional pressure for Germanization. The seventeenth-century commander against the Turks in Transylvania, Prince Eugene of Savoy, is said to have insisted on 75 to 80 percent Germans among his officers. In 1790 even the army of the kingdom of Hungary was incorporated in the general military establishment with German as the language of command.[84] More significant as a reflection of noble-bourgeois cleavage was the legitimizing ideology. Whereas nobles readily accepted archaicizing styles, bourgeois officials played a considerable role during the late seventeenth century in elaborating a "Machiavellian-Roman law" concept of the general good to be furthered by a powerful, "progressive" state. The Roman legal doctrines inculcated by the German universities where most had trained stressed monarchical rights against particularism, and the "science" of cameralistics provided an early theory for centralized economic development. It is significant that the Jesuits who conducted the Maria Theresa Knights' Academy and the Piarist Order that supervised the Savoy Knights' Academy distrusted both these disciplines, although the clerics were obliged to provide some instruction in law and economics for their aristocratic students.[85]

Under Joseph II the bourgeois "modernizing" trend triumphed. Lower- and middle-level administrators took the lead in an enhanced centralization. C. A. Macartney has cogently remarked that such modernizing trends inevitably implied the selection of a single modern language for internal communication throughout the administration "to satisfy the new and fussy insistence of the bureaucrats that everything possible must be in writing, so that it could be checked centrally." A Magyar historian supplements this analysis by pointing out that the Enlightenment ideal of education likewise required a choice of language.[86] But centralization itself was also based on conscious application of Enlightenment ideas, including anticlericalism. Joseph intended to replace the various local languages, except Italian, by German in the law courts and in fact did succeed in doing away with the vestiges of Czech in the Bohemian nobles' assemblies.[87] Apparently, though, he and his high officials were not more biased in favor of German culture than their predecessors. In 1783, Joseph issued an instruction emphasizing that "nationality and religion must make no difference [in appointing and evaluating officials]. All must be employed as brothers in the monarchy and all must be useful."[88]

Nevertheless, the policy makers considered use of German to be the only available method for efficient centralization by promoting communication among the groups salient for modernization—officials, lawyers, bourgeois. French, dominant at Court under Maria Theresa, was already on the wane. For Joseph's officials, German was also a desirable substitute for clerical Latin. Opposition, notably by the Magyar nobility, made Joseph retreat. His successors, alarmed by the French Revolution, tried to reverse some modernizing trends by reemphasis on noble origins for high office. Nikolaus von Preradovich calculates that in 1804 only one of the top administrative officers was bourgeois, as contrasted to five from the old Austrian nobility. Most of the others were from other noble backgrounds.

Table 2. University Students in Austrian Empire, 1851

	Total Number	Percent of Total	Jurisprudence Number	Percent
By Religion				
Roman Catholic, Latin Rite	8,421	88	4,303	93
Protestant	202	2	87	2
Jewish	463	5	116	3
Other (mostly Uniate Catholic)	460	5	131	3
By Language				
German and Yiddish	2,589	27	1,331	29
Slavic	2,995	31	1,402	30
Magyar	585	6	250	5
Other (mostly Italian)	3,377	35	1,654	36

Source: Constructed from data in Hain, 2:682. Jurisprudence includes students in five law academies in addition to the law faculties of the ten universities. Of the latter, two were located in the Italian provinces that Austria still retained at that date.

By 1829, one-fourth of the officials were bourgeois. By 1847, however, reflecting recruitment during the later French revolutionary period, the bourgeois filled only one-fifth of these offices, compared to one-tenth from the old Austrian nobility and no fewer than 35 percent from other German nobilities. Preradovich's data suggest that nearly all bourgeois were actually Germans, thus their proportionate increase, added to the surprisingly high influx of German nobles at those late dates, implies that up to the period of industrialization the high Austrian administration was overwhelmingly German in background. It was, indeed, more German— though less aristocratic—than the group of army generals.[89]

Many lower officials continued to adhere, tacitly, to the principles of the "good" Enlightenment, notably anticlericalism.[90] Such small but symbolic steps as the effort to design a single great seal for all the Habsburg lands had long been pushed by the centralizing administration, even before Joseph II. The formation in 1804 of an Austrian, as contrasted to the defunct Holy Roman empire, though nominally diminishing the dynasty's attachments to German, was actually used by the Vienna administration to further erode particularistic privileges in a manner that inevitably promoted German culture. By 1851, Austrian higher education had developed sufficiently to provide the great majority of the monarchy's administrative recruits. Table 2 suggests the extent to which Germans and Catholics (the sum of the two categories cannot be precisely calculated from the available aggregate data) remained the mainstay of the system. Legal study constituted the usual qualification for entry to the administration; consequently, the significantly greater enrollment of Germans and Catholics in law as contrasted to a relatively strong position of different religioethnic elements in other disciplines appears to be important. The *Ausgleich* of 1867 with Hungary effectively removed half of the Habsburg domains from such Germanizing influence. Nevertheless, despite its openness to recruits who were prepared to acculturate completely, the Austrian administration remained a powerful force for Germanization.

The slow but inexorable drift toward an administrative elite unified around a single ethnic identity in Austria presents a superficial contrast to the sharp, brittle reaction of Spanish administrators against Habsburg efforts at constructing a supranational elite. In the final analysis, though, both branches of the Habsburgs, despite efforts that must be evaluated as entirely sincere, reasonable, generally consistent, and occasionally imaginative, failed to arrest trends toward homogeneous ethnic identities. In both cases the long-run development undermined the broader imperial polities which the dynasts envisaged. In Spain the last Habsburgs presided over an exhausted kingdom divided by strong regional ethnic identities. Much later, the fall of the eastern branch of the dynasty coincided with a complete imperial catastrophe that left as a souvenir only the rump Austrian republic. In the short run, large administrative apparatuses that were relatively efficient for their time had accomplished a great deal in promoting ethnic identity and some measure of modernization, but the cost was ultimate failure.

A serious question remains that cannot be fully treated within the framework of this study. Were the Austrian and Spanish administrative experiences essentially different from those of France or England, where administrators acted as major forces for achieving unified national identities? The argument that the latter were successful because they operated in an earlier historical period must confront the fact that Spanish identity was promoted by an equally precocious administrative elite; yet that identity remains less solid. One can advance, without much assurance, the counterargument that the overwhelming imperial aspirations of sixteenth-century Spanish elites impaired thorough amalgamation of some areas like Catalonia and the Basque country. Timing is more evidently significant in the Austrian case. Nevertheless, the seeds of Magyar resistance to the constitution of a unified ethnic identity for the Habsburg lands were sown not later than the sixteenth-century Turkish invasion, that is, by the Moslem-Christian frontier experience. I am left wondering if there is not something older and more fundamental in Western civilization, perhaps related to the tension between ecclesiastical and secular universalisms, that undermines efforts to develop supranational identity. It is beyond dispute, however, that the evolution of centralized bureaucracies in the West, in contrast to Islam, made identity problems salient. No administrative elite unified in recruitment, socialization, and esprit de corps can be neutral on ethnic issues for long, especially as pressures of modernization increase. For effective socialization, an administrative elite must imbibe and propagate a single myth associated with a single linguistic vehicle; and this myth acquires the force of ethnic identity.

Summary and Conclusions

Regarded purely as a concept, the universal terrestrial empire reflecting the order of heaven is compatible with a hierarchy of respect in which the emperor merely presides over rulers of lesser polities. Such a limited empire, however, accords neither with the usual trend of politics nor with the historical origins of compound polities. If it is to reflect divine harmony, terrestrial order requires complicated institutions to assure the supremacy of centralized authority. In practice, emperors have relaxed their demand for complete authority only in circumstances (such as the decline of Byzantium) that manifestly deprived them of the power to subordinate other rulers, or when (as in West Europe) the ecclesiastical guardians of the universal myth maneuvered to maintain a balance among secular rulers.

Establishment of a fixed capital has been a significant institutional mechanism for enhancing central power. Memories of the city-state, the predecessor of the compound imperial polity, also required symbolic transfer of affect to a single superordinate city. In some situations, notably the Holy Roman empire, Spain, and most Moslem polities, practical considerations and the inertia of tradition thwarted this recourse. The recurring need to symbolize the splendor of a new dynasty led Moslem rulers to change seats of government, or at least to build new palace quarters in the same capital. In medieval northern Europe, economic inability to support a large royal entourage persisted long enough to enable the entrenchment of particularistic interests working for peripatetic government. Neither supreme rulers nor elites were rational actors. Usually they perpetuated arrangements made familiar by custom, whether original circumstances had produced a single capital as in Byzantium or the inefficient perambu-

lation of Burgundy and Spain. Sudden moves, such as Charles IV's effort
to center the Holy Roman imperial government on Prague, were rarely
enduring.

In the long run, nevertheless, fixation of the capital or even incremental
restriction of perambulation to a small district like the Ile de France facilitated institutionalization of administrative recruitment and socialization.
Such centralized patterns were strengthened by a dynasty's reliance on
particular elements of the population, such as the South German Catholics
recruited by the Habsburgs. The institutional patterns associated with the
capital developed their own inertia, including esprit de corps centering on
metropolitan styles, pride in administrative efficacy, and acceptance of the
dynasty's *mythomoteur*. To become fully effective, socialization required a
well-developed cultural tradition. One that accorded with preentry socialization of elite recruits (particularly their identity myths) was most effective. In early Byzantium, for example, the prestige of Greek language and
culture was sufficient to displace early formal adherence to Latin; during
the course of many centuries, a Hellenic identity myth also replaced the
myth of Rome. In European polities like Poland and Hungary where sharp
differences between gentry and burgher myths and culture persisted, or
(as in Russia) were revived as an unanticipated consequence of imperial
policy, formation of a uniform governing elite remained incomplete. Elite
segmentation impeded the development of strong centralized polities,
although in the Russian case an exceptionally powerful *mythomoteur* partially overcame this impediment.

For Moslem polities, elite segmentation by ethnic identity myth—
Arabic, Persian, Turkic—was the norm. It is remarkable that such segmentation reached its apex in Mameluke Cairo and Ottoman Constantinople,
the principal instances of stable Islamic capitals. The longevity of the
empires based on these capitals suggests that stable compound polities are
compatible with multiethnic administrations, although the social costs are
high. It must be recalled, however, that a common core of Islamic values
united these segmented elites. Moreover, all Islamic imperial polities relied, in varying degrees, on non-Moslems for administrative or para-
administrative tasks, a practice that eventually reduced governmental
efficacy.

Conversely, in European centralized administrations the myth adopted
by the governing elite gradually imbued larger elements of the population
of the compound polity. When, as in France, the popularized *mythomoteur*
and standardized linguistic patterns penetrated most of the population
before the era of nationalism, a "nation-state" arose. Where major elite or
potential elite elements remained attached to other myths and linguistic

patterns, on the other hand, conflict with the centralized administrative elite became a major source of tension.

Although it is difficult to express these complicated differences in imperial polity development in typological form, the following propositions (less formally integrated than those presented at the end of chapter 4) provide a useful summary.

A. The effects of the three basic mythic types on ethnic identification have been modified by
   1. The type of capital city, its role as a communications center, and the symbolic attraction it exerts.
   2. The type of imperial bureaucratic administrations, where such centralized bureaucracies have developed.
B. Islamic polities are characterized by
   1. Capitals that have frequently shifted. Even where a single city has remained the capital for a long time, its segmented nature and frequent additions of new palace or garrison quarters dilute its potential for communicating symbols of identity.
   2. Administrations that are segmented functionally, with a single ethnoreligious group assuming each function; consequently, the bureaucracy does not develop and propagate a unified identity myth.
   3. The two factors just listed, combined with the low concern of the Islamic myth for specific imperial polities (especially after the end of the caliphate) have led to low propensity of Islamic polities to create ethnic identity. Conversely, Islamic polities rarely develop myths strong enough to prevent the emergence of such identities.
C. Byzantium and Russia (the two Orthodox imperial polities) are characterized by
   1. A single capital, the city-state writ large, communicating intense affect symbolism transcending all local myths, although this effect is somewhat attenuated in Russia since the seventeenth century.
   2. In Byzantium, a single, unified administration strongly propagating the imperial identity myth; in Russia a weaker administration (because of relative economic underdevelopment) tending toward ethnic segmentation.
   3. The factors just listed, plus very strong imperial myths, have produced somewhat divergent results in the two polities:
      a. A Byzantine polity producing intense neo-Hellenic identity as the prospects for universal rule declined.
      b. A Russian polity producing intense Russian national identity at a relatively early stage, but with a segmented elite.

D. Western Christendom has been characterized by three sharply differing types of polities:
   1. Imperial polities (the Carolingian and the Holy Roman empires) with diminishing quasi-universalist claims characterized by
      a. Late, insecure emergence of capitals, which are unable to communicate symbols transcending local myths.
      b. Unified bureaucracies in which a single ethnic element tends to predominate in spite of the universalist aspect of the original polity myths.
      c. A consequent tendency of the imperial polity to break up or decline as the prospects of universal rule diminish.
   2. Large polities (such as France) with myths ascribing to each a specific, limited, but quasi-sacral mission, such as defense of the ecclesiastical vicar of Christ, capable of transcending local myths. These polities are characterized by
      a. Slow but definite emergence of capitals that gradually communicate strong affect symbols.
      b. Unified bureaucracies gradually assuming a specific ethnic coloration.
      c. A consequent tendency to produce a "national state," with France as prototype and model.
   3. Polities characterized primarily by a strong *Antemurale* legitimization myth, but lacking one of the characteristics listed under 2 above, namely either
      a. A capital communicating strong affect symbols (Spain).
      b. A unified bureaucracy (Poland, Hungary).

CHAPTER SEVEN

Religious Organizations and Communication

Religious and Ethnoreligious Identities

So much attention has already been devoted to the influence of religion on ethnic identity that one may well ask if any aspects of this relationship remain unconsidered. The unifying theme of the present chapter is, however, rather different from the earlier discussion of religions, namely, the penetrative power of religious organizations. Ecclesiastical structures and imperial myths, as discussed in the preceding chapter, have been intimately related. Left to their own resources, large polities in the premodern period often had a low capacity to communicate their legitimizing myths to the masses. This limitation had not much affected the city-state, which could depend on immediate visual effects and face-to-face communication, at least among the portion of the urban population admitted to citizenship. For imperial polities the problem of disseminating myths and symbols was of a different order of magnitude. In earlier chapters, attention was concentrated on elites, such as aristocracies and administrative officials, because these elements were the custodians of, and hence, by definition, were penetrated by the myths. In the Byzantine case, where a high proportion of the affairs of the polity was concentrated in a single large city, a sizable elite of officials could communicate the legitimizing myth to a considerable fraction of the total population. Even in Byzantium, however, ratios of communicators to masses are disconcerting. Warren T. Treadgold estimates that there were three thousand fully educated persons active professionally at any one time. If one may assume that the literate body of minor officials and professionals was thirty times as large (Treadgold makes no numerical estimate at this level), the total apparatus capable of following the literary evolution (exceptionally significant in Byzantium) of the myth was only on the order of 2 percent of the adult male population. The proportion of fully literate Castilian males was not a great deal larger: 5.4 percent of eighteen-year-olds matriculated in the universities at the end of the sixteenth century, declining to 2.2 percent by 1750, with many entering the church during both periods.[1] Moreover, direct contacts between the lay elite of officials and professionals and the masses of artisans, shop-

keepers, and peasants were not highly conducive to propagating an identity message. Apart from directing military activities, the aspect of the
official role that brought bureaucrats into direct contact with the masses
was, usually, tax-collecting.

A majority, probably, of literate Byzantines and a high proportion of
literate Spaniards were not laymen, however. A special feature of most
Christian churches has been preparation of a body of clergy to convey the
religious message to all social strata and to the most remote corners of a
polity. The Byzantine church, with its relatively strong educational system,
was an early leader in this effort. Certainly such an objective took a long
time to attain, especially in the rural West. But in the most thickly settled
West European regions, the end was attained in purely quantitative terms
during the ninth century through the establishment of a network of contiguous parishes. Probably a similar network covered the central Byzantine
territories of Thrace and Asia Minor somewhat earlier, though city parishes were relatively more important. Extension of the parochial networks
to outlying areas of both divisions of Christendom took longer. Surely,
moreover, the mere existence of parishes did not assure communication of
uniform, intelligible messages. The recurrent efforts of monastic orders to
establish centralized discipline and spiritual vigor testify to the deficien-
cies. Clearly, though, the Christian ecclesiastical network constituted a far
more effective penetrative organization than did the administrations of
large premodern polities.

The penetrative capacities of certain religions lacking centralized hierarchies directing parochial networks were not less effective. Uniform communication and zeal in communicating could be assured by a common
socialization and community pressures as well as by explicit authority,
although some authoritative tribunals appeared. Both Islam and Judaism
lack the sacral priesthoods present in most traditional Christian churches
and in Zoroastrianism, but the respect accorded men exactingly prepared
in religious law guarantees a considerable measure of uniformity in authoritative opinions. As F. E. Peters has recently explained, the relationship between Moslem and Jewish "men of the law" is not accidental. The
tradition of relying on a religious law school rather than on a hierarchic, officially appointed religious authority began with the Babylonian captivity and
was revived even before the Roman destruction of Jerusalem in A.D. 70:

> Johannan bar Zakkai left Jerusalem and founded a school (*beth
> ha-midrash*) at Jabneh on the coast. The type was absolutely new in
> the Mediterranean. . . . What was novel in Johannan's institution was
> the combination of a learned and a religious tradition, and whatever the
> title—theological school, catechetical school or *madrasah*—it was to

have an impressive history. . . . The *beth ha-midrash* also arrogated to itself most of the prerogatives of the *beth ha-din*, the "House of the Law" that regulated the external affairs of the Jewish community.[2]

Although Islam is usually regarded as nonhierarchic, the presence of central Islamic authorities in Cairo (one grand *cadi* for each law school) and Constantinople (the *sheikh ul-Islam*) has already been noted. Less personalized structures of earlier centuries were probably as effective in promoting uniformity. Similarly, Judaism under the Abbasids, as previously under Roman rule, had a nominal head, the Babylonian exilarch, but his authority declined after a few centuries. Large subdivisions of the Jewish diaspora had their separate heads, such as the *gaon* of Egypt. Each community resorted to one of three *yeshivas* in Baghdad for appeals from the local tribunal. These superior religious law authorities bear a remarkable resemblance to the "mother cities" of German city law. Moreover, as in the Lübeck system, a community confronting a problem in the application of law was not allowed to approach two authoritative bodies (*yeshivas*) simultaneously.[3] As will shortly become apparent, Christian churches were also able to adapt to circumstances in which regular hierarchical communication was impracticable without losing the power to communicate a considerable number of messages regularly and uniformly to lay members.

The penetrative power of religious organizations has important implications for formation of ethnic identity. When the ecclesiastical structure (as in Byzantium, medieval France, or the Abbasid caliphate) is closely associated with the large polity, their activities become complementary, indeed almost inextricably mingled. The identity fostered by the polity elite is immeasurably strengthened by the network of local religious organizations or, in Islam and often in Christianity, by itinerant preachers. Recurrent gatherings in churches, synagogues, or mosques, such as the Friday prayer in central mosques or special liturgical celebrations in cathedrals, provide effective forums for conveying symbolic as well as explicit messages. Catechetical instruction, although vestigial during much of the Middle Ages, conveyed messages that (because the receiver was bound to respond) could not be ignored. A leading authority on the reception of Roman law points out, for example, that the 1215 requirement for annual confession led to the issuance of preparatory handbooks based on canon law. Instruction based on these manuals eventually imbued the average German's mind so deeply with Roman law principles that she or he was prepared later to accept Roman private law.[4]

As this instance suggests, the effects of ecclesiastical communications were often unanticipated. Such, particularly, were the effects of religious administrative divisions upon linguistic usage, hence indirectly but very strongly on ethnic identity. Whereas administrative officers frequently went about their business without exerting a strong impact on clients' language patterns, religious usage in liturgy, sermons, and legal proceedings was rarely neutral. Symbolic associations derived from use of a special sacral script were often as influential as instrumental communication. So strong were such associations that a change of script or alphabet was a normal concomitant of religious conversion. Thus in the seventh century the replacement of the Pahlevi script by the Arabic alphabet sealed the conversion of Persia from Zoroastrianism to Islam. In Western Christianity nine hundred years later, Lutherans adopted "Gothic" script in place of the "cursive" handwriting which Catholics and Calvinists used.[5] Conversely, retention of a highly distinctive sacral script is a prime boundary-maintaining symbol for an isolated ethnoreligious group.

Before proceeding to consider such diasporas, a few words on the significance of the earliest divisions of Christianity will be useful, for they not only exerted a lasting influence on varieties of Christian identity but through their perpetuation under Islam significantly affected interaction of the two great universal religions. Scholars of the early Christian era have exhibited a remarkable interest in the ethnic implications of these sectarian divisions. In contrast to the general consensus (which I share) that adherence to Islam or to Christianity constituted the overriding identification for medieval man, the primacy of religion or of "national" identification among early Christians has been hotly debated. The mere existence of such alternation of debate and consensus suggests that in the phenomenon of ethnicity historiography may be encountering—as I observed tentatively in chapter 1—a phenomenon that is cyclical.

A stimulating essay by the ancient historian A. H. M. Jones asks: "Were ancient heresies national or social movements in disguise?" Without entering into the theological implications of Jones's question, I shall retain his usage by referring to sects outside the mainstream of Christianity during the first five or six centuries as "heresies." Jones answers his own question by concluding that the interpretation of heresies as "national" is a projection of present-day nationalism into the past. He is concerned, obviously, to refute oversimplifications as in E. L. Woodward's *Christianity and Nationalism.*[6] But Jones poses his more specific queries in a manner that, given the ambiguities of an earlier age, cannot fail to support his thesis: "Did the average Copt say to himself, 'I am an Egyptian and proud of it. . . . I do not know or care whether Christ has one or two natures, but as the Romans insist on the latter view, I hold the former,'" or even that the Copt reflected, "'I will firmly reject any compromise which the Romans may offer, and even if they accept our view I will never be reconciled with them.'"[7]

The lengthy discussions of the relation of myth to identity in preceding chapters have, I hope, prepared the reader to reply that such unambiguous rational responses would be hard to elicit even today in matters like religion and ethnicity that involve strong affect. Endre Ivánka's genetic approach appears to be a more promising way of demonstrating that the heresies were only superficially involved with ethnic identity. "In the multiple distortions (heresies) in which the proclamation and formulation of Christian teachings arose are reflected basic tendencies of ancient Hellenic intellectual life as these had developed before the appearance of Christianity and during the conflict with it."[8] Gilbert Dagron, specifically considering the Christian community of Constantinople, agrees: "After the Arian crisis, Christianity there had become the language by which the people expressed its opposition and obedience, its good and bad political humor and its imaginings."[9] Quarrels about heresies had taken the place, he continues, of earlier polytheistic rivalries.

Ivánka sharply rejects the theory that rivalry between the Monophysite heresy and the Nestorian heresy, for instance, reflected an old antagonism of Egyptian and Syrian views; he demonstrates that the dispute really reflected pre-Christian differences between the Alexandrine and the Antiochian schools of Greek philosophy. Insofar as any regional or ethnic distinctions tinged this philosophical polarity, they arose from the circumstances in which Hellenization had taken place in the two cities. In Alexandria, Hellenic culture was so strong that it attracted the local Jewish community. Hence opposition to Neo-Platonic, anthropomorphic Christianity had to be recruited among the un-Hellenized Coptic monks, whereas Antioch was purely Greek. Nevertheless, Ivánka insists, it is most likely that the different heresies are to be explained by "the special intellectual attitudes of the Greeks in each city, from the special direction and colorations which Hellenic thought and philosophy, the Hellenic religion and world view, had assumed in each city; in the final analysis, from a polarity in *Hellenic* modes of thought."[10]

It may appear, therefore, that by a different route the Hungarian scholar has demonstrated Jones's principal thesis. But are Ivánka's conclusions truly probative as far as the ethnic issue is concerned? To assume that they are is, I think, once again to treat the nature of identity superficially. Most characteristics of ethnic myths, as noted time and time again, are diffused from various centers rather than invented by the group that ultimately accepts them as part of its own core identity. The key factor is persistence. As Ivánka himself notes, Monophysitism, wherever it may have originated, persisted almost exclusively (in Egypt) among Copts.[11] In fact, the Monophysite interpretation of Christ's nature has constituted the core identifying element not only of the diminished number of Egyptian Christians (who have given up their ancient language for everyday use in favor of Arabic) but of the Amharic (Ethiopian) nation. The latter retains a distinctive language partly because it is preserved in Monophysite literature. It seems to me that Dagron more accurately reflects the real intermingling of religious and ethnic considerations in his remarks on the accidental provincialization of heresies:

> One cannot say that Orthodoxy was favorable to the expansion of the Greek language and that this or that heresy put a brake on it. But one must acknowledge that heretical denunciations of whatever doctrine had the effect of provincializing heresy and driving it out of the capital, thereby de-Hellenizing it to the extent that the provincial churches became less and less Greek-speaking. There was a correlation between the unity of Orthodoxy, the single Empire, and the unifying Greek language; conversely, there was a correlation between the pluralism of the heresies (which constitutes their very definition), political particularism, and diversity of national languages, including the Greek of the schools of Athens and Alexandria.[12]

When ethnicity and religion mix, one will always encounter a large element of confusion. It seems desirable, therefore, to turn now to historical phenomena where the congruence of ethnicity and religion is so obvious that one can proceed immediately to analyzing the nature of the relationship rather than debating its existence. After some of the problems have been identified in these more clear-cut cases, certain more typical interconnections of religion and ethnicity under medieval and modern conditions can, perhaps, be untangled.

Archetypal Diasporas

Many investigations of modern nationalism, in seeking to explain its manifestations in nineteenth-century philological myths, find diaspora nations hard to interpret. There are, to be sure, modern versions of Jewish and Armenian nationalism based ostensibly on linguistic distinctiveness. Even these versions are more concerned with adapting ancient myths to the currently dominant assumption that a nation must be territorial. I do not intend to criticize resort to such fashionable secular myths; under certain conditions it constitutes an indispensable defensive reaction to others' xenophobia. All the same, it is crucial to be clear about the essential difference between a collectivity that has maintained a sharp identity for centuries or millennia and one that is the product of the diffusion of nationalist ideology. The intensity of identity produced by older sacral myths—based on but not always coextensive with distinctive religions—has never been exceeded by modern secular myths.

Elsewhere I have termed diaspora ethnic collectivities that have maintained such persistent sacral myths "archetypal diasporas." Archetypal diasporas that have survived (including the remnant of Parsees, mainly in India, but retaining sacral centers in Iran) have been sustained by the highly concrete component of their myth that points to their sacral locus of origin as well as by a distinctive alphabet.[13] The ambiguous circumstances of David's founding of Jerusalem as a sacral capital for a hitherto nomadic people were noted in chapters 2 and 6. Perhaps the tensions involved in Jewish adaptation to an urban center made nostalgic attachment to it stronger after its destruction by the Romans. Thenceforward dispersed Jews could perceive Jerusalem not as an urban life style but as a purely sacral symbol. One small indication of the intensity of identification with Jerusalem will suffice. The Chinese, like late medieval Western aristocrats, identify a family by the location of its ancestral graveyard. Over the centuries, Jews have been just as concerned with their burial places, hoping to rest in Jerusalem. When, as was usually the case, this turned out to be impracticable, they avoided referring in their epitaphs to any other place of origin, preferring to stress instead the solidarity of all Jews.[14]

Armenians created a similar center of intense attachment in Echmiadzin, a small city near Yerivan in what is now Soviet Armenia. They assert that the head of their distinctive church, the Catholicos, has been consecrated in Echmiadzin (originally called Vagharshapat) ever since the fourth century. Repeated attempts—by Byzantines, Ottomans, and most recently by anti-Soviet Armenians—to establish rival sacral centers have never succeeded.

As is the case for other theological aspects of ecclesiastical history, exploration of the doctrinal bases of the Gregorian church, as the Armenians' faith came to be known, would exceed the scope of this work. Given the paucity of general knowledge on the subject, however, some reference to the issues that divided Gregorians from larger Christian bodies is indispensable. The main divergence from the neighboring Christian church of Byzantium was a peculiar formula concerning the relationship between the divine and the human natures of Christ. Some observers have termed this formula "Monophysite." Historically, it is true, Armenians have preferred symbols near to the latter belief. For example, the sixth-century Gregorian church, like St. Hripsimeh's near Echmiadzin, originally had a single apse window; during the seventh century, Byzantine occupying forces introduced three windows to symbolize the triumph of the orthodox doctrine of the Holy Trinity. Later, popes seeking church unification urged Gregorians to mix water with the wine of consecration to symbolize the two natures of Christ.[15] Armenian theological scholars reject the Monophysite label, in contrast to the Copts, pointing out that Gregorians admit Christ's real human nature, although not the true mortality of his body. Gregorian rejection of the Council of Chalcedon (451), Armenian scholars contend, came about because the council confused the two natures. In any case, a schism had arisen between the Gregorians and the orthodox Byzantine church decades before this doctrinal divergence when the former insisted on consecrating its own ecclesiastical head. The Gregorians argued—there is a parallel to French rejection of the "Donation of Constantine"—that because Armenia had never belonged to the Roman empire, it need not recognize Constantinople's ecclesiastical jurisdiction.[16]

It is striking to observe how, in its origin, the Armenian ethnoreligious myth endeavored to assimilate components of the established Jewish identity. The surviving branch of the Arsacid dynasty in Armenia claimed ancient Jewish origin. St. Gregory the Enlightener apparently came from this family. About A.D. 300, when Roman Christians were still subject to persecution, he collaborated with his lay relatives in a manner familiar from Central European experience to impose Christianity from above. Church leadership (which also was almost hereditary) at first was designated by the title *kahanaiapet*, derived from Hebrew for "high priest." Many Armenian nobles, such as the Bagratids, also asserted descent from Jews deported to Armenia in the first century B.C. by the Armenian pagan king Tigranes, who had carried out an ephemeral conquest of Syria. St. Gregory also endeavored to relate earlier Armenian history to the Jews in order to share their role as God's Chosen People. Old Testament models of belief, hope, and conduct were frequent sermon themes. A high place was accorded a warrior saint such as Judas Maccabeus, and the prominence of liturgical prayers for Armenian victory is notable. Perhaps alone among Christian churches, the Gregorians have maintained the custom of ritual sacrifice of lambs in centers such as Geghard Monastery in a remote mountain district of Soviet Armenia.[17]

When one scrutinizes the history—as far as it can be known—of both Jews and Armenians, one detects curious parallels, even if the ancestral relationship is fictitious. Jews were seminomadic; Armenians apparently were sedentary in their earliest period. Both areas of settlement, however, lay athwart the great trade routes from the Mediterranean area to farther Asia. Their location constituted at once the curse and the opportunity of both peoples. Situated in hardly defensible positions between the Persian empires and the Hellenistic polities, both were exposed to repeated devastation. Ultimate subjugation for Jews came from the Roman Hellenistic side, for the Armenians from the Moslem Turkic successors of the Persians. Both Jews and Armenians developed large diaspora elements long before foreign force compelled complete dispersion. Some accounts place the number of Jews in Egypt at one million (14 percent of the total population), and there were other large colonies throughout the Mediterranean world before it was united by Rome. Armenians moved in very large numbers to the Byzantine empire before their country was crushed between it and the Moslems. It is significant that at the start of their history both ethnic groups were renowned as warriors. Jewish mercenaries enjoyed some prominence in the early Middle East; Armenians constituted the best recruiting base for Byzantium in the seventh century A.D. A recent Soviet study identifies some thirty-eight Armenian families among the three hundred top aristocratic families of tenth- to eleventh-century Byzantium. Almost all of the Armenian elite began as military commanders and regional governors, although many families then moved into Byzantine civil administration.[18]

After the final subjugation of their home territories, neither Jews nor Armenians had opportunities for prominent military careers—in fact, they became so well known as extremely unmilitary peoples that the Ottomans exempted both from the *devshirme*. Only after the holocausts suffered by both groups in the twentieth century did they revert, with remarkable distinction, to military traditions. During the long intervening period, Armenians and Jews alike turned to commercial occupations, that is, to roles usual for groups denied access to governing and military command positions. The extraordinary accumulation over the centuries of skills and aptitudes required in modernizing polities has led me to categorize such groups as "mobilized diasporas."[19] Both Jews and Armenians had obtained a long head start in acquiring commercial skills before their ultimate dispersions at times when other occupations were still open to them. No doubt most Jews—about one hundred thousand—in the great commercial metropolis of the Roman empire, Alexandria, were in commerce or liberal professions. Before the Persian Shah Abbas deported them to his capital in the sixteenth century, the Armenians of Julfa in the Transcaucasian homeland for several centuries had constituted the focal point for Armenian trading colonies stretching from Lvov to India.

Nevertheless, the dispersions accelerated the process by which both groups became "middleman minorities." For the Armenians, to be sure, final dispersion never took place in the sense that they ceased to occupy a small, fairly compact territory, although since 1915 this area has existed only within the Russian polity. In retrospect, one can locate the initial step that reduced the Armenian homeland to this vestige in the 1830–40 Ottoman implantation among sedentary Armenian peasants of Kurdish semi-nomadic mountaineers. The latter were entitled as Moslems to bear arms, in contrast to the Armenians, who were left almost defenseless.[20] The sources of the Armenian Holocaust, therefore, are closely related to the age-old incompatibility of nomadic and sedentary ways of life and the recurrent temptation of Islamic regimes to resort to nomadic auxiliaries.

In chapter 4 some account was presented of the extraordinary utility of Jews and Armenians to multiethnic polities lagging in modernization, like Poland-Lithuania and the Ottoman empire. Much of this usefulness derived from the diasporas' technological knowledge in fields as diverse as medicine, luxury goods artisanry, and shipbuilding. Unquestionably, however, their greatest utility was for long-distance commerce. Both Jews and Armenians derived considerable advantages from their ability to cross the Islamic-Christian frontier. As long as they were widely tolerated, Jews performed a major service in exchange of knowledge as well as ideas between the two civilizations. Later, Armenians enjoyed a similar precarious toleration because their "heretical" position kept them from being identified with either Orthodox or Catholics.[21] It appears that both Jews and Armenians were more highly appreciated as middlemen by Moslem than by Christian elites. For example, the Armenian community in the Crimea was instrumental in capturing the Black Sea commerce for the Ottomans from Italian merchants.[22]

Factors generated by their special backgrounds as diasporas were also important in enabling Armenians and Jews to conduct trade in diverse, often hostile environments. A network of protective family relationships provided contacts and shelter along the trade routes. Usually the solidarity engendered by such contacts was sufficient to make business dealings among diaspora members predictable.[23] If necessary, however, each community had its religious tribunals (usually recognized by the authorities of the broader polity for cases internal to the diaspora) to enforce probity. The Ottoman *millet* system extended such broad jurisdictional, welfare, and taxation authority to Armenian and Jewish communities that a narrow elite control emerged among them. In the first half of the nineteenth century, for example, Ottoman policy enabled the 7 percent of the Armenian *millet* residing in Constantinople to dominate all major institutions of the ethnic group.[24]

It is important to emphasize, however, that even when effective communications with the church hierarchy was impracticable the Gregorian Christian church appears to have been able to maintain uniformity almost entirely through community tribunals and informal pressures. Even less formally centralized subsystems enabled archetypal diasporas to maintain, through intensive communication networks, a high degree of uniformity in ethical expectations. Such uniformity was, in turn, a strong force for perpetuating identity.[25]

The degree to which both Jews and Armenians acquired a polyglot capacity was an extremely important factor in their usefulness to large polities. Part of their linguistic ability arose from their international contacts; it was also fostered by the requirement at any early age to adjust to a difficult sacral written language that was not commonly spoken. So important were linguistic skills that, for example, the 1569 treaty between France and the Ottoman sultan was composed by the interpreters for both sides in Hebrew. In circumstances like the sixteenth-century conflict between the Habsburgs and the Ottomans, a Jew such as Joseph of Nasi, who understandably hated the former, could become indispensable as diplomatic adviser to the sultan by use of a network of Jewish informants attached to the European Courts.[26]

Ethnoreligious identity was certainly prior to and more important than occupational roles. Nevertheless, such roles became so involved with identity that whole ranges of activity were excluded, whereas other activity was accepted by the diaspora communities as unavoidable. The special occupational roles held by Armenians and Jews were critically important for the exchange relationships that elites of both groups maintained with dominant polity elites. From the point of view of this section, however, the main issue is the effect of separate occupational niches upon the identities of the diasporas themselves. The circumstances of Islamic and Christian environments appear to have affected the diasporas differently. Islamic society, especially in cities, was not only highly segmented; this segmentation was accepted as the natural order of things. More specifically, as S. D. Goitein points out, the lack of strict territoriality in jurisdiction of the Islamic law schools made a nonterritorial Jewish religious law system seem natural. Conversely, even in Carolingian West Europe after the disappearance of the Syrian commercial colonies, "Jews" and "merchants" became synonomous terms, just as "Jews" and "moneylenders" were synonomous in eighteenth-century England.[27] Consequently, Jews in the West and both Jews and Armenians in Poland were the objects of harsh stereotyping. In Moslem countries, both diasporas were prominent in specific roles, but other ethnic groups also had their allocated places in the occupational spectrum. Some diaspora roles in Islam incurred opprobrium from other minorities—for example, the requirement that Jews dispose of bodies of executed persons. The Ottoman requirement that Jews throw the ecumenical patriarch's body in the Golden Horn during the Phanariot massacre of 1821 led, for example, to violent Greek reprisals against Jews.[28] Generally, however, neither role opprobrium nor role competition appears to have been as intense in Moslem societies as in European Christian environments even where the latter (as in Poland-Lithuania) had many occupational niches for different groups.

Apparently, a major factor prior to industrialization—which increased tensions in many modernizing societies—was the agrarian ethos of both nobles and peasants in Christian countries. This ethos tended to stereotype townsmen, especially those who were alien in belief and appearance, as parasites. Such stereotypes of Germans were apparent in Poland and Hungary before Jews were prominent there and in Spain were directed against Genoese. Of course, Moslem nomads also had their stereotypes of cowardly, grasping, talkative townsmen. But the overwhelmingly urban model for Islamic religion and culture precluded such feelings from emerging as dominant trends except during periods of nomadic incursion when all city dwellers suffered alike.[29]

Religious belief remained the heart of diaspora identity. Complete adherence to boundary mechanisms in matters like endogamy was strongly enforced by the same system of community tribunals that adjudicated commercial quarrels. The development of a distinctive Armenian alphabet about a century after the adoption of Christianity meant that Armenians were isolated from the propaganda of Zoroastrians using Pahlevi texts and Nestorian heretics using the Syriac alphabet. Theological communication with Byzantium, although constant until Chalcedon, was rendered more difficult.[30]

In later periods, the peculiar languages of the diasporas were often reduced to symbols of religious identity, for members usually conversed in adaptations of foreign languages. Hebrew had been replaced by Aramaic before the first-century dispersion from Palestine. After the Arab conquest, Jews throughout the Islamic world shifted to Arabic, whereas those in the northern Mediterranean areas adopted variants of Romance. Most of the latter, moving northward, developed Yiddish from Old High German, whereas the Iberian Jews at some point during the *reconquista* shifted to variants of the Spanish dialects. Somewhat divergent from standard Castilian, a form of this language (Ladin) for centuries remained the speech of Jewish refugees in the Ottoman empire. Armenians adopted languages like Polish when they were distant from their rural ethnic area. Throughout these processes of linguistic shift, Scriptures and liturgy remained in the original sacral languages. Strong border guard mechanisms were retained against employing foreign linguistic elements, however convenient or prestigious they might be, that suggested deviation in the direction of a hostile faith. One case of such a border guard in Yiddish was noted in chapter 1. Very probably a less obvious resort to linguistic boundary mechanisms appeared in the perpetuation among Jewish physicians in Poland of Arabic (regarded as the vehicle of a relatively tolerant faith) and

Greek instead of the Latin medical terms current among Christian physicians.[31] Latin might have opened doors to communication with the dominant elites, but, as Joseph II's effort to "make the Jews regular citizens" (that is, to Germanize them by eliminating their Yiddish "jargon") demonstrated, their identity would have been imperiled by such intercourse. Indeed, Jews in the Habsburg dominions encountered strong Jewish community opposition when they wished to enter general schools or universities.[32] Armenians reacted in much the same way; children were forbidden to learn Latin which was identified with the dreaded "Latin" church. "Better the Armenian faith in Hell than to get to Heaven with the Latin."[33]

There is considerable merit to Joseph Laurent's generally sympathetic criticism of the Gregorian church:

> Because it had become exclusively Armenian in its recruitment, the dedication of its members, its faith, and its tendencies, it lacked the power to struggle against national customs, being unable to invoke against their recalcitrance the authority of a general Christian organization above the very concept of nationality. At every level of the hierarchy, the Armenian church was the prisoner of those whom it had to direct or combat, because the church was merely for them and of them.[34]

Certainly the Armenian ecclesiastical organization has been identified for fifteen hundred years with a single ethnic group. Although unable to engage in extensive proselytizing, the church, like Judaism, Islam, and larger Christian denominations, has persisted in its concept of a worldwide mission in the divine plan. For the Gregorians, this mission was in practice largely confined to the Caucasus region, "Iberia" (Georgia), and "Albania" (present-day Dagestan).[35] Given the way the universal missions of larger religious bodies have occasionally been diverted—not necessarily perverted, for the balance of human values achieved through national identity has not yet been determined—it would be imprudent to reject the peculiar combinations of religion and ethnicity that diasporas have achieved.

The Rift between Eastern and Western Churches

To analyze the subtle theological reasons why the Eastern ("Orthodox") and the Western ("Catholic") churches drifted apart would transcend my design even more than consideration of doctrinal divergences of such "heretics" as the Gregorians. The sole purpose of my examination of the Orthodox-Catholic divergence is to supplement the discussion of imperial polity factors outlined earlier and to explain how this rift affected the linguistic and religious composition of East Europe. As numerous scholars with broader aims than mine have emphasized, the most fundamental division in Europe has been between Byzantium and its heirs and Rome and its secular progeny. Cultural and doctrinal differences interacted to set intangible boundaries. A basic factor was the extent to which the Greek language was regarded by its speakers as superlative. Probably no modern culture except the French has devoted so much of its energy to style and precision in linguistic usage, or has so consistently made correct usage the prime criterion for ethnic identity. As a recent writer puts it, "Many a Byzantine Greek was no doubt the product of a mixture, but whether the product of a mixture or not, he was a Greek nevertheless."[36]

The emphasis on Greek began long before Byzantium. Caesar, Brutus, and Cicero went to Greek centers like Rhodes to learn rhetoric in its original speech. Emperors, including Marcus Aurelius, prided themselves on their ability to converse in Greek, yet its forms were so demanding that they usually spoke from prepared texts in public.[37] It was scarcely avoidable that a Christian church centered on Constantinople should inherit this conviction of linguistic superiority. Indeed, once Hellenic culture had reasserted itself there, two factors tended to make Christians even more concerned with language than pagan rhetoricians had been. The culture of Hellenistic antiquity was essentially oral. This oral tradition survived in Byzantium, especially among laymen; but the possession of the Word in its original written form in the New Testament constituted a powerful motivation for considering Greek not merely superior but sacral—perhaps *the* sacral language. To the extent to which Christian theological disputes reflected pre-Christian philosophical divergences, precise formulation in the language of philosophy was essential to orthodox belief and ecclesiastical unity. To be sure, the task of accommodating Christianity and the pagan cultural heritage was at least as complicated as the process, discussed in chapter 5, by which the secular imperial myth and Christian universalism were accommodated. The fundamental issue was Christian acceptance of the classical rhetorical education even for boys destined for the clergy. Christian leaders indignantly rejected suggestions by the Emperor Julian "the Apostate" and his followers that Christians, having rejected the ancient religion, were unfit to study classics like the works of Homer.[38]

The process by which Christians trained in the classics adapted them to doctrine has continued through the centuries. Pagan myths are reinterpreted as allegories of Christian truths or of biblical figures. In Byzantine times the process was primarily literary, but it is most striking in its graphic manifestations. Three examples will suffice: angels supporting the throne or emblem of Christ were modeled on the Greek *Nikēs* (Victories); Euripides' "Telephus" was drawn upon to portray Isaac fleeing from Abraham; in the Anastasis, Christ pulling Adam out of Limbo (as in the mosaics of Hosios Lukas and Daphni monasteries) is modeled on Hercules dragging Cerberus from Hades.[39] Armed with such an elaborate symbolic repertory, the Byzantine church tried to express all Christian teaching in Hellenic forms. The customary interpretation of the Pentecostal "speaking in tongues" was that Byzantine Christians should do their best to evangelize all men by first teaching them Greek.[40]

It is possible, as one historian suggests, that consideration for the ancient traditions of the Egyptians, Iranians, and Semites—and indeed Jesus' own use of Aramaic—restrained the Byzantine church from demanding that these peoples learn Greek. Still, as discussed above, persistence among these groups of specific heresies of Greek origin that gradually became identified with different languages suggests that Greek linguistic intolerance was a factor even in the ancient Middle East. To counter such pressure, one early Christian writer demanded that Egyptian and Syriac be accepted as sacral languages along with the three (Greek, Hebrew, and Latin) ultimately canonized as holy languages by the dominant Christian tradition. By the seventh century, dissatisfaction with Greek linguistic demands played a part in the low level of resistance to Islam; in Palestine, for example, only Greek-speaking *poleis* held out for a long time.[41]

A common opinion that the Eastern in contrast to the Western church readily admitted diverse liturgical languages is, therefore, exaggerated. Karl Holl's summation is worth extended consideration:

> The official Christian church of the early ages was based everywhere on cultured languages and shoved the popular languages aside or encroached upon them both in the East and in the West. One should not be misled by the numerous Eastern translations of the Bible. Certainly there were Syrian, Coptic, Gothic, Armenian, Iberian [i.e., Georgian] translations, eventually even a Nubian translation. But all of them taken together do not imply that the Greek-speaking half of the Christian church was less averse to national speeches than was the Latin. None of these translations arose in the way that our missionaries create them today. No Greek ever learned a foreign dialect for Christianity's sake, in order to translate the Bible for another people. Early Christians never understood Paul's words (that there is neither Greek nor Jew, neither Barbarian nor Scythian) in that way. To be sure, when the members of a people translated the Bible themselves and thereby raised their national language to a written cultural language, the church accepted it—but no

more than that. Nowhere did the church ever further the development or even the persistence of a popular language. It was not the great flexibility of the church but rather the strong self-consciousness of the peoples which provided the East with its rich garland of Bible translations.[42]

Not only were concessions to Middle Eastern languages few and reluctant; the seventh- and eighth-century reconquest of Balkan areas of the empire overrun by Slavs proceeded not merely with compulsory Christianization but with as complete cultural Hellenization as was feasible.[43]

Nevertheless, the nuances of difference between Eastern and Western ecclesiastical practice in the linguistic field played a critical role in the eventual division between the two church-civilizations. The most generally accepted scholarly position seems to be that no doctrinal or even disciplinary grounds appeared for considering Latin to be the unique Western liturgical language until the eighth century. As late as 370, according to one scholar, the Roman church used Greek. Afterward, for reasons very similar to those that led Greek ecclesiastics to make an accommodation with Hellenic culture, the Roman church sought to reinterpret Latin classics in a Christian manner. Because the bishops and their staffs constituted the only considerable body of educated men, they naturally followed Roman administrative practice in using Latin. The great mass of the indigenous Christian population was slowly moving from Low Latin dialects to varieties of Romance. The value of a single ecclesiastical language for maintaining doctrinal unity was, as in the East, evident. But not until Charlemagne was exclusive use of the Latin liturgy made a matter of church discipline, not doctrine. By the tenth century, papal adherents called Latin one of the three holy languages, destined for use in the northern and western regions of the world.[44] Presented in such terms, the claims for Latin encountered very little opposition because Romance-speakers still regarded their dialects as, at best, colloquial forms of the superior literary Latin, and Germanic groups did not often consider their tongues to be competitors for liturgical usage.

A more basic problem arose from Greek unwillingness to accept Latin as a peer. Despite the imperial prestige of Latin, few Greeks learned it until Diocletian's reign, shortly before the triumph of Christianity.[45] At that point, the principal motives for learning Latin were study of law, military command, and above all the desire to perpetuate the imperial myth of eternal Rome. Dagron contends that certain subjects related to the polity were thought in Latin. In principle, therefore, the ideal Roman citizen was bilingual, with separate "linguistic codes" (see chapter 8): Latin for power, Greek for culture, the civilizing work of Athens providing moral force for Rome in return for protection, as Greek rhetoricians liked to envisage the accommodation.[46]

Obviously, such a division put intellectual subjects, philosophy and theology, for example, squarely in the Hellenic sphere. Byzantine theologians often dismissed Latin as impoverished, asserting that it lacked words to express theological concepts precisely.[47] Early Western Christian thinkers tended to accept this verdict. Being middle class, most of them lacked the polish in Greek that slave tutors sometimes imparted to the pagan senatorial aristocracy. Very often Western theologians simply used calques of Greek terms out of fear of mistranslating in a freer manner. The same practice was followed later in transmitting theological concepts from Latin to the Western vernaculars.[48] By 449, the Greek spoken by Roman representatives at church synods was so inadequate that they could not follow the proceedings. The urgent desire of the Roman church to present its claims effectively was a major reason, apparently, for the election of eleven Sicilian Greeks and Greek-speaking refugees from the East among the thirteen popes chosen during 678–752.[49] Nevertheless, the gap in linguistic knowledge kept growing, leading to independent development of philosophical and theological thought in the West and in the East.[50]

These divergences, a recent Catholic commentary suggests, resulted in an almost insurmountable phenomenological barrier by the ninth century. The doctrinal issue revolved around the *filioque* clause in the Latin version of the Nicaean Creed. The Western church understood the formula to imply that the Holy Spirit proceeds from the Father and the Son, whereas Greeks took the Latin *ex* ("from") to convey the much stronger relationship of the Greek *ékh*.[51] The semantic misunderstanding may have been manipulated by the ecumenical patriarch Photios; parallel misunderstandings of Greek formulas alienated the Latin clergy. Byzantine spokesmen reproached the popes for failing to understand the language of the New Testament and of most of the Church Fathers, whereas popes criticized Byzantium for claiming to be the Roman empire without knowing the Roman language.

One should not, of course, ascribe the schism that led in 1054 to formal mutual excommunications to phenomenological barriers alone. There were very real clashes of interest, most apparent when Byzantine authority was still strong in central Italy. The art historian Otto von Simson has detected a covert conflict between papal and Byzantine imperial symbols in the mosaic scenes of late sixth-century Ravenna.[52] At one point during the seventh century, the partially Latin army of the Ravenna exarchate rescued a pope from arrest by the emperor's representatives.[53] The way Byzantine omissions led popes to rely on the Franks and ultimately to crown a separate Western emperor has already been recounted. Certainly funda-

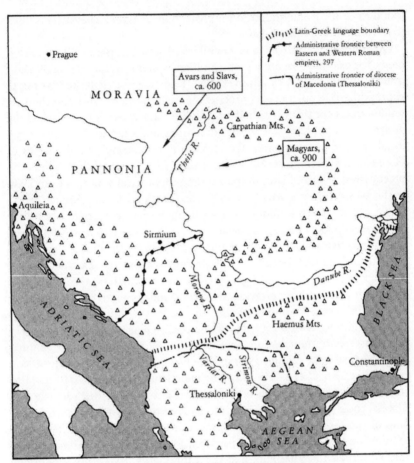

MAP 4. Frontiers between Eastern and Western Christendom

mental differences on the position of the papacy itself constituted a barrier to continued unity; nor were other doctrinal differences entirely the result of verbal misunderstandings. Nevertheless, it is noteworthy that the sharpest conflicts between the Western and the Eastern civilizations did not occur along a frontier zone of perpetual warfare, as occurred between Christians and Moslems, but in increasingly intemperate long-distance exchanges. Not until the mid-eleventh century did these disputes culminate in major armed clashes, when popes (mainly because of their conflicts with the Holy Roman emperors) entered an alliance with the aggressive Sicilian Norman kingdom. The violent rupture culminated in the crusaders' conquest of Constantinople in 1204. In between there were not only attempts at reconciliation by negotiation but spontaneous expressions of Christian solidarity, for example, in joint services in Syria and Palestine.

The basic reasons why an intra-Christian frontier of conflict did not develop were, nevertheless, geopolitical. In the late Roman empire, a fairly well-defined linguistic boundary between Latin- and Greek-language spheres existed in the continuously settled agricultural areas of the southern Balkans. This boundary was understood by contemporaries to be equivalent to the division between *pars occidentalis* and *pars orientalis*, West and East.[54] Latin prevailed south of the Danube as far as the Haemus Mountains, then down the Morava-Vardar valley toward the Aegean Sea. First- and second-century emperors tried to extend the area of Latin speech southward to the sea by settling veterans in the towns. Located, as the urban colonies were, in the midst of Greek-speaking peasants, they gradually disappeared as migration from the West diminished, leaving Thessaloniki and its vicinity entirely Greek in language.[55]

Although recognized by contemporaries, the linguistic boundary was less important practically than imperial and ecclesiastical frontiers that ran close to it. But these administrative divisions (which ordinarily coincided, although the "diocese" in imperial usage was a larger unit than the bishop's jurisdiction later given that title) deviated from the linguistic boundary at a few significant points. In 297, Diocletian—who certainly gave no thought to Christian divisions and very little to language—transferred two Latin-speaking provinces (upper Moesia and Praevalitana, roughly equivalent to present-day Montenegro and northern Serbia) from the prefecture of Italy to the Greek-speaking prefecture of Illyricum. The Western empire continued to claim not only these provinces, but the entire prefecture of Illyricum, whereas as the authority of the West declined the Eastern Roman empire asserted claims to the diocese of Illyria, a distinct area farther north under the prefecture of Italy.[56] In 421, Theodosius II, exercising the power he claimed as head of the entire Christian church, transferred the disputed areas from the jurisdiction of the pope (as patriarch of the West) to that of the patriarch of Constantinople. Theodosius extended the archepiscopal province of Thessaloniki as far north as Pannonia, part of which had been overrun by German invaders.[57]

Jurisdictional disputes over the lower Balkans, especially Thessaloniki, continued for centuries. The devastating Slavic invasions of the sixth and seventh centuries reduced the Latin and possibly the Greek rural populations of the Balkans to vestiges and drove the ecclesiastical organizations into the few remaining cities. Byzantine recolonization enlisted the active cooperation of the bishops of the southern part of the prefecture of Illyricum, that is, of Greece proper. Conversion of the Slavs during the ninth century was accompanied, approximately as far north as the present

Greek border, by cultural and linguistic Hellenization.[58] During this process, the Thessaloniki archbishops and their suffragans appear to have become integral parts of the Constantinople patriarchate, although some lingering attachments to the Roman patriarchate were evident in sentiment and in artistic styles. Apart from the practical exigencies of alliance with Byzantine power, the extreme difficulty of communication with Rome made this transfer of jurisdiction (which implied no doctrinal shift) almost inevitable. Instead of a continuous linguistic boundary between Greek and Latin or a definite ecclesiastical frontier, an immense wedge of Slavic and Turkic groups, still pagan, covered the northern and central Balkan peninsula. Consequently, until the ninth century there was no real disputed frontier between East and West, except for intermittent minor clashes. Even the earlier conditions for such a frontier zone had vanished; but they left behind sentiments and legalistic issues that were to exert considerable influence in the future.

Before examining the sequel, it is important to note that there was another putative frontier between Eastern and Western Roman empires and between Eastern and Western Christian churches in southern Italy. Nominally, there was a third—the desert frontier in Libya—but that never became significant and was overrun by Islam during the seventh century. The weight of scholarship is clear that in Christian times the southern Italian frontier never corresponded to a real linguistic boundary. Although Greek colonies in Sicily and southern Italy had been important earlier, the rural population was overwhelmingly Latin-speaking by the fourth century A.D.[59] Consequently, rivalries revolved around Greek cultural influences in the cities, churches, and monasteries and were made salient by Byzantine imperial and ecclesiastical pretensions. As suggested earlier, these two bases for dispute did not always coincide because many Greek-speaking ecclesiastics were firm adherents of Rome. But the desires of the Byzantine emperors to retain their Italian possessions as part of their claim to universal dominion led them, especially the iconoclast Leo the Isaurian, to integrate the southern Italian areas administratively into the Constantinople patriarchate. Leo decreed the introduction of the Byzantine liturgy in Illyricum and in Italy, though apparently without much effect in the latter. After 800 the emperors also confiscated papal estates in Italy. Late in the ninth century, the introduction of the Greek liturgy was actually implemented in Sicilian and Calabrian churches through the assistance of Greek monks who had originally fled from iconoclast emperors. Basilian monks even kept Greek liturgical practices alive in cities like Naples beyond Byzantine jurisdiction. Some Apulian dioceses, on the other hand, remained Latin, although Constantinople influenced the appointment of their bishops.[60] The military successes of Byzantium against the Moslems in southern Italy down to the early eleventh century enhanced the diffusion of Greek culture.

As Marc Bloch has noticed, even in that early period the linguistic division was not wholly irrelevant to jurisdictional claims. In the tenth century, a Lombard bishop argued that all Romance-speaking areas of southern Italy should belong to the kingdom of Italy (under the Holy Roman empire) rather than to Byzantium.[61] Very soon after the culmination of Byzantine reconquests, however, Norman forces advanced against Byzantines and Moslems alike. An exceedingly complicated situation arose. As Byzantine areas were conquered, their Greek (or Greek-rite) bishops accepted Norman rule in accordance with the Eastern tradition of bowing to a new secular authority. Insecure in their first capital (Mileto in Calabria), however, the Normans desired a Latin bishop. The popes—whom the Greek bishops were reluctant to acknowledge anyway—were ready to accept their Norman allies' requests for new bishops in accordance with the papal custom of appointing bishops acceptable to any new Western rulers. "The preponderance of a Latin bishop was essential in this official and administrative milieu, where the influence of a Greek hierarch would have been dissipated because the Normans would have mistrusted the influence of such a stranger—who would always have been suspected of nationalism," writes a historian of the church dispute.[62] The Normans also turned over abandoned monasteries to the Latin Benedictines and subordinated remaining Greek monks to them. All of these measures suggest a clear awareness of the penetrative power of the church organization, as compared to the transitory impact of a polity swollen by rapid military conquest.

As the Norman conquests—from Moslems—proceeded in Sicily, the new rulers installed additional Latin bishops. Sometimes, however, the Normans for a while acceded to the urban populations' desires for Greek prelates, as long as they accepted Roman patriarchal jurisdiction. Once their kingdom was secure, in fact, the Normans often appear to have preferred Greek secular clergy and Byzantine-rite monks under Roman jurisdiction, in line with the Norman kings' practice of balancing Greek, Latin, and even Moslem elements in their administration. The noncelibate Greek parish clergy posed more of a problem for the secular order of the kingdom than for the papacy, however. Priests' sons who did not enter holy orders remained free, an anomaly in the feudal countryside.[63] In Apulia, the primarily Latin dioceses were placed under a new Latin archbishop of Otranto; but at the parish level Greek priests and the Byzantine liturgy were not disturbed for a long time.

To sum up, there never was a real frontier zone between Eastern and Western Christian churches in southern Italy. Shifts in authority took place quickly, as often as not through conflict with Moslems rather than the other Christians. Both Byzantines and Normans were anxious to maintain the complete loyalty of church authorities, whom they correctly perceived —as explained earlier in this chapter—as potent influences on the masses of the population. As long as such loyalty was assured, language and liturgical rite had little immediate significance. Doctrinal issues were hardly present. The dispute over the pope's jurisdiction as patriarch of the West did not directly affect the broader question of papal authority in the universal church. Nevertheless, as Bernard Leib writes, Byzantine efforts to remove areas from papal jurisdiction and the papal alliance to the aggressive Normans exacerbated the long-standing cleavage: "In the eyes of the Byzantines this dispossession indicated Norman distrust of their rites, and, additionally, preponderance of the Latin liturgy. In southern Italy peoples of very different civilizations, each proud of its culture, confronted each other."[64]

Triangular Ecclesiastical Competition in East Central Europe

Neither in the southern Balkans nor in southern Europe did friction between the Eastern and the Western churches result in a real frontier conflict zone. Consequently, such friction as existed produced no lasting effect on ethnic identities. Conversely, in a broad region from the Adriatic to the Baltic, contact between these branches of Christianity constituted the strongest formative influence in determining ultimate ethnic boundaries, particularly among Slavic groups. Yet one should not regard this process as either simple or continuous. In chapter 3, I noted how the emergence of the Austrian military frontier with Islam in the sixteenth century immensely complicated what had been a relatively clear frontier between Orthodox Serbs and Catholic Croats. Elsewhere in East Central Europe, complicating factors, although appearing earlier, were no less intense. The principal complication was the existence not merely of an intensifying rivalry between Eastern (Orthodox) and Western (Catholic) churches as a whole, but the increasing awareness of the popes from the ninth century on that the German Holy Roman emperors and their specific church organization might present as strong a challenge to papal authority as the Byzantine imperial-church combination.

The first major manifestation of this triangular conflict appeared in the famous episode of the mission of Constantine (Cyril) and Methodius to the Danubian and Moravian Slavs. The history has been discussed at such length that I hesitate to try to sum it up. Nevertheless, precisely because conflicting interpretations have produced a wealth of complementary evidence, the episode is exceptionally useful for understanding the fundamental boundary-setting mechanisms at work.

Mission activity is especially important for ethnic identity because it unavoidably poses the question of which language is to be used for proselytizing. By the mid-ninth century, both the Western and the Eastern churches, as indicated above, strongly preferred to maintain the three holy languages—or rather the one that appealed to each church. A striking feature of the Western church was the willingness of the Frank rulers and the entire ecclesiastical organization associated with them to endorse Latin as the exclusive liturgical language and vehicle for internal ecclesiastical communication. Although German monks at times cultivated their vernacular in preserving sagas and other literature, Alcuin and Charlemagne had been, at the least, ambiguous about such pagan survivals. As the recent treatment by A. P. Vlasto concludes, "There is much in favor of the view that Charlemagne's personal enthusiasm for Latin culture and imposition of Latin uniformity on the Frankish church put an end to its further Germanization; no German dialect was accepted as a liturgical language."[65] Consequently, wherever German missions appeared, although they preached and taught in the vernacular, Latin dominated. That situation in no way precluded German penetration in customs, personnel, and life style, but it did imply a sharp separation of linguistic from other identity factors, especially at the ecclesiastical level.

Fear of heresy or pagan relapse also affected the Byzantine church's opposition to a Slavic liturgy, although the consistent conviction that Greek was the only language really fitted for theology played a part. Up to the 860s, as in the reconquest of the Aegean area, any use of Slavic in church affairs was regarded merely as a measure transitional to Hellenization, which ultimately (in contrast to German advancement of Latin) meant use of Greek in all spheres of life.[66] By the mid-ninth century, however, the Byzantine church and polity confronted a formidable adversary in the Turkic Bulgar khans ruling a large Slavic population just north of the Aegean Sea. Their "tsar," Boris, although accepting baptism, was impatient at Patriarch Photios's delay in conceding a hierarchy. Consequently, Boris secured the promise of an archepiscopal province from Pope Nicholas I. This gesture seems to have brought the Byzantines around, and Boris was content to return to their ecclesiastical aegis.[67] This sequence of events had repercussions far away on the middle Danube. Rostislav, prince of the large Slavic group in Moravia, was also seeking to establish an autonomous church. Ever since Charlemagne had defeated the Turkic Avar overlords of the Danubian Slavs in 796, missionaries from Bavaria (Salzburg and Passau) had been penetrating the region as well as Slovene-inhabited areas farther south. In 855, however, Rostislav drove out the Bavarian priests while retaining missionaries, possibly Italians from the patriarch of Aquileia, although it was also under Frank suzerainty. Later the Aquileia patriarchate was dominated by a series of German incumbents, but during the ninth century, at least, both Slovenes and Danubian Slavs regarded Aquileian missionaries as more tolerant of their ethnic identity.[68]

Like the Bulgars, Rostislav turned to Nicholas I (861–62) to obtain an ecclesiastical structure independent from overweening neighbors. In 863, apparently Nicholas dispatched two missionaries from the Thessaloniki vicariate, Constantine and Methodius; but by then Rostislav had been defeated and compelled to readmit the German missionaries.[69] Hence Constantine and Methodius turned southward to a Slavic prince in Pannonia. There their efforts became embroiled in the complicated legal position of the area. As noted above, the region had regularly been part of the Western Roman empire and the patriarchate of the West. Diocletian's transfers, however, had brought Eastern imperial jurisdiction very close to the Pannonian diocese's capital, Sirmium. Leo the Isaurian, during his quarrels with the papacy, had consigned all of Pannonia to the Constantinople patriarch. The question was practically moot, nevertheless, until Charlemagne's recovery of Pannonia from the Avars. Instead of returning Sirmium, which apparently was in ruins, and the surrounding region either to Byzantium or to the pope, he assigned it to German ecclesiastical jurisdiction.[70] The stage was set, therefore, for a triangular struggle for missionary activity that became the prelude to centuries of conflict in East Central Europe. For the moment, the new pope (Hadrian II) seized the opportunity presented by Constantine and Methodius to make the latter archbishop of a revived Sirmium see under his papal jurisdiction.

The complicated situation was still further exacerbated by the question of liturgical language. The two "apostles to the Slavs," as they became known, had developed a Slavic (Cyrillic) alphabet and liturgy based on dialects spoken by the Slavic groups near their home base of Thessaloniki. Later, these dialects became known as Bulgarian, hence the term "Old Bulgarian" sometimes used for this liturgical language, otherwise known as "Church Slavonic." Both missionaries were completely orthodox in the form and content of their liturgical innovation. Apparently, the Byzantine emperor had finally sanctioned the vernacular liturgy, which offered the only chance for the relatively weak Byzantine mission effort to compete in Central Europe. Constantine himself defended it strongly on the basis of the words of St. Paul: "There are doubtless many languages in the world and none is without meaning; but if I do not know the meaning of a language, I shall be a foreigner to the speaker, and the speaker a foreigner to me" (1 Corinthians 14:10–11).[71] His principal critics, or rather fierce attackers, were the German bishops, who had Methodius imprisoned. A new pope, John VIII, sent a legate to have him released. Methodius moved on to Moravia, briefly again in a position to welcome him. It now seems fairly certain that while publicly instructing Methodius to be prudent in his orthodoxy John also dispatched a letter authorizing the Slavonic liturgy as long as the Gospel was read in Latin. As a Catholic historian of the episode judiciously remarks, "the Pontiff's plan was to enlighten the Moravians without informing the Romans, to get Methodius out of trouble without getting into it himself."[72] One version of the papal bull "*Industriae tuae*" does appear to endorse Constantine's argument for a vernacular liturgy. The missive was apparently falsified, however, before it could be implemented. Stephen V, John's successor, was persuaded by the version he saw that the Slavic missions should be terminated, and in 885 he forbade their liturgy. By the time a true version had reappeared four centuries later, the entire project for a separate liturgy had long been buried.[73]

In the meantime, the new Moravian ruler and the papacy alike were seeking reconciliation with the Germans and probably with the Byzantines as well. Neither of Methodius's allies, therefore, wanted to pursue the tactic of endorsing a "third force" in Central Europe. Before the tactical situation could again alter, the Magyar invasion overran Moravia and Pannonia, confronting both Byzantium and the Holy Roman empire with extreme difficulties.

Once again a pagan invasion had decisively separated the rival churches. Gradually, the Roman church acquired a dominant position along the Adriatic coast.[74] Despite their subsequent ability to carry out military campaigns on the lower Danube and even to invade Hungary shortly after its conversion to Latin Christianity, Byzantines were unable to penetrate Central Europe via mission activity after the ninth century. Consequently, a fairly stable frontier developed between the two churches, or, indeed, Eastern and Western Christian civilizations. This frontier lasted until the Ottoman invasion, except for a zone in Bosnia inhabited for several centuries by Bogomil "heretics."

Termination of the last major pagan menace to East Central Europe through conversion of the Magyars did not, therefore, restore a meaningful triangular competition such as had prevailed during the ninth century. Instead—to oversimplify a bit—two separate areas of rivalry developed. Byzantine-Western rivalry shifted to the border zones of Rus, with the papacy, the German church, and other Latin Christian organizations usually in alliance. In the Danube basin and other regions in the confines of the Holy Roman empire, on the other hand, the practical exclusion of major Byzantine intervention left a tacit struggle between the papacy and the German ecclesiastical organizations.

This struggle rarely even attained the level of overt verbal denunciation; it was usually conducted instead by symbolic acts in relation to East Central European rulers. The nuances of the struggle cannot be followed here, but the main outlines appear to be fairly clear. Walter Ullmann argues that "because created by the papacy, the Western Roman emperor was a reflexion of the universality which was epitomized in the Roman Church."[75] Hence the emperor was impelled to combine missionary activity and military expansion to sustain his pretensions to universality. The tenth-century victories of the German kings—several did not even claim the title of emperor—over the Magyars immensely enhanced their prestige and opened the way for a revival of the Western empire. By the reign of Otto I ("the Great," 962–73) the eastern relationships of Christianity had once again altered drastically. Certainly the Ottonian echo of the old Roman slogan, "the army creates the emperor," designed to emphasize independence from the pope, would not have enjoyed even the limited success it attained except for the aura of victory in the east.[76] Instead of a semicircle of aggressive pagans extending from Scandinavia, through the Wends of the Elbe-Oder region, to the Magyars of the Danube, Western Christendom confronted, except for the remaining Wends, putative polities eager to acquire a higher civilization. As Herbert Ludat writes, "Acceptance of Christianity became a requirement of political wisdom for many princes, for along with modernizing their states, Christianity decisively strengthened the princes' domestic and internal positions. It was the sole guarantee of political freedom."[77]

With the important exception of the Přemyslid dynasty in Bohemia, which had already been converted by German missionaries and continued to rely on German settlers, the established Christian forces along this open frontier zone were German. Otto I was determined to create a broad imperial polity; there were powerful German ecclesiastical authorities also eager to extend their control. On the other hand, the papacy was evolving a broader, more consistent policy out of its hesitant ninth-century efforts to avoid complete German ecclesiastical domination of Central Europe. Consequently, the papal offices opposed efforts by German archbishops to subordinate bishops of the emerging polities beyond the Holy Roman imperial frontier.

The first major attempt was by the archbishop of Magdeburg, a new creation fostered by Otto I in his residential seat. Under the very confused circumstances of the 960s, Otto and his prelate apparently helped found a Polish church center at Poznan or nearby Gniezno; there were implications that the Polish King Mieszko I as well as his church were subordinated to their imperial patrons. About 1000, however, the papacy intervened to secure the independence of both Polish institutions. Instead, Poland became a nominal fief of the papacy itself, with its own archbishop at Gniezno.[78] Nevertheless, no open break with the emperor of that time, Otto III, occurred. Influenced by his Byzantine maternal heritage, Otto evidently considered a "family of kings" with himself at the pinnacle to be his goal. He entitled himself the "Thirteenth Apostle," dreamed of reuniting Christendom, and actually dispatched a mission to Rus.[79] For the moment, the Curia could cooperate with such grandiose but nebulous schemes, which coincided with papal efforts to expand Rome's authority eastward. At the same time, the Curia strengthened its direct supervision of East Central European churches. In 1000, St. Stephen of Hungary brought about the conversion of his country, relying on Cluniac advisers but like the Polish kings accepting Otto III's nominal suzerainty.

Stephen and his successors had more pressing problems, arising from the domestic turbulence and Byzantine attacks, just as the Polish kings had to face internal pagan reaction, Wend incursions, and possible invasion by Rus princes. It would be very misleading to suggest, therefore, that there was a fixed papal-Polish-Hungarian alignment against the Germans even during the periods when popes and emperors were at loggerheads. A generation later, when the papacy refused to approve the Hamburg-Bremen Archbishop Adalbert's proposal for a "Nordic patriarchate" including Scandinavia, he withdrew it gracefully. About the same time, the Polish King Boleslaw Chrobry openly renounced the emperor's suzerainty. In 1133, on the other hand, one finds Innocent II, for ephemeral political reasons, granting Magdeburg ecclesiastical jurisdiction over all Poland.[80]

In some ways, symbolic acts appear to have been more consistent than jurisdictional decrees. Not only was the Magyar Stephen canonized; in 1254 the Poles were granted a second patron saint (Stanislaus) to replace an earlier one (Adalbert) whose revered body had been stolen by the Czechs. Through the Stanislaus legend, the Polish people were elevated to the sacral status attained earlier by the French. In a way reminiscent of the doctrine that the church is the Mystical Body of Christ, Poland was identified with Stanislaus's body; from the thirteenth century on partitioning Poland was considered equivalent to dismembering the saint.[81] Similar cults, extremely important as unifying symbols for dynasties and subsequently for peoples, were recognized in Scandinavia, Bohemia, and England. Where once pagan adversaries confronted the Germans, an intangible crescent of sacral attractions hemmed them in on their eastern and northern frontiers. Conversely, although the Ottonians honored Charlemagne as a saint, in contrast to northern and East European heroes, he was never recognized as such by the papacy, then or during more formal Hohenstaufen efforts (1165) to canonize him.[82] Gradually, the example of French independence as a sacral monarchy, supported by the Curia and French monastic orders, became a model for the East European monarchs.

Throughout the periods just sketched, friction between the large Orthodox polities in the Black Sea river valleys and the papal-sponsored kingdoms that had also arisen about 1000 was slight, for great forests separated their settlements. Up to the Mongol invasions even the relatively weak Rus trading polities near the Baltic were able to hold their own against Scandinavian and Teutonic Order expansion along the coast. The Mongol disruption destroyed the main Rus Orthodox center in Kiev and pushed the surviving Rus principalities in different directions. Those established in the northwest fell initially under the control of pagan Lithuania. The number of East Slavs absorbed by this incipient polity was so great and their cultural level so relatively advanced that in the early fourteenth century absorption of the Lithuanian elite in a new Orthodox polity appeared probable. Like the Magyars, however, native Lithuanians were bolstered by a peculiar prephilological myth. They believed that their Baltic tongue was derived from Latin via Roman colonists along the Niemen River. Consequently, Lithuanians looked down on both Polish and East Slavic languages—although the Lithuanian epic claiming Roman origin was actually preserved in Church Slavonic, the only written language at the nobles' disposal.

During the fifteenth century, about half of the Lithuanians were converted to Orthodoxy and absorbed among the Slavic population.[83] The western portion became Catholic, however, as did the Jagiellonian dynasty. This conversion, along with the increased Polish noble influence after the two polities were joined in personal union in 1386, was decisive. Although the union was motivated primarily by dynastic reasons (the Poles required a strong ruler like the recently baptized Wladislaw Jagiello to repulse partition schemes advanced by Brandenburg and Hungary), it also represented a culmination of Curia efforts to expand eastward.[84] The last Piast king, Casimir the Great (1333–70), had welcomed Curia financial support against the still-pagan Lithuanians, the infidel Tatars, and especially the *Impios Ruthenorum*—the successful local Orthodox East Slav missions. As yet Moscow was too remote to be considered seriously. Casimir actually acquired the southwestern principality of Halich, until then almost wholly Ruthenian, that is, Orthodox East Slav. He was conciliatory toward its nobility; although a few decades later a Catholic hierarchy was introduced, the Polish kings continued to tolerate the Orthodox hierarchy.[85] Eleven years after Casimir died, this group of bishops was even placed under the metropolitan of Kiev "and All Russia," by then resident in Moscow.

The position of the Kiev metropolitanate was, in fact, one of the most sensitive indicators of Orthodox-Catholic rivalry. As the sole central institution surviving from the period of Kievan Rus, the metropolitanate exerted a strong appeal to the nostalgia of the East Slavs for their period of glory. Alexandre Eck summarizes the situation as follows:

> The princes represented in medieval Russian society the centers of territorial organization around which the elements of defense crystallized. Another organizing force functioned alongside them, the church, whose activity extended without distinction to all the principalities at once. The religious organization was at that time the only centralized institution common to all Russia. The church acted as the only cement tying together the separated parts of the dismembered territory and the thinly spread-out nation.[86]

For half a century (1240–99) following the Mongol catastrophe, the metropolitan resided in the principality of Halich in the Carpathian foothills. For approximately twenty-eight years (1299–1327) more he lived in Vladimir, at the time the strongest of the principalities in the northeast forests. From 1371 on the metropolitanate (replaced by the patriarchate at the end of the sixteenth century) was in Moscow. Establishment of the metropolitans there constituted a significant step toward that principality's assumption of the leadership of Orthodox Russia. During 1354–81 and 1416–19, however, the Lithuanians insisted on a separate metropolitan as highest ecclesiastical authority, directly under the Constantinople patriarch, for their Orthodox subjects. Moscow, however, refused to recognize the Lithuanian institution of a metropolitan in Kiev during 1458–1596 who maintained relations with the pope.[87] A third Orthodox metropolitanate existed in Halich for a time after 1302 and again after 1539 under Polish aegis.

Orthodox bishops in union with Constantinople generally were prepared to recognize Polish secular authority, and (see chapter 8) as the prestige of the Polish language increased, even to employ it for all except liturgical purposes. The pressures resulting from the Counter-Reformation led a significant minority of the Orthodox clergy (mostly in Halich or, as it came to be known, Galicia) to adhere to Rome while retaining a Ruthenian (Uniate) rite. These priests were allowed to marry; both they and their bishops continued to use a Church Slavonic liturgy. Lack of education kept the Uniate clergy's prestige low, and the problem of finding a place in feudal society for priests' sons who did not take holy orders was solved by reducing them to serfs. Polish Jesuits, eager to absorb the Galician East Slavs completely, continued to emphasize educating the Orthodox in their schools. Orthodox Ruthenians considered the Uniates worse than Latin-rite proselytizers, preferring cultural Polonization to religious conversion.[88] After the Polish Partitions, the Austrian government in Galicia significantly improved the educational standards of the Uniate clergy, whom it regarded as a useful barrier to Polish hegemony and Russian attraction.[89] The large bodies of Uniates in the kingdom of Hungary (some Ruthenian, or Ukrainian, as they became known in the nineteenth century, most Rumanian) remained a neglected part of the Catholic majority of the Habsburg empire.[90] By the nineteenth century, Uniate Ukrainians began to play an important role in national consciousness. The Ukrainian movement derived its principal myth, however, from the cossack experience on the Islamic-Christian frontier rather than from the Catholic-Orthodox frontier within old Poland.

Reformation and Ethnicity

A detailed exposition of the influence of the Protestant Reformation and the Catholic Counter-Reformation on ethnicity would require volumes. Although all religious divisions produce complex effects, the ultimate results of the religious conflicts of the sixteenth to seventeenth centuries were so contradictory as almost to defy analysis. Peculiar examples of the apparently capricious effects on identity appear in the East Central European areas just considered. In Poland, for example, Orthodox Ruthenian nobles could rarely be converted by Catholic proselytizers. A moderately large number became Lutheran during the first wave of the Reformation, however; after that experience, many of the converts were induced without much difficulty to join Catholicism rather than return to Orthodoxy. In Transylvania a mirror-image effect is observable. Rumanians could be converted to Protestantism only after having become Catholic at some time in the past.[91] The explanation in both cases appears to be the loss of continuity in identity, a complete break with the Greco-Slavonic tradition, which made further change easy.[92]

Hermann Aubin and his associates emphasize the cross-cutting effects of Lutheran and Catholic influences in central Germany.[93] For centuries German historians have complained, with good reason, that the Reformation division of their country delayed its unity, as contrasted to polities like England, France, and Spain, where one side or the other won a decisive victory in the sixteenth century. Given the extreme weakness of the Holy Roman empire just before the Reformation, however, one may wonder whether religious strife was the cause or the effect. In Germany proper, the religious wars and the principle *cuius regio eius religio* (whoever rules determines the religion) unquestionably reinforced particularist tendencies. On the other hand, the Habsburgs temporarily overcame particularism under the banner of religious unity. One may wonder, again, whether any stronger German state than theirs could have emerged during that period without Catholic religious legitimization and concrete assistance from Spanish arms.

Certainly the events of the Reformation period eliminated some polities that appeared to be developing strong ethnic myths. The English-speaking reader will think immediately of the independent kingdom of Scotland and the vestiges of native rule in Ireland. The case of Bohemia has already been mentioned several times. It is important here to recall that the proto-Reformation Hussite movement was highly ambiguous in its ethnic implications. Insofar as it brought the issue of language to the forefront, the Hussite movement undoubtedly constituted a precociously "modern" movement, possibly because of the peculiar intensity of linguistic distinctions in Bohemia. Ecclesiastical organization in Bohemia had derived from the Mainz archdiocese rather than from the more aggressively German Hamburg, Magdeburg, or Salzburg authorities. Moreover, the missionaries arrived under the aegis of the native Přemyslid dynasty, which had brought in so many German colonists and burghers that their kingdom was thoroughly mixed in background by the fourteenth century. After that, Bohemia was inherited by several primarily German dynasties. At least by 1294 there was enough local aristocratic reaction against "foreigners" to delay (until 1348) foundation of the University of Prague. Even earlier Bohemian priests, whether Czechs or Germans, had resented the influx of outsiders as competitors.[94]

Both German and Czech historians disagree on the extent to which John Hus and his followers were opposed in 1409 to Germans as such or simply as foreigners. He is said to have remarked that he preferred good Germans to bad Bohemians and desired a nation including both ethnic elements. But Hus certainly identified Rome with foreigners, apparently burning only Germans as "heretics," during his few years of power. It is not surprising that most of the university student body and professors, together with many German bourgeois, left Prague. In some measure, however, the opposition to Hus was a class conflict between the learned and wealthy half of the population and the Czech artisans who demanded exclusive use of their language in preaching, but tolerated Germans who had been settled in Bohemia a long time and had absorbed the Czech language.[95]

There is considerable irony in the repetition of the religious conflict in

Bohemia nearly two centuries later, though the tragic violence of the seventeenth-century struggle renders inappropriate Karl Marx's dictum that history repeats itself as farce. Although they made the myth of the Hussites their central ideology, the Protestant nobility and bourgeoisie were reluctant to resist to the bitter end for fear of unleashing a Czech peasant uprising. Furthermore, although this time the only available allies for the Protestants were Germans, the Czech anti-Habsburg party was just as determined as the Hussites to roll back German immigration and cultural influence. This ideological aspect of their linguistic emphasis is indicated by the fact that most Protestant Bohemian noble families, according to a sympathetic historian, had not spoken Czech for generations. As in the earlier conflict, however, the anti-Catholic party began, in 1609, by demanding that all learn Czech. In 1615, the Bohemian Diet provided that inheritances should go to younger children who had learned Czech if their elder siblings had not; nor was an immigrant family to be allowed to hold office until after three generations' residence and attainment of proficiency in Czech.[96] As noted in chapter 6, the Habsburgs and their imported nobility practically reversed such provisions after winning complete victory in the Thirty Years' War. Consequently, Bohemia provides a fairly clear case of Reformation and Counter-Reformation leading to the submergence for centuries of a "historic nation" identified with a long-established polity and its symbols.

It can also be argued that an incipient Flemish nation was aborted by the Reformation division between the United Netherlands and the Spanish Netherlands. In this instance, of course, a new Dutch nation based on an intense elite Calvinist religious identification offset in a certain sense the submergence of the incipient Flemish identity. The development had extremely significant implications for the ultimate division of the German-language sphere. Consequently, it is better considered in chapter 8.

More generally, one may conclude that the strongest effect of the Reformation and Counter-Reformation on ethnicity was heightening of awareness of its linguistic component. The sixteenth century can be seen as a high point in the cycle of ethnic consciousness in contrast to preceding medieval unity based on common use of Latin as an elaborated code and the subsequent dominance of French styles and language under Absolutism. But the phase was not simple. Effects were cross-cutting; the strongest manifestations of concern for the vernaculars arose not as special features of Protestantism or Catholicism as such, but as artifacts of the struggle between the two religious movements. In the final analysis, one must recognize that a mass trait like language will come to the fore, as it did both during the period of the ancient heresies and again in ninth-century East Central Europe, whenever religious competition is intense. That this is so may be disquieting; but to recognize the phenomenon is to acknowledge the high penetrating power of religious organizations, which inevitably activate latent mass characteristics.

Organizational Rifts in Islam

The virtual disregard, up to this point, of Islam as an example of cleavage in organized religion may appear to belie my concern for comparing Moslem and Christian trends. But what has appeared in earlier chapters concerning Islam's minimalization of the significance of specific polities applies here, too. The dominant trend of the religion is to regard political structures as unimportant as long as the basic needs of the faith are safeguarded. Consequently, one would not expect religious structures to exert strong influences on more restricted kinds of identity within the common Islamic identity, either directly or by influencing myths of particular polities. On the other hand, symbols and myths tend to develop lives of their own, even in a system that ostensibly rejects the significance of symbolic communication. It should not, therefore, be surprising that the first decades of the sixteenth century, the very period when Western Christendom witnessed the start of its most divisive religious quarrel, also saw the most extreme and persistent schism in Islam.

The coincidence in the timing of the Protestant Reformation and the establishment of the Shia was very likely accidental. Both Protestantism and the Shia resulted in extreme persecution by secular rulers based— though neither the Shiites nor their Sunni opponents knew the phrase— on the principle *cuius regio eius religio*. But the end results differed sharply. Whereas in the West certain incipient nations were submerged and others arose out of the religious conflict, a single cleavage quickly assuming the force of ethnic identity severed the Persians from the remainder of the Moslem world. Which factors led to this separation, why it had not appeared earlier, and why the special circumstances of the sixteenth century rendered it possible are all questions requiring a survey of the rich scholarly literature.

Lacking a fixed structure with authoritative internal relationships, Moslem teaching authorities probably have less incentive to expand their spheres at the expense of other teaching bodies than do Christian hierarchies and certainly lack the organizational capacity for such expansion. The general principles of Islamic teaching authority are simple. Each Sunni

Moslem—the Shiite system is somewhat less formalized in this respect—is obliged to adhere to a single school of "law," that is, of religious norms. The four recognized schools go back to the mid-ninth century, three others having died out by 1300. Named after the scholars who founded them at a time when orthodox Sunni Moslems recognized that the "gates of the law" were open to wider-ranging interpretation than is permissible now, the schools are the Hanafi, the Malikite, the Hanbali, and the Shafi. As suggested below, in most regions of the Moslem world a single school predominates. In such a case, the man (a woman is rarely in a position to voice a preference) who lives in the region all his life has no real choice. Similarly, any Moslem who settles for a long time in a given area usually adheres to the dominant school there, for any problem requiring a judgment must be referred to the available *cadi*. Such problems may be entirely questions of conscience; they may involve intimate family disputes; or they may concern any manner of neighborhood or business transaction such as the civil tribunals of a Western society would adjudicate.[97]

There have been, however, major exceptions to the regional predominance of a single school. Abbasid Baghdad had several schools, and Isfahan continued to be split by strong factional rivalry between Hanafis and Shafis down to the deeper Shiite-Sunni split of the sixteenth century. Mameluke Egypt and Syria were most catholic in their approach to the schools. Four pyramids of judges were tolerated, each culminating in a grand *cadi* of Cairo. At the religious judge level, adherence was usually determined by where the *cadi* had studied. Many *medressas* had instructors for all four schools. As a result, the students intermingled; quarrels that arose appear to have been based on distinctive living quarters for men from different regions rather than on law adherence.[98]

The Ottomans preferred the Hanafi school, which was more flexible in accommodating to the needs of the political rulers. As a result, it was "established" throughout their empire, with more or less compulsory transfer of *cadis* to it in Iraq, but continued tolerance (without the earlier formal equality) of other schools in Egypt. Only in Malikite North Africa (Tunisia and Algeria; the Ottomans did not acquire suzerainty over Morocco) did establishment of a Hanafi school lead to anything approaching ethnic cleavage. Turk administrators and soldiers insisted on importing their school, complete with new mosques equipped with Turkish domes or at least with octagonal minarets, whereas the indigenous Moslems clung to the Malikite school with its square Almohad minaret. Several scholars have attributed the triumph of the Malikite school throughout the Maghreb by the eleventh century to the puritanism of the Berbers, as contrasted to Arabs who had originally preferred the Hanafis. It seems more likely that this puritan impulse was ingrained in North Africans during the rule of the Almohads, who taught distrust of the worldly culture of the Moslem East. In any case, by the time of the Ottoman arrival both Berbers and Arabs were united in loyalty to the Malikite school. Indeed, the strength of this adherence is said to have been so great that it resulted in a "rehabilitation" of the despised Arab nomads as defenders of distinctive Maghreb tradition.[99]

Whether there has been a true Maghreb identity as opposed to the Turks, or whether the maintenance of Maghreb distinctiveness is primarily a result of its extreme isolation (for Moslem peoples are not much inclined to the sea) is uncertain. The *sufi* movements, prominent throughout the Moslem world after 1100, had an even more dubious role as producers of identity, with the single exception of the Safavids discussed below. Generally, these popular religious movements (*sufi* means a "coarse wool garment") appealed to nomadic groups rather than to city dwellers or peasants, although at times the movements united the three life-style groups.[100] As a reaction against official, urban Islam the *sufis* tended to stress folk customs and languages in contrast to Arabic and formal literary styles. In Anatolia, at least, the very widespread *sufi* (dervish) orders contributed to the maintenance of a popular Turkish different not only from Arabic and Persian but from the peculiar Ottoman Turkish Court linguistic code.[101]

The only *sufi* order that produced a real ethnic identity did so in very indirect ways. Safi ad-Din took over leadership of a *sufi* order in Azerbaijan about 1300. His descendants ascribed to him a genealogy going back, in the twenty-first generation, to a South Arabian, who in turn was supposed to be related to the Shiite Seventh Imam. The latter was descended from Mohammed's grandson Ali. This complicated history, resembling (not by coincidence) the "begats" of Genesis, does not prevent one scholar from suspecting that Safi was really an offspring of the neighboring Kurds. Like other Azerbaijani dervishes, he spoke Turkic and Persian.[102] The Safavid *sufi* chiefs, who established a tiny theocracy in Ardebil, apparently received favors from the Il Khans and Tamerlane. Their main entry into politics occurred in the late fifteenth century, however, through a complicated marriage and tutelage relationship with the prince of the "White Sheep" Turkic regime in Azerbaijan. In 1499, Ismail, descendant and heir both of the *sufi* order and of the Turkic ruler, began expansion. His legitimizing myth was a typical amalgam of *ghazi* themes (directed against the Christian Caucasus), *mahdi* puritanism (directed against the "decadent" urban Ottomans), and Turkic nomad appeals. The myth complex was, in fact, not very different from the myths used by the Ottomans themselves a century or two earlier. By 1499, however, Ismail and his *sufi* order had become Shiite, along with many Turkic elements in Azerbaijan and eastern Anatolia.[103] Although the eponymous ancestor and his immediate descendants had almost certainly been Sunnis, from the end of the fifteenth century the Safavid dynasty was, therefore, identified with the Shia and bitterly opposed to the Sunni ascendancy in Islam.

Apparently, Ismail hoped to overthrow Ottoman power in Anatolia as well as to defeat the lesser regimes in Iran. Shiite strength was probably greater in eastern Anatolia than in eastern Iran. As Michel M. Mazzaoui points out, however, "the boundaries between Īrān and Anatolia can at no time be definitely drawn during this period. . . . This ['open society of free movement and intercourse'] . . . was perhaps the most important single factor which helped in the dissemination of the religious ideas." The Shiite sect was weak in urban areas generally—the proportion estimated for the partly Turkic city of Tabriz in Azerbaijan is one-third.[104] Some historians have nevertheless believed that Persia had deep inclinations toward the Shia. A large element of this interpretation seems to have been based on earlier historiography that exaggerated the roles of Persians and Shiites alike in the eighth-century accession to power of the Abbasid dynasty. Some further consideration of the cultural and linguistic implications of this episode will appear in chapter 8. Here it need only be pointed out that, whatever temporary use the first Abbasids may have made of Shiite opposition to the Umayyad caliphs, the followers of the sect whom the Abbasids utilized in Khurasan and Iraq were mainly Arabs.[105]

Intransigence toward Sunni regimes usually characterized later Shiite leaders, some of whom urged the Mongol invaders to seize Baghdad from the last Sunni caliph. A few centuries earlier, certain Fatimid caliphs had been equally intransigent. The Shiite Buyid polity in northern Iraq, however, exercised a tolerant protectorate over the Abbasid caliphate from 932 to 1055. The Ismaili Shiite sect ("Assassins"), which survived the Fatimid regime, is noted for its fanatic opposition to Mongols and crusaders and was prepared to serve Sunni regimes like the Mamelukes.[106] The Ismaili stronghold was not far from Ardebil. Some scholars see significance in the fact that Safi was ascribed descent from the Seventh Imam, the mythical Hidden Imam of both Ismailis and Fatimids, rather than from the Twelfth Imam honored in Iran since 1499. At that time, Ismail's advisers had to conduct a protracted search to find written evidence of the Twelfth Imam doctrine. Ismail's claim to be the Hidden Imam is uncertain; in any case, his *sufi* followers asserted that Ismail "himself used to abide with God, but now he appeared in the world."[107] Consequently, the Shiite clergy never regarded even the Safavid polity as a culmination of their history.

Like previous conquerors, Shah Ismail and his immediate successors surrounded themselves with Persian advisers, not all Shiite, and Arabian Shiite *mullahs*. The shah's concern for doctrinal legitimacy probably made

such staffs trained in urban traditions necessary. Shah Ismail's unprecedented step consisted of mass persecution of the large Sunni elements in
the Persian cities. Many fled to the Ottoman empire. Although occasional
Fatimid caliphs had persecuted non-Moslems fiercely, generally the Fatimids recognized the unfeasibility of putting excessive pressure on their
predominantly Sunni subjects.

By the seventeenth century, Persia, apart from minorities such as the
Kurds and Turkomans, was homogeneously Shiite to a degree never before attained by any Shiite regime. Indeed, such doctrinal solidarity had
rarely been present in Sunni polities. The Ottoman response to Shah
Ismail's fanaticism, however, was to enforce Sunni orthodoxy. Tens of
thousands of Anatolian Shiites were executed and many more fled to
Persia. The brunt of the persecution was directed against the Kizilbash
Shiite dervishes whom Ismail hoped to use to gain power there, whereas
urban Shiites, less receptive to Safavid claims, were generally tolerated,
though discouraged.[108]

The emergence within a century of two homogeneously sectarian Islamic polities confronting each other did not immediately result in anything resembling Western national identity. At most, as the English literary
historian Edward G. Browne puts it, the Safavids "produced that homogeneity which is the basis of national sentiment."[109] A sixteenth-century
German traveler noted that Ottomans considered Persians to be less faith-
ful than Christians.[110] It is true that Persian merchants visiting Constantinople were required to renounce the Shia before being permitted to enter
mosques. The Ottoman rulers did not, however, consider their conflict to
be with Persians as such.[111] Sultan Selim I compared himself to Firdawsi's
mythical Iranian king combating the Turanian (Turkic) Afrasiyab (Ismail).
In fact, the sultans and their courtiers spoke Persian about as much as
Ottoman Turkish, and Azerbaijani Turkic remained the Safavid Court
language until the seventeenth century.[112] Moreover, there was an element
of grudging respect in Ottoman antagonisms toward the Safavids, curiously
resembling the Byzantine attitude toward the Sassanids. For example, the
Persian regime was the only one with which the Ottoman sultans ex-
changed real ambassadors. Antagonism between Safavids and the Sunni
Uzbeks to the northeast was fiercer; Ismail referred to their ruler as a
"branch of the Genghisid tree of unbelief."[113]

Gradually, the Safavids ceased to rely on their turbulent seminomadic
retainers, who were incapable of facing the Janissaries. Regular troops,
like civilian advisers, tended to use Persian rather than Turkic. Nevertheless, Persian culture, especially poetry, appears to have declined under the Safavid regime as a result of emigration and Shiite suspicion of
heterodoxy.[114]

Summary and Conclusions

Religious organizations are important for ethnic identity because in premodern conditions such organizations penetrate the masses of a population to a degree that few administrations of large polities can attain. Penetrative force is most evident in two circumstances: (1) missionary activity characteristic of the two great universal religions; and (2) sectarian disputes within each of them. Because both Islam and Christianity assert a duty to proselytize, both missionary activity and sectarian advocacy require forms of communication accessible to the masses. Although most Christian churches have relied heavily on nonverbal symbolism (which Islam unavowedly employs), communication by the word has always been the principal vehicle for both religions, which assert that their essential truths are contained in scriptures. Whereas many theological controversies have resorted to exegesis in linguistic codes available only to elites, preaching and written exhortations have necessarily been in popular languages. Religious activity therefore contrasts with the heavy emphasis on high cultural values embodied in traditional elite languages used by imperial administrative personnel.

As a result of these factors, religious organizations are not only more penetrative than imperial administrations; the former greatly stimulate the use and written codification of popular languages, especially during periods of intense sectarian controversy. This phenomenon is especially noticeable during two periods of European history: early doctrinal disputes among Christians producing ethnoreligious identities centering on languages such as Armenian, Nestorian Syriac, and Coptic; and the Reformation and Counter-Reformation, which transformed several modern languages into written cultural vehicles.

Armenians, ever since the fifth-century emergence of their distinctive Gregorian Christian church, and Jews for twice that length of time, have maintained highly distinctive ethnoreligious identities despite dispersion over vast reaches of the Middle East and Europe. Observation of these diasporas, and others now less prominent, provides a key to understanding how persistent religious distinctiveness and ethnic identity tend to become an inseparable identity complex. The archetypal diasporas also exemplify the crucial but ambiguous relationship of language to ethnicity. Although highly distinctive linguistic codes, which they preserved from their early period of territorial settlement, continue to constitute vehicles for the Jewish and the Gregorian sacral myths, everyday use of the languages has not been essential for preservation of identity. The origin myth itself acts as the essential *mythomoteur*, focusing on a specific geographic sacral center.

Throughout most of their history, as was briefly discussed in chapter 4, distinctive legal codes, religious in origin and regulating the most intimate spheres of life, have been important institutional mechanisms for preserving Jewish and Armenian identities. It is interesting to note that, whereas Armenian codes have been supported (often ineffectively) by a hierarchy, Jewish codes have depended on community pressure institutionalized in a tribunal system that included certain optional appeal instances. This institutional distinction between the two most prominent archetypal diasporas parallels the two types of legal control mechanisms established throughout the major universal religions. Most traditional Christian churches have relied on formal hierarchies, in contrast to the tribunals supported by popular pressures throughout Islam and among many smaller Christian sects. Both mechanisms can be effective for communication, social control, and maintenance of doctrinal regularity. Thus both contribute to a strong penetrative potential of the religious organizations.

Hierarchical organizations almost by definition are more inclined to jurisdictional disputes than are autonomous community organizations. Such disputes not only characterized early Christian experience with "heresies," but were most important at the beginning of the cleavage between Eastern and Western churches. The latter dispute paralleled and reinforced a growing cultural division, after the fourth century, between the Greek-language portions of the Roman empire and the Latin West. The Germanic invasions directly impeded East-West communications and indirectly undermined the Western ability to communicate with the Greeks by disrupting the educational system. A significant phenomenological barrier arose to reinforce the jurisdictional cleavages. Neither Eastern nor Western hierarchs were able to comprehend fully the others' doctrinal formulations, not only because of strictly semantic differences but because modes of thought had diverged. As a result, the inertia of jurisdictional conflict and the political interests that developed around it were exacerbated by doctrinal schism.

Missionary competition in East Central Europe, involving political as well as ecclesiastical interests, complicated the cultural and linguistic aspects of the conflict. After the crusader capture of Constantinople in 1204, the East-West (or Orthodox-Catholic) divergence took on many aspects of an ethnic conflict. It strongly influenced late Byzantine reidentification as "Hellene" and divided most East and South Slavs from Catholic Slavs. In many respects, the civilizations based on Orthodoxy and on Latin Catholicism became as distinct as Islam and Christendom. In contrast to the cleavage between the latter civilizations, however, no geographical frontier of incessant conflict developed between the two Christian civilizations. The reasons are partly fortuitous: the great distance between the West and the Orthodox centers (Constantinople, Kiev, Moscow) and the intrusion of external forces like steppe nomads between the two civilizations. But the absence of the peculiar combination of Islamic and steppe nomad values discussed in chapter 3 also obviated such an unstable frontier between the two branches of Christendom.

Instability of the frontier between Iran and Sunni Moslem polities derived, as late as the nineteenth century, in some measure from nomadic values. The basis for a distinctive Iranian identity was the most significant, persistent doctrinal cleavage within the Moslem civilization. The fact that the cleavage between Sunni versions and the Shia did not become identified with distinctive ethnic cultures until the sixteenth century suggests that the eventual relation of doctrine to ethnicity may have been a historical accident. Early Safavid and Ottoman governing elites were not separated by culture—or rather such differences as did exist cut across lines of incipient polity formation. Intense political efforts to produce territorially unified polity bases, combined with certain latent cultural and linguistic differences between the core areas of Anatolia and Iran, however, eventually transformed Shiite distinctiveness into the most stable ethnic identity within Islam.

The transforming force of religion, immensely enhanced by the penetrative power of religious organizations, has made doctrinal differences very important for ethnicity. This importance was relatively greater before the late modern development of highly penetrative political mechanisms. Nevertheless, the potency of ethnoreligious identity continues to rival the more widespread contemporary ethnolinguistic identity.

CHAPTER EIGHT

Language: Code and Communication

Linguistic Codes in Segmented Polities

Language has been left to the last not because it is the least important among factors affecting ethnic identity, but because it is the most likely to be misunderstood. The undue emphasis placed on linguistic aspects of ethnicity both by nationalists and by scholars who have analyzed nationalism was discussed at the start of this study. By first considering other factors and gradually increasing attention to linguistic questions, I have tried to avoid such overemphasis, but at the same time not to neglect language as one important element in the intricate pattern of ethnic identity. The treatment of territorial attachment, nomads, and genealogical groupings in chapter 2 prescinded as much as possible from language in order to emphasize that early ethnic alignments could arise without much attention to linguistic affiliations. Emphasis in subsequent chapters on politics as an independent variable suggested that language was more often the product than the cause of polity formation; but cause and effect were rarely unidirectional. The penetrative capacity of religious organizations rendered linguistic factors more significant in their activities, but basic religious cleavages were not often due primarily to language.

The special position of linguistics among the social sciences also appeared to be a good reason for postponing consideration of language until other factors had been clarified. As Lévi-Strauss writes, linguistics "is not merely a social science like the others, but, rather, the one in which by far the greatest progress has been made."[1] Apart from anthropologists, however, few social scientists have undertaken the basic task of linking linguistic theory to their own disciplines.[2] In delimiting as precisely as possible the aspects of linguistics relevant to ethnic identity, Fredrik Barth is, once again, an invaluable guide: "Socially relevant factors alone become diagnostic for membership, not the overt, 'objective' differences which are generated by other factors. It makes no difference how dissimilar members may be in their overt behaviour—if they say they are A, in contrast to another cognate category B, they are willing to be judged as A's and not as B's; in other words, they declare their allegiance to the shared culture of A's."[3] This distinction concerning ethnic membership, together with Barth's emphasis on boundary mechanisms, requires concentration on linguistic elements that serve as "border guards," not on the innumerable other aspects of language that professional linguists rightly stress.

Among linguistic theories, those derived from investigations of bilingualism and linguistic codes have been most instructive for me. Concrete research by linguists on language as code has been largely restricted to contemporary situations where speakers can be observed directly. There is always an element of risk in extending generalizations derived from such observation to remoter periods. Such striking congruence appears between certain of the linguists' propositions and the findings of philologists, however, that it seems appropriate to use the theory of language codes to clarify important historical linguistic relationships.

The concept of linguistic codes is also intimately related to the myth-symbol complex. Some of the most sophisticated studies of ethnicity, such as Karl Deutsch's, emphasize the instrumental communications aspect of language.[4] Density of road networks, frequency of messages, proximity of individuals in urban settings, even the monetary value of commercial exchanges have been used as indicators of communication densities that produce or transform ethnic identities. In examining social modernization, a process salient for analysts such as Deutsch, these relatively precise indicators may be appropriate. Deutsch's own earlier analysis of medieval patterns suggests, however, that less tangible indicators are required in different historical circumstances. As Otto Jespersen points out, language cannot be fully understood as a means of communication, for its "original" function was to serve "as an outlet for intense feelings [rather] than for an intelligible expression of them."[5] To put the matter slightly differently, it is the high affect potential of language that requires that the greatest attention be directed to its use in myths and symbols.

Many studies of bilingualism have focused on diglossia, that is, the relation of an elaborated code used for "high" cultural purposes to a restricted code employed for intimate relationships involving high affect content. This distinction can be highly significant for ethnic identity, but it is important to envisage the coexistence of several elaborated codes as well. Joshua Fishman suggests that a more general way to look at bilingual or multilingual social settings is to refer to "domains" of each language. The dominance or rank-ordering of the languages is primarily a question of each individual's use of them in such a setting, rather than the status position of the group to which he belongs.[6] I think it is possible, following Fishman's suggestion, to envisage a social setting in which the domains of several distinctive languages, although separate, are perceived as equal in many respects. In effect each language constitutes an equally elaborated code, but the social contexts in which they are employed overlap only a little. Individuals acquire prestige from fluent and correct use of any one of the languages. For some roles, full command of a single code is sufficient; for other roles, complete bilingualism or even multilingualism is required to attain high status. Such conditions require that considerable numbers of speakers of all the codes reside in proximity to each other. Certain geographical regions in contact with the multilingual social setting, perhaps even within the same polity, may be monolingual as far as their elaborated codes are concerned. In addition, isolated groups and lower-status elements within the multilingual setting may employ only restricted codes. The relationships among all of the codes present in such a social setting or polity are dynamic; consequently, their relative status or extent of usage may alter considerably.

The model I have just elaborated is, I believe, remarkably applicable to the segmented Islamic polities reviewed in chapter 6. Peripheral groups such as Berbers and Nubians often used only restricted linguistic codes. The dominant elites, however, frequently employed no fewer than three elaborated codes: Arabic, Persian, and Turkish. For a few decades, Arabic was the only high-status code for Moslems, and Turkic did not become such a code until about 1000. Neither Turkic nor Persian ever became common in parts of the Islamic world like Morocco, and use of Arabic was rare in Central Asian Genghisid polities. For many regions and for most of Islamic history, however, three elaborated codes coexisted. A fundamental reason why, after the brief dominance of Arabic, no single language acquired a unique position as a high-status vehicle, was that few Moslem polities were stable enough to promote such ascendancy. Polities like the Mamelukes' and the Ottomans' that might have done so preferred, for reasons suggested in chapter 6, to maintain segmented elites. Consequently, at an early stage Persian became the "domain" of men of the pen. Although in some polities this occupational elite used Arabic almost exclusively, Persian concepts and terminology were used in Islamic administrations everywhere. Turkic was the linguistic domain of powerful if uncultured men of the sword; later its elaborated versions in the Mameluke and Ottoman polities became veritable arcana of rule. Arabic remained the essential language of men of the law, although it is said that a high religious official under the Mamelukes, a Persian from Herat, could not speak it. Many Shiite *mullahs* repeat the Koran by rote, using popular manuals in Persian. Nevertheless, prior to the twentieth century, even Shiite theology was usually written in Arabic.[7]

Everything else being equal, men of the pen were most in need of knowing the other two languages. Their association, in the *medressas* and elsewhere, with men of the law tended to produce bilingualism (in Arabic and Persian) among both occupational groups. Men of the sword prided themselves on command of a linguistic domain in addition to the Turkic they usually employed. Consequently, intercourse was multilingual to an extent that few citizens of the larger contemporary national states can appreciate. Polyglot accomplishment was facilitated by lexical interpenetration; the Persian vocabulary of culture and administration was transferred into Arabic, as were a relatively restricted number of Turkic terms. Persian borrowed a small number of terms from Turkic, whereas both Turkic and Persian absorbed an immense body of religious terminology from Arabic. The Ottoman Court language became so synthetic that a sixteenth-century German observer could write: "In the Court at Constantinople they have a mass of Arabic and Persian words mixed with Turkish as the German has Latin. But the Asiatic Turks who live in the mountains speak nothing but pure Turkish and do not mix other languages, so that when they come to Constantinople they cannot understand the language well."[8]

Perhaps the most remarkable characteristic of this interplay of languages is that each of the three represents a distinct linguistic group: Arabic is Semitic, Persian is Indo-European, and Turkic belongs to the widespread Altaic group. Moreover, the relatively slight internal dialect differentiation of Arabic and Turkic (as nomad languages) made their contrast to each other and to Persian sharper. Each language's grammatical structure and basic vocabulary required great efforts to master, yet a large portion of the educated strata did acquire two or more of them. Some comprehension of how this could occur can be derived from a brief look at the backgrounds of each language.

Perhaps no ancient people except the Greeks attached as much importance to language as did the Arabs. In contrast to the Greeks, however, Arabic was catapulted into quasi-universal ascendancy not after centuries of literary maturation but at a stage resembling the Greek "heroic" epoch before Homer or Hesiod. The question, as Marshall Hodgson poses it, is "how the Arabic language and with it so much of the Arabian background managed to emerge as a cultural framework in a society where they were so greatly disadvantaged?"[9] One answer is that Arabic, as the language of long-distance merchants and nomads, was more highly unified than Greek had been. By the sixth century, Arabic already had its *koine*, and the circumstances of the conquest amalgamated residual dialects. The quickest acceptance of Arabic was in the Syria-Mesopotamia region, where a closely related Semitic *koine*, Aramaic, already prevailed. Given the long-standing penetration of Arab elements into this area, the transition must have been relatively easy.[10]

Even more important was the fact that the Umayyad dynasty and, to a considerable extent, the Abbasids during their first centuries behaved in ways strikingly similar to modern nationalist conquerors. Instead of following the ancient and medieval custom of accepting the high cultural language of the conquered, they insisted on establishing Arabic as the administrative language, effectively in Syria, nominally in Egypt and Mesopotamia, within two generations. To the north, general use of Arabic soon coincided with the earlier range of the entire Semitic language group up to the boundary with Greek and the languages of Asia Minor, closely approximating the northern frontier of the Roman imperial diocese of the East. Linguistic assimilation by peasants was hardly more escapable than conversion to Islam if they were to overcome the stigma of being "Nabateans." Knowledge of Arabic very quickly became a prime requisite for imputation to oneself of a prestigious Beduin lineage, within a social order centered, during the first two centuries, almost entirely on genealogical claims. Like many other languages, Arabic was considered to be the first human speech. A myth that God had forbidden Adam to speak it after his expulsion from Eden, requiring him to use Syriac until he repented, expresses the superiority complex of the Arabic speaker. There is no doubt that possession of the Koran, the highest revelation of God, available in Arabic alone, "the chosen language, that all of them may taste the name of the Lord, and serve Him together with one consent," was crucial.[11] It gave the Arab conquerors the confidence they required to press their relatively undeveloped language on others. Egyptian resistance to Islam, based on the village Coptic church, could not be overcome until the Abbasids disrupted the rural organizations after a tax rebellion. Thereafter even the remaining Coptic Christians gradually adopted Arabic. In effect, resistance to Arabic required resistance to Islam.

Concern for the purity of the Koran, which led all law schools except the Hanafis to forbid its recitation in translation, also lay at the bottom of Arab elites' insistence on linguistic purity. Ibn Khaldun wrote that the first caliph, Omar, tried to preserve Arabic purity by forbidding use of non-Arabic dialects.[12] The rapid success achieved by Arabic following the conquest did threaten to turn the language into a restricted code pidgin usable only for instrumental communication. Jews quickly learned to use Arabic in place of Aramaic for the vastly expanded Mediterranean trade that the conquest opened up. During the eighth century, both Christians and Jews who had adopted Arabic simplified its grammar to make it more convenient for commercial purposes. Even for the Abbasid Court, however, such a procedure was anathema, for pure Arabic constituted a fundamental boundary mechanism for maintaining the identity of the Islamic elite. Court poetry clung to the nostalgia for Beduin life; speaking Arabic "like a Beduin" was a status symbol.[13] When poets disagreed on the admissibility of a locution, they asked any available Beduin to settle the dispute. The difficulty with this course was the unadaptability of Beduin Arabic to patterns of urban thinking and behavior embraced by an imperial Court and wealthy merchants. In the meantime, the Beduin dialects and poetry were evolving away from the Koranic style. Consequently, by the tenth century the effort to preserve purity was hopeless for the living language.[14] Further change was precluded, moreover, by the fact that the Beduin dialects, on which literary Arabic had been based, themselves had changed. Lacking living influence from these dialects, it could henceforward be standardized throughout the Moslem world as a dead language.

Johann Fück's analysis just summarized supports the newer scholarly consensus that far more profound forces than the replacement of Umayyads by Abbasids gradually dethroned Arabic as the unique elaborated code of Islam. As briefly indicated in chapter 7, the Abbasids did use Shiite dissidents, but they soon cast them off. Recent scholarly opinion doubts that there was a significant ethnic element involved in the dynastic change either. Although up to their overthrow the Umayyad Court and the principal officers remained Arab, the last rulers of the dynasty were moving in a direction of egalitarianism to replace superior status for born Arabs. The Persian aristocrats of Khurasan, where the revolt began, apparently favored the Umayyads and their Arab garrisons who might be induced to extend the Islamic empire into Central Asia. On the other hand, poorer Iranians and long-established Arab colonists in Khurasan suffered from the impositions of the Umayyad regime. The principal rebel leaders were Khurasan Arabs, hence there was no question of an anti-Arab movement as such.[15] But the overthrow of the Umayyad dynasty facilitated the rapid spread of Islam, especially in the east.[16] The vexing requirement that converts be attached to an Arab "tribe" was dropped, but full equality was still not conceded to converts until the third generation. The process of assimilation of Arabs to such Persian customs as wearing trousers and sometimes to the Persian language began in Iran and by the ninth century was common in Iraq, too.[17] The far more developed culture of the Persians permeated the Abbasid Court, but it was nearly always written in Arabic. The Courtly *adab* literature was fundamentally Persian in inspiration, as were tracts on history, religion, and ethics. So were administrative documents, based on a full acquaintance with Persian tax regulations but composed in literary Arabic.[18]

The renaissance of Persian as a language, although employing the Arabic script and heavily infiltrated by Arabic vocabulary, began in the Samanid Central Asian polity, which made Persian the official language in the ninth century. Its greatest monument, Firdawsi's *Shahname* ("Book of Kings"), glorified the pre-Islamic Persian past. Persians, who had denigrated the nomadic customs of the Arabs, by that time more or less openly rejected the nostalgic Beduin ideal in favor of the old Iranian cow-herder hero, Rustam. Mercantile and urban themes were subordinated to royal and aristocratic motifs. Even the populist *sufi* movement was heavily Persian, with Persian dervishes predominating as far west as Egypt.[19] But the cleavage was by no means always determined by background. By the ninth century, many Arabs were bilingual. Conversely, an Iranian scholar contemporary to Firdawsi wrote that "I must confess I would prefer invective in Arabic to praise in Persian [which is not clear enough for science]. . . . The purpose of the Persian language is to perpetuate historical epics dealing with the kings of yesteryear and to provide stories for evening social gatherings."[20]

No doubt much resentment of this type toward Persian existed among the Arabs themselves; but the *hadith* they found to express their change of status reflected resignation: "If scholarship hung suspended at the highest parts of heaven, the Persians [people of Fars] would take it."[21] Arabs continued to rank Persians far above Turks. Ibn Khaldun considered Turkish nomads to be worse than the Arab Beduins, to whom he attributed much of the degradation of Islamic civilization. Persians and even cultivated Ottoman urbanites referred derogatorily to "Turk" nomads and peasants. Thus the last reigning Abbasid caliph very rashly called the Mongol Hulagu a "Turkish dog."[22] Conversely, there is an ironic parallel to Germans, who were contemptuous of the "Welsch" while avidly aping Romance manners, in Turkic scorn of the unwarlike, sedentary "Tajik" who spoke Persian. Yet it was the Turkic regimes, notably the Seljuks, that completed the process of installing Persian as the most prestigious cultural language. It is said that the rigidification of Arabic legal texts in the *medressa* instruction hastened the language's decline for cultural purposes. These schools did insist on a knowledge of Arabic for administrators as well as *ulema*, however. As noted in chapter 6, Arabic was taught even in the Ottoman Seraglio schools. The Mameluke empire, although ruled by Turks and heavily influenced by Persians, constituted virtually a "universal state" for the Arabs, embracing the entire Arabic-speaking region except the Maghreb, Iraq, and the southern parts of the Arabian peninsula. Arab cultural influences via the Indian Ocean reached as far as Canton, whereas Persian styles predominated along the northern, overland route through Central Asia. It is hardly surprising that an Arabic renaissance occurred in Mameluke Egypt during the fourteenth and fifteenth centuries.[23]

The linguistic position of the Mameluke regime itself was peculiar. Early Mamelukes had Kipchak Turkic as their native tongue and required their Egyptian scribes to know it. Later Mamelukes, including the Circassians whose native languages were entirely different from Turkic, preserved it as a secret language. The Mameluke sultans were accused of having "despised those who bore the names of the prophets and friends of Mohammed, preferring those with Mameluke names."[24] On the other hand, Arab writers glorified the Mameluke victories over non-Moslems in a way that explicitly recognized their Turkic valor: "It was the fierce Turks of Egypt who exterminated and dispersed the Tatars in Syria. . . . Since they have set out on their campaign, the Turks have sworn not to leave any domain to the Franks." In other words, the "Turk lions" were recognized as the sword of Islam by its men of the pen and of the law.[25] Turkic military regimes as far apart as the pre-Seljuk Karakhanids in Khurasan and the thirteenth-century Moslem principalities in India gladly accepted the role as men of the sword, identifying with Firdawsi's Afrasiyab.[26] In Seljuk Anatolia the Turks explained Persian reluctance to join the *jihad* against the crusaders by saying, "Whoever learns Persian has lost half his faith."[27]

Nevertheless, apart from the Mamelukes, whose secret Turkic language was influenced by Persian, and the minor Karamanli principality in Anatolia, all Turkic regimes used Persian as their Court language, although Tamerlane maintained a Turkic chancery as well. The Ottoman empire's break with this high cultural tradition in its diplomatic correspondence cost it influence in other Moslem Courts. The Sunni Persian poets who needed imperial patronage in Constantinople, whether they were refugees from the Safavids or attracted by Ottoman magnificence, learned the "mysteries and refinements" of Court Ottoman, the principal language of communication. Even in the second generation, however, they often identified themselves as Persians. As noted in chapter 7, sultans such as Selim I also used Persian and did not try to prove the superiority of Turkic elements.[28] Yet, as long as they remained victorious in war, the Ottomans, like other Turks, continued to say, "we are all sons of princes," in that manner, as Gustave Von Grunebaum remarks, abstracting their destiny from that of Islam as a whole. No doubt Turkic consciousness of being part of an immense, triumphant group heightened this sense of destiny.[29]

Ordinarily, all three linguistic groups among the Islamic elites, like other Moslems, placed their religious identity far above language considerations. Unity of religion despite disparity of languages was symbolized by the use of a single sacral alphabet, Arabic, to write all three languages. At a more intimate level, genealogical alignments were also more important than language. Precisely because they were intensely concerned with their lineages, Turks, Persians, and Arabs appreciated their cultural backgrounds. When a family like the Safavids claimed descent from the Prophet, it did not of course mean that they were really Arabicized. Assertions of descent from less exalted figures of clans (like Berber claims to Arab lineages), however, usually implied a propensity to adopt Arabic. Consequently, although Persian and Turkic elite members fairly often claimed Arab descent, they combined this assertion with other claims, such as Sassanid ancestry, that emphasized their non-Arab heritage. For example, a Soviet scholar found that twenty-four of forty-one notable families in a thirteenth-century Khurasan city claimed Arab ancestry, as compared to twelve of putative Iranian descent. Most of the "Arabs," however, were supposed to be descendants of Ali, the Shiite ancestor, suggesting a strong religious motivation for the genealogy.[30]

As noted at many points above, a general eagerness to learn Arabic and Persian, along with resigned determination to acquire the more developed Turkic codes, was evident. But an elite member's identity was bound up with his occupational code as well as his family background. Consequently, he cherished the language associated with both these elements of his identity just as a diaspora member clung to his community tribunals, which were indispensable both to his religious identity and to his occupational role.

Grammatical and lexical differences among the three Islamic elaborated codes were so great that multilingual speakers required conscious and protracted efforts to employ them fluently and accurately. Especially in later centuries, even native speakers of an Arab dialect required considerable training to use standardized Arabic properly. Similar requirements prevailed for literary Persian and Ottoman Turkish. It is evident that a very large portion of a young man's time was devoted to acquiring linguistic proficiency. As Hodgson notes, such heavy investment in literary skills is a not uncommon "luxury" for agrarian societies. The investment paid large dividends by producing elites who could travel throughout Islam, assuming high posts requiring fluent and socially acceptable communication in almost any polity that needed their skills. Linguistic differences as barriers to communication, in contrast to their influence as affect and status symbols, were not significant for most Moslem elite members. For less educated Moslems, communications barriers arose almost as often in the nearby *suk* or bazaar or in communicating with local religious or civil authorities as in travel to distant parts of the *Dar ul-Islam*. Curiously enough, the Moslem elites, who were willing to devote immense effort to acquiring their own elaborated codes, were virtually incapable, as noted in the preceding chapter, of acquiring European languages. Consequently, they depended on mobilized diasporas whose internal life the Moslem elites, completely untutored in such languages as Hebrew, Ladin, and Armenian, could never penetrate. Conversely, as a matter of necessity, multiple codes prevailed among the non-Moslem minorities. For example, Christian Andalusians employed Latin for church affairs, Arabic for written literature, and Romance for oral communication.[31] The overall effect of the Islamic segmented polity was very broad promotion of multilingualism.

European Linguistic Barriers: The Germanic-Romance Case

Elaborate linguistic codes in Europe developed in a very different direction from those in Islam. Greek literary men occasionally suggested that Greek become the language of culture, Latin the language of governance in the Roman empire. Fundamental Hellenic self-sufficiency prevented such proposals for bilingualism from reaching fruition even during the centuries of imperial grandeur. During the Byzantine empire's later centuries, emphasis on Greek precluded a domain for any other linguistic code, whereas ignorance of Greek in the West was a significant factor in the development of separate polities. Although both languages are Indo-European, Greek and Latin were too distinct to permit communication except by those who had invested great efforts in acquiring the others' language. Language barriers constantly reinforced political rivalries and ecclesiastical frictions.

Similar recognition of strong linguistic barriers without corresponding efforts to elaborate their native languages prevailed among Magyars (see chapter 2), Lithuanians (see chapter 7) and other Baltic speakers, Celts, Basques, and northern Finnic elements. The great language boundaries of medieval Europe ran, however, between three major Indo-European language families—the Romance, the Germanic, and the Slavic. Because the area of Romance-Slavic confrontation is very small, consideration can be limited to the Germanic-Romance and the Germanic-Slavic boundaries.

The most striking feature of these boundaries is the sharp, virtually immovable linguistic division between Germanic and Romance tongues from a point about fifty miles inland from Boulogne east to Liège, then southeast almost to the Rhine River. On that language boundary a change in linguistic affiliation (during the past millennium) more than a single commune in depth is exceptional. Farther west, on the Flanders coast, French has gained sharply, and farther southeast, in the Swiss valleys, German has advanced. Even in the latter region, however, the area of change is clearly delimited, with few mixed zones except in cities.[32] A necessary condition for such an unusual boundary is thick settlement; one reason why the Swiss linguistic boundary has shifted more than the average is the relatively scattered settlement. As noted earlier, contiguous

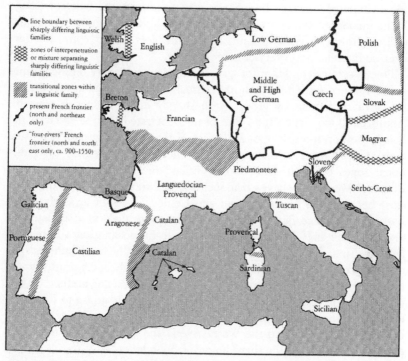

MAP 5. European Linguistic Families (early twentieth century)

village settlement was attained by the eleventh century in the area between the Loire and the Scheldt, embracing most of the sharp section of the Germanic-Romance boundary. On the other hand, where wastelands persist, movements by different linguistic groups inevitably entail considerable changes in the zone dividing them.

A second striking aspect of the Germanic-Romance boundary is that never, for any major portion of its course, has it coincided with a political frontier. The present French frontier still includes a small Flemish enclave, whereas Belgium has a very large Romance (Walloon) population. Throughout almost its entire length, the Franco-German frontier lies east of the linguistic boundary. Not only is Switzerland a multilingual country; the linguistic boundary cuts across several of its cantons. Farther east the linguistic boundary lies well south of the Italo-Austrian frontier. Political frontiers were in very different locations in earlier periods. Nevertheless, the highly stable "four-rivers" frontier of France lay far west of the linguistic boundary, leaving the important *Reichsromanen* in the Holy Roman empire. It is possible to argue, therefore, that a certain consciousness of the stability of language boundaries associated with the fixity of village limits influenced the concept, so prominent in West Europe, of definite political frontiers. The two kinds of fixed borders did not coincide, however, so the relationship is not demonstrable.

One necessary condition for a sharp linguistic boundary on the ground was density of settlement. Another, usually, was the coming together of waves of settlement by groups with sharply differing speech patterns. About 2000 B.C., when Indo-Europeans penetrated Europe as far as the Seine, they presumably spoke dialects of the same language. The usual developments from the disintegration of such a language family are transitional zones between dialects. Line boundaries are completely absent. Reinhard Wenskus believes that such a broad transitional zone did once exist between the Germanic and the Celtic dialects of an early Indo-European language family, but that intermediate dialects assimilated to one or the other.[33] Alternatively, if two Indo-European groups instead of being separated by such a transitional zone actually lived hundreds of miles apart for centuries, their dialects would have become mutually unintelligible. This is the hypothesis which Maurits Gysseling prefers: "It was the emigration of the dialects which formed the Italic group to Italy, followed by Germanization of one portion of their original territory [roughly between the Canche and the Weser rivers] and Celtization of the other portion, which caused the sharp linguistic boundaries."[34]

Either hypothesis can explain why two strongly distinguished linguistic groups became neighbors, but neither explains why the boundary became immobile as well as sharp. The Celts who came up from the south were conquered by Rome, adopted Latin, and subsequently developed Romance dialects that apparently perpetuate the Celtic side of the division with Germanic tongues.[35] A German advance between the Rhine and the Scheldt during Roman times is generally accepted by scholars. One view, developed mainly by German investigators, holds that a broad bilingual zone, extending down to the Seine or even the Loire, persisted until the Carolingian period.[36] Recent French and Belgian scholarship rejects this position, finding little evidence that Germans (as agricultural settlers) penetrated much south of the present linguistic boundary.[37] Partly as a result of such disagreement, several incompatible theories have been advanced to explain the location of that boundary. The nonspecialist is reduced to agreeing with an expert, Jean Stengers, that almost any explanation is possible and that one would do better to recognize the extent of our ignorance of early developments than to try to provide consistent generalizations.[38] There is broad agreement, however, that the present boundary has existed at the very least since about 1000.

To the east, Celtic settlement, transformed into Romance, apparently extended to the Roman *limes* on the Danube. In that area there seems to be little doubt that Germans advanced during the fifth to sixth centuries approximately to the Alps. A large Romance population persisted in northern Switzerland and in southern Germany for several more centuries, however, especially in remaining urban centers on trade routes. Apparently, adherence of the bishops, the principal cultural figures, to the Frank church tended to promote use of German along with liturgical Latin. The influence of religious divisions was also notable in German penetration of the Swiss Alpine valleys, although economic factors such as the mobility of German cow herders were significant. Still farther east, the isolated Rhaeto-Romansch, a group closer to Gallic Romance dialects than to the neighboring Italians to the south, were more easily assimilated by Germans. Because the Rhaeto-Romansch lay between Germans and Italians until quite late in the Middle Ages, there was no linguistic contact boundary between Germans and Italians.[39]

Along the boundaries just analyzed, local people were well aware at all times that a sharp linguistic division existed between them and villages only a few miles away. Some sophisticated travelers also noted the difference in crossing such a boundary. Most travelers, including many educated persons, had little occasion to remark on the languages used in a village they passed through, however, for they were accustomed to using a single elaborated code, Latin, for communicating with other educated persons. Down to the twelfth century, this prevalence of a single elaborated code set Western Christendom apart from the multiple elaborated codes of Islam. The Western situation bore a certain resemblance to Byzantium, but the differences were significant. Uneducated people in the Byzantine core areas (Asia Minor, Thrace, and peninsular Greece) spoke Greek dialects intelligible to the educated Constantinopolitan. Moreover, the proportion literate in Greek, including numerous laymen, was far larger than Latin literates in the early medieval West. The Greek *koine* remained cultivated in syntax and vocabulary, but Latin degenerated. The warrior ruling stratum of West Europe remained, as a rule, unable to speak Latin throughout the Middle Ages; when the stratum did become literate, it was in vernacular languages. During the Carolingian period, there had been a brief flowering of German manuscripts (old poems, new religious verses), but from then until about 1100 scarcely anything written in German has survived.

Several scholars note the decline of Latin as early as the second century.[40] As Ferdinand Lot trenchantly remarks, after 600 people did not again dare to write the way they customarily spoke until the tenth century in France and much later in other European countries. Moreover, Lot points out, the only men who could write had little occasion to converse with other educated men in Latin, for ecclesiastical gatherings were rare.[41]

Nevertheless, the Latin liturgy, mandatory north of the Pyrenees after Charlemagne, and the pressing requirements for uniform record-keeping and communication, demanded continued cultivation of Latin. The evidence is strong that clerics thought in their respective vernaculars, then crudely translated into the written language. At times, two types of Latin were recognized: a relatively correct church style (*Latin obscurum*) and notarial Latin (*Latin circa romanicum*), a crude form mixed with the vernacular.[42] But the small staffs of educated ecclesiastics provided the entire apparatus of record-keeping for ecclesiastical administration and secular polities alike. The first lay scribe appeared in the French royal chancery as late as 1298, later in many other chanceries.

A single elaborated code inevitably coincided with a class division. Such class division has continued to set the Western world apart from the ethno-religious segmentation prevalent in Islam and in some East European countries. At an early stage, however, an accommodation between the Latin of the clergy and the speeches of the predominantly Germanic aristocracy had to be attained. In some respects, the relationship of Latin clerics to Germanic warriors resembled the coexistence of Persian or Arab "men of the law" with untutored Turkic warriors. Very quickly, however, priest and aristocrat were conversing in a common vernacular, although the former alone possessed an elaborated written code. The large component of Romance nobles and nobles of mixed descent among the Franks, as compared to the Visigoths, Burgundians, and Lombards, probably facilitated such growth of vernacular communication. Even in France, however, the Carolingian kings spoke German; Hugh Capet (987) was the first monarch to speak Romance alone. Strong memories of Germanic descent persisted among the Francian, Italian, Provençal, and "Gothic" Castilian nobilities; but it appears that by about 1000 all use of Germanic speeches had ceased in what is now Romance Europe. Two generations later, the Norman Conquest—although carried out by a group with vivid recollection of Germanic origins—for two centuries added the nobility of England to the Romance-speaking world.[43]

From about 1000 on, therefore, contact between the Romance and the Germanic spheres consisted of an intercourse between two territorially distinct groups. Apart from England, such contacts as persisted had the quality of visitations rather than day-to-day contact. Nobles, townsmen, and peasants in each smaller European area all tended to speak similar dialects affording a rough means of mutual comprehensibility. Most of the clergy commonly used the dialect for day-to-day communication, although their travels (especially for monks) were broader. Whether in Romance countries Latin was usually perceived as more familiar, hence less a special code for sacral usage and long-distance communication, than in Germanic countries is debatable. In 813, nearly two centuries before Romance became the sole language of the Francian Court, the Carolingian church required sermons in Romance as well as in Germanic ("*Theoticam*"). A few written documents appeared in each language; even in Italy, religious instruction in the vernacular was required by 1000.[44]

During the high Middle Ages, Italy received numerous German influences from trade, pilgrimages, and imperial visitations. Only the latter appear to have aroused widespread concern, related more to the imperial impact on factional struggles than to ethnic perceptions. Occasionally, an Italian town accepted a German *podestà* (temporary dictator) as "neutral." Italian dismay at German "barbarism" was aroused by Frederick I's repression in Milan in 1162.[45] By the fourteenth century, however, writers such as Dante praised the German rulers and claimed German descent. Petrarch, also claiming German ancestry, referred (as did the Roman leader Cola di Rienzo) to the *furor theutonicum*. In contrast to Italy, there was practically no German political or military presence in France or Iberia during the high Middle Ages. As noted earlier, there was considerable rivalry between French and Germans for the Frank heritage and thus for predominance in Europe. Some of this was expressed in terms of linguistic and cultural resentment. For the most part, the prestigious French epic and romantic literature simply "naturalized" Germanic themes, while discussing the peoples usually identified as German in stereotypes ranging from admiration for courage to contempt for drunkenness.[46] As a German scholar warned seventy years ago, however, one should not exaggerate the ethnic significance of such stereotypes: "In those times, the troubadours, strong in their faith, distinguished parties less by nationality than by religion. For the troubadours the opponents are not primarily Germans, Slavs, Arabs; they are enemies of the Christian religion."[47]

Germanic reactions were sharper because of increasing feelings of cultural inferiority.[48] In Court society, French influence increased until the fifteenth century, but the burgher culture of the German cities was more resistant.[49] As Friedrich Heer points out, even the *Minnesingers* were modeled on Provençal troubadour styles, and the strongest exponents of imperial claims, such as Frederick I, introduced the most French culture.[50]

On the actual boundary, relations do not appear to have become exacerbated, when compared to the numerous local quarrels of feudal lords. Bloch contends that by the twelfth century French-speaking crusading knights from the Holy Roman empire were drawing closer to knights from the French kingdom than to Germans from the empire. Germans, on the other hand, had begun to refer to Lorraine as "non-German Germany."[51]

On the threshold of the modern period, awareness of linguistic divergence increased to a degree that makes even a survey impracticable here.

One development that turned out to be decisive for the German sphere internally requires attention, however. As was noted in chapter 5, the French culture of the French kingdom exercised a strong attraction on the fifteenth-century Burgundian polity. All of its institutions were based on French, the sole language of the elite. Charles the Bold called himself a "Portugalois" after his mother and frequently spoke English, but the basic identity of the dynasty was also French. The peasants and townspeople of Burgundy on both sides of the imperial frontier were solidly French, as was a notable portion of the Burgundian southern Netherlands. The greater part of Flanders, Brabant, and the northern Netherlands, commercially the most important parts of the Burgundian polity, had French-speaking nobles and Low German (Flemish)-speaking peasants. These areas were anomalous in West Europe, where, by the fifteenth century, the vernacular of nobles and their peasants was usually identical.[52] The critical balance in Flanders was held by the bourgeoisie. By 1300, Bruges patricians (still nominally within the French kingdom) used French, whereas Antwerp and Louvain tended to retain Flemish, perhaps because of influences from the administration of the Cologne archepiscopal province. Brussels apparently became more French under the influence of the Burgundian Great Court of Justice located there. In the fourteenth and fifteenth centuries, use of Flemish became a symbol of resistance to both Burgundian and French kingdom Courts. Moreover, a literature, most brilliantly represented by the poet Maerlant, unified the diverse Low German dialects of the area during the thirteenth century, followed by a popular devotional movement of the fourteenth century using the vernacular.[53]

By the sixteenth century, the Low German speech area under Burgundy might have gone in either of two directions. Continuation of the trends just outlined might have produced unity around a Flemish elaborated code prevailing from Boulogne almost to the present northern boundary of the Netherlands. If dynastic and historical accidents had united this region to a purely German ruling house that thereafter became Lutheran, these "Netherlands" might ultimately have accepted High German as did the Low German Hansa cities farther east. If that had occurred, the entire modern Germanic region (except Scandinavia, where languages had become sharply differentiated from German before the invasion period, and England) might have adhered to the same literary language. Instead, the effect of the Reformation was to produce a distinctive Netherlands culture in the Dutch United Provinces.

Most authorities agree that the actual division between the present-day Netherlands and Belgian Flanders is almost entirely the product of military operations. Both Protestantism and anti-Spanish sentiment were at least as influential in southern Flanders and Brabant at the start of the Reformation as in the less-developed northern provinces. Moreover, the Frisian and Gelderland gentry in the latter area were more closely connected to eastern Low Germans than to the seaport areas of the United Provinces, which had the same literary speech as southern Flanders. Relying on natural water barriers and their own naval prowess, the Calvinists were able to control Amsterdam and other northern coastal towns despite opposition from a Catholic bourgeois majority, whereas in the south Spaniards could not be resisted.

Subsequent consolidation strangely resembled the way Safavids and Ottomans produced ethnically unified polities during the same period. Calvinists fled to the northern towns they controlled, providing much of the cultural and political leadership there and ruthlessly suppressing local Catholics. William the Silent introduced Flemish (Dutch) as the official language, although Latin was retained for scholarly use and connections with French-Calvinist Geneva were close. The Calvinist Bible translation tended to separate Dutch from High German, whereas Luther's Bible had unified the latter and eastern Low German.[54] The Spanish based their power on French-speaking Artois and Walloonia. They used French or Spanish for official communications, depending on which language their chancery secretaries knew best. Neither Spanish nor Austrian Habsburg rulers in the southern Netherlands actively opposed use of Flemish in the communes.[55] All the weight of cultural institutions and prestige favored French, however. Southern Flemish did not revive, as an expression of lower-class efforts to turn a restricted code into an elaborated code (almost identical with written Dutch), until the nineteenth century.

Down to the modern period, perception of linguistic differences between Romance and Germanic languages, although always latent, rarely produced sharp friction. Even when such friction arose, as in the Netherlands, it was resolved by circumstances fundamentally unrelated to language cleavage. Friction was minimalized in the West because at a very early period the principal bodies of Germanic and Romance speakers were territorially distinct. Hence, despite vicious dynastic rivalries, the consciousness of divergent cultural and linguistic interests was low except in a few areas like Flanders where language and class cleavage coincided.

European Linguistic Barriers: The Germanic-Slavic Case

In East Central Europe, reinforcing cleavages along linguistic and class lines was the rule rather than the exception. Most aspects of Slavic-Germanic contact have been treated in preceding chapters, so the linguistic element can be treated summarily here. Where German peasants settled in large numbers near the German linguistic boundary, it appeared for many centuries that a stable division had arisen, resembling the persistent boundaries in West Europe. This was notably true of the Bohemian plateau, where during the twelfth through the fourteenth centuries streams of German settlers moving across the mountains from all directions except the east encountered Czech-speaking peasant settlements moving outward from the central river valleys.[56] Most areas where the Germans settled on invitation of the Czech Přemyslid kings had been virtually untouched by Czechs, though a few Czech settlers may have been Germanized. Hence there was no overlap of villages. Only 1.3 percent of the inhabitants of German communes were Czech in the late nineteenth century, only 88 of 7,063 Bohemian communes were mixed in ethnic background, and only half of these 88 were on the linguistic boundary. Apparently, this sharp division had existed for many centuries, producing a line boundary comparable to the Germanic-Romance boundary in Belgium.[57] Although far from straight, the boundary was clear and continuous and, like other linguistic boundaries, it disregarded shifting modern economic requirements. But German-Slavic contact in Bohemia was complicated by several other factors. First, awareness of linguistic differences was intense, although many Czechs perforce learned to communicate in German. Perhaps awareness was intensified because German settlers had no contact with other speakers of Germanic dialects too different from theirs for easy communication, whereas Czech speakers had almost no boundaries with other Slavic speakers. Hence consciousness of a communications barrier was focused entirely on the German-Czech difference. Moreover, although villages were separate, the two linguistic groups were heavily intermingled in Prague and other large towns located deep in the Czech countryside. After 1620 the German urban majority included the entire bourgeoisie and upper classes; hence a class cleavage was added to the linguistic awareness. The kingdom of Bohemia constituted a geographic and strategic "natural" unit, with an unusually long history of stable political frontiers. Consequently, both German and Czech inhabitants (an unchanging ratio of about one to two from the fifteenth century until the mid-twentieth century) regarded Bohemia as a unity that must be preserved.[58]

The long history of violent quarrels—the Hussite rebellion, the early seventeenth-century anti-German measures, the sweeping suppression of the Bohemian nobility a few years later, continuing pressures against the Czech language—all contributed to extreme antipathies. The nineteenth-century Czech movement, like Flemish nationalism along an equally stable linguistic boundary, was motivated by class feeling, for Germans comprised almost all of the nobles, the wealthier bourgeois, and higher officials. The culmination, Adolf Hitler's seizure of the entire country in 1939, was followed six years later by complete expulsion of the German population. The historical position of the Slovenes, although they were weaker and less subject to violent reversals than the Czechs, was similar.

The lack of direct relationship between sharpness of linguistic boundaries and the ultimate intensity of ethnic conflict is suggested by the fact that in 1945 Germans were expelled by all the other Central East European states. Expellees included the large German peasant populations of East Prussia and Silesia, the fringes of Brandenburg, West Prussia, and Poznan. Some of these territories had been so long and intimately connected with German rule and were so solidly settled by groups considering themselves German that it is pointless to discuss their "reversion" after eight centuries to Poland as a result of ethnic friction. Silesia and East Prussia, on the other hand, represented historic provinces somewhat resembling Bohemia, where streams of German and Slavic colonization had met along fairly continuous, although sinuous, lines. In East Prussia the considerable Slavic population considered itself, as Lutheran, closer to Germans than to Poles. In Silesia, on the other hand, Poles were a minority in a province that (although the political frontiers were unstable) had been under German rule for centuries. Taken as a whole, however, the problems posed by these territories were not different from irredentas in the West.

Beyond these areas of compact settlement adjoining Germany proper, German-speaking peasants, as discussed in chapter 4, constituted numerous small islands of settlement in Poland. Because so much of the population of the kingdom of Hungary was Slavic, it is convenient to point out that a somewhat similar situation prevailed there. In addition, most of the urban populations in both kingdoms during the Middle Ages was German. Rural Germans had, in many cases, been assimilated by the end of the Middle Ages, but newer peasant settlements in the Banat of Temesvar remained distinct, as did the old Transylvanian "Saxon" colony and a number of small "islands" near the frontier of the Holy Roman empire in Poland. These exceptions caused occasional uneasiness among ruling groups in Poland and Hungary and among the settlers themselves, who, like other distinctive groups, clung to their particularistic "privileges." German-language islands in the cities were scarcely more directly important for Poland; even those in Hungary, which did maintain their German speech, became assimilated in other ways, as discussed in chapter 4. But there were more indications of friction between these diasporas and the environing populations than appeared among the geographically separated Germanic and Romance populations. Concern of Germans for their diaspora position, combined with a consciousness of cultural and economic superiority, gave rise to such expressions as the following commentary in a 1798 survey of Hungarian statistics: "No nation, either of the old or the new world, is as scattered over the continents and in every climate as the German, and none thinks and acts in such a situation more cosmopolitanly."[59]

Part of the difficulty, of course, was that by no means all German minorities "thought cosmopolitanly." Intransigent insistence on their own privileges (against fellow Germans like the Lübeck-law cities and against Catholic Poles, as well as against pagan Old Prussians, Lithuanians, Estonians, and Latvians) characterized the various German orders of crusading knights. Whereas in 1237 Polish lords gave the Knights Hospitallers, identified as the *curus Theutonicus*, the right to settle on Polish territory, shared antagonism to the Teutonic Order was a major factor behind the Polish-Lithuanian personal union a century and a half later. One move of the new king, Jagiello, was to expel the *"natio Teutonica"* from his combined realm. During the same period, Poland vainly claimed Pommerelia (much later known as the "Polish corridor") from the Teutonic Order on the ground that the territory was Polish-speaking.[60] In the most celebrated clash, the battle of Tannenberg in 1410, royal Polish forces defeated the Teutonic Order's knights. Down to the Partitions, however, such extreme antagonism between Polish elites and Germans was rare. A parallel did not arise in Hungary until the Habsburg centralizing measures, which began in some respects as early as the sixteenth century.

Ordinarily, the rural-based Polish and Magyar elites found the symbiosis with "useful" burgher Germans too valuable to jeopardize. Friction with neighboring German territorial polities was less marked than with polities ruled by Orthodox or pagan Slavs, pagan Lithuanians, Moslem or pagan Turks. The strong identities of the Polish and Hungarian kingdoms backed by papal policy acted as a barrier to high-level German plans for expansion. But the sacral myths and symbols of these East Central European polities rested on a Catholicism shared with Germans, a factor that muted hostility toward them as a cultural and linguistic group. All circumstances considered, language was probably not much stronger as a force for antagonism between Germans and Slavs than between Germanic and Romance peoples. The principal difference between the two types of contact was that when modern linguistic nationalism did arise, a basis for irreconcilable antagonisms was present in the inextricably intermingled populations of East Central Europe in contrast to the linguistically separable Western territories.

Transitional Linguistic Differentiation: The Romance Case

A major obstacle to understanding the latent significance of language differentiation in Europe has arisen from failure to distinguish between obvious barriers created by geographical juxtaposition of very different languages and the lack of perceptible dividing lines among transitional dialects of the same language family. In the first case, unavoidable perception of movement from a given language area to a very different one may constitute merely a latent factor for identity. Even during periods of latency, however, consciousness of differences from neighbors was always more acute in boundary districts than in the interior of a language family. When such differences became salient for speakers of a given language group, leaders of the ethnic movement that arose came disproportionately from such boundary districts.[61] Moreover, the latent linguistic differences between speakers of sharply differing language families was always available for mobilization if (as in Bohemia) factors such as political rivalries, religious cleavages, or class differentiation produced the appropriate conditions. But such mobilizing conditions have almost always been the direct consequence, often unintended, of the operation of political or religious organizations.

Conversely, the Germanic, Romance, and Slavic languages that gradually emerged from imperceptible transitions among the peasant dialects within each of the three language families did not necessarily constitute latent factors available for identity mobilization, although specific historical circumstances might make particular dialects available for such manipulation. Medieval observers were occasionally aware of this fundamental distinction between sharply distinguished language families on the one hand and mutually intelligible dialect divisions within a single family on the other. Significantly, expression of such awareness occurred when an observer was confronted by a very alien situation that he perceived as parallel. For example, a papal envoy to the Mongols, C. de Bridia, recognized their internal linguistic differentiation as resembling the dialect divisions he knew in Europe: "There are four, namely, Moal, Zumoal, Merkit, and Mecrit, constituting a single language, but differentiated from one another in the same manner as the Bohemians, Poles, and Ruthenians [i.e., Slavs]; or as Romans, Lombards, and Friulians [i.e., Italians]; or as East Franks, Thuringians, and Suabians [i.e., Middle Germans]; or as Saxons, Flemings, and Westphalians [i.e., Low Germans]."62 De Bridia took for granted major discontinuities in European language families similar to those accepted by linguists today, except that he apparently considered the differences between Middle and Low German to be equivalent to the barriers setting off the Germanic family from the Slavic and the Romance families. For the purposes of this study, further exploration of differentiation within the Germanic group is unnecessary. Close examination of dialect differentiation within the Romance and Slavic families, however, which present remarkable parallels, is highly instructive.

In its origins, differentiation among Romance dialects followed an unusual pattern, namely, disintegration of a language that had already been standardized by an elaborated code, Latin. During the Roman Republican age, the Italic dialects that contributed to Latin were unified both in writing and in stylized rhetoric for the predominantly oral culture. Such incisive forms of expression were produced that they have continued to shape "the molds of a uniform thought" even for Germans and Englishmen.63 Just as this highly elaborated code was reaching perfection, however, it began (like the Roman legal system and the Roman economy) to submit to particularistic influences. Although it is hard to prove a negative, most scholars reject the older view that the development of provincial forms of Latin (any more than particularist forms of Roman law) was significantly influenced by "underlying strata" of influences from the pre-Roman populations. Scholars—with notable exceptions—also reject the notion that Germanic influences strongly affected Romance differentiation. Walther von Wartburg, for example, finds an unusually strong Germanic influence on French; but a detailed examination of vocabulary shows that during its formative period French accepted as many words (four hundred) from a single related Romance speech, Languedocian, as from German and Celtic together, to say nothing of numerous direct borrowings from Latin.64

In any case, Wartburg and other scholars find the principal source of Romance differentiation to have been early varieties of colloquial speech current among Romans, or at the most Italian speakers of Latin, before Rome Latinized immense areas of Europe. Similarly, an Italian scholar concludes that "the entire history of Italian, and, unless I am mistaken, long periods of the history of Spanish and French, can be subsumed under the history of the solution of a contrast, from the beginning, between cultural and vulgar language, prolonging into the modern era a condition which, as we have seen, was inherent in the history of Latin."65 The fundamental dividing line was between areas Latinized by "patrician" influences, disseminated primarily by the municipal school system, and areas receiving Latin from uncultivated garrisons. The latter included most of the Balkans as well as all Italy south of the Appenines. Of contemporary languages, only Rumanian and Italian derive from this eastern garrison influence. The western "patrician" influence dominated northwest Africa, Iberia, Gaul, Britain, the Alps-Danube area, and the Po valley. Today western Latin is represented by French, Spanish, and Portuguese, but the group also included very important medieval dialects that have since declined.

Within the Western Latin sphere, standardization by schools and the constant movement of elites and military units maintained the elaborated code in the towns. Some tendency toward dialects of Latin may, however, have arisen from the differing points (Trier, Lyons, and others) from which Latin was diffused. As urban life declined, schools closed, and each little countryside became isolated, it developed its own *patois*. Scholars such as Ferdinand Brunot regard the transitions between such *patois* as distinguishable only by trained linguists attuned to the minor variations in word usage and pronunciation. Over a long distance such differences accumulate; but the choice of a line dividing one dialect grouping from another is, according to this view, essentially arbitrary.[66] Other scholars, although recognizing that variations among *patois* within a given dialect are very small, believe that determinable zones—certainly not line boundaries—always existed between dialects. Marcel Cohen, a leading exponent of this position, basically agrees with Brunot, however, on the lack of clear boundaries:

All things considered, there were no sharp boundaries between spoken languages having the same origin in a relatively recent past and contiguous on the ground. A true linguistic frontier forms later when languages that had started out from points more or less distant from one another and had spread like spots of oil finally converged. . . . Thus one can speak of the frontiers of "official" French, Italian, and Spanish; but that does not prevent there being, at many points, an insensible transition of the languages spoken as *patois* by the [nominal] adherents of these [official] languages.[67]

Probably within the Romance area completely transitional dialects and dialects marked by slightly more precise limits both existed. In the cases where the latter appear, there is considerable scholarly agreement on the influence of earlier Roman administrative limits, indigenous "tribal" divisions that preceded the Romans, and ecclesiastical divisions that generally coincided with the Roman limits. The principal mechanism for establishing a *patois* zone, Marcel Cohen suggests, was communication in an administrative-market center, and these centers tended to remain the same for pre-Roman groups, Romans, and the church.[68]

The most significant dialect boundary—apart from the Appenines zone dividing eastern and western Latin—appears to have been the zonal boundary between Francian and Languedocian. As Cohen points out, this boundary was older and more durable than the boundary between the Frank and the Visigoth kingdoms. André Piganiol traces it to Diocletian's division of A.D. 298 between Aquitania–Gallia Narbonensis on the one hand and Gallia Lugudunensis on the other.[69] South of that line, all the way to the Appenines and eastern Iberia was a region more united in peasant linguistic patterns than any other in West Europe. These dialects, called Languedocian or Provençal—the terms are nearly interchangeable—acquired a literary language in the late eleventh century. But there is strong evidence, at least for the high Middle Ages, that common people within the large region could communicate with each other with only moderate difficulty.

The life of the fourteenth-century itinerant Catalan preacher, St. Vincent Ferrer, illustrates this unity. The following account, though admiring, tries to provide a linguistic explanation for his legendary "gift of tongues":

> Catalan-Valencian is a *langue d'oc* like Provençal. In our time a Catalan can make himself understood to an Auvergnat or a Piedmontese. In the midst of the Middle Ages the various dialects of *oc*, less remote from their Latin base than at present, were less differentiated among themselves. The speech of Limoges was so close to that of the Balearic Islands and of Valencia that they called the latter "*Lémosin*." The medieval Valencian language is neither more nor less than the troubadours' language. It was even so close to the Old French of the Loire and the Seine regions that one can read Master Vincent's Catalan sermons right off without noticing that they are written in a foreign language, which in rigorous logic one should be ignorant of. This Valencian also contained numerous Castilian terms, and it was easy for the preacher to learn Castilian enough to make himself understood. Apart from Castile, where he did not encounter insurmountable obstacles, one may therefore assert that in the region from Murcia in Spain up to the Loire our pilgrim found a vast "France" in which, still only slightly differentiated, a Romance speech of the *langue d'oc* prevailed.[70]

A glance at the map of contemporary Europe will demonstrate that this remarkable zone of intercommunication does not now correspond—and has not for many centuries—to any unity at the political level. Certainly the political developments are evidence that language as communication is not decisive for constituting identity. The reasons why a common linguistic communication vehicle did not become a set of unifying identity symbols are complex; but they do a great deal to elucidate the whole problem of language and identity.

Down to 1258, Catalonia and Languedoc-Provence were united in many ways: marriage networks, architectural styles, dynastic aspirations for a larger polity, all tended to draw the regions on both sides of the Pyrenees together. Even the church on both sides of the mountains was directed from Narbonne. But the symbolic network that bound the two sides together was related to the myth of Charlemagne as liberator from the Moslems. That is, instead of isolating the identity of the Languedoc-Catalan region, its myth incorporated the region in a larger identity, the Frank empire, or, more cogently, France. No better description of the power of an identity myth to organize a complex of symbols has been written than the following passage by J. Lee Shneidman, although he does not explicitly employ these analytic terms:

> Despite their proximity to Aragon, the Catalans behaved more like Frenchmen than like Aragonese. Their ideals were Carolingian or Capetian. As long as the Frankish state was the *reference*, all Catalan action was predicated by it. . . . For all practical purposes, then, there was no physical connection between the March and the Frankish state after the latter date [1088], yet for the next two centuries the Catalans acted as if they were still part of France. This is evident in their foreign policy, their marriage alliances—which were a particular form of foreign policy—and their method of dating documents. In examining these factors we shall have a clue to the Catalan's sense of national identity.[71]

Late in the eleventh century, Catalonia was detached from the archepiscopal province of Narbonne. The papacy at first wished to place the Catalan dioceses under the archbishop of Toledo, but in the mid-thirteenth century was persuaded to unite them with Aragon in a revived archepiscopal province of Tarragona, although the coastal districts had a dialect very distinct from Aragonese. By that time the destruction of Languedoc society, centered on the county of Toulouse, by the northern French crusade against the Albigensians completed the reorientation of the Catalans. Shneidman writes, "Basically the direction of Catalan foreign involvement depended upon the Catalans' psychological identity. . . . when the Catalan nobility reidentified themselves as purely Catalan, the merchants were able to enroll them in their cause and the province's full power became engaged in economic imperialism."[72]

This alteration was not wholly the result of dynastic politics. It coincided with the opening of opportunities in the Mediterranean such as that which led the quasi-sovereign Company of Catalans to dominate, briefly, large parts of the Aegean. The mercenary group used Aragonese for its chronicles and "Aragon" for its war cry.[73] The shift in Catalan identity also meant participation in Aragonese royal conquests from the Moslems in the western Mediterranean. From these adventures a *conquistador* (the term is Aragonese as well as Castilian) mentality developed. In other words, a version of the Christian frontier myth that formed the Castilian identity also reoriented Catalan identity away both from the greater France and the lesser France of Languedoc.

By the thirteenth century, when the Castilian and the Catalan myths converged, however, the two Iberian groups were very different. Some note was made in chapter 3 of the differences in visual symbols derived from Moslem styles. Much earlier, Castile had gone over to Mudejar architecture while Catalonia preserved a very early form of Romanesque shared with Languedoc. The forms of Gothic (earlier in Catalonia) that invaded the peninsula were also very different; Catalonia drew on the Cistercian Order, Castile on Cluny. There is little resemblance between the Cathedral of Barcelona and the Cathedral of Seville.

The strongest boundary mechanisms had arisen in the field of language. In many respects, Castilian, isolated from West Europe by its military and geographic circumstances, is the most idiosyncratic of Romance languages. Precisely because of this isolation, Castilian developed precociously, with the kings trying to use it as an elaborated code for administration as early as the thirteenth century. It is conceivable that their numerous educated Jewish and Moslem subjects, willing to speak Romance but averse to Latin, had something to do with the kings' efforts. At the overt level, Castilian elites assimilated use of their language to a divine mission confirmed by the final defeat of the Moors in Granada and the simultaneous discovery of America. A Castilian grammar—the first systematic work for a modern European language—was also completed in 1492. Praising it, the bishop of Avila told Queen Isabella: "Your Majesty, language is the perfect instrument of empire." Other Castilians claimed that their language would be the successor of the three holy languages, to express the heroic deeds of their kings and their world mission, with barbarians subdued by Isabella learning Castilian just as the Spaniards' barbarian forebears had learned Latin.[74] Despite such grandiose expectations, Castilian has never even been able to become fully "Spanish." There are many reasons why the Catalans retained a separate identity, but undoubtedly the emergence of Castilian and Catalan as two very distinct Romance languages before the union of the crowns was crucial. Charles V's abdication decree of 1556 was issued in Castilian throughout Spain except in Aragon and its dependencies, where Latin—the last refuge for Habsburg tergiversation there as in Hungary—was used. During the following century, Castilian *letrados* (lawyers) who poured into Catalonia were especially hated, probably because their status depended on linguistic manipulation in Castilian, because after 1620 Latin usage became a barrier rather than an asset in social mobility. At the same time, Catalans were virtually excluded from imperial assignments and the prestigious military orders.[75]

The analysis of why Catalan identity broke away from the broader Languedocian sphere has carried the account of Romance differentiation well beyond the Middle Ages; but developments in the medieval period provide the key to understanding this differentiation. Beginning in the tenth century and accelerating down to the fourteenth, large numbers of West Europeans traveled about the Continent. Crusaders, clerics, merchants, pilgrims to shrines like Santiago de Compostella—all contributed to merging the very small linguistic units noted above. Probably professional manipulators of the vernaculars were most important, however. Because, except for extraordinary preachers such as St. Vincent Ferrer, clergymen were able to satisfy their communication needs by using Latin when far from home, these new communications specialists consisted of Court troubadours and the more popular minstrels. Both, as Karl Vossler has brilliantly stated the problem, had to find ways to overcome the differences of Romance dialects they encountered after traveling a hundred or so miles.

> Generally neither the minstrels nor the troubadours, neither clerical teachers and pupils nor humanists were sedentary. Throughout the entire Middle Ages and Renaissance the arts of singing and speech were best represented by "traveling" people. . . . The individual poets could proceed in two ways. Adapting their hereditary speech sounds and accents to the ears of listeners in neighboring areas and wandering from market to market and Court to Court they might form an adapted, mixed type of speech which was not entirely at home anywhere. Or they could seek a higher set of rules like those of Latin grammar as an ideal for writing and for art.[76]

In other words, the troubadours developed for the Court aristocracies elaborated codes that were potential rivals of Latin. The content of such a "vehicular language," as Marcel Cohen terms the troubadours' elaborated code, probably developed through interaction of men from a broad area, each retelling (for the culture was still predominantly oral) each others' romances in their own words. In this way, they gradually produced a common vocabulary.[77]

The earliest major development along these lines was in Languedoc about 1100. The troubadour genre was virtually identified with Langue-doc, and troubadour speech was adopted as the Court language as far away as the Piedmont, with its closely related dialect. After the Hohenstaufen loss of Sicily, the Provençal Angevin dynasty introduced Provençal to the Sicilian Court as well. Meanwhile, Sicilian poets traveling with Frederick II's Court had produced a Court vernacular (*vulgare aulicum*) incorporating some Provençal and French features, but based on the Tuscan dialect derived from eastern Latin.[78] This language was not often written until after 1300, when the immense prestige of Dante, Petrarch, and Boccaccio suddenly catapulted Tuscan into prominence as a European literary language.

In the meantime, during the tenth to twelfth centuries, Old French had developed from the dialects spoken in the densely populated region between the Loire and the Aisne rivers that constituted the heart—indeed, for practical purposes, the entire body—of the French kingdom. Paris, an early stronghold for Latin schools, played no significant role in this development until the twelfth century. There is considerable uncertainty concerning the initiatory role of the royal Court, for German was spoken there until 987. The masterpiece of French epic poetry, the "Song of Roland," appeared in 1080, thus influences other than the Court's must have been formative. For the next two generations (until the rise of the troubadours) Old French, disseminated through the crusades, became the preferred elaborated code of the Romance nobility.[79] By the late eleventh century, the Court, peripatetic in the region of closely related dialects from Orleans to Laon, played a very strong part in standardizing and popularizing the new linguistic form, as evidenced by its rapid spread to Champagne after that area was added to the royal domains in 1300.[80]

Court French still had to compete with Norman French, which prevailed in England after the French king forced many English vassals to choose between his suzerainty and the English king's, resulting in a considerable resettlement in England. In the most significant symbol of identification, their preferred burial place, many Anglo-Norman aristocrats remained attached to France until the fourteenth century. Norman French prevailed in law courts in England until 1362 and to some extent in the English royal Court until 1500.[81] A more serious obstacle to standardizing French was Picard, which may have been based on a Romance dialect area corresponding to the old Gallic division of the Belgae; or Picard may have derived from a different center of Latinization (Trier) than central French, which had received its Latin via Lyons. The prosperous towns of Picardy and Artois fostered the local dialect, in spite of aristocratic scorn, through institutions like the religious comic theater. As late as the seventeenth century, local peasants could not speak standard French.[82]

It would be a long time before French replaced Latin for official purposes in the French kingdom: 1250 in the royal chancery, 1539 in the law courts. The wars of religion hastened the turn to French as the language of civilization, despite the Catholic Ligue's effort, for a time, to emphasize Latin as the language it shared with its Spanish allies: "They are not foreigners to us in the church, where they use the same ceremonies and the same language."[83] The prestige of French usage at Court and by great nobles gave it, however, a European reputation as the language in which stirring secular themes, whether verse or prose, should be written. The most famous example is Marco Polo's *Merveilles du Monde* (1298). The elevation of French to the pinnacle of the European vernaculars was only part of a development by which the traveling poets and chroniclers of the high Middle Ages treated each of the new languages as a semielaborated code suited to specific literary genres. Along with the local language of communication, one or more genre codes were used in each major cultural center.[84] These languages included Castilian for solemn prose, Galician-Portuguese for lyrics, Provençal for lyric romances, Picard for satire, Norman for didactic works.

Both the royal consolidation of French and Castilian and the sudden vogue of Italian appear to have undermined this incipient development of elaborated codes among the lay literati of Western Europe. If the level of political organization had remained as low as it was during the twelfth and thirteenth centuries, it is conceivable that the cosmopolitan writers would have produced a general Romance language by the same process by which they had amalgamated dialects to produce specific languages. It is perhaps significant that separate terms for the languages commonly called *Romanice* or *volgare* appeared only at the end of the Middle Ages (*français, provençal, italiano, catalan, castellano, español,* and others).[85] But the influence of the emerging polities and the Italian bourgeoisie was too strong to await such necessarily slow development. Italian remained (apart, of course, from Latin, which still preempted truly "serious" international scholarship) the principal vehicle for humanism from the fourteenth century down to the early sixteenth century. By the latter period, even papal envoys used Italian in correspondence with the Curia. Then Castilian, fortified by the power and prestige of the Iberian monarchy, assumed the ascendancy, with almost as sudden a burst of energy as Italian had exhibited.[86] Throughout the two centuries, French had maintained such a high level of prestige that it is questionable to speak of its ever having been surpassed. After the decline of Spanish following the Thirty Years' War, French regained unquestioned superiority during the century of Absolutism. Even in defeat, the French saw their language replace Latin for the first time as the inter-

270 270 / Nations before Nationalism

Table 3. The Rise of the Romance Elaborated Codes

Language	First Written Text	Conversion of Private Documents to Vernacular	Major Usage in Administration	Earliest Literary Prestige
Provençal		1102	ca. 1150	ca. 1100
French	842	1204	1250	1080
Castilian	1145	1173	ca. 1250	ca. 1250
Italian	964	1193	ca. 1300	1300
Portuguese	1192			ca. 1450
Rumanian	late 15th c.			ca. 1850

Sources: Column 1, Cohen, *Histoire d'une Langue*, p. 51 (except Provençal). Column 2, Schmitt, p. xxix; Wartburg, *Problems . . . in Linguistics*, p. 222 (Provençal). Column 3, Cohen, *Histoire d'une Langue*, p. 88 (Provençal, French Royal Chancery); Hillgarth, p. 13 (Castilian). Column 4, see text; on Rumanian developments, see Turczynski, pp. 223ff. Column 5, Curtius, pp. 383ff. Column 6, Yardeni, p. 48; Gilbert, in Ranum, p. 38; Vossler, *Aus der romanischen Welt*, p. 283.

national diplomatic vehicle at the Treaty of Rastatt in 1714.[87] What Europe witnessed, therefore, was a relay of brilliant Romance linguistic achievements rather than a unified elaborated code.

Even in the sixteenth century, all three languages (together with Portuguese, which alone of the promising genre codes of the thirteenth century secured an independent political base) still suffered from the humanists' charges that their irregular grammar made them inferior to Latin. Local feeling and princes' pride led to efforts to refine the vernaculars. In Florence the Accademia della Crusca, in Rome the Accademia dei Lincei, worked on philology and dictionaries during the sixteenth century. The Académie Française (1635) and the Réal Academia Española (1713) used these Italian models to develop their languages as symbols of unified polities. As a result, the principal Romance polities entered the age of nationalism with fully elaborated linguistic codes. Because all of these had begun outside the great central Languedocian sphere and continued to base their elites in capitals outside that sphere (Paris, Madrid, Florence, Rome, Naples) the diversity was far greater than one might have anticipated from observing the original mutual comprehensibility of the Romance dialects. As the literary languages were spread by conscription, mass education, and mass media during the late eighteenth and nineteenth centuries, they produced sharp language boundaries (for all speakers ex-

Period of Ascendancy	Academy for Standardization
1150–1250	
1050–1150	1635
1258–1300	
1650–1762	
1530–1650	1713
1300–1530	1582

cept a sparse frontier peasant population) on the Alps and Pyrenees, where once imperceptible transitional forms had united the peoples on both sides of the mountains. This development played a significant part in sealing the territorial division of the European nations. By the sixteenth century, in France at least, every time anyone wanted to emphasize that an event concerned people of that country and them alone, he started by referring to the linguistic criterion.[88]

Along with this conjunction of territorial and linguistic principles went an accentuation of internal class division. As noted in chapter 4, class divisions as well as territorial identity have distinguished West Europe from many other parts of the world ever since the early Middle Ages. The development of a standardized national language, according to the French linguist Antoine Meillet, accentuated class barriers:

Today France has a democratic political organization and all her citizens have access to a certain measure of culture, often very mediocre, even for most who get through secondary education. But she has a refined language made for an aristocracy, which can be fluently and correctly handled only by a small class of society. . . . All the common languages which began to become precise during the Renaissance period are, in varying degrees, similar in this regard. Like French, sometimes almost as much as French, English, Italian, Spanish, Portuguese, German, and Polish are traditional languages created by elites for elites, which one can readily employ and write only at the price of a difficult apprenticeship and as part of a high culture.[89]

Transitional Linguistic Differentiation: The Slavic Case

Whereas the transformation of Latin into a plurality of Romance languages can be clearly traced despite the obscurities of the Middle Ages, the change from a "common Slavic" to the separate contemporary languages left few written records. In this respect, Slavic differentiation resembles the prehistoric differentiation of Indo-European languages or of the early Germanic differentiation that separated the Scandinavian speeches from "West Germanic." Such resemblances are apparent because Slavic evolution represented a particularistic elaboration of a "primitive" language base rather than, as was the case with Romance differentiation, the disintegration of an elaborated code. But the Slavic process occurred so late—apparently during or shortly after the Avar domination of the seventh to eighth centuries—that fairly sophisticated observers were present. Moreover, using philological methods, it is possible to trace many of the features, over such a short period of time, back to a common source. Consequently, one can compare the differentiation of Slavic to that of Latin with sufficient detail to permit some inferences concerning the impact of institutional and political factors.

The common Slavic language, which certain scholars locate on the middle Dnieper River, others farther west, evidently became somewhat differentiated under the impact of mass migrations during the Avar period. At that time the East Slav dialects became differentiated from those farther west and south, although apparently only to a minor extent. Moreover, a new *koine* developed in the Dnieper area among the urbanized Kievan Slavs. In the extreme northwest (Novgorod and Pskov), the dialect of the East Slavs was noticeably different from that of Kiev, and there was probably some differentiation between the extreme southwest (Halich) and the far northeast (Vladimir-Suzdal).[90]

Along with their conversion, these Kievan Rus Slavs obtained a developed literary language, a version of Constantine's Church Slavonic based on Bulgarian. Because the new language had been used in the Bulgarian church since 893, a wide range of religious translations was already available. Most of these translations had been written under the influence of strict Byzantine monastic circles who feared the Hellenic classics. Consequently, from the start the Rus (East Slavs) were equipped with a ready-made literature which their teachers, Bulgarian and Greek ecclesiastics, contended embraced all that was necessary for salvation. This initial situation developed a momentum that discouraged extensive translation from ancient Greek or secular Byzantine works, especially those produced during the revival under the Macedonian dynasty.[91]

The East Slavs also became convinced that Slavic, specifically the Bulgarian ecclesiastical version, was preferred by God because a saint had created it. Even in the ninth century the Slavs had begun to think of themselves as "a new people speaking the same tongue" and praising God in it.[92] Efforts to introduce the classics through instruction in Greek increasingly encountered another obstacle as the various East Slav vernaculars as well as the South Slav developed languages departed from the Old Bulgarian Church Slavonic. Learning the latter required a very great effort, comparable to that required for Latin by Romance youths. When the Constantinople patriarchate did make a strong effort to promote Greek in schools founded by Orthodox laymen in sixteenth-century Kiev, resistance by students facing the task of learning two difficult dead languages proved to be insurmountable.[93] The sacral quality of Church Slavonic required that, if a choice was indispensable, it remain the sole elaborated code.

Adoption of Church Slavonic as the elaborated code for liturgy and literature in Kievan Rus did not, therefore, bring about a cultural symbiosis with Byzantium comparable to the attachments of the Germanic, much less the Romance peoples, to Latin culture. Instead, Church Slavonic became the elaborated code for the entire Orthodox Slavic world. Despite some residual Cyrillic learning in Bohemia and southern Poland, this code did not extend to Catholic Slavs, whether the western branch (Poles, Czechs, Slovaks, and the Lusatian Sorbic remnant of the Wends) or to the northernmost members of the South Slavic group (Slovenes, Croats). How much difficulty these Catholic Slavs experienced in practical communication with one another—the educated, of course, used Latin—or with the Orthodox Slavs is hard to estimate. Certainly they had an awareness of linguistic similarity. Until the fourteenth century the patterns of settlement in East Central Europe were so sparse that large forests separated most groups. For example, it is said that the Severiane of the Chernigov-Seversk region east of the middle Dnieper had been regarded as "Liaki" (Poles) by other East Slavs, but after conversion to Eastern Christianity the Liaki rapidly assimilated. At a somewhat later period, as streams of settlers met, Polish and East Slavic villages became to some extent intermingled in a broad belt consisting of the Lublin, Sanok, and Podlachia districts.[94]

The political division of the Rus peoples caused by the Mongol invasion was outlined in chapter 7. From the linguistic standpoint, the results of this catastrophe somewhat resemble the collapse of the Roman empire for the Latin-speaking peoples. Like the great "Romania" of the Western Middle Ages, there was a great "Ruthenia" in which common linguistic origin and some measure of mutual comprehensibility was assumed. Of course, Latin was stronger than Church Slavonic from the point of view of its literary accomplishments, the considerable number of people literate in it, and the lingering prestige of the empire that had once used it as its vehicle. Moreover, whereas uneducated citizens of the western parts of the Roman empire had used restricted codes that varied, all were offshoots of a single Latin language. The various East Slavic dialects, on the other hand, had never actually been a part of the Old Bulgarian from which Church Slavonic was derived, although doubtless at one time their ancestors and those of the Bulgarians had spoken very closely related languages. For all of these reasons, one might anticipate that it would be harder either to preserve Church Slavonic as an adequate elaborated code or to develop vernacular elaborated codes using it as a model. Church Slavonic did enjoy, however, the advantage of a unified church organization determined to preserve it for liturgical use and suspicious of any substitutes even for secular purposes.

As indicated earlier, most Slavs dispersed by the Mongol invasion were eventually ruled by the Lithuanians. The latter, down to their conversion to Catholicism in 1386, had no more reason to interefere with Church Slavonic than with the Orthodox church. Even after some interest in converting the Orthodox appeared, the Jagiellonian dynasty respected use of Church Slavonic as the traditional right of their eastern subjects. In 1390, Jagiello even recruited a special group of Benedictine monks from Prague who still used the Slavonic liturgy to proselytize his eastern lands.[95] On the other hand, the Polish-Lithuanian polity did not exert itself to develop and standardize either Church Slavonic or the East Slav dialects. The cities the kings encouraged did not help the local languages either, for they were inhabited by elements alien to the Orthodox countryside. Given the relatively low level of rural economic development, transportation, and contiguous settlement, therefore, East Slavic in Lithuania-Poland became fragmented to an extent resembling that of the Romance dialects about 1000.

Scribes, whether for church or government, could understand each other's writing all the way from Vilna to Lvov (as far as from Paris to Milan), for they used a traditional orthography that took no account of varying local pronunciations. The chancery of the Grand Duchy of Lithuania employed this "Russian language" (*russky yazyk*), learned in special schools for scribes with terms derived from local dialects and Polish, when the Church Slavonic vocabulary did not suffice.[96] In other words, the chancery scribes used a practical though corrupted code that perhaps resembled the *Latin circa romanicum* employed by early medieval notaries. The latter, like chancery scribes, did not have many occasions to travel far enough to experience the need for an oral communications medium. But the higher classes, whether nobles (largely illiterate until the sixteenth century) or clerics, did travel; they could not readily communicate with each other when they came from distant districts. Moreover, the lack of a classical literature or even authoritative texts made even the written chancery language so unstandardized that communication of precise meanings was uncertain beyond the realm of the fixed formulas of theology and liturgy. The first Church Slavonic grammar appeared in Vilna in 1586, followed by a Greek-Slavonic comparative grammar in Lvov five years later.[97] The critical issue, which Continental West European polities avoided during the long transition to elaborated vernacular codes by retaining Latin in their law courts, was precision in legal expression. As a contemporary anthropologist puts it, "Writing is for the law, the law inhabits writing; to be acquainted with the latter is to be no longer unable to know the former."[98] A major basis for identity for rural East Slavs, nobles and peasants alike, moreover, was retention of their ancestral legal system, based on the *Pravda Russkaya*, in contrast to Polish law or Magdeburg city law. As a translator of East Slav law remarked to the Polish King Stephen Batory (1516), however: "Either the Lithuanians should have their laws written in Latin *or they should make precise rules and laws for speaking and for writing the language in which the laws are written.* Indeed, so long as this [Slavic] language has not been reduced to a precise norm it will be licit for anyone to interpret its words as he likes and deviate from their meaning, something which the numerous rules of the grammarians forbid for those who speak and write in Latin."[99]

The solution the translator recommended was already obsolescent, however, for the commonwealth neighbors of the Grand Duchy were already abandoning for administrative purposes the Latin associated with Catholicism. The most pertinent example was Galicia. As noted earlier, in the 1340s the old East Slav principality of Halich fell directly to Poland rather than to Lithuania. In 1434–35 Polish law (with proceedings in Latin) was introduced for Galician nobles, although peasants and other commoners (apart from those under Magdeburg law) remained under the *Pravda Russkaya*. The Polish kings were especially eager for uniformity in administrative proceedings, which meant using Latin as the sole official language after 1435.[100] But there had been no chancery documents in Cyrillic since the fourteenth century, and even then they were only a little more numerous than papers in German. In the sixteenth and early seventeenth centuries, however, all educated people in Galicia, including the remaining Orthodox nobility and eventually much of the Orthodox clergy, adopted Polish as a living language adaptable for all communication needs that also had a high status value. In 1633, 81 of 208 signatures nominating candidates for the Orthodox bishopric of Przemysl were in Polish, including about 70 percent of the lay nobles signing, but only a few of the clergy.[101]

Symbolically, signing one's name in Latin script probably represented a greater shift in identity than using Polish for oral communication, for the holy alphabet was the precious possession of the Orthodox. In Lithuanian territories, Slavonic formulas written in Cyrillic script were never abandoned as symbolic opening passages of official documents even when the rest of the text was in Polish. Yet the attraction of Polish was very strong there, too.[102] The "weight" of Polish civilization was derived from an intense cultural flowering such as French had experienced repeatedly and Italian and Spanish enjoyed in their golden ages. For Polish, the golden century began with printing and the ferment of the Reformation and Counter-Reformation, which terminated quickly enough to avoid the trauma experienced by German culture. The first Polish grammar appeared in 1568; thereafter, although the nobility continued to use Latin, an impressive outpouring of poetry and memoirs raised Polish to the level of the advanced European vernaculars. Coming as it did only a century after subjugation of Byzantium and the South Slavs, Polish literary splendor combined with considerable military success for the Polish-Lithuanian polity made many Slavs regard it as the natural leader of their world. The defeat of the Bohemian Slavs in 1620 further confirmed Poland's position as the only Slavic power in Europe. Her attraction for the other Slavs was almost comparable to the aura of French culture among the Romance peoples of the crusading epoch. Despite the geographically peripheral position of Polish, Antoine Martel, a most perceptive historian of these language interactions, considered that the language was prestigious enough and sufficiently close in form to the East Slav dialects to have had a real chance to become the literary language of the Middle Dnieper.[103] In Martel's appraisal, as in evaluations of the prospects of the Romance language family, the assumption is apparent that a single elaborated code might eventually have prevailed for each family of languages.

By the late seventeenth century, even the Orthodox clergy of Lithuania, if permitted to retain its religion, was prepared to express all but the liturgy in Polish. By 1670, the Kiev Orthodox confraternities conducting the Greek-Slavonic schools established in 1585 were using mainly Polish textbooks.[104] In fact, so many errors had crept into the manuscript copies of the Slavonic Bible that the Orthodox clergy had to use parallel texts in order to comprehend the scriptures. A Jesuit Pole advised them to use Greek. The clergy, however, continued to assert (echoing the Armenians and Jews cited in the preceding chapter) that God prefers Slavonic—but the devil loves Latin. Consequently, Polish seemed to be the least offensive auxiliary, both for biblical study and for defensive polemics. During the sixteenth and seventeenth centuries, little lay literature appeared in the East Slavic dialects except for a few pieces virtually transliterated from Polish or Latin because the educated Orthodox laity had adopted these languages.[105] The strong appeal of the "Sarmatian" life style of the Polish gentry—an "equestrian" society with frequent visiting within a single, enormous family—was a factor favoring adoption of Polish. As noted earlier, this was a "family" that distrusted outsiders; by adopting its language if not its religion, the Orthodox petty nobility would gain some access to the comfortable life style.[106]

The Orthodox East Slav elites had, in principle, a living alternative to Polish, namely, adherence to a single East Slavic vernacular raised to the level of an elaborated code. The problem was that their own dialects had been drifting apart. Kiev, the symbol of resurrection, became the principal cultural center in the seventeenth century, but it could not displace Vilna, the capital of the Grand Duchy. The Orthodox nobility of the southern regions of Lithuania (especially Volhynia) had strongly resisted the 1569 Lublin Union, which replaced the loose personal union of 1386 between Lithuania and Poland. But the danger of Tatar and Muscovite attacks in the mid-sixteenth century had already compelled the Volhynians to accept Polish penetration. Moreover, even during the preceding century, these southern regions had had a closer relationship to Poland, through the joint crown, than had the northern regions centering on Vilna.[107] Although the precise effects of these administrative relationships on the differentiation of East Slavic are unknown, it seems almost certain that the influence of different administrative centers was not negligible. It is essential to recall, however, that the entire region from Vilna to Kiev is occupied by *patois* differing from their neighbors in such insignificant ways that only experts can assign them (perhaps, as Brunot suggests, only nominally) to a given dialect or its neighbor. Experts admit a large zone of transitional speech in the Pripet area between Belorussian and Ukrainian. In the seventeenth century, in any case, the terms "Ukrainian" and "Belorussian" were rarely used. The East Slavic peoples of the Polish-Lithuanian commonwealth continued to call themselves collectively *"russky," "rossky,"* or *"rossiisky."* The latter term, developed in these western regions, was later adopted by the Russian empire to signify "all-Russian."[108] East Slav reality, however, was linguistic fragmentation and a declining capacity for intercommunication.

In the meantime, a very different development was occuring among the northeastern East Slav principalities. In 1386, Moscow seemed far away, separated as it was from Lithuania-Poland by several minor principalities. Although Moscow absorbed them, the Lithuanian frontier remained stable for nearly three centuries except for certain shifts in control of the Smolensk district. The Smolensk area constitutes a zone of transitional dialects like those between the Romance languages, although an authoritative Russian linguistic investigation considered Smolensk speech to be closer to Belorussian than to Russian.[109] Whereas the western frontier and the linguistic boundary of the Russian area remained essentially unaltered, however, Moscow (see chapter 5) developed an intensely powerful *mythomoteur* identifying its imperial mission with Orthodoxy and calling for the "ingathering" of the Russian lands once ruled by the Kievan Rurikid dynasty. The holy Slavic speech was a prime symbol of this claim. Some scholars contend that clerics of the northeastern principalities, although the vernacular there was more distant from Church Slavonic than that of the Kiev area, reverted to the ecclesiastical language for literary purposes while under Mongol suzerainty.[110] Others point out that Muscovites asserted that the Old Russian language they used in their chancery and church affairs actually was nearly identical with Church Slavonic, although in fact Old Russian was more distant from the liturgical language (and nearer the Moscow vernacular) than was the Lithuanian Slavonic chancery writing. Genuine Church Slavonic, according to the latter view, was used in fourteenth- and fifteenth-century Moscow almost exclusively by the numerous South Slav refugees.[111] The question is not salient in considering Moscow's appeal to the East Slavs of Lithuania. Neither the cossack accession of 1654 nor the Partitions of Poland at the end of the eighteenth century rested to any appreciable degree on linguistic arguments of an instrumental nature, whereas appeals to Slavic brotherhood, common Orthodoxy, and possession of the sacral Cyrillic script did legitimize the Russian acquisitions. Such appeals by Russia were so strong, in fact, that after 1721 they attracted South Slavs to Kiev for theological training. Through these students, a Church Slavonic coloration was reintroduced into the new South Slavic languages, which had long outgrown Old Bulgarian.[112]

The significance of the relation of Church Slavonic to the Old Russian of the Moscow chancery became important during the eighteenth century for other reasons. Using two elaborated codes, neither fully attuned to contemporary speech or sufficiently precise, was so awkward that many Russians, like other East Slavs, resorted to Latin or Polish as auxiliaries. In the mid-eighteenth century, however, the Russian literary language was fundamentally reshaped—in a manner comparable to Dante's transformation of Italian or the standardization of French by the Académie Française. The Russian process, associated with the poet-philologist Mikhail Lomonosov, produced a language much closer to Church Slavonic than Old Russian had been. Some scholars consider New Russian more Church Slavonic than Russian. According to Aleksei Shakhmatov, for example, "Its fatherland is Bulgaria."[113] Apparently, this development explains why contemporary writers of forceful, popular Russian such as Alexander Solzhenitsyn inject so many colloquial terms and frequently produce new words from them in ways inconsistent with the formal rules of Russian derivation adapted from Church Slavonic. Nevertheless, as the Russian empire expanded during the late eighteenth century to include nearly all of the Orthodox East Slav regions, New Russian became the dominant elaborated code for all of them.

Any comparison of Slavic developments to West European linguistic evolution is somewhat misleading; but perhaps it is as though a dialect derived from East Latin, like Tuscan, had triumphed (as it did in fact) in Italy, then gone on to become the dominant elite code for the entire Romance world. Pursuing this analogy, one can generalize that there has been a tendency in both great European spheres of transitional dialects for dialects based on powerful, eccentrically located polities to triumph. Resistance—by Catalan speakers in the west and Ukrainians (whose literary spokesmen deliberately employed calques from Polish to accentuate its distance from Russian) in the east—has never ceased.[114]

Summary and Conclusions

In modernized polities, mass education and communcations tend to make language usage the most salient identity criterion; but relationships in the premodern polities of the Middle East and Europe were very different. At times, language did become symbolically important for identity, but it rarely became the prime identity criterion. The important linguistic requirements discussed in chapter 6 mainly affected elites. Religious proselytizing did bring the issue of mass language usage to the fore, but in a context that made religious identification the salient criterion. In the premodern polity, communication at the mass level over long distances was usually too slight to make the language issue crucial for the average person.

Throughout the Islamic civilization, identification with the religion was dominant. Nevertheless, a number of factors, particularly the intense concern for genealogy, produced a general awareness of the differences between the three major linguistic and cultural elements—Arabic, Persian, and Turkic. Although language was an important symbolic component of this consciousness of difference, which determined ethnic boundaries, identity myths based on historical differences were more significant. Character stereotypes, not very different from the stereotypes that attributed specific personality traits to peoples of antiquity and of medieval Europe, were common in Islam. Often these characterizations acted as expressions of friction among the three major ethnic groups. Nevertheless, in Moslem polities two or three elaborated linguistic codes coexisted among governing elites as well as at the mass level. Such elite coexistence rested on an assumption, derived from early practice but self-perpetuating, that each of the three cultural identity types, or rather the bearers of the three cultural-linguistic traditions, was particularly suited to specific functional areas of government: Arabic for religious law, Persian for central administration, and Turkic for military command. As a result, the governing elite was segmented. This segmentation was enhanced by the tendency to use still more diverse ethnic and cultural elements for functions such as diplomatic contact with non-Moslem powers. Elites controlling each segment possessed a distinctive identity; but they rarely considered that that identity should be expressed by exclusive control of a polity. Very frequently, officials in the multiethnic segmented administration had mastered one or both of the languages used in the other principal segments. This practice imposed considerable educational costs on the societal elites, but adequately assured communication within governing circles.

Eastern Christian imperial polities, principally Byzantium and Russia, associated a single elaborated language with a unique strong identity myth. Whereas the Byzantine association of the Greek language, the Orthodox church, and the myth of empire as a terrestrial reflection of divine order was intense, several factors tended to weaken this association of factors in Russia. Attachment to Slavic as a holy tongue constituted a major part of the *mythomoteur*; but a standardized literary language was slow in emerging even in the core Russian regions. As discussed in chapter 4, the early Russian polity relied for several functions on urban elements attached to diverse languages and identity myths. Heavy recruitment of Baltic Germans and Poles for elite activities renewed this reliance in the late eighteenth century.

In West European polities, the importance of centralization has tended to produce a single elite administrative language even when (as among the Habsburgs) the imperial *mythomoteur* rejected reliance on a particular culture. Diffusion of this single elaborated code from the capital has constituted a significant by-product of the imperial centralizing imperative.

At the mass level, it is important to distinguish two very different kinds of language differentiation in Europe. Barriers to communication among the major language families are so high that awareness of linguistic differences has always been present though not necessarily salient in men's consciousness. As a result of early compact territorial settlement, the boundary between the Romance family and the Germanic family has been a fixed geographical line ever since the early Middle Ages. Although populations on both sides of the line were aware of the unusual barrier to communication, the language boundary rarely coincided with polity frontiers. Only when speakers of the two language families were intermingled on the same territory, with speakers of one family occupying higher social status, did perception of language differences cause political cleavage. In Continental West Europe, such intermingling was exceptional; the most important case was Flanders. Along the Germanic-Slavic boundary in Central Europe, such cases were more frequent. Although the linguistic boundary often (as in Bohemia) included line segments, certain rural boundaries consisted of intermingled zones. Still more important was the predominance of Germans among burghers in Bohemia, Hungary, and Poland; the resulting linguistic difference between town and countryside tended to correlate with a class division. Even in East Central Europe, however, major language divisions—which often diminished over time—did not constitute the salient aspect of ethnic identity until the modern period.

A different kind of development characterized the interior of the regions occupied by the three great European language families. Until late in the Middle Ages, clear internal linguistic divisions did not arise. Instead, local *patois* shaded off into one another. Consequently, the ordinary traveler did not experience linguistic changes as sharp breaks between patterns but as the accumulation of minor variations, none of which was crucial in itself. The ability of individuals to communicate with one another throughout very large regions was considerable, as long as neither legal precision nor literary elegance was demanded. Such intercommunication especially characterized huge central regions of the Romance and the Slavic language families—Piedmont, Provence, Languedoc, and Catalonia for the former, the Dnieper valley and adjoining areas for the latter. Throughout the Romance region, the requirement of precision in legal and theological affairs was met by the persistence of Latin as the sole elaborated code of the learned. Each incipient Romance elaborated code tended to become the special vehicle of a literary genre. Because it was not standardized, Church Slavonic could not provide an adequately precise code; yet its ecclesiastical prestige hindered the development of more popular linguistic vehicles.

In both the Romance and the Slavic regions, complicated political and religious circumstances eventually secured the predominance of elaborated codes diffused from peripherally located capitals. For the Dnieper Slavs, these codes were, successively, Polish and Russian; for the Romance, the prevailing codes became, simultaneously, the French *langue d'oïl*, Tuscan Italian, and Castilian. If other combinations of political and ecclesiastical forces had prevailed, different modern language divisions, or conceivably, a single Romance elaborated code and a single code for northern Slavs might have emerged.

One must, therefore, conclude that politics, in the broad sense of the term, precipitated the development of specific elaborated language codes from among the range of possible linguistic vehicles present at an early stage. In other words, in the long run politics and religion have been the independent variables in the linguistic interaction within each European language family. For somewhat different reasons and with considerably different effects, politics and religion also constituted the principal formative variables in Islam. Certainly these generalizations do not preclude the existence of complex causal interaction, nor do they fully apply to European conditions where strong barriers to communication between linguistic families prevailed. Generally, nevertheless, premodern experience demonstrates that the significance of language for ethnic identity is highly contingent.

CHAPTER NINE

Nations in the Perspective of Time

Comparison over the *Longue Durée*

Like any other major element of human experience, ethnic identification is so closely associated with other components of society that analysis of the part necessarily involves interpretation of the whole. This book has deliberately left aside most of the questions usually considered to constitute the philosophy of history. In stressing that ethnic identity is an attitude, I do not purport to show that it is unaffected by geography, technology, or relationships of production. At the least, such factors impose severe limits on human activities. In discussing the sharply differing ways of life in chapter 2 and in examining the effects of terrain and techniques on the relations between Islam and Christendom, these limits become salient. Group interests of an economic or status nature are rather more briefly introduced at several points, especially in relation to mercantile burghers, administrative elites, and the nomad-merchant symbiosis. But respect for a multifactor interpretation does not change my conviction that the historical record reaffirms the ways in which the human psyche shapes, for better or worse, its own fate. Whatever the ultimate source of the myths, symbols, and patterns of communication that have constituted ethnic identity, their persistence is impressive. The ways modern technology has reshaped myths are beyond the scope of this work; but I do not think that the force of myths has been diminished.

At the other end of the spectrum of the philosophy of history, the transcendental significance of many myths is inescapable. As indicated at several points, use of the term "myth" does not imply falsity in a historical sense, much less a theological one. Many if not most of the *mythomoteurs* or constitutive myths discussed have major religious components. Such could hardly fail to be the case in a consideration of ideas that moved man before the age of nationalism, which is also the age of secularism. Not only did ecclesiastical organizations dominate the penetrative aspects of ethnic myth propagation; in most cases the notion of compartmentalization of religious and secular beliefs was inconceivable. Obviously, the larger question of whether such myths reflect a divine plan in history is outside the scope of my work. All the same, to the extent that this book recalls man's abiding concern for the divine—however narrow or even perverted his interpretation of the divine intention may have been—the work may serve to restore a more balanced sense of the forces behind historical development.

The examination brings together evidence, hitherto widely scattered in specialized secondary treatments, on contacts among civilizations that are based on the values of the universal religions. Consideration of Protestant-Catholic confrontation has been limited because its effects on national consciousness, important as they were in a few cases, did not fundamentally transform the *mythomoteurs* of the most important Western nations. The relationships between Eastern and Western Christian civilizations, formed a millennium earlier, affected ethnic identity more profoundly despite lesser divergences in doctrine. Although phenomenological barriers to communication rather than underlying theological disputes were more important at the start, the fundamental distinction between the emperor as vicar of Christ in the Orthodox sphere and the peculiar Western relationship between pope and secular rulers became a crucial distinction. "Accidents" like the geographical separation between the two Christian religious spheres produced by Germanic and subsequent invasions, as well as conscious manipulation of differences by hierarchs and rulers, accelerated the process of estrangement. Most notable in the long perspective is the emphasis on separation of the two spheres rather than constant hostility along a common frontier.

From the start, such hostility was a striking aspect of Islamic-Christian contact. Surely, the hostile relationship suggests the presence of irreconcilable doctrinal differences. Some observers have suggested an underlying clash between Western and "Oriental" civilizations reappearing in a new guise. At times, such a "revenge of the Orient" thesis has appealed both to Christians on the defensive and to Moslem expansionists. Considering the heterogeneity of the adherents of the two religions, the early salience of anti-Islamic tendencies among Eastern Mediterranean Christian spokesmen, and the fluctuations in intensity of the animosity, I do not find the thesis convincing. It may conceal, though, an appreciation of the fact that Islam's origins as a latecomer propelled it toward militancy in relations with the established Christian polities. When, in contrast to the "Oriental" Sassanid regime, these polities (Byzantine, Frank, and lesser Iberian and Caucasian kingdoms) did not collapse at the first impact, a spiral of hostility was hardly avoidable. Nevertheless, the initial and persistent symbiosis between Islam and nomadism appears to have done more to produce unremitting hostility along a physical frontier zone between Islam and Christendom. Islamic legitimization of specific nomadic values, notably sexual conspicuous consumption, constituted (almost accidentally from the doctrinal standpoint) a significant part of the symbiosis. But the interest complex that perpetuated slave raiding along an unstable frontier zone was only partly due even to peripherally important Islamic values. More specific nomadic cultural patterns, such as the unreliable nature of extended kin support for Islamic ruling families, made a constant supply of male slaves for military and administrative service important. The overriding significance of such interest complexes became evident after the spectacular infusion of more ruthless Eurasian steppe nomadic values began in the eleventh century.

Broad historical questions cannot be avoided in this exploratory study. This is particularly true when, as in the Islamic-Christian conflict, a kind of supraethnicity nominally based on religious adherence arose. The way adherents of each of the two universal religions defined their collective identity by reference to the opposed civilization closely resembles the way boundaries of smaller ethnic groups are determined by a process of excluding outsiders. In treating such questions, the perspective of *longue durée* is useful principally for showing persistence of certain underlying values together with their occasional reinforcement or alteration by injection of new elements.

Just as frequently, I have brought together for comparison historical cases that are analogous rather than parts of an evident continuum. Such, notably, has been the interpretation of the persistence of multiethnic polities such as Poland and Hungary. Considered in isolation, the multiethnic nature of these polities has often appeared to be a concomitant of the "island" nature of the East Central European town. A longer perspective (chapter 4) suggests that the ethnic separation of town and countryside was by no means an inevitable result of the infusion of distinctive urban settlers or even of early provisions for particularistic legal codes. Catholic townsmen of varied origins could eventually become assimilated. But myths of gentry superiority, which arose during the initial ethnic diversity, persisted. Combined with the precedents for legal particularism, these myths turned out to be incompatible with rural-urban integration once town populations had been transformed by immigrating elements unassimilable by Catholicism.

This conclusion might have been reached through a diachronic comparison limited to the East Central European region. Cross-cultural comparison with West European and Russian Orthodox experience is required, however, to reveal how the persistence of unassimilated rural elements (gentry and peasants) is the indirect consequence of the incapacity of the multiethnic towns to act as centers of integration. In West Europe, weaker but discernible linguistic barriers to communication between bourgeois and countrymen persisted well into modern times; yet linguistic differences were overcome by powerful unifying myths. The early clerical propagators of these identity myths were frequently based on towns, particularly such embryonic capitals as Saint-Denis, Reims, and Paris. As lay burghers educated in communication skills, especially in the legal sphere, became more important, they assumed the integrating task of myth propagation. The recurrent ethnic division between town and countryside in East Central Europe, reinforced by gentry antiurban myths, precluded such an integrative role for burghers there.

Because I have devoted half a lifetime to study of East Central Europe, I feel moderately confident about asserting the importance of the comparative perspective for understanding that ethnic shatter zone. As any area specialist knows, though, no scholar can be fully competent in more than limited aspects of his region. Dependence on specialists is obviously greater when one explores an enormous range of time and space. This is a good point to stress my gratitude to such specialists as Pierre Guichard, Marshall Hodgson, and Joseph Strayer, whose insights transcend their monographic research. Explicitly or implicitly, wholly or in part, such insights reflect the comparative range of the authors' vision. Guichard, for example, evidently derives his understanding of the effect of Islamic cultural patterns upon expansion from broad comparisons in the Mediterranean region. I hope that still broader comparisons, embracing the impact of steppe nomads and Islamic cultures in Russia, may have deepened this understanding a little more.

Cross-cultural and diachronic comparisons have been especially relevant for consideration of diffusion and mimesis. One topic affected by these factors is the process of imperial centralization. Imperial structures are illuminated by consideration of Mesopotamian experience in evolving a transcendental myth in which the compound polity is the terrestrial reflection of a divine hierarchy. The lengthy chain connecting this early mythic version and similar manifestations in medieval Islam and early modern Europe has not been fully established. Particular aspects of the myth of terrestrial reflection have been strikingly documented, however, by art historians, ecclesiastical historians, and medievalists. Considered in the light of anthropological theory, this evidence justifies advancing the hypothesis that the Mesopotamian prototypical myth acquired a remarkable potency. At a different level of comparative analysis, diffusion of administrative organizational features, if not fully documented in its details, is indisputable in its tendency to perpetuate the centralization imperative. Were it not for repeated mimesis of administrative forms traceable to Diocletian and beyond, the structures of recruitment, socialization, and formal organization that tended to produce ethnically homogeneous European imperial elites might not have prevailed.

Issues like those just mentioned, where diffusion and innovation provide alternative interpretations, could be examined most revealingly in a comparative perspective that included civilizations outside the cognate European-Middle Eastern group. Others, I hope, may extend the comparative approach to include the Far East, the Indic, and the pre-Columbian experiences of identity.

I do not think that a summation, in numerical or other form, of all ethnic experiences in Europe and the Middle East prior to the age of nationalism is what is most urgently needed to facilitate further comparison. Instead, I have concentrated on experiences that seem to have been salient in the overall emergence of nations. Two criteria have guided this selection. On the one hand, I have tried to understand patterns of identity that directly affected developments through long periods of time, such as the Turkish, the Russian, and the Jewish. No observer of the present international scene can doubt the significance of these identities; I believe a sufficiently informed observer a half-millennium ago would have been impressed by their importance. Moreover, the reasons why such nations as the French, the Spanish, and the Persian exist today is intrinsically important—the most important aspect of this book for many readers. How these rather than other nations came to form the polities that today share the map of Europe and the Middle East is a fascinating topic, too. I do not pretend to explain all of this process. The side of state formation I do explore is long overdue for extended consideration. My second criterion, only partially distinguishable from the first, is the significance of a particular ethnic experience as a model. Here the city-states, ancient and early modern, the millennial prestige of Byzantium, and the position of France as the legitimizing model for many European polities, come to mind.

The aim throughout this book has been to present experiences salient for national emergence. It has not appeared desirable to follow a method of exposition that considers each ethnic case separately. Instead, I have examined sets of factors, such as the nomad-sedentary interaction, the impact of centralizing imperial polities, and linguistic patterns. As the differential impact of these factors on ethnic identities was explored, specific identities emerged as types. In the conclusions of chapters 4 and 6, types of identity related to a particular factor complex were presented. The former constituted a formal typology of urban identity, the latter a less precise typology of centralization in compound polities. I hope these limited typologies will be especially useful for other investigators.

SCHEMA: EMERGENCE OF NATIONAL IDENTITY

UNDERLYING ATTACHMENTS (II)
1. Latency: *Language* (VIII) 2. Conditioning: *Nomad Nostalgia*   *Sedentary Nostalgia*
                 3. Frameworks: *Genealogical Framework*   *Territorial Framework*

FUNDAMENTAL LEGITIMIZING MYTHS:
1. Polis (IV.A):   2. Universal Religion: *Islam*
Sedentary + territorial +
unified elite +   Tension Relationship: Legitimizing Relationship:
single language   *Genealogical Identity*   *Nomad Nostalgia* (II)
                               Frontier Insecurity (III)

	Islam	*Archetypal Diasporas*		
RELIGIOUS ORGANIZATIONS (III, VII)	Community Tribunal Network under Theocracy (VII)	Community Tribunal Network without Polity (with Hierarchy: *Armenians*; without Hierarchy: *Jews*) (VII)	Hierarchy under Imperial Vicariate (VII)	
MYTHOMOTEURS:	Universal Theocracy; Frontier Ghazi (III); Steppe Conquest Agglomeration (III)	Sacral Center (Echmiadzin, Jerusalem); Symbolic Language (Armenian, Hebrew)	Terrestrial Reflection Polity (Byzantium) as Polis Writ Large (IV.A, V); Vicariate (V); Antemurale (III)	Terrestrial Reflection Polity (Russia) as Vicariate Substitute (V); Antemurale (III); Steppe Successor (III)
POLITY STRUCTURE:	Low Stability (VI.B, VII); Compound or Shifting Capital (e.g., Baghdad) (VI.B.1); Segmented Elite (e.g., Mameluke) (VI.B.2)	- None -	High Stability; Single Capital (Constantinople) (VI.C.1); Unified Elite (VI.C.2)	Moderate Stability; Single Capital (St. Petersburg replacing Moscow) (VI.C.1); Elite tending toward Segmented (VI.C.2)
RECIPROCAL INFLUENCES:	Segmented Urban united with Rural (IV.D); Multiple Elaborated Codes from Diverse Linguistic Families (VIII)	Tending toward Urban Occupational Niches (IV.D, IV.F, VII); Successive Secular Elaborated Codes from Diverse Linguistic Families (VII)	Unified Urban united with Rural (IV.A); Single Elaborated Code (VIII)	Segmented Urban Elite tending toward united with Rural (IV.E); Multiple Elaborated Codes from Diverse Linguistic Families (VIII)
ULTIMATE ETHNIC IDENTITY:	Weak (Persian Exception) (V, VII); Low Penetration	Very Strong, High Penetration (VII)	Very Strong, High Penetration (VI.C.3.a)	Very Strong, Low Penetration (VI.C.3.b)

Key: Roman numerals refer to chapters; capital letters refer to categories in chapter conclusions.

	Christianity		
...lationship: ...*algia* (II)	Tension Relationship: *Terrestrial Reflection of Heaven* *Territorial—Class Division* (V)		

	Christendom		

Separate Hierarchy Constituting a Vicariate (VII)

	Terrestrial Reflection as Limited-Objective Polity (V.B.3)		
...tion ...ial ...empire) (V) ...icariate ...I)	Antemurale (Poland, Hungary)	Antemurale (Spain)	Protector of Pope-Vicar (France)
...y ...na) ...ard ...l.b)	Moderate Stability Single Capital (Cracow; Ofen-Pest) (VI.D.2.a) Segmented Elite (VI.D.3.b)	High Stability Shifting Capital (Toledo to Seville to Madrid) (VI.D.3.a) Elite tending toward Unified (VI.D.2.b)	High Stability Single Capital (Paris) (VI.D.2.a) Unified Elite (VI.D.2.b)
...arate ...B) ...placed ...ated	Segmented Urban Elite separate from Rural (IV.F) Multiple Elaborated Codes partly derived from Transitional Lin- guistic Family (VIII)	Declining Segmented Urban Elite separate from Rural (IV.C) Single Elaborated Code derived from Tran- sitional Linguistic Family (VIII)	Unified Urban Elite separate from Rural (IV.B) Single Elaborated Code derived from Transitional Linguistic Family (VIII)
...D.1.c)	Very Strong, High Penetration (VI.D.3.b)	Very Strong, High Penetration (VI.D.3.a)	Very Strong, Low Penetration (VI.D.2.c)

Toward a Typology of Emerging Nations

At this stage, a more general typology providing a schematic overview of the interrelation between major factors and specific identity types is in order. The types I present are neither exhaustive categories nor statistical central tendencies, but abstractions from the historical record. It is desirable, therefore, to keep close to that record in the following presentation. Consequently, each type is designated not merely as an abstract category, but by explicit reference to the historical case or cases from which the type is derived. Such references somewhat complicate the schematic overview, but I believe they enhance its comprehensibility.

The types presented in the schema, "Emergence of National Identity," are closely related to concrete historical phenomena; therefore, it would be misleading to imply that their characteristics exist in isolation from one another. The ubiquitous causal interaction has been noted in earlier chapters and requires emphatic attention here. Although the tabular arrangement begins with broad underlying factors and proceeds to specific ethnic identity types, it should not be regarded as suggesting unidirectional influences. The label "Reciprocal Influences" applied to the fifth major horizontal category merely stresses the special importance of such influences at that level. Urban and linguistic factors, for example, are intensely affected by myths and organizational structures as well as by each other. Moreover, such factors as "Mythomoteurs" and "Religious Organizations" interact almost as strongly.

"Underlying Attachments" are those factors that frequently shape the expression of ethnic identity but do not in themselves constitute such identities. Among the most significant attachments are the conditioning attachments of nomad and sedentary nostalgia. Nostalgia can be diverted into various channels or suppressed for long periods. A specific type of nostalgia can be produced among peoples who have not experienced the corresponding way of life only through the impact of religious or political structures operating throughout long periods of history. For example, after centuries of Arabicization carried out under the aegis of Islam, some Fertile Crescent peasants who never had nomadic ancestors express nostalgia for the desert. Magyars, whose forebears were nomads, adhere to the sedentary images associated with the Christian cycle of liturgical celebrations. But such cases are exceptional. Usually the attachments based on underlying ways of life act almost exclusively as independent variables.

Basic identity frameworks, genealogical and territorial, although highly persistent, are somewhat more frequently altered by drastic upheavals in civilizations and belief systems. For example, Persians abandoned much of their territorial attachment on becoming Moslem, turning instead to genealogical emphasis. Nevertheless, it has been far easier for groups like the Berbers, predisposed through their nomadic and genealogical patterns, to make fundamental identity changes by adopting new genealogies, usually Arab in origin. Germanic groups with sedentary backgrounds tended under the impact of Christian ethos to modify their legitimization to emphasize family attachments to fixed territorial locations in place of their original *Geblütsrecht* legitimizing myth. The process required some seven centuries, however—another instance for which an extended time perspective is indispensable.

The latent effects of communications barriers posed by highly diverse language families is sufficiently persistent to warrant treating such patterns as underlying factors comparable to life styles. But even the most fundamental language affiliation can be completely altered. The Latin-speaking population of North Africa became Arabic, as did a high proportion of speakers of Berber and the Coptic version of ancient Egyptian. The Greek-speaking population that remained in Anatolia adopted the utterly alien Turkic language, as did most of the large Iranian-speaking population of the Amu Darya and the Sir Darya valleys. Similarly, a large majority of the Celtic speakers of Western Europe has become Germanic or Romance in language. The historical evidence of such drastic shifts should suggest great caution in attributing independent influence to language as a communication barrier or as a persistent set of symbolic attachments.

My approach to the ethnic phenomenon has stressed its boundary properties instead of the "essence" of ethnic identity that some analysts have sought. Identity, in my approach, constitutes an intense affect phenomenon, hence a value in itself rather than a definer of a wide range of general values. Indeed, as has been noted several times—especially in relation to the diffusion of French identity models to other parts of Europe—ethnic values and even the forms of ethnic myths often vary surprisingly little. Only the perception of group differences, of insiders and outsiders, as formulated in mythic substance separates many ethnic alignments. It is a commonplace that groups with very similar general values often engage in the most violent clashes. On the other hand, as between Islamic and Christian groups, underlying value differences that produce distinctive civilizations may produce sharp conflict.

Religions, especially the great universal religions, have been the major forces producing broad value differentiation. Nevertheless, even very strong religious affiliations are sometimes surrendered as the price for retaining ethnic or national identity. Consequently, the "Fundamental Legitimizing Myths," which constitute the second major category in my scheme, are even less likely than language to remain independent variables conditioning nostalgia, or basic identity frameworks. Today the phenomenon of sacrificing religion to nationalism is not uncommon. It appears in the rejection of missionary efforts by Third World nationalists or Marxists, even in countries like China or India where missions had achieved great success. Ostensible renunciation of religion to preserve ethnic identity demonstrably occurred among Moslems of the Soviet North Caucasus during the 1930s and is probably widespread under Leninist regimes. Certainly the phenomenon was far rarer in premodern times, when religion usually constituted the central factor in consciousness of identity. Nevertheless, examples do exist, such as the Persian converts to Islam who retained intense pride in their Sassanid ancestors or the Jewish *conversos* who believed that as Catholics they could assume a major position in the politics of fourteenth-century Spain.

Two types of relations between legitimizing myths (I repeat that I employ "myth" only to signify a coherent, strongly held identity belief, without implication as to its truth or falsity) are derived from universal religions and the attachments noted above. Although nostalgia is not a core aspect of either Islam or Christianity, these religions do provide a kind of legitimization for nomadic and sedentary nostalgia, respectively. But there is an inherent tension between universal religions as transcendental faiths and the support each has indirectly provided for more specific identifying myths. Christian churches have frequently endorsed claims of particular polities to reflect in this terrestrial sphere the order of heaven; but this ancient Mesopotamian myth is hard to accommodate to Christian universalism. More direct Christian endorsement of territorial alignments and class divisions arising from sedentary identities is still harder to square with universalism. In a somewhat similar fashion, Islam endorses the *jihad*; yet the actual conditions of frontier warfare, accentuated by Central Asian conquest agglomerations, coexist uneasily with the Moslem faith. The fundamental genealogical identity principle, dominant nearly everywhere that Islam prevails, clashes with Moslem egalitarian beliefs. When carefully circumscribed for defensive purposes, the *Antemurale* myth of several Christian polities has accorded with dominant interpretations of the Christian ethic; but such militant myths have frequently been transformed into the un-Christian excesses associated with several crusades. Recognition of tension as well as reciprocal influence is, therefore, essential to comprehension of the values underlying the principal organizational structures involved in myth elaboration.

The *polis* as producer of a fundamental identifying myth deserves treatment in its own right, for in rather different ways the *polis* influenced both Christian and Islamic identity. Whereas urbanism as such is essential to the ideal Moslem identity, attachment to specific cities has rarely if ever been prominent enough to provide the basis for civic consciousness in Islam. In Christian societies, on the other hand, the intense experience of the *polis* has never lost its potential for transfer to broader ethnic identity. Religious organizations as such can be treated briefly. The Moslem community tribunal network is coordinated by the theocratic polity. Diasporas, lacking such polities, have relied on networks of tribunals that are largely self-coordinating but nonetheless effective as ethnic boundary mechanisms. The hierarchic Byzantine and Russian churches were headed by rulers who assumed the role of vicar of Christ. Catholic church organizations always had an ecclesiastical pyramid headed by the pope outside the full scope of secular authority. The significance of these differences becomes evident in considering the *mythomoteurs* that have characterized Eastern and Western Christendom.

The *mythomoteur*, as Abadal i de Vinyals's felicitous term implies, is what sustains a polity and enables it to create an identity beyond that which can be imposed by force or purchased by peace and prosperity. At this level of the scheme I present, underlying attachments and vaguer myth components come to focus on the identities of specific polities. The treatment, although still skeletal, is correspondingly complex. Certainly awareness of the significance of the mythic factor in the emergence of nations is not novel. But concern for myth as a major formative factor has often been absent from analyses where it might have been most appropriate, for example, in interpretations noted earlier in this chapter. Emphasis on the critical role of myths does not imply a single-factor interpretation, however. Discussion (in chapter 5 and below) of the complicated factors producing a strong identity in the kingdom of France is intended to bring out the importance of considering material circumstances as well as legitimizing myths.

Components of the Islamic *mythomoteur* are directly deducible from the fundamental Islamic legitimizing myths: universal theocracy (any polity is a contingent structure); *ghazi* struggle against the infidel; injection of inflammatory steppe conquest values. The *mythomoteur* of the archetypal diaspora, which lacks a polity, must focus entirely on religion. The sacral center, a vestigial city, and the symbolic language, often hardly more than a sacred alphabet and the scriptures encoded in it, are indispensable symbols.

For the *mythomoteurs* of all Christian imperial types, the polity as a reflection of heavenly order is fundamental. In the "Polis Writ Large" (Byzantium and to a degree Trebizond) the ruler as universal vicar of Christ is central. Concentration of affect on the capital city, however, makes the empire an enlarged city-state. *Antemurale* myth components are secondary, arising primarily from the continued need for defense against

Islam. For the "Vicariate Substitute" type (Russia, the Bulgar tsardoms) the emperor as vicar of Christ remains central, but lacks truly universal pretensions. On the other hand, the *Antemurale* component is stronger because it was present from the beginning of the polity. The vicariate substitute myth legitimizes the empire as "ingatherer of the peoples" of the same faith. Both Russia and the original Turkic Bulgar khans also claimed to succeed defeated steppe conquest agglomerations, thereby introducing a myth component that tended to legitimize enhanced autocracy.

The Western emperor occupies a peculiar position. He cannot be the vicar of Christ because the pope occupies that role. Instead, the emperor is the pope's protector and is under his tutelage. But very quickly the Western emperors—Frank, Holy Roman, and Habsburg—acquired a strong secondary legitimizing myth theme as *Antemurale* defenders of Christendom, at first against heathens, then against Islam. But the geographical extent of the imperial polities combined with their own weakness and papal balancing politics prevented the emperors from becoming the unique *Antemurale* defenders. Rather, in Western Christendom as in Islam, the role of defender of the faith has been widely diffused. A major difference between Christian and Islamic civilizations, however, is that whereas every *ghazi* defender was potentially the legitimate ruler of all Islam, in principle no success against the infidel entitled a Christian monarch to usurp the Holy Roman imperial crown. On the other hand, Western legitimizing principles guaranteed the coexistence of the Christian empire and powerful polities based on *Antemurale* myths, such as Castile, Aragon, Poland, and Hungary. Each of these, therefore, developed a strong ethnic identity.

A very different type of legitimizing myth sustained the kingdom of France, which because of its geographical position was relatively insignificant in *Antemurale* defense. Instead, through clever royal policy and papal acquiescence, France succeeded in inheriting a special aspect of the Frank role as protector of the vicar of Christ. This special myth, more than the *Antemurale* themes that partly reflected unavoidable necessities of defense, became the legitimizing basis for a European multipolity system.

Structural effects relate to the imperatives of centralization. One must be cautious, of course, in attributing basic characteristics of a regime to a single organizational factor, but significant correlations are worth noting. In the short run, centralization promotes stability. But centralization also tends to produce intense ethnic identity. The effect is minimal in Islamic polities where, with certain notable exceptions, shifts in capitals or at least palace quarters by each dynasty lower the stability of centralized polities. The segmented nature of Islamic elites also minimizes the effect of polity centralization. Conversely, concentration of life in a single capital with a unified elite facilitated high stability in Byzantium, whereas the Russian branch of Eastern Christendom, with a segmented elite and a somewhat less continuous capital, was less stable. A frequently shifted capital plus unified elites facilitated a comparable, moderate level of stability in Western imperial systems. In Poland and Hungary an infrequently shifted capital plus segmented elites also accompanied moderate stability. In Spain, on the other hand, a unified elite was present, along with high stability, despite a shifting capital, but at the cost of internal debilitation and colonial losses. Finally, France attained high stability in the fifteenth century shortly after a fixed capital became the symbolic center of the regime and the base of a unified elite.

The specific reciprocal influences can be briefly summarized. For Islam, segmented cities controlling the countryside matched an elite segmented in language. For the diasporas, occupation of urban occupational niches was feasible partly because community tribunal discipline facilitated long-distance commerce and partly because successive elaborated codes produced a precocious level of literacy and multilingual experience. Almost exactly the opposite situation prevailed in Byzantium. Using a single, elaborated code, a unified urban population extended control (although with decreasing effectiveness) into the countryside. All factors, notably the strong church organization, tended to reinforce a strong identity penetrating most parts of the empire. A precocious Greek nationalism shaped the identity of the populations of peninsular Greece, Thrace, and Western Asia Minor. Conversely, Byzantine rule of un-Hellenized regions, mostly rural areas in the central Balkans, Armenia, and Italy, was shaky and temporary.

The Russian heir to Byzantium exhibited considerable similarity as well as certain interesting contrasts. After the late sixteenth century, the Russian polity gradually extended its rule to considerable populations which the Russian imperial myth could not penetrate because of their different religions. The Russian language eventually became the common elaborated code for the East Slavs, but cities throughout the western portions of the empire (which contained the bulk of the urban population) remained essentially alien in myth and language. As a result, a very strong Russian core identity coexisted with low penetration of much of the empire's population.

A similar but more acute cleavage characterized the Western empires. Ethnically unified cities predominated, at least in core areas, producing a strong identity for the dominant elites using a single elaborated linguistic code. Such elites were present in the Germanic-Romance mixture of the Frank nobility, the French-speaking nobility of the Burgundian realm, the Castilian-Aragonese gentry of sixteenth-century Habsburg Iberia, and the German cities of the later Habsburg empire in the Danubian basin. In all of these cases—and still more in the medieval Holy Roman empire—the Western empires also ruled cities of a unified but quite different ethnic complexion, Italian, *Reichsromanen*, Catalan. It was not the alien nature of these peripheral cities, however, but ethnically distinct countrysides that sapped the unity of Western imperial systems. Rural alienation, of gentry and peasantry, from urban administrative bureaucracies imposing the languages and myths of major ethnic elements constituted increasingly disruptive forces in all of these Western imperial polities. France, on the other hand, managed to overcome most such difficulties at an early stage. Its cities, generally unified ethnically after the Albigensian crusade, readily transferred the strong civic loyalty they had inculcated to the kingdom. Despite the low penetrative power of the French elaborated linguistic code among peasants until the nineteenth century, rapid adoption of the standard language by the rural nobility made it difficult for dialects to resist long.

Consideration of the French case raises the question of why so many factors working for strong ethnic identity coincided. A complete reply is impossible within the scope of this work. Certainly, early contiguous settlement provided resources for a relatively manageable administrative center, but in fact a fixed capital was slow in developing. The sense of territorial identity that arose from this contiguous settlement fostered concern for fixed language boundaries and political frontiers, which in turn contributed to polity stability. Indirectly, perhaps, one can trace the superior capacity of France's tenth-century bishops and subsequent royal insistence on male primogeniture to the precocious sense of territoriality, but the evidence is fragile. At an early date the French kingdom produced prestigious linguistic, architectural, and aristocratic styles that later provided strong symbolic support for a centralized polity. When French cultural ascendancy was established during the eleventh and twelfth centuries, however, there was little in the way of a polity to support. A reciprocal relation with other factors supporting the growth of identity is also hard to demonstrate. Certainly the Court eventually promoted the French language to replace Provençal, but the decisive event was the Albigensian crusade. One impulse behind the crusade was the interest of northern French nobles, but the instigating personality was Pope Innocent III. Only when the long ordeal was well under way did the French monarchy intervene and reap many of the benefits. The key factor, as in other steps that indirectly strengthened the French polity, was papal interest in alliance with a French elite that usually, but not always, included the monarch. The French elite had the unique advantage of being powerful and orthodox enough to subdue the pope's foes, but far enough away to preclude, during most periods, threats to papal independence. From Pepin to Louis XI, this symbiotic relationship, which provided the core of the French *mythomoteur*, apparently operated independently of the other factors strengthening French identity; but the French would not have been attractive allies if they had not enjoyed an inherently strong position.[1]

Papal alliance with France not only enabled the French kingdom to establish the strongest identity in Europe; the papacy in effect turned on a *mythomoteur* that drew the majority of European elites into the process of developing separate ethnic identities. Papal influence worked directly to encourage Hungary, Poland, and the northern polities to assume independent stances and indirectly through encouraging them to emulate the French experience. Indeed, it is not too fanciful to suggest that the French *mythomoteur*—in the course of centuries rather than decades—resembles contemporary national economic "motors" in initiating development. Just as West Germany after 1948 acted as the economic motor for European economic recovery, the French *mythomoteur* set in motion similar forces in Poland, Hungary, Spain, and other peripheral European polities. In both cases, there was evident a mixture of unconscious, incremental use of opportunities revealed by the first initiative; conscious emulation of specific features of the "motor"; and above all the confidence, engendered by the initial success, that development was legitimate and feasible. It appears possible, therefore, to specify both the pattern that produced the French *mythomoteur* and the effects of this phenomenon. Because the pattern was so complex, however, it is impossible to indicate how it might be replicated at other times and in other places. Perhaps the only generalization to be derived from this historical experience is that if a polity endowed with a very powerful *mythomoteur* appears in a cultural region, it may produce a demonstration effect vigorous enough to transform identity throughout the region. In other words, the appearance of a legitimized independent polity, if it happens to represent a prestigious culture like the French, tends to encourage the emergence of a system of polities characterized by national consciousness.

Clearly the European multilateral state system could hardly have developed, however favorable the geopolitical circumstances may have been, without myths powerful enough to sustain independent polities within the recognized frontiers of Western Christendom. The Islamic *mythomoteur* appears to have influenced developments in almost the opposite direction. Islam created a civilization of extraordinary force and cultural unity. At the cultural level it tolerated, if it did not encourage, ethnic identities of extraordinary diversity and persistence. This is true not only of the three great identities—Arab, Persian, and Turk—that have dominated Islamic polities, but of a number of persistent non-Moslem identities, including Copts, Christian Syrians, Armenians, and Jews. As a demonstration of the ability of ethnic identity to persist without a territorial base, the experience of such groups in Islamic polities conveys invaluable lessons for the contemporary world. But Islamic accomplishments were not accompanied either by a real theory of universal theocracy or by legitimization of a plurality of polities. The fate of the Mameluke empire exemplifies the ineradicable problem of legitimacy in Islam. Enduring nearly three centuries, that polity presided over a cultural and commercial renaissance. Its peculiar elite was renowned as the defender of Islam against vicious attacks from the Central Asian steppes as well as against sporadic West European crusade ventures. The Mameluke regime was highly orthodox and generally restrained in its relations with other Moslem polities.[2] Yet when the Ottoman empire was ready to destroy it, only scattered, impotent religious protests appeared. Once accomplished, the deed was accepted as additional evidence of a legitimate Ottoman ascendancy in Sunni Islam. Without assessing the ethical implications of this history, I think it is fair to point out that it had no parallel within the framework of well-established, religiously orthodox Western polities down to the Polish Partitions—and everyone is aware how persistent if ineffectual the "bad conscience" caused by the Partitions has appeared among the vestiges of Western Christendom.

International relations in the Eastern Christian sphere were more straightforward. The goal of a single empire "ingathering" the Christian peoples effectively precluded a legitimate multilateral state system, although the principle of *oikhonomia* frequently produced a de facto international balance. The historical imagination cannot avoid being impressed with Justinian's scheme for a thalassocracy extending to the Atlantic or even the stubborn twelfth-century Byzantine efforts to reunite Christendom on the Italian and the Black Sea coasts. With its deliberately more restricted objectives, the Russian Orthodox monarchy proved able to provide a Christian supranational empire for a huge region that just previously had been subjected to extreme disruption. In both the Byzantine and the Russian empires, the ingathering process, though never carried to a conclusion, tended toward cultural homogenization that would have left little place for either distinctive ethnic identities or independent polities.

In Western Europe, tension between pope and emperor precluded such a process of ingathering. Despite repeated efforts to assert their primacy, Western imperial rulers could not reject the legitimacy of independent secular polities. Although for centuries the fluid, multiform nature of medieval polities ranging from local baronies to city-states obscured the presence of a legitimate multilateral international order, it was present in the West at least from the tenth century on. Down through the age of Absolutism, this plural international order was accompanied by increasing authoritarian centralization within many of its component polities. The authoritarian heritage, along with the legacy of frequent, legitimized warfare, has constituted a heavy burden for the modern system of national states. On the other side of the ledger, a plural international order has perpetuated a diffusion of power that, except for brief intervals, has precluded a single imperial tyranny throughout the West. This environment has made it possible for the nations we know to emerge and to persist in their inexhaustible variety.

Notes

Chapter 1

1. Examination of polities necessarily includes some of the factors treated in such recent works as the collective volumes sponsored by the Committee on Comparative Politics of the Social Science Research Council, which I assisted in minor ways. See especially Grew; Tilly.

2. See especially Becker, *Islamstudien*; E. Werner; Hodgson, vol. 1; and Patai, *Golden River*, on the importance of combining studies of the European and the Middle Eastern past.

3. Hayes, p. 44. Cf. Kohn, p. 17, and Meinecke, *Cosmopolitanism*, p. 10.

4. See especially Elias, *Ueber den Prozess der Zivilisation*, 1:116. Cf. Elias, *Die höfische Gesellschaft*; Bidermann, "Die staatsrechtlichen Wirkungen"; Braudel, *The Mediterranean*; Lhotsky; P. Anderson.

5. Barth, *Ethnic Groups*, pp. 9–10. See also LeVine and Campbell, pp. 82–83, 102.

6. Wenskus, *Stammesbildung*, pp. 210, 252. Cf. Jespersen, p. 9; Graus, "Die Entstehung der mittelalterlichen Staaten," p. 60.

7. Hüsing, "Völkerschichten," p. 199.

8. Benveniste, 1:368.

9. See R. Anderson on a separate peasant culture in medieval Europe. Cf. Varagnac, p. 21.

10. See especially Geertz, pp. 45, 209; Cassirer, *Language and Myth*, p. 91; Firth, p. 40; Lasswell.

11. Suzanne K. Langer, "On Cassirer's Theory of Language and Myth," in Schlipp, p. 386; Max Weinrich, "The Reality of Jewishness versus the Ghetto Myth: The Sociolinguistic Roots of Yiddish," in *To Honor Roman Jakobson*, p. 2209.

12. Brandi, p. 265; Heer, p. 218.

13. Lévi-Strauss, *Structural Anthropology*, p. 210. Cf. Lévi-Strauss, *The Savage Mind*, p. 254; Deutsch, *Nationalism*.

14. Abadal i de Vinyals, p. 584.

15. Dardel, p. 38.

16. Hroch, p. 30. For other pertinent discussions of symbolism and identity, see especially John A. Wilson, "Egypt," in Frankfort, p. 41; Kaerst, *Die Antike Idee der Oekumene*, pp. 7ff; Corbin, pp. 39, 160; Buccellati; Simson.

17. Yardeni, p. 5. Cf. Huizinga, *Patriotisme en Nationalisme*, pp. 23–32.

18. Bernard Lewis, "Islam," in Sinor, *Orientalism*, p. 16.

19. Vossler, *Aus der romanischen Welt*, p. 399; Dunbar, pp. 72, 132.

20. Ullmann, *The Carolingian Renaissance*, p. 100.

21. Henri Terrasse, "Classicisme et Décadence dans les Arts," in Brunschvig and Von Grunebaum, p. 71. Cf. Brunschvig in ibid., pp. 35ff.; Marçais, *Manuel d'Art Musulman*, vol. 2; O. Grabar, p. 81.
22. Strayer, *Medieval Statecraft*, p. 369.

Chapter 2

1. Varagnac, pp. 21ff.; Hodgson, 1:31.
2. Schier, pp. 8ff., 17.
3. Weiss, p. 99.
4. Schier, p. 20. For additional details on the Germanic-Slavic interaction see ibid., pp. 65, 374; Kötzschke, "Salhof und Siedelhof," pp. 36ff.
5. Dauzat, *Le Village*, pp. 43, 179. Cf. chapter 8 below.
6. Gautier, *Les Siècles Obscurs*, p. 236. For a somewhat similar division in Morocco, see Bourrilly, p. 177.
7. Wirth, "Zur Sozialgeographie," pp. 266-68.
8. R. Williams, p. 12; Vossler, *Aus der romanischen Welt*, p. 90.
9. Baudet, p. 38.
10. Montagne, p. 47.
11. Miquel, *L'Islam et Sa Civilisation*, p. 37.
12. Ibid., p. 154.
13. Gautier, *Moeurs et Coutumes*, p. 68.
14. Gustave E. Von Grunebaum, "The Cultural Function of Dreams," in Von Grunebaum and Caillois, pp. 6ff.
15. Kirk, p. 272.
16. Toufy Fahd, "The Dream in Medieval Islamic Society," in Von Grunebaum and Caillois, p. 357.
17. Saladin, p. 271.
18. Giamatti, p. 11; Corbin, p. 39; Brandenburg, *Samarkand*, p. 210, considers "paradise" reached the Arabs via Greek.
19. Brandenburg, *Samarkand*, p. 210.
20. See Marguerite Gautier-Van Berchem, "Mosaics of the Dome of the Rock in Jerusalem and of the Great Mosque in Damascus," in Creswell, pp. 326-27, 339.
21. At least that is the Shiite tradition. See Corbin, p. 225n.
22. Quoted in Marçais, *Manuel de l'Art Musulman*, 1:206. Cf. Spuler, *The Muslim World*, 1:103.
23. Von Grunebaum, *Medieval Islam*, p. 260.
24. Wiet, "L'Empire Néo-Byzantine des Omayyades," p. 67.
25. Translated in F. Rosenthal, 1:250, 274.
26. Weulersse, p. 69. Cf. Hodgson, 1:239.
27. Planhol, "Caractères Généraux de la Vie Montagnarde," p. 120.
28. Commeaux, p. 28.

29. Ibid., p. 241.
30. H. and H. A. Frankfort, "Conclusion," in Frankfort, p. 246.
31. Flight, p. 162. Cf. Campbell, pp. 141–54.
32. Flight, pp. 211–13.
33. Nyström, pp. 83–95, 123–32.
34. Inability to resist sedentary ways of life, connected with a relative absence of nostalgia for the pastoral life, apparently characterizes most mountaineer populations and other groups on the margins of well-established sedentary cultures. Braudel, *The Mediterranean*, 1:25ff., points to the importance of mountaineer populations; but only rarely (as in Switzerland) did they become the basis for persistent polities.
35. Grenier, p. 314.
36. Kirk, p. 153. See also Peters, pp. 201–2, and chapter 4 below.
37. Weulersse, pp. 70–71. Cf. Haussig, p. 345.
38. G. Williams, p. 97.
39. Giamatti, p. 184. See also Gerhardt, p. 32.
40. Elias, *Die höfische Gesellschaft*, pp. 321–22.
41. Lévi-Strauss, *Structural Anthropology*, p. 292.
42. Buccellati, pp. 19, 31, 56–72.
43. Commeaux, p. 9.
44. Benveniste, 1:310–11. Varagnac, p. 190, considers emphasis on the house threshold to be a general sedentary characteristic, but he advances only French (i.e., Indo-European) evidence.
45. Millar, p. 435.
46. Juster, 1:390ff.
47. Dion, p. 11.
48. Benveniste, 1:160.
49. Gagé, *Les Classes Sociales*, pp. 178–81; Petit-Dutaillis, p. 11.
50. Bauer, p. 470.
51. Dion, p. 27; Lemarignier, pp. 6ff.
52. Ullmann, *The Carolingian Renaissance*, p. 39; Chaunu, *L'Espagne*, 1:65–66. Cf. Lemarignier, pp. 6ff.
53. Paul Bonenfant, "A Propos des Limites Médiévales," in *Eventail de l'Histoire*, p. 79.
54. Bloch, *Feudal Society*, 2:382; Haller, p. 413; Girard d'Albissin, pp. 24, 371ff.
55. Bloch, *Feudal Society*, 2:382. See also Sugar, p. 151, for the peculiar exception of Transylvania in early modern Europe.
56. Girard d'Albissin, pp. 23, 27.
57. Ibid., pp. 160, 252.
58. Graus, "Die Entstehung der mittelalterlichen Staaten," p. 48.
59. Karp, pp. 74, 100; E. Schwarz, pp. 667ff.
60. Karp, p. 13.
61. Eck, p. 84.
62. Ibid., p. 87.
63. Ibid., p. 97.
64. Poliakov, *The Aryan Myth*.

65. Lemberg, p. 148.

66. Wenskus, *Stammesbildung*, pp. 74, 81, 398. Cf. Schlesinger, "Herrschaft und Gefolgschaft," pp. 238ff.; Hóman, pp. 28ff.

67. Wenskus, *Stammesbildung*, pp. 62, 339, 349, 440; Schlesinger, "Herrschaft und Gefolgschaft," p. 270.

68. Dannenbauer, 1:31; Altheim, *Niedergang der alten Welt*, 1:99, 112ff.; Vernadsky, "Der sarmatische Hintergrund," p. 348.

69. Previté-Orton, 1:84.

70. Wenskus, *Stammesbildung*, p. 75; Josef Matl, "Die Slawen auf den Balkan," in Šaria, p. 69.

71. Cipolla, pp. 370ff.; Petri, p. 95; Musset, p. 235. On the numerical decline of the Roman armies, see Dannenbauer, 1:229.

72. Stroheker, p. 270.

73. Wenskus, *Stammesbildung*, pp. 54, 57, 62; Deér, p. 118.

74. Wenskus, *Stammesbildung*, p. 486; Zöllner, *Die politische Stellung*, p. 47.

75. Wenskus, *Stammesbildung*, p. 78.

76. Schenk von Stauffenberg, p. 11.

77. Tellenbach, *Königtum und Stämme*, p. 6.

78. Wenskus, *Stammesbildung*, pp. 75ff. Cf. Young, p. 35, for analogous "tribal" formations in colonial Africa.

79. Sinor, "Central Eurasia," in Sinor, *Orientalism*, p. 91.

80. Wenskus, *Stammesbildung*, p. 75.

81. On totems, see especially Deér, p. 52. For the persistence of the Genghisid myth, see Alderson, p. 15; Allen, p. 48n.; Hodgson, 3:104.

82. Brandenburg, *Samarkand*, pp. 94, 132.

83. Wenskus, *Stammesbildung*, p. 440.

84. Schlesinger, "Herrschaft und Gefolgschaft," p. 267.

85. Wenskus, *Stammesbildung*, pp. 373-90, 445-46, 478.

86. Ibid., p. 446; Musset, pp. 56, 235-37; Vogt, *The Decline of Rome*, p. 220; DeVries, p. 102.

87. Kurth, "La France et les Francs," p. 358.

88. Schenk von Stauffenberg, pp. 28ff.; Stroheker, pp. 12, 20.

89. Karl F. Werner, "Important Noble Families in the Kingdom of Charlemagne," in Reuter, pp. 140ff.; cf. Schlesinger, "Herrschaft und Gefolgschaft," p. 248.

90. Schenk von Stauffenberg, p. 156.

91. Zöllner, *Die politische Stellung*, p. 85; Kurth, "La France et les Francs," p. 398; Bergengrün, p. 31; Chaume, pp. 196, 210ff.

92. Stroheker, p. 55; K. Schmidt, p. 84.

93. Stroheker, pp. 119, 155. For precedents before Rome, see Schubart, p. 17; Jouguet, p. 89. On the complicated legal evolution in the early Middle Ages, see Stroheker, pp. 124ff., 155ff.; Mayer-Homberg, pp. 13, 275ff.; Sohm, p. 8; Kiener, pp. 85ff; García Gallo, pp. 249, 259ff.; Reinhart, pp. 350ff.; Bloch, *Feudal Society*, 1:111; Schlesinger, "Herrschaft und Gefolgschaft," p. 267; Goubert, "Byzance et l'Espagne," p. 21.

94. Koschaker, pp. 57, 87, 111, 120; Sohm, pp. 26ff.; Below, *Territorium und Staat*, p. 194.

95. Gagé, *Les Classes Sociales*, p. 92; Peters, p. 311.

96. Tellenbach, *Königtum und Stämme*, pp. 56ff.; Graus, *Volk, Herrscher und Heiliger*, p. 273.

97. Guichard, chart on p. 19.

98. Heers, p. 15.

99. Tellenbach, *Studien . . . frühdeutschen Adels*, introduction, p. 5; Sablonier, pp. 27ff., 68ff.; Eck, pp. 186ff.; Heers, p. 25; K. Schmid, "Zur Problematik von Familie," pp. 13, 23.

100. Tellenbach, *Studien . . . frühdeutschen Adels*, p. 5; K. Schmid, "Zur Problematik von Familie," pp. 30-34; K. Werner, "Die Entstehung des *Reditus*," pp. 37, 58.

101. Josef Fleckenstein, "Ueber die Herkunft der Welfen," in Tellenbach, *Studien . . . frühdeutschen Adels*, p. 132.

102. Heers, p. 29.

103. Zöllner, *Die politische Stellung*, p. 137. A superficially different evaluation of the lingering importance of the *Stämme* is presented by Kienast, *Studien über . . . Volkstämme*, especially pp. 5ff., 73ff., 95ff., 130ff., 173ff. Kienast contends explicitly that the *Stämme* in both the western and eastern Frank realms remained equally important until the ninth or tenth century. But his basis for admitting groups like the Catalan and the Aquitainians to the *Stamm* category is his contention that regional particularism, promoted by dynastic and other political forces, produced an identity *similar* to that of the sedentarized Germanic *Stämme* east of the Rhine. In other words, Kienast identifies as a "later" kind of *Stamm* consciousness precisely the kind of territorial identity which I (following numerous other authors) contrast to the real *Stamm*, which is based on a fundamentally different genealogical myth. To be sure, Kienast does regard even territorial identities as reinforced by some cohesion derived from pre-Roman Celtic groups that may have resembled the Germanic *Stämme*; but he recognized that all mythic bases for such identity had vanished long before the period he treats. For a balanced critique emphasizing Kienast's rather idiosyncratic use of "*Stamm*," see Ganshof, "Stämme als Träger," pp. 147ff.; and Ganshof, "A Propos de Ducs," pp. 16-17.

104. Zöllner, *Die politische Stellung*, p. 50; Kirn, pp. 69ff.

105. Wenskus, *Sächsischer Stammesadel*, pp. 464ff., 471, 474.

106. Wilhelm Berges, "Das Reich ohne Hauptstadt," in "Das Hauptstadtproblem," p. 1.

107. Rosenstock, p. 116; Keutgen, p. 119.

108. Rörig, "Territorialwirtschaft," p. 458.

109. Schöffler, p. 18; Sohm, p. 26. Cf. Wenskus, *Stammesbildung*, p. 38, but note that he is discussing references to *Stämme* in the "Sachsenspiegel," not to the legal basis of the *Stamm*. As Hugelmann, "Studien zum Recht der Nationalitäten," p. 277, had shown earlier, the "Sachsenspiegel" unquestionably reflects the German myth of *Stamm* differentiation, whether or not this differentiation remained truly significant by the thirteenth century. As he points out (ibid., pp. 285ff.), by then

Frank (Salic) law, like the "Sachsenspiegel," was tending to become purely territorial.

110. Graus, "Die Entstehung der mittelalterlichen Staaten," p. 13; Tellenbach, *Königtum und Stämme*, p. 6; Wolowski, p. 52.

111. Musset, p. 208; Heinrich Mitteis, "Der Vertrag von Verdun im Rahmen der Karolingischen Verfassungspolitik," in Mayer, *Der Vertrag von Verdun*, p. 90.

112. Remppis, pp. 80ff.; E. Schubert, pp. 316ff. For an argument for the continuity of some such territorial designations and earlier *Stamm* divisions, see Kienast, *Studien über . . . Volkstämme*, pp. 145ff.

113. Schramm, *Herrschaftszeichen*, 3:846. Cf. Vasiliev, *History of the Byzantine Empire*, 1:268. See also K. Werner, "Die Entstehung des *Reditus*," p. 25, for the view that *Rex Francorum, Rex Franciae*, and similar terms were interchangeable. For the considerably earlier evidence of the concept of territorial empire, see chapter 5.

114. Roux, *Les Traditions des Nomades*, p. 37. See also Bacon, p. 54; Commeaux, pp. 87–88; Montagne, pp. 25ff.; Eydoux, p. 74; Woods, p. 187; and Vladimirtsov, *Le Régime Social*, pp. 51, 207.

115. Gautier, *Les Siècles Obscurs*; Poncet, "Le Mythe de la 'Catastrophe' Hilalienne," pp. 1100–1114.

116. LeStrange, p. 323.

117. Marçais, *La Berbérie*, p. 203; Deverdun, p. 525; Poliak, "Le Caractère Colonial," p. 247.

118. Guichard, p. 70.

119. Laroui, 1:135–43. Laroui regards the nomadic disruption as a consequence rather than a cause of economic depression. From my point of view this causal issue is not crucial, because the effect on boundaries is apt to be the same in either case.

120. Sarkisyanz, p. 226; Grousset, p. 218.

121. Weulersse, p. 86.

122. Rabinow, pp. 46–47. For the pre-Islamic nomad frontier, see Moret and Davy, p. 177; and Gagé, *Les Classes Sociales*, p. 276. For interesting parallels concerning the defense of the Caucasus frontier, see Peters, pp. 522n., 712; Previté-Orton, 1:192. Much the most detailed account of the Caucasus frontier is in Gadlo, pp. 28ff.

123. Ayalon, p. 116; Sivan, pp. 165ff. On the Transoxanian *limes*, see Barthold, pp. 180ff.; Hodgson, 1:493; Altheim, *Niedergang der alten Welt*, 1:43.

124. P. P. Tolochko, "Kievskaya Zemlya," in Besrovny, p. 13; M. P. Kuchera, "Pereyaslavskoye Knyazhestvo," in ibid., pp. 124ff.; Obolensky, *The Byzantine Commonwealth*, p. 229; Eck, pp. 24ff.

125. Amélineau, p. 2.

126. Fasoli, "Points de Vue sur les Incursions Hongroises," p. 28; Lüttich, p. 163; Bagalei, p. 82; Nolde, 2:61ff.; Eck, p. 33.

127. Vladimirtsov, *Gengis-Khan*, p. 117.

128. Woods, pp. 194ff.

129. Vladimirtsov, *Gengis-Khan*, p. 117; Bloch, *Feudal Society*, 1:56.

130. Nyström, p. 41; Guichard, pp. 71, 209; Miquel, *L'Islam et Sa Civilisation*, p. 29.

131. Rabinow, p. 38. See also Patai, *Golden River*, p. 179; Menendez Pidal, *The Cid*, p. 220.

132. Gautier, *Moeurs et Coutumes*, p. 53.

133. Dussaud, p. 11.

134. Guichard, pp. 22–23.

135. Holt, p. 53; Mez, p. 149; Hodgson, 2:88; Patai, *Society, Culture and Change*, p. 161.

136. Laroui, 1:72. Cf. Julien, p. 22.

137. Guichard, p. 209. Cf. Montagne, p. 53; Baron, *A Social and Religious History*, p. 41.

138. Patlagean, p. 71. Cf. Guichard, p. 96.

139. R. Anderson, p. 31.

140. Guichard, p. 85.

141. Ibid., p. 94.

142. Bacon, p. 68.

143. Sarkisyanz, p. 218.

144. Ibid., p. 23; Palmov, p. 10; Commeaux, p. 112.

145. Hudson, p. 22.

146. Gurliand, p. 82.

147. Roux, *Les Traditions des Nomades*, p. 325; Sohrweide, "Der Sieg der Safaviden," p. 136.

148. Laroui, 1:72; Krader, "Principle . . . Asiatic Steppe-Pastoralists," p. 78.

149. Wilson, in Frankfort, p. 47; Kortepeter, p. 30.

150. Benkö and Imre, pp. 269, 274.

151. Harold Steinacker, "Das Wesen des Madjarischen Nationalismus," in Walter and Steinacker, p. 54.

152. The theory is trenchantly advanced in Macartney, *The Magyars*, pp. 122ff.

153. Vladimirtsov, *Le Régime Social*, p. 40; Sinor, "The Outlines of Hungarian Prehistory," p. 521.

154. Marquardt, p. 33; Thomas von Bogyay, "Die Reiternomaden im Donauraum," in Šaria, pp. 100–103.

155. Deér, pp. 44ff.

156. Fasoli, *Le Incursioni Ungare*, pp. 25ff.

157. Schünemann, *Die Entstehung des Städtewesens*, 1:17. Cf. Richard, p. 26, on later church efforts to sedentarize the Cumans.

158. Hóman, 2:249.

159. Schünemann, *Die Deutschen in Ungarn*, pp. 24ff., 106; Hóman, 1:273ff.; Karajan, pp. 491ff.

160. Hóman, 2:240.

161. Ibid., pp. 244ff.

Chapter 3

1. Toynbee, pp. 14–20, 555. Because I argue that each religion shaped the central values of a civilization, I shall use "Islam" to refer to both the religion and the civilization, for there is no convenient term like "Christendom" to distinguish the civilization as such.

2. Bulliet, *The Camel*, pp. 221ff.; Lombard, *Espaces et Réseaux*, pp. 14–18.

3. Hodgson, 2:81ff.; Altheim, *Alexander*, pp. 15ff.

4. Watt, p. 247; Sohrweide, "Der Sieg der Safaviden," pp. 116, 163.

5. Hodgson, 1:307; Weulersse, p. 71.

6. Ganem, 1:11.

7. Becker, *Islamstudien*, p. 417.

8. Patai, *Golden River*, p. 49; Hodgson, 2:515.

9. Hodgson, 3:11.

10. Ibid., 2:556–58.

11. Watt, p. 197.

12. Djaït, p. 100.

13. Hodgson, 2:537.

14. Wright, p. 118.

15. Gardet, p. 346; Amélineau, p. 10. See also Schacht, *An Introduction to Islamic Law*, pp. 130, 187, for the formal restrictions.

16. Lane-Poole, *A History of Egypt*, p. 127.

17. Becker, *Islamstudien*, p. 398.

18. Daniel, p. 147; Eickhoff, pp. 49, 66ff.

19. Dannenbauer, 1:183. Cf. Altheim, *Niedergang der alten Welt*, 2:60ff.; Garsoïan, "Armenia," pp. 347–49; Stroheker, p. 219.

20. Erdmann, pp. 1ff.

21. Güterbock, pp. 25ff.

22. Vasiliev, *History of the Byzantine Empire*, 1:310.

23. Bréhier, *Vie et Mort de Byzance*, 1:190; Dölger, *Byzanz*, p. 331. Theophilus also, however, sought to enlist the aid of the Umayyad rivals of the Abbasids.

24. Eickhoff, p. 66.

25. Sivan, p. 80; Werblowsky, pp. 5ff. See Eickhoff, p. 227; Erdmann, pp. 1ff., 79; Franz Irsigler, "On the Aristocratic Character of Early Frankish Society," in Reuter, p. 118, on the general setting of the crusades.

26. Lotter, pp. 11ff.

27. Daniel, pp. 264ff.; Remppis, pp. 53ff.; Erdmann, pp. 60, 87; Beumann, *Das Kaisertum Ottos*, p. 552.

28. Lotter, p. 20. See also Dempf, p. 220, on Bernard as the "unique public voice" of his time.

29. See especially Gadlo, p. 27.

30. Heers, p. 73; Claude Cahen, "Les Facteurs Economiques et Sociaux," in Brunschvig and Von Grunebaum, p. 206.

31. Miquel, *L'Islam et Sa Civilisation*, p. 128. See Crone, *Slaves*, p. 81, on the unique "moral gap" associated with slavery in Islamic civilization.
32. Nyström, p. 171.
33. Goitein, *A Mediterranean Society*, 1:134–35. See Braudel, *Civilisation Matériélle*, 2:450; ibid. 3:350, for the difference in tacit public acceptance—not display—of slave mistresses in an early modern Ibero-American society as contrasted to the clandestine behavior of North American slaveowners in the same period. Balard, 2:821–22, in his minutely documented examination, reaches similar conclusions concerning the Genoese, the most important Western Christian slave traders of the late Middle Ages.
34. M. Lombard, *L'Islam dans Sa Première Grandeur*, pp. 198, 211.
35. Guichard, p. 78.
36. Arié, pp. 257, 320; Pelenski, *Russia and Kazan*, pp. 232, 295.
37. Ganem, 2:9. See also Wiesflecker, 3:43.
38. Stökl, *Die Entstehung des Kosakentums*, p. 54; Ferguson, p. 141.
39. Sugar, pp. 105–7.
40. Hodgson, 3:71; Sarkisyanz, p. 224.
41. Daniel, p. 45.
42. Braudel, *The Mediterranean*. See also Dufourcq, *L'Espagne Catalane*; Kortepeter; Angyal; McNeill.
43. Eickhoff. See also Ahrweiler; Labatut, p. 153.
44. Honigmann, pp. 39ff.; Shaban, *Islamic History*, p. 129; Laurent, *Byzance et les Turcs*, pp. 103ff.; Laurent, *L'Arménie*, pp. 243ff.; Vasiliev, *History of the Byzantine Empire*, 1:272; LeStrange, p. 137.
45. Sivan, p. 9; Canard, p. 45; Ahrweiler, p. 40; Hodgson, 2:273; Fattal, p. 50; Laurent, *L'Arménie*, pp. 118, 157, 169, 188, 221.
46. Planhol, "Géographie Politique," p. 547.
47. Grenier, pp. 293ff. .
48. Dubler, pp. 186–96, and map; Burns, *Islam under the Crusaders*, pp. 67ff.
49. Julien, p. 84; Bulliet, *The Camel*, p. 229; Lombard, *L'Islam dans Sa Première Grandeur*, p. 82.
50. Abadal i de Vinyals, p. 584; J. Perez de Urbel, "La Reconquista de Castilla y León," in *La Reconquista Española*, pp. 129ff.
51. Chaunu, *L'Espagne*, 1:123.
52. See especially Dubler, p. 186, and map. Defourneaux, p. 9; Klein, p. 7; Lombard, *L'Islam dans Sa Première Grandeur*, p. 171, agree on the Berber origin of the Mesta. Charles J. Bishko, "The Castilian as Plainsman," in Lewis and McGann, p. 56, however, believes the institution originated much later.
53. Menéndez Pidal, *The Cid*, p. 288; Richard Konetzke, "Probleme der Beziehungen zwischen Islam und Christentum im spanischen Mittelalter," in Wilpert, p. 221.
54. Hillgarth, p. 321.
55. Carande, p. 381. See also Konetzke, in Wilpert, p. 224.
56. Verlinden, *L'Esclavage*, 1:103ff. Some other Christian groups, notably the Genoese, found slave-trading more profitable than the use of slaves.

57. Sanchez-Albornoz, pp. 123ff.; Perez de Urbel, in *La Reconquista Española*, pp. 151ff.

58. Burns, *Islam under the Crusaders*, p. 157.

59. Braudel, *Capitalism*, p. 24.

60. F. Yndurain, "Relaciones entre la Filologia y la Historia," in *La Reconquista Española*, p. 238.

61. Bevan, p. 107.

62. Arié, pp. 230ff.

63. Dufourcq, *L'Espagne Catalane*, pp. 105ff.; Julio Gonzalez, "Reconquista y Repoblacion," in *La Reconquista Española*, p. 194; Defourneaux, pp. 143, 171; Lourie, p. 68; Burns, *The Crusader Kingdom*, p. 173.

64. Yardeni, p. 271. See also Elliott, *Imperial Spain*, p. 381; Chaunu, *L'Espagne*, 1:39–40.

65. Burns, *Islam under the Crusaders*, p. 301; Burns, *The Crusader Kingdom*, pp. 13, 19.

66. Burns, *The Crusader Kingdom*, p. 19.

67. Castro, pp. 76, 591; Hillgarth, p. 381; Angyal, p. 220; Peristiany, p. 123; Boswell, p. 344; Vicens Vives, 3:116; Elliott, *Imperial Spain*, p. 46; Thomas F. Glick, "Ethnic Systems of Pre-Modern Spain," in Tomassin, p. 165.

68. Carande, p. 384.

69. Young, pp. 429ff.

70. Chaunu, *L'Espagne*, 1:33.

71. I. P. Petrushevsky, "Iran i Azerbaidzhan," in Tikhvinsky, p. 237. The famous Khan Berke's earlier conversion did not have much immediate impact.

72. L. V. Cherepin, "Mongoly-Tatary na Rusi," in Tikhvinsky, pp. 202–6.

73. Eck, p. 43. See also Bezzola, p. 41.

74. Bächtold, pp. 134ff.

75. Yakubovsky, pp. 30–36.

76. Kortepeter, pp. 38ff., 110.

77. Calculated on the basis of data in McNeill, p. 29n.; Stökl, *Die Entstehung des Kosakentums*, p. 147; Ernst, pp. 3ff.

78. Bagalei, p. 85; Ernst, p. 19.

79. Nolde, 1:161.

80. Stökl, *Die Entstehung des Kosakentums*, pp. 140ff.; S. A. Pletneva, "Polovetskaya Zemlya," in Besrovny, p. 269; Bagalei, p. 36; Eck, p. 293; Ferguson, pp. 139ff.

81. Ibid., p. 142; Bagalei, pp. 36ff.; Kortepeter, p. 36n.; Stökl, *Die Entstehung des Kosakentums*, pp. 85, 140.

82. Nolde, 1:14. See also Gaudefroy-Demombynes and Platonov, p. 485.

83. Courant, p. 42; Sarkisyanz, pp. 22ff.

84. Nolde, 1:161ff.; 2:220.

85. Pelenski, *Russia and Kazan*, p. 4.

86. Nolde, 1:36, 117.

87. Ferguson, pp. 139–41; Nolde, 2:7ff.

88. Nolde, 2:135, quoting an Imperial Rescript of 16 January 1774.

89. Nolde, 2:170.

90. Ibid., pp. 220ff.

91. Ibid., pp. 364ff.

92. Ibid., pp. 182ff., 220ff.

93. Ibid., pp. 173ff.; Burns, *Islam under the Crusaders*, pp. 49ff.; Chaunu, "Minorités et Conjuncture," pp. 90ff.; Sarkisyanz, pp. 289ff.

94. Spuler, *The Muslim World*, 2:186. See also Spuler, *Die Mongolen*, end map; Hodgson, 3:221.

95. McNeill, pp. 26–36.

96. Ibid., p. 41, and the critique by Sugar, p. 191.

97. Walter, *Österreichische . . . Verwaltungsgeschichte*, p. 49.

98. Iorga, 2:220ff.; Rothenberg, pp. 1, 6.

99. Rothenberg, p. 27.

100. Ibid., p. 15; Schwicker, pp. 4ff.; Bidermann, *Geschichte der . . . Gesammt-Staats-Idee*, 1:24ff.

101. Angyal, p. 228.

102. Schwicker, pp. 16ff.; Rothenberg, pp. 26ff.

103. Valjavec, *Geschichte . . . Südosteuropa*, 3:75ff.; Schwicker, p. 52; Turczynski, pp. 51ff.

104. Schwicker, pp. 171ff.; Rothenberg, p. 123.

105. Schwicker, pp. 52, 78; Turczynski, p. 114.

106. Ferguson, p. 148; Rothenberg, p. 123; Schwicker, p. 185.

107. E. Werner, p. 19; Ercümend Kuran, "The Impact of Nationalism on the Turkish Elite of the Nineteenth Century," in Polk and Chambers, pp. 109ff.

108. Ranke; Hammer (Purgstall), *Geschichte des osmanischen Reiches*; Zinkeisen.

109. E. Werner, p. 37.

110. See especially Cahen, *Pre-Ottoman Turkey*.

111. Sa'd Al-Din, p. 5.

112. Paul Wittek, "Le Rôle des Tribus Turques dans l'Empire Ottoman," in *Mélanges Georges Smets*, p. 673. See also Woods, p. 357.

113. Lybyer, p. 88; Iorga, 1:149; Wittek, *The Rise of the Ottoman Empire*, p. 50.

114. Wittek, *The Rise of the Ottoman Empire*, pp. 21ff.; cf. Wittek, "Deux Chapitres . . . Turcs de Roum," p. 294. Giese, pp. 248, 249, 253, stresses the Moslem character of the new immigrants, whereas E. Werner, p. 47, emphasizes shamanist survivals.

115. Birge, pp. 16ff.

116. E. Werner, p. 89.

117. Ibid., p. 63.

118. Grenard, p. 52; E. Werner, p. 220; Kortepeter, p. 74.

119. Ranke, p. 35.

120. Wittek, *The Rise of the Ottoman Empire*, p. 14.

121. Giese, pp. 253ff.

122. McNeill, p. 132.

123. See especially Hodgson, 3:106–7, on the accommodation of the *ghazi* and the High Islamic myths.

124. Sugar, p. 27.
125. Giese, pp. 253ff.; Wittek, "Deux Chapitres . . . Turcs de Roum," p. 309.
126. Zinkeisen, p. 857.

Chapter 4

1. Braudel, *Capitalism*, p. 399.
2. Benveniste, 1:364.
3. Braudel, *The Mediterranean*, 1:351.
4. Goitein, "The Rise of the Near-Eastern Bourgeoisie," p. 596.
5. W. Fischel, "Über . . . Karimi-Kaufleute," p. 82.
6. Harmand, p. 293.
7. Harris, pp. 283–88. See also Leitsch, "Remarques Comparatives sur le Développement des Villes en Russie et dans les Balkans," in *Structure Sociale*, p. 132.
8. R. Williams, p. 1.
9. Braudel, *Capitalism*, p. 376; Rörig, *Die europäische Stadt*, p. 75.
10. Waley, pp. 7ff.
11. Brunner, "Europäisches und russisches Bürgertum," p. 16.
12. Lévi-Strauss, *Structural Anthropology*, p. 292.
13. Geertz, p. 222.
14. Vernant, pp. 594–95.
15. Bernand, p. 58.
16. Claude, p. 103.
17. Simson, p. 119. See also Galassi, 1:161.
18. Claude, pp. 41ff.; Sauvaget, "Equisse . . . Damas," p. 454; Sauvaget, *Alep*, pp. 52, 63–68; Wulzinger and Watzinger, pp. 30ff.
19. Brunschvig, "Urbanisme Médiéval," pp. 131ff.; Hodgson, 2:116.
20. Gautier, *Moeurs et Coutumes*, p. 83; Gabriel, *Religionsgeographie*, p. 119; Hans Hogg, "Istanbul: Stadtorganismus und Stadterneuerung," in Bachteler, p. 282; Gönol Tankut, "The Spatial Distribution of Urban Activities in the Ottoman City," in *Structure Sociale*, p. 258; Clerget, 1:282; Busch-Zantner, pp. 3, 8, 11.
21. Antonio Garcia y Bellido, "La Edad Antigua," in Garcia y Bellido, p. 30.
22. Jouguet, pp. 204–5.
23. Leopold Torres Balbas, "La Edad Medici," in Garcia y Bellido, p. 99; Hillgarth, p. 67.
24. Heers, p. 173; Sjoberg, p. 100. For the opposing view, which seems more plausible to me, see, in addition to the authors cited above, Mols, p. 153.
25. Quoted in Waley, p. 148.
26. Ibid., p. 159.
27. Quoted in ibid., p. 99, from Sienese regulations.
28. Ibid., p. 163.

29. Kirsten, p. 64.
30. Benveniste, 1: 367.
31. Kirsten, p. 67.
32. Vetruvius, as quoted in Bernand, p. 58.
33. Friedrich Vittinghoff, "Die Struktur der spätantiken Stadt," in Jankuhn, Schlesinger, and Steuer, p. 94; Kirsten, p. 64; Claude, p. 12.
34. Waley, p. 7; Chiapelli, 6:18ff.
35. Waley, pp. 35ff.; Rörig, *Die europäische Stadt*, p. 34; Ennen, *Frühgeschichte*, p. 262; Heers, p. 43.
36. Chaunu, *L'Espagne*, 1:270; Waley, pp. 7, 21, 35ff., 71, 222.
37. Schramm, *Herrschaftszeichen*, 3:861; Kantorowicz, pp. 62, 81.
38. Waley, p. 104.
39. Weulersse, p. 87.
40. Bourrilly, p. 200; Le Tourneau, *Fez . . . Merinides*, pp. 27ff.
41. Marçais, "La Conception des Villes," pp. 524, 533; Eugen Wirth, "Die soziale Stellung und Gliederung der Stadt im Osmanischen Reich," in *Untersuchungen . . . der mittelalterlichen Städte*, pp. 408ff.; J. Aubin, "Comment Tamerlan," p. 95; Le Tourneau, *Fès avant le Protectorat*, pp. 230ff.; Weulersse, p. 83. On abortive movements toward urban independence in medieval Syria, see Ashtor, pp. 226ff.
42. Marçais, "La Conception des Villes," p. 533.
43. Labib, p. 494; Miquel, *L'Islam et Sa Civilisation*, p. 203.
44. Petrushevsky, "Gosudarskaya Znat," p. 109; Ashtor, pp. 258, 322; Lapidus, p. 69; Claude Cahen, "Mouvements et Organisations Populaires dans les Villes de l'Asie Musulman au Moyen Ages," in *Recueils . . . Bodin*, pp. 275ff.; Crone, *Slaves*, p. 86.
45. Planitz, *Die deutsche Stadt*, pp. 55ff., 99ff., 113, 190ff.; Rörig, *Die europäische Stadt*, pp. 8ff., 24ff.; Marguerite Boulet-Sautel, "La Formation de la Ville Médiévale dans les Régions du Centre de la France," in *Recueils . . . Bodin*, pp. 357–70; Hektor Ammann, "Von Städtewesen Spaniens und Westfrankreichs," in Constance, Institut . . . Bodenseegebietes, pp. 109ff., 123ff.; Ewig, pp. 588–94.
46. Ennen, *Frühgeschichte*, pp. 41ff. See also Ennen, *The Medieval Town*, p. 46.
47. See Philippe Dollinger, "Les Villes Allemandes au Moyen Age," in *Recueils . . . Bodin*, pp. 371–401, and all the works cited in note 45 above.
48. Ennen, *The Medieval Town*, p. 99. Cf. Heers, pp. 19ff.; Gerard Dilcher, "Rechtshistorische Aspekte des Stadtbegriffs," in Jahnkuhn, Schlesinger, and Steuer, p. 29.
49. Kirsten, p. 63.
50. Heers, p. 154; Rörig, *Die europäische Stadt*, p. 31.
51. Rörig, *Die europäische Stadt*, p. 113. This exceptionally extensive territory may be compared to the one hundred-square mile territory of a small Roman *polis* in the declining phase of the empire. See Claude, p. 12. The average *polis* territory, as indicated in Table 1, was some seven hundred square miles. On Amsterdam as the "last *polis* of Europe," see Braudel, *Civilisation Matérielle*, 2:437.
52. Bader, *Der deutsche Südwesten*, p. 134.

53. Ahasver von Brandt, "Die gesellschaftliche Struktur des spätmittelalterlichen Lübeck," in *Untersuchungen . . . der mittelalterlichen Städte*, p. 217; Ebel, p. 9. I use the date of Lübeck's legal foundation in Schubart-Fikentscher, p. 383; some sources give a somewhat earlier year.

54. Halban, pp. 45ff.; Bächtold, pp. 51, 106; Schubart-Fikentscher, pp. 31ff.

55. Bächtold, p. 51; Harold Steinacker, "Die geschichtlichen Voraussetzung des österreichischen Nationalitätenproblems," in Hugelmann, *Das Nationalitätenrecht*, pp. 11ff.; Künssberg, "Rechtssprachgeographie," p. 46.

56. Manfred Hellmann, "Probleme früher städtischer Sozialstruktur Osteuropas," in *Untersuchungen . . . der mittelalterlichen Städte*, pp. 395ff.; Heinrich Appelt, "Die mittelalterliche deutsche Siedlung in Schlesien," in *Deutsche Ostsiedlung*, pp. 15–18; Hans Thieme, "Die Magdeburger und Kulmer Stadtrechte," in ibid., pp. 151–57; H. Aubin, *Grundlagen . . . Kulturraumforschung*, p. 579; Koebner, pp. 328, 341; Lynnychenko, p. 30; Schmalfuss, pp. 1, 3, 8.

57. Ebel, pp. 9, 11; Thieme, in *Deutsche Ostsiedlung*, p. 155; Schubart-Fikentscher, p. 33.

58. Schubart-Fikentscher, p. 33; Ebel, pp. 9, 11; Samsonowicz, pp. 10ff.; Braudel, *Civilisation Matérielle*, 2:424.

59. Koschaker, pp. 241ff.

60. Below, "Die städtische Verwaltung," pp. 438ff., 462.

61. Berges, in "Das Hauptstadtproblem," p. 22; Bader, *Der deutsche Südwesten*, p. 154.

62. Stein Rokkan, "Dimensions of State-Formation and Nation-Building," in Tilly, p. 576.

63. Ennen, *Frühgeschichte*, p. 267. See Sablonier, pp. 74ff., for somewhat different conditions in Switzerland.

64. Ennen, *Frühgeschichte*, p. 147.

65. Goitia, in Garcia y Bellido, p. vi.

66. R. Williams, pp. 2, 266.

67. Quoted in Hôman, 1:187. Cf. W. Kuhn, "Die Erschliessung," pp. 416, 472.

68. Appelt, in *Deutsche Ostsiedlung*, pp. 2ff.

69. W. Kuhn, "Die deutschrechtlichen Städte," pp. 279ff., 319, 334.

70. Herbert Ludat, "Zum Stadtbegriff im osteuropäischen Bereich," in Jahnkuhn, Schlesinger, and Steurer, pp. 78ff. (including map); Herbert Ludat, "Frühformen des Städtewesens in Osteuropa," in Constance, Institut . . . Bodenseegebietes, pp. 538ff.

71. W. Kuhn, "Die deutschrechtlichen Städte," p. 285.

72. Ibid., p. 711; Schubart-Fikentscher, pp. 227ff., 267.

73. Valjavec, *Geschichte . . . Südosteuropa*, 1:73, 80; 2:26; Schünemann, *Die Entstehung des Stadtwesens*, pp. 79ff.; Hôman, 1:417; 2:154.

74. Valjavec, *Geschichte . . . Südosteuropa*, 3:103; Sugar, p. 88; Schwartner, pp. 89, 92, 94.

75. Schubart-Fikentscher, pp. 237ff.; Jaffé, pp. 329ff.; Martel, p. 198.

76. Brawer, p. 40; Angyal, p. 210; Wolowski, pp. 45, 57.

77. Kopchak, p. 65; Brawer, pp. 28ff.; Baron, *A Social and Religious History*, pp. 4, 209.

78. Bächtold, p. 55; Lynnychenko, p. 226.
79. Auerbach, p. 260; Petrowicz, pp. 323ff.; Wojciechowski, *L'Etat Polonais*, p. 237. Cf. Richard, p. 267, on intermittent efforts to secure the union of the Lvov Armenians with Rome.
80. Brawer, p. 91; Bächtold, p. 54.
81. Baron, *A Social and Religious History*, pp. 182ff.; Brawer, pp. 40ff.
82. Halban, p. 43.
83. Martel, p. 195; Bächtold, p. 54; Wolowski, p. 99.
84. Hellmann, in *Untersuchungen . . . der mittelalterlichen Städte*, p. 384. Cf. Hittle, p. 26.
85. Lombard, *Espaces et Réseaux*, p. 84.
86. Ludat, in Constance, Institut . . . Bodenseegebietes, pp. 532–37; Tikhomirov, pp. 55ff., 168, 240ff.
87. Eck, p. 14; Hellmann, "Stadt und Recht," pp. 52ff.
88. Halban, pp. 19, 31; Lynnychenko, pp. 19ff.
89. Miliukov, pp. 131ff.
90. Eck, p. 328; Hittle, pp. 30ff.
91. Baron, *A Social and Religious History*, p. 242; Tushin, pp. 62ff.
92. John A. Armstrong, "Mobilized Diaspora in Tsarist Russia: The Case of the Baltic Germans," in Azrael, pp. 63–104, and works cited there.
93. Leitsch, in *Structure Sociale*, p. 132.
94. Ewig, p. 591; Musset, pp. 203–5; Dannenbauer, 2:88; Demougeot, p. 534. Slouschz, pp. 187ff., 302, suggests that the Syrians became Jews; this theory appears highly improbable to me.
95. Geanakoplos, p. 177; Lane, pp. 300ff.; Jacoby, *Société et Démographie*, p. 186; Schaube, pp. 236, 246.
96. Brawer, pp. 28, 43.
97. Vicens Vives, 2:13 (map); Burns, *Islam under the Crusaders*, pp. 149ff.; Ammann, in Constance, Institut . . . Bodenseegebietes, pp. 109ff.
98. Christensen, *L'Iran*, p. 379; Bell, *Egypt*, pp. 43, 52; Bernand, p. 241.
99. Miquel, *L'Islam et Sa Civilisation*, p. 31.
100. Hodgson, 1:208.
101. Wittek, in *Mélanges Georges Smets*, p. 673; Marçais, "La Conception des Villes," pp. 526ff.; Hautecoeur and Wiet, 1:20; Golvin, p. 70.
102. Bulliet, *The Camel*, pp. 172ff., 224ff.
103. Thoumin, p. 250.
104. Goodwin, p. 446; Odile Daniel, "Le Procès d'Islamisation," in *Structure Sociale*, p. 242; Tankut, in ibid., pp. 252ff.
105. D. and J. Sourdel, *La Civilisation de l'Islam*, p. 431.
106. Clarke, p. 267; Franco, p. 174; Mantran, pp. 53ff., 451ff.
107. Lapidus, pp. 185–86.
108. Another hypothetical type (+a, +b, +c) appears very unlikely in practice, because strong civic consciousness and territorial extension can hardly coexist with ethnic segmentation.

Chapter 5

1. Eisenstadt, p. 10.
2. Ibid., p. 11.
3. See Benveniste, 2:19, on the Achemenid origin of "King of Kings," made familiar in Greek as *"Basileus Basileon."*
4. Buccellati, p. 63.
5. Kampers, p. 30; Thorkild Jacobsen, "Mesopotamia," in Frankfort, p. 200.
6. Hammond, pp. 53–54. Cf. Benveniste, 2:19–20.
7. Kaerst, *Studien . . . Altertum*, p. 56; Altheim, *Alexander*, pp. 115–17.
8. Kaerst, *Die antike Idee*, pp. 23ff.; Dannenbauer, 1:183; Stein, 1:7. Cf. Altheim, *Niedergang der alten Welt*, 1:52ff., who considers that the Sassanids gave up the concept of world dominion ("King of Kings of Iran and non-Iran") only after defeat by the Romans.
9. Garsoïan, "Le Rôle de l'Hiérarchie Chrétienne," p. 119; Dölger, *Byzanz*, pp. 51, 60; Gagé, *Les Classes Sociales*, p. 211; Gagé, "L'Empereur Romain," p. 260.
10. Vasiliev, *History of the Byzantine Empire*, 1:199.
11. Ovid, *Fasti*, 2:683–84, as quoted in Hammond, p. 278.
12. Hunger, p. 106.
13. Gagé, *Les Classes Sociales*, p. 260; Hussey, p. 106.
14. Paschoud, pp. 20, 31, 153.
15. Dannenbauer, 1:14.
16. Demougeot, p. xiii. See also Latouche, p. 31; Steinacker, p. 276; Hammond, pp. 302, 315; Storoni Mazzolani, p. 190.
17. Seel, p. 79.
18. Djaït, p. 129. Cf. Crone, *Slaves*, p. 83.
19. See especially Shaban, *Islamic History*, p. 72.
20. Gibb, "Arab-Byzantine Relations," p. 232.
21. Wiet, "L'Empire Néo-Byzantine," p. 66.
22. Shaban, *Islamic History*, pp. 19, 72ff.; Bertold Spuler, "Iran," in Von Grunebaum, *Unity and Variety*, pp. 172–79; Hodgson, 1:282, 348–50; Haussig, p. 203.
23. Von Grunebaum, *Medieval Islam*, p. 33; Miquel, *La Géographie Humaine*, p. 99. Of course, the central role of the Arabian Holy Cities continued to be emphasized. Moreover, as Jacob Lassner, pp. 170ff., emphasizes, direct Sassanid influences have often been exaggerated. But he fully agrees with the importance of Baghdad as a symbol of centralized rule (ibid., pp. 244ff.).
24. Schacht, "Zur soziologischen Betrachtung," pp. 227ff.; Gardet, pp. 165ff.; D. and J. Sourdel, *La Civilisation de l'Islam*, pp. 370ff.; D. Sourdel, *Le Vizirat*, 2:647ff.
25. Hodgson, 1:347. See also Miquel, *La Géographie Humaine*, pp. 261, 269, 309; Miquel, *L'Islam et Sa Civilisation*, p. 9; Marçais, *Manuel de l'Art Musulman*, 2:469; Becker, "Bartholds Studien," pp. 351ff., 358, 363; Wiet, *L'Egypte*, p. 437;

Eickhoff, p. 291; Anwar G. Chejne, "Islamicization and Arabicization in Al-Andalus," in Vryonis, *Islam and Cultural Change*, p. 72.

26. Wiet, *L'Egypte*, p. 437.

27. Gardet, p. 179.

28. Kern, *Gottesgnadentum und Widerstandsrecht*, p. 257, on the phrase "Grace of God."

29. Quoted in Gibb, "Luftī Paşa," p. 290. Cf. Hodgson, 2:453.

30. Nolde, 2:117.

31. Von Grunebaum, *Modern Islam*, p. 206.

32. Wittek, *The Rise of the Ottoman Empire*, p. 48; Becker, "Bartholds Studien," p. 390; Shay, pp. 91ff.

33. Von Grunebaum, *Medieval Islam*, p. 113; Turan, "The Ideal," p. 83.

34. Turan, "The Ideal," p. 78.

35. Kirsten, p. 35.

36. Spuler, *The Muslim World*, 2:4, 5.

37. Quoted in Commeaux, p. 126.

38. N. P. Shastina, "Obraz Chingiskhana v Srednevekhovoi Literature Mongolov," in Tikhvinsky, p. 477. Cf. Franke, p. 104, on continuation of Chinese styles and titles by Chagatays and Il Khans.

39. Courant, p. 126; Vladimirtsov, *Le Régime Social*, p. 242.

40. Palmov, pp. 35, 42.

41. Ayalon, p. 177; Gurliand, pp. 14, 40ff.; Woods, p. 17.

42. I. P. Petrushevsky, "Pokhod Mongolskikh Voisk v Srednyuyu Aziyu," in Tikhvinsky, pp. 118–21, 131–32; E. Werner, p. 170.

43. Grousset, p. 513; J. Aubin, "Comment Tamerlan Prenait les Villes," p. 86.

44. Grousset, p. 437; Abu-Lughod, p. 31; Ayalon, pp. 128–38; Poliak, "Le Caractère Colonial," pp. 232ff.

45. Sivan, p. 177.

46. Ayalon, p. 138; Poliak, "Le Caractère Colonial," pp. 233. On the mythic origins of the Black Banner, see Lassner, p. 28.

47. Vacalopoulos, p. 257.

48. Ganem, 1:201.

49. Hanson, in Bachteler, p. 262. The same point is made by Charles, pp. 321–44. For an example of the works Hanson criticizes, see Aga-Oglu, pp. 183ff. For a layman like me it is difficult, after spending many hours in the Hagia Sophia and the Ottoman imperial mosques, and more time scrutinizing plans and photographs of them, to see how anyone could contest their relationship.

50. Dölger, *Byzanz*, p. 80. See also Lechner, p. 303; Schenk von Stauffenberg, p. 113.

51. Heldmann, p. 189.

52. Stroheker, pp. 207ff.

53. Ahrweiler, pp. 10, 231ff., 252; Ostrogorsky, p. 342.

54. Stroheker, pp. 19ff.; Piganiol, p. 193; Paschoud, pp. 211ff., 229, 269.

55. Helbling, p. 9.

56. Schenk von Stauffenberg, pp. 96ff.

57. Folz, *The Concept of Empire*, p. 6.

58. Dölger, *Byzanz*, p. 310.

59. Uspensky, pp. 64ff.; see also Obolensky, *The Byzantine Commonwealth*; Deér, p. 113.

60. Peters, p. 580.

61. See especially Hunger, pp. 61ff. Cf. Folz, *The Concept of Empire*, p. 7; Anton Michel, "Die Kaisermacht in der Ostkirche," in Šaria p. 128; Schenk von Stauffenberg, pp. 112–13.

62. Altheim, *Niedergang der alten Welt*, 2:200; A. Grabar, p. 153.

63. Geanakoplos, p. 132. Cf. Simson, pp. 2ff.

64. Diez and Demus, p. 42. Cf. Simson, pp. 112ff.; Cutler, pp. 106ff.

65. Geanakoplos, p. 132. Cf. Vossler, *Medieval Culture*, 2:97.

66. Kantorowicz, pp. 62–81; Haussig, p. 121; Schenk von Stauffenberg, p. 113; Kaerst, *Studien . . . Altertum*, p. 49.

67. Michel, in Šaria, p. 137.

68. Baynes and Moss, introduction p. xxviii; and Wilhelm Ensslen, "The Emperor and the Imperial Administration," in ibid., p. 274.

69. Haussig, pp. 186ff., 201; Previté-Orton, 1:268.

70. Michel, in Šaria, p. 135.

71. That is, no alien was actually recognized by Byzantines as their ruler. Germanic leaders claimed the Roman throne in the West, and in 1204 West European crusaders installed their "emperor" in Constantinople.

72. Michael Cherniavsky, "Khan or Basileus," in Cherniavsky, *The Structure of Russian History*, p. 67.

73. Pelenski, "The Origins of the Official Muscovite Claims," p. 40; Stökl, "Die Begriffe Reich," p. 104.

74. Pelenski, *Russia and Kazan*, pp. 115ff., 178.

75. Ibid., p. 8.

76. Michael Cherniavsky, "Russia," in Ranum, pp. 127, 133.

77. Obolensky, *The Byzantine Commonwealth*, pp. 129, 223; Soloviev, p. 460. At that date (972) the Rus were allies of the Christian Bulgars who, as noted below, persisted in intermittently attacking Byzantium.

78. Cherniavsky, in Cherniavsky, *The Structure of Russian History*, p. 67.

79. Medlin, pp. 67ff.

80. Obolensky, *The Byzantine Commonwealth*, pp. 108, 113.

81. Ibid., pp. 115, 242ff., 366; Medlin, pp. 75ff.

82. Michel, in Šaria, pp. 136–37.

83. Medlin, pp. 116ff.; Olšr, p. 373.

84. Olšr, p. 373.

85. Duchhardt, p. 128.

86. Walicki, p. 147. Cf. Armstrong, in Azrael.

87. Medlin, pp. 226ff.

88. Chayev, p. 23. Peter I had also explicitly advanced Russia's role as an *Antemurale* defense of Christendom. Winter, *Russland und das Papsttum*, 2:33.

89. Mohr, p. 17; Kern, *Gottesgnadentum und Widerstandsrecht*, pp. 10, 13, 25.

90. Mohr, pp. 17, 28.

91. Heldmann, pp. 68ff., 234ff.; Kantorowicz, pp. 62, 129.

92. Heldmann, pp. 268ff.

93. Ullmann, *The Carolingian Renaissance*, pp. 83, 85, 91; Kern, *Gottesgnadentum und Widerstandsrecht*, pp. 45, 84.

94. Ullmann, *The Carolingian Renaissance*, p. 178.

95. Heldmann, p. 107.

96. Vasiliev, *History of the Byzantine Empire*, 1:268.

97. Ullmann, *The Carolingian Renaissance*, pp. 136, 139.

98. Mohr, p. 7; Kern, *Gottesgnadentum und Widerstandsrecht*, p. 13; Tellenbach, "Die Unteilbarkeit des Reiches," p. 25.

99. Schlierer, pp. 49ff., 91.

100. Mohr, p. 176.

101. K. Werner, "Die Entstehung des *Reditus*," p. 25; Kern, *Die Anfänge . . . Ausdehnungspolitik*, pp. 16ff.; Folz, *The Concept of Empire*, p. 19; Zeller, p. 275.

102. Folz, *Le Souvenir . . . de Charlemagne*, pp. 191ff.; Heer, pp. 85ff.

103. Strayer, *Medieval Statecraft*, p. 311.

104. Ullmann, *The Carolingian Renaissance*, p. 125.

105. Mohr, pp. 28, 170; Schramm, *Der König von Frankreich*, 1:71, 84, 112, 266. See Schneidmüller, pp. 179–80, on initial papal claims.

106. Schramm, *Der König von Frankreich*, 1:232; Previté-Orton, 1:469; Ullmann, *The Carolingian Renaissance*, p. 109. Cf. K. Werner, "Die Entstehung des *Reditus*," p. 37, on the role of female descent.

107. Ullmann, *The Carolingian Renaissance*, pp. 108, 126ff.; Mohr, p. 116. See Reuling, pp. 70ff., 102–104, 200–206, on French and imperial developments.

108. Kern, *Gottesgnadentum und Widerstandsrecht*, p. 60.

109. Zeller, p. 290ff.

110. Wieruszowski, p. 143.

111. Zeller, p. 299.

112. Schramm, *Der König von Frankreich*, 1:4.

113. Joseph R. Strayer, "France: The Holy Land, the Chosen People, and the Most Christian King," in Rabb and Seigel, pp. 5, 16.

114. K. Werner, in Reuter, pp. 247ff.

115. Dhondt, *Etudes . . . des Principautés Territoriales*, p. 256; critique by K. Werner, in Reuter, pp. 247ff.

116. K. Werner in Reuter, pp. 247ff.

117. Strayer, *Medieval Statecraft*, pp. 311–13. I have no intention of implying that a direct connection between the Mesopotamian concept and the medieval French view can be established. Such remote relationships of symbols have been noted before, however; for example, between the seven mythical Zoroastrian viceroys and the seven Electors of the Holy Roman empire. See Hammer (Purgstall), *Geschichte des osmanischen Reiches*, 2:3. On the other hand, see Lassner, p. 270, for a detailed critique of unwarranted attribution of Abbasid practices to the terrestrial reflection tradition.

118. Kern, *Die Anfänge . . . Ausdehnungspolitik*, p. 16. Cf. Kienast, *Deutschland*, 1:6.

119. Ullmann, *The Carolingian Renaissance*, p. 165; Deér, pp. 23, 33.

320 / Notes to Pages 159–69

120. Ullmann, *The Carolingian Renaissance*, p. 1.
121. Koenigsberger, *The Practice of Empire*, p. 11.
122. Folz, *The Concept of Empire*, p. 167. On practical limitations of imperial authority, see Kienast, *Deutschland*, 2:417, 465; Sommerfeldt, p. 194; Reimann, pp. 362, 374.
123. Duchhardt, p. 4; Danvila y Collado, 2:245; Kantorowicz, pp. 139ff.
124. Quoted in Hauser and Renaudet, p. 405.
125. Heinrich Sproemberg, "Das Erwachen des Staatsgefühl in den Niederlanden," in *L'Organisation Corporative*, p. 87; Lhotsky, p. 31.
126. Quoted in Calmette, p. 173.
127. Brandi, pp. 260–61; Wiesflecker, 1:238; Walther, p. 60; Huizinga, "Burgund," p. 25.
128. Chaunu, *L'Espagne*, 1:60–73.
129. M. Philippson, p. 7; Häbler, p. 34.
130. Walser, pp. 171ff.
131. Brandi, p. 263.
132. Polišenský, pp. 84ff. On the strength of the Germanic *Geblütsrecht* principle in Austrian law until 1521, see Winkler, *Studien über Gesamtstaatsidee*, p. 41.
133. Quoted in M. Philippson, pp. 27, 231; Helmut Koenigsberger, "Spain," in Ranum, p. 163.
134. Koenigsberger, *The Practice of Empire*, pp. 56ff.; M. Philippson, p. 571; Meinecke, *Machiavellism*, pp. 105–6. For additional evidence on the importance of the imperial concept during the early modern period, see Folz, *The Concept of Empire*, pp. 15, 41, 54ff.; Schramm, *Herrschaftszeichen*, 2:481ff.; 3:1055; Duchhardt, pp. 69, 120ff., 128, 153, 171; Hüffer, pp. 441ff. On the eventual demise of the imperial concept in West Europe, see Duchhardt, pp. 311ff.; Srbik, pp. 10ff., 19; Mitrofanov, 1:256; and Redlich, 1:2.
135. Tezner, p. 369; Srbik, pp. 31ff., 50.
136. Redlich, 1:2, 7; Bidermann, *Geschichte ... Gesammt-Staats-Idee*, 1:1, 3; Walter, *Österreichische ... Verwaltungsgeschichte*, pp. 25ff.
137. Winkler, *Studien über Gesamtstaatsidee*, pp. 22ff., 37ff.; Lhotsky, p. 117.
138. Redlich, 1:11ff.; Sturmberger, pp. 20ff.; Bidermann, *Geschichte ... Gesammt-Staats-Idee*, 1:50, 92n., 93n.
139. Bidermann, *Geschichte ... Gesammt-Staats-Idee*, 1:24ff.; Redlich, 1:7ff.

Chapter 6

1. See "Das Hauptstadtproblem"; Peyer, pp. 1–21. In addition to these works devoted explicitly to the historical role of capitals, Hammond, and Elias, *Ueber den Prozess der Zivilisation*, pp. 131ff., are suggestive.
2. Flight, p. 202; Nyström, pp. 83ff.; Buccellati, p. 94.
3. Petrushevsky, in Tikhvinsky, p. 237.

4. Hammond, pp. 311, 326; Millar, pp. 15ff.; Gagé, *Les Classes Sociales*, pp. 190ff.

5. Demougeot, p. 7. See Luttwak, p. 56.

6. Peyer, pp. 4, 15; Juliusz Bardach, "L'Etat Polonais," in Polish Academy of Sciences, pp. 292, 301; Guenée, pp. 746–49; Graus, "Die Entstehung der mittelalterlichen Staaten," p. 53.

7. Grundmann und Heimpel, p. 49.

8. Yardeni, p. 209; Prinz, p. 59; Gustaff Roloff, "Hauptstadt und Staat in Frankreich," in "Das Hauptstadtproblem," pp. 234, 249, 257ff.

9. Berges, in "Das Hauptstadtproblem," pp. 1ff.; Heer, pp. 33ff.

10. Vossler, *Medieval Culture*, 2: 69; Sproemberg, "Residenz und Territorium," p. 119.

11. Press, p. 153.

12. Schmitt, p. 118.

13. Calmette, pp. 325ff.; Walther, pp. 11, 41; Brandi, p. 261; Wiesflecker, 1:240.

14. Luis Cervera Vera, "La Epoca de los Austrias," in Garcia y Bellido, p. 176; Elliott, *Imperial Spain*, p. 132; Hillgarth, p. 10.

15. Cervera Vera, in Garcia y Bellido, pp. 176, 206.

16. On the pre-Habsburg efforts to make Prague a real center for the Holy Roman empire, see Spěváček, p. 130.

17. Adler, p. 31; Fellner, 1:79–82; Lhotsky, p. 83; Toman, p. 7; Otto Brunner, "Hamburg und Wien," in *Untersuchungen*, p. 288.

18. Kruedener, p. 75.

19. Elias, *Die höfische Gesellschaft*, pp. 73ff.; see also p. 322.

20. F. Rosenthal, 2:288ff.

21. Krebs, p. 157; McNeill, p. 41; Sugar, p. 191; Iorga, 2:205; Goodwin, p. 446.

22. Quoted in Ahrweiler, p. 303.

23. Dölger, *Byzanz*, p. 71.

24. Dagron, *Naissance d'une Capitale*, pp. 27, 48, 318ff., 541; Hunger, pp. 41ff.; Hussey, p. 357; A. Philippson, pp. 445ff.

25. Hunger, p. 50; Dagron, *Naissance d'une Capitale*, p. 389.

26. Uspensky, pp. 4, 14.

27. Pelenski, *Russia and Kazan*, pp. 178ff.

28. The monk Philotheos, quoted in Schaeder, *Moskau das dritte Rom*, p. 55. Cf. ibid., p. 100; Zabelin, p. 52.

29. V. Martin, p. 7.

30. Ibid., p. 17; Bell, "The Byzantine Servile State," pp. 87–91; Jones, *The Greek City*, pp. 18ff., 273; Johnson, p. 494.

31. Altheim, *Alexander*, p. 115.

32. Hirschfeld, p. 469.

33. A. H. M. Jones, "The Social Background of the Struggle between Paganism and Christianity," in Momigliano, p. 35.

34. Piganiol, p. 395. Cf. ibid., pp. 383, 387; Dagron, *Naissance d'une Capitale*, p. 146.

35. André Andreades, "La Recrutement des Fonctionnaires," in *Mélanges . . . Corneil*, p. 27. See also Ensslen, in Baynes and Moss, p. 282; Ostrogorsky, p. 243; Kazhdan, pp. 136ff.; D. Miller, p. 97.

36. Dagron, "Aux Origines de la Civilisation Byzantine," pp. 25, 40ff.

37. Zilliacus, p. 37.

38. Dagron, "Aux Origines de la Civilisation Byzantine," p. 40; Kunkel, p. 168.

39. Zilliacus, pp. 37, 67, 86, 100; Dagron, "Aux Origines de la Civilisation Byzantine," p. 40.

40. Hunger, pp. 349ff.; Weitzmann, pp. 45, 57ff.; Fuchs, pp. 22ff.; Ensslen, in Baynes and Moss, p. 294.

41. Wieacker, p. 174; Andreades, in *Mélanges . . . Corneil*, pp. 30–31.

42. Millar, p. 346.

43. Palm, pp. 7, 130ff.

44. Hussey, p. 81.

45. Vacalopoulos, pp. 173ff.

46. Ibid., p. 30; Moles, p. 107. For an opposing view, see Thiriet, pp. 110ff.

47. Dagron, "Aux Origines de la Civilisation Byzantine," p. 40.

48. Armstrong, in Azrael; Armstrong, *The European Administrative Elite*, pp. 134–35, 224–27, 253–62; Armstrong, "Administrative Elites," pp. 115–19.

49. Gaudefroy-Demombynes, *La Syrie*, p. xix; Björkmann, pp. 2ff.; Wiet, *L'Egypte*, p. 159; Lane-Poole, *A History of Egypt*, pp. 35ff.; Spuler, in Von Grunebaum, *Unity and Variety*, pp. 169ff.; D. Sourdel, *Le Vizirat*, 2:580; D. and J. Sourdel, *La Civilisation de l'Islam*, pp. 370–72; Christensen, *L'Iran*, pp. 315, 508.

50. Hammer (Purgstall), *Geschichte des osmanischen Reiches*, 2:3. See also Frye, pp. 17ff.; Christensen, *L'Iran*, pp. 128, 396.

51. Quoted in Spuler, *The Muslim World*, 1:52. See also Sourdel, *Le Vizirat*, 1:127ff.; Crone, *Slaves*, pp. 70ff.

52. Woods, p. 14; Spuler, *The Muslim World*, 1:82; D. and J. Sourdel, *La Civilisation de l'Islam*, p. 372; B. Miller, p. 13.

53. Gaudefroy-Demombynes, *La Syrie*, pp. lxivff.; Ashtor, p. 282; Ziadeh, p. 107; W. Fischel, "Ueber die Gruppe der Karimi," pp. 78–82.

54. B. Miller, p. 20.

55. Gladden, pp. 188–89; B. Miller, p. 127; Lybyer, p. 51.

56. Quoted in Babinger, p. 461. See also Mouradja d'Ohsson, pp. 153ff.

57. Wright, pp. 65, 94.

58. Itkowitz, pp. 77ff., 85; Sugar, p. 56.

59. Mouradja d'Ohsson, pp. 77ff. Cf. Lybyer, p. 232; B. Miller, pp. 31ff.; Lhotsky, p. 60.

60. B. Miller, pp. 6ff. Very recently Findley (see especially pp. 46ff.) has discussed in detail the complicated phases of the Ottoman administrative system. His treatment is essential for an understanding of chronological differences that I could only suggest in passing.

61. Mouradja d'Ohsson, pp. 165ff.; 500. Cf. Iorga, 2:438ff.

62. Mouradja d'Ohsson, pp. 203, 287; Wright, p. 52; Tavernier, pp. 156ff.

63. Tavernier, p. 27.

64. I have dealt with this aspect of the Ottoman situation in "Mobilized and Proletarian Diasporas" and in "Administrative Elites" and shall only summarize it here.

65. Ashtor, p. 282.

66. See Spěváček, p. 156, on underestimation by emperors (even one as capable as Charles IV) of the significance of a strong, centralized administration.

67. Hintze, pp. 54ff. Shneidman, 1:125; Walther, p. 41. On papal models for administration, see Jordan, pp. 99ff.

68. Walser, pp. 30, 196ff., 246.

69. Quoted in Ranke, p. 161.

70. Walser, pp. 194ff.; Kagan, pp. 43ff., 63, 65, 71, 132. See also chapter 7, n. 1.

71. Walther, pp. 27, 38.

72. Walser, pp. 198–99.

73. Walther, p. 8.

74. Walser, pp. 38, 127.

75. M. Philippson, pp. 7ff.; Walser, pp. 1, 161ff., 179, 254.

76. Bidermann, "Die staatsrechtlichen Wirkungen," p. 346.

77. Ibid., p. 345.

78. Lhotsky, pp. 140, 149; Bidermann, *Geschichte . . . Gesammt-Staats-Idee*, 1:15, 18ff.; Makkai, pp. 12ff.

79. Lhotsky, pp. 94, 137.

80. Fellner, 5:43; Redlich, 1:28. See Stroheker, p. 55, on Roman practice.

81. Polišenský, pp. 210ff. For the older view, see Denis, 1:50ff., 123; Redlich, 1:10.

82. Roscher, p. 31; Bidermann, *Geschichte . . . Gesammt-Staats-Idee*, 1:15.

83. Kübeck von Kübau, pp. 37ff.; Beidtel, 1:79, 2:47; Kornis, pp. 55ff.

84. H. Aubin, *Grundlagen . . . Kulturraumforschung*, p. 594; Bader, *Der deutsche Südwesten*, p. 161; Bidermann, *Geschichte . . . Gesammt-Staats-Idee*, 1:39ff., 278; Beidtel, 1:65, 79, 182; Wiesflecker, 3:249; Eisenmann, p. 6.

85. Redlich, 1:17, 20, 49; Haussherr, p. 80; A. Martin, pp. 155ff.

86. Macartney, *The Habsburg Empire*, p. 89; Kornis, pp. 25ff.

87. A. Fischel, pp. xxiiiff.; Beidtel, 1:79, 203.

88. Quoted in Winter, *Der Josephinizmus*, p. 187.

89. Preradovich, *Die Führungsschichten*, pp. 8, 26ff., 43; Preradovich, "Südslawen," pp. 285, 291; Beidtel, 1:203.

90. Valjavec, *Der Josephinismus*, p. 19.

Chapter 7

1. Treadgold, p. 1250; Kagan, pp. 199, 225ff. See Prinz, pp. 62–63, on the Capetian French church as a penetrative mechanism.

2. Peters, pp. 532–33. Cf. Baron, *Modern Nationalism*, pp. 215–16.

3. Goitein, *A Mediterranean Society*, 2:9.

4. Trusen, pp. 135ff.

5. Dhalla, p. 278; Mieses, p. 7.

6. Jones, "Were Ancient Heresies National?" p. 290; Woodward.

7. Jones, "Were Ancient Heresies National?" pp. 280–81.
8. Ivánka, p. 7.
9. Dagron, *Naissance d'une Capitale*, p. 378.
10. Ivánka, pp. 71–72.
11. Ibid., p. 69.
12. Dagron, "Aux Origines de la Civilisation Byzantine," p. 54.
13. Another diaspora important during the Middle Ages was the Nestorian Christian community, which one fifteenth-century traveler considered as important in "the Indies" as Jews were in the West. Nau, p. 210. See also Richard, pp. 9ff.; Joseph, pp. 10ff., 42ff.; Dauvillier, p. 70; Commeaux, pp. 294, 307.
14. Juster, 1:418.
15. Yeremian, p. 264; Richard, p. 201.
16. Der Nersessian, pp. 25–37; Ter-Minassiantz, pp. 91ff.; Ter-Mikelian, pp. 14, 40, 75; Weber, pp. 354ff.; Laurent, *L'Arménie*, pp. 133ff.
17. I rely on Laurent, *L'Arménie*, pp. 133ff., and on recent personal observations, for the ritual sacrifice. On other points, see Sarkisyanz, pp. 46ff.; Weber, pp. 229ff.; Christensen, *L'Iran*, pp. 13, 230; H. Gelzer, "Die Anfänge der armenischen Kirche," pp. 130–32.
18. Kazhdan, pp. 146–50.
19. See Armstrong, "Mobilized . . . Diasporas," for additional bibliographical references and analysis of the exchange relationship between diasporas and dominant elites.
20. Planhol, "Géographie Politique et Nomadisme," p. 552. Cf. Nalbandian, p. 26. Kurds had been infiltrating the Armenian area since the thirteenth century. Cahen, "Le Problème Ethnique en Anatolie," pp. 352ff.
21. Vyronis, *The Decline of . . . Hellenism*, p. 199.
22. Inalcik, p. 129; Nolde, 2:141.
23. W. Fischel, *Jews . . . Islam*, p. 30; Baron, *A Social and Religious History*, p. 41; Deverdun, p. 277; Sharf, pp. 98–99; Brawer, pp. 82–91.
24. Atamian, p. 44; Grigorian, pp. 2ff.; Nalbandian, pp. 43ff., 71ff.
25. On differences in diaspora adaptability to peculiar ethical contexts, see Turczynski, p. 71; McCagg, p. 53. Braudel, *Civilisation Matérielle*, 2:100, 127; 3:415.
26. Roth, pp. 19, 67; Gerlach, p. 155.
27. Kisch, *The Jews in Medieval Germany*, p. 318; Goitein, *A Mediterranean Society*, 1:66.
28. Argenti, p. 172; Franco, pp. 132, 160ff.
29. Wilber, *The Architecture*, p. 13; W. Fischel, *Jews . . . Islam*, p. 110; Brunschvig, *La Berbérie Orientale*, 1:397; Mendelssohn, pp. 10, 81; Schlumberger, 2:444. As discussed in chapter 3, the Castilians, despite their normal Mediterranean inclination to town life, adopted an antiurban ideology. The strong urban preference of Italians, on the other hand, may have influenced their tolerance of Jews.
30. Laurent, *L'Arménie*, p. 133; Weber, p. 405.
31. Valjavec, *Der Josephinismus*, p. 32; Brawer, pp. 104ff.
32. Beidtel, 2:170; Mitrofanov, 1:267; Kisch, *Die Prager Universität*, p. 53.

33. Wallach, p. 49.
34. Laurent, *L'Arménie*, p. 145.
35. Weber, p. 515; but see Richard, p. 92, on Gregorian efforts to proselytize Turkic groups.
36. Charanis, *Studies . . . Demography*, p. 19.
37. Millar, pp. 206, 208; Peters, p. 380; W. Schmid, p. 9.
38. Hunger, p. 346; Piganiol, p. 434; F. Fuchs, pp. 35ff.; Dagron, "Aux Origines de la Civilisation Byzantine," p. 47.
39. Weitzmann, pp. 57, 63; A. Grabar, pp. 172ff.
40. Dagron, "Aux Origines de la Civilisation Byzantine," p. 48.
41. Franz Cumont, "Pourquoi le Latin Fut la Seule Langue Liturgique en Occident," *Mélanges Paul Frédéricq*, pp. 63ff.; Previté-Orton, 1:231–32.
42. Holl, pp. 249–50. Cf. Obolensky, *The Byzantine Commonwealth*, p. 151.
43. Haussig, pp. 208ff.
44. Cumont, in *Mélanges Paul Frédéricq*, pp. 63–67; Vogt, *The Decline of Rome*, p. 230; Wallach, p. 14.
45. Marrow, p. 257.
46. Dagron, "Aux Origines de la Civilisation Byzantine," pp. 23, 25.
47. Anton Michel, "Sprache und Schisma," in *Festschrift Kardinal Faulhaber*, p. 46.
48. Eggers, 1:96; Marrow, pp. 257ff.
49. Jules Gay, "Quelques Remarques sur les Papes Grecs et Syriens," in *Mélanges . . . Schlumberger*, pp. 40ff.; Leib, p. 65.
50. Michel, in *Festschrift Kardinal Faulhaber*, p. 65.
51. Ibid., pp. 66, 68.
52. Simson, pp. 12ff.
53. Guillou, p. 172.
54. Harmand, pp. 11–12.
55. Dagron, "Aux Origines de la Civilisation Byzantine," p. 34; Balduin Šaria "Die antiken Grundlagen," in Šaria, p. 11; Günter Reichenkron, "Das Ostromanische," in ibid., pp. 154–57.
56. Dagron, "Aux Origines de la Civilisation Byzantine," p. 34; Goubert, *Byzance avant l'Islam*, 2:24 (map); Šaria, in Šaria, pp. 3ff., 14; Van der Meer and Mohrmann, map 19.
57. Tafrali, *Thessalonique: Des Origines*, pp. 251ff.; Demougeot, p. 337.
58. Tafrali, *Thessalonique au Quatorzième Siècle*, pp. 86, 91.
59. Sestan, p. 650; Gay, p. 8.
60. Gay, pp. 8, 12, 188ff., 243, 350ff.
61. Bloch, *Feudal Society*, 2:435.
62. Leib, p. 129.
63. Ibid., pp. 105, 122, 135; Gay, pp. 350ff.; Haussig, pp. 247ff.; Delvoye, p. 259.
64. Leib, p. 141.
65. Vlasto, p. 46; Hauck, 2:191.
66. Vlasto, p. 12.
67. Nový, pp. 173ff.; Lapôtre, pp. 46ff., 64, 95, 110.

68. Valjavec, *Geschichte . . . Südosteuropas*, 1:10–13; Kuhar, p. 127.

69. On the complicated relations of Constantine and Methodius to Byzantium and the papacy, see Dvornik, pp. 164, 200; H. von Schubert, pp. 12ff.; Vavřinek, pp. 34–45; Hynek Bulín, "Aux Origines des Formations Etatiques des Slaves," in Polish Academy, pp. 183–90.

70. Vavřinek, pp. 43, 45.

71. Obolensky, *The Byzantine Commonwealth*, pp. 139ff.

72. Lapôtre, pp. 155ff.

73. Ibid., pp. 160–69; Nový, p. 184. Vavřinek thinks that Pope John actually took two separate decisions, the first against a Slavic liturgy, the second, in 880, in favor of it (p. 49).

74. Obolensky, *The Byzantine Commonwealth*, p. 99; Stökl, "Die Begriffe Reich," p. 107; Bréhier, *Vie et Mort de Byzance*, 1:111; Vlasto, pp. 188ff., 211; Šišić, pp. 108ff., 229ff.

75. Ullmann, *The Carolingian Renaissance*, p. 170.

76. Schramm, *Kaiser*, 1:79–80.

77. Ludat, p. 13.

78. Vlasto, p. 119; Ebert, pp. 71ff.; Brackmann, pp. 13, 18; Schubart-Fikentscher, p. 58; Lanckorońska, pp. 36ff., 147, 155; Schramm, *Herrschaftzeichen*, 3:940; Wojciechowski, *L'Etat Polonais*, pp. 40, 54; Wojciechowski, "La Condition des Nobles," pp. 54ff.; Beumann, "Das Kaisertum Ottos," pp. 566–72; Helmut Beumann, "Das päpstliche Schisma," in *Deutsche Ostsiedlung*, pp. 20ff.; Juliusz Bardach, "L'Etat Polonais," in Polish Academy, pp. 301–4; Herbert Ludat, "Piasten und Ottonen," in ibid., pp. 330ff.

79. Schramm, *Kaiser*, 1:138; Folz, *The Concept of Empire*, pp. 45ff.

80. Deér, pp. 33ff.; Bloch, *Feudal Society*, 1:34; Beumann, in *Deutsche Ostsiedlung*, pp. 20, 28, 41–43.

81. Schaeder, *Geschichte der Pläne zur Teilung*, pp. 23ff.

82. Schramm, *Kaiser*, 1:138ff.; Folz, *Le Souvenir . . . Charlemagne*, 191ff.; Graus, "Die Entstehung der mittelalterlichen Staaten," p. 57.

83. Martel, pp. 51, 161ff., 171.

84. Schaeder, *Geschichte der Pläne zur Teilung*, pp. 41ff.

85. Rhode, p. 64; Bächtold, pp. 14ff., 25.

86. Eck, p. 122.

87. Ibid., ; Seton-Watson, p. 490, n. 2; Bächtold, p. 59; Martel, p. 15.

88. Martel, pp. 241ff., 289; Brawer, p. 103.

89. Valjavec, *Der Josephinismus*, pp. 152ff.

90. Turczynski, pp. 145ff., 167ff.

91. Martel, p. 217; Valjavec, *Geschichte . . . Südosteuropas*, 2:33.

92. Martel, p. 217.

93. Aubin, Frings, and Müller, p. 91. The relationship of the Reformation to the consolidation of the English nation has been debated. Recently Fernand Braudel, *Civilisation Matérielle*, 3:312, has concluded that England, prior to 1453, acted as a province of the "Anglo-French space." During the following century, England "became an island" partly as a result of the Reformation, but mainly because of military exclusion from the Continent.

94. Graus, "Die Entstehung der mittelalterlichen Staaten," p. 61. See especially Spěváček, pp. 67, 116ff., 186, 191, on the Luxemburg dynasty's encouragement of Czech traditions, language, and ecclesiastical organization a generation before Hus.
95. Rádl, pp. 45ff.; Koppelmann, pp. 217ff.; Czuczka, pp. 78ff.; Höfler, pp. 131, 280ff., 323ff.
96. Denis, 1:148; A. Fischel, pp. xvff.; Rádl, p. 73.
97. Schacht, "Zur soziologischen Betrachtung," pp. 229-36; Schacht, An Introduction to Islamic Law, pp. 65ff.; Fattal, p. x; Hodgson, 1:335-45. Bulliet, Conversion, p. 61, points out that departure from a family tradition of adherence to a law school is rare.
98. Hodgson, 3:30; Hautecoeur and Wiet, 1:101; Darraj, p. 340; Miquel, L'Islam et Sa Civilisation, p. 193.
99. Laroui, 1:109-10; Hodgson, 2:271; Julien, pp. 279, 292; Miquel, L'Islam et Sa Civilisation, p. 184.
100. Julien, p. 197; Hodgson, 2:206ff.
101. Birge, p. 16.
102. Hinz, pp. 12ff., 49ff.; Mazzaoui, pp. 45ff.; Molé, p. 63; Efendiyev, p. 60.
103. Mazzaoui, pp. 14ff., 62ff., 72; Hinz, pp. 26, 73.
104. Mazzaoui, p. 14; Grenard, p. 137; Savory, "The Consolidation of Safawid Power," pp. 84ff.; Spuler, Die Mongolen, end map.
105. Shaban, Islamic History, p. 163. For a somewhat different interpretation, see Corbin, pp. 99ff.
106. Hodgson, 1:495; Spuler, Die Mongolen, p. 236.
107. Mazzaoui, p. 85; Woods, pp. 337-38; Sohrweide, "Der Sieg der Safaviden," pp. 97-109, 123-24, 141, 197; Savory, Iran, p. 23.
108. E. Werner, p. 47; Hasluck, 1:139, 172.
109. Browne, A Literary History, 4:15.
110. Gerlach, p. 191.
111. Sohrweide, "Dichter und Gelehrte," pp. 295ff.
112. Browne, A Literary History, 4:13, 25; Efendiyev, p. 9.
113. Woods, p. 233.
114. Browne, A Literary History, 4:25. Cf. Minorsky, p. 125.

Chapter 8

1. Lévi-Strauss, Structural Anthropology, p. 31.
2. I have found Schmidt-Rohr; Fishman, "A Systematization . . . Whorfian Hypothesis"; and Wartburg, Problems . . . in Linguistics, especially useful as theoretical introductions.
3. Barth, Ethnic Groups, p. 15.
4. Deutsch, Nationalism, pp. 44-45, 49ff., 123ff.
5. Jesperson, p. 5; Deutsch, "Medieval Unity," pp. 23ff.

6. Fishman, *Sociolinguistics*, p. 78; W. P. Robinson, "Restricted Codes," in Whiteley, pp. 90ff.; Fishman, "Language Maintenance," p. 41; Bernstein, pp. 57ff.

7. Lane-Poole, *A History of Egypt*, p. 327; Gabriel, *Religionsgeographie*, p. 91; Browne, *A Literary History*, 4:359.

8. Gerlach, p. 301.

9. Hodgson, 1:43.

10. Miquel, *L'Islam et Sa Civilisation*, p. 39; Dussaud, p. 21; Poliak, "L'Arabisation," pp. 45ff.

11. Quoted in Von Grunebaum, *Medieval Islam*, p. 37. Cf. ibid., p. 38; Hönigmann, p. 39; Crone and Cook, *Hagarism*, pp. 89, 112; Wiet, *L'Egypte*, p. 47.

12. F. Rosenthal, 2:300ff.

13. Fück, pp. 2, 46. Cf. Frye, p. 124.

14. Fück, p. 39. See also ibid., p. 131.

15. Shaban, *The 'Abbāsid Revolution*, pp. xiv, 35ff., 53ff., 57ff. An earlier work that takes much the same position is Nöldeke, pp. 70ff. For opposing views, see Wellhausen, pp. 247, 307ff., 331, 347; Van Vloten, pp. 11ff., 70ff.

16. Shaban, *The 'Abbāsid Revolution*, p. 168.

17. Hodgson, 1:273-76; Von Grunebaum, *Medieval Islam*, p. 201; Fück, p. 71.

18. Miquel, *La Géographie Humaine*, pp. 340ff.; D. Sourdel, *Le Vizirat*, 1:177ff.; Gardet, p. 346.

19. Watt, pp. 117ff.; Hodgson, 2:156; Wellhausen, p. 307.

20. Alexander Bausani, "Muhammad or Darius," in Vryonis, *Islam*, p. 56; Duchesne-Guillemin, p. 237; Fück, p. 71; Frye, pp. 16, 122-23.

21. Khaldun, in F. Rosenthal, 3:313.

22. Hodgson, 3:29; A. Galstyan, "Zavoyevaniye Armenii," in Tikhvinsky, p. 176.

23. Charles Pelliot, "Les Etapes de la Décadence Culturelle," in Brunschvig and Von Grunebaum, pp. 88-89; P. Pelliot, p. 185.

24. Poliak, "Le Caractère Colonial," p. 235.

25. Sivan, p. 177.

26. Sarkisyanz, pp. 173, 314; Annemarie Schimmel, "Turk and Hindu," in Vryonis, *Islam*, pp. 113ff.

27. E. Werner, p. 47.

28. Sohrweide, "Dichter und Gelehrte," pp. 293-96. See also Findley, pp. 34, 87, 91.

29. Roux, *Les Traditions des Nomades*, p. 357; Von Grunebaum, *Modern Islam*, p. 70.

30. Petrushevsky, p. 88. Cf. his report (ibid., p. 91) on a somewhat similar situation among the notables of a central Iranian city. See also Spuler, *Die Mongolen*, end map, for the prevalence of Shiites in Khurasan at that time.

31. Hodgson, 3:289; Lambert, p. 80. According to Cohen, *Pour une Sociologie*, p. 533, Mongolia under the Manchu dynasty also had three elaborated codes: classic Mongolian for literary purposes, Manchu for official usage, and Tibetan for religion.

32. Musset, p. 136. For examples of the numerous scholars supporting the generalization concerning the linguistic boundary, see Steinbach, *Studien . . . Volksge-*

schichte, p. 178; Geyl, p. 25; and the map in Kurth, *La Frontière Linguistique*; Southern, p. 16.

33. Wenskus, *Stammesbildung*, pp. 161, 210, 219.

34. Gysseling, p. 7. Meillet, p. 133, seemed to support this hypothesis as early as 1928.

35. Morf, p. 33.

36. Wartburg, "Umfang . . . der germanischen Siedlung," pp. 33ff.; Steinbach, *Studien . . . Volksgeschichte*, pp. 155ff., 176ff.; Kienast, *Deutschland*, 1:2ff.; Kienast, *Studien . . . Volkstämme*, pp. 13ff.; Petri, pp. 56ff., 95.

37. H. Aubin, Frings, and Müller, pp. 18ff., 34ff., is a major earlier German work that, although not directly confronting the questions treated later by the "Bonn School" just cited, seems to assume slight Germanic penetration south of the present linguistic boundary. See also Folz, *De l'Antiquité*, p. 94; Verlinden, *Les Origines de la Frontière Linguistique*, p. 95; Dhondt, "Essai . . . Frontière Linguistique," p. 275; Kurth, *La Frontière Linguistique*, pp. 398, 417.

38. Stengers, p. 5.

39. Hauck, 1:308; Dopsch, pp. 121ff.; Weiss, pp. 100ff.

40. Mohrmann, "Le Latin Commun," p. 9; Mohrmann, "Linguistic Problems," pp. 16ff.; Bloch, *Feudal Society*, 1:76; Lot, "A Quelle Epoque . . . Latin?" p. 146; Terracini, p. 80; Haussig, p. 30.

41. Lot, "A Quelle Epoque . . . Latin?" pp. 103, 143.

42. Riché, pp. 130ff.; Vossler, *Aus der romanischen Welt*, p. 331.

43. R. Anderson, p. 84, contends that there were two aristocratic marriage networks, one among Romance-speakers, the other among Germanic-speaking nobles and other Catholics in East Central Europe. Cf. Southern, pp. 20ff., 76. Schramm, *Herrschaftszeichen*, 3:1084, on the other hand, refers to the readiness of the thirteenth-century nobility to enter into very distant marriages.

44. Cohen, *Histoire d'une Langue*, p. 69; Wartburg, *Problems . . . in Linguistics*, p. 216; Vossler, *Medieval Culture*, 2:5.

45. Heer, p. 131; Costa, pp. 17ff., 48; E. Jordan, p. 65.

46. Remppis, pp. 115, 146ff.; Zimmermann, pp. 300ff.

47. Zimmermann, p. 257.

48. See especially Grundmann and Heimpel, pp. 5ff., 95.

49. Rosenqvist, pp. 21ff.

50. Heer, pp. 121, 272, 275.

51. Bloch, *Feudal Society*, 2:436; E. Schubert, pp. 230ff.

52. Kern, *Die Anfänge . . . Ausdehnungspolitik*, p. 16; Kurth, *La Frontière Linguistique*, pp. 40ff.

53. H. Aubin, Frings, and Müller, pp. 45, 192; Geyl, pp. 25, 29, 43, 75; Kurth, *La Frontière Linguistique*, pp. 40ff.

54. Geyl, pp. 16ff., 29, 62, 105, 131, 171; Huizinga, *Dutch Civilization*, pp. 10, 26, 35; Huizinga, *Patriotisme en Nationalisme*, pp. 45, 60.

55. Geyl, pp. 178, 258; Kurth, *La Frontière Linguistique*, pp. 50ff.

56. Uhlemann, p. 545.

57. Haussen, "Die vier deutschen Volkstämme," p. 183; Auerbach, pp. 148ff.

58. Koppelmann, pp. 217ff.; A. Fischel, p. ix.

59. Schwartner, p. 94.

60. Vigener, p. 95; Daube, p. 28; Maschke, p. 38.

61. Graus, "Die Entstehung der mittelalterlichen Staaten," p. 60.

62. Quoted in Bezzola: Latin text, p. 214; German text, pp. 129–30.

63. Harmand, p. 448.

64. Wartburg, *Die Ausgliederung*, p. 50; Cohen, *Histoire d'une Langue*, p. 128.

65. Terracini, p. 202; Wartburg, *Problems . . . in Linguistics*, p. 26; Wartburg, *Die Ausgliederung*, p. 20.

66. Brunot, p. 297.

67. Cohen, *Histoire d'une Langue*, p. 82.

68. Ibid., pp. 78–79.

69. Ibid., p. 80; Piganiol, p. 72.

70. Zananiri, p. 170, quoting M. M. Gorch, "Saint Vincent Ferrier" (doctoral dissertation, University of Clermont-Ferrand, 1923). Cf. Burns, *Islam*, pp. 19ff., on the predominance of settlers from Catalonia and Languedoc in Valencia after its reconquest from the Moslems; and Shneidman, 2:298, on the similarity of Languedocian, Provençal, and Catalan.

71. Shneidman, 2:288, 291. Cf. Kienast, *Studien . . . Volkstämme*, pp. 90ff.

72. Shneidman, 2:286–87.

73. Jacoby, *Société . . . à Byzance*, pp. 85–88.

74. Elliott, *Imperial Spain*, p. 117; Bevan, pp. 71, 88; Meier, pp. 10, 16ff.

75. Kagan, pp. 58–60; Elliott, *Revolt of the Catalans*, p. 73.

76. Vossler, *Aus der romanischen Welt*, p. 328.

77. Cohen, *Histoire d'une Langue*, pp. 84ff.

78. Vossler, *Medieval Culture*, 2:71.

79. Wartburg, *Problems . . . in Linguistics*, p. 219.

80. Cohen, *Histoire d'une Langue*, p. 84. Cf. Cohen, *Pour une Sociologie*, pp. 141–42; Prinz, p. 54.

81. Cohen, *Histoire d'une Langue*, p. 139; Dauzat, *Histoire de la Langue Française*, pp. 542ff.; Brunot, p. 367; Curtius, p. 35.

82. Dauzat, *Le Village*, p. 179; Morf, pp. 24ff., 33.

83. Quoted in Yardeni, p. 56; Brunot, pp. 326ff.; Cohen, *Histoire d'une Langue*, p. 88.

84. Vossler, *Aus der romanischen Welt*, p. 331; Terracini, p. 57.

85. Vossler, *Aus der romanischen Welt*, p. 108. Cf. Curtius, p. 32.

86. Curtius, pp. 587ff. Cf. the abundant footnotes in Duchhardt for examples of Curia use of Italian.

87. Meillet, p. 161. Cf. Brunot, pp. 300–301.

88. Yardeni, p. 48; Gilbert, in Ranum, p. 38; Vossler, *Aus der romanischen Welt*, p. 283.

89. Meillet, p. 175.

90. Haussig, p. 257; Shakhmatov, pp. 18ff.; Hensel, pp. 17, 49, 70; Trautmann, p. 139.

91. Vlasto, p. 295.

92. Obolensky, *The Byzantine Commonwealth*, pp. 323, 335; Haase, p. 5.
93. Martel, pp. 153, 269.
94. Bächtold, pp. 96, 187; Martel, p. 18.
95. Lanckorońska, p. 144.
96. Martel, pp. 39, 42–45.
97. Ibid., pp. 80, 153.
98. Clastre, p. 152. Cf. Schmitt, pp. 137ff., on the need for standardized Latin legal formulas in late medieval Germany.
99. Quoted in Martel, p. 45.
100. Bächtold, pp. 25, 32, 105; Martel, p. 36.
101. Martel, p. 59.
102. André Mazon, in introduction to ibid., p. 9.
103. Ibid., p. 176. Cf. Balazs, "Der Einfluss des polnischen Humanismus," in *La Renaissance et la Réformation*, pp. 290–96.
104. Martel, pp. 252ff.
105. Ibid., pp. 71, 146; Trautmann, p. 155.
106. Angyal, p. 210.
107. Martel, pp. 22–25.
108. Ibid., pp. 15ff. Cf. Bächtold, p. 7.
109. Martel, p. 18; Trautmann, p. 141.
110. Trautmann, p. 170; Haase, pp. 65ff.
111. Unbegaun, "Le Russe Littéraire," pp. 21ff.
112. Turczynski, pp. 16ff.; Trautmann, p. 45; Haase, p. 5.
113. Shakhmatov, p. 80; Unbegaun, "Le Russe Littéraire," pp. 22ff. Cf. Trautmann, p. 172, for the contrary view that New Russian exhibits less Church Slavonic influence except in words related to ecclesiastical affairs. Unbegaun's newer and highly circumstantial argument appears convincing to me.
114. See Unbegaun, "Le Calque dans les Langues Slaves," p. 45.

Chapter 9

1. See especially Prinz, pp. 62–63, 67–68, on the sacral ideology relating the king to the papacy and on royal control of ecclesiastical preferment, which provided communication channels for disseminating that ideology.
2. Darraj, pp. 389ff.

Bibliography

Abadal i de Vinyals, Ramon d'. "A Propos du Legs Visigothique en Espagne." *Settimane di Studio del Centro Italiano di Studi sull'Aït. Medioevo* 2 (1958): 541–85.

Abu-Lughod, Janet L. *Cairo: 1001 Years of the City Victorious*. Princeton: Princeton University Press, 1971.

Adams, Robert M. *Land behind Baghdad: A History of Settlement on the Diyala Plains*. Chicago: University of Chicago Press, 1965.

Adler, Sigmund. *Die Organisation der Centralverwaltung unter Kaiser Maximilian I.* Leipzig: Duncker & Humblot, 1886.

Adontz, Nicolas. *Armeniya v Epokhu Yustiniana: Politicheskoye Sostoyaniye na Osnove Nakharskago Stroya*. St. Petersburg: Tipografiya Imperatorskoi Akademii Nauk, 1908.

———. *Etudes Arméno-Byzantines*. Lisbon: Bertrand, 1965.

Aga-Oglu, Mehmet. "The Fatih Mosque at Constantinople." *Art Bulletin* 12 (1930):179–95.

Ahrweiler, Hélène. *Byzance et la Mer: La Marine de Guerre, La Politique, et les Institutions Maritimes de Byzance aux VIIe–XVe Siècles*. Paris: Presses Universitaires, 1966.

Alderson, A. D. *The Structure of the Ottoman Dynasty*. Oxford: Clarendon, 1956.

Alexander, Paul J. "The Strength of Empire and Capital as Seen through Byzantine Eyes." *Speculum* 37 (1962):339–57.

Ali-Zade, Abdul Kerim. *Sotsialno-Eknomicheskaya i Politicheskaya Istoriya Azerbaidzhana XIII–XIV VV*. Baku: Akademiya Nauk Azerbaidzhanskoi SSSR, 1956.

Allen, William E. D. *Problems of Turkish Power in the Sixteenth Century*. London: Central Asian Research Centre, 1963.

Alteuropa und die moderne Gesellschaft: Festschrift für Otto Brunner. Göttingen: Vandenhoeck & Ruprecht, 1963.

Altheim, Franz. *Alexander und Asien: Geschichte eines geistigen Erbes*. Tübingen: Niemeyer, 1953.

———. *Niedergang der alten Welt: Eine Untersuchung der Ursachen*. 2 vols. Frankfurt/M.: Klostermann, 1952.

———, ed. and co-author. *Geschichte der Hunnen*. Vol. 2. Berlin: De Gruyter, 1960.

Amedroz, Henry F., and Margoliouth, David S., ed. and trans. *The Eclipse of the 'Abassid Caliphate: Original Chronicles of the Fourth Islamic Century*. Vol. 5. Oxford: Blackwell, 1921.

Amélineau, Emile. "La Conquête de l'Egypte par les Arabes." *Revue des Questions Historiques* 119 (1914):273–314; 120 (1915):1–25.

Anderson, Perry. *Lineages of the Absolutist State*. London: NLB, 1974.

Anderson, Robert T. *Traditional Europe: A Study in Anthropology and History.* Belmont, Calif.: Wadsworth, 1971.

Andreotti, Roberto. "Die Weltmonarchie Alexanders des Grossen in Ueberlieferung und geschichtlicher Wirklichkeit." *Saeculum* 8 (1957):120–66.

Angyal, Andreas. *Die slawische Barockwelt.* Leipzig: Seemann, 1961.

Arensberg, Conrad M. "The Old World Peoples: The Place of European Cultures in World Ethnography." *Anthropological Quarterly* 36 (1965):75–99.

Argenti, Philip P. *The Religious Minorities of Chios.* Cambridge: Cambridge University Press, 1970.

Arié, Rachel. *L'Espagne Musulmane au Temps des Nasrides (1232–1492).* Paris: Boccard, 1973.

Armstrong, John A. "Administrative Elites in Multiethnic Polities." *International Political Science Review* 1 (1980):107–28.

_____. *The European Administrative Elite.* Princeton: Princeton University Press, 1973.

_____. "Mobilized and Proletarian Diasporas." *American Political Science Review* 70 (1976):393–408.

Ashtor, E. *A Social and Economic History of the Near East in the Middle Ages.* Berkeley: University of California Press, 1978.

Atamian, Sarkis. *The Armenian Community.* New York: Philosophical Library, 1955.

Atiya, Aziz Suryal. *The Crusade in the Later Middle Ages.* London: Methuen, 1938.

Aubin, Hermann. *Grundlagen und Perspektiven Geschichtlicher Kulturraumforschung und Kulturmorphologie.* Bonn: Röhrscheid, 1965.

_____, Frings, Theodor, and Müller, Josef. *Kulturströmungen und Kulturprovinzen in den Rheinlanden.* 1926. Reprint. Bonn: Röhrscheid, 1966.

Aubin, Jean. "Comment Tamerlan Prenait les Villes." *Studia Islamica* 19 (1953):83–122.

_____. "Etudes Safavides I: Šāh Ismāʿīl et les Notables de l'Iraq Persan." *Journal of the Economic and Social History of the Orient* 2 (1959):37–81.

Auerbach, Bertrand. *Les Races et les Nationalités en Austriche-Hongrie.* 2d ed. Paris: Alcan, 1917.

Aulard, A. *Le Patriotisme Français de la Renaissance à la Révolution.* Paris: Chiron, 1921.

Ayalon, David. "The Great Yāsa of Chingis Khān." *Studia Islamica* 34 (1971):151–80; 35 (1972):113–58; 38 (1973):107–56.

Azrael, Jeremy R., ed. *Soviet Nationality Policies and Practices.* New York: Praeger, 1978.

Babinger, Franz. *Mehmed the Conqueror and His Times.* Trans. Ralph Manheim. Princeton: Princeton University Press, 1978.

Bachteler, Kurt, ed. *Istanbul: Geschichte und Entwicklung der Stadt, Festschrift zum 60. Geburtstag von Dr. Kurt Albrecht.* Ludwigsburg: Karawane, 1967.

Bächtold, Rudolf. *Südwestrussland im Spätmittelalter.* Basel: Helbing und Lichtenhahn, 1951.

Bacon, Elizabeth E. "Types of Pastoral Nomadism in Central and Southwest Asia." *Southwestern Journal of Anthropology* 10 (1954):44–65.

Baddeley, John F. *Russia, Mongolia, China: Being Some Record of the Relations between Them from the Beginning of the XVIIth Century to the Death of Tsar Alexei Michailovich, A.D. 1602–1676.* 2 vols. New York: Franklin, n.d.

Bader, Karl S. *Der deutsche Südwesten in seiner Territorialstaatlichen Entwicklung.* Stuttgart: Koehler, 1950.

————. "Territorialbildung und Landeshoheit." *Blätter für Deutsche Landesgeschichte* 40 (1953):109–31.

Baer, Yitzhak. *A History of the Jews in Christian Spain.* 2 vols. Philadelphia: Jewish Publication Society of America, 1966.

Bagalei, D. I. *Ocherki iz Istorii Kolonizatsii Stepnoi Okrainy Moskovskago Gosudarstva.* Moscow: Universitetskaya Tipografii M. Katkov, 1887.

Balard, Michel. *La Romanie Génoise: XIIe–Début du XVe Siècle.* 2 vols. Genoa: Società Ligure di Storia Patria, 1978.

Balazs, Etienne. *Chinese Civilization and Bureaucracy.* New Haven: Yale University Press, 1964.

Banniza von Bazan, Heinrich, and Müller, Richard. *Deutsche Geschichte in Ahnentafeln.* Vols. 1, 2. Berlin: Metzner, 1943, 1942 *(sic).*

Barany, George. *Stephen Széchenyi and the Awakening of Hungarian Nationalism, 1791–1841.* Princeton: Princeton University Press, 1968.

Barkan, O. Lufti. "L'Organisation du Travail dans le Chantier d'une Grande Mosquée à Istanbul au XVIe Siècle." *Annales* 17 (1962):1093–1106.

Baron, Salo W. *Modern Nationalism and Religion.* New York: Harper, 1947.

————. *A Social and Religious History of the Jews.* 2d ed. Vol. 16. New York: Columbia University Press, 1976.

Barth, Fredrik. "On the Study of Social Change." *American Anthropologist* 69 (1967):661–69.

————, ed. *Ethnic Groups and Boundaries.* Bergen: Universitetsforlaget, 1969.

Bartha, Antal. *Hungarian Society in the 9th and 10th Centuries.* Budapest: Akadémiai Kiadó, 1975.

————. "Hungarian Society in the Tenth Century and the Social Division of Labor." Budapest: Akadémiai Kiadó, *Acta Historica* 9 (1963):333–69.

Barthold, Vasily. *Turkestan down to the Mongol Invasions.* Trans. H. A. R. Gibb. London: Luzac, 1928.

Basil, Anne. *Armenian Settlements in India: From the Earliest Times to the Present Day.* Calcutta: Armenian College, n.d.

Baudet, Henri. *Paradise on Earth: Some Thoughts on European Images of Non-European Man.* Trans. Elizabeth Wentholt. New Haven: Yale University Press, 1965.

Bauer, Clemens. "Die Epochen der Papstfinanz." *Historische Zeitschrift* 128 (1928):457–503.

Baynes, Norman H., and Moss, H. St. L. B., eds. *Byzantium: An Introduction to East Roman Civilization.* Oxford: Clarendon, 1948.

Becker, Carl H. "Bartholds Studien über Kalif und Sultan." *Der Islam* 6 (1916):350–412.

————. *Islamstudien: Vom Werden und Wesen der islamischen Welt.* Vol. 1. Leipzig: Quelle & Meyer, 1924.

Beidtel, Ignaz. *Geschichte der österreichischen Staatsverwaltung, 1740–1848.* 2 vols. Innsbruck: Wagner, 1896, 1898.

Belenitsky, A. M. "K Voprosu o Sotsialnykh Otnosheniyakh v Irane v Khulaguidskuyu Epokhu." *Sovetskoye Vostokovedeniye* 5 (1948):111–28.

Bell, H. Idris. "The Byzantine Servile State in Egypt." *Journal of Egyptian Archaeology* 4 (1917):86–106.

———. *Egypt from Alexander the Great to the Arab Conquest: A Study in the Diffusion and Decay of Hellenism.* Oxford: Clarendon, 1948.

Beloch, Julius. "Die Bevölkerung Europas im Mittelalter." *Zeitschrift für Sozial Wissenschaft* 3 (1900):405–23, 765–86.

Below, Georg von. "Die städtische Verwaltung des Mittelalters als Vorbild der späteren Territorialverwaltung." *Historische Zeitschrift* 75 (1895):396–463.

———. *Territorium und Staat.* Osnabrück: Teller, 1965.

———. *Die Ursachen der Rezeption des Römischen Rechts in Deutschland.* Munich: Oldenbourg, 1905.

Bémont, Fredy. *Les Villes d'Iran: Des Cités d'Autrefois à l'Urbanisme Contemporain.* Paris: n.p., 1969.

Ben-Ami, Aharon. *Social Change in a Hostile Environment: The Crusader's Kingdom of Jerusalem.* Princeton: Princeton University Press, 1969.

Benkö, Lorand, and Imre, Samu, eds. *The Hungarian Language.* The Hague: Mouton, for Akadémiai Kiadó, 1972.

Benveniste, Emile. *Le Vocabulaire des Institutions Indo-Européennes.* 2 vols. Paris: Editions de Minuit, 1969.

Bergengrün, Alexander. "Adel und Grundherrschaft im Merowingerreich." *Vierteljahrschrift für Sozial- und Wirtschaftsgeschichte*, Beiheft 41 (1958).

Bernand, André. *Alexandrie la Grande.* Paris: Artaud, 1966.

Bernard, Augustin, and Lacroix, N. *L'Evolution du Nomadisme en Algérie.* Algiers: Jourdan, 1906.

Bernstein, Basil. "Elaborated and Restricted Codes." *American Anthropologist* 66 (1964), no. 6, pt. 2, pp. 55–69.

Besrovny, L. G., ed. *Drevnerusskiye Knyazhestva X–XIII vv.* Moscow: "Nauka," 1975.

Bettelheim, Bruno, and Janowitz, Morris. *Dynamics of Prejudice.* New York: Harper, 1950.

Beumann, Helmut. "Das Kaisertum Ottos des Grossen." *Historische Zeitschrift* 194 (1962):529–73.

———. *Das Kaisertum Ottos des Grossen: Zwei Vorträge.* Constance: Konstanzer Arbeitskreis für Mittelalterliche Geschichte, n.d. [1962].

———. "Kreuzzugsgedanke und Ostpolitik im hohen Mittelalter." *Historisches Jahrbuch* 72 (1953):112–32.

Bevan, Bernard. *History of Spanish Architecture.* London: Batsford, 1938.

Bezzola, Gian Andri. *Die Mongolen in Abendländischer Sicht (1220–1270): Ein Beitrag zur Frage der Völkerbegegnungen.* Bern: Francke, 1974.

Bidermann, Hermann J. *Geschichte der österreichischen Gesammt-Staats-Idee, 1526–1804.* 2 vols. Innsbruck: Wagner, 1867, 1889.

———. "Die staatsrechtlichen Wirkungen der österreichischen Gesammtsstaats-idee." *Zeitschrift für das Privat- und Öffentliche Recht* 21 (1894):339–429.

Birge, John Kingsley. *The Bektashi Order of Dervishes*. 1937. Reprint. London: Luzac, 1965.

Birot, Pierre, and Dresch, Jean. *La Meditérranée et le Moyen-Orient*. 2 vols. Paris: Presses Universitaires, 1953, 1956.

Bischoff, Ferdinand. "Das alte Recht der Armenier in Lemberg." *Sitzungsberichte der Philosophisch-Historischen Classe*. Vienna: Akademie der Wissenschaft 40 (1862):255–302.

Bisinger, J. C. *General-Statistik des österreichischen Kaiserthumes: Ein Versuch*. 2 vols. Vienna: Geistinger, 1807, 1808.

Björkmann, Walther. *Beiträge zur Geschichte der Staatskanzlei im islamischen Aegypten*. Hamburg: Friedrichsen, De Gruyter, 1928.

Block, Marc. *Feudal Society*. Trans. L. A. Manyon. 2 vols. Chicago: University of Chicago Press, 1961.

———. *Mélanges Historiques*. Vol. 1. Paris: S.E.V.P.E.N., 1963.

Blum, Jerome. *Noble Landowners and Agriculture in Austria, 1815–1848: A Study in the Origins of the Peasant Emancipation of 1848*. Baltimore: Johns Hopkins Press, 1948.

Boba, Imre. *Nomads, Northmen and Slavs*. The Hague: Mouton, 1967.

Bock, Friedrich. *Reichsidee und Nationalstaaten: Vom Untergang des alten Reiches bis zur Kündigung des deutsch-englischen Bündnisses im Jahre 1341*. Munich: Callwey, 1943.

Boehm, Laetitia. "Gedanken zum Frankreich-Bewusstsein im frühen 12. Jahrhundert." *Historisches Jahrbuch* 74 (1955):681–87.

Böhm, Jaroslav, et al. *La Grande Moravie: Tradition Millénaire de l'Etat et de la Civilisation*. Prague: Československé Akademie Věd, 1963.

Bosch-Gimpera, Pedro. *Les Indo-Européens: Problèmes Archéologiques*. Trans. R. Lantier. Paris: Payot, 1961.

Bosl, Karl. *Die Gesellschaft in der Geschichte des Mittelalters*. Göttingen: Vandenhoeck and Ruprecht, 1966.

———. "Das grossmährische Reich in der politischen Welt des 9. Jahrhunderts." Bayerische Akademie der Wissenschaften, Philosophisch-Historische Klasse, *Sitzungberichte*, 1966, Heft 7.

Boswell, John. *The Royal Treasure: Muslim Communities under the Crown of Aragon in the Fourteenth Century*. New Haven: Yale University Press, 1977.

Bourrilly, Joseph. *Elements d'Ethnographie Marocaine*. Paris: Larose, 1932.

Bousquet, G. H. "Nature et Causes de la Conquête Arabe." *Studia Islamica* 6 (1956):37–52.

Brackmann, Albert. *Magdeburg als Hauptstadt des deutschen Ostens*. Leipzig: Schmidt & Günther, 1937.

Brandenburg, Dietrich. *Islamische Baukunst in Aegypten*. Berlin: Hessling, 1966.

———. *Samarkand: Studien zur islamischen Baukunst in Uzbekistan (Zentralasien)*. Berlin: Heisling, 1972.

Brandi, Karl. "Der Weltreichgedanke Karls V." *Ibero-Amerikanisches Archiv* 13 (1913):259–69.

338 / Bibliography

Brătianu, G. I. *Etudes Byzantines d'Histoire Economique et Sociale.* Paris: Geuthner, 1938.

Braudel, Fernand. *Capitalism and Material Life, 1400–1800.* Trans. Miriam Kochan. London: Weidenfeld & Nicolson, 1973.

_____. *Civilisation Matérielle, Economie et Capitale, XV–XVIIIᵉ Siècle.* Vols. 2 and 3. Paris: Colin, 1979.

_____. *Ecrits sur l'Histoire.* Paris: Flammarion, 1969.

_____. *The Mediterranean and the Mediterranean World in the Age of Philip II.* Trans. Sian Reynolds. 2 vols. New York: Harper, 1972, 1973.

Brawer, Abraham Jakob. *Galizien wie es an Oesterreich kam: Eine historisch-statistiche Studie über die inneren Verhältnisse des Landes im Jahre 1772.* Leipzig: Freytag, 1910.

Bréhier, Louis, "Les Colonies des Orientaux en Occident au Commencement du Moyen-Age; Vᵉ–VIIIᵉ Siècle." *Byzantinische Zeitschrift* 12 (1903):1–39.

_____. "L'Origine des Titres Impériaux à Byzance." *Byzantinische Zeitschrift* 15 (1906):161–78.

_____. *Vie et Mort de Byzance.* 2 vols. Paris: Albin, 1946, 1949.

Briggs, Lloyd C. *Tribes of the Sahara.* Cambridge: Harvard University Press, 1960.

Briggs, Martin S. *Muhammadan Architecture in Egypt and Palestine.* Oxford: Clarendon, 1924.

Brown, L. Carl, ed. *From Madina to Metropolis.* Princeton: Darwin, 1973.

Browne, Edward G. "Account of a Rare Manuscript History of Isfahan Presented to the Royal Asiatic Society on May 19, 1827 by Sir John Malcolm." *Journal of the Royal Asiatic Society*, London, July 1901, pp. 411–46; October 1901, pp. 661–89.

_____. *A Literary History of Persia.* Vols. 1, 4. Cambridge: Cambridge University Press, 1908, 1928.

Bruhl, Adrien. "Souvenir d'Alexandre le Grand et les Romains." *Mélanges d'Archéologie et d'Histoire* 47 (1930):202–21.

Brunner, Otto. "Europäisches und russisches Bürgertum." *Vierteljahrschrift für Sozial- und Wirtschaftsgeschichte* 40 (1953):1–27.

_____. *Neue Wege der Verfassungs- und Sozialgeschichte.* Göttingen: Vandenhoeck & Ruprecht, 1968.

Brunnhofer, Hermann. *Iran und Turan: Historisch-geographische und ethnologische Untersuchungen über den altesten Schauplatz der indischen Urgeschichte.* Leipzig: Friedrich, 1889.

Brunot, Ferdinand. *Histoire de la Langue Française des Origines à 1900.* Vol. 1. Paris: Colin, 1905.

Brunschvig, Robert. *La Berbérie Orientale sous les Hafsides: Des Origines à la Fin du XVᵉ Siècle.* 2 vols. Paris: Adrien-Maisonneuve, 1940, 1947.

_____. "Urbanisme Médiéval et Droit Musulman." *Revue des Etudes Islamiques* 15 (1947):127–55.

_____, and Von Grunebaum, George E., eds. *Classicisme et Déclin Culturel dans l'Histoire de l'Islam: Actes du Symposium International d'Histoire de la Civilisation Musulmane, Bordeaux, 25–29 Juin 1956.* Paris: Besson-Chantemerle, 1957.

Brutails, J. A. "La Géographie Monumentale de la France." *Moyen Age* 34 (2d série, 35) (1923):1–31.

Buccellati, Giorgio. *Cities and Nations of Ancient Syria: An Essay on Political Institutions with Special Reference to the Israelite Kingdoms*. Rome: University of Rome, Instituto di Studi de Vicino Oriente, 1967.

Budinszky, Alexander. *Die Ausbreitung der lateinischen Sprache über Italien und die Provinzen des Römischen Reiches*. Berlin: Hertz, 1881.

Bulliet, Richard W. *The Camel and the Wheel*. Cambridge: Harvard University Press, 1975.

————. *Conversion to Islam in the Medieval Period*. Cambridge: Harvard University Press, 1979.

Burns, Robert I. *The Crusader Kingdom of Valencia: Reconstruction of a Thirteenth-Century Frontier*. Cambridge: Harvard University Press, 1967.

————. *Islam under the Crusaders: Colonial Survival in the Thirteenth-Century Kingdom of Valencia*. Princeton: Princeton University Press, 1973.

Bury, J. B. *The Imperial Administrative System in the Ninth Century: With a Revised Text of the Kletorologion of Philotheos*. London: Henry Frowde, Oxford University Press, 1911.

Busch-Zantner, Richard. "Zur Kenntnis der osmanischen Stadt." *Geographische Zeitschrift* 38 (1932):1–13.

Butler, Alfred J. *The Arab Conquest of Egypt and the Last Thirty Years of the Roman Dominion*. Oxford: Clarendon, 1902.

Cahen, Claude. "L'Evolution Sociale du Monde Musulmane jusqu'au XIIᵉ Siècle face à Celle du Monde Chrétien." *Cahiers du Civilisation Mediévale* 2 (1959):451–63.

————. "Mouvements Populaires et Autonomisme Urbain dans l'Asie Musulmane du Moyen Age." *Arabica* 5 (1958):225–50; 6 (1959):25–56, 233–65.

————. *Pre-Ottoman Turkey*. Trans. J. Jones-Williams. London: Sidjwick & Jackson, 1968.

————. "Le Probleme Ethnique en Anatolie." *Cahiers d'Histoire Mondiale* 2, no. 2 (1954):347–62.

————. "Le Régime de la Terre et l'Occupation Turque en Anatolie." *Cahiers d'Histoire Mondiale* 2 (1955):566–80.

Calasso, Francesco. "Il Problema Storico del Diritto Comune e i Suoi Riflessi Metodologici nella Storiografia Guiridica Europea." *Archives de l'Histoire du Droit Oriental* 2 (1953):441–63.

Calmette, Joseph. *Les Grands Ducs de Bourgogne*. Paris: Michel, 1949.

Cameron, George G. *History of Early Iran*. Chicago: University of Chicago Press, 1969.

Campbell, Edward F., Jr. "Moses and the Foundations of Israel." *Interpretation* 29 (1975):141–54.

Canard, Marius. "Les Relations Politiques et Sociales entre Byzance et les Arabes." *Dumbarton Oaks Papers* 18 (1954):33–56.

Carande, Ramon. "Der Wanderhirt und die überseeische Ausbreitung Spaniens." *Saeculum* 3 (1952):373–87.

Cardona, George, ed. *Indo-European and Indo-Europeans*. Philadelphia: University of Pennsylvania Press, 1970.

Carney, T. F. *Bureaucracy in Traditional Society: Romano-Byzantine Bureaucracy Viewed from Within*. Lawrence, Kan.: Coronado, 1971.

Cassirer, Ernst. *Language and Myth*. Trans. Suzanne K. Langer. New York: Harper, 1945.

———. *The Myth of the State*. New Haven: Yale University Press, 1946.

Castro, Americo. *The Spaniards: An Introduction to Their History*. Trans. Willard F. King and Selma Margaretten. Berkeley: University of California Press, 1971.

Charanis, Peter. "The Armenians in the Byzantine Empire," *Byzantinoslavica* 22 (1961):196–240.

———. *Studies on the Demography of the Byzantine Empire*. London: Variorum Reprints, 1972.

Charles, Martin A. "Hagia Sophia and the Great Imperial Mosques." *Art Bulletin* 12 (1930):321–44.

Chaume, Maurice. "Le Sentiment National Bourguignon de Goudebaud à Charles le Téméraire: Essai de Synthèse sur l'Histoire de la Bourgogne, Royaumes, Duchés, Comtés." *Mémoires de l'Académie des Sciences, Arts et Belles-Lettres de Dijon*, 5e Série, 4 (1922):195–308.

Chaunu, Pierre. *L'Espagne de Charles Quint*. Vols. 1, 2. Paris: Société d'Edition d'Enseignement Supérieur, 1973.

———. "Minorités et Conjuncture: L'Expulsion des Moresques." *Revue Historique* 225 (1961):81–98.

Chavannes, Edouard, ed. *Documents sur les Tou-Kiue (Turcs) Occidentaux*. St. Petersburg: Imperatorskaya Akademiya Nauk, 1903.

Chayev, N. S. "Moskva-Trety Rim v Politicheskoi Praktike Moskovskogo Pravitelstva XVI Veka." *Istoricheskiye Zapiski* 17 (1945):3–23.

Chejne, Anwar G. *Muslim Spain*. Minneapolis: University of Minnesota Press, 1974.

Chenon, Emile. *Histoire Générale du Droit Français Public et Privé des Origines à 1815*. 2 vols. Paris: Sirey, 1926, 1929.

Cherniavsky, Michael, ed. *The Structure of Russian History: Interpretive Essays*. New York: Random House, 1970.

Chiappelli, Luigi. "Formazione Storica de Comune Cittadino in Italia." *Archivo Storico Italiano*, 7th ser., 6 (1926):3–59; 10 (1928):3–89; 13 (1930):3–59.

Chimitdorzhiyev, Sh. B. *Vsaimootnosheniya Mongolii i Rossii v XVII–XVIII vv.* Moscow: "Nauka," 1978.

Chłebowczyk, Jòsef. *Procesy Narodotworcze we wschodniej Europie Srodkowej w Dobie Kapitalizmu*. Warsaw: Wydawnictwo Naukowe, 1975.

———. "Die Madjarisierungs- und die Germanisierungspolitik im 18.–19. Jahrhundert und um die Jahrhundertwende: Versuch einer Konfrontation." *Acta Poloniae Historica* 3 (1974):163–86.

Christensen, Arthur. *L'Iran sous les Sassanides*. Copenhagen: Munksgaard, 1936.

Ciccoti, Ettore. "Motivi Demografici e Biologici nella Rovina della Civiltà Antica." *Nouva Rivista Storica* 14 (1930):29–62.

Cipolla, Carlo. "Della Supposta Fusione degli Italiani coi Germani nei Primi Secoli del Medioevo." *Reale Accademia dei Lincei, Classe di Scienze, Morale, Storiche e Filologiche* 5th ser, 9 Rendiconti (1900):329–69, 1369–1422.

Clarke, Hyde. "On the Supposed Extinction of the Turks." *Journal of the Statistical Society* 28 (1865):261–82.

Clastre, Pierre. *La Société contre l'Etat: Recherches d'Anthropologie Politique.* Paris: Editions de Minuit, 1974.

Claude, Dietrich. "Die byzantinische Stadt im 6. Jahrhundert." *Byzantinisches Archiv* 13 (1969):1–257.

Clerget, Marcel. *Le Caire: Etude de Géographie Urbaine et d'Histoire Economique.* 2 vols. Cairo: Schendler, 1934.

Cohen, Marcel. *Histoire d'une Langue: Le Français, des Lointaines Origines à Nos Jours.* Paris: Editions Hier et Aujourd'hui, 1947.

———. *Pour une Sociologie du Langage.* Paris: Michel, 1956.

Coing, Helmut. "Römisches Recht in Deutschland." *Ius Romanum Medii Aevi* 5, pt. 6 (1964):3–212.

Commeaux, Charles. *La Vie Quotidienne chez les Mongols de la Conquête (XIIIᵉ Siècle).* Paris: Hachette, 1972.

Confino, Michael. "A propos de la Noblesse Russe au XVIIIᵉ Siècle." *Annales* 22 (1967):1163–1205.

Congrès International des Sciences Historiques, 7 (1933). *La Pologne.* Vol. 3. Warsaw: Société Polonaise d'Histoire, 1933.

Constance. Institut für Geschichtliche Landforschung des Bodenseegebietes. *Studien zu den Anfängen des europäischen Stadtewesens.* Lindau: Thorbecke, 1956.

Corbin, Henry. *Terre Céleste et Corps de Résurrection: De l'Iran Mazdéen à l'Iran Shi'ite.* Paris: Buchet-Chastel, 1960.

Costa, Gustavo. *Le Antichita Germaniche nella Cultura Italiana da Machiavelli a Vico.* Naples: Bibliopolis, 1977.

Coulton, G. G. "Nationalism in the Middle Ages." *Cambridge Historical Review* 5 (1935):15–40.

Courant, Maurice. "L'Asie Centrale aux XVIIᵉ et XVIIIᵉ Siècles: Empire Kalmouk ou Empire Mantchou?" *Annales de l'Université de Lyon,* Nouvelle Série 2, Droit, Lettres 26 (1912).

Courcelle, Pierre. *Histoire Littéraire des Grandes Invasions Germaniques.* 3d ed. Paris: Etudes Augustiniennes, 1964.

Creswell, K. A. C., ed. *Early Muslim Architecture: Umayyads, A.D. 622–750.* Oxford: Clarendon, 1969.

Crone, Patricia. *Slaves on Horses: The Evolution of the Islamic Polity.* Cambridge: Cambridge University Press, 1980.

———, and Cook, Michael. *Hagarism: The Making of the Islamic World.* Cambridge: Cambridge University Press, 1977.

Curtius, Ernst R. *European Literature and the Latin Middle Ages.* Trans. Willard R. Trask. London: Routledge & Kegan Paul, 1953.

Cutler, Anthony. *Transfigurations: Studies in the Dynamics of Byzantine Iconography.* University Park: Pennsylvania State University Press, 1975.

Czuczka, Ernst. *Die kulturgemeinschaftlichen Beziehungen der Deutschen und Tschechen.* Weinböhla bei Dresden: "Aurora," 1923.

Dagron, Gilbert. "Aux Origines de la Civilisation Byzantine: Langue de Culture et Langue d'Etat." *Revue Historique* 241 (1969):23–56.

_____. *Naissance d'une Capitale: Constantinople et Ses Institutions de 330 à 451.* Paris: Presses Universitaires, 1974.

Daniel, Norman. *Islam and the West: The Making of an Image.* Edinburgh: The University Press, 1960.

Dannenbauer, Heinrich. *Die Entstehung Europas.* 2 vols. Stuttgart: Kohlhammer, 1959.

Danvila y Collado, Manuel. *El Poder Civil en España.* 2 vols. Madrid: Tello, 1885.

Dardel, Eric. "The Mythic: According to the Ethnological Works of Maurice Leenhardt." *Diogenes*, 1954, no. 7, pp. 33–51.

Darko, Eugene. "Le Rôle des Peuples Nomades Cavaliers dans la Transformation de l'Empire Romain au Premiers Siècles du Moyan Age." *Byzantion* 18 (1948):85–97.

Darraj, Ahmad. *L'Egypte sous le Règne de Barsbay, 825–841/1422–1438.* Damascus: Institute Français de Damas, 1961.

Daube, Anna. *Der Aufstieg der Muttersprache im deutschen Denken des 15. und 16. Jahrhunderte.* Frankfurt a/M.: Diesterweg, 1940.

Dauvillier, Jean. "Byzantins d'Asie Centrale et d'Extreme-Orient au Moyen Age." *Revue des Etudes Byzantines* 11 (1953):62–87.

Dauzat, Albert. "Le Déplacement des Frontières Linguistiques du Français de 1806 à Nos Jours." *La Nature* 55, no. 2775, 15 December 1927, pp. 329–35.

_____. *Histoire de la Langue Française.* Paris: Payot, 1930.

_____. *Le Village et le Paysan de France.* Paris: Gallimard, 1941.

Dawn, C. Ernest. *From Ottomanism to Arabism: Essays on the Origins of Arab Nationalism.* Urbana: University of Illinois Press, 1973.

Dawson, Christopher. *The Making of Modern Europe: An Introduction to the History of European Unity.* Cleveland: Meredian, 1966.

Deér, Josef. *Heidnisches und Christliches in der altungarischen Monarchie.* 1934. Reprint with postscript. Darmstadt: Wissenschaftliche Buchgesellschaft, 1969.

Defourneaux, Marcelin. *Les Français en Espagne aux XIe et XIIe Siècles.* Paris: Presses Universitaires, 1949.

Delvoye, Charles. *L'Art Byzantin.* Paris: Arthaud, 1967.

Demougeot, Emilienne. *De l'Unité à la Division de l'Empire Romain, 395–410.* Paris: Maisonneuve, 1951.

Dempf, Alois. *Sacrum Imperium: Geschichts- und Staatsphilosophie des Mittelalters und der politischen Renaissance.* Munich: Oldenbourg, 1929.

Demus, Otto. *Byzantine Mosaic Decoration: Aspects of Monumental Art in Byzantium.* London: Kegan Paul, 1947.

Denifle, Heinrich. *Die Entstehung der Universitäten des Mittelalters bis 1400.* Berlin: Weidmann, 1885.

Denis, Ernest. *La Bohème depuis la Montagne Blanche.* 2 vols. Paris: Leroux, 1903.

Der Nersessian, Serarpie. *Armenia and the Byzantine Empire.* Cambridge: Harvard University Press, 1945.

Deutsch, Karl W. "Medieval Unity and Its Economic Conditions." *Canadian Journal of Economic and Political Science* 10 (1944):18–35.

―――. *Nationalism and Social Communication: An Inquiry into the Foundations of Nationality.* Cambridge: M.I.T. Press, 1953.

Deutsche Ostsiedlung in Mittelalter und Neuzeit. Vienna: Böhlau, 1971.

Deverdun, Gaston. *Marrakech: Des Origines à 1912.* Vol. 1. Rabat: Editions Techniques Nord-Africaines, 1959.

DeVries, Jan. *Kelten und Germanen.* Bern: Francke, 1960.

Dhalla, Maneckji N. *Zoroastrian Civilization: From the Earliest Times to the Downfall of the Last Zoroastrian Empire, 651 A.D.* London: Oxford University Press, 1922.

Dhondt, Jan. "Essai sur l'Origine de la Frontière Linguistique." *Antiquité Classique* 16 (1947):263–86.

―――. *Etudes sur la Naissance des Principautés Territoriales en France: IXe–Xe Siècle.* Bruges: "De Tempel," 1948.

Dickinson, Robert E. *City and Region.* London: Routledge & Kegan Paul, 1964.

―――. *The West European City.* London: Routledge & Kegan Paul, 1951.

Dietrich, Karl. "Römer, Romäer, Romanen." *Neue Jahrbücher für das Klassische Altertum, Geschichte und Deutsche Literatur* 9 (1907):482–99.

Diez, Ernst, and Demus, Otto. *Byzantine Mosaics in Greece: Hosios Lucas and Daphni.* Cambridge: Harvard University Press, 1931.

Dimaros, C. T. *La Grèce au Temps des Lumières.* Geneva: Droz, 1969.

Dion, Roger. *Les Frontières de la France.* Paris: Hachette, 1947.

Djaït, Hichem. *L'Europe et l'Islam.* Paris: Editions du Seuil, 1978.

Dölger, Franz. *Beiträge zur Geschichte der byzantinischen Finanzverwaltung besonders des 10. und 11. Jahrhunderts.* Leipzig: Teubner, 1927.

―――. *Byzanz und die europäische Staatenwelt.* Speyer: Ettal, 1953.

Dopsch, Alfons. *Wirtschaftliche und soziale Grundlagen der europäischen Kulturentwicklung aus der Zeit von Cäsar bis auf Karl den Grossen.* Vol. 1. Vienna: Seidel, 1918.

Dubler, C. E. "Ueber Berbersiedlungen auf der iberischen Halbinsel." *Romania Helvetica* 20 (1943):182–97.

Dubois, Charles. "L'Influence des Chaussées Romaines sur la Frontière Linguistique de l'Est." *Revue Belge de Philologie et d'Histoire* 9 (1930):455–94.

Duchesne-Guillemin, Jacques. *Religion of Ancient Iran.* Trans. K. M. Jamasp Asa. Bombay: Tata, 1973.

Duchhardt, Heinz. *Protestantisches Kaisertum und altes Reich: Die Diskussion über der Konfession des Kaisers in Politik, Publizistik und Staatsrecht.* Wiesbaden: Steiner, 1977.

Duda, Herbert W. "Zur Lage der christlichen Untertanen der Pforte." *Wiener Zeitschrift für die Kunde des Morgenlandes* 5 (1948):56–63.

Dufourcq, Charles E. "Berbérie et Ibérie Mediévale: Un Problème de Rupture." *Revue Historique* 240 (1968):293–328.

———. *L'Espagne Catalane et le Maghreb.* Paris: Presses Universitaires, 1966.

Dumézil, Georges. *Les Dieux Indo-Européens.* Paris: Presses Universitaires, 1952.

———. *L'Idéologie Tripartite des Indo-Européens.* Vol. 1. Brussels: Latomus, Revue d'Etudes Latines, 1939.

Dunbar, Helen Flanders. *Symbolism in Medieval Thought and Its Consummation in the Divine Comedy.* New Haven: Yale University Press, 1929.

Dunlop, D. M. *The History of the Jewish Khazars.* Princeton: Princeton University Press, 1954.

Dupront, Alphonse. "Problèmes et Méthodes d'une Histoire de la Psychologie Collective." *Annales* 16 (1961):3–11.

Dussaud, René. *Les Arabes en Syrie avant l'Islam.* Paris: Leroux, 1907.

Dvornik, Francis. *Les Slaves, Byzance et Rome au IXᵉ Siècle.* Paris: Champion, 1926.

Dwight, Henry O. *Constantinople and Its Problems.* New York: Revell, 1901.

Ebel, Wilhelm. *Forschungen zur Geschichte des lübischen Rechts.* Vol. 1. Lübeck: Schmidt-Römhild, n.d.

Ebert, Wolfgang, et al. *Kulturräume und Kulturströmungen in mitteldeutschen Osten.* Halle: Niemeyer, 1936.

Eck, Alexandre. *Le Moyen Age Russe.* 1933. 2d ed. The Hague: Mouton, 1968.

Efendiyev, O. A. *Obrazovaniye Azerbaidzhanskogo Gosudarstva Sefavidov v Nachale XVI Veka.* Baku: Izdatelstvo Akademii Nauk Azerbaidzhanskoi SSR, Institut Istorii, 1961.

Eggers, Hans. *Deutsche Sprachgeschichte.* 3 vols. Munich: Rowohlt, 1970.

Eickhoff, Ekkehard. *Seekrieg und Seepolitik zwischen Islam und Abendland.* Berlin: De Gruyter, 1966.

Eisenbach, Arthur, and Grochulska, Barbara. "La Population de la Pologne au Confins du XVIIIᵉ et du XIXᵉ Siècle." *Annales de Démographie Historique,* 1965, pp. 105–25.

Eisenmann, Louis. *Le Compromis Austro-Hongrois de 1867: Etude sur le Dualisme.* Paris: Société Nouvelle de Librairie et d'Edition, 1904.

Eisenstadt, Shmuel N. *The Political System of Empires.* Glencoe: Free Press, 1963.

Elias, Norbert, *Die höfische Gesellschaft.* Neuwied: Luchterhand, 1969.

———. *Ueber den Prozess der Zivilisation: Soziogenetische und Psychogenetische Untersuchungen.* Vol. 1. Basel: Haus zum Falken, 1939.

Elliott, John H. *Imperial Spain, 1469–1716.* London: Penguin, 1970.

———. *Revolt of the Catalans: A Study in the Decline of Spain, 1598–1640.* Cambridge: Cambridge University Press, 1963.

Elvin, Mark. *The Pattern of the Chinese Past.* Stanford: Stanford University Press, 1973.

Encyclopedia of the Social Sciences. Vol. 14. New York: Macmillan, 1934.

Ennen, Edith. *Frühgeschichte der europäischen Stadt.* Bonn: Röhrscheid, 1953.

———. *The Medieval Town.* Trans. Natalie Fryde. Amsterdam: North Holland Publishing Co., 1979.

Erdmann, Carl. *Die Entstehung des Kreuzzugsgedankens.* Stuttgart: Kohlhammer, 1955.

Ernst, Nikolaus. "Die ersten Einfälle der Krymtataren in Südrussland." *Zeitschrift für Osteuropäische Geschichte* 3 (1913):1–59.

Eventail de l'Histoire Vivante: Offert par l'Amitié d'Historiens, Linguistes, Géographes, Economistes, Sociologues, Ethnologues à Lucien Febvre. 2 vols. Paris: Colin, 1953.

Ewig, Eugen. "Volkstum und Volksbewusstsein im Frankenreich des 7. Jahrhunderts." *Settimane di Studio del Centro Italiano di Studi sull'Alto Medioevo* 2 (1958):587–648.

Eydoux, Henri-Paul. *L'Homme et le Sahara.* 2d ed. Paris: Gallimard, 1943.

Fasoli, Gina. *Le Incursioni Ungare in Europa nel Secolo X.* Florence: Sansoni, 1945.

———. "Points de Vue sur les Incursions Hongroises en Europe au Xe Siècle." *Cahiers du Civilisation Médiévale* 2 (1959):17–35.

Fattal, Antoine. *Le Statut Légal des non-Musulmans en Pays d'Islam.* Beirut: Imprimerie Catholique, 1958.

Feine, Hans E. "Vom Fortleben des römischen Rechts in der Kirche." *Zeitschrift der Savigny Stiftung für Rechtsgeschichte,* Kanonistische Abteilung 42 (1956): 1–24.

Fellner, Thomas (ed. posthumously by Heinrich Kretschmayer). *Die österreichische Zentralwaltung: Von Maximilian I bis zur Vereinigung der österreichischen und böhmischen Hofkanzlei, 1749.* Vols. 1, 5. Vienna: Holzhausen, 1907.

Fényes, Alexius. *Ungarn im Vormärz nach Grundkräften, Verfassung, Verwaltung und Kultur.* Trans. from Hungarian. Leipzig: Herbig, 1851.

Ferguson, Alan D. "Russian Landmilitia und Austrian Militärgrenze." *Südostforschungen* 13 (1954):138–59.

Festschrift Kardinal Faulhaber zum achtzigsten Geburtstag: Dargebracht vom Professorcollegium der Philosophisch- Theologischen Hochschule Freising. Munich: Pfeiffer, 1949.

Festschrift Meinhof. Glückstadt: Augustin, 1927.

Ficker, Julius. *Forschungen zur Reichs- und Rechtsgeschichte Italiens.* 4 vols. Innsbruck: Wagner, 1868, 1869, 1872, 1874.

———. *Das Deutsche Kaiserreich in seiner universalen und nationalen Beziehungen.* 2d ed. Innsbruck: Universitäts Buchhandlung, 1862.

Findley, Carter V. *Bureaucratic Reform in the Ottoman Empire: The Sublime Porte, 1789–1922.* Princeton: Princeton University Press, 1980.

Fine, John V. A., Jr. *The Bosnian Church: A New Interpretation.* Boulder: East European Quarterly, 1975.

Firth, Raymond. *Symbols: Public and Private.* London: Allen & Unwin, 1973.

Fischel, Alfred. *Das oesterreichische Sprachenrecht: Eine Quellensammlung.* 2d ed. Brünn: Irrgang, 1910.

Fischel, Walter J. *Jews in the Economic and Political Life of Medieval Islam.* London: Royal Asiatic Society for Great Britain and Ireland, 1937.

———. "Über die Gruppe der Karimi-Kaufleute." *Studia Arabica* 1 (1937):65–82.

Fishman, Joshua. *Essays by Joshua A. Fishman.* Ed. Anwar S. Dil. Stanford: Stanford University Press, 1972.

———. "Language Maintenance and Language Shift." *Linguistics* 9 (1964):32–70.

———. *Sociolinguistics.* Rowley: Newbury House, 1970.

———. "A Systematization of the Whorfian Hypothesis." *Behavioral Science* 5 (1960):323–39.

Flamand, Pierre. *Un Mellah en Pays Berbère: Demnate.* Paris: Librairie Générale du Droit, 1952.

Flight, John W. "The Nomadic Idea and Ideal in the Old Testament." *Journal of Biblical Literature* 42 (1923):158–226.

Fodor, István. *The Rate of Linguistic Change: Limits of the Application of Mathematical Methods in Linguistics.* The Hague: Mouton, 1965.

Folz, Robert. *The Concept of Empire in Western Europe.* Trans. Sheila A. Ogilvie. London: Arnold, 1969.

———. *Le Souvenir et la Légende de Charlemagne dans l'Empire Germanique Médiéval.* Paris: "Les Belles Lettres," 1950.

———, et al. *De l'Antiquité au Monde Médiéval.* Paris: Presses Universitaires, 1972.

Franco, Moise. *Essai sur l'Histoire des Israélites de l'Empire Ottoman.* 1897. Reprint. Hildesheim: Olms, 1973.

Frank, Tenney. "Race Mixture in the Roman Empire." *American Historical Review* 21 (1916):689–708.

Franke, Herbert. "Westöstliche Beziehungen im Zeitalter der Mongolen." *Saeculum* 19 (1968):91–106.

Frankfort, Henry, et al. *Before Philosophy: The Intellectual Adventure of Ancient Man.* London: Penguin, 1963.

Fritsch, Erdmann. *Islam und Christentum im Mittelalter: Beiträge zur Geschichte der muslimischen Polemik gegen das Christentum in arabischer Sprache.* Breslau: Müller & Seiffert, 1930.

Fry, Richard N. *The Golden Age of Persia: The Arabs in the East.* New York: Barnes & Noble, 1975.

Fuchs, Frederich. *Die höheren Schulen von Konstantinopel im Mittelalter.* Leipzig: Teubner, 1926.

Fuchs, Harold. *Das geistige Widerstand gegen Rom in der antiken Welt.* Berlin: De Gruyter, 1938.

Fück, Johann. *'Arabīya: Recherches sur l'Histoire de la Langue et du Style Arabe.* Trans. Claude Denizeau. Paris: Didier, 1955.

Gabriel, Alfons. *Die religioese Welt des Iran: Entstehung und Schicksal von Glaubensformen auf persischem Boden.* Vienna: Böhlau, 1974.

———. *Religionsgeographie von Persien.* Vienna: Hollenek, 1971.

Gadlo, A. B. *Etnicheskaya Istoriya Severnogo Kavkaza, IV–X vv.* Leningrad: Izdatelstvo Leningradskogo Universiteta, 1979.

Gagé, Jean. *Les Classes Sociales dans l'Empire Romain.* Paris: Payot, 1964.

———. "L'Empéreur Romain et les Rois: Politique et Protocole." *Revue Historique* 221 (1959):15–60.

Gaillard, Henri. *Fès: Une Ville d'Islam.* Paris: André, 1905.

Galassi, Giuseppe. *Roma o Bizanzio: I Musaici di Ravenna e le Origini dell'Arte Italiana.* 2 vols. 1929. New ed. Rome: Libreria dello Stato, 1953.

Ganem, Halil. *Les Sultans Ottomans.* 2 vols. Paris: Chevalier-Marescq, 1901, 1902.

Ganshof, François L. "A Propos de Ducs et Duchés au Haut Moyen Age." *Journal des Savants* 1972, pp. 13–24.

———. "Stämme als 'Träger des Reiches'?" *Zeitschrift der Savigny Stiftung für Rechtsgeschichte,* Germanistische Abteilung 89 (1972):147–60.

Garcia y Bellido, Antonio, et al. *Resumen Historico del Urbanismo en España.* 2d ed. Madrid: Instituto de Estudios de Administracion Local, 1968.

García Gallo, Alfonso. "Nacionalidad y Territorialidad del Derecho en la Epoca Visigoda." *Annuario de Historia del Derecho Español* 13 (1936–41):168–254.

Gardet, Louis. *La Cité Musulmane.* Paris: Librairie Philosophique, 1954.

Garnsey, P. D. A., and Whittaker, C. R., eds. *Imperialism in the Ancient World.* Cambridge: Cambridge University Press, 1978.

Garsoïan, Nina G. "Armenia in the Fourth Century." *Revue des Etudes Arméniennes,* new series 8 (1971):341–52.

———. "Politique ou Orthodoxie? L'Arménie au Quatrième Siècle." *Revue des Etudes Arméniennes,* new series 4 (1967):297–320.

———. "Le Rôle de l'Hiérarchie Chrétienne dans les Rapports Diplomatiques entre Byzance et les Sassanides." *Revue des Etudes Arméniennes,* new series 10 (1973–74):119–38.

Gaudefroy-Demombynes, Maurice. *La Syrie à l'Epoque des Mamelouks d'après les Auteurs Arabes: Description Géographique, Economique et Administrative Précédée d'une Introduction sur l'Organisation Gouvernmentale.* Paris: Geuthner, 1923.

———, and Platonov, S. F. *Le Monde Musulman et Byzantin jusqu'aux Croisades.* Paris: Boccard, 1931.

Gautier, Emile F. *Moeurs et Coutumes des Musulmans.* Paris: Payot, 1931.

———. *Les Siècles Obscurs du Maghreb.* Paris: Payot, 1927.

Gay, Jules. *L'Italie Méridionale et l'Empire Byzantin: Depuis l'Avénement de Basile 1ᵉʳ jusqu'à la Prise de Bari par les Normands, 867–1071.* Paris: Fontemoing, 1904.

Geanakoplos, Deno J. *Interaction of the "Sibling" Byzantine and Western Cultures in the Middle Ages and Italian Renaissance (330–1600).* New Haven: Yale University Press, 1976.

Geertz, Clifford. *The Interpretation of Cultures: Selected Essays.* New York: Basic Books, 1973.

Gellner, Ernest, and Micaud, Charles. *Arabs and Berbers: From Tribe to Nation in North Africa.* Lexington, Mass.: Lexington Books, Heath, 1972.

Gelzer, Heinrich. "Die Anfänge der armenischen Kirche." Königlich-Sächische Gesellschaft der Wissenschaft zu Leipzig. Philologisch-Historische Klasse. *Berichte über die Verhandlungen* 65 (1895):109–74.

———. *Geistliches und Weltliches aus dem türkisch-griechischen Orient.* Leipzig: Teubner, 1900.

Gelzer, Mathias. *Studien zur byzantinischen Verwaltung Aegyptens.* Leipzig: Quelle & Meyer, 1909.

Genicot, Leopold. "La Noblesse au Moyen Age dans l'Ancienne 'Francie'." *Annales* 17 (1962):1–22.

Gerhardt, Mia Irene. "Essai d'Analyse Littéraire de la Pastorale dans les Littératures Italienne, Espagnole et Française." Doctoral dissertation, Leiden University, n.d.

Gerlach, Stephan. *Tage-Buch.* Ed. Samuel Gerlach. Frankfurt a/M: Zunners, 1674.

348 / Bibliography

Geyl, Pieter. *The Revolt of the Netherlands, 1555–1609*. London: Williams & Norgate, 1932.

Giamatti, A. Bartlett. *The Earthly Paradise and the Renaissance Epic*. Princeton: Princeton University Press, 1966.

Gibb, Hamilton A. R. "Arab-Byzantine Relations under the Umayyad Caliphate." *Dumbarton Oaks Papers* 12 (1958):219–33.

———. *The Arab Conquests in Central Asia*. 1923. Reprint. New York: AMS Press, 1970.

———. "Lutfî Paşa on the Ottoman Caliphate." *Oriens* 15 (1962):287–95.

———, and Bowen, Harold. *Islamic Society and the West*. Vol. 1, pt. 2. London: Oxford University Press, 1957.

Giese, Friedrich. "Das Problem der Entstehung des osmanischen Reiches." *Zeitschrift für Semitistik und Verwandte Gebiete* 2 (1924):246–71.

Girard d'Albissin, Nelly. *Genèse de la Frontière Franco-Belge: Les Variations des Limites Septentrionales de la France de 1659 à 1789*. Paris: Picard, 1970.

Gladden, E. N. "Administration of the Ottoman Empire under Suleiman." *Public Administration* 16 (1937):187–93.

Glück, Heinrich. "Das kunstgeographische Bild Europas am Ende des Mittelalters und die Grundlagen der Renaissance." *Monatshefte für Kunstwissenschaft* 15, Bd. 2 (Nov. 1921–22):161–80.

Godechot, Jacques. "Nation, Patrie, Nationalisme et Patriotisme en France au XVIIIᵉ Siècle." *Annales Historiques de la Revolution Française* 63 (1971): 480–501.

Goerlitz, Theodor. "Das flämische und das fränkische Recht in Schlesien und ihr Widerstand gegen das sächsische Recht." *Zeitschrift der Savigny-Stiftung für Rechtsgeschichte* Germanistische Abteilung 57 (1957):138–81.

Goetz, Walter. "Das Wiederaufleben des römischen Rechtes im 12. Jahrhundert." *Archiv für Kulturgeschichte* 10 (1912):25–40.

Goitein, S. D. "Artisans en Méditérranée Orientale au Haut Moyen Age." *Annales* 19 (1964):847–68.

———. *A Mediterranean Society: The Jewish Communities of the Arab World as Portrayed in the Documents of the Cairo Geniza*. 2 vols. Berkeley: University of California Press, 1967, 1971.

———. "The Rise of the Near-Eastern Bourgeoisie in Early Islamic Times." *Revue d'Histoire Mondiale* 3 (1957):583–604.

Göller, Emil. *Die Periodisierung der Kirchengeschichte und die epochale Stellung des Mittelalters zwischen dem christlichen Altertum und der Neuzeit*; together with Karl Heussi, *Altertum, Mittelalter und Neuzeit in der Kirchengeschichte: Ein Beitrag zum Problem der historischen Periodisierung*. Darmstadt: Wissenschaftliche Buchgesellschaft, 1969. Reprints of 1919 and 1921, respectively.

Golvin, Lucien. *Essai sur l'Architecture Religieuse Musulmane*. Vol. 3. Paris: Klincksieck, 1974.

Goodblatt, Morris S. *Jewish Life in Turkey in the 16th Century*. New York: Jewish Theological Seminary of America, 1952.

Goodwin, Godfrey. *A History of Ottoman Architecture*. London: Thames & Hudson, 1971.

Gottschalk, H. L. "Die Autad Šaih Aš-šuyūk." *Zeitschrift für das Kunde des Morgenlandes* 53 (1956):57–87.

Goubert, Paul. *Byzance avant l'Islam*. 2 vols. (2d vol. in 2 parts). Paris: Picard, 1951, 1955, 1965.

———. "Byzance et l'Espagne Wisigothique, 554–711." *Revue des Etudes Byzantines* 2 (1944):5–78.

Grabar, André. *L'Empereur dans l'Art Byzantin*. 1936. London: Variorum Reprints, 1971.

Grabar, Oleg. "Islamic Art and Byzantium." *Dumbarton Oaks Papers* 18 (1964):67–88.

Graham, George. "On the Progress of the Population of Russia." *Journal of the Statistical Society* 7 (1844):243–50.

Graus, František. "Die Entstehung der mittelalterlichen Staaten in Mitteleuropa." *Historica* 10 (1965):5–65.

———. *Volk, Herrscher und Heiliger im Reich der Merowinger: Studien zur Hagiographie der Merowingerzeit*. Prague: Československé Akademie Věd, 1965.

Greene, Frederick D. *The Armenian Crisis in Turkey: The Massacre of 1894, Its Antecedents and Significance*. New York: Putnam, 1895.

Grenard, Fernand. *Grandeur et Décadence de l'Asie: L'Avénement de l'Europe*. Paris: Colin, 1939.

Grenier, Albert. "La Transhumance des Troupeaux en Italie et Son Rôle dans l'Histoire Romaine." Ecole Française [d'Athenes et] de Rome, *Mélanges d'Archéologie et d'Histoire* 25 (1905):293–328.

Grew, Raymond, ed. *Crises of Political Development in Europe and the United States*. Princeton: Princeton University Press, 1978.

Grigorian, Mesrop G. *Armenians in the Service of the Ottoman Empire, 1860–1908*. London: Routledge & Kegan Paul, 1977.

Grosjean, Georges. *Le Sentiment National dans la Guerre de Cent Ans*. Paris: Bossard, 1928.

Grousset, René. *L'Empire des Steppes*. Paris: Payot, 1939.

Grundmann, Herbert. *Das deutsche Nationalbewusstsein und Frankreich: Vom Antichristspiel bis zu Alexander von Roes*. Düsseldorf: A. Bagel, 1936.

———, and Heimpel, Hermann, ed. and trans. *Die Schriften des Alexander von Roes*. Weimar: Böhlau Nachfolger, 1949.

Gudian, Gunter. *Die Begründung in Schöffensprüchen des 14. und 15. Jahrhundert*. Darmstadt: Rinck, 1960.

Guenée, Bernard. "Espace et Etat dans la France du Bas Moyen Age." *Annales* 23 (1968):744–58.

Guichard, Pierre. *Structures Sociales "Orientales" et "Occidentales" dans l'Espagne Musulmane*. Paris: Mouton, 1977.

Guilland, Rodolphe. *Etudes Byzantines*. Paris: Presses Universitaires, 1959.

Guillou, André. "Régionalisme et Indépendance dans l'Empire Byzantin au VIIe Siècle: L'Example de l'Exarchate et de la Pentapole d'Italie." *Studi Storici*, Fasc. 75–76 (1969):1–348.

Gurliand, Ilya I. *Stepnoi Zakonodatelstvo Drevneishikh Vremen po 17-oe Stoletiye*. Kazan: Tipo-litografiya Imperatorskago Universiteta, 1904.

Gürtler, Alfred. *Die Volkszählungen Maria Theresias und Josef II, 1753–1790*. Innsbruck: Wagner, 1909.

Güterbock, Carl. *Der Islam im Lichte der byzantinischen Polemik*. Berlin: Guttentag. 1912.

Gysseling, Maurits. "La Genèse de la Frontière Linguistique dans le Nord de la Gaule." *Revue du Nord* 44 (1962):5–37.

Haase, Felix. *Die Religiöse Psyche des russischen Volkes*. Leipzig: Teubner, 1921.

Häbler, Konrad. *Geschichte Spaniens unter den Habsburgern*. Vol. 1. Gotha: Perthes, 1907.

Hahn, Ludwig. *Rom und Romanismus im griechisch- römischen Orient: Mit besonderer Berücksichtigung der Sprache bis auf die Zeit Hadrians*. Leipzig: Dieterich, 1906.

Hain, Joseph. *Handbuch der Statistik des österreichischen Kaiserstaates*. 2 vols. Vienna: Tendler, 1852, 1853.

Hajnal, Etienne. "Le Rôle Social de l'Ecriture et l'Evolution Européenne." Université Libre de Bruxelles, Institut de Sociologie Solvay, *Revue de l'Institut de Sociologie* 4 (1934):23–53, 253–82.

Halban, Alfred. *Zur Geschichte des deutschen Rechtes in Podolien, Wolhynien und der Ukraine*. Berlin: Praeger, 1896.

Haller, Johannes. "Der Reichsgedanke der staufischen Zeit." *Die Welt als Geschichte* 5 (1939):399–417.

Hamdan, G. "The Pattern of Medieval Urbanism in the Arab World." *Geography* 47 (1962):121–34.

Hamm, Michael F., ed. *The City in Russian History*. Lexington: University Press of Kentucky, 1976.

Hammer, Joseph von (Purgstall). *Geschichte des osmanischen Reiches*. 2d ed. 4 vols. Budapest: Hartleben, 1834, 1835, 1836.

———. *Des osmanischen Reichs Staatsverfassung und Staatsverwaltung*. Vienna: Camesina, 1815.

Hammond, Mason. *The City in the Ancient World*. Cambridge: Harvard University Press, 1972.

Handelsman, Marcel. "Le Rôle de la Nationalité dans l'Histoire du Moyen Age." *Bulletin of the International Committee of Historical Sciences*, 2, pt. 1, no. 6 (May 1929) (Sixième Congrès International des Sciences Historiques, Oslo, 1928: Actes du Congrès). N.p. (Le Comité Organisateur du Congrès), pp. 235–47.

Hanslik, Erwin. "Kulturgeographie der deutsch-slawischen Sprachgrenze." *Vierteljahrsschrift für Sozial- und Wirtschaftsgeschichte* 8 (1910):103–27.

Harmand, Louis. *L'Occident Romain: Gaule, Espagne, Bretagne, Afrique du Nord (31 av. J.C. à 235 ap. J.C.)*. Paris: Payot, 1960.

Harmatta, Janos. "The Dissolution of the Hun Empire." *Acta Archaeologica* 2 (1952):277–304.

Harris, Marvin. *Town and Country in Brazil*. New York: Columbia University Press, 1956.

Hasluck, F. W. *Christianity and Islam under the Sultans.* 2 vols. Oxford: Clarendon, 1929.

Hauck, Albert. *Kirchengeschichte Deutschlands.* Vols. 1–3. 9th ed., 1922. Reprint. Berlin: Akademie Verlag, 1958.

Hauptmann, L. "Les Rapports des Byzantins avec les Slaves et les Avares pendant la Seconde Moitié du VIᵉ Siècle." *Byzantion* 4 (1927–28):137–70.

"Das Hauptstadtproblem in der Geschichte: Festgabe zum 90. Geburtstag Friedrich Meineckes." *Jahrbücher für die Geschichte des deutschen Ostens* 1 (1952):1–308.

Hauser, Henri, and Renaudet, Augustin. *Les Débuts de l'Age Moderne.* Paris: Presses Universitaires, 1956.

Haussen, Adolf. "Die vier deutschen Volkstämme in Böhmen." Verein für Geschichte der Deutschen in Böhmen, *Mitheilungen* 34 (1896):181–210.

———. "Zur Geschichte der deutschen Universität in Prag." Verein für Geschichte der Deutschen in Prag, *Mitheilungen* 38 (1900):110–27.

Haussherr, Hans. *Verwaltungseinheit und Ressorttrennung: Vom Ende des 17. bis zum Beginn des 19. Jahrhundert.* Berlin: Akademie Verlag, 1953.

Haussig, H. W. *A History of Byzantine Civilization.* Trans. J. M. Hussey. London: Thames & Hudson, 1971. (German ed. 1966.)

Hautecoeur, Louis, and Wiet, Gaston. *Les Mosquées du Caire.* 2 vols. Paris: Leroux, 1932.

Hayes, Carlton J. H. *Essays on Nationalism.* New York: Macmillan, 1933.

Heer, Friedrich. *Die Tragödie des Heiligen Reiches.* Zurich: Europa Verlag, 1952.

Heers, Jacques. *Le Clan Familial au Moyen Age: Etude sur les Structures Politiques et Sociales des Milieux Urbains.* Paris: Presses Universitaires, 1974.

Heidborn, A. *Manuel de Droit Public et Administratif de l'Empire Ottoman.* Vol. 1. Vienna: Stern, 1908.

Helbig, Herbert. "Deutsche Siedlungsforschung im Bereich der mittelalterlichen Ostkolonisation." *Jahrbüch für die Geschichte Mittel und Ostdeutschlands* 2 (1953):283–345.

Helbling, Hanno. *Goten und Wandalen: Wandlung der historichen Realität.* Zurich: Fretz and Wasmuth, 1954.

Heldmann, Karl. *Das Kaisertum Karls des Grossen: Theorien und Wirklichkeit.* Weimar: Böhlau, 1928.

Helfert, Joseph A. von. *Die österreichische Volksschule: Geschichte, System, Statistik.* 2 vols. Prague: Tempsky, 1860, 1861.

Hellbling, Ernst C. *Österreichische Verfassungs- und Verwaltungsgeschichte.* Vienna: Springer, 1956.

Hellmann, Manfred. "Stadt und Recht in Altrussland." *Saeculum* 5 (1954):41–64.

Hensel, Witold. *La Naissance de la Pologne.* Wrocław: Institut d'Histoire de la Culture Matérielle, 1966.

Herklots, G. A., ed. *Islam in India or the Qanun-i-Islam: The Customs of the Musalmans of India by Ja'far Sharif.* 1863. New ed. by William Crooke. London: Oxford University Press, 1921.

Hess, Andrew C. *The Forgotten Frontier: A History of the Sixteenth Century Ibero-African Frontier.* Chicago: University of Chicago Press, 1978.

Heyd, Uriel. *Foundations of Turkish Nationalism: Ziya Gökalp*. London: Luzac, 1950.

——. "The Jewish Communities of Istanbul in the 17th Century." *Oriens* 6 (1952):299–314.

Heyd, Wilhelm. *Histoire du Commerce du Levant au Moyen Age*. 2 vols. Trans. Furcy Raynaud. 1885–86. Reprint. Amsterdam: Hakkert, 1967.

Hillgarth, J. N. *The Spanish Kingdoms, 1250–1516*. Oxford: Clarendon, 1976.

Hintze, Otto. "Die Entstehung der modernen Staatsministerien." *Historische Zeitschrift* 100 (1908):53–111.

Hinz, Walther. *Irans Aufstieg zum Nationalstaat im fünfzehnten Jahrhundert*. Berlin: De Gruyter, 1936.

Hirschberg, H. Z. "The Jewish Quarter in Muslim Cities and Berber Areas." *Judaism* 17 (1968):405–21.

Hirschfeld, Otto. *Die kaiserlichen Verwaltungsbeamten bis auf Diocletian*. 2d ed. Berlin: Weidmann, 1905.

Hittle, J. Michael. *The Service City: State and Townsman in Russia, 1600–1800*. Cambridge: Harvard University Press, 1979.

Hodgson, Marshall G. S. *The Venture of Islam*. 3 vols. Chicago: University of Chicago Press, 1974.

Höfler, Karl A. *Magister Johannes Hus und der Abzug der deutschen Professoren und Studenten aus Prag, 1409*. Prague: Temsky, 1864.

Holl, Karl. "Das Fortleben der Volkssprachen in Kleinasien in nachchristlicher Zeit." *Hermes* 18 (1908):240–54.

Hollingsworth, T. H. *Historical Demography*. Ithaca: Cornell University Press, 1969.

Holt, P. M. *Egypt and the Fertile Crescent, 1516–1922: A Political History*. Ithaca: Cornell University Press, 1966.

Hóman, Bálint. *Geschichte des ungarischen Mittelalters*. 2 vols. Trans. Hildegard von Roosz and Lothar Saczek. Berlin: De Gruyter, 1940.

Honigmann, Ernst. *Die Ostgrenze des byzantinischen Reiches: Von 363 bis 1071*. Brussels: Editions de l'Institut de Philologie et d'Histoire Orientale, 1935.

Howorth, Henry H. "The Westerly Drifting of Nomades: From the Fifth to the Nineteenth Century." *Journal of the Anthropological Institute of Great Britain and Ireland* 1 (1872):226–53; 2 (1873):205–27; 3 (1874):145–72.

Hroch, Miroslav. *Die Vorkämpfer der Nationalenbewegung bei den kleinen Völkern Europas: Eine vergleichende Analyse zur gesellschaftlichen Schichtung der patriotischen Gruppen*. Prague: Universita Karlova, 1968.

Huart, Clement, *Histoire de Bagdad dans les Temps Modernes*. Paris: Leroux, 1901.

Hudson, Alfred E. *Kazak Social Structure*. 1938. Reprint. New Haven: Yale University Publications in Anthropology, No. 20, 1964.

Hübinger, Paul E., ed. *Bedeutung und Rolle des Islam beim Uebergang von Altertum zum Mittelalter*. Darmstadt: Wissenschaftliche Buchgesellschaft, 1968.

——. *Kulturbruch oder Kulturkontinuität im Uebergang von der Antike zum Mittelalter*. Darmstadt: Wissenschaftliche Buchgesellschaft, 1968.

Hüffer, Hermann J. "Die mittelalterliche spanische Kaiseridee und ihre Probleme." *Saeculum* 3 (1952):425–43.

Hugelmann, Karl G. "Die deutsche Nation und der deutsche Nationalstaat im Mittelalter." *Historisches Jahrbuch* 51 (1931):1–29, 445–84.

———. "Studien zum Recht der Nationalitäten im deutschen Mittelalter." *Historisches Jahrbuch* 47 (1927):275–96.

———, ed. *Das Nationalitätenrecht des alten Oesterreich*. Vienna: Universitäts-Verlagsbuchhandlung, 1934.

Huizinga, Jan H. "Burgund: Eine Krise des romanisch-germanischen Verhältnisses." *Historische Zeitschrift* 198 (1925):1–28.

———. *Dutch Civilization in the Seventeenth Century and Other Essays*. Ed. Peter Geyl and F. W. N. Hugenholtz. Trans. Arnold J. Pomerans. London: Collins, 1968.

———. *Patriotisme en Nationalisme in de Europeesche Geschiedenis tot het Einde der 19ᵉ Eeuw*. Haarlem: Tjeenk Willenk, 1940.

Hunger, Herbert. *Reich der neuen Mitte: Der christliche Geist der byzantinischen Kultur*. Graz: Styria, 1965.

Hüsing, Georg. *Iranische Ueberlieferung und das arische System*. Leipzig: Henrich, 1909.

———. "Völkerschichten in Iran." *Mitteilungen der Anthropologischen Gesellschaft in Wien* 46 (1916):199–250. (3d series, 16).

Hussey, J. M., ed. *The Byzantine Empire. Cambridge Medieval History*, vol. 4, pt. 2. Cambridge: Cambridge University Press, 1967.

Inalcik, Halik. *The Ottoman Empire: The Classical Age, 1300–1600*. London: Weidenfeld & Nicolson, 1973.

Institute for Balkan Studies, Thessalonica. *Symposium "L'Epoque Phanariote," 21–25 Octobre 1970: A la Mémoire de Cléobule Tsourkas*. Thessalonica: Institute for Balkan Studies, 1974.

International Congress of Historical Sciences, Oslo, 1928. *Bulletin of the International Committee of Historical Sciences*, No. 7 (October 1929), La Nationalité et l'Histoire.

Iorga, Nicolae. *Geschichte des osmanischen Reiches*. 3 vols. Gotha: Perthes, 1908–1910.

Isbert, O. A. "Zur Psychologie der Madjarisierung." *Deutsches Grenzland*, 1936, pp. 59–71.

Itkowitz, N. "Eighteenth Century Ottoman Realities." *Studia Islamica* 16 (1962):73–94.

Ivánka, Endre. *Hellenisches und Christliches im frühbyzantinischen Geistesleben*. Vienna: Herder, 1948.

Jacoby, David. "La Population de Constantinople à l'Epoque Byzantine: Un Problème de Démographie Urbaine." *Byzantion* 31 (1961):81–100.

———. *Société et Démographie à Byzance et en Romanie Latine*. London: Variorum Reprints, 1975.

Jaffé, Moritz. "Wie kam die deutsche Ausbreitung nach Osten zum Stillstand?" *Archiv für Sozialwissenschaft* 59 (1928):322–39.

Janin, R. *Constantinople Byzantine: Développement Urbaine et Répertoire Topographique*. Paris: Institut Français d'Etudes Byzantines, 1950.

Jankuhn, Herbert, Schlesinger, Walter, and Steuer, Heike, eds. *Vor- und Frühfor-*

354 / Bibliography

men der europäischen Stadt in Mittelalter: Bericht über ein Symposium in Reinhausen bei Göttingen in der Zeit von 18. bis 24. April 1972. Part 1. Göttingen: Vandenhoeck & Ruprecht, 1973.

Jażdżewski, Konrad. "Das gegenseitige Verhältnis slawischer und germanischer Elemente in Mitteleuropa seit dem Hunneneinfall bis zur awarischen Landnahme an der mittleren Donau." *Archaeologia Polona* 2 (1958):51–70.

Jeanton, Gabriel, ed. "Enquête sur les Limites des Influences Septentrionales et Méditérranéenes en France." *Mémoires de la Société pour l'Histoire du Droit et des Institutions des Anciens Pays Bourguignons, Comtois et Romands* 4 (1937):168–84.

Jespersen, Otto. *Mankind, Nation and Individual from a Linguistic Point of View.* London: George Allen & Unwin, n.d.

Jettmar, Karl. "The Altai before the Turks." Ostasiatiska Samlingarna (Stockholm, The Museum of Far Eastern Antiquities), *Bulletin*, no. 23 (1951), pp. 135–223.

Joachimsen, Paul. *Vom deutschen Volk zum deutschen Staat: Eine Geschichte des deutschen Nationalbewusstseins.* 3d ed. Göttingen: Vandenhoeck & Ruprecht, 1956.

Johnson, Allan C. *Roman Egypt to the Reign of Diocletian.* Vol. 2. Baltimore: Johns Hopkins Press, 1936.

Jones, A. H. M. *The Greek City from Alexander to Justinian.* Oxford: Clarendon, 1940.

———. "Were Ancient Heresies National or Social Movements in Disguise?" *Journal of Theological Studies* 10 (1959):280–98.

Jonquière, [Vicomte] de la. *Histoire de l'Empire Ottoman depuis Son Origines jusqu'à Nos Jours.* 2 vols. [Paris]: Hachette, 1914.

Jordan, Edouard. *L'Allemagne et l'Italie aux XIIe et XIIIe Siècles.* Paris: Presses Universitaires, 1939.

Jordan, Karl. "Die entstehung der römischen Kurie." *Zeitschrift der Savingny-Stiftung für Rechtsgeschichte*, Kanonistische Abteilung 28 (1939):97–152.

Joseph, John. *The Nestorians and Their Muslim Neighbors: A Study of Western Influence on Their Relations.* Princeton: Princeton University Press, 1961.

Jouguet, Pierre. *La Vie Municipale dans l'Egypte Romaine.* Paris: Fontemoing, 1911.

Julien, Ch.-André. *Histoire de l'Afrique du Nord: Tunisie, Algérie, Maroc, de la Conquête Arab à 1830.* 2d ed. Paris: Payot, 1969.

Juster, Jean. *Les Juifs dans l'Empire Romain: Leur Condition Juridique, Economique et Sociale.* 2 vols. Paris: Geuthner, 1914.

Kaerst, Julius. *Die antike Idee der Oekumene in ihrer politischen und kulturellen Bedeutung.* Leipzig: Teubner, 1903.

———. *Studien zur Entwicklung und theoretische Begründung der Monarchie im Altertum.* Munich: Oldenbourg, 1898.

Kagan, Richard L. *Students and Society in Early Modern Spain.* Baltimore: Johns Hopkins University Press, 1974.

Kaindl, Raimund F. *Geschichte der Deutschen in Ungarn: Ein deutsches Volksbuch.* Gotha: Perthes, 1912.

Kampers, Franz. *Vom Werdegange der abendländischen Kaisermystik.* Leipzig: Teubner, 1924.

Kann, Robert. "German-Speaking Jewry during Austria-Hungary's Constitutional Era, 1867–1918." *Jewish Social Studies* 10 (1948):239–56.

————. "Hungarian Jewry during Austria-Hungary's Constitutional Period, 1867–1918." *Jewish Social Studies* 7 (1945):357–86.

————. *The Multinational Empire: Nationalism and National Reform in the Hapsburg Monarchy, 1848–1918.* 2 vols. New York: Columbia University Press, 1950.

Kantorowicz, Ernst H. *Laudes Regiae: A Study in Liturgical Acclamations and Medieval Ruler Worship.* Berkeley: University of California Press, 1958.

Karajan, M. Th. von. "Ueber den Leumund der Oesterreicher, Böhmen und Ungern in den heimischen Quellen des Mittelalters." Vienna, Akademie der Wissenschaften, Philosophisch-Historische Klasse, *Sitzungsberichte* 42 (1863):447–531.

Karayannopulos, Johannes. *Das Finanzwesen des frühbyzantinischen Staates.* Munich: Oldenbourg, 1958.

Karp, Hans-Jürgen. *Grenzen in Ostmitteleuropa während des Mittelalters: Ein Beitrag zur Entstehungsgeschichte der Grenzlinie aus dem Grenzsaum.* Cologne: Böhlau, 1972.

Karpat, Kemal. *An Inquiry into the Social Foundations of Nationalism in the Ottoman State.* Princeton: Princeton University Press, 1973.

Kaser, Kurt. *Politische und soziale Bewegungen im deutschen Bürgertum zu Beginn des 16. Jahrhunderts: Mit besonderer Rücksicht auf den Speyeres Aufstand im Jahre 1512.* Stuttgart: Kohlhammer, 1899.

Katz, Jacob. *Tradition and Crisis: Jewish Society at the End of the Middle Ages.* New York: Free Press, 1961.

Kazhdan, A. P. *Armyane v Sostave Gospodstvuyushchego Klassa Bizantiiskoi Imperii v XI–XII vv.* Yerevan: Akademiya Nauk Armenskoi SSR, 1975.

Kern, Fritz. *Die Anfänge des frانzözischen Ausdehnungspolitik bis zum Jahre 1308.* Tübingen: Mohr, 1910.

————. *Gottesgnadentum und Widerstandsrecht im früheren Mittelalter: Zur Entwicklungsgeschichte der Monarchie.* 3d ed. Darmstadt: Wissenschaftliche Buchgesellschaft, 1962.

Kerner, Robert J. *Bohemia in the Eighteenth Century: A Study in Political, Economic, and Social History with Special Reference to the Reign of Leopold II, 1790–1792.* New York: Macmillan, 1932.

Keutgen, F. *Der deutsche Staat des Mittelalters.* Jena: Fischer, 1918.

Kienast, Walther. *Deutschland und Frankreich in der Kaiserzeit, 900–1270.* 2 vols. Stuttgart: Hiersemann, 1914–15.

————. *Studien über die fransözischen Volkstämme des Frühmittelalters.* Stuttgart: Hiersemann, 1968.

Kiener, Fritz. *Verfassungsgeschichte der Provence seit der Ostgothenherrschaft bis zur Errichtung der Konsulate, 510–1200.* Leipzig: Dyk, 1900.

Kirk, G. S. *Myth: Its Meaning and Functions in Ancient and Other Cultures.* Cambridge: Cambridge University Press, 1970.

356 / Bibliography

Kirn, Paul. *Aus der Frühzeit des Nationalgefühls.* Leipzig: Koehler & Amelang, 1943.

Kirsten, Ernst. *Die griechische Polis als historisch-geographisches Problem des Mittelmeerraumes.* Bonn: Dümmler, 1956.

Kisch, Guido. *Forschungen zur Rechts- und Sozialgeschichte der Juden in Deutschland während des Mittelalters.* Zurich: Europa, 1955.

——. *The Jews in Medieval Germany: A Study of Their Legal and Social Status.* Chicago: University of Chicago Press, 1949.

——. *Die Prager Universität und die Juden, 1348–1848: Mit Beiträgen zur Geschichte des Medizinstudium.* Mährisch-Ostrau: Kittl, 1935.

Klein, Julius. *The Mesta: A Study in Spanish Economic History, 1273–1836.* Cambridge: Harvard University Press, 1920.

Koczy, Leon. "The Holy Roman Empire and Poland." *Antemurale* 2 (1955):50–65.

Koczyński, Stefan. "Osteuropäischer Handel im XV. Jahrhundert." *Jahrbücher für Nationalökonomie und Statistik* 34 (1879):498–502.

Koebner, Richard. "Deutsches Recht und deutsche Kolonisation in den Piastenländern." *Vierteljahrsschrift für Sozial- und Wirtschaftsgeschichte* 25 (1932):313–52.

Koenigsberger, H. G. *The Practice of Empire.* Ithaca: Cornell University Press, 1969.

Kohn, Hans. *The Idea of Nationalism: A Study in Its Origins and Background.* New York: Macmillan, 1944.

Kopanov, A. I. "Naseleniye Russkogo Gosudarstva v XVI V." *Istoricheskiye Zapiski* 54 (1959):233–54.

Kopchak, S. I. *Naseleniya Ukrayinskoho Prikarpattya.* Lvov: "Vyshcha Shkola," 1974.

Koppelmann, H. L. *Nation, Sprache und Nationalismus.* Leiden: Sijthoff, 1956.

Kornis, Gyula. *Ungarische Kulturideale, 1777–1848.* Leipzig: Quelle & Meyer, 1930.

Kortepeter, Carl Max. *Ottoman Imperialism during the Reformation: Europe and the Caucasus.* New York: New York University Press, 1972.

Koschaker, Paul. *Europa und das römische Recht.* Munich: Biederstein, 1947.

Kötzschke, Rudolf. "Salhof und Siedelhof im älteren deutschen Agrarwesen." Sächische Akademie der Wissenschaften zu Leipzig, Philologisch-Historische Klasse, *Berichte über die Verhandlungen*, Heft 5, 1953.

——, and Ebert, Wolfgang. *Geschichte der ostdeutschen Kolonisation.* Leipzig: Bibliographisches Institut, 1937.

Kovačević, Esref. *Granice Bosanskog Pašaluka Prema Austriji i Mletačkoj Republici po Odredbama Karlovčkg Mira.* Sarajevo: Svjetlost, 1973.

Krader, Lawrence. "Feudalism and the Tatar Polity of the Middle Ages." *Comparative Studies in Society and History* 1 (1958):76–99.

——. *Formation of the State.* Englewood Cliffs: Prentice-Hall, 1968.

——. "Principle and Structure in the Organization of the Asiatic Steppe-Pastoralists." *Southwestern Journal of Anthropology* 11 (1955):67–92.

Kralik, Richard. *Oesterreichische Geschichte.* Vienna: Holzhausen, 1913.

Kramer, Hans. *Die Italiener unter der österreichisch-ungarischen Monarchie.* Vienna: Herold, 1954.

Kramer, J. H. "La Sociologie de l'Islam." *Acta Orientalia* 21 (1953):243–53.

Krebs, Norbert. "Die geographische Struktur des osmanischen Reiches." *Geographische Zeitschrift* 25 (1919):156–66.

Krischen, Fritz. *Die griechische Stadt: Wiederherstellungen.* Berlin: Mann, 1938.

Kruedener, Jürgen von. *Die Rolle des Hofes im Absolutismus.* Stuttgart: Fischer, 1973.

Krymsky, A. Y. *Istoriya Persii, Yeya Literatury i Dervisheskoi Teosofii.* New ed. with K. Freit. Moscow: Gattsuk, 1909.

Kübeck von Kübau, Carl F. *Tagebücher des Carl Friedrich Freiherrn Kübeck von Kübau.* Ed. Max Freiherr von Kübeck. Vol. 1. Vienna: Herold, 1909.

Kuhar, Aloysius. "The Conversion of the Slovenes and the German-Slav Ethnic Boundary in the Eastern Alps." *Studia Slovenica* 2 (1959).

Kuhn, Hans. "Die Grenzen der germanischen Gefolgschaft." *Zeitschrift der Savigny-Stiftung für Rechtsgeschichte,* Germanistische Abteilung, 73 (1956):1–83.

Kuhn, Walter. "Die deutschrechtlichen Städte in Schlesien und Polen in der ersten Hälfte des 13. Jahrhunderts." *Zeitschrift für Ostforschung* 15 (1966):278–337, 457–510, 704–43.

————. "Die Erschliessung des südlichen Kleinpolen im 13. und 14. Jahrhundert." *Zeitschrift für Ostforschung* 17 (1968):401–80.

Kulisher, Alexander and Kulisher, Eugen. *Kriegs- und Wanderzüge: Weltgeschichte als Völkerbewegung.* Berlin: De Gruyter, 1932.

Kunkel, Wolfgang. *An Introduction to Roman Legal and Constitutional History.* 2d ed. Trans. J. M. Kelly. Oxford: Clarendon, 1973.

Künssberg, Eberhard von. *Rechtsgeschichte und Volkskunde.* Ed. Pavlos Tzermias. Cologne: Böhlau, 1965.

————. "Rechtssprachgeographie." Heidelberger Akademie der Wissenschaften, Philosophisch-Historische Klasse, Jahrgang 1926–27, vol. 27. *Sitzungsberichte* (1. Abhandlung), pp. 3–48.

Kupper, Jean R. *Les Nomades en Mésopotamie au Temps des Rois de Mari.* Paris: "Les Belles Lettres," 1957.

Kurth, Godefroid. "La France et les Francs dans la Langue Politique du Moyen Age." *Revue des Questions Historiques* 57 (new series 13) (1895):337–99.

————. *La Frontière Linguistique en Belgique et dans le Nord de la France.* Brussels: Académie Royale des Sciences, des Lettres et des Beaux-Arts de Belgique, 1895.

Labatut, Jean-Pierre. *Les Noblesses Européennes de la Fin du XVe Siècle à la Fin du XVIIIe Siècle.* Paris: Presses Universitaires, 1978.

Labib, Subhi Y. "Handelsgeschichte Aegypten im Spätmittelalter (1171–1517)." *Vierteljahrschrift für Sozial- und Wirtschaftsgeschichte,* Beiheft 46 (1965).

Lambert, Elie. *L'Art Musulman d'Occident des Origines à la Fin du XVe Siècle.* Paris: Société d'Edition d'Enseignement Supérieur, 1966.

Lambton, Ann. *Landlord and Peasant in Persia.* London: Oxford University Press, 1969.

Lammens, Henri. *Le Berceau de l'Islam: L'Arabie Occidentale à la Veille de l'Hégire.* Vol. 1. Rome: Sumptibus Pontificii Instituti Biblici, 1914.

Lanckorońska, Karolina. *Studies in the Roman-Slavonic Rite in Poland.* Rome: Pont. Institutum Orientalium Studiorum, 1961.

Landau, Georg. *Die Territorien in Bezug auf ihre Bildung und ihre Entwicklung.* Hamburg: Perthes, 1854.

Landau, Richard. *Geschichte der jüdischen Aerzte: Ein Beitrag zur Geschichte der Medicin.* Berlin: Karger, 1895.

Lane, Frederic C. *Venice: A Maritime Republic.* Baltimore: Johns Hopkins University Press, 1973.

Lane-Poole, Stanley. *A History of Egypt in the Middle Ages.* 2d ed. London: Methuen, 1914.

_____. *Medieval India under Mohammaden Rule, A.D. 712–1764.* London: Fisher Unwin, 1903.

Lang, C. L. "Les Minorités Arménienne et Juive d'Iran." *Politique Etrangère* 26 (1961):460–72.

Langhans-Ratzeburg, Manfred. "Geographische Rechtswissenschaft." *Zeitschrift für Geopolitik* 5 (1928):89–98.

Lapidus, Ira M. *Muslim Cities in the Later Middle Ages.* Cambridge: Harvard University Press, 1967.

Lapôtre, Arthur. *L'Europe et le Saint-Siège à l'Epoque Carolingienne.* Part 1. Paris: Picard, 1895.

Laroui, Abdallah. *L'Histoire du Maghreb: Un Essai de Synthèse.* 2 vols. Paris: Maspero, 1975.

Larson, Gerald J. *Myth in Indo-European Antiquity.* Berkeley: University of California Press, 1974.

Lassner, Jacob. *The Shaping of 'Abbāsid Rule.* Princeton: Princeton University Press, 1980.

Lasswell, Harold D., with Fox, Merritt B. *The Signature of Power.* New Brunswick: Transaction Books, 1979.

Latouche, Robert. *Les Grandes Invasions et la Crise de l'Occident au Vᵉ Siècle.* Paris: Aubier, 1946.

Laurent, Joseph. *L'Arménie entre Byzance et l'Islam depuis la Conquête Arabe jusqu'en 886.* Paris: Fontemoing, 1919.

_____. *Byzance et les Turcs Seldjoucides dans l'Asie Occidentale jusqu'en 1081.* Nancy: Berger-Levrault, 1913.

Lazarev, V. N. *Drevnerusskiye Mozaiki i Freski: XI–XV vv.* Moscow: "Iskusstvo," 1973.

Lechner, Kilian. "Byzanz und die Barbaren." *Saeculum* 6 (1955):291–306.

Lederer, E. *La Structure de la Société Hongroise du Début du Moyen-Age.* Budapest: Akadémiai Kiadó, 1960.

LeGoff, Jacques. "Culture Cléricale et Traditions Folkloriques dans la Civilisation Mérovingienne." *Annales* 22 (1967):781–91.

Leib, Bernard. *Rome, Kiev et Byzance à la Fin du XIᵉ Siècle: Rapports Réligieux des Latins et des Gréco-Russes sous le Pontificat d'Urbain II (1088–1099).* Paris: Picard, 1924.

Lemarignier, Jean-François. "Recherches sur l'Hommage en Marche et les Frontières Feodales." *Travaux et Mémoires de l'Université de Lille,* Nouvelle Série, Droit et Lettres 24 (1945):1–191 + vii–xx.

Lemberg, Eugen. *Geschichte des Nationalismus en Europa.* Stuttgart: Schwab, 1950.

Lemerle, Paul. "Invasions et Migrations dans les Balkans depuis la Fin de l'Epoque Romaine jusqu'au VIIIe Siècle." *Revue Historique* 211 (1954):265–308.

LeStrange, Guy. *The Lands of the Eastern Caliphate: Mesopotamia, Persia, and Central Asia from the Moslem Conquest to the Time of Timur.* Cambridge: Cambridge University Press, 1930.

Lestschinsky, Jakob, ed. *Schriften für Wirtschaft und Statistik.* Berlin: Yiddish Scientific Institute, Section für Wirtschaft und Statistik, 1928.

Le Tourneau, Roger. *Fès avant le Protectorat: Etude Economique et Sociale d'une Ville de l'Occident Musulman.* Casablanca: Société Marocaine de Librairie et d'Editions, 1949.

————. *Fez in the Age of the Merinides.* Norman: University of Oklahoma Press, 1961.

Levine, Donald N. *Greater Ethiopia: The Evolution of a Multiethnic Society.* Chicago: University of Chicago Press, 1974.

LeVine, Robert A., and Campbell, Donald T. *Ethnocentrism: Theories of Conflict, Ethnic Attitudes and Group Behavior.* New York: Wiley, 1972.

Lévi-Strauss, Claude. *The Savage Mind.* Chicago: University of Chicago Press, 1966.

————. *Structural Anthropology.* Trans. Claire Jacobson and Brooke G. Schoepf. New York: Basic Books, 1963.

Levshin, Aleksei. *Déscription des Hordes et des Steppes des Kirghiz-Kazaks ou Kirghiz-Kaïssaks.* Paris: Imprimerie Royale, 1860.

Lewis, Archibald R., and McGann, Thomas F., eds. *The New World Looks at Its History.* Proceedings of the Second International Congress of Historians of the United States and Mexico. Austin: University of Texas Press, 1963.

Lewis, Bernard. *The Emergence of Modern Turkey.* 2d ed. London: Oxford University Press, 1968.

————. *Islam in History.* London: Alcove Press, 1973.

————. "The Islamic Guilds." *Economic History Review* 8 (1937):20–37.

Lézine, Alexandre. *Deux Villes d'Ifriqiya: Sousse, Tunis, Etudes d'Archaéologie, d'Urbanisme, de Démographie.* Paris: Geuthner, 1971.

Lhotsky, Alfhons. *Das Zeitalter des Hauses Österreich: Die ersten Jahre der Regierung Ferdinands I in Österreich (1520–1527).* Vol. 4. Vienna: Böhlau, 1971.

Lipshits, Elena Emmanuilovna. *Ocherki Istorii Vizantiiskogo Obshchestva i Kultury: VIII–Pervaya Polovina IX veka.* Moscow: Izdatelstvo Akademii Nauk SSSR, 1961.

Lomax, Derek W. *The Reconquest of Spain.* London: Longman, 1978.

Lombard, Jacques. *Autorités Traditionelles et Pouvoirs Européens en Afrique Noire.* Paris: Colin, 1967.

Lombard, Maurice. *Espaces et Réseaux du Haut Moyen Age.* Paris: Mouton, 1972.

————. *L'Islam dans Sa Première Grandeur.* Paris: Flammarion, 1971.

————. *Monnaie et Histoire d'Alexandre à Mohamet.* Paris: Mouton, 1971.

Lončar, Dragotin. *The Slovenes: A Social History from the Earliest Times to 1910.* Trans. Anthony J. Klancar. Cleveland: American Jugoslav Printing and

Publishing Co., 1939.

Lopez, R. S. "Byzantine Law in the Seventh Century and Its Reception by the Germans and the Arabs." *Byzantion* 16 (1942–43):445–61, Fasicule 1.

Lot, Ferdinand. "A Quelle Epoque A-t-On Cessé de Parler Latin?" *Bulletin de Cange* 6 (1931):97–159.

————. *Les Invasions Barbares et le Peuplement de l'Europe: Introduction à l'Intelligence des Derniers Traités de Paix.* 2 vols. Paris: Payot, 1937.

Lotter, Friedrich. *Die Konzeption des Wendenkreuzzugs: Ideengeschichtliche, kirchenrechtliche und historisch-politische Voraussetzungen der Missionierung von Elb- und Ostseeslawen um die Mitte des 12. Jahrhunderts.* Sigmaringen: Thorbecke, 1977.

Lourie, Elena. "A Society Organized for War: Medieval Spain." *Past and Present* 35 (1966):54–76.

Ludat, Herbert. *Der europäische Osten in abendländischer und sovjetischer Sicht.* Cologne: Müller, 1954.

Łukasik, Stanislas. *Pologne et Roumanie: Aux Confins des Deux Peuples et des Deux Langues.* Paris: Librairie Polonaise, 1938.

Lukeš, J. *Militärische Maria-Theresien-Orden: Ueber Autorisation des Ordens nach authentischen Quellen verfasst und angeordnet.* Vienna: Kaiserliche-Königliche Hof- und Staatsdrückerei, 1890.

Lüttich, Rudolf. *Ungarnzüge in Europa im 10. Jahrhundert.* Berlin: Ebering, 1910.

Luttwak, Edward N. *The Grand Strategy of the Roman Empire.* Baltimore: Johns Hopkins University Press, 1976.

Lybyer, Albert H. *The Government of the Ottoman Empire at the Time of Suleiman the Magnificent.* Cambridge: Harvard University Press, 1913.

Lynnychenko, Ivan. *Suspilni Verstvy Halytskoyi Rusy XIV–XV V.* Lvov: Naukovo Tovarystvo imeny Shevchenka, 1899.

Macartney, C. A. "The Eastern Auxiliaries of the Magyars." *Journal of the Royal Asiatic Society of Great Britain and Ireland* (1969):49–58.

————. *The Habsburg Empire, 1790–1918.* London: Weidenfeld & Nicolson, 1968.

————. *The Magyars in the Ninth Century.* Cambridge: Cambridge University Press, 1930.

Makkai, L. *Die Entstehung der gesellschaftlichen Basis des Absolutismus in den Ländern der österreichischen Habsburger.* Budapest: Akadémiai Kiadó, 1960.

Mal, Josip. *Uskochke Seobe i Slovenske Pokrajjne povest Naseobina s Kulturno-Istorijskim Prikazom.* Ljubljana: Jugoslovanska Tiskarna, 1924.

Mantran, Robert. *Istanbul dans la Seconde Moitié du XVIIe Siècle.* Paris: Maisonneuve, 1962.

Marçais, Georges. *La Berbérie Musulmane et l'Orient au Moyen Age.* Paris: Aubier, n.d.

————. "La Conception des Villes dans l'Islam." *Revue d'Alger* 2 (1945):517–33.

————. *Manuel d'Art Musulman: L'Architecture, Tunisie, Algérie, Maroc, Espagne, Sicile.* 2 vols. Paris: Picard, 1926, 1927.

Marczali, Henry. *Hungary in the Eighteenth Century.* Cambridge: Cambridge University Press, 1910.

Marías, Julián. *Generations: A Historical Method*. Trans. Harold C. Raley. University, Ala.: University of Alabama Press, 1967.

Marquardt, J. *Osteuropäische und ostasiatische Streifzüge: Ethnologische und historisch-topographische Studien zur Geschichte des 9. und 10. Jahrhunderts, ca. 840–940*. Leipzig: Dieterich, 1903.

Marrow, Henri I. *A History of Education in Antiquity*. Trans. George Lamb. London: Sheed & Ward, 1956.

Martel, Antoine. "La Langue Polonaise dans les Pays Ruthènes: Ukraine et Russie Blanche, 1569–1667." *Travaux et Mémoires de l'Université de Lille*, Nouvelle Série, Droit et Lettres, No. 20, 1938.

Martin, Alfred von. "Zur soziologie des höfischen Kultur." *Archiv für Sozialwissenschaft* 64 (1930):155–65.

Martin, Victor, *La Fiscalité Romaine en Egypte aux Trois Premiers Siècles de l'Empire: Ses Principes, Ses Méthodes, Ses Résultats*. Geneva: Georg, 1926.

Maschke, Erich. *Das Erwachen des Nationalbewusstseins im deutsch-slavischen Grenzraum*. Leipzig: Hinrich, 1933.

Mayer, Theodor. "Die Ausbildung der Grundlagen des modernen deutschen Staates im hohen Mittelalter." *Historische Zeitschrift* 159 (1939):457–87.

———, ed. *Der Vertrag von Verdun, 843: Neun Aufsätze zur Begründung der europäischen Völker- und Staatenwelt*. Leipzig: Koehler & Amelang, 1943.

Mayer-Homberg, Edwin. *Die fränkischen Volksrechte im Mittelalter: Eine rechtsgeschichtliche Untersuchung*. Vol. 1. Weimar: Böhlau, 1912.

Mazzaoui, Michel M. *The Origins of the Safawids: Šī'ism, Sūfism, and the Gulāt'*. Wiesbaden: Steiner, 1972.

McCagg, William O., Jr. *Jewish Nobles and Geniuses in Modern Hungary*. Boulder: East European Quarterly, 1972.

McNeill, William Hardy. *Europe's Steppe Frontier, 1500–1800*. Chicago: University of Chicago Press, 1964.

Mears, Elliot, ed. *Modern Turkey*. New York: Macmillan, 1924.

Medlin, William K. *Moscow and East Rome: A Political Study of the Relations of Church and State in Muscovite Russia*. Geneva: Droz, 1952.

Meier, Harri. "Spanische Sprachbetrachtung und Geschichtsschreibung am Ende des 15. Jahrhundert." *Romanische Forschungen* 49 (1935):1–20.

Meillet, Antoine. *Les Langues dans l'Europe Nouvelle*. Paris: Payot, 1928.

Meinecke, Friedrich. *Cosmopolitanism and the National State*. Trans. Robert B. Kimber. Princeton: Princeton University Press, 1970.

———. *Machiavellism: The Doctrine of Raison d'Etat and Its Place in Modern History*. Trans. Douglas Scott. London: Routledge & Kegan Paul, 1957.

Meitzen, August. *Siedlung und Agrarwesen der Westgermanen und Ostgermanen: Der Kelten, Römer, Finnen und Slawen*. Berlin: Hertz, 1895.

Mélanges de Droit Romain Dédiées à Georges Corneil. Vol. 1. Ghent: Vanderpoorten, 1926.

Mélanges Georges Smets. Brussels: Librairie Encyclopédique, 1952.

Mélanges Offerts à M. Gustave Schlumberger: A l'Occasion du Quatre-Vingtième Anniversaire de Sa Naissance, 17 October 1924. Vol. 1. Paris: Geuthner, 1924.

362 / Bibliography

Mélanges Paul Frédéricq: Homage de la Société pour le Progrès des Etudes Philosophiques et Historiques. 1904. Reprint. Geneva: Slatkins Reprints, 1975.

Mendelssohn, Sidney. *The Jews of Asia: Especially in the Sixteenth and Seventeenth Centuries.* London: Kegan Paul, Trench, Trubner & Co., 1920.

Menéndez Pidal, Ramón. *The Cid and His Spain.* Trans. Harold Sunderland. London: Cass, 1971.

———. *The Spaniards in Their History.* Trans. Walter Starkie. New York: Norton, 1950.

Merk, Walther. "Die deutschen Stämme in der Rechtsgeschichte." *Zeitschrift der Savigny-Stiftung für Rechtsgeschichte,* Germanistische Abteilung 85 (1938):1–41.

Meyer, Paul M. *Das Heerwesen der Ptolemäer und Römer in Aegypten.* Leipzig: Teubner, 1900.

Meynial, Edouard. "Remarques sur la Réaction Populaire contre l'Invasion du Droit Romain en France aux XII⁰ et XIII⁰ Siècles." *Romanische Forschungen* 23 (1907):557–84.

Mez, Adam. *The Renaissance of Islam.* Trans. Salahuddin Khuda Buksh. London: Luzac, 1937.

Mieses, Matthias. *Die Gesetze der Schriftgeschichte: Konfession und Schrift im Leben der Völker.* Vienna: Braumüller, 1919.

Miliukov, Peter. "Die Entwicklung des russischen Städtewesens." *Vierteljahrschrift für Sozial- und Wirtschaftsgeschichte* 14 (1916):130–46.

Millar, Fergus. *The Emperor in the Roman World, 31 BC–AD 337.* Ithaca: Cornell University Press, 1977.

Miller, Barnette. *The Palace School of Muhammad the Conqueror.* Cambridge: Harvard University Press, 1941.

Miller, Dean A. *Imperial Constantinople.* New York: Wiley, 1979.

Miller, Randall M., and Marzik, Thomas D. *Religion and Immigrants in Rural America.* Philadelphia: Temple University Press, 1977.

Millet, Gabriel, ed. *L'Art Byzantin chez les Slavs.* 2 vols. Paris: Geuthner, 1930, 1932.

Minorsky, Vladimir. *La Perse au XV⁰ Siècle entre la Turquie et la Venise.* Paris: Leroux, 1933.

Miquel, André. *La Géographie Humaine du Monde Musulman jusqu'au Milieu du 11⁰ Siècle.* Paris: Mouton, 1967.

———. *L'Islam et Sa Civilisation, VII⁰–XX⁰ Siècles.* Paris: Colin, 1968.

Mitrofanov, Pavel. *Joseph II: Seine politische und kulturelle Tätigkeit.* 2 vols. Trans. V. von Demelič. Vienna: Stern, 1910.

Mitzka, Walther. "Mundart und Verkehrsgeographie." *Zeitschrift für Mundartforschung* 11 (1935):1–5.

Mohr, Walter. *Die karolingische Reichsidee.* Münster: Aschendorff, 1962.

Mohrmann, Christine. "Le Latin Commun et le Latin des Chrétiens." *Vigiliae Christianae* 1 (1947):1–12.

———. "Linguistic Problems in the Early Christian Church." *Vigiliae Christianae* 11 (1957):11–36.

Molé, Marijan. "Les Kubrawija entre Sunnisme et Shiisme aux Huitième et Neuvième Siècles de l'Hégire." *Revue des Etudes Islamiques* 29 (1961):61–142.

Moles, Ian N. "Nationalism and Byzantine Greece." *Greek, Roman and Byzantine Studies* 10 (1969):95–108.

Mols, Roger. *Introduction à la Démographie Historique des Villes d'Europe du XIVᵉ au XVIIIᵉ Siècles*. Vol. 2. Louvain: Duculot, 1955.

Momigliano, Arnaldo, ed. *The Conflict between Paganism and Christianity in the Fourth Century*. Oxford: Clarendon, 1963.

Montagne, Robert. *La Civilisation du Désert*. Paris: Hachette, 1947.

Moret, Alexandre. *Histoire de l'Orient*. Vol. 1. Paris: Presses Universitaires, 1936.

———, and Davy, Georges. *From Tribe to Empire: Social Organization among Primitives and in the Ancient East*. London: Kegan Paul, Trench, Trübner, 1926.

Morf, Heinrich. "Zur sprachlichen Gliederung Frankreichs." Berlin, Preussische Akademie der Wissenschaften, Philosophisch-Historische Klasse, *Abhandlungen*, 1911.

Morgan, Jacques de. *The History of the Armenian People: From the Remotest Times to the Present Day*. Trans. Ernest F. Barry. N.p., n.d. (ca. 1918).

Mouradja d'Ohsson. *Tableau Général de l'Empire Ottoman*. Paris: Didot, 1824.

Mühlmann, W. E. "Ethnologie als soziologische Theorie der interethnischen Systeme." *Kölnisches Zeitschrift für Soziologie und Sozialpsychologie* 8 (1956):186–205.

———. "Pseudologische Gleichsetzung mit Fremdgruppen: Ein Teilfrage aus dem Problemkreis der ethnischen Assimilation." *Kölnisches Zeitschrift für Soziologie und Sozialpsychologie* 1 (1948–49),410–20.

Müller, Johannes. *Quellenschriften und Geschichte des deutschsprachlichen Unterrichtes bis zur Mitte des 16. Jahrhunderts*. Gotha: Thienemann, 1882.

Mülverstedt, G. A. von. "Ueber die Nationalität der Ritterbrüder des deutschen Ordens in Preussen im 15. Jahrhundert." *Correspondenzblatt des Gesamtvereines der deutschen Geschichts- und Alterthumsvereine* 19 (1871):17–22.

Münz, Isak. *Ueber die jüdischen Aerzte im Mittelalter*. Berlin: Driesner, 1887.

Musset, Lucien. *Les Invasions*. Paris: Presses Universitaires, 1965.

Musulin vom Gomirje, Alexander. *Das Haus am Ballplatz: Erinnerungen eines österreich-ungarischen Diplomaten*. Munich: Verlag für Kulturpolitik, 1924.

Nalbandian, Louise. *The Armenian Revolutionary Movement*. Berkeley: University of California Press, 1963.

Nau, François. "L'Expansion Nestorienne en Asie," *Annales du Musée Guimet, Bibliothèque de Vulgarisation* 40. Paris: Hachette, 1913.

Neuman, Abraham A. *The Jews of Spain*. 2 vols. Philadelphia: Jewish Publication Society of America, 1942.

Newman, William M. *American Pluralism: A Study of Minority Groups and Social Theory*. New York: Harper & Row, 1973.

Nolde, Boris. *La Formation de l'Empire Russe: Etudes, Notes et Documents*. 2 vols. Paris: Institut d'Etudes Slaves, 1952, 1953.

364 / Bibliography

Nöldeke, Theodor. "Zur Ausbreitung des Schiitismus." *Der Islam* 13 (1923):70–81.

Norberg, Dag. "A Quelle Epoque A-t-On Cessé de Parler Latin en Gaule?" *Annales* 21 (1966):346–56.

Nouvelles Etudes Historiques: Publiées à l'Occasion du XIIᵉ Congrès International des Sciences Historiques par la Commission Nationale des Historiens Hongrois. Vol. 1. Budapest: Akadémiai Kiadó, 1965.

Novak, Viktor. "The Slavonic-Latin Symbiosis in Dalmatia during the Middle Ages." *Slavonic and East European Review* 32 (1953):1–28.

Nový, Rostislav. *Die Anfänge des böhmischen Staats.* Part 1: *Mitteleuropa im 9. Jahrhundert.* Prague: Universitata Karlova, 1968.

Nyström, Samuel. *Beduinentum und Jahwismus: Eine soziologischreligions-geschichtliche Untersuchung zum Alten Testament.* Lund: Gleerup, 1946.

Obolensky, Dmitri. *The Byzantine Commonwealth: Eastern Europe 500–1453.* London: Weidenfeld & Nicolson, 1971.

————. "Nationalism in Eastern Europe in the Middle Ages." *Transactions of the Royal Historical Society,* 5th series 22 (1972):1–16.

Oestrich, Gerhard. *Geist und Gestalt des frühmodernen Staates.* Berlin: Duncker & Humblot, 1969.

Ohmann, Emil. *Ueber den italienischen Einfluss auf die deutsche Sprache bis zum Ausgang des Mittelalters.* Helsinki: Suomalaisen Tiedeakatemian Tvimituksia, 1942.

Olschki, Leonardo. *Geschichte der neusprachlichen wissenschaftlichen Literatur.* Vol. 1, Heidelberg: Carl Winter's Universitätsbuchhandlung, 1919; Vol. 2, Leipzig: Leo S. Olschki, 1922. Vaduz: Kraus reprint, 1965.

Olšr, P. Giuseppe, S.J. "Gli ultime Rurikidi e le Basi Ideologiche della Sovranità della Stato Russo." *Orientalia Christiana Periodica* 12 (1946):322–73.

L'Organisation Corporative du Moyen Age à la Fin de l'Ancien Régime. Etudes Presentées à la Commission Internationale pour l'Histoire des Assemblées d'Etats. Vol. 3. Louvain: Bibliothèque de l'Université, 1939.

Ostrogorsky, George. *History of the Byzantine State.* Trans. Joan Hussey. Oxford: Blackwell, 1956.

Pallas, P. G. *Reise durch verschiedene Provinzen des russischen Reichs.* 3 vols. (Vol. 1 in 2 parts.) St. Petersburg: Imperial Academy of Sciences, 1770, 1771, 1776.

Palm, Jonas. *Rom, Römertum und Imperium in der griechischen Literatur der Kaiserzeit.* Lund: Gleerup, 1959.

Palmov, N. N. *Etyudy po Istorii Privolzhskikh Kalmykov XVII i XVIII Veka.* Chast Pervaya. Astrakhan: Kalmytsky Oblastnoi Ispolitelny Komitet, 1926.

Panofsky, Erwin. *Renaissance and Renascences in Western Art.* 2 vols. Stockholm: Almqvist & Wiksell, 1960.

Paret, Rudi. *Der Islam und das griechische Bildungsgut.* Tübingen: Mohr, 1950.

Parker, Geoffrey. "Spain, Her Enemies and the Revolt of Netherlands." *Past and Present* 49 (1970):72–95.

Parkes, James. *The Jew in the Medieval Community: A Study of His Political and Economic Situation.* London: Soncino, 1938.

Parvan, Vasile. *Die Nationalität der Kaufleute im römischen Kaiserreiche*. Breslau: Fleischmann, 1909.

Paschoud, François. *Roma Aeterna: Etudes sur le Patriotisme dans l'Occident Latin à l'Epoque des Grandes Invasions*. Geneva: Institut Suisse de Rome, 1967.

Patai, Raphael. *Golden River to Golden Road: Society, Culture, and Change in the Middle East*. 3d ed. Philadelphia: University of Pennsylvania Press, 1969.

————. "Nomadism: Middle Eastern and Central Asia." *Southwest Journal of Anthropology* 7 (1951):401–14.

————. *Society, Culture and Change in the Middle East*. Philadelphia: University of Pennsylvania Press, 1971.

Patlagean, Evelyne. "Le Représentation Byzantine de la Parenté et ses Origines Occidentales." *L'Homme* 6, no. 4 (Oct.–Dec. 1966):59–81.

Patzelt, Erna. *Die fränkische Kultur und der Islam: Mit besonderer Berücksichtigung der nordischen Entwicklung*. Baden: Rudolph M. Rohrer, 1932.

Paul, Ulrich. *Studien zur Geschichte des deutschen Nationalbewusstseins im zeitalter des Humanismus und der Reformation*. Berlin: Ebering, 1936.

Peake, Harold, and Fleure, Herbert. *The Steppe and the Sown*. New Haven: Yale University Press, 1928.

Pelenski, Jaroslaw. "The Origins of the Official Muscovite Claims to the 'Kievan Inheritance.'" *Harvard Ukrainian Studies* 1 (1977):29–52.

————. *Russia and Kazan: Conquest and Imperial Ideology (1438–1560s)*. The Hague: Mouton, 1974.

Pelliot, Paul. "Les Plus Anciens Monuments de l'Ecriture Arabe en Chine." *Journal Asiatique*, 11ᵉ série, 2 (1913):177–91.

Peristiany, J. G., ed. *Honour and Shame: The Values of Mediterranean Society*. Chicago: University of Chicago Press, 1966.

Pervolf, Yusif. *Slavyane, Ikh Vzaimnyya Otnoshennya i Svyazi*. Vol. 1. Warsaw: Kovalevsky, 1886.

Peters, F. E. *The Harvest of Hellenism: A History of the Near East from Alexander the Great to the Triumph of Christianity*. London: Allen & Unwin, 1972.

Petit-Dutaillis, Charles. *The Feudal Monarchy in France and England from the Tenth to the Thirteenth Century*. London: Kegan Paul, Trench, Trübner, 1936.

Petri, Franz. *Zum Stand der Diskussion über die fränkische Landnahme*. Darmstadt: Wissenschaftliche Buchgemeinschaft, 1954.

Petrowicz, Greg. "L'Organisation Juridique des Arméniens sous les Monarques Polonais." *Revue des Etudes Arméniennes*, new series, 4 (1967):321–54.

Petrushevsky, I. P. "Gosudarskaya Znat v Gosudarstve Khulaguidov: K Istorii Vnutrennogo Stroya Gorodov Irana i Sopredelnykh Stran v Epokhu Mongolskogo Vladychestva." *Sovetskoye Vostokovedeniye* 5 (1948):85–110.

Peyer, Hans C. "Das Reisekönigtum des Mittelalters." *Vierteljahrschrift für Sozial- und Wirtschaftsgeschichte* 51 (1964):1–21.

Philippson, Alfred. "Das byzantinische Reich als geographische Erschienung." *Geographische Zeitschrift* 60 (1934):441–55.

Philippson, Martin. *Ein Ministerium unter Philip II: Kardinal Granvella am spanischen Hofe, 1579–1586*. Berlin: Cronbach, 1895.

Pierling, Paul. "Un Protagoniste du Panslavisme au XVIIᵉ Siècle: Mémoire Inédite du Iouri Krejanitch." *Revue des Questions Historiques* 49 (nouvelle série 15) (1896):186–200.

Pierson, Peter. *Philip II of Spain.* London: Thames & Hudson, 1975.

Piganiol, André. *L'Empire Chrétien, 325–395.* Paris: Presses Universitaires, 1972.

Pigulevskaya, Nina V. *Byzanz auf den Wegen nach Indien: Aus der Geschichte des byzantinischen Handels mit dem Orient vom 4. bis 6. Jahrhundert.* Trans. from Russian. Berlin: Akademie Verlag, 1969.

Planhol, Xavier de. "Caractères Généraux de la Vie Montagnarde dans le Proche-Orient et dans l'Afrique du Nord." *Annales de Géographie* 71 (1962):113–30.

———. "Géographie Politique et Nomadisme en Anatolie." *Revue Internationale des Sciences Sociales* 11 (1959):547–53.

———. *Le Monde Islamique: Essai de Géographie Réligieuse.* Paris: Presses Universitaires, 1957.

Planitz, Hans. *Die deutsche Stadt von der Römerzeit bis zu den Zunftkämpfen.* Graz: Böhlau, 1924.

———. *Germanische Rechtsgeschichte.* Berlin: Weidmann, 1936.

Plaumann, Gerhard. *Ptolemais in Oberägypten: Ein Beitrag zur Geschichte des Hellenismus in Aegypten.* Leipzig: Quelle & Meyer, 1910.

Poliak, Abraham N. "L'Arabisation de l'Orient Sémitique." *Revue des Etudes Islamiques* 12 (1938):35–63.

———. "Le Caractère Colonial de l'Etat Mamelouk dans Ses Rapports avec la Horde d'Or." *Revue des Etudes Islamiques* 9 (1935):231–48.

———. *Feudalism in Egypt, Syria, Palestine, and the Lebanon, 1250–1900.* London: The Royal Asiatic Society, 1939.

Poliakov, Léon. *The Aryan Myth: A History of Racist and Nationalist Ideas in Europe.* Trans. Edmund Howard. New York: Basic Books, 1974.

———, Delacampagne, Christian, and Girard, Patrick. *Le Racisme.* Paris: Seghers, 1976.

Polišenský, J. V. *War and Society in Europe, 1618–1648.* Cambridge: Cambridge University Press, 1978.

Polish Academy of Sciences. *L'Europe aux IXᵉ–XIᵉ Siècles: Aux Origines des Etats Nationaux.* Warsaw: Panstwowe Wydawnictwo Naukowe, 1968.

Polk, William R., and Chambers, Richard L., eds. *Beginnings of Modernization in the Middle East: The Nineteenth Century.* Chicago: University of Chicago Press, 1968.

Poncet, Jean. "L'Evolution des 'Genres de Vie' en Tunisie: Autour d'une Phrase d'Ibn Khaldoun." *Les Cahiers de Tunisie* 2 (1954):315–23.

———. "Le Mythe de la 'Catastrophe' Hilalienne." *Annales* 22 (1967):1099–1120.

Prawer, Joshua. *The World of the Crusaders.* London: Weidenfeld and Nicolson, 1972.

Preradovich, Nikolaus von. *Die Führungsschichten in Oesterreich und Preussen (1804–1918): Mit einem Ausblick bis zum Jahre 1945.* Wiesbaden: Steiner, 1955.

———. "Südslawen als Inhaber des österreichischen Militär-Maria-Theresien Ordens." *Südost-Forschungen* 13 (1954):285–91.

Presnyakov, A. E. *The Formation of the Great Russian State: A Study of Russian History in the Thirteenth to Fifteenth Centuries.* Trans. A. E. Moorhouse. Chicago: Quadrangle Books, 1970.

Press, Volker. *Calvinismus und Territorialstaat: Regierung und Zentralbehörden der Kurpfalz, 1559–1619.* Stuttgart: Klett, 1970.

Previté-Orton, C. W. *The Shorter Cambridge Medieval History.* 2 vols. Cambridge: Cambridge University Press, 1975.

Prinz, Friedrich. "Zur französischen Nationswerdung." *Bohemia* 16 (1975):51–69.

Quirin, Karl H. *Die deutsche Ostsiedlung im Mittelalter.* Göttingen: Musterschmidt, 1954.

Rabb, Theodore K., and Seigel, Jerrold E. *Action and Conviction in Early Modern Europe: Essays in Memory of E. H. Harbison.* Princeton: Princeton University Press, 1969.

Rabinow, Paul. *Symbolic Domination: Cultural Form and Historical Change in Morocco.* Chicago: University of Chicago Press, 1975.

Rachfal, Felix. "Die niederländische Verwaltung des 15./16. Jahrhunderts und ihr Einfluss auf die Verwaltungsreforme Maximilian I in Österreich und Deutschland." *Historische Zeitschrift* 110 (1913):1–66.

———. "Der Ursprung der monarchischen Behördenorganisation Deutschlands in der Neuzeit." *Jahrbücher für Nationalökonomie und Statistik* 105 (1915): 433–83.

Rádl, Emanuel. *Der Kampf zwischen Tschechen und Deutschen.* Trans. from Czech by Richard Brandeis. Reichenberg (Bohemia): Stiepel, 1928.

Ramsay, William M. "The Intermixture of Races in Asia Minor: Some of Its Causes and Effects." *Proceedings of the British Academy,* 1915–16, pp. 359–422.

Ranke, Leopold. *Histoire des Osmanlis et de la Monarchie Espagnole pendant les XVIᵉ et XVIIᵉ Siècles.* Trans. J. B. Haiber. Paris: Debécourt, 1839.

Ranum, Orest, ed. *National Consciousness, History, and Political Culture in Early Modern Europe.* Baltimore: Johns Hopkins University Press, 1975.

Rashdall, Hastings. *The Universities of Europe in the Middle Ages.* New ed. by F. M. Powicke and A. B. Emden. 3 vols. London: Oxford University Press, 1936.

Rassow, Peter. "Forschungen zur Reichs-Idee im 16. und 17. Jahrhundert." *Arbeitsgemeinschaft für Forschung des Landes Nordrhein-Westfalen, Geisteswissenschaften,* Heft 16. Cologne: Westdeutscher Verlag, 1955.

La Reconquista Española y la Repoblacion del Pais: Conferencia del Curso Celebrado en Jaca en Agosto de 1947. Zaragoza: Cursos del Instituto de Estudios Pirenaicos, 1951.

Recueils de la Société Jean Bodin. Vols. 6–7, *La Ville.* Brussels: Librairie Encyclopédique, 1954–55.

Redlich, Josep. *Das österreichische Staats- und Reichsproblem: Geschichtliche Darstellung der inneren Politik der habsburgischen Monarchie von 1848 bis zum Untergang des Reiches.* 2 vols. Leipzig: Der Neue Geist, 1920, 1926.

Rehfeldt, Bernhard. *Grenzen der vergleichenden Methode in der rechtsgeschichtlichen Forschung.* Bonn: Scheur, 1942.

Reichard, Hans. *Die deutschen Stadtrechte des Mittelalters in ihrer geographischen, politischen und wirtschaftlichen Begründung.* Berlin: Heymann, 1930.

Reimann, E. "Das Verhalten des Reiches gegen Livland in den Jahren 1559-1561." *Historische Zeitschrift* 53 (1876):346-80.

Reinhart, W. "Ueber die Territorialität der westgotischen Gesetzbuches." *Zeitschrift der Savigny Stiftung für Rechtsgeschichte*, Germanistische Abteilung, 68 (1951):348-54.

Remppis, Max. "Die Vorstellungen von Deutschland im altfranzösischen Heldenepos und Roman und ihre Quellen." *Zeitschrift für Romanische Philologie*, Beiheft 34, 1911.

La Renaissance et la Réformation en Pologne et en Hongrie. Budapest: Akadémiai Kiadó, 1963.

Reuling, Ulrich. *Die Kur in Deutschland und Frankreich: Untersuchungen zur Entwicklung des rechtförmlichen Wahlaktes bei der Königserhebung im 11. und 12. Jahrhundert.* Göttingen: Vandenhoeck & Ruprecht, 1979.

Reuter, Timothy, ed. and trans. *The Medieval Nobility: Studies on the Ruling Classes of France and Germany from the Sixth to the Twelfth Century.* Amsterdam: North Holland Publishing Co., 1978.

Rhode, Gotthold. "Die Ostgrenze Polens im Mittelalter." *Zeitschrift für Ostforschung* 2 (1953):15-65.

Ricard, Robert. "Destin et Problèmes de la Langue Espagnole." *Annales* 3 (1948):401-8.

Richard, Jean. *La Papauté et les Missions d'Orient au Moyen Age, XIII-XV Siècle.* Rome: Ecole Française de Rome, 1977.

Riché, Pierre. *Education et Culture dans l'Occident Barbare, VIe-VIIe Siècles.* Paris: Editions du Seuil, 1962.

Rörig, Fritz. *Die europäische Stadt und die Kultur des Bürgertums im Mittelalter.* Göttingen: Vandenhoeck & Ruprecht, 1953.

––––––. "Territorialwirtschaft und Stadtwirtschaft." *Historische Zeitschrift* 150 (1934):457-84.

Roscher, Wilhelm. "Die österreichische Nationalökonomik unter Kaiser Leopold I." *Jahrbücher für Nationalökonomie und Statistik* 2, vol. 1, Heft 1 (1864):25-59, 105-22.

Rosenqvist, Arvid. *Der französische Einfluss auf die mittelhochdeutsche Sprache in der ersten Hälfte des XIV. Jahrhunderts.* Helsinki: Philosophische Fakultät, Helsinki University, 1932.

Rosenstock, Eugen. *Königshaus und Stämme in Deutschland zwischen 911 und 1250.* Leipzig: Meiner, 1914.

Rosenthal, Eduard. *Die Behördenorganisation Kaiser Ferdinands I: Das Vorbild der Verwaltungsorganisation in den deutschen Territorien, Ein Beitrag zur Geschichte des Verwaltungsrechts. Archiv für Oesterreichische Geschichte* 69 (1887), pt. 2, pp. 53-316.

Rosenthal, Franz, trans. and ed. *Ibn Khaldûn, the Muqaddemah: An Introduction to History.* 3 vols. London: Routledge & Kegan Paul, 1958.

Roth, Cecil. *The House of Nasi: The Duke of Naxos.* Philadelphia: Jewish Publication Society of America, 1948.

Rothenberg, Gunther E. *The Austrian Military Border in Croatia, 1522-1747.* Urbana: University of Illinois Press, 1960.

Rothkirch, Wolfgang Graf von. *Architektur und monumentale Darstellung im hohen Mittelalter, 1100–1250.* Leipzig: Seemann, 1938.

Rouillard, Germaine. *L'Administration Civile de l'Egypte Byzantine.* Paris: Presses Universitaires, 1925.

Roux, Jean-Paul. "Le Chameau en Asie Centrale." *Central Asiatic Journal* 5 (1959):35–76.

———. *Les Traditions des Nomades de la Turquie Méridionale: Contribution à l'Etudes des Représentations Réligieuses des Sociétés Turques d'après les Enquêtes Effectuées chez les Yörük et les Tahtaci.* Paris: Maisonneuve, 1970.

Rozman, Gilbert. *Urban Networks in Russia, 1750–1800, and Premodern Periodization.* Princeton: Princeton University Press, 1976.

Rubin, Berthold. *Das Zeitalter Justinians.* Vol. 1. Berlin: De Gruyter, 1960.

Rudolph, Hans. *Stadt und Staat in römischen Italien.* Leipzig: Dieterich, 1935.

Runciman, Steven. *The Great Church in Captivity.* Cambridge: Cambridge University Press, 1968.

Russell, Josiah C. *Medieval Regions and Their Cities.* Bristol, Eng.: David & Charles, 1972.

———. "The Metropolitan City Region of the Middle Ages." *Journal of Regional Science* 2 (1960):55–70.

Sablonier, Roger. *Adel im Wandel: Eine Untersuchung zur sozialen Situation des ostschweizerischen Adels um 1300.* Göttingen: Vandenhoeck & Ruprecht, 1979.

Sa'd Al-din, Ibn Hassanjān. *Chronica dell'Origine e Progressi della Casa Ottomona.* Part 1. Trans. Vincenzo Bratutti. Vienna: Ricio, 1649.

Saladin, Henri. *Manuel d'Art Musulman.* Vol. 1, *L'Architecture.* Paris: Picard, 1907.

Salzmann, Philip C. "Political Organization among Nomadic Peoples." American Philosophical Society *Proceedings* 3 (1967):115–31.

Samsonowicz, Henryk. "Les Liens Culturels entre les Bourgeois du Littoral Baltique dans le Bas Moyen Age." *Studia Maritima,* 1 (1978):9–28.

Sanchez-Albornoz, Claudio. *Despoblacion y Repoblacion del Valle del Duero.* Buenos Aires: Instituto de Historia de España, Universidad de Buenos Aires, 1966.

Sanjian, Avedis K. *The Armenian Communities in Syria under Ottoman Dominion.* Cambridge: Harvard University Press, 1965.

Sarafian, Vahe A. "Turkish Armenian and Expatriate Population Statistics." *Armenian Review* 9 (1956):118–28.

Šaria, Balduin, ed. *Völker und Kultur Südosteuropas: Kulturhistorische Beiträge.* Munich: Südosteuropa-Gesellschaft, 1959.

Sarkisyanz, Emanuel. *Geschichte der orientalischen Völker Russlands bis 1917: Eine Ergänzung zur ostslawischen Geschichte Russlands.* Munich: Oldenbourg, 1961.

Saunders, John J. "The Nomad as Empire Builder: A Comparison of the Arab and Mongol Conquests." *Diogenes,* no. 52 (1965):79–103.

Sauvaget, Jean. *Alep: Essai sur le Développement d'une Grande Ville Syrienne des Origines au Milieu du XIXᵉ Siècle.* Paris: Geuthner, 1941.

———. "Esquisse d'une Histoire de la Ville de Damas." *Revue des Etudes Islamiques* 8 (1934):421–80.

370 / Bibliography

_____. *Introduction to the History of the Muslim East: A Bibliographical Guide.* Berkeley: University of California Press, 1965.

Savickij, P. N. "Les Problèmes de la Géographie Linguistique du Point de Vue du Géographie." *Travaux du Cercle Linguistique de Prague* 1 (1929):145–56.

Savory, R. M. "The Consolidation of Safawid Power in Persia." *Der Islam* 41 (1965):71–94.

_____. *Iran under the Safavids.* Cambridge: Cambridge University Press, 1980.

Sazonova, Julia. "The German in Russian Literature." *Slavic Review* 4 (1945): 51–79.

Schacht, Joseph. *An Introduction to Islamic Law.* Oxford: Clarendon, 1966.

_____. "Zur soziologischen Betrachtung des islamischen Rechts." *Der Islam* 22 (1935):206–38.

Schaeder, Hildegard. *Geschichte der Pläne zur Teilung des alten polnischen Staates seit 1386.* Vol. 1. Leipzig: Hirzel, 1937.

_____. *Moskau das dritte Rom: Studien zur Geschichte der politischen Theorien in der slawischen Welt.* Hamburg: Friedrichsen, De Gruyter, 1929.

Schaube, Adolf. *Handelsgeschichte der romanischen Völker des Mittelmeergebiets bis zum Ende der Kreuzzüge.* Munich: Oldenbourg, 1906.

Scheel, Helmut. "Die Staatsrechtliche Stellung der ökumenischen Kirchenfürsten in der alten Türkei." Preussische Akademie der Wissenschaften, Philosophisch-Historische Klasse, *Abhandlungen*, Jahrgang 1942, no. 9.

Scheffer-Boichorst, Paul. "Zur Geschichte der Syrer in Abendlande." *Mitteilungen des Instituts für Oesterreichische Geschichtsforschung* 5 (1884): 521–50.

Schemmel, Fritz. *Die Hochschule von Konstantinopel vom V. bis IX. Jahrhundert.* Berlin: Trowtsch, 1912.

Schemsi, Kara Safvet Bey. *Turcs et Arméniens devant l'Histoire.* Geneva: Imprimerie Nationale, 1919.

Schenk von Stauffenberg, Alexander. *Das Imperium und die Völkerwanderung.* Munich: Rinn, n.d.

Schier, Bruno. *Hauslandschaften und Kulturbewegungen im östlichen Mitteleuropa.* 2d ed. Göttingen: Schwartz, 1966.

Schlesinger, Walter. "Die deutsche Kirche im Sorbenland und die Kirchenverfassung auf westslawischem Boden." *Zeitschrift für Ostforschung* 1 (1952): 345–71.

_____. "Herrschaft und Gefolgschaft in der germanisch-deutschen Verfassungsgeschichte." *Historische Zeitschrift* 176 (1953):225–75.

Schlierer, Richard. *Weltherrschaftsgedanke und altdeutsches Kaisertum: Eine Untersuchung über die Bedeutung des Weltherrschaftsgedankens für die Staatsidee des deutschen Mittelalters vom 10. bis 12. Jahrhundert.* Darmstadt: Wissenschaftliche Buchgesellschaft, 1968.

Schlipp, Paul A., ed. *The Philosophy of Ernst Cassirer.* Evanston: Library of Living Philosophers, 1949.

Schlumberger, Gustave. *L'Epopée Byzantine à la Fin du Dixième Siècle.* 3 vols. Paris: Hachette, 1896–1905.

Schmalfuss, A. "Das deutsche Städtewesen und sein politischer und sozialer

Einfluss auf Land und Volk im Böhmen und seinen Nebenländern." *Mittheilungen des Vereines für Geschichte der Deutschen in Böhmen* 3 (1865):1-12.

Schmid, Heinrich F. "Das Recht der Gründung und Ausstattung von Kirchen im Kolonialen Teile der Magdeburger Kirchenprovinz während des Mittelalters." *Zeitschrift der Savigny Stiftung für Rechtsgeschichte*, Kanonistische Abteilung, 13 (1924):3-214.

———. "Die sozialgeschichtliche Erforschung der mittelalterlichen deutschrechtlichen Siedlung auf polnischem Boden." *Vierteljahrschrift für Sozial- und Wirtschaftsgeschichte* 20 (1927):301-55.

Schmid, Karl. "Zur Problematik von Familie, Sippe und Geschlecht, Haus und Dynastie beim mittelalterlichen Adel." *Zeitschrift für Geschichte des Oberrheins*, Neue Folge, 66 (1957):1-62.

Schmid, Wilhelm. *Ueber den kulturgeschichtlichen Zusammenhang und die Bedeutung der griechischen Renaissance in der Römerzeit.* Leipzig: Dieterich, 1898.

Schmidt, Berthold. *Die späte Völkerwanderungszeit im Mitteldeutschland.* Halle: Niemeyer, 1961.

Schmidt, Kurt D. *Die Bekehrung der Germanen zum Christentum.* Göttingen: Vandenhoeck & Ruprecht, n.d. (ca. 1941).

Schmidt-Rohr, Georg. *Die Sprache als Bilderin der Völker.* Jena: Diederich, 1932.

Schmitt, Ludwig E. *Untersuchungen zu Entstehung und Struktur der "Neuhochdeutschen" Schriftsprache.* Vol. 1. Cologne: Böhlau, 1966.

Schnee, Heinrich. *Die Hoffinanz und der moderne Staat.* Vol. 1. Berlin: Duncker & Humblot, 1953.

Schneider, Fedor. *Rom und Romgedanke im Mittelalter: Die geistigen Grundlagen der Renaissance.* Munich: Drei Masken, 1926.

Schneidmüller, Bernd. *Karolingische Tradition und frühes französisches Königtum.* Wiesbaden: Steiner, 1979.

Schöffler, Herbert. *Abendland und Altes Testament: Untersuchung zur Kulturmorphologie Europas, inbesondere Englands.* Bochum-Langendreer: Poppinghaus, 1937.

Schramm, Percy E. *Herrschaftszeichen und Staatssymbolik: Beiträge zu ihrer Geschichte vom dritten bis zum sechszehnten Jahrhundert.* 3 vols. Stuttgart: Hiersemann, 1954, 1955, 1956.

———. *Kaiser, Rom und Renovation: Studien und Texte zur Geschichte des römischen Erneuerungsgedankens vom Ende des karolingischen Reiches bis zum Investiturstreit.* 2 vols. Leipzig: Teubner, 1929.

———. *Der König von Frankreich: Das Wesen der Monarchie vom 9. zum 16. Jahrhundert.* 2 vols. Weimar: Böhlau, 1960.

Schröder, Richard. "Die Franken und ihr Recht." *Zeitschrift der Savigny Stiftung für Rechtsgeschichte*, Germanistische Abteilung, 2 (1881):1-82.

Schubart, Wilhelm. "Die Griechen in Ägypten." *Beihefte zum "Alten Orient,"* Heft 10 (1927), pp. 5-54.

Schubart-Fikentscher, Gertrud. *Die Verbreitung der deutschen Stadtrechte in Osteuropa.* Weimar: Böhlau, 1942.

Schubert, Ernst. *König und Reich: Studien zur spätmittelalterlichen deutschen Verfassungsgeschichte.* Göttingen: Vandenhoeck & Ruprecht, 1979.

Schubert, Hans von. "Die sogennanten Slavenapostel." Heidelberg, Akademie der Wissenschaften, Philosophisch-Historische Klasse, *Sitzungberichte* 1 (1916):3–32.

Schulze, Eduard O. *Die Kolonisierung und Germanisierung der Gebiete zwischen Saale und Elbe.* Leipzig: Hirzel, 1896.

Schünemann, Konrad. *Die Deutschen in Ungarn bis zum 12. Jahrhundert.* Berlin: De Gruyter, 1923.

——. *Die Entstehung des Städtewesens in Südosteuropa.* Vol. 1. Breslau: Priebatsch, n.d.

——. *Oesterreichs Bevölkerungspolitik unter Maria Theresia.* Vol. 1. Berlin: Deutsche Rundschau, n.d. (ca. 1930).

——. "Zur Geschichte des deutschen Landesausbaus im Mittelalter." *Südostdeutsche Forschungen* 1 (1936):30–46.

Schwarber, Karl, ed. *Festschrift Gustav Binz.* Basel: Schwabe, 1935.

Schwartner, Martin. *Statistik des Königreichs Ungern: Ein Versuch.* Pest: Trattner, 1798.

Schwarz, Ernst. "Bairische und ostfränkische Ostsiedlung im Mittelalter." Munich, *Deutsche Akademie zur Wissenschaftlichen Erforschung* 1 (1935):661–72.

Schwarz, Henry F. *The Imperial Privy Council in the Seventeenth Century.* Cambridge: Harvard University Press, 1943.

Schwicker, J. H. *Geschichte des oesterreichischen Militärgrenze.* Vienna: Prochaska, 1883.

Sebeok, Thomas A., ed. *Myth: A Symposium.* Bloomington: Indiana University Press, 1974.

Seel, Otto. *Römertum und Latinität.* Stuttgart: Klett, 1964.

Seipel, Ignaz. *Nation und Staat.* Vienna: Bräumüller, 1916.

Sestan, Ernesto. "La Composizione Etnica della Società in Rapporto allo Svolgimento della Civiltà in Italia nel Secolo VII." *Settimane di Studio del Centro Italiano di Studi sull'Alto Medioevo* 5, pt. 2 (1957):649–77.

Seton-Watson, Hugh. *Nations and States.* Boulder: Westview Press, 1977.

Setton, Kenneth M. *A History of the Crusades.* 4 vols. Madison: University of Wisconsin Press, 1969–77.

Shaban, M. A. *The 'Abbāsid Revolution.* Cambridge: Cambridge University Press, 1970.

——. *Islamic History, A.D. 600–750 (A.H. 132): A New Interpretation.* Cambridge: Cambridge University Press, 1971.

Shakhmatov, Aleksei. *Korotkyi Naris Istoriyi Ukrayinskoyi Movy.* Trans. from Russian by Vasyl Demyanchuk. Kiev: Istorychny-Filologichny Vidil Ukrayinskyi Akademiyi Nauk, 1934.

Sharf, Andrew. *Byzantine Jewry from Justinian to the Fourth Crusade.* London: Routledge & Kegan Paul, 1971.

Shay, Mary L. *The Ottoman Empire from 1720 to 1734 as Revealed in Despatches of the Venetian Baili.* Urbana: University of Illinois Press, 1944.

Shneidman, J. Lee. *The Rise of Aragonese-Catalan Empire, 1200–1350.* 2 vols. New York; New York University Press, 1970.

Sieger, Robert. *Die geographischen Grundlagen der Oesterreichisch-Ungarischen*

Monarchie und ihrer Aussenpolitik. Leipzig: Teubner, 1915. (Offprint of *Geographische Zeitschrift* 21.)

Simson, Otto G. von. *Sacred Fortress: Byzantine Art and Statecraft in Ravenna.* Chicago: University of Chicago Press, 1948.

Sinor, Denis, ed. *Orientalism and History:* Cambridge: Heffer, 1954.

———. "The Outlines of Hungarian Prehistory." *Journal of World History* 4 (1958):513–40.

Šišić, Ferdinand von. *Geschichte der Kroaten.* Zagreb: "Matica Hrvatska," 1917.

Sivan, Emmanuel. *L'Islam et la Croisade: Idéologie et Propagande dans les Réactions Musulmanes aux Croisades.* Paris: Maisonneuve, 1968.

Sjoberg, Gideon. *The Preindustrial City: Past and Present.* Glencoe: Free Press, 1960.

Slouschz, Nahum. *Hébraeo-Phéniciens et Judéo-Berbères: Introduction à l'Histoire des Juifs et du Judaisme en Afrique.* Paris: Leroux, 1908.

Smith, E. Baldwin. *The Dome: A Study in the History of Ideas.* Princeton: Princeton University Press, 1950.

Sohm, Rudolph. "Fränkisches Recht und römisches Recht." *Zeitschrift der Savigny Stiftung für Rechtsgeschichte,* Germanistische Abteilung 1 (1880):1–84.

Sohrweide, Hanna. "Dichter und Gelehrte aus dem Osten im osmanischen Reich (1453–1600)." *Der Islam* 46 (1970):263–302.

———. "Der Sieg der Safaviden in Persien und seine Rückwirkungen auf die Shiiten Anatoliens im 16. Jahrhundert." *Der Islam* 41 (1965):95–223.

Soloviev, Alexander V. "Der Einfluss des byzantinischen Rechts auf die Völker Osteuropas." *Zeitschrift der Savigny Stiftung für Rechtsgeschichte,* Romanistische Abteilung 76 (1959):432–79.

Sommerfeldt, Gustav. "Die Beratungen über eine gegen Russland und die Türkei zu genährende Reichshilfe, 1560–1561." *Historische Vierteljahrschrift* 13 (1910):191–200.

Somssich, Paul von. *Das Legitime Recht Ungarns und seines Königs.* Vienna: Jasper, Hügel & Manz, 1850.

Sorel, Albert. *L'Europe et la Révolution Française.* Vol. 1. Paris: Plon, n.d.

Sourdel, Dominique. *Le Vizirat 'Abbāside de 749 à 936 (132 à 324 de l'Hégire).* 2 vols. Damascus: Institut Français de Damas, 1959, 1960.

———, and Sourdel, Janine. *La Civilisation de l'Islam Classique.* Paris: Arthaud, 1968.

Southern, R. W. *The Making of the Middle Ages.* 1953. Rev. ed. New Haven: Yale University Press, 1965.

Spěváček, Jiří. *Karl IV: Sein Leben und seine staatsmännische Leistung.* Prague: Akademia, Nakladelstvi Československé Akademie Věd, 1978.

Sproemberg, Heinrich. "Residenz und Territorium im niederländischen Raum." *Rheinische Vierteljahrsblätter* 6 (1936):113–39.

Spuler, Bertold. *Die Mongolen in Iran: Politik, Verwaltung und Kultur der Ilchanzeit, 1220–1350.* Leipzig: Hinrich, 1939.

———. *The Muslim World: A Historical Survey.* Trans. F. R. C. Bagley. 2 vols. Leiden: Brill, 1960.

Srbik, Heinrich von. *Das Oesterreichische Kaisertum und das Ende des Heiligen*

374 / Bibliography

Römischen Reiches, 1804–1806. Berlin: Deutsche Verlagsgesellschaft für Politik und Geschichte, 1927.

Steen de Jehay, F. van den. *De la Situation Légale des Sujets Ottomans Non-Musulmans*. Brussels: Schepens, 1906.

Stein, Ernest. *Histoire du Bas-Empire*. Trans. from German by Jean-Remy Palanque. 2 vols. N.p.: Desclée de Brouwer, 1949, 1959.

Steinacker, Harold. "Volk, Staat, Heimat und ihre Verhältnis bei den romanisch-germanischen Völkern." *Bulletin of the International Committee of Historical Sciences* 2, pt. 1, no. 6 (May 1929). Sixième Congrès International des Sciences Historiques, Oslo, 1928: Actes du Congrès. N.p.: Le Comité Organisateur du Congrès, pp. 273–301.

Steinbach, Franz. "Gibt es ein lotharingisches Raum?" *Rheinische Vierteljahrsblätter* 9 (1939):52–66.

_____. *Studien zur westdeutschen Stamm- und Volksgeschichte*. Jena: Fischer, 1926.

Stengel, Edmund E. *Regnum und Imperium: Engeres und weiteres Staatsgebiet im alten Reich*. Rede bei der akademischen Reichsgründungsfeier am 18. Januar 1930 in der Aula der Universität Marburg. Marburg: Elwert, 1930.

Stengers, Jean. *La Formation de la Frontière Linguistique en Belgique: Ou de la Légitimité de l'Hypothèse Historique*. Brussels: Latomus, Revue d'Etudes Latines, 1954.

Stoianovich, Traian. "The Conquering Balkan Orthodox Merchant." *Journal of Economic History* 20 (1960):234–313.

_____. *French Historical Method: The Annales Paradigm*. Foreword by Fernand Braudel. Ithaca: Cornell University Press, 1976.

Stökl, Günther. "Die Begriffe Reich, Herrschaft und Staat bei den orthodoxen Slawen." *Saeculum* 5 (1954):104–18.

_____. *Die Entstehung des Kosakentums*. Munich: Isar, 1953.

_____. "Die politische Religiosität des Mittelalters und die Entstehung des Moskauer Staates." *Saeculum* 2 (1951):393–415.

Storoni Mazzolani, Lidia. *The Idea of the City in Roman Thought: From Walled City to Spiritual Commonwealth*. Trans. S. O'Donnell. London: Hollis & Carter, 1970.

Strayer, Joseph R. *Medieval Statecraft and the Perspectives of History*. Princeton: Princeton University Press, 1971.

Stroheker, Karl F. *Germanentum und Spätantike*. Zurich: Artemis, 1965.

Structure Sociale et Développement Culturel des Villes Sud-Est Européennes et Adriatiques aux XVIIe–XVIIIe Siècles. Bucharest: Association Internationale d'Etudes du Sud-Est Européen, 1975.

Strzygowski, Josef. *Origin of Christian Church Art: New Facts and Principles of Research*. Trans. O. M. Dalton and H. J. Braunholtz. Oxford: Clarendon, 1923.

Sturmberger, Hans. *Kaiser Ferdinand II und das Problem des Absolutismus*. Munich: Oldenbourg, 1957.

Sugar, Peter F. *Southeastern Europe under Ottoman Rule, 1354–1804*. Seattle: University of Washington Press, 1977.

Suolahti, Hugo. *Der französische Einfluss auf die deutsche Sprache im dreizehnten Jahrhundert*. Helsinki: Société Néo-Philologique, 1929.

Svoronos, Nicholas G. *Le Commerce de Salonique au XVIII Siècle*. Paris: Presses Universitaires, 1956.

Swift, Emerson H. *Roman Sources of Christian Art*. New York: Columbia University Press, 1951.

Tafrali, Oreste. *Thessalonique au Quatorzième Siècle*. Paris: Guethner, 1913.

————. *Thessalonique: Des Origines au XIVᵉ Siècle*. Paris: Leroux, 1919.

Tamrati, Michel. *L'Eglise Géorgienne des Origines jusqu'à Nos Jours*. Rome: Société Typographico-Editrice Romaine, 1910.

Tavernier, J. B. *Nouvelle Rélation de l'Intérieur du Serrail du Grand Seigneur: Contenant Plusieurs Singularitéz Qui jusqu'icy n'Ont Point Esté Misés en Lumière*. Paris: Varennes, 1675.

Tellenbach, Gerd. *Königtum und Stämme in der Werdezeit des deutschen Reiches*. Weimar: Böhlau, 1939.

————. "Die Unteilbarkeit des Reiches: Ein Beitrag zur Entstehungsgeschichte Deutschlands und Frankreiches." *Historische Zeitschrift* 163 (1940):20–42.

————, ed. *Studien und Vorarbeiten zur Geschichte des grossfränkischen und frühdeutschen Adels*. Freiburg im Breisgau: Albert, 1957.

Ter-Mikelian, Aršak. *Die armenische Kirche in ihren Beziehungen zur byzantinischem: Vom IV. bis zum XII. Jahrhundert*. Leipzig: Gustav-Fock, 1892.

Ter-Minassiantz, Erwand. *Die armenische Kirche in ihren Beziehungen zu den syrischen Kirchen bis zum Ende des 13. Jahrhunderts: Nach dem armenischen und syrischen Quellen*. Leipzig: Hinrich, 1904.

Terracini, Aron Benvenuto. *Conflitti di Lingue et di Cultura*. Venice: Pozza, 1957.

Tezner, Friedrich. "Der österreichische Kaisertitel, seine Geschichte und seine politische Bedeutung." *Zeitschrift für das Privat- und Öffentliche Recht* 25 (1898):357–428.

Thiriet, Freddy. *La Romanie Vénitienne au Moyen Age*. Bibliothèque des Ecoles Françaises d'Athènes et de Rome, 183 (1959).

Thoumin, Richard. *Géographie Humaine de la Syrie Centrale*. Paris: Leroux, 1936.

Tikhomirov, M. N. *The Towns of Ancient Rus*. Moscow: Foreign Languages Publishing House, 1959.

Tikhvinsky, S. L., ed. *Tataro-Mongoly v Asii i Evrope: Sbornik Statei*. 2d ed. Moscow: "Nauka," 1977.

Tilly, Charles, ed. *The Formation of National States in Western Europe*. Princeton: Princeton University Press, 1975.

To Honor Roman Jakobson. Vol. 3. The Hague: Mouton, 1967.

Todorov, N. *Balkansky Gorod XV–XIX Vekov*. Moscow: "Nauka," 1976.

Toman, Hugo. *Das böhmische Staatsrecht und die Entwickelung des österreichischen Reichsidee vom Jahre 1527 bis 1848*. Prague: Calve, 1872.

Tomassin, Richard F., ed *Comparative Studies in Sociology: An Annual Compilation of Research*. Vol. 1. Greenwich, Conn.: JAI Press, 1978.

Toynbee, Arnold J. *A Study of History*. Abridgement of vols. 1–6 by D. C. Somervell. New York: Oxford University Press, 1947.

Trautmann, Reinhold. *Die slavischen Völker und Sprachen*. Göttingen: Vandenhoeck & Ruprecht, 1947.

Treadgold, Warren T. "The Revival of Byzantine Learning and the Byzantine State." *American Historical Review* 84 (1979):1245–66.

Treitinger, Otto. *Die oströmische Kaiser- und Reichsidee nach ihrer Gestaltung im höfischen Zeremoniell*. Jena: Biedermann, 1938.

Tritton, A. S. *The Caliphs and Their Non-Muslim Subjects*. 1930. Reprint. London: Cass, 1970.

Trusen, Winfried. *Anfänge des gelehrten Rechts in Deutschland: Ein Beitrag zur Geschichte der Frührezeption*. Wiesbaden: Steiner, 1962.

Tscherikower, Avigdor V. "Die hellenistischen Städtegründungen von Alexander dem Grossen bis auf die Römerzeit." *Philologus*, Supplement vol. 19 (1927), Heft 1.

Turan, Osman. "The Ideal of World Domination among the Medieval Turks." *Studia Islamica* 4 (1955):76–90.

————. "L'Islamisation dans la Turquie du Moyen Age." *Studia Islamica* 10 (1959):137–52.

Turck, Rudolph. *Die frühmittelalterlichen Stammegebiete in Böhmen*. Prague: Československá Společnost Archeologická při Československe Akademii Věd v Praze, 1957.

Turczynski, Emanuel. *Konfession und Nation: Zur Frühgeschichte der serbischen und rumänischen Nationalbildung*. Düsseldorf: Schwann, 1976.

Tushin, Yu. P. *Russkoye Moreplavaniye na Kaspiiskom, Azovskom i Chernom Moryakh, XVII Bek*. Moscow: "Nauka," 1978.

Uebersberger, Hans. *Österreich und Russland seit dem Ende des 15. Jahrhunderts*. Vol. 1. Vienna: Braumüller, 1906.

Uhlemann, Walter. "Zur Frage nach dem Ursprung und der Herkunft der Deutschen in Böhmen und Mähren." *Historische Vierteljahrschrift* 22 (1924–25):541–49.

Ullmann, Walter. *The Carolingian Renaissance and the Idea of Kingship*. London: Methuen, 1969.

————. *Law and Politics in the Middle Ages: An Introduction to the Sources of Medieval Political Ideas*. London: The Sources of History, 1975.

Unbegaun, Boris O. "Le Calque dans les Langues Slaves Littéraires." *Revue des Etudes Slaves* 12 (1932):19–48.

————. "Le Russe Littéraire Est-il d'Origine Russe?" *Revue des Etudes Slaves* 64 (1965):19–28.

Untersuchungen zur gesellschaftlichen Struktur der mittelalterlichen Städte in Europa: Reichenau Vorträge, 1963–64. Constance: Thorbecke, 1966.

Uspensky, F. I. *Ocherki iz Istorii Trapezuntskoi Imperii*. Leningrad: Akademiya Nauk SSSR, 1929.

Vacalopoulos, Apostlos E. *Origins of the Greek Nation*. Trans. Ian Moles. New Brunswick: Rutgers University Press, 1970.

Valjavec, Fritz. *Geschichte der deutschen Kulturbeziehungen zu Südosteuropa*. Munich: Oldenbourg. Vol. 1, 1953; vol. 2, 1955; vol. 3, 1958; vol. 4, 1965; vol. 5, 1970.

_____. *Der Josephinismus: Zur geistigen Entwicklung Oesterreichs im achtzehnten und neunzehnten Jahrhundert.* 2d ed. Munich: Oldenbourg, 1945.

van der Meer, F., and Mohrmann, Christine. *Atlas of the Early Christian World.* Trans. Macy F. Hedlund and H. H. Rowley. London: Nelson, 1959.

Van Vloten, Gerlof. *Recherches sur la Domination Arabe, le Chiitisme et les Croyances Messianiques sous le Khalifat des Omayades.* Amsterdam: Müller, 1894.

Varagnac, André. *Civilisation Traditionnelle et Genres de Vie.* Paris: Michel, 1948.

Vasiliev, A. A. *Byzance et les Arabes.* Ed. and trans. from Russian by Henri Grégoire and Marius Canard. Brussels: Université Libre de Bruxelles, 1935.

_____. *History of the Byzantine Empire, 324–1453.* 2 vols. Madison: University of Wisconsin Press, 1958.

Vasmer, Max. "Die Slaven in Griechenland." Berlin: Preussische Akademie der Wissenschaften, Philosophisch-Historische Klasse, *Abhandlungen*, 1941, no. 12.

Vaughn, Dorothy M. *Europe and the Turk: A Pattern of Alliances, 1350–1700.* Liverpool: Liverpool University Press, 1954.

Vavřinek, Vladimir. "Die Christianisierung und Kirchenorganisation Grossmährens." *Historica* 7 (1963):5–56.

Verlinden, Charles. *L'Esclavage dans l'Europe Médiévale.* Vol. 1, Bruges: "De Tempel," 1955; vol. 2, Ghent: Riksuniversitet te Gent, 1977.

_____. *Les Origines de la Frontière Linguistique en Belgique et la Colonisation Franque.* Brussels: La Renaissance de la Livre, 1955.

Vernadsky, George. *The Origins of Russia.* Oxford: Clarendon, 1959.

_____. "Der sarmatische Hintergrund der germanischen Völkerwanderung." *Saeculum* 2 (1951):340–92.

Vernant, Jean-Pierre. "Espace et Organisation Politique en Grèce Ancienne." *Annales* 20 (1965):576–95.

Veyne, Paul. *Comment On Ecrit l'Histoire: Essai d'Epistémologie.* Paris: Seuil, 1971.

Vicens Vives, Jaime, ed. *Historia Social y Economica de España y America.* 5 vols. Barcelona: Tiede, 1957–59.

Vigener, Fritz. *Bezeichungen für Volk und Land der deutschen vom 10. bis zum 13. Jahrhundert.* Heidelberg: Winter, 1901.

Vildomec, Věroboj. *Multilingualism.* Leyden: Sythoff, 1963.

Vinski, Zdenko. *Die südslavische Grossfamilie in ihrer Beziehung zum asiatischen Grossraum.* Zagreb: Tiskara Kuzmi Rožmanić, 1938.

Vladimirtsov, Boris. *Gengis-Khan.* Trans. Michel Carsow. Paris: Maisonneuve, 1948.

_____. *Le Régime Social des Mongols.* Paris: Maisonneuve, 1948.

Vlasto, A. P. *The Entry of the Slavs into Christendom: An Introduction to the Medieval History of the Slavs.* Cambridge: Cambridge University Press, 1970.

Vogt, Joseph. *Ancient Slavery and the Ideal of Man.* Trans. Thomas Weidemann. Cambridge: Harvard University Press, 1975.

_____. *The Decline of Rome: The Metamorphosis of Ancient Civilization.* Trans. Janet Sondheimer. London: Weidenfeld & Nicolson, 1967.

Vom Deutschen Osten: Max Friedrichsen zum 60. Geburtstag. Breslau: Marcus, 1934.

378 / Bibliography

Von Grunebaum, Gustave E. *Islam: Essays in the Nature and Growth of a Cultural Tradition.* 2d ed. London: Routledge & Kegan Paul, 1961.

———. *Medieval Islam: A Study in Cultural Orientation.* 2d ed. Chicago: University of Chicago Press, 1953.

———. *Modern Islam: The Search for Cultural Identity.* Berkeley: University of California Press, 1962.

———. "The Spirit of Islam as Shown in Its Literature." *Studia Islamica* 1 (1953):101–19.

———, ed. *Unity and Variety in Muslim Civilization.* Chicago: University of Chicago Press, 1955.

———, and Roger Caillois, eds. *The Dream and Human Societies.* Berkeley: University of California Press, 1966.

Vossler, Karl. *Aus der romanischen Welt.* Karlsruhe: Stahlberg, 1948.

———. *Medieval Culture: An Introduction to Dante and His Times.* Trans. William C. Lawton. 2 vols. New York: Harcourt, Brace, 1929.

Vryonis, Speros, Jr. *The Decline of Medieval Hellenism in Asia Minor and the Process of Islamization from the Eleventh through the Fifteenth Century.* Berkeley: University of California Press, 1971.

———, ed. *Islam and Cultural Change in the Middle East.* Wiesbaden: Harrassowitz, 1975.

Wächter, Albert. *Der Verfall des Griechentums in Kleinasien im XIV. Jahrhundert.* Leipzig: Teubner, 1902.

Walek-Czernecki, M. T. "La Rôle de la Nationalité dans l'Histoire de l'Antiquité." *Bulletin of the International Committee of Historical Sciences* 2, pt. 1, no. 6 (1929):303–20.

Waley, Daniel. *The Italian City Republics.* London: Weidenfeld & Nicolson, 1969.

Walicki, Andrzej. *The Slavophile Controversy: History of a Conservative Utopia in Nineteenth-Century Russian Thought.* Oxford: Clarendon, 1975.

Walker, Mack. *German Home Towns: Community, State, and General Estate, 1648–1871.* Ithaca: Cornell University Press, 1971.

Wallach, Richard. *Das abendländische Gemeinschaftsbewusstsein im Mittelalter.* Leipzig: Teubner, 1928.

Walser, Fritz. *Die spanischen Zentralbehörden und der Staatsrat Karls V.* Ed. and expanded by Rainer Wohlfeil. Göttingen: Vandenhoeck & Ruprecht, 1959.

Walter, Friedrich. *Österreichische Verfassungs- und Verwaltungsgeschichte von 1500–1955: Aus dem Nachlass herausgegeben von Adam Wandruszka.* Vienna: Böhlau, 1972.

———, and Steinacker, Harold. *Die Nationalitätenfrage im alten Ungarn und die Südostpolitik Wiens.* Munich: Oldenbourg, 1959.

Walther, Andreas. *Die burgundischen Zentralbehörden unter Maximilian I und Karl V.* Leipzig: Duncker & Humblot, 1909.

Wartburg, Walther von. *Die Ausgliederung des romanischen Sprachräume.* Bern: Francke, 1950.

———. *Problems and Methods in Linguistics.* Rev. ed. in collaboration with Stephen Ullman. Oxford: Blackwell, 1969.

Bibliography / 379

———. "Umfang und Bedeutung der germanischen Siedlung in Nordgallien im 5. und 6. Jahrhundert." Berlin: Deutsche Akademie der Wissenschaften, *Vorträge und Schriften*, Heft 36, 1950.

Watt, H. Montgomery. *Islam and the Integration of Society*. Evanston: Northwestern University Press, 1961.

Weber, Simon. *Die katholische Kirche in Armenien: Ihre Begründung und Entwicklung vor der Trennung, Ein Beitrag zur christlichen Kirchen- und Kulturgeschichte.* Freiburg im Breisgau: Herder, 1903.

Weigle, Fritz. *Die Matrikel der deutschen Nation in Siena, 1573–1738.* 2 vols. Tübingen: Niemeyer, 1962.

Weinreich, Uriel. *Languages in Contact.* 1963. Reprint. The Hague: Mouton, 1970.

Weiss, Richard. "Sprachgrenzen und Konfessiongrenzen als Kulturgrenzen: Auf Grund des Atlases der schweizerischen Volkskunde." *Laos* 1 (1951):96–110.

Weitzmann, Kurt. "The Survival of Mythological Representations in Early Christian and Byzantine Art and Their Impact on Christian Iconography." *Dumbarton Oaks Papers* 14 (1960):43–68.

Wellhausen, Julius. *Das arabische Reich und sein Sturz.* Berlin: Reimer, 1902.

Wenger, Leopold. "Volk und Staat in Aegypten am Ausgang der Römerherrschaft." Bayerische Akademie der Wissenschaft, Historische Klasse, *Sitzungsberichte*, 1921.

Wenskus, Reinhard. *Sächischer Stammesadel und fränkischer Reichadel.* Göttingen: Vandenhoeck & Ruprecht, 1976.

———. *Stammesbildung und Verfassung: Das Werden der frühmittelalterlichen gentes.* Cologne: Böhlau, 1961.

Werblowsky, R. J. Z. *The Meaning of Jerusalem to Jews, Christians and Muslims.* Jerusalem: Israel Universities Study Group for Middle Eastern Affairs, 1977.

Werner, Ernst. *Die Geburt einer Grossmacht—Die Osmanen (1300–1481): Ein Beitrag zur Genesis des türkischen Feudalismus.* Berlin: Akademie Verlag, 1966.

Werner, Karl F. "Die Entstehung des *Reditus Regni Francorum ad Stirpem Karoli*." Doctoral dissertation, Ruprecht-Karl University, Heidelberg, 1955.

Westermarck, Edward. *Survivances Païennes dans la Civilisation Mahométane.* Trans. from German by Robert Godet. Paris: Payot, 1935.

Weulersse, Jacques. *Paysans de Syrie et du Proche-Orient.* 6th ed. Paris: Gallimard, 1946.

Whiteley, W. H., ed. *Language Use and Social Change: Problems of Multilingualism with Special Reference to Eastern Africa.* Oxford: Oxford University Press, 1971.

Wieacker, Franz. *Vom römischen Recht: Wirklichkeit und Ueberlieferung.* Leipzig: Köhler & Amelang, 1944.

Wieczynski, Joseph L. *The Russian Frontier: The Impact of Borderlands upon the Course of Early Russian History.* Charlottesville: University Press of Virginia, 1976.

Wieruszowski, Hélène. "Vom Imperium zum nationalen Königtum: Vergleichende

380 / Bibliography

Studien über die publizistischen Kämpfe Kaiser Friedrichs II. und König Philippe des Schönen mit der Kurie." *Historische Zeitschrift*, Beiheft 30 (1933).

Wiesflecker, Hermann. *Kaiser Maximilian I: Der Reich, Oesterreich und Europa an der Wende zur Neuzeit.* Vols. 1, 3. Vienna: Verlag für Geschichte und Politik, 1971, 1977.

Wiet, Gaston. *L'Egypte Arabe de la Conquête Arabe à la Conquête Ottomane, 642–1517 de l'Ere Chrétienne.* Paris: Plon, n.d. (1937).

———. "L'Empire Néo-Byzantine des Omayyades et l'Empire Néo-Sassanide des Abbassides." *Cahiers d'Histoire Mondiale* 1 (1953):63–71.

Wilber, Donald N. *The Architecture of Islamic Iran: The Il Khānid Period.* New York: Greenwood, 1955.

———. "The Development of Mosaic Faïence in Islamic Architecture." *Ars Islamica* 6 (1939):16–74.

Williams, George H. *Wilderness and Paradise in Christian Thought: The Biblical Experience of the Desert in the History of Christianity and the Paradise Theme in the Theological Idea of the University.* New York: Harper, 1962.

Williams, Raymond. *The Country and the City.* London: Chatto & Windus, 1973.

Wilpert, Paul, ed. *Antike und Orient im Mittelalter: Vorträge der Kölner Mediaevalistentagungen, 1956–1959.* Berlin: De Gruyter, 1962.

Winkler, Arnold. *Oesterreichs Weg: Die ideellen und geschichtlichen Grundlagen des Staates.* Vienna: Manzsche, 1936.

———. *Studien über Gesamtstaatsidee, Pragmatische Sanktion und Nationalitätenfrage im Majorat Oesterreich: Die Grundlage der Habsburger Monarchie.* Leipzig: Schmid, 1915.

Winter, Eduard. *Der Josephinizmus und seine Geschichte: Beiträge zur Geistesgeschichte Oesterreich, 1740–1848.* Brunn: Rohrer, 1943.

———. *Russland und das Papsttum.* 3 vols. Berlin: Akademie Verlag, 1960, 1961, 1972.

Wirth, Eugen. "Damaskus-Aleppo-Beirut: Ein geographischer Vergleich dreier nahöstlicher Städte im Spiegel ihrer sozial und wirtschaftlich tonangebenden Schichten." *Die Erde* 97 (1966):96–137, 166–202.

———. "Zur Sozialgeographie der Religionsgemeinschaft im Orient." *Erdkunde* 19 (1965):265–84.

Wittek, Paul. "Deux Chapitres de l'Histoire des Turcs de Roum." *Byzantion* 11 (1934):285–319.

———. *The Rise of the Ottoman Empire.* London: Royal Asiatic Society, 1938.

———. "Türkentum und Islam, I." *Archiv für Sozialwissenschaft und Sozialpolitik* 59 (1928):489–525.

Wittschewsky, Valentin. *Russlands Handels- Zoll- und Industriepolitik von Peter dem Grossen bis auf die Gegenwart.* Berlin: Mittler, 1905.

Wojciechowski, Zygmunt. "La Condition des Nobles et le Problème de la Féodalité en Pologne au Moyen Age." *Revue Historique de Droit Français et Etranger*, Série 4, 15 (1936):651–700; 16 (1937):20–76.

———. *L'Etat Polonais au Moyen Age.* Trans. Bernard Hamel. Paris: Sirey, 1949.

Wolf, G. "Zur Geschichte jüdischer Aerzte in Oesterreich." *Monatsschrift für Geschichte und Wissenschaft des Judentums* 13 (1864):194–200.

Wolowski, Alexandre. *La Vie Quotidienne en Pologne au XVIIᵉ Siècle.* Paris: Hachette, 1972.

Woltmann, Ludwig. *Die Germanen und die Renaissance in Italien.* Leipzig: Thüringische Verlagsanstalt, 1905.

Woods, John E. "The Āqqūyanlū: Clan, Confederation and Empire." Ph.D. dissertation, Princeton University, 1974.

Woodward, E. L. *Christianity and Nationalism in the Later Roman Empire.* London: Longmans, Green, 1916.

Wright, Walter L., Jr., ed. and trans. *The Book of Councel for Vezirs and Governors of Sari Mehmed Pasha, the Defterdar.* Princeton: Princeton University Press, 1935.

Wulzinger, Karl, and Watzinger, Carl. *Damaskus: Die islamische Stadt.* Berlin: De Gruyter, 1924.

Yakubovsky, A. "Iz Istorii Padeniya Zolotoi Ordy." *Voprosy Istorii,* 1947, no. 2, pp. 30–45.

Yaney, George L. *The Systematization of Russian Government: Social Evolution in the Domestic Administration of Imperial Russia, 1711–1905.* Urbana: University of Illinois Press, 1973.

Yardeni, Myriam. *La Conscience Nationale en France pendant les Guerres de Réligion (1559–1598).* Louvain: Nauwelaerts, 1971.

Yavuz, Kerim. *Der Islam in Werken moderner türkischer Schriftsteller (Islamkundliche Untersuchungen,* Vol. 26). Freiburg im Breisgau: Klaus Schwarz, 1974.

Yeremian, A. B. "Sur Certaines Modifications Subies par les Monuments Arméniens au VIIᵉ Siècle." *Revue des Etudes Arméniennes* 8 (1971):251–66.

Young, M. Crawford. *The Politics of Cultural Pluralism.* Madison: University of Wisconsin Press, 1976.

Zabelin, Ivan. *Istoriya Goroda Moskvy: Sochineniye Napisannoye po Porucheniyu Moskovskoi Gorodskoi Dumy.* Vol. 1. Moscow: Mamontov, 1902.

Zananiri, Gaston. *L'Eglise et l'Islam.* Paris: SPES, 1969.

Zehntbauer, Richard. *Gesamtstaat, Dualismus und Pragmatische Sanktion.* Freiburg/Schweiz: Gschwend, 1914.

Zeller, Gaston. "Les Rois de France Candidats à l'Empire: Essai sur l'Idéologie Impériale en France." *Revue Historique* 173 (1934):273–311, 497–534.

Zernov, Nicolas. *Moscow the Third Rome.* London: Society for Promoting Christian Knowledge, 1937.

Ziadeh, Nicola A. *Urban Life in Syria under the Early Mamluks.* Beirut: American Press, 1953.

Zilliacus, Henrik. *Zum Kampf der Weltsprachen im östromischen Raum.* 1935. Reprint. Amsterdam: Hakhert, 1965.

Zimmermann, Karl L. "Die Beurteilung der Deutschen in der französischen Literatur des Mittelalters mit besonderer Berücksichtigung des *chansons de geste.*" *Romanische Forschungen* 29 (1911):222–316.

Zinkeisen, Johann W. *Geschichte des osmanischen Reiches in Europa.* Vol. 1. Hamburg: Perthes, 1840.

Zöllner, Erich. *Die politische Stellung der Völker im Frankenreich*. Vienna: Universum Verlag, 1950.

――――. "Zur Siedlungs- und Bevölkerungsgeschichte des österreichischen Frühmittelalters." *Österreich in Geschichte und Literatur* 5 (1961):113–26.

Index

America: Spanish in, xxxiii, xxxiv, 74,
161, 266; nomad tactics in, 41; isola-
tion of, 56; slavery in, 62, 309 (n.
33); United States politics in, 192; pre-
Columbian, 287
Amharic, xv, 206
Amsterdam, 257, 313 (n. 51)
Amu Darya valley, 291
Anatolia, xxxii, xxxiii, 42, 46, 68, 69,
85, 86, 89, 92, 103, 185, 202,
235–37, 244–45, 248, 253, 291, 295
Andalusia, xxix, xxx, 64, 70, 73, 105,
183, 249. See also Spain
Angevins, 268
Anglo-Saxons, xxviii
Annales school, 4
Antemurale myth, xv, 91, 288–89,
292–94; Polish aristocracy and, 35;
Magyars and, 49, 50; and Islamic
frontier, 65; in Iberia, 73–75, 82,
123; Poland-Lithuania and, 76–78,
123, 200; Habsburgs and, 82, 84,
163, 167; in Russia, 318 (n. 88)
Anthropologists, 4, 5, 21, 241, 286
Antioch, xxvii, xxx, 68, 170, 205
Antwerp, 256
Apulia, 220
Aquileia, xxix, 224
Aquitania, xxvii, 37, 264, 305 (n. 103)
Arabia, xviii, xix, 19, 42, 94, 137, 235,
236, 316 (n. 23)
Arabic, xv, 10, 15, 72, 186, 198, 204,
206, 243–49, 280, 290, 291; verse
in, 17; Egypt as center for, 144; Jews
and, 212; and urban Moslems, 235
Arabs, xvi, xx, xxiv, xxviii, xxix, 144,
255, 297, 302 (n. 18); house forms
of, 15; genealogical myths of, 15, 42,
43, 46, 248–49; and Islam, 16, 17,
54, 55, 58; and Berbers, 15, 43, 291;
nostalgia of, 17, 18, 20; in steppe
warfare, 30; and Baluchis, 38; as
nomads, sedentaries, and merchants,
39, 41, 49, 55, 94, 141; in Central
Asia, 40; comitatus among, 45;

endogamy among, 52; caliph's style
among, 64; in Anatolia, 68, 69, 71; in
Sicily and Sardinia, 69; in Iberia,
69–75; urbanism of, 124, 125; concept of honor of, 125; in Moslem
empires, 137; conquests of, 138,
183; in Egypt, 173; Karimi as, 184; in
North Africa, 234; 235; importance
of language to, 244; and Abbasids,
246; and Persians, 247–54
Aragon, xvi, 72–75, 78, 79, 80, 81, 91,
104, 163, 189–91, 251, 265–66, 294
Aramaic, 212, 215, 244–45
Archaicizing elements, 161, 193, 194
Archetypal diasporas, xv, 207, 238,
288, 293
Architectonic, xv, 96–101, 168–69,
171, 173
Architecture: as border guard, 6; as Islamic symbol, 11, 188; quality of in
Rome, 134; as terrestrial myth rep-
resentation, 147; in Russia, 149; and
Islamic law schools, 234; Catalan and
Castilian, 265; French, 296; in Ottoman imperial mosques, 317 (n. 49)
Ardebil, 235
Arians (disciples of Arius), xxviii, 32,
123, 146, 206
Ark, xv, 105
Armenians, xv, xviii, xix, xxvii, xxxi,
xxxiii, xxxvi, 57, 206, 238–39, 249,
288, 297; as slave traders, 63; and
Russia, 80, 122, 188; and Ottomans,
88, 209–10; and Poland, 118–19,
128, 277, 319 (n. 79); in Venice, 123;
in Moslem cities, 126, 128, 174; and
Byzantium, 146, 179, 207, 208, 210;
and Soviet Union, 207, 209; alphabet
of, 212; Bible among, 215; religion
among, 324 (n. 17); and Kurds, 324
(n. 20)
Arpads, xv, 48, 49
Arsacids, xv, 208
Artois, 257, 268
Asabiya, xv, 18, 45

and East Europe, 114; and urbanism,
123, 127; universal claims of, 133,
144–48, 150, 152, 153, 165–66; architecture of, 147; and Russia,
150–51, 181; and Western empire,
152–54, 162; capital city of, 174–75,
199; administration of, 178–81, 182,
190, 197, 198; education for, 201;
and religious organization, 203, 293;
and Armenians, 207, 209, 212; and
popes, 217–18; and Italy, 220–22;
and Sassanids, 237; and Greek language, 250, 253, 280; and Church
Slavonic, 273; and South Slavs, 276;
and Germanic elements, 318 (n. 71);
and crusaders, 318 (n. 71); and Bulgarians, 318 (n. 77)
Byzantium, before Constantinople, 176

Cadaster, xvi, 177
Cadi, xvi, 55, 140, 184, 203, 234
Caesar, Julius, xxvii, 214
Caesaropapism, xvi, 148, 151
Cairo, 11, 100, 125, 126, 138, 174,
198, 203, 234
Calabria, 220–21
Calatrava, Order of, 73
Caliph, xvi, xix, xxx, xxxii, 137–44,
182–83, 199. See also names of indi-
vidual caliphs and dynasties
Calque, xvi, 115, 217, 279
Calvinists, 171, 204, 232, 256–57
Camel, as symbol, 18, 19, 124
Cameralistics, xvi, 194
Campanella, Thomas, 163
Cantabrians, 70
Canton, 247
Capa media, xvi, 190
Capa y espada, 190
Capet, Hugh, xxx, 155, 254
Capetians, xvi, 155–57, 265, 323 (n. 1)
Capital city, 17, 127, 168–76, 197–
200, 286, 288–89, 294, 320 (n. 1);
Moslem, 105–6, 124, 173–74;
Rome as, 134–35; Baghdad as,

136–37; Ottoman, 144; Byzantine,
144–45, 148, 174–75; Carolingian,
155, 200; Russian, 176, 181; and language, 282; sacral, 293; symbolic,
295
Carolingians, xvi, xviii, xix, xxi, xxix,
xxx, 160, 166, 171, 252, 254, 257;
origins of, 32; myth of, 33, 159, 200;
aristocratic families and, 34, 35, 36,
45; law of, 37, 211; and papacy,
152–54; and France, 154–56, 158;
and Catalonia, 265
Carthage, xxvii, 131, 133
Casa de Austria, xvi, 160, 162–63, 172
Casimir the Great, xxxii, 228
Castilian language, xx, xxxi, xxxiii, 73,
212, 251, 257, 262–67, 269–72,
276, 282
Castilians, xvi, xviii, xxx, xxxii, xxxiv,
294; nobility of, 35, 254; Islamic
frontier and, 71, 73, 78, 81, 82, 91,
163–64; ideas of, 73–75, 201, 324
(n. 29); towns of, 101; in Sicily and
Naples, 163; capital of, 172; under
Habsburgs, 189–91
Catalonia, xxx, xxxii, 75, 80, 104, 196,
251, 264–67, 279, 281, 296, 305 (n.
103), 330 (n. 70)
Cataphract, xvi, 28, 31, 49, 71
Catherine II, xxxv, 79
Catholic, xvi, xviii, xxi, xxv, xxviii, xxix,
xxxiii, xxxiv, xxxv, 204; liturgy and
organization, 11, 123–24; conversion
of Franks, 32, 152; marriage regulations, 44, 329 (n. 43); conversion of
Magyars, 47–51, 307 (n. 157); relation to crusades, 60–61; monarchs
as, 80; Habsburgs as, 81–84, 91,
162–64, 193, 198; relation to Serbs,
83, 84; assimilation effect in Poland
and Hungary, 116, 260; relation to
Russia, 149, 151; role of Paris, 170;
element in Austrian service, 195–96;
Lithuanians as, 228; Ruthenians as,
228–30; Rumanians as, 230; relation

298; and face-to-face contact, 13, 201; in Roman empire, 22–23, 97, 135; in Italy, 101, 102, 127; myths of, 130–31; as empire component, 132–35, 168, 169; in Mesopotamia, 165; Rome as, 180

Civilization: and religion, 3, 4, 12, 54, 55, 90; defined, 4; and nomad-sedentary dichotomy, 12, 54; as burden, 16; nostalgia in, 16–19; urban, 93; in ancient Middle East, 132, 136, 165; Chinese, 141; of Islam and Christendom, 70, 210, 291, 297, 308 (n. 1); of Eastern and Western Christianity, 216, 225–26, 239–40; Polish, 276; and universal religions, 284. See also *Civitas*; *Polis*

Civis, xvi, 103

Civitas, xvi, xxii, 23, 102–3

Clan, 131; among steppe nomads, 30, 31, 45, 46, 52, 77, 142–43; Ottomans and, 86, 87, 185; and Islam, 125, 138; and Berbers, 148

Class, 112, 123, 127, 289; as part of identity continuum, 6, 7; in Austrian administration, 193–95; in Bohemia, 231, 258–59, 261, 281; in Flanders, 251; and European languages, 271–72. *See also* Bourgeoisie; Nobility; Peasants

Claude, Dietrich, 97, 98

Claudius (emperor), 179

Clovis (king), xxviii

Cluny, xvi, 72, 227, 266

Cognatic, xvi, 34, 35. *See also* Genealogy

Cohen, Marcel, 263–64, 267

Colbert, J. B., 158

Colchis. *See* Trebizond

Cologne, 110, 256

Comitatus, xvi, xvii, xviii, 28, 32, 45, 48–49, 86, 87, 120, 189

Common fate, 9

Communication, 13, 253, 264, 283; primitive, 5; symbolic content of, 8,

204; and nationalism, 14; in exchange relationships, 44; administrative, 107, 178, 180, 201; religions and, 201, 212, 223, 233, 238, 267, 280, 331 (n. 1); phenomenological problems, 214, 216–18, 239, 284; instrumental and affect, 242, 249; Greek and Latin in, 250; long and short-range, 254–55; between language families, 259, 261, 281, 282

Comnenes, xvi, 175, 178

Comparative approach, 3, 4, 12

Compound polity. *See* Empire

Conquest agglomeration, 29, 30, 31, 38, 45, 51, 86, 87, 141–42, 288, 292, 294

Conquistador, xvi, 69, 74, 266

Conseil d'Etat, xvi, 190

Consejo de Estado, xvi, 189, 191

Conspicuous consumption, sexual, 62–63, 85, 91, 284, 309 (n. 33)

Constantine I, xxviii, 145, 149, 174, 176, 180

Constantine XI, 179

Constantine, St. (Cyrill), xxix, 222, 224–25, 272, 326 (n. 69)

Constantinople, xvii, xx, xxiii, xxiv, xxviii, xxix, xxxiii, 18, 64, 77, 80, 144, 147, 148, 150, 174–76, 178, 180, 208, 239, 240, 248, 253, 288–89; and Germanic forces, 146; Byzantine layout of, 100; Ottomans in, 126, 174, 187, 198, 203; and Umayyads, 137; Armenians in, 210; crusaders and, 218, 318 (n. 71)

Constitutive myth. *See* *Mythomoteur*

Converso, xvi, 190–91, 292

Copts, xvi, 58, 106, 136, 184, 204, 205, 206, 208, 215, 238, 245, 291, 297

Cordova, 74

Corregidor, xvi, xvii, 190

Cossacks, xvii, xxxv, 78–80, 278

Counter-Reformation, 4, 229–30, 238, 276

Coutumes, xvii, 33, 112, 170

288-90; and civilization, 12; and sedentaries, 12, 15, 40-43, 46, 47, 210-11, 287; way of life of, 15, 95; nostalgia for, 16-19, 288, 290, 292; and genealogy, 17, 18, 34, 40, 42, 43; and Russia, 27, 75-81; and *Stamm*, 30, 31; and space, 38-39; Berbers as, 39; Arabs as, 39, 247; Central Asians as, 39; of hot-desert regions, 39, 52; Magyars as, 47-51; as *grands nomades*, 51, 70, 169; Germanic groups and, 52; and Islam, 61, 62, 90-92, 284; in Balkans, 69; in Spain, 69-75, 81; in Anatolia, 68, 79; on Croatian frontier, 82; and empire, 130, 141; Genghisids as, 142-43; Ottomans and, 144, 188, 235; and *sufi* movement, 235; in Safavid myth, 235; steppe values of, 285, 286; and ethnic boundary, 306 (n. 119)

Nome, 100, 128
Nordic patriarchate, 227
Normandy, 33
Normans, xxx, xxxi, 35, 37, 60, 155, 189, 210, 221-23, 268-69
North Africa, xv, xvii, xxi, xxx, 43, 64, 124, 234-35, 263, 291. *See also* Maghreb
Nostalgia, xxii, 51, 288, 289, 290, 292; and group identity, 15, 16; nomadic themes in, 17, 18, 19, 69; sedentary themes in, 19; Arabs and, 60; Turkic groups and, 88; for Rome, 135; in Islamic politics, 136; of Charles V, 160; of Court nobility, 173; for Constantinople, 174; of mountaineers, 303 (n. 34)
Novgorod, 75, 121, 272
Nubian, 243
Nuclear family, 44
Nur al-Din, 60
Nuremberg, 108

Obolensky, Dmitri, 150
Occupational differentiation, 6-7, 118,

209, 249, 295
Ofen. *See* Budapest
Oghuz. *See* Turkic
Oikhonomia, xxii, 146, 298
Old Testament references, 19, 20, 29, 60, 61, 86, 147, 159, 160, 174, 235, 245
Omar, caliph, xxviii, 42
Oppidum, xvi, xviii, xxii, 107, 115, 120. See also *Burg*; *Gorod*
Orel, 77
Orleans, 268
Ormuz (divinity), 182
Orthodox, xviii, xix, xxii, xxxi, xxxii, xxxiv, 199, 260, 280, 284-85, 298; liturgy, 11; and "heretics," 58; 204-6; Russia as, 80-81, 149-51, 166, 187, 228-29, 280; Serbs as, 83, 84, 91, 116; Rumanians as, 84, 91; in Hungary, 116; in Poland, 118-19; in Venice, 123; emperor as, 151, 152; South Slavs as, 151, 239; and Greek language, 204-11, 280; East Slavs as, 228-30, 239, 273-77. *See also* Byzantines, Eastern Christianity
Osmanli. *See* Ottomans
Ostmark, 36
Ostrogoths, 29
Otranto, 221
Otto I, xxx, 60, 226
Otto III, 154, 227
Ottomans, xvii, xviii, xix, xx, xxi, xxii, xxiii, xxiv, xxxii, xxxiii, xxxiv, xxxv, xxxvi, 55, 159; warfare by, 41; and Hungary, 50, 116-17; and Christians, 58, 185, 187; as slave market, 64, 77; and Crimean Tatars, 77-81; and Habsburgs, 81-84, 162, 164, 173, 193-94; myths of, 85-90, 91, 144, 184-86, 188; and Armenians, 118, 210; urbanism of, 125, 126; and caliphate, 138-40, 144; and Mamelukes, 140, 298; mosques of, 144, 317 (n. 49); and Byzantium, 150, 179; and Constantinople, 174;

administration of, 184–88, 322 (n. 60); language of, 186, 235, 243–44, 247–49; Jews and, 187, 210–12; and Kemalists, 188; *millet* system of, 210; and Safavids, 237–40, 257; Turkic recruits of, 311 (n. 114)
Ottonians, xxii, 154, 159, 226–27
Our Lady of the Golden Dome, 175
Ovid (poet), 133

Padishah, xxii, 86, 138, 143
Paganism, xxviii, 55, 58, 60, 123, 134, 136, 146, 180, 214, 220, 223, 225, 227, 260
Pagus, xxii, 23
Pahlevi, xxii, 204, 212
Palatinate, 171
Palermo, xxx, 171
Palestine, xviii, xix, xxxi, 60, 61, 153, 212, 215, 219
Pannonia, 219, 224
Pantokrator, xxii, 147
Paradise (as image), 17, 18, 20, 174, 302 (n. 18)
Paris, xvii, xxiii, 33, 112, 170, 173, 174, 270, 274, 286
Parish, 24, 202, 221
Parlement, xxii, 170
Parsees, 207
Parthia, xv, xxvii
Partitions of Poland, xxii, 181, 227, 230, 260, 278, 298
Paschoud, François, 134
Pasha, xxii, 186, 188
Passarowitz, Peace of, xxxv
Passau, 224
Pastoral nomads, xxii, 19, 42, 69, 72, 96, 141, 208, 302 (n. 34). See also Nomads
Patois, xxii, 263, 277, 282
Patria, xxii, 93, 102, 135, 173
Patriarch, xxii, xxxiv, xxxv, 151, 175, 219–22, 227. See also Ecumenical patriarch
Patriotisme de clocher, xxii, 24, 44

Paul I, 153
Paul, St., xxvii, 215, 224–25
Pays, xxiii, 26
Peasants, 96, 202, 212, 288–89, 290, 301 (n. 9); and ethnic consciousness, 7; house forms of, 14–15; Chinese as, 19, 142; in West Europe, 20, 24; and territoriality, 21; burial places of, 35; under Islam, 40, 42, 47, 55, 56, 105–6, 142, 245; and symbols, 51, 55; in Brazil, 94; in *polis*, 102–4; and Italian city, 104, 108; under Mongols, 106; and northern European city, 108, 109; French, 158, 268, 296; and Court nobility, 173; in Egypt, 177; as bound to soil, 177, 235; Armenian, 210; as linguistically absorbing city, 219; Czech, 232, 259; in Low Countries, 250; and dialect differentiation, 261
Pelenski, Jaroslaw, 79, 149
Peloponnesian wars, xxvii
Penetration by myth-symbol complex, 130, 167, 169, 239, 241, 283, 290, 295, 323 (n. 1)
Pepin, xxix, 152–53, 157, 296
Pereyaslav, 77
Persians, xv, xix, xxii, xxiii, xxiv, xxxiv, xxxv, xxxvi, 11, 124, 143, 287, 297, 328 (n. 30); language of, 10, 186, 235, 291; gardens of, 17; as pastoral, 20; and nomads, 39; and Islam, 55, 56, 204, 291, 292; and Sassanids, 59, 141; and Uzbeks, 65; urbanism among, 94, 95; and Il Khans, 106, 142–43; and Armenians, 118, 209; in Astrakhan, 121; administration of, 137, 182–83, 198, 280; as Shiites, 140; and universal rule, 141, 144; and Mesopotamia, 173; and Turkic regimes, 184; as Parsees, 207; as Christians, 215; Safavid and Ottoman relation to, 237, 240, 243–49, 254
Personal law, xxiii. See also Law
Peter I, xxv, 79, 122, 151, 176, 181,

5765370R00262

Printed in Great Britain
by Amazon.co.uk, Ltd.,
Marston Gate.